The Routledge Applied Linguistics Reader

Blackwell.

The Routledge Applied Linguistics Reader is an essential collection of readings for students of applied linguistics. Featuring 26 carefully selected readings, the Reader focuses on the topics and issues to which applied linguistics research has made a significant contribution, in particular:

- Reconceptualizing the native speaker and the language learner
- Reconceptualizing language in language learning and practice
- Critical issues in applied linguistics
- Applied linguistics in a changing world

The selection comprises seminal articles from leading researchers, as well as fresh perspectives from new voices in the field, and takes a broad interpretation of applied linguistics from its traditional foundations in language teaching and learning to the newer sub-disciplines such as corpus linguistics, lingua franca communication, language planning and language policy, language and politics, language and the law, language and commerce, and language in the workplace.

These readings are amplified by a critical introduction, a detailed discussion of methodological issues, as well as study questions, recommended further reading and a resource list.

Readings

Douglas Biber, Susan Conrad and Randi Reppen • David Block • Deborah Cameron • Suresh Canagarajah • Ronald Carter and Michael McCarthy • Guy Cook, Matt Reed and Alison Twiner • Vivian Cook • Alan Davies • Patricia Duff, Ping Wong and Margaret Early • John Flowerdew • Christina Higgins • Nancy Hornberger • Ken Hyland • Claire Kramsch and Anne Whiteside • Ryuko Kubota • Constant Leung • Constant Leung, Roxy Harris and Ben Rampton • Angel Lin, Wendy Wang, Nobuhiko Akamatsu and A. Mehdi Riazi • Enric Llurda • Tim McNamara • Janet Maybin and Joan Swann • Aneta Pavlenko • Alastair Pennycook • Bonny Norton Peirce • Christina Schäffner • Barbara Seidlhofer

Li Wei is Professor of Applied Linguistics at Birkbeck College, University of London, UK. He is editor of *The Bilingualism Reader*, second edition (Routledge, 2007) and *Bilingualism and Multilingualism: Critical Concepts in Linguistics*, four volumes (Routledge, 2009).

The Routledge
Applied Linguistics Reader

Edited by

Li Wei

Routledge
Taylor & Francis Group

LONDON AND NEW YORK

First published 2011
by Routledge
2 Park Square, Milton Park, Abingdon, Oxon OX14 4RN

Simultaneously published in the USA and Canada
by Routledge
711 Third Avenue, New York, NY 10017

Routledge is an imprint of the Taylor & Francis Group, an informa business

British Library Cataloguing in Publication Data
A catalogue record for this book is available from the British Library

Library of Congress Cataloging in Publication Data
The Routledge applied linguistics reader / edited by Li Wei.
   p. cm.
   1. Applied linguistics. 2. Language and languages—Study and teaching.
   I. Wei, Li, 1961-
   P51R68 2011
   418—dc22   2010044326

ISBN: 978–0–415–56619–3 (hbk)
ISBN: 978–0–415–56620–9 (pbk)

Typeset in Perpetua and Bell Gothic by
Florence Production Ltd, Stoodleigh, Devon
Printed and bound in Great Britain by TJ International Ltd, Padstow, Cornwall

Contents

Illustrations

Figures

Tables

Contributors

Nobuhiko Akamatsu is Professor of English at Doshisha University, Japan. E-mail: nakamats@mail.doshisha.ac.jp

Douglas Biber is Regents' Professor of Applied Linguistics at Northern Arizona University, USA. Email: Douglas.Biber@nau.edu

David Block is Professor of Languages in Education at the Institute of Education, University of London, UK. Email: d.block@ioe.ac.uk

Deborah Cameron is Rupert Murdoch Professor of Language and Communication at Oxford University, UK. Email: Deborah.Cameron@ell.ox.ac.uk

Suresh Canagarajah is William J and Catherine Craig Kirby Professor in Language Learning at Pennsylvania State University, USA. Email: asc16@psu.edu

Ronald Carter is Professor of English Language Studies at Nottingham University, UK. Email: ronald.carter@nottingham.ac.ukfax

Guy Cook is Professor of Education at the Open University, UK. E-mail: g.cook@open.ac.uk

Vivian Cook is Professor of Applied Linguistics at Newcastle University, UK. Email: vivian.cook@ncl.ac.uk

Susan Conrad is Professor of Applied Linguistics at Portland State University, USA. Email: conrads@pdx.edu

Alan Davies is Professor Emeritus of Applied Linguistics at Edinburgh University, UK. Email: a.davies@ed.ac.uk

Patricia Duff is Professor of Language and Literacy Education at the University of British Columbia, Canada. Email: patricia.duff@ubc.ca

Margaret Early is Associate Professor of Language and Literacy Education at the University of British Columbia, Canada. Email: margaret.early@ubc.ca

John Flowerdew is Professor in the Department of English at the City University of Hong Kong, China. Email: enjohnf@cityu.edu.hk

Roxy Harris is Senior Lecturer in Language in Education at King's College, University of London, UK. Email: roxy.harris@kcl.ac.uk

Christina Higgins is Assistant Professor in Second Language Studies at the University of Hawai'i at Manoa, USA. Email: cmhiggin@hawaii.edu

Nancy Hornberger is Goldie Anna Professor of Education at the University of Pennsylvania, USA. Email: nancyh@gse.upenn.edu

Ken Hyland is Professor of Applied Linguistics at Hong Kong University, China. Email: khyland@hku.hk

Claire Kramsch is Professor of German at University of California, Berkeley, USA. Email: Email: ckramsch@berkeley.edu

Ryuko Kubota is Professor in the Department of Language and Literacy Education at the University of British Columbia, Canada. Email: ryuko.kubota@ubc.ca

Constant Leung is Professor of Educational Linguistics at King's College, University of London, UK. Email: constant.leung@kcl.ac.uk

Li Wei is Professor of Applied Linguistics at Birkbeck College, University of London, UK. Email: li.wei@bbk.ac.uk

Angel Lin is Associate Professor in the Faculty of Education, University of Hong Kong, China. E-mail: angellin@hku.hk

Enric Llurda (Giménez) is Professor of English Philology at the University of Lleida, Catalan, Spain. Email: ellurda@dal.udl.es

Michael McCarthy is Professor Emeritus of Applied Linguistics at Nottingham University, UK. Email: Michael.McCarthy@nottingham.ac.uk

Tim McNamara is Professor of Applied Linguistics at the University of Melbourne, Australia. Email: tfmcna@ unimelb.edu.au

Janet Maybin is Senior Lecturer in Education at the Open University, UK. E-mail: j.maybin@open.ac.uk

Aneta Pavlenko is Professor in the College of Education at Temple University, USA. Email: aneta.pavlenko@temple.edu

Bonny Peirce Norton is Professor and Distinguished University Scholar in the Department of Language & Literacy Education at the University of British Columbia, Canada. Email: bonny.norton@ubc.ca

Alastair Pennycook is Professor of Language Studies at the University of Technology Sydney, Australia. Email: Alastair.Pennycook@uts.edu.au

Randi Reppen is Professor of Applied Linguistics at Northern Arizona University, USA. Email: randi.reppen@nau.edu

Ben Rampton is Professor of Applied and Socio-Linguistics at King's College, University of London, UK. Email: ben.rampton@kcl.ac.uk

Matt Reed is a Research Fellow at the Countryside and Community Research Institute in Cheltenham, UK. Email: mreed@glos.ac.uk

A. Mehdi Riazi is Associate Professor in the Department of Linguistics at Macquarie University, Australia. Email: mehdi.riazi@mq.edu.au

Christina Schäffner is Professor of Translation Studies at Aston University, Birmingham, UK. E-mail: c.schaeffner@aston.ac.uk

Barbara Seidlhofer is Professor of English and Applied Linguistics at the University of Vienna, Austria. Email: barbara.seidlhofer@univie.ac.at

Joan Swann is Senior Lecturer in Education at the Open University, UK. E-mail: j.swann@open.ac.uk

Alison Twiner is a Research Assistant at the Open University, UK. Email: a.j.twiner@open.ac.uk

Wendy Wang is Associate Professor in the Department of World Languages at Eastern Michigan University, USA. Email: wwang@emich.edu

Anne Whiteside is Professor of ESL at City College of San Francisco, USA. Email: awhitesi@ccsf.edu

Ping Wong (Deters) is a professor at the English Language Institute at Seneca College, Toronto, Canada. Email: ping.deters@senecac.on.ca

Zhu Hua is Professor of Applied Linguistics and Communication at Birkbeck College, University of London, UK. Email: zhu.hua@bbk.ac.uk

Preface and how to use the Reader

The Reader is intended for use as a teaching text, either on its own or as a secondary source-book, on a variety of applied linguistics courses. Postgraduates may use it for research training, and undergraduates can use it to survey the field of applied linguistics. All the reprinted articles are selected from journals and edited volumes. No extracts from single authored monographs are included here. The papers are grouped into different parts, each having a brief introduction highlighting its theme. Within each part, the papers are arranged, as far as possible, in a chronological order.

The general introduction aims to place the reprinted articles in context, and thus should be read first. Users can then choose to read the papers in different parts which interest them most, although I have organized the papers in such a way that the focus of discussion moves naturally from one to another. I have followed the model of other successful Readers and provided a set of Study Questions and Study Activities at the end of each part. The Study Questions are intended for reviewing some of the essential concepts in the individual articles and can be used on under-graduate courses or for self study. The Study Activities aim to extend reading by generalization to the user's own locality or experience. Some of the activities require research, and may be used as topics for essays or dissertation projects. These are particularly suitable for use at an intermediate or advanced level. There is also a short list of Further Reading at the end of each part, which lists other relevant publications by the authors of the reprinted articles and will be useful for those who are interested in following up particular issues and ideas. Most of the publications in the Further Reading lists are monographs or edited volumes, as they give a more extended treatment of the topics the authors deal with in the reprinted articles. The methodology chapter highlights some of the key issues in applied linguistics research. Although it is placed at the end of the volume, it can (and perhaps should) be read before reading the individual papers. The Resources section contains key references, textbooks, handbooks, book series, journals, corpora and professional associations, as well as key websites. The key references are listed in thematic groupings, containing mainly monographs, edited volumes and special journal issues. They complement the Further Reading sections in the different parts of the Reader.

Li Wei
Russell Square, London
September, 2010

Acknowledgements

The editor and the publisher gratefully acknowledge the permission by the copyright holders to reprint the following material:

Davies, Alan (2004). The native speaker in applied linguistics. In A. Davies and C. Elder (eds) *Handbook of Applied Linguistics*. Oxford: Blackwell, pp. 431–449.

Leung, C., Harris, R. and Rampton, B. (1997). The idealised native speaker, reified ethnicities and classroom realities. *TESOL Quarterly*, 31: 543–560.

Higgins, Christina (2003). "Ownership" of English in the Outer Circle: an alternative to the NS-NNS Dichotomy. *TESOL Quarterly*, 37(4): 615–644.

Llurda, Enric (2004). Non-native speaker teachers and English as an international language. *International Journal of Applied Linguistics*, 14(3): 314–323.

Cook, Vivian (2007). The nature of the L2 user. In L. Roberts, A. Gurel, S. Tatar and L. Marti (eds) *EUROSLA Yearbook*, 7: 205–220.

Lin, A. M. Y., Wang, W., Akamatsu, A. and Riazi, M. (2002). Appropriating English, expanding identities, and re-visioning the field: from TESOL to Teaching English for Globalized Communication (TEGCOM). *Journal of Language, Identity and Education*, 1(4), 295–316.

Pennycook, A.D. (2007). Language, localization, and the real: hip-hop and the global spread of authenticity. *Journal of Language, Identity, and Education*, 6(2): 101–116.

Seidlhofer, Barbara (2001). Closing a conceptual gap: the case for a description of English as a lingua franca. *International Journal of Applied Linguistics*, 11: 133–158.

Canagarajah, Suresh (2007). Lingua Franca English multilingual communities and language acquisition. *Modern Language Journal*, 91: 923–939.

Hyland, Ken (2002). Authority and invisibility: authorial identity in academic writing. *Journal of Pragmatics*, 34: 1091–1112.

Biber, D., Conrad, S. and Reppen, R. (1994). Corpus-based approaches to issues in applied linguistics. *Applied Linguistics*, 15(2): 169–189.

Carter, Ronald and McCarthy, Michael (2004). Talking, creating: interactional language, creativity and context. *Applied Linguistics*, 25(1): 62–88.

Norton Peirce, B. (1995). Social identity, investment, and language learning. *TESOL Quarterly*, 29(1): 9–31.

Block, David (2006). Identity in applied linguistics. In Tope Omoniyi and Goodith White (eds) *Sociolinguistics of Identity*. Continuum, pp. 34–49.

Kubota, Ryuko (2003). New approaches to gender, class, and race in second language writing. *Journal of Second Language Writing*, 12(1): 31–47.

Leung, Constant (2005). Convivial communication: recontextualizing communicative competence. *International Journal of Applied Linguistics*, 15(2): 119–144.

Kramsch, Claire and Whiteside, Anne (2008). Language ecology in multilingual settings: towards a theory of symbolic competence. *Applied Linguistics*, 29: 647–671.

Cameron, Deborah (2002). Globalization and the teaching of "communication skills". In David Block and Deborah Cameron (eds) *Globalization and Language Teaching*. Routledge, pp. 67–82.

Flowerdew, John (2000). Discourse community, legitimate peripheral participation and the non-native-English-speaking scholar. *TESOL Quarterly*, 34(1): 127–150.

McNamara, Tim (2001). Language assessment as social practice: challenges for research. *Language Testing*, 18(4): 333–349.

Duff, P., Wong, P. and Early, M. (2000). Learning language for work and life: the linguistic socialization of immigrant Canadians seeking careers in healthcare. *Canadian Modern Language Review*, 57: 9–57.

Hornberger, Nancy (2002). Multilingual language policies and the continua of biliteracy: an ecological approach. *Language Policy*, 1(1): 27–51.

Schäffner, Christina (2004). Political discourse analysis from the point of view of Translation Studies. *Journal of Language and Politics*, 3(1): 117–150.

Maybin, Janet and Swann, Joan (2007). Everyday creativity in language: textuality, contextuality, and critique. *Applied Linguistics*, 28(4): 497–517.

Pavlenko, Aneta (2008). Non-native speakers of English and the Miranda warnings. *TESOL Quarterly*, 42(1): 1–30.

Cook, G., Reed, M. and Twiner, A. (2009). 'But it's all true!' Commercialism and commitment in the discourse of organic food promotion. *Text & Talk*, 29(2): 151–173.

Every effort has been made to obtain permission to reproduce copyright material. If any proper acknowledgement has not been made, or permission not received, we would like to invite copyright holders to inform the publisher and the editor of that oversight.

The original articles are reproduced as faithfully as possible. The authors' original writing styles and conventions, whether in British or North American norms, have been kept. The numbering of sections, subsections, examples, tables and figures is reformatted according to the sequence of the chapters in this Reader. Given the inevitable restrictions of space and the need to produce a coherent and readable collection, the editor has changed or omitted references to other articles in the same original collection (e.g. 'see Chapter 6 of this volume' has been changed 'see xxx, date'), and put all the bibliographical details of the original articles at the end of the Reader. Other minor textual changes and omissions are indicated by the insertion of [. . .] in the text. For journal articles, the original abstracts are not reproduced but have been incorporated into the Part introductions. Acknowledgements in the original articles, unless integral to the contents of the articles, are omitted.

The editor is especially gratefully to Vivian Cook for his contribution to the last section of the General Introduction. Part of the text is taken from Vivian Cook and Li Wei (2009).

Zhu Hua co-authored the chapter on methodology and made valuable comments on the editorial material. Special thanks go to Brigid O'Connor, who proofread a significant amount of the editorial material very quickly and efficiently. The reviewers commissioned by the publisher made valuable suggestions and comments on the selection of articles as well as the editorial material written by the editor, which greatly enhanced the quality of the final product. Similarly, David Block, Constant Leung, Jean-Marc Dewaele, Bonny Norton, Aneta Pavlenko, Bernard Spolsky and Terry Wiley gave the editor important advice on various aspects of the Reader. As always, the Routledge editorial team, led by Louisa Semlyen, has been a real pleasure to work with. David Cox has been a patient and helpful textbook development editor. Rosie White and the team at Florence Production Ltd did a very professional job of typesetting and project management. The editor is most grateful for their hard work. The book is dedicated to the editor's two sons, Andrew and Timothy, whose contribution to proofreading and indexing was invaluable.

LI WEI

FROM PEDAGOGICAL PRACTICE TO CRITICAL ENQUIRY
An introduction to Applied Linguistics

I T WAS MONDAY 9 NOVEMBER 2009 in a Chinese restaurant in Russell Square, London. I was having lunch with Ofelia Garcia and Ricardo Otheguy who were visiting London. Ofelia had recently moved from Columbia University's Teachers' College to the Graduate Center of City University of New York. And my department, the Department of Applied Linguistics and Communication at Birkbeck College, University of London, had just moved from the School of Arts to the School of Social Sciences. We were happily exchanging news about our moves. I was especially very proud to tell Ofelia and Ricardo about what I knew of the history of our department: the fact that it was the first university department with applied linguistics in its name in England and that it played an instrumental role in the establishment of the British Association of Applied Linguistics, etc., when Ricardo, in his usual calm and thoughtful voice, asked me, 'Are you happy with the name of the department?' I had to pause a while. Nobody had asked me such a question before. And coming from Ricardo, I knew the question was not simply about the name of the department but about the nature of the discipline. A chain of other questions came to mind: Can it not be, simply, Linguistics? What does 'applied' mean in this context? Indeed, what is applied linguistics anyway?

None of these questions have straightforward answers, and our lunch was certainly not ruined by a heated discussion of them. But Ricardo's question has been on my mind ever since. I have been reading the various histories of applied linguistics as a discipline, including histories of professional bodies in different countries of the world, accounts of the development of the field, and personal views on what applied linguistics meant for them from a career development perspective. It is quite obvious that there is no uniform view on what the discipline stands for, or on how it came to be seen as a separate field of enquiry. In what follows, I will try to outline the main developmental pathways of applied linguistics, the practical and theoretical concerns that have provided the impetus for the development of applied linguistics over time, the key achievements of applied linguistics so far, and where the field is heading. The objective of this chapter is to map out the general background and context for the papers to be presented later in this Reader.

Initial impetus: language teaching and learning, and professional development

Those who have studied the history of applied linguistics seem to agree that the term, applied linguistics, came to prominence after the Second World War, especially in the United States of America, in specialized language teaching programmes. *Language Learning*, which was founded in 1948 and published from the University of Michigan, was the first academic journal in the world to carry the term applied linguistics in its subtitle. In the first few years, the articles published in *Language Learning* were all concerned with issues such as the contrasts between sounds in English and in other languages, the importance of native language in learning new sounds and other linguistic structures, oral practice, literacy and alphabet learning, medium of instruction, the use of the dictionary, and note-taking. A central concern at the time appears to be developing pedagogies for teaching linguistic structures to foreign learners. And describing and analysing both the target language and the learner's native language, and contrasting their differences, were believed to be particularly helpful in understanding the difficulties learners might have. This in some sense was an extension of the traditional grammar-translation method in language teaching where the ability to analyse the target language was seen to be a pre-requisite for using the language. The descriptions and analyses of language were heavily influenced by the structural linguistics in North America at the time. With direct involvement of linguists such as Leonard Bloomfield, Charles C. Fries and Robert Lado, applied linguistics in those days was very much what Davies (1999 and 2003) described as 'linguistics applied'.

Even though professional associations for applied linguists were developed much later in Europe and Australia, the early days of applied linguistics in countries outside the USA were very much similar in its orientation, i.e. linguistics applied. People tried to find solutions to problems they faced in language teaching by applying methods and findings of linguistics. There was a view that to do applied linguistics, one had to study linguistics first. Indeed, many people who were entering the profession as language teachers had studied aspects of linguistics and knew a great deal about the structures of language. The main activity of applied linguistics then was centred around describing the formal structures of the target language and contrasting them with those of the learners' native languages, in order to predict difficulties in teaching and learning and develop ways of overcoming the difficulties.

In the 1950s, language laboratories began to emerge. The learners could listen to recordings of native speakers' speech repeatedly and even record their own speech to contrast with that of the native speaker. The field of language teaching began to diverge into those who were primarily concerned with analysing the learner's errors and helping them to overcome any difficulties to achieve a high level of proficiency and those who were interested in developing new material for teaching as well as new teaching methods. In fact, a myriad of new teaching material and methods were developed in the subsequent decade. New audio-visual material emerged all the time, and classroom teaching gradually shifted its focus from structural differences between the target and the learner's native language to what was known as the notional-functional syllabus where the context in which people communicate and the purpose for a speaker in a given context were emphasized over grammatical structures.

The Chomskyan revolution: modern linguistics and the development of SLA research

In the meantime, as technology transformed the language teaching profession, revolutionary changes were taking place within linguistics itself. Chomsky's attack on behaviourism threw much of what lay behind language teaching and learning at the time into question. Language learning was no longer seen as simply drilling, repetition and habit formation. Instead, it was understood as a process that involved innovation and generation of new structures in accordance with rules of great abstractness and intricacy. Formal linguistics began to focus almost exclusively on expounding the abstract rules that were assumed to be underlying the speaker's generation and transformation of grammatical structures. In terms of describing the structures of either the target language or the learner's language, generative linguistics, as it became known, had a limited direct impact on language teaching. But in terms of setting the agenda for modern linguistics, Chomsky's ideas have had a huge influence. He defined three fundamental questions for linguistics (e.g. Chomsky, 1964, 1976, 1986):

- What constitutes knowledge of language?
- How is knowledge of language acquired?
- How is knowledge of language put to use?

Vivian Cook later reformulated these questions for applied linguistics (e.g. Cook, 1993):

- *What constitutes knowledge of multiple languages?* If a person learns another language in addition to his or her native language, he or she would have two grammars. In other words, one mind possesses two systems of language knowledge. What then is the nature of the knowledge of more than one language? How does it differ from that of a monolingual speaker? How do two systems of linguistic knowledge co-exist and interact in one mind?
- *How is knowledge of multiple languages acquired, either simultaneously or sequentially?* Some speakers have acquired multiple languages at the same time from birth, because they are brought up in a bilingual or multilingual environment. Others may have learned additional languages later in life. Either way, how does the mind acquire two or more grammars? Does second language acquisition differ from first language acquisition, or are they different aspects of a single process? Does bilingual and multilingual first language acquisition, i.e. simultaneous acquisition of two or more languages, differ from either unilingual first language acquisition or sequential second language acquisition?
- *How is knowledge of multiple languages put to use?* If a speaker knows two or more languages, he or she can decide when to use which one according to the situation they find themselves in and the people they are talking to. How does the same speaker utilize knowledge of two or more languages for different functions? How do they manage the selection of language? And why do some speakers switch between languages in the same interaction?

Questions such as these gave rise to Second Language Acquisition (SLA), which gradually became rather independent of the main agenda of applied linguistics. Many SLA researchers have come into the field from linguistics or psychology without professional experience as a language teacher or any real interest in language teaching practices. Like modern linguistics, the core of SLA is busy building closer connections with cognitive science and is increasingly informed by theoretical and methodological developments in psychology, neurology and computer science. Likewise, research on bilingual and multilingual first language acquisition, which has expanded significantly in recent years, is seeking to address a similar research agenda.

The communicative turn and the diversification of the linguistics applied

The rejection of behaviourism in modern linguistics did have an impact on the language teaching profession. Listening repeatedly to recordings of conversations in the language lab and mimicking the pronunciation and grammatical structures in these dialogues were no longer regarded as adequate or appropriate. A new approach that placed emphasis on teaching the functions of language and helping the learner to use the target language in different contexts was developed, as a further extension of the notional-functional syllabus. This new approach became known as Communicative Language Teaching (CLT). It was clearly influenced by the notion of *communicative competence*, which was developed by the American anthropological linguist Dell Hymes in response to Chomsky's (1965) distinction between *competence* (and *performance*) (Hymes, 1966, 1971) and which refers to a language user's grammatical knowledge as well as social knowledge about how and when to use utterances appropriately. CLT is more of a broad approach to teaching, rather than a specific method with a clearly defined set of classroom practices. As such, it is most often defined as a list of general principles or features. Nunan (1991), for example, describes five key features of CLT:

1   An emphasis on learning to communicate through interaction in the target language.
2   The introduction of authentic texts into the learning situation.
3   The provision of opportunities for learners to focus not only on language but also on the learning management process.
4   An enhancement of the learner's own personal experiences as important contributing elements to classroom learning.
5   An attempt to link classroom language learning with language activities outside the classroom.

Under the CLT umbrella, any teaching practice that helps students develop their communicative competence in an authentic context is deemed appropriate and beneficial. In the actual language classroom, CLT often takes the form of pair or group work requiring negotiation and cooperation between learners, fluency-based activities that encourage learners to develop their confidence, role-plays in which students practise and develop language functions, as well as judicious use of grammar and pronunciation focused activities.

While continuing in the linguistics applied tradition, language teaching professionals began to draw insights and inspirations from approaches to linguistics other than the generative-transformational paradigm. For example, Halliday's Systemic Functional Grammar (SFG) gave CLT theoretical motivation for its emphasis on the functions of language. The term *systemic* refers to the view that language is a network of systems or interrelated sets of options for making meaning, and *functional* indicates that the approach is concerned with the contextualized, practical uses to which language is put. These choices relate the language users' intentions to the concrete forms of a language. According to SFG, the functional bases of grammatical phenomena are divided into three broad areas: the *ideational*, the *interpersonal* and the *textual* (e.g. Halliday, 1973). SFG led to a large number of studies of language functions by learners and users from a variety of backgrounds, including young children, second language learners and people with special language and communication needs. It later provided impetus to multimodality analyses of language and communication from a social semiotic point of view.

Similarly, the discourse analysis model developed by a group of linguists at the University of Birmingham in Britain extended the structural analysis of language beyond the unit of sentence to what they called "transactions" between language users. These transactions consist of units of exchanges, moves and acts. Using classroom interaction as an example, Sinclair and Coulthard (1975) proposed the so-called IRF structure, i.e. Initiation–Response–Follow-up. It was argued that language in the classroom followed a rather rigid sequence, and that the speaking patterns of the teacher and the pupils were highly structured. Drawing on insights from Speech Act Theory, Sinclair and Coulthard created a structural description of classroom discourse according to the functions of the moves. This work later evolved and expanded to allow the investigation of less rigidly structured discourse, through the works of Coulthard and Montgomery (1981), Sinclair and Brazil (1982), and Sinclair and Coulthard (1992).

The learner takeover and the birth of contemporary applied linguistics

By the late 1970s and early 80s, yet another fresh approach to language teaching began to dominate the profession, namely the learner-centred approach. Initially concerned with curriculum development and, somewhat ironically, the teacher's planning process, the learner-centred approach highlighted the need for a detailed, systematic analysis of the learner's needs and characteristics. These included not only what native languages the learner may have, but also their motivations for learning new languages, learning styles, context of learning, and access to learning resources (Nunan, 1988). All these factors would need to be taken into consideration in selecting the tasks to be used in teaching and the way teaching is conducted.

It soon became clear that no two learners were exactly the same, in background, need, motivation and style. Different material and methods would be needed for different learners. This realization led to a further separation between those who are primarily concerned with curriculum design, material development and efficacy evaluation for language teaching and those interested more in studying the learners' characteristics, their process of learning new languages, the role of prior knowledge of other languages (and indeed other kinds of knowledge) in learning new languages, and the outcome of learning, i.e. production in the new language. There are of course issues that are of concern to researchers working in both of these broad areas – for instance, language testing. While many researchers were engaged in developing new language testing regimes, some began to ask critical questions about the assumptions of the learner behind some of the tests, and social as well as pedagogical implications of language testing for policy and practice.

The impact of the learner-centred approach to language teaching on applied linguistics generally was way beyond what those people who advocated it could ever have imagined. In fact, once the learner took centre stage, the identity of applied linguistics changed forever. It was no longer simply linguistics applied. Indeed, people began to realize that many questions and issues that they were concerned with could not be dealt with satisfactorily by borrowing methods and findings from mainstream linguistics. One example is the nature of the learner's L2 production. Although there were, and still are, many researchers trying to characterize it in Chomskyan linguistics terms, from Universal Grammar to the Minimalist Programme, others began to conceptualize it as a distinctive and dynamic system. This led to the notions of *interlanguage* (Selinker, 1972, 1992) and later *multicompetence* (Cook, 1991, 1992, 2007). Still others began to borrow insights from sociology and other social science disciplines and asked questions about the socio-cultural and political dimensions of language teaching and learning, the role of learner identity and motivations, the effects of language policies, and the politics of knowledge, expertise and difference.

Methodologically, applied linguistics also began to make distinctive innovations. Cook, for example, challenged what he called the 'comparative fallacy', where the native speaker was posited as the norm with which the L2 learner was compared; any difference would be regarded as deviation, deficiency or disorder, which had to be treated and overcome (e.g. Cook, 1999). As some of the articles reprinted in this Reader show, the notion of 'the native speaker' is imagined and idealized. There is a whole variety of language users with their distinctive identities, attitudes, abilities, motivations and access to resources. This realisation of the diversity of language users has attracted people who are not language teachers and who do not necessarily have an interest in language teaching *per se* to applied linguistics as a field of enquiry. Their work tends to focus on issues of identity, the conceptualization of competence, and language policy and practice beyond the conventional classroom context.

Another methodological innovation that was brought about in great part by the increasing focus on the learner is the development of language corpora. Indeed, corpus linguistics is often seen as a major contribution by applied linguists including not only those working with second language learning but also first language, monolingual as well as multilingual speakers. In terms of second language learning, corpus linguistics has demonstrated the complex and dynamic systems of the L2 learner's production. As for first language and multilingual speakers, corpus linguistics has provided much needed resources for the investigation of stylistic and genre differences, individual variations, cross-linguistic differences, and quantitative analyses.

Further diversification and consolidation of applied linguistics as a field of critical enquiry

For applied linguistics, the 1990s was a very significant decade. It not only saw further expansion of the range of topics applied linguists tried to address through their empirical and theoretical work, but also the beginning of critical self-reflections of the history and key achievements of applied linguistics in the previous decades, what it stood for and where the field would go in the new millennium. A number of historical accounts of applied linguistics in different parts of the world emerged (e.g. Catford, 1998; articles in Grabe, ed. 2000, and papers presented at the 2001 American Association of Applied Linguistics Colloquium on the Roots of Applied Linguistics in Different Contexts), and a new generation of introductory textbooks, a dictionary and several state-of-the-art handbooks were compiled (e.g. Davies, 1999; Pennycook, 2001; McCarthy, 2001; Schmitt, 2002; Cook, 2003; Johnson and Johnson, 1999; Davies and Elder, 2004; Kaplan, 2005). But more importantly perhaps were the exchanges between some of the leading researchers in the field debating over the identity and the directions of applied linguistics (Brumfit, 1997; Rampton, 1997; Widdowson, 2000; articles in the Applied Linguistics Association of Australia Newsletter, new series 44, 2001). These together give the field of Applied Linguistics a sense of maturity.

In terms of the scope of applied linguistics, researchers went well beyond their traditional territory – the language classroom – and started to investigate systematically and critically the multilingual workplace, new learning environments, new media and professional contexts. Many of the new research sites came to the attention of applied linguists because of the intensification of global migration and contacts between people of different linguistic and cultural backgrounds. The applied linguists' traditional focus on the language learner gradually expanded to the diversity of language user groups. Globalization and language contact also motivated some to raise questions of access to linguistic resources. Increasingly influenced by the work of social scientists such as Bourdieu, applied linguists argued, along with their colleagues in socio-linguistics, that language should be seen as a resource rather than purely as a system of abstract codes, and access to linguistic resources was affected by a variety of historical and political factors. Thus, a speaker's apparent lack of competence in a particular language may have nothing to do with his or her cognitive capacity but be the result of a lack of opportunity to learn and use the language in particular ways. Such issues manifest themselves not only in language teaching classrooms, but also in the workplace as well as health and legal contexts.

Increased contacts between people of different linguistic backgrounds, either through global migration or information and communication technology, also lead to situations where the majority of the participants in a communicative event are not native or first language speakers of the language being used. Beyond the practical issue of how the co-interactants cope with each other's different linguistic proficiencies in such situations, applied linguists have asked questions such as how a language is chosen to be the lingua franca; what political, economic and cultural reasons might there be for the choice of the lingua franca and for the different roles of different languages; are there language policies, explicit or implicit, at work; and what are the consequences of linguistic franca communication on the individuals' identity and self-confidence.

For all such questions, the increasingly mentalistic orientation of formal linguistics with its focus on the so-called I-language is seen by applied linguists as irrelevant. Applied linguistics has become a broad field of study of language learning and language use by different learner and user groups as well as wider social issues such as language planning, language ideology and language and social (dis)advantage. It is no longer focused on applying any specific linguistic theory or model, but on developing a critical perspective on language in everyday social life. Methodologically, applied linguistics has adopted a broad-based discourse analysis, complemented by multimodality analysis.

By the end of the twentieth century, applied linguistics had become a diverse, inter-disciplinary field. While language teaching and learning remained the core to applied linguistics, the actual focus shifted considerably. The acquisition and learning of specific domains of language, e.g. phonology, vocabulary, pragmatics, had become central issues for SLA, and teacher development, material and syllabus design had become core areas for TESOL and language education. What remained under the rubric of applied linguistics were descriptions of learner language, often with corpora; classroom discourse; motivation; learner strategy; content and task-based learning; and language testing. In the meantime, new areas were opened up for applied linguists to explore. For example, intercultural stereotype; intersections between translation and politics and law; media discourse, forensic linguistics, deaf studies, and language planning and language policy. Some of these areas have long and well-established histories. But a new generation of applied linguists joined the established researchers to raise new questions and develop new perspectives.

So, what are the major achievements of applied linguistics as a field of enquiry? We have seen different teaching methods come and go. All experienced language teaching professionals know that successful teaching depends very heavily on the match between the learner's needs and the teaching style. In the meantime, we know a great deal more about the language learning process, either by young children learning one or more languages from birth or adults learning additional languages later in life. We also know quite a lot about speech and language disorders, i.e. problems and difficulties in the language learning process, in some populations. Language acquisition and speech and language disorders are very lively fields. We will no doubt learn more about these processes with technological advances such as brain imaging. To me the key achievements of applied linguistics so far, which have helped to build the identity of the field, are:

- a critical reconceptualization of the native speaker and the language user;
- a critical reconceptualization of language in language learning and language use;
- a critical examination of issues of identity and competence in the context of language learning and use;
- a critical examination of language practices in real-life contexts, focusing particularly on how linguistic resources are manipulated by various agencies, e.g. the media, government, law.

The articles reprinted in this Reader will showcase these achievements. The Introductions to each part of the Reader will discuss the four themes in more detail.

Applied linguistics for the twenty-first century

Going back to the question posed to me by Ricardo Otheguy, which is really about the identity of applied linguistics especially in relation to linguistics, the field has moved a very long way from the earlier concerns with professional issues in language teaching and attempts to find solutions in structural linguistics to much broader social issues that are related to language learning and language use and a critical approach to such issues. The most widely accepted definition of applied linguistics nowadays is Brumfit's (1995: 27): 'The theoretical and empirical investigation of real-world problems in which language is a central issue.' Linguistics plays a minimal role in applied linguistics today, whether in terms of current linguistic theories or descriptive tools. Linguistic theories of the past twenty years are barely mentioned in training courses on applied linguistics. Contemporary applied linguists feel free to draw on almost any field of human knowledge, from psychological models such as declarative/procedural memory and emergentism, mathematical models such as dynamic systems theory or chaos theory and early Soviet theories of child development such as Vygotsky, to French thinkers such as Foucault and Bourdieu, feminist philosophy, and post-modernism. However, as Cook and Li Wei (2010) point out, the term 'problem' in Brumfit's definition raises two questions:

1   What is the nature of the problem, and whose problem is it anyway? In one sense the problem can be a research question posed in a particular discipline; in another sense it is something that has gone wrong which can be solved. Talking about the problem of multilingualism, say, is ambiguous between defining it as a research area and claiming that it is in some way defective. Calling areas 'problems' fosters the attitude that there is something wrong with them. Bilingualism is no more intrinsically a problem to be solved than is monolingualism. Applied linguists have to be clear that they are solving problems within an area of language acquisition or use, not regarding the area itself as a problem, except in the research question sense. Language teaching is not itself a problem to be solved; it may nevertheless raise problems that applied linguists can resolve.

2   In reality, what problems can applied linguists actually solve? If you are worried about your child's speech, you are more likely to go to a speech therapist than to an applied linguist. If your country is torn by civil war between people who use two scripts, you ask for a United Nations Peacekeeping Force. If you are drafting a new law, you go to a constitutional lawyer or a civil servant. The problem-solving successes of applied linguistics have included devising orthographies for languages that have no written form and inventing simplified languages for mariners; applied linguists have played a part in EU projects on translation and on linguistic diversity. But the most notable success of applied linguistics has to do with language teaching, such as the syllabuses and methods that swept the world from the 1970s onwards. Outside language teaching, applied linguists have taken important roles behind the scenes as advisors to diverse governmental and inter-governmental bodies. But they have had relatively little impact on public debate or decision-making for most language problems. The point is that problems are not solved by talking about them at applied linguistics conferences; the solutions have to be taken out into the world to the language users. Take the political correctness issue of avoiding certain terms for reasons of sexism, racism and so on. This is based on one inter-pretation of the relationship between language and thinking: not having a word means you cannot have the concept, as George Orwell suggested with Newspeak. Yet applied linguists have been reluctant to contribute their expertise to this debate, despite the extensive research into linguistic relativity of the past decade. Public discussion of language issues is as ill-informed about language as it was fifty years ago at the dawn of applied linguistics.

It seems important, therefore, to reassert the focus on language in applied linguistics. The unique selling point of applied linguistics that distinguishes it from the many domains and sub-domains of sociology, economics, politics, law, management and neuroscience has to be language. At its core applied linguistics needs a coherent theory of language, whether this comes from linguistics or from some other discipline, a set of rigorous descriptive tools to handle language, and a body of research relevant to language practice. This is not to say that the language element has to dominate or that a particular linguistics theory or model has to feature. But it does not count as applied linguistics:

1   *If there is no language element.* Many of the concerns applied linguists have are also concerns of sociologists, neuroscientists and other professional researchers. Crucially, however, applied linguists focus on the role of language in the broad issues of sociological or neurological concern. Why call it applied linguistics if it has no language content?
2   *If the language elements are handled without any theory of language.* The theory of language does not need to come from linguistics but might be philosophy, history, social theory or literary theory. Yet applied linguistics cannot treat language as if there were no traditions of language study whatsoever. Nor can the language elements be based solely on folk ideas from the school tradition of grammar or the practical EFL teaching tradition, which would be rather like basing physics on folk beliefs or alchemy. Indeed, one of the responsibilities of the applied linguist should be to challenge both the folk notions of language and grammar and the theoretical linguists' models of how language works.
3   *If the research base is neither directly concerned with language issues nor related to them in a demonstrable way.* That is to say, a theory from other disciplines cannot be applied without a clear chain showing how and why it is relevant. An idea from mathematical theory, computer simulation or the neural network needs to show its credentials by proving a/the

practical solution of real-life language problems (e.g. how bilingual speakers with aphasia process sentences), not by imposing itself by fiat, by analogy, or by sheer computer modelling. This is an area where there is huge potential for further development, as more and more applied linguists become attracted by theories and ideas from other disciplines.

Over the last two decades, there have been a number of attempts to reconceptualize applied linguistics as part of social science (e.g. Brumfit, 1997; Rampton, 2000; and most explicitly, Sealey and Carter, 2004). What this means essentially is to view language practices, including language teaching and learning, language planning, language testing, etc., as social practices and empirical analysis of social practices as social science. Along with some of their sociolinguist colleagues, applied linguists have borrowed theories and approaches from sociologists such as Durkheim, Parsons and Levi-Strauss, as well as Bourdieu and Giddens, and highlighted the differential distributions of linguistic resources in society. One outcome of such work is an increased awareness among applied linguists that failure to achieve a certain standard in second and additional language learning, for example, is not simply a linguistic or psychological matter but a much broader socio-political issue. Different (varieties of) languages carry different historical and cultural meanings to different groups of people, resulting in different attitudes towards the learning and use of the languages in specific contexts. Learners' apparent difficulties in learning certain languages may well be due to their deliberate rejection of the socio-cultural values the languages represent.

Nevertheless, the social science perspective on applied linguistics has had disappointingly little impact on the broad field that it aspires to be part of. An admirable exception is perhaps Critical Discourse Analysis (CDA), where some of the language it uses has been taken up by generic social scientists who are interested in social change. One could say, of course, that much of the social science research is critical analyses of public discourses. But the question remains as to how applied linguists can have their work taken more seriously at both theoretical and practical levels by social scientists generally, rather than having it seen as providing empirical support for existing models or policies on a limited scale.

There are a number of possible ways forward: one is to come up with some alternative theories of society and social structures. This would, however, risk endangering the future of applied linguistics as a discipline, as language does not have to feature at all in theories of society and social structures. Applied linguistics would then submerge under any other branch of social science. Alternatively one could argue that language is integral, even essential, to everything in society. Language is certainly a critical part of the social life of individual members of society. There is no doubt that applied linguists can make a major contribution to social science by focusing on how members of society use the social resources, which include languages that are available to them to create, maintain and change social relationships and social structures.

Perhaps the most important way forward for applied linguistics is the development of a multi-strategy approach in applied linguistic research methods (see also, Sealey and Carter, 2004). I am not talking here about the combination of what might be called qualitative and quantitative methods, or the macro and the micro analysis. We need an approach that goes beyond the traditional dichotomies, that is critical of existing theories and models including existing theories of language and of society; and that sees the social world as stratified and social phenomena as related to one another in complex ways. In other words, applied linguistics research needs to develop further its critical perspective and establish itself as a field of critical enquiry with a focus on language in the real world.

References

Brumfit, Christopher, 1995, Teacher professionalism and research. In G. Cook and B. Seidlhofer (eds), *Principle and Practice in Applied Linguistics*. Oxford University Press, pp. 27–42

Brumfit, Christopher, 1997, How applied linguistics is the same as any other science. *International Journal of Applied Linguistics*, 7(1): 86–94

Catford, John, 1998, Language learning and applied linguistics: a historical sketch. *Language Learning*, 48(4): 465–496

Chomsky, Noam, 1964, *Current Issues in Linguistic Theory*. The Hague: Mouton

Chomsky, Noam, 1965, *Aspects of the Theory of Syntax*. Cambridge, MA: MIT Press

Chomsky, Noam, 1976, On the nature of language. In S. R. Harnad, H. D. Steklis and J. Lancaster (eds), *Origins and Evolution of Language and Speech*. Annals of the New York Academy of Sciences, Volume 280, pp. 46–57

Chomsky, Noam, 1986, *Knowledge of Language*. New York: Praeger

Cook, Guy, 2003, *Applied Linguistics*. Oxford: Oxford University Press

Cook, Vivian, 1991, The poverty-of-the-stimulus argument and multi-competence. *Second Language Research*, 7(2), 103–117

Cook, Vivian, 1992, Evidence for multi-competence. *Language Learning*, 42(4): 557–591

Cook, Vivian, 1993, *Linguistics and Second Language Acquisition*. Basingstoke: Macmillan

Cook, Vivian, 1999, Going beyond the native speaker in language teaching. *TESOL Quarterly*, 33(2): 185–209

Cook, Vivian, 2007, Multi-competence: black hole or wormhole for Second Language Acquisition research? In Han, Z-H (ed.), *Understanding Second Language Process*. Clevedon: Multilingual Matters, pp. 16–26

Cook, Vivian and Li Wei (eds), 2010, *Contemporary Applied Linguistics*, Volume 1, *Language Teaching and Learning*, Volume 2, *Linguistics for the Real World*. London: Continuum

Coulthard, Malcolm and Montgomery, Martin (eds), 1981, *Studies in Discourse Analysis*. London: Routledge

Davies, Alan, 1999, *An Introduction to Applied Linguistics: from practice to theory*. Edinburgh: Edinburgh University Press

Davies, A., 2003, *The Native Speaker: myth and reality*. Clevedon, UK: Multilingual Matters

Davies, Alan and Elder, Catherine (eds), 2004, *Handbook of Applied Linguistics*. Oxford/Malden, MA: Blackwell

Grabe, William (ed.), 2000, Applied Linguistics as an emerging discipline. *Annual Review of Applied Linguistics*, Volume 2

Halliday, M.A.K., 1973, *Explorations in the Functions of Language*. London: Edward Arnold

Hymes, Dell, 1966, Two types of linguistic relativity. In W. Bright (ed.), *Sociolinguistics*. The Hague: Mouton, pp. 114–158

Hymes, Dell, 1971, *On Communicative Competence*. Philadelphia: University of Pennsylvania Press

Johnson, Keith and Johnson, Helen, 1999, *Encyclopedic Dictionary of Applied Linguistics*. Oxford: Blackwell

Kaplan, Robert, 2005, *The Oxford Handbook of Applied Linguistics*. Oxford: Oxford University Press

McCarthy, Michael, 2001, *Issues in Applied Linguistics*. Cambridge: Cambridge University Press

Nunan, David, 1988, *The Learner-Centred Curriculum*. Cambridge: Cambridge University Press

Nunan, David, 1991, *Language Teaching Methodology*. New York: Prentice Hall

Pennycook, Alastair, 2001, *Critical Applied Linguistics: a critical introduction*. London: Lawrence Erlbaum Associates

Rampton, Ben, 1997, Retuning in applied linguistics? *International Journal of Applied Linguistics*, 7(1): 3–25

Rampton, Ben, 2000, Continuity and change in views of society in applied linguistics. In H. Trappes-Lomax (ed.), *Change and Continuity in Applied Linguistics*. Clevedon: Multilingual Matters, pp. 97–114

Schmitt, Norbert, 2002, *An Introduction to Applied Linguistics*, London: Arnold

Sealey, Alison, and Carter, Bob, 2004, *Applied Linguistics as Social Science*. London: Continuum

Selinker, Larry, 1972, Interlanguage. *IRAL – International Review of Applied Linguistics in Language Teaching*, 10: 209–232

Selinker, Larry, 1992, *Rediscovering Interlanguage*. Harlow: Longman

Sinclair, John and Brazil, David, 1982, *Teacher Talk*. Oxford University Press

Sinclair, John and Coulthard, Malcolm, 1975, *Towards an Analysis of Discourse*. Oxford: Oxford University Press

Sinclair, John and Coulthard, Malcolm, 1992, Toward an analysis of discourse. In M. Coulthard (ed.), *Advances in Spoken Discourse Analysis*. Routledge, pp. 1–34

Widdowson, Henry, 2000, On the limitations of linguistics applied. *Applied Linguistics*, 21(1): 3–25

NOTES FOR STUDENTS AND INSTRUCTORS

Study questions

1 What is the learner-centred curriculum? What are the basic principles of a learner-centred approach to language teaching?
2 What does Vivian Cook (1999) refer to when he talks about the 'comparative fallacy'? And why do you think it is a fallacy?
3 What are the key differences between linguistics applied and applied linguistics according to Alan Davies (e.g. 1999; Davies and Elder, 2004)?
4 What are the topics recent articles in *Applied Linguistics* and *International Journal of Applied Linguistics* deal with? What theories and models outside linguistics have been applied in these studies?
5 What core issues does critical applied linguistics aim to address (Pennycook, 2001)?

Study activities

1 Pick a recent newspaper or magazine and find one article that either talks about a language or language-related problem. What is the problem? To whom is it a problem? How can descriptive linguistics help? To what extent is the problem also related to historical, political, cultural and policy issues?
2 Reflecting on your own language learning or teaching experience, how much did linguistics help you? Were there any issues for which you had to go to other disciplines such as psychology, sociology, cultural studies, to find possible solutions or ideas and inspirations? What are these disciplines?
3 Keep a diary for a week and see how many events you have experienced are related to language and communication issues. What are the issues? Are there practical solutions to any of them? What research questions can be formulated about the issues for further investigation?

Further reading

Davies, Alan, 1999, *An Introduction to Applied Linguistics: from practice to theory*, Edinburgh: Edinburgh University Press, surveys the history and definitions of the field and discusses issues such as applied linguistics and language learning and teaching, applied linguistics and language use, and the professionalising of applied linguistics.

Cook, Guy, 2003, *Applied Linguistics,* Oxford: Oxford University Press, is a concise but comprehensive overview of the central issues in applied linguistics.

McCarthy, Michael, 2001, *Issues in Applied Linguistics*, Cambridge: Cambridge University Press, outlines the historical roots of the field and its major developments over the years. It also examines issues such as language modelling and the analysis of discourse.

Schmitt, Norbert (ed.), 2010, *An Introduction to Applied Linguistics*, second edition, London: Hodder Education, provides a comprehensive survey of the key topics in applied linguistics. It contains three parts, focusing on the description of language and language use, essential areas of enquiry in applied linguistics, and language skills and assessment.

Hunston, Susan and Oakey, David, 2009, *Introducing Applied Linguistics: concepts and skills*, Oxford: Routledge, is a short, introductory text that introduces students to the key concepts faced when studying applied linguistics, as well as the study skills needed for academic reading and writing.

Pennycook, Alastair, 2001, *Critical Applied Linguistics: a critical introduction*, Mahwah, NJ: Lawrence Erlbaum Associates, discusses an alternative approach to critical questions in language education, literacy, discourse analysis and language in the workplace, translation and other language-related domains.

Sealey, Alison and Carter, Bob, 2004, *Applied Linguistics as Social Science*, London: Continuum, shows how social theory and applied linguistics share common concerns and argues that a social scientific account of applied linguistics is needed to explain the interaction between social structures, human agents and language.

Cooke, Melanie and Simpson, James, 2008, *ESL: a critical guide*, Oxford: Oxford University Press, is aimed at English language teachers and teacher-educators who wish to extend their understanding of the issues and debates surrounding English for speakers of other languages (ESOL) in an age of globalization and mass migration.

Seidlhofer, Barbara (ed.), 2003, *Controversies in Applied Linguistics*, Oxford: Oxford University Press, reprints the exchanges between some of the leading applied linguists on controversial issues, such as the global spread of English, corpus linguistics and language teaching, Critical Discourse Analysis, second language acquisition and the nature of applied linguistics.

Cook, Vivian and Li Wei (eds), 2010, *Contemporary Applied Linguistics*, Volume 1 *Language Teaching and Learning*, Volume 2 *Linguistics for the Real World*, London: Continuum, consist of twenty-four introductory chapters, showcasing cutting edge research in applied linguistics. The contributors in the first volume present current research in areas such as multilingualism, language education, teacher-learner relationships and assessment. Chapters in volume 2 present an overview of new and interdisciplinary fields such as language and economics, language and the law, language and religion, language and tourism, language and the media, and language and health.

Two handbooks provide comprehensive and in-depth surveys of the field:

Davies, A. and Elder, C. (eds), 2004, *Handbook of Applied Linguistics*, Oxford: Blackwell.
Kaplan, Robert, 2010, *The Oxford Handbook of Applied Linguistics*, second edition, Oxford: Oxford University Press.

Other useful references include:

Johnson, Keith and Johnson, Helen (eds), 1999, *Encyclopedic Dictionary of Applied Linguistics*, Oxford: Blackwell.
Davies, Alan, 2005, *A Glossary of Applied Linguistics*, second edition, Edinburgh: Edinburgh University Press.
Richards, Jack and Schmidt, Richard (eds), 2010, *Longman Dictionary of Language Teaching and Applied Linguistics*, fourth edition, Harlow: Longman.
Spolsky, Bernard and Hult, Francis M., 2007, *Handbook of Educational Linguistics,* Oxford: Blackwell.

PART I

Reconceptualizing the native speaker and the language learner

Introduction

AS WE DISCUSSED in the General Introduction, language teaching and learning have been the main concern of applied linguistics from the very beginning till this day. And one of the key assumptions in language teaching and learning has been the existence of a native speaker who acts as the model for the learners. The language produced by the native speaker is the standard norm, which the teacher will teach and the learner will learn. Until the 1980s, rarely did applied linguists and language teaching professionals question the notion of the native speaker or the norm that the native speaker supposedly produced. But who is the native speaker? And what kind of language does the native speaker actually produce?

Sociolinguists often remind us, with their research evidence, that:

- No-one is born to speak a standard language. First language acquisition takes place first and foremost in informal settings, and young children are exposed to informal and non-standard language most of the time. Standard languages are artificial constructions, and they are usually learned through formal instructions in institutional contexts.
- No-one speaks one single language style all the time. As part of their communicative competence, speakers adapt their language according to who they are talking to, what the setting is and what they are talking about.

The notion of the native speaker in applied linguistics is in fact an ideological construct. It has no linguist or psychological reality. It has had a divisive effect in that native-speaker teachers are often assumed to represent a Western culture from which spring the ideals both of the language, especially English, and of language teaching methodology (Holliday, 2006). The language learner by implication is put in a position where he or she is expected to follow the native speaker's model. Their own linguistic knowledge and resources are often made irrelevant, even counter-productive.

One of the key achievements of applied linguistics is the critique of the concept of the native speaker, as the articles in this part of the Reader demonstrate. In unpicking the ideological underpinnings and the implications of the concept for the characterisation of the language learner, the critique simultaneously raises our awareness of the diversity of language users.

This part opens with an article by Alan Davies, who has been a leading critic of the concept of the native speaker. His article provides a comprehensive and critical survey of the various interpretations of the concept. It begins with the issue of the native speaker as identity. After considering the different definitions of the concept by other researchers, Davies examines the relation between the native speaker and the non-native speaker, and raises the question of whether a second or foreign language learner who starts learning after puberty can become a native speaker of the target language. This brings us back to the issue of identity, and Davies considers four ways of coping with the issue of loss of identity as a native speaker. He concludes that the native speaker concept is both myth and reality, both metaphor and embodiment of the language-parole and of the competence-performance distinctions, and therefore lies at the heart of applied linguistics.

Chapter 2 by Constant Leung, Roxy Harris and Ben Rampton is a much cited article that questions the relevance of the notion of the native speaker in English as a Second Language (ESL) teaching. Drawing directly from examples of TESOL classrooms in urban schools in England, the authors challenge what they see as an idealised and neat one-to-one correspondence between ethnicity and language which tends to conceptualise L2 learners as a linguistically diverse group but with similar language learning needs. As they point out, demographic and social changes, particularly in the past three decades, have rendered such correspondence and conceptualisation inadequate and misleading, especially in multi-ethnic urban settings. They argue that the linguistic profile and language learning needs of ESL students in contemporary multilingual schools are not easily understood in terms of fixed concepts of ethnicity and language. Adopting a critical cultural studies perspective and focusing on the shifting and changing relationship among ethnicity, social identity and language use in the context of the postcolonial diaspora, the authors urge applied linguists and language teaching professionals to ask questions about language expertise, language inheritance and language affiliation.

The existence of the notion of the native speaker automatically entails an othering of groups of language users who are somehow judged to be non-native. There is a group of language users whose identity may be ambiguous in this native-speaker and non-native-speaker (NS-NNS) dichotomy, namely, speakers of distinctive varieties of a language: for example, Indian, Malaysian and Singaporean speakers of English. Their English is often considered non-native; yet many of them are brought up speaking it as their primary language that they have been using from birth. Christina Higgins in Chapter 3 addresses the issue of the linguistic classification of English speakers from the so-called outer-circle countries (Kachru, 1986), its implications for policy and practice in language learning. Using an acceptability judgment test, she provides evidence that demonstrates variations among both the outer-circle and inner-circle users of English and similarities across the two groups. She interprets the findings in terms of *ownership*, that is, the degree to which the language user projects him or herself as a legitimate speaker with authority over the language, which she argues is a better alternative to the NS-NNS dichotomy.

Chapter 4 by Enric Llurda turns the attention to non-native-speaker teachers and their role in the context of the global need for English language education. This is a review article of relevant literature on teaching English as an international language (EIL). The author argues that there is an increasing appreciation of non-native-speaker teachers, both in English as a second language (ESL) and in English as a foreign language (EFL) contexts. This, together with the growing interest in EIL, creates the right conditions for the gradual acceptance of English as a lingua franca (ELF). One of the consequences of the acceptance of ELF is a decrease in the role of native-speaker teachers in setting the principles and norms on which the lingua franca is taught.

This part concludes with Vivian Cook's well-known position paper on the nature of the L2 user. Cook raises three key questions:

1   Who are the second language users?
2   What is the language they know?
3   What is the community they belong to?

Approaching the questions from the multicompetence perspective (e.g. Cook, 1992), Cook argues that the so-called L2 users are a highly diverse group, whose language ranges from developing to relatively static to reducing. He discusses five meanings of *language*: as a human representational system, as an institutional object, as a set of sentences, as a community possession, and as an individual possession. He argues that the language systems of the individual and of the community need to be treated as a whole. L2 users belong to diverse communities of their own, both local and global. Applied linguists need to explore the nature of these communities rather than assuming that L2 users wish to be part of native monolingual communities.

References

Cook, Vivian, 1992, Evidence for multi-competence, *Language Learning*, 42(4): 557–591
Holliday, Adrian, 2006, Native-speakerism, *ELT Journal*, 60(4): 385–387
Kachru, Braj, 1986, *The Alchemy of English: the spread, functions, and models of non-native Englishes*. Urbana: University of Illinois Press

Chapter 1

ALAN DAVIES

THE NATIVE SPEAKER IN APPLIED LINGUISTICS (2004)

Introduction

IN **THIS CHAPTER**, I discuss the role of the native speaker in applied linguistics and set out the different interpretations of the concept. I begin with the issue of the native speaker as identity; then I consider various definitions of the concept. I then examine the relation between the native speaker and the non-native speaker and raise the question of whether a second or foreign language learner who starts learning after puberty can become a native speaker of the target language. This brings us back to the issue of identity: I consider four ways of coping with the issue of loss of identity as a native speaker. I conclude that the native speaker concept remains ambiguous, necessarily so, since it is both myth and reality.

Native speaker as identity

The concept of native speaker occupies a curious position in applied linguistics. On the one hand it is widely used as a benchmark for knowledge of a language (and as such attracts opposition because it excludes those who are not native speakers), and as a criterion for employment; on the other hand a definition of the native speaker is elusive. How useful is the concept of native speaker to applied linguistics? That is the theme of this chapter.

Ferguson comments: "Linguists . . . have long given a special place to the native speaker as the only true and reliable source of language data" (Ferguson, 1983, p. vii). He continues:

> much of the world's verbal communication takes place by means of languages which are not the users' mother tongue, but their second, third or nth language, acquired one way or another and used when appropriate. This kind of language use merits the attention of linguists as much as do the more traditional objects of their research.
>
> (p. vii)

This is a plea from sociolinguistics. But is Ferguson right to conclude as follows: "In fact the whole mystique of native speaker and mother tongue should preferably be quietly dropped from the linguist's set of professional myths about language" (p. vii). As my discussion shows, there is no doubt about the myth-like properties of the native speaker idea. The question remains, however, of whether it is also a reality. I attempt to answer that question.

Theoretically, as we shall see, the native speaker concept is rich in ambiguity. It raises, quite centrally, the issue of the relation between the particular and the universal. Chomsky, as a protagonist of the universalist position, conveys to Paikeday's questioning approach about the status of the native speaker (Paikeday, 1985) the strongest possible sense of the genetic determinants of speech acquisition which, as he sees it, must mean that to be human is to be a native speaker.

What Chomsky does is to equate language development with other normal human development, finding no value in questions about developmental states or stages which he regards as contingent and essentially of no theoretical interest. In the same vein Chomsky finds distinctions between synchronic states of language or languages and dialects uninteresting, "the question of what are the 'languages' or 'dialects' attained, and what is the difference between 'native' and 'non-native' is just pointless" (Chomsky quoted in Paikeday, 1985, p. 57). Chomsky's whole argument depends on a rationalist opposition to "incorrect metaphysical assumptions: in particular the assumption that among the things in the world there are languages or dialects, and that individuals come to acquire them" (Paikeday, 1985, p. 49). This is the argument from psycholinguistics (or cognitive linguistics).

And so Chomsky must conclude that "everyone is a Native Speaker of the particular language states that the person has 'grown' in his/her mind/brain." In the real world, that is all there is to say" (p. 58). Chomsky's view is uninfluenced by any social factor or contextual constraint. Variety and context; he seems to argue, are trivial. This is a thoroughgoing unitary competence view of language in which language use is contingent and the native speaker is only a realization of that competence at a linguistic and not a language-specific level. For Chomsky, like many theoretical linguists, is not interested in languages: what he studies is language.

For our present purpose, however, we note that Chomsky does in fact acknowledge the real individual, living, as he says, in the real world, whose speech repertoire is multiple. His view may take no account of social or sociolinguistic analysis or parameters, but he is not unaware that the real world consists of complex variation. Our concern in this chapter is to explore the real-world parameters of the native speaker since it is there that applied linguistics has its role.

The native speaker/non-native speaker distinction is hardly as dramatic as the difference between the sexes; and it does not contain the crucial genetic difference. If we accept the model of Universal Grammar (UG), different languages are the same language (or set of principles) but with different parameter settings. From this point of view it has been maintained that languages differ essentially in terms of vocabulary. I can express the argument as follows. A child draws on UG to construct his/her first language (L1) on the basis of input from parents or other caretakers using their L1. The child is then in time socialized into a standard language (see below). Parameters are set and reset at all points. The same procedure is said to apply to the second language (L2) learner, who first regresses to UG and then adds or exchanges one L1 for another L1 through resetting of parameters.

A child may be a native speaker of more than one language as long as the acquisition process starts early and necessarily prepuberty. After puberty (Felix, 1987), it becomes difficult—not impossible, but very difficult (Birdsong, 1992)—to become a native speaker. Unlike male/female differences, native speaker/non-native speaker differences are not innate but learnt, but the learning is so well imprinted that the "membership" it bestows is real and fixed. What this means is that the concept of the native speaker is not a fiction, but has the reality that "membership," however informal, always gives. The native speaker is relied on to know what the score is, how things are done, because she/he carries the tradition, is the repository of "the language." The native speaker is also expected to exhibit normal control especially in fluent connected speech (though in writing only after long schooling), and to have command of expected characteristic strategies of performance and of communication. A native speaker is also expected to "know" another native speaker, in part because of an intuitive feel, like for like, but also in part because of a characteristic systematic set of indicators, linguistic, pragmatic, and paralinguistic, as well as an assumption of shared cultural knowledge.

The native speaker, who remains a learner of new words and new registers (not to mention additional languages) and who is able to balance that role with the proper authority role necessarily attained, can only be a valued resource for others. McCawley (1986) notes the difference between the native and the non-native speaker as learner since the native speaker has to combine being also the authority. Indeed, we might hazard that a non-native speaker can claim that they have achieved the steady state of being a native speaker in the second language when they are prepared to accept the fragility of the knowledge they have so carefully acquired, acknowledging that there is always more to learn. Adulthood as a native speaker is no different from being an adult in any other field.

By remaining a learner, the native speaker gains access to the standard language. Note that it is membership of the group of native speakers that determines behaviour; in this case, adoption of the standard language, rather than the other way round of behaviour determining membership. And it is membership as a native speaker that determines the choice of the code to be used in an encounter, including the standard language.

Such a stress on identity relates this view of the native speaker to the work in social identity theory of Henri Tajfel. His comment on the typical majority-minority situation is relevant: "minorities are often defined on the basis of criteria originating from, and developed by, the majorities. They are different from something which, itself, need not be clearly defined" (Tajfel, 1981, p. 317). There is a relief in this saving comment that allows us to admit that a failure to define the native speaker may indicate that, like other majorities, native speakers define themselves negatively as not being non-native speakers. To be a native speaker means not being a non-native speaker. Such a conclusion reminds us of the central importance to all discussions of language behaviour of the non-native speaker. Before we consider the non-native speaker, what is it we know about the native speaker?

Definitions of the native speaker

Let us rehearse what seems to be agreed about the native speaker:

- Everyone is a native speaker of his/her own unique code: this allows us to reject as illogical the notion of semilingualism (Martin-Jones & Romaine, 1986).
- Everyone accepts and adheres to the norms of a standard language either an informal (standard) language, which might be a dialect, or a codified standard (typically called a language). The relation between informal (standard) languages and a codified standard is that the codified standard is flexible enough to permit a good deal of tolerance to the informal (standard) language(s), except in situations where for extraneous cultural or political or religious reasons there is norm conflict leading to misunderstandings and refusal to communicate. Examples of informal (standard) languages might be Singapore English and Newfoundland English.
- Those near what Bartsch (1988) called the "point," that is the centre or model of the standard language, are favored and advantaged. They suffer less from insecurity, are less likely to

practice hypercorrection, and above all have less of a learning problem in using the standard language for public purposes (for example in education) because their home language use is nearer to the standard language. Meanwhile those near the extremes are disfavored and disadvantaged, they are more likely to feel insecure and to have their version of the standard language stigmatized, as well as to stigmatize it themselves. In public uses (such as education) they have more of a learning problem. It is possible (though this is quite unclear) that they may also have a cognitive problem because they have learnt to think in their own variety of the standard language, a difficulty compounded by possible lack of intelligibility of input by teachers whose standard language may be nearer the point. Nevertheless, this is the situation of social life and of a non-homogeneous community and it is possible, if difficult, for those disadvantaged initially by their own L1 to accumulate and later gain full access to a more central version.

- Native speakers all do indeed have intuitions about their standard language, but in those cases where there is tolerance but flexibility it is likely that their knowledge of and performance in those norms will be shaky. And where they are uncertain they will guess, or admit ignorance, or fall back on some basic UG principle. What this means is that intuitions are learnt not innate: the grammar of the standard language is not built into the head of the child any more than is the grammar of his/her own individual idiolectal version of the standard language.
- All native speakers have access to some kind of language faculty, which may be called UG and which has to operate at a very high level of abstraction. The apparent polar arguments seeking to explain acquisition, whereby the learner moves across from an L1 (some version of the old contrastive analysis model) or regresses to the primary UG state and then moves forward again into an L2, are in a serious sense non-arguments since both must be true. Since the L1 grammar is a version of UG and underlying it is UG, then it is a matter of generative arrangement how I draw the connection between L1 and L2 since UG must occur there somewhere.

The native speaker (and this means all native speakers) may be defined in the following six ways (Davies, 1991, 2003):

1   The native speaker acquires the L1 of which she/he is a native speaker in childhood.
2   The native speaker has intuitions (in terms of acceptability and productiveness) about his/her idiolectal grammar.
3   The native speaker has intuitions about those features of the standard language grammar which are distinct from his/her idiolectal grammar.
4   The native speaker has a unique capacity to produce fluent spontaneous discourse, which exhibits pauses mainly at clause boundaries (the "one clause at a time" facility) and which is facilitated by a huge memory stock of complete lexical items (Pawley & Syder, 1983). In both production and comprehension the native speaker exhibits a wide range of communicative competence.
5   The native speaker has a unique capacity to write creatively (and this includes, of course, literature at all levels from jokes to epics, metaphor to novels).
6   The native speaker has a unique capacity to interpret and translate into the L1 of which she/he is a native speaker. Disagreements about the deployment of an individual's capacity are likely to stem from a dispute about the standard or (standard) language.

Native speaker or native speaker-like?

To what extent can the L2 learner become a target language native speaker? We will consider this question in relation to L2 learners in general. Let us again consider the six criteria listed above:

1   *Childhood acquisition.*   No, the second language learner does not acquire the target language in early childhood. If she/he does, then she/he is a native speaker of both L1 and the target language (TL), or in her/his case of L1x and L1y; that is, she/he is a bilingual native speaker.

2   *Intuitions about idiolectal grammar.*   Yes, it must be possible, with sufficient contact and practice, for the second language learner to gain access to intuitions about his/her own idiolectal grammar of the target language (although, as I will show, this makes an important assumption about criterion 1, childhood acquisition).

3   *Intuitions about the standard language grammar.*   Yes again, with sufficient contact and practice the second language learner can gain access to the standard grammar of the target language. Indeed in many formal learning situations it is exactly through exposure to a target language standard grammar that the target language idiolectal grammar would emerge, the reverse of L1 development.

4   *Discourse and pragmatic control.*   In practice it is very difficult for a non-native speaker to gain the discourse and pragmatic control of a native speaker; difficult but not impossible in special cases.

5   *Creative performance.*   Yes again, with practice it must be possible for a second language learner to become an accepted creative artist in the target language. Among writers, there are of course well-known examples of such cases—Conrad, Becket, Senghor, Narayan. There is also the interesting problem of the acceptability to the L1 community of the second language learner's creative writing; this is an attitudinal issue, but so too is the question of the acceptability to the same community of a creative writer writing not in the standard language but in a non-codified (standard) language, e.g., Scots. Equally in doubt is the acceptability of a standard variety of a language to readers from other standard varieties: too American or too Australian, a Brit might say; and, of course, the reverse.

6   *Interpreting and translating.*   Yes again, this must be possible although international organizations generally require that interpreters should interpret into their L1. (It remains, of course, unclear what judgments are made of an applicant for an interpreter's post; no doubt proficiency tests are carried out, but it might be difficult to deny the claim of an applicant that she/he is a native speaker.)

All except (1) are contingent issues. In that way the question: Can a second language learner become a native speaker of a target language? reduces to: Is it necessary to acquire a code in early childhood in order to be a native speaker of that code? Now the answer to that question, and this is where the circularity lies, is to ask a further question: What is it that the child acquires in acquiring his/her L1? But I have already answered that question in my criteria (2)–(6) above, and so the question again becomes a contingent one.

We need in (2) and (3) above to ensure a cultural dimension since the child L1 acquirer has access to the resources of the culture attached to the language and particularly to those learnt and encoded or even imprinted early. The post-puberty second language learner does not have this experience, which puts a question mark against my assertion about gaining access to intuitions about the idiolectal grammar if those intuitions lack a childhood cultural component. Still, having said that, what of sub-cultural differences between, far example, the Scots and the

English; of different cultures with the same standard language (for example the Swiss, the Austrians, the West Germans, and the East Germans); or of different cultures with different standard languages (for example the British and the American)? What too of International English and of an isolated L1 in a multilingual setting (for example Indian English)?

Given the interlingual differences and the lack of agreement on norms that certainly occur among such groups it does appear that the post-pubertal second language learner has a difficult but not an impossible task to become a native speaker of a target language which can contain such wide diversities. The answer to the question of whether L2 learners can evolve into native speakers of the target language must therefore be, "Yes": but the practice required, given the model of the child L1 acquirer who for five to six years spends much of his/her time learning language alone, is so great that it is not likely that many post-pubertal second language learners ever become native speakers of their target language. The analogy that occurs to me here is that of music, where it is possible to become a concert performer after a late start but the reality is that few do. The more exact analogy of learning to play the piano as a child and switching to, say, the cello later on is common and is perhaps more relevant.

Coppieters' empirical investigation (Coppieters, 1987) into the differences between native speakers of French and advanced learners of French in grammatical judgments produced results which indicated a significant difference between the two groups: She concluded that the difference between native speakers and non-native speakers repeats the elaborated/restricted code difference which Bernstein (1971–5) reported and with the same implication. For what holds back the non-native speaker (like the speaker of a restricted code) is the early acquired generalizing capacity.

It is difficult for an adult non-native speaker to become a native speaker of a second language precisely because I define a native speaker as a person who has early acquired the language. However, the limitations imposed by the later acquisition, when it is very successful, are likely to be psycholinguistic rather than sociolinguistic. The adult non-native speaker can acquire the communicative competence of the native speaker; she/he can acquire the confidence necessary to membership. Leaving aside the matter of accentual difference, what is more difficult for the non-native speaker is to gain the speed and the certainty of knowledge relevant to judgments of grammaticality. But as with all questions of boundaries (for the native speaker is a boundary that excludes), there are major language differences among native speakers. Native speakers may be prepared to make judgments quickly about grammaticality but they do not necessarily agree with one another. And so I am left asking to what extent it matters. If a non-native speaker wishes to pass as a native speaker and is so accepted, then it is surely irrelevant if she/he shows differences on more and more refined tests of grammaticality. That may be of interest psycholinguistically, but for applied linguistic purposes I maintain that it is unimportant.

The differing positions of the psycholinguistic and the sociolinguistic are probably irreconcilable. For the psycholinguist no test is ever sufficient to demonstrate conclusively that native speakers and non-native speakers are distinct: once non-native speakers have been shown to perform as well as native speakers on a test, the cry goes up for yet another test. For the sociolinguist there is always another (more) exceptional learner who will, when found, demonstrate that (exceptional) non-native speakers can be equated to native speakers on ultimate attainment. The problem is that we cannot finally and absolutely distinguish non-native speakers from native speakers except by autobiography. So Cook (1999) is right to make a strong case for the native/non-native speaker distinction being one above all of biography. However, making the cut by biography shows only some problems and hides away the exceptions, the bilinguals, the movers away, the disabled intellectually, the exceptional learners. The fact is that mother tongue is not gender, it is not a given from the womb. It is, classically, social, just as culture is.

We cannot distinguish between native speakers and non-native speakers because our premises are inherently flawed, as Hyltenstam and Abrahamsson (2000) point out, since there are different views of what being a native speaker means. They include:

1   native speaker by birth (that is by early childhood exposure),
2   native speaker by virtue of being a native user,
3   native speaker (or native speaker-like) by being an exceptional learner,
4   native speaker through education in the target language medium,
5   native speaker through long residence in the adopted country.

What is at issue is whether claiming to be a native speaker, to "own" the language, requires early childhood exposure. Let us consider this issue of ownership with regard to English.

Losing a native speaker identity

The global expansion of English in the twentieth century has been widely discussed and analyzed (Crystal, 1997; Holborow, 1999; Graddol, 1999). It has been seen in both a favourable and in a critical light. Those who regard the expansion favourably (Fishman, Cooper & Conrad, 1975; MacArthur, 1999) comment on the empowering role of English, the values of openness it brings, the access it provides both to knowledge and to markets. Those who regard the expansion negatively discuss the hegemonizing of the weak by the strong, the ways in which English is used by the powerful west and their allies to dominate through globalization, much as they dominate through economic and military means. They also point to the loss of choice, first linguistic, and then, inevitably it is suggested, cultural. What the spread of English does, it is argued (Phillipson, 1992), is to squeeze other languages into less and less central roles, eroding their functions until eventually they are marginalized to the private and the home and finally lost. That, it is suggested, is what is happening in a society such as Singapore where English is now the only school medium of instruction for all Singaporeans. It is what has already happened in Guyana. And this destruction of the local languages is not confined to the Third World, to poor countries which do not have the resources at hand to combat the rise of English. It applies equally to the developed world, where it remains for the present possible to operate a language policy of the local language plus English in countries such as Denmark, the Netherlands, Sweden. Such countries are often held up as models of successful language learning and teaching: successful because they succeed in acquiring the foreign language, English, and becoming proficient in it while at the same time not losing their first language, Danish, Swedish, Dutch, and so on. But the picture of easy (and stable) bilingualism in these western countries is queried by observers such as van Els (2000), who take the view that English in these settings could well be the cuckoo in the European nest, meaning that in another couple of generations, these local languages could be in terminal decline. That, of course, is the problem with the argument from function: if language is primarily a matter of functional distinction and adequacy, then once a world language such as English starts to encroach on the local language functions, there is really nothing to stop it from taking over all functions. Except sentiment of course, except the sense of distinctness, except the concern that it is possible to be truly oneself (a Dane, a Swede, a Singaporean) only in the local language or in one of the local languages (Holborow, 1999; wa' Thiongo, 1986). At the back of such a sentiment is the two-fold awareness of language in personal and in group identity. On one side there is the central role accorded to language as the transmitter and carrier of the sense of self, both inclusiveness to the in-group and exclusiveness to those who are seen to belong to other ethnicities. On the other side is the meaning attached to the local language itself, meaning that derives from its cognitive and psychological importance in the ontogenetic growth of cognition and other aspects of "normal" development. The first of these concerns what you do with language, its sociolinguistics, the second with what language does to you, its psycholinguistics.

Both have to do with the sense of self which is, or seems to be, bound up with the language in which one grew up as a child, one's first language, mother tongue. The sense of self, one's personal identity is, on this basis, closely associated with the power that being a native speaker gives. Such power is very hard to attain in any additional acquired language, however successful the acquisition.

And that identity is threatened by the sense of not being valued for one's self (one's language is perceived as not good enough), of someone else's language being presented not just as different (so much is obvious), but as better than yours, and of the pervading feeling that whatever you do you will never achieve "proper" command over the incoming language, that "inferiority complex" of which Medgyes (1994, p. 10) wrote.

One's personal sense of identity is bound up with one's language: this is true both for the social aspects—sharing being a native speaker with others (and the opposite, not sharing it with those who do not belong) and the psycholinguistic aspects—mapping one's way through the basic interpersonal communicative skills (BICS) and cognitive/academic language proficiency (CALP) that are claimed to be necessary to effective cognitive development (Cummins, 1984).

This being so, or rather if this is so, then we would expect the growth of English to be condemned as an aspect of postcolonial imperialism because it erodes the pride of native speakerness appertaining to local languages and never somehow replaces it with the gift (or the attainment) of being a native speaker in the acquired and desired English. Here, the stereotyped attitude of the excolonialists to themselves, native speakers of English, is not dissimilar to the attitude the British took in their colonial heyday: the attitude that allowed the "natives" to remain native, that accorded them large measures of local autonomy (indirect rule) but which took for granted that it was never going to be possible for the colonized to become British.

Underlying many of the remarks by postcolonial apologists is their failure to acknowledge that English in the world at the start of the twenty-first century is a special case, if only because the inferiority complex, to which we have referred, is more likely to be found in relation to a global language such as English than to a language of more limited provenance. This denial of a special status for native speakers of English is surely ideological, belonging to an argument about the role of English in a world filled with new or world Englishes, where most speakers of English are second language learners. In this context there is a political point to be made in comparing the privileged position of the Old Variety of English (OVE) speaker, say of British or American English, and the New Variety of English (NVE) speaker, say of Nigerian or Indian English. Rajagopalan maintains that: "the quest for the pure native is part of a larger agenda that in other epochs manifested itself—and in some quarters still does – as the quest for the pure race" (1997, p. 229). Since there are no "viable and fool-proof criteria for identifying a native" (p. 228), then all that is left is the "myth of nativity" (p. 229).

Are such sentiments specific to English because English is a special case? Or are the sentiments generalizable? Would these critics make the same point about Welsh or Basque or Menomini or Kikuyu? Clearly they are making a political point and an understandable one, given the inequities of the world. It is worth remembering that English is not itself a cause of those inequities, rather, it is a correlative. There are after all countries and societies with high levels of English (e.g., Kerala) which remain very poor. But that said, if native speakers' privilege is controlled, by for example choosing a different language for schooling, as happened in Malaysia in the 1970s, English still appears today to enjoy a special status. True, Graddol writes of the "decline of the native speaker" and asks the "tantalising question: . . . large numbers of people will learn English as a Foreign Language in the 21st century . . . But will they continue to look towards the native speaker for authoritative norms of usage?" (1999, p. 68).

It is this question of authority that worries Greenbaum when he writes of the inherent instability of a New Variety of English (NVE) and wonders whether the real question is the acceptance of the national characteristics and their institutionalization (Greenbaum, 1985).

Where does this leave the postcolonial English speaker, such as the native speaker/user of Singaporean English? James (1999) maintains that there is good documentary evidence for the existence of Singapore English, a view attested to by Gupta (1994). Surely, the answer is that it leaves Singapore English exactly where it leaves, say, Glasgow English. Singapore is in fact in a stronger position: it has statehood and therefore is a centralizing force for language planning and norms. We might speculate on what would be the position of English if Scotland became independent. Would there be a deliberate scotizing of norms? Or would Scotland go the way of Ireland? There, the rich vein of creative writing in English has never been supported by—or itself supported—the demand for the development of a Standard Irish English. True, there has been research into and discussion of Hiberno-English (Harris, 1985), but little sign of different norms for education and publishing and the media (as in the USA, Australia). Perhaps Ireland – the oldest British colony—has had enough confidence not to insist on making that difference explicit. Or perhaps the presence of the Irish Gaelic language has provided a sufficiently separate identity and taken up the space that a Standard Irish English movement might have filled.

The theoretical debate about native speakers may be unresolved, but in the daily practice of language teaching and testing resolution is necessary and agreement on a model and a goal required. Even so, Leung, Harris, and Rampton (1997, p. 1) argue for flexibility: "Little development of such an expanded pedagogy is possible without the displacement of conventional notions of the 'native speaker' of English (what we here label the 'idealized native speaker')." While this approach makes sense for individuals it is hard to see how it would lead to a language teaching policy for whole populations. Cook (1999) argues for the second language (the non-native speaker) model to replace the native speaker in order to consider the harmful effects of privileging an inappropriate communication model in countries such as Japan.

What both Rajagopalan (1999) and Canagarajah (1999) helpfully do is to argue strongly (as Medgyes, 1999, does) for the valorizing of the L2 teacher of English while at the same time reassuring professional colleagues that in teaching English as a Foreign Language (or indeed English as a Second Language) they are not acting as instruments of linguistic imperialism. Rajagopalan attacks the "alarmist thesis that the teaching of English to speakers of other languages is an outrageous act of aggression" (1999, p. 202). And Canagarajah, a doughty critic of the power of English in the periphery, makes very clear that scholars and teachers in the periphery are not dupes, that they are perfectly capable of operating "subtle forms of resistance to English," appropriating from it what they need (1999, p. 3). And he puts a question mark against the absolutist strategy advocated by the Kenyan writer James Ngugi (Ngugi wa' Thiongo) who renounced English as his medium in order to write in his first language, Kikuyu: "there are many reason why [his] oppositional strategy may be ill conceived . . . this is not a solution to the ideological challenges, but an escape from it" (Canagarajah, 1999, p. 177). This is the argument presented by Agnihotri and Khanna (1997) following their survey of young people in India's views on "the space of English in tomorrow's India" (p. 50). They conclude that English is indeed an Indian language and needs to be problematized in the Indian context, that it must be accorded its proper role within the "complementarity" of the English language (p. 139).

Four ways of coping with loss

This sense of loss of identity as a native speaker of one's own language through domination by English (or, of course, of any other widely spoken language) attracts four kinds of comment. The first is that of the attack on the cult of the native speaker, usually as teacher of his/her L1. This reminds us of the Paikeday argument (1985) and is presented typically by those who have suffered from discrimination on the grounds of themselves not being regarded as native speakers. The second comes from the special case of so-called world Englishes, the term used to legitimate the Englishes spoken in the British non-white colonies (Indian English, Malaysian English, Kenyan English, and so on). The position taken up here is again one that complains of discrimination against users of world Englishes by those who are native speakers of metropolitan English varieties (British English, American English, and so on). The third concern with identity takes the world English critique further. It presents the linguistic imperialism argument which states that English (and by implication any world language) rides roughshod over all local languages with which it comes in contact and particularly those in the ex-colonies: so now the critique is not just of the attitude of native speakers of metropolitan English to new Englishes, but also to all other languages. These three attacks are all on the sociolinguistic side, claiming that belonging to desired groups is made difficult by the loss of or denial of native speaker status. The fourth attack takes on the psycholinguistic argument and concerns the claimed need for all normal development to take place in the language of the home. It is an argument for the rewarding of first language importance in child development and therefore may be regarded as a claim not just for the fact of native speaker status but for its pre-eminence.

Commentators take up very different positions on the issue of native speaker power. But we can, I think, postulate that they separate into those writing from the foreigner perspective and those writing from the "other-native" perspective. The foreigner view is of two kinds, "traditional" and "revisionist": The traditional view is that native speakers have special advantages but that these advantages are not unfair, just given; and in any case it is possible for non-natives working in professions such as language teaching to gain high levels of proficiency and to use their own learner background to deploy particularly relevant pedagogic skills. Medgyes (1999) provides an excellent summary of this type of view, as do several of the contributors to Braine (1999). They argue that being a non-native-speaking teacher of English is a powerful position to be in.

The traditional foreigner

Medgyes looks for cooperation between native and non-native-speaking teachers: "The ideal NEST [native English-speaking teacher] and the ideal nonNEST arrive from different directions but eventually stand quite close to each other" (Medgyes, 1999, p. 74). Or as Kramsch and Lam (in Braine, 1999) make clear from the title of their chapter ("Textual identities: the importance of being non-native") being a non-native has advantages. This is an appealing view, given the fact that by far the majority of the world's language teachers are teaching what is to them a foreign language. A supportive view, though not directly concerned with the language of teachers, is found in Mohanan (1998), who takes a very traditional line: "For a given speaker, a non-native system is one that s/he has acquired after the acquisition and stabilisation of some other linguistic system" (p. 50). And he challenges those who argue the issue from the position of righting social justice: "the plea for 'endonormative' standards as a means of preventing social injustice contains a logical contradiction. We should be willing to abolish all standards or to accept exonormative standards" (p. 53).

What Mohanan is drawing our attention to here is how even a variety which is subordinate to a distant standard (say Singapore English to British English) has the tendency to assume a dominant normative status with respect to some marginalized speakers (e.g., of Singlish) in Singapore. And Annamalai makes a similar point with regard to the relation between Telugu and Tamil in India and ponders whether bilingual speakers of both may be regarded as native speakers of Tamil: "Nativity . . . is a shifting construct and is correlated with political perceptions" (Annamalai, 1998, p. 154).

Holborow (1999) offers a similar argument from a Marxist perspective. "Often attempts to revive and impose a former national language can be a nationalist cloak under which new rulers' interests are hidden" (Holborow, 1999, p. 79). The traditional foreigner view is, at bottom, an acceptance of the strong view, that the native speaker is so by virtue of early childhood experience. That is seen to be an inescapable fact and it is pointless to pretend otherwise.

The revisionist foreigner

Observing the sense of deprivation of which Medgyes writes, Seidlhofer (2000) takes the bold step of recommending the abandonment of the traditional native speaker model, echoing Kramsch who suggests that it is time to "take our cues not from monolingual native speakers . . . but from the multilingual non-native speakers that constitute the majority of human beings on the planet" (1993, p. 49). The problem with such boldness is that it takes learners into a mapless setting. For indeed the state of mind she describes among non-native speakers of English as a lingua franca is surely one of anomie. Seidlhofer quotes Medgyes on non-native-speaking teachers of English: "We suffer from an inferiority complex caused by glaring defects in our knowledge of English. We are in constant distress as we realize how little we know about the language we are supposed to teach" (Medgyes, 1994, p. 10). (Skeptics among us might wonder how far this lament applies to native speakers also.) But the point Medgyes is making is that native speakers do not need this knowledge in an explicit form, while non-native speakers do because that is their way into the language.

And so Seidlhofer recommends that attention be given to the variety of English used by speakers of English as a Lingua Franca (EliF) communicating with one another. She claims that the appeal to the native speaker as model for all English is not appropriate now that the numbers of EliF speakers far outnumber the English L1 speakers, especially since the L1 model is neither desired by nor relevant to communication between EliF speakers, "it is important to realize that native-speaker language use is just one kind of reality, and not necessarily the relevant one for lingua franca contexts" (Seidlhofer, 2000, p. 54). So it is English as a lingua franca that needs to be investigated and described, now that EliF is spreading "with a great deal of variation but enough stability to be viable for lingua franca communication" (p. 54).

Seidlhofer proposes a research project which works toward "mapping out and exploring the whole spectrum of Englishes across the world" (p. 65). Such a project may be thought timely now that the methodology exists for the compilation of a corpus of English as a lingua franca. Indeed, work on such a corpus (the Vienna EliF corpus) has already begun. The end point of the research is to provide a description of EliF use which "would have potentially huge implications for curriculum design and for reference materials and textbooks."

It is understandable that Seidlhofer should wish to overturn the native speaker model. "There is," she claims, "really no justification for doggedly persisting in referring to an item as 'an error' if the vast majority of the world's L2 English speakers produce and understand it" (p. 65). As she points out, her iconoclasm is widely shared in the linguistic imperialism English postcolonialist literature (Paikeday, 1985; Phillipson, 1992; Medgyes, 1994; Canagarajah, 1999).

The other native

The "other native" view is very well represented in both the Braine (1999) and Singh (1998) volumes. A number of the contributors to the Braine volume are involved in teaching English in North America where they have met with prejudice about their lack of native speaker status. And so the prevailing theme of the book is critical, protesting at not being accorded the same status as native speakers. This was, it will be remembered, the complaint of Thomas Paikeday (1985), pointing to his experience of job discrimination. But it is worth noting that such discrimination is typically found in mother tongue English settings. In the great majority of situations where English (or any language) is taught, the teachers are not native speakers, but members of the local community who themselves have acquired the language they teach as a foreign language. What the argument is really about is whether language use in a NVE setting, which involves English and no doubt other languages as well, provides participants with sufficient exposure to English to make them native users and furthermore in so doing gives them everything that the traditional native speaker has acquired in absorbing the language from childhood. Such native users – this is agreed – speak a different variety of English, a NVE, but this is, it is argued, in no way inferior to the variety spoken by those brought up in the UK or in any other setting Kachru (1982) has called the inner circle. And it therefore follows, so the argument runs, that there should be no discrimination (in teaching or in any other occupation) on the grounds of group membership of such NVEs.

This is the argument that Singh (1998) puts forward. It is the postcolonial argument. It is the argument that says that American English is different from British English and yet is not regarded as being full of errors. Therefore, Indian English (etc.) should be considered different, not inferior. It is an argument that appeals to social justice. So much is clear. But is it an argument that convinces in applied linguistic terms?

Singh (1998) is not comfortable with the term "native speaker," preferring to speak of "native user." In this his approach is similar to that of Ikome (1998) and Kandiah (1998). For Ikome, "native speaker" is a political designation for social empowerment or for peer recognition (p. 37). Kandiah attacks: "the mainstream discourse on the native speaker (which) can be seen to be a strongly normative discourse that is heavily invested ideologically against considerable numbers of people on our globe" (1998, p. 92). He insists that "it ought not to be necessary to repeat here the demonstration that these varieties of English [the NVEs] are the equal of any other variety of the language, being not mere hodge-podges of errors, mere deviations from the norms of the 'mother' language, but viable rule-governed systems in their own right which sustain and are sustained by speech communities of their native users" (p. 93).

He admits that the argument is not fundamentally about what distinguishes one variety from another, nor about whether a variety of native users (rather than native speakers), maintained by a speech community largely made up of non-monolingual speakers of English whose English has not necessarily been acquired as their first childhood language, should be regarded as "the equal of any other variety." What the argument is about is whether the boundary between the NVE and the OVE is seen to be a real boundary by the NVE native users.

This is the appeal to the Barth social boundary theory (Barth, 1970) and ultimately is about the attitudes of native users to their own NVE: "The critical feature of the group then becomes self-ascription and ascription by others on the basis of features, signs, signals, value orientations and standards which the actors themselves regard as significant and by which they judge themselves and expect others to judge them" (1970, p. 96). Barth's model of ethnicity *is* helpful here, since what it does is to emphasize, as Kandiah realizes, membership before content. This is the conclusion that Medgyes comes to, quoting Davies (1991, pp. 8, 16): "I believe that (native speaker) membership is largely a matter of self ascription, not of something being given . . . We should bear in mind, however, that such a choice carries responsibilities in terms of confidence and identity."

Medgyes is concerned with the status of an individual near-native speaker, unlike Kandiah whose concern is for group membership. The confidence Medgyes refers to applies equally to both. But while the Medgyes individual near native needs to identify with the norms of English, both in a linguistic and a cultural sense, which in his case means the norms of OVEs, the identity Kandiah is concerned with is identity with the NVE group; and confidence for him means asserting that the English variety which his NVE members speak relates to the norms of their own NVE. This is the postcolonial imperative, that just as the Australian native speaker of English no longer admits allegiance to the norms of British English, similarly the NVE native user (say of Singapore English) no longer takes account of the norms of British English.

How far the norms differ is an empirical question, but it seems likely that as far as the written language is concerned, the differences are minimal. I am still of the opinion I expressed in 1991, that: "on linguistic grounds Singaporean English does not exist, but nor of course does British English . . . what does exist is the individual speaker. If a speaker identifies him/herself as a native speaker of Singaporean English then that is a sociolinguistic decision" (Davies, 1991, p. 67). Which means, of course, that it is a decision about identity.

International English

We have considered three ways of coping with the sense of losing one's identity as a native speaker—the traditional foreigner, the revisionist foreigner, and the other native. There is a fourth way, that of a globalized international language. One approach would be via an artificial language such as Esperanto or Idaho, where everyone gives up their national identity (or adds to it) for the sake of an international ideal of community. The other approach is via an existing lingua franca, such as English, and here we are close to the revisionist foreigner position where we discussed the proposal of Seidlhofer. The difference between that and what has come to be known as International English is that International English is not just for L2 users, but for all. The question which arises for applied linguistics is whether International English (Smith, 1983; Kachru, 1985; Davies, 1989) means a special variety of English with its own norms which are distinct from any national official standard English, or whether it means a use of English in international conferences and settings for example the United Nations, academic conferences, trade missions, business negotiations. If the latter, then International English becomes like EliF. My own view is that International English usually means using one or the other standard English in international settings. Therefore, from an applied linguistic point of view, it is more appropriate to designate the activity as English as an International Language rather than as International English. The emphasis is then firmly put on the use of English and not on a separate language.

Conclusion

Disputes and differences of opinion about the native speaker arise because the concept is interpreted differently. That is why it has been referred to as both myth and reality (Davies, 2003). Discussions of the native speaker concept get trapped in the very different ideas of what is being talked about. One main type of approach sees the native speaker as the repository and guardian of the true language—this is the linguistic view; the other, the social view, concerns the native speaker as the standard setter. The two views are related and merge into one another. But what they reflect is that different positions can be taken on the basis of interest in and concern for the same phenomenon, because what is at issue is the individual speaker in relation to his/her social group, and to its community norms, i.e., the standard language. At bottom the native speaker is both metaphor and embodiment of the language/parole and of the competence/performance distinctions.

References

Agnihotri, R. K. & Kanna, A. Y. (1997) *Problematizing English in India.* New Delhi: Sage.

Annamalai, E. (1998) Nativity of language. In R. Singh (ed.), *The native speaker: multilingual perspectives* (pp. 148–57). New Delhi: Sage.

Barth, F. (ed.) (1970) *Ethnic groups and boundaries.* London: George, Allen & Unwin; Bergen: Universitets Forlaget.

Bartsch, R. (1988) *Norms of language.* London: Longman.

Bernstein, B. (1971–5) *Class, codes and control* (vols 1–5). London: Routledge & Kegan Paul.

Birdsong, D. (1992) Ultimate attainment in second language acquisition. *Language*, 68, 706–55.

Braine, G. (ed.) (1999) *Non-native educators in English language teaching.* Mahwah, NJ: Lawrence Erlbaum.

Canagarajah, S. (1999) *Resisting linguistic imperialism in English teaching.* Oxford: Oxford University Press.

Cook, V. (1999) Going beyond the native speaker in language teaching. *TESOL Quarterly*, 33(2), 185–209.

Coppieters, R. (1987) Competence differences between native and nearnative speakers. *Language*, 63, 544–73.

Crystal, D. (1997) *English as a global language.* Cambridge: Cambridge University Press.

Cummins, J. (1984) *Bilingualism and special education: issues on assessment and pedagogy.* Clevedon, UK: Multilingual Matters.

Davies A. (1989) Is international English an interlanguage? *TESOL Quarterly*, 23(3), 447–67.

Davies, A. (1991) *The native speaker in applied linguistics.* Edinburgh: Edinburgh University Press.

Davies, A. (2003) *The native speaker: myth and reality.* Clevedon, UK: Multilingual Matters.

Felix, S. W. (1987) *Cognition and language growth.* Dordrecht: Foris.

Ferguson, C. (1983) Language planning and language change. In H. Cobarrubias & J. Fishman (eds), *Progress in language planning: international perspectives* (pp. 29–40). Berlin: Mouton.

Fishman, J. A., Cooper, R. L., & Conrad, A. W. (1975) *The spread of English.* Rowley, MA: Newbury House.

Graddol, D. (1999) The decline of the codification and sociolinguistic native speaker. In D. Graddol & U. H. Meinhof (eds), *English in a changing world* (pp. 57–68). *AILA Review*, 13.

Greenbaum, S. (1985) Commentary on Braj B. Kachru "Standards, codification and sociolinguistic realism: the English language in the outer circle". In R. Quirk & H. G. Widdowson (eds), *English in the world: teaching and learning the language and literatures* (pp. 31–2). Cambridge: Cambridge University Press and the British Council.

Gupta, A. F. (1994) *The step-tongue: children's English in Singapore.* Clevedon, UK: Multilingual Matters.

Harris, J. (1985) *Phonological variation and change: studies in Hiberno-English.* Cambridge: Cambridge University Press.

Holborow, M. (1999) *The politics of English: a marxist view of language.* London: Sage.

Hyltenstam, K. & Abrahamsson, N. (2000) Who can become native-like in a second language? All, some or none? On the maturational constraints controversy in second language acquisition. *Studia Linguistics*, 54(2), 150–66.

Ikome, Otto M. (1998) Language "nativization" in West Africa: acculturation and acquisition of "native" speakers in Cameroon. In R. Singh (ed.), *The native speaker: multilingual perspectives* (pp. 62–78). New Delhi: Sage.

James, J. (1999) Linguistic realities and pedagogical practices in Singapore: another perspective. In Gopinathan et al., *Language, society and education in Singapore: issues and trends* (2nd edn.) (pp. 99–116). Singapore: ASEAN/RELC.

Kachru, B. B. (ed.) (1982) *The other tongue: English across cultures.* Urbana, IL: University of Illinois Press.

Kachru, B. B. (1985) Standards, codification and sociolinguistic realism: the English language in the outer circle. In R. Quirk & H. G. Widdowson (eds), *English in the world: teaching and learning the language and literatures* (pp. 11–30). Cambridge: Cambridge University Press and the British Council.

Kandiah, T. (1998) Epiphanies of the deathless native user's manifold avatars: a post-colonial perspective on the native speaker. In R. Singh (ed.), *The native speaker: multilingual perspectives* (pp. 79–100). New Delhi: Sage.

Kramsch, C. (1993) *Context and culture in language teaching.* Oxford: Oxford University Press.

Kramsch, C. & Lam, W. S. E. (1999) Textual identities: the importance of being non-native. In G. Braine (ed.), *Non-native educators in English language teaching* (pp. 57–72), Mahwah, NJ: Lawrence Erlbaum.

Leung, C., Harris, R., & Rampton, B. (1997) The idealised native-speaker, reified ethnicities, and classroom realities: contemporary issues in TESOL. *Working papers in urban language and literacies*, no. 2. King's College, London.

MacArthur, T. (1999) On the origin and nature of Standard English. *World Englishes*, 18(2), 61–170.

Martin-Jones, M. & Romaine, S. (1986) Semilingualism: a half-baked theory of communicative competence. *Applied linguistics*, 7(1), 26–38.

McCawley, J. D. (1986) Review of *The native speaker is dead!* by T. M. Paikeday. *Linguistics*, 24(6), 1137–41.

Medgyes, P. (1994) *The non-native teacher*. London: Macmillan.

Medgyes, P. (1999) *The non-native teacher* (revised 2nd edn.). Ismaning, Germany: Hueber Verlang.

Mohanan, K. P. (1998) On new/non-native Englishes: a quartet: second response. In R. Singh (ed.), *The native speaker: multilingual perspectives* (pp. 50–3). New Delhi: Sage.

Paikeday, T. M. (1985) *The native speaker is dead!* Toronto and New York: Paikeday Pub. Co.

Pawley, A. & Syder, F. H. (1983) Two puzzles for linguistic theory: naturelike selection and naturelike fluency. In J. C. Richards & R. Schmidt (eds), *Language and communication* (pp. 191–226). Harlow: Longman.

Phillipson, R. (1992) *Linguistic imperialism*. Oxford: Oxford University Press.

Rajagopalan, K. (1997) Linguistics and the myth of nativity: comments on the controversy over "new/non native" Englishes. *Journal of Pragmatics*, 27, 225–31.

Rajagopalan, K. (1999) Of EFL teachers, conscience and cowardice. *ELT Journal*, 53(3), 200–6.

Seidlhofer, B. (2000) Mind the gap: English as a mother tongue versus English as a lingua franca. University of Vienna Department of English, *Views*, 9(1), 51–68.

Singh, R. (ed.) (1998) *The native speaker: multilingual perspectives*. New Delhi: Sage.

Smith, L (ed.) (1983) *Readings in English as an international language*. Oxford: Pergamon Press.

Tajfel, H. (1981) *Human groups and social categories*. Cambridge: Cambridge University Press.

van Els, T. J. M. (2000) The European Union, its institutions and its languages: some language political observations. Final Public lecture University of Nijmegen, The Netherlands, 22 September.

wa' Thiongo, N. (1986) *Decolonising the mind: the politics of language in African literature*. London: Heinemann.

Chapter 2

CONSTANT LEUNG, ROXY HARRIS, AND BEN RAMPTON

THE IDEALISED NATIVE SPEAKER, REIFIED ETHNICITIES AND CLASSROOM REALITIES (1997)

when I encounter rural area students

TESOL PRACTICE WITHIN THE SCHOOLING SECTOR in England has been mainstreamed.[1] Historically this represents a major advance in terms of pedagogical relevance and equality of access, but our current research (Rampton, Harris, & Leung, 1997) and our recent experience in working with teachers have suggested that mainstreaming itself has generated a number of new and unresolved issues in relation to language use, ethnicity, and social identity. This article seeks to advance a number of propositions.

1. Socially and ideologically inspired conceptualisations of the language learner and the associated language pedagogies in England over the past 40 years are no longer adequate to cope with the range of what are termed *bilingual learners*[2] typically encountered in classrooms, particularly in urban settings.
2. Some of the recent developments in cultural theory assist a critical analysis of the prevailing thinking. They also contribute to an understanding of the changing nature of the linguistic formation and social identity of the bilingual learner and of the resulting need to develop an expanded notion of TESOL pedagogy.
3. In the specific arena of language, little development of such an expanded pedagogy is possible without displacing conventional notions of the *native speaker* of English (what we label here *the idealised native speaker*). This can be accomplished by asking about the language expertise, language inheritance, and language affiliation of all learners of English in the classroom (Rampton, 1990), regardless of the language attributed to them.
4. Language use and notions of ethnicity and social identity are inextricably linked. Because of this, specific attention must be paid to the way that many bilingual learners actively construct their own patterns of language use, ethnicity, and social identity. These patterns can often be in strong contradiction to the fixed patterns and the reified ethnicities attributed to bilingual learners by many of those attempting to develop effective TESOL pedagogies.

The current historical moment of profound change and flux is not a time for the pronouncement of grand strategies or solutions but rather an opportunity to engage in open analysis and questioning as a first step towards a better understanding of some of the problems encountered in classrooms and the possible development of an expanded and more responsive TESOL pedagogy. We stress that in this article we are writing specifically of the English urban context, although we hope that some of what we say will have a resonance for colleagues working on TESOL questions in major urban centres in other locations.

Background and prevailing assumptions about TESOL in England

An important element in understanding both the historic and current TESOL context in England is the nature of the post-1945 inward migration of peoples and languages. Martin-Jones (1989) characterises these migrations as principally of people entering England as either migrant workers or refugees. At the same time she sees a significant divide between those entering from other parts of Europe and those entering from former colonies and third-world nations. Historically, it has been the latter who have had the greatest interaction with TESOL policy and practice in England—people who migrated to England in relatively large numbers from India, Pakistan, Bangladesh, the Caribbean, Hong Kong, East Africa (principally Kenya, Tanzania, and Uganda), West Africa (mainly Nigeria and Ghana), Vietnam, Ethiopia and Eritrea, Somalia, and Cyprus (see Peach, 1996), bringing with them languages such as Panjabi, Urdu, Gujerati, Hindi, Bengali and Sylheti, Cantonese and Hakka Chinese, Caribbean Creoles, Yoruba, Twi, Cypriot Greek and Turkish, Kurdish, Tigrinya, Amharic, and Somali (see Alladina & Edwards, 1991; Inner London Education Authority, 1989).

Space constraints prohibit a detailed critical analysis of the historical development and limitations of TESOL in England (see Leung, 1993, 1996; Leung, Harris, & Rampton, 1997; Rampton, 1985, 1988; Rampton, Harris, & Leung, 1997). At present, however, TESOL practitioners urgently need to take account of social and demographic changes that pose troubling questions about the ways in which TESOL pedagogy classifies and conceptualises the large numbers of bilingual learners who are the children and grandchildren of the migrants of the 1950s, 1960s, 1970s, and 1980s. A highly significant factor has been the historical racism and disdain for the peoples and languages emanating from former English colonies and third-world countries. Over the past 40 years, this attitude has tended to lead to TESOL approaches bounded at first by overtly assimilationist approaches (Department of Education and Science, 1971) and then, after assimilationism was dropped as an official approach (Swarm, 1985), by a tendency not to take a proper account of the complexities of language learning and language use in contemporary multiethnic urban settings. (For a fuller discussion of the tenets of the current practice see Edwards & Redfern, 1992.) In fact, we would summarise the current configuration of L2 education goals and practices in England in terms of three implicit assumptions:

1.   that linguistic minority pupils are, by definition, bilingual, having an ethnic minority language at home while at school they are learning and using English;
2.   that these pupils' language development needs can be understood and categorised broadly in the same way; that is, there is a universal L2 learner phenomenon, which, since the 1960s and despite the mainstreaming initiative, has been conceptualised as someone learning English as a social and linguistic outsider; and
3.   that there is an abstracted notion of an idealised native speaker of English from which ethnic and linguistic minorities are automatically excluded.

In fact, we agree with Garcia's (1996) conclusion from North American experience that for many teachers it has become necessary to cope with a process of change whereby the ethnolinguistic identity of children is itself undergoing rapid change . . . . The greatest failure of contemporary education has been precisely its inability to help teachers understand the ethnolinguistic complexity of children, classrooms, speech communities, and society, in such a way as to enable them to make informed decisions about language and culture in the classroom. (p. vii)

In the next section, we try to explore approaches to this complexity that might be more productive.

Contemporary realities of TESOL

To adjust to the complex realities of contemporary urban multilingualism, we would suggest at least three strategies. First, it is worth attending closely to recent developments in cultural theory and research that offer ways of accommodating patterns of change in language use and social identity. Second, educators need to address the actual rather than the presumed language use, ethnicity, and culture of the bilingual learner. And third, they need to draw on the first two strategies to develop more specific, precise, and differentiated English language pedagogies, spanning a range of practice from the pupil who is a recent arrival and early English user to the pupil who is a settled bilingual in the mainstream class. In the process, teachers will need to engage properly with the hitherto unresolved (and now virtually invisible) issues surrounding the language needs of speakers of Creole-influenced language and Black English. The question of similarities and differences in L2 and Creole-influenced language continues to be unresolved in the English educational literature.[3] One reason why this is important is that in recent years the English-born children of other settled migrant minority groups, like their Caribbean-descended peers from an earlier period, have become much more difficult to separate into clearly bounded ethnic and linguistic categories that neatly divide them from ownership of English ethnicity, standard English, and local urban vernacular Englishes. (See Voices from the classroom below for some evidence of the salience of this observation in the contemporary multiethnic classroom.)

Developments in cultural theory

One of the key questions addressed in an innovative way in British cultural studies is this: At what point are the people involved in migration to be considered as a permanent and integral part of the host nation and not as part of a kind of permanent "otherness"? For TESOL, this question is important for curriculum organisation and for classroom pedagogy because it paves the way for a better understanding of two further challenging questions:

1. Why do many bilingual learners, especially those in adolescence, actively seek to escape the essentialising linguistic and ethnic categories within which their English language teaching takes place?
2. What are TESOL teachers to do when the actual language use and language expertise of the young learners whom they daily observe confound the commonsense, fixed, and clearly bounded notions of language and ethnicity?

We would suggest that TESOL practitioners who wish to make progress with these and allied questions have much to gain from studying the thinking emanating from cultural theory and research in the late 1980s and early 1990s. Bhabha (1994), for instance, in a detailed theoretical treatment, gives an insight into the ways in which particular ethnic groups come to be constructed into a permanent otherness: "An important feature of colonial discourse is its dependence on the concept of 'fixity' in the ideological construction of otherness" (p. 66). Meanwhile, Gilroy (1987) analyses the processes in the British nation-state that construct notions of Englishness or Britishness that permanently exclude certain minority groups. He identifies the role played by what he calls *ethnic absolutism*, a perspective that "views nations as culturally homogeneous communities of sentiment" (pp. 59–61). As Hall (1988) suggests, members of minority groups are not simple inheritors of fixed identities, ethnicities, cultures, and languages but are instead engaged in a continual collective and individual process of making, remaking, and negotiating these elements, thereby constantly constructing dynamic new ethnicities.

Writing more specifically of language, Hewitt (1991) identifies the significant ways in which urban youth participate in the "destabilisation of ethnicity" (p. 27) in their routine language use. He further suggests that an important but often overlooked part of their language use is what he describes as a local multiethnic vernacular, a community English. This language use is "the primary medium of communication in the adolescent peer group in multi-ethnic areas" (p. 32). There is also relevance in the associated notion of *language crossing*, which involves the use of minority languages by members of ethnic out-groups (e.g., Creole used by White and Asian adolescents or Panjabi used by Whites and African Caribbeans—see Rampton, 1995, 1996). Among other things, crossing draws attention to the existence of many cross-ethnic friendships, to the fact that "there can be a strong interest in minority languages by majority group peers," and to the reality that "adolescents do not necessarily require *all* members of their peer group to speak *all* its languages with *equal* proficiency" (Rampton, 1995, p. 328). It also emphasises the intractable problems associated with the term *native speaker* in relation to the speaking of English.

It is not necessary to accept these contributions in their entirety in order to argue for their potential relevance. This is neatly and vividly illustrated in an article by a multilingual Indian-born teacher about himself and his British-born son (Hallan, 1994).

As a British person I have lived 33 of my 40 years in England. So I should not have been surprised when, on a recent educational visit to the USA, I was constantly referred to as "our English guest" or "our English visitor." I was amazed at how much they admired my English accent and confused when, on a formal occasion, I received the compliment: "you English always dress so well."

I was puzzled because in all my 33 years in England nobody had ever referred to me in those terms. In England I am always referred to as Indian. Why was my "Englishness" so prominent in the USA and so unrecognised here? . . . . The real surprise came last Christmas when, having left at the age of seven, I returned to India for a holiday. . . . My eight year old son, who is not fluent in Panjabi, suddenly found himself in an environment that he did not fully comprehend, where customs and traditions were not always familiar. There was a different emphasis on food, particularly towards vegetarianism, and fast food was a rarity. He was constantly looking for the "safe" and familiar. The street games played by the children of his age were new to him and, as he spoke little Panjabi and no Hindi, and they spoke only Hindi and no English, it was clear from day one that to stay within the bounds of the safe, he would be spending most if not all of his stay, with me and my parents or with other English speakers. He spent his spare time watching English language broadcasts on cable TV, MTV and BBC Asia, and after the first few days he was missing his Big Mac, chips and bacon sandwiches, and he was bored.

In my son I was witnessing an amplification of my "Englishness" and a reduction of my "Indianness." As he was only fluent when communicating in English, it was no surprise when some of my relatives began to call him "Angrez"—the "Englishman." But here lies the dilemma experienced by English people whose parents originate from outside Europe, particularly those who do not have a white skin and therefore do not "blend in" with most of the British population. In England he is seen as an outsider, an Indian, but in India he is seen as an outsider, the "*Angrez*." So where does his ethnic identity lie, and what epithet correctly describes his ethnicity?

what community do they belong to? (pp. 14–15)

Cultural theorists provide theoretical frameworks that help clarify phenomena like this. For instance, Mercer (1994) is one of many writers to redeploy the concept of diaspora to show that many people in minority groups in Britain can retain both real and imaginary global African, Asian, Caribbean, and other affiliations, combining them with definite British identities. His notion of "emerging cultures of hybridity, forged among the overlapping African, Asian and Caribbean diasporas" (p. 3) could also help make sense of what this teacher and his son have been experiencing. As Mercer further observes, "in a world in which everyone's identity has been thrown into question, the mixing and fusion of disparate elements to create new, hybridized identities points to ways of surviving, and thriving, in conditions of crisis and transition" (pp. 4–5).[4]

Voices from the classroom: making sense of experience

In contemporary English urban environments, issues like these are commonly exemplified in the lived linguistic and cultural experience of young bilingual and multilingual learners. This is illustrated in the following written extracts, drawn from some 13- and 14-year-old pupils in one class of a London secondary school in 1996.[5]

M.T. (female): I've lived in London all my life. The two main languages that I speak everyday are English and Gujarati . . . . When I was little I went to India. My mum's family were teaching me how to speak standard Gujarati, but I was too young and not interested. Now I am 13 I wish I had learnt how to speak proper Gujarati. Now at school I learn German. I can read, write, listen and speak German o.k., better than my home language Gujarati where I can only understand and speak it . . . . I don't like speaking it (Gujarati) a lot mainly because I can speak English better. I have to speak Gujarati with my mum—sometimes when I don't know how to say a thing or object in Gujarati, I say the word in English, but with a Gujarati accent . . . my dad is always telling me to speak proper English so that I don't get in the habit of speaking slang all the time.

A.T. (female): When I was young I was unable to speak another language like Hindi. My mother spoke to me all the time in Hindi hoping that I would pick it up, but however hard I tried to speak it, I did it all wrong and I was only able to understand. But when I went to India I felt really awkward. There all the children all spoke in Hindi and I was the only one who spoke English and so with me being young I had to fit in. I had felt so left out. I was only there for a month.

N.K. (female): My first language is English. I read, write, speak and think in English. I also speak Gujarati because my mum and dad are Gujarati first language speakers.

At home we mostly speak English, but my mum speaks to me in Gujarati, and I answer back in English which is common . . . . My own language style is using a lot of slang and not enough Standard English. I have tried to speak Standard English . . . but I can't. I can't because I am used to speaking slang. . . . In Gujarati I can only speak a few sentences and words. I only know some numbers and none of the alphabet in Gujarati . . . . People said that I should try to speak proper English not slang or cockney. My parents say that my English is not that good because I speak too much slang.

D.C. (female): I was born in London. I speak Gujarati and English. My mother tongue is Gujarati but I mainly speak English. I can understand other languages such as Punjabi, Urdu and Hindi but I can't speak, read or write them. I can speak Gujarati and English fluently, but there are some words in Gujarati which I can't pronounce. I also can't read or write Gujarati. I've tried learning Gujarati but I can't seem to remember it. I have been learning German for nearly 3 years. I can read, write and speak, but there are still lots of things I don't know. I've been speaking Gujarati for all my life but I still can't read or write it . . . when I'm with my friends I speak London English including slang.

P.M. (male): My family religion is Sikh. My Mum was born in Nairobi, Kenya, and came to this country when she was three years old. My Dad was born in Madras, India, and came to this country when he was twenty years old. I myself was born in England . . . . As I started out in High School, I had to develop a cockney accent of speaking in order to fit in with the rest of my friends. I kept on speaking London English to the point where I spoke it naturally . . . . When I'm with my mates you'll hear me say things like "easy' or "awight" instead of "hello" . . . or "send it here" instead of "pass it here," or "nasty" instead of "disgusting" . . . or "laters" instead of "bye" or "bad" or "wicked" instead of "cool," or "gwan there" instead of "well done," and "relax" instead of "don't worry". . . . When I'm speaking to people like my uncle on my dad's side of the family and my grandparents I speak Punjabi . . . people in my class think of me as normal, whereas my parents think that I talk like a "Gangsta."

S.K. (female): I know Punjabi, Urdu, Swahili, German, English and Arabic. I can speak Punjabi perfectly and understand it very well. I know a lot of German, and I know how to speak it, and understand it and write it mainly. I know Arabic very little but can write a little bit of it. I know how to speak, write and understand English.

The pupils quoted above were attempting to describe, indirectly and delicately, the difference between their experience and the linguistic and ethnic categories imposed on them. Hall (1992) perceives that perhaps

> everywhere, cultural identities are emerging which are not fixed, but poised, *in transition* between different positions; which draw on different cultural traditions at the same time; and which are the product of those complicated cross-overs and cultural mixes which are increasingly common in a globalised world.
>
> (p. 310)

Along with the concept of transition, Hall presents that of *translation*, which

> describes those identity formations which cut across and intersect natural frontiers, and which are composed of people who have been dispersed forever from their homelands.

Such people retain strong links with their places of origin and their traditions, but they are without the illusion of a return to the past. They are obliged to come to terms with the new cultures they inhabit, without simply assimilating to them and losing their identities completely. They bear upon them the traces of the particular cultures, traditions, languages and histories by which they were shaped. The difference is that they are not and will never be *unified* in the old sense, because they are irrevocably the product of several interlocking histories and cultures, belong at one and the same time to several "homes" (and to no one particular "home"). People belonging to such *cultures of hybridity* have had to renounce the dream or ambition of rediscovering any kind of "lost" cultural purity, or ethnic absolutism. They are irrevocably *translated* . . . . They are the products of the new *diasporas* created by the post-colonial migrations. They must learn to inhabit at least two identities, to speak two cultural languages, to translate and negotiate between them. Cultures of hybridity are one of the distinctly novel types of identity produced in the era of late-modernity, and there are more and more examples of them to be discovered.

(p. 310)

The relevance of Hall's ideas stands out in these pupils' writing.

- M.T. has experienced family support in developing her bilingualism but has rejected it. On the other hand, she depicts both her schooled German and her schooled English as languages in which she has a dramatically higher level of competence than she does in Gujarati, her supposed mother tongue.
- A.T. demonstrates what is true for many other bilingual learners in the class, namely, that she feels "other," a linguistic and cultural outsider, not in relation to the English language and Britain but in relation to the Hindi language and India. At the same time she nevertheless retains a definite relationship with both Hindi and India. In this example the notion of diaspora is particularly useful.
- N.K. seems to claim only a minimum attachment to her family language; even when it is spoken to her she has neither the desire nor the level of competence to sustain a spoken response in it. This pattern was characteristic of several of her classmates. Like many other pupils, she identified her usual language use as slang. Are she and her colleagues referring to Hewitt's (1991) local multiethnic vernacular or community English?
- P.M.'s parents' different birthplaces and his own birthplace raise the question of what ethnic category he would be classified under. In his language use, he clearly places Panjabi in a relatively restricted domain while demonstrating his identification and comfort with London English and a kind of Black London English with Jamaican Creole undertones. This situation may link into Hewitt's local multiethnic vernacular as well as Rampton's concept of language affiliation (to which we will later return).
- S.K. would be defined by the school as having Panjabi as her mother tongue, but she claims no literacy in it (see also D.C.). In fact, like a lot of other pupils at the school, she seems to feel that curriculum languages—here German—are rated more highly, and the fragility of describing her as a Panjabi-English bilingual is demonstrated elsewhere in her writing when she illustrates her discussion with examples that include confident German sentences alongside the full Arabic alphabet, Gujarati script, Gujarati sentences, and Swahili expressions.

These pupils seem to be struggling to understand the impact on themselves and their families of the processes that Hall describes, and the discovery of these processes by their teachers may well be an urgent prerequisite to the development of more sophisticated pedagogic strategies. Certainly, when approached with sensitivity, these students were perfectly willing to assist the enquiring teacher in gaining a better understanding of the effects of global social change on language use. But what kind of school language policy planning and pedagogy could exist for pupils with this kind of capability? Of course, the examples just cited contain all the weaknesses associated with self-report, and we have no room here for more than a brief, oversimplified discussion. Even so, this class is not highly atypical[6] and yields enough evidence to show that there are serious problems with current routine practices in the education of bilingual learners. Such pupils are frequently attributed a kind of romantic bilingualism and turned into reified speakers of community languages, and in the process their ethnicities are also reified.

Such then is the mismatch between the realities of urban multilingualism and the educational classification of students' language identities and backgrounds. On the other side are the prevailing views of English.

The Swann Committee (1985) and National Curriculum documents (from 1988 to date) officially accept ethnic and linguistic diversity in society, but they nevertheless insist on cultivating English as the universal medium defining the nation-state and as a principal instrument for achieving social cohesion. In doing so, the population of England is for practical purposes cast as a homogenous community with one language and one culture. According to Anderson (1991), this situation is typical of the way a nation comes to be artificially constructed as an imagined community, and one dimension can be seen in the way bilinguals are taught as if only one English mattered. This English is seen as the province of the idealised native speaker, something that he or she already possesses and that the outsider imperfectly aspires to. A more accurate picture of English language realities in Britain emerges from scholars whose work is more empirically oriented.

The British education system rests on the assumption that teachers and pupils will use the grammar of standard English. However, the majority of British children are speakers not of standard English but of a non-standard variety of English (a dialect), and this has been recognised as posing extremely important problems concerning language in education (Cheshire, Edwards, & Whittle, 1993, p. 54).

This view is endorsed in a recent piece of empirical national research in England, which concluded that a minimum of 68% of 11- to 16-year-olds did not habitually use only standard English speech forms (Hudson & Holmes, 1995). The following piece of writing shows an attempt to write in standard English by a White, monolingual English-speaking 7-year-old child.

> We find a car wive grnsu on it . . . aw no they cacht us. They wolt to the dunjoon. We hewd aw bref . . . wen we opoed awe iys we was in the diynjoon . . . we slept in the dungeon for friy nights . . . we only had 10 pans left. We farad 10,000 Pans on the suit Pavmot . . . we was wocen olog the rode . . . John basht into the wole . . . we got att . . . they ran away they was nevu to bey sene a gen . . . Tony foth for a mirait . . . Tony foth we can put a are money in the bank.
>
> (Harris, 1995)

> [We found a car with guns on it . . . oh no they caught us. They walked to the dungeon. We held our breath . . . when we opened our eyes we were in the dungeon . . . we slept in the dungeon for three nights . . . we only had 10 pounds left. We found 10,000 pounds on the street pavement . . . we were walking along the road . . . John crashed into the wall . . . we got out . . . they ran away they were never to be seen again . . . Tony thought for a minute . . . Tony thought we can put all our money in the bank.]

Reasons of focus and space prohibit a full analysis, but the key point is that even so-called native speakers do not necessarily use standard forms. In the example above, the child is showing that the language use he finds most natural is in fact London English and not standard English.

These findings, we would suggest, are true not only for those pupils of White British descent but also for a large proportion of the descendants of the migrant groups to whom we have been referring. Either many of the pupils defined as bilingual learners are most comfortable linguistically with either a local urban spoken English vernacular, or, alternatively, a nonstandard variety of this kind serves as their first spoken entry into English in the local community context. This reflects

> the obliteration of pure language forms deriving from a single cultural source, evident in some inner city areas (in the U.K.) and . . . the diasporic distribution of com- municative forms which, whilst generated from and based in local communities, nevertheless reach out and extend lines of connection in a global way. The local penetration and mixing of language forms evident in some urban settings in the U.K. should, in fact, be seen perhaps as a reflex of the broader linguistic diasporic pro- cesses.
>
> (Hewitt, 1995, p. 97)

Again, it is important to ask what consideration traditional TESOL pedagogic approaches give to these factors.

Language expertise, affiliation, and inheritance: an educational response to linguistic and ethnic diversity

So far, we have suggested that the conceptual frameworks of contemporary TESOL provide little leverage on the classroom realities created by the linguistic and ethnic composition of the pupil population. This lack of analytic clarity has led both TESOL practitioners and mainstream teachers to feel paralysed in their ability to respond to pupils' language needs, as seen, for example, in the constant struggle to develop adequate pedagogies for the large numbers of bilingual pupils who are no longer at an early stage of learning English, who have spent a significant proportion of their lives in Britain, and who use everyday colloquial English with ease (often referred to as the *plateau effect*, in which the pupil does not seem to be able to make any further progress in English language development).

In this context, Rampton (1990) offers a framework that may offer one or two ways forward. He suggests that "language education [is seen] as a social activity in which efforts are made to manage continuity, change and the relationship between social groups" (p. 100; also see Rampton, 1995, chap. 13). Rampton suggests replacing the terms *native speaker* and *mother tongue* with the notions of *language expertise, language inheritance,* and *language affiliation.* In a slight reworking of Rampton's original formulation, the term *language expertise* refers to how proficient people are in a language; *language affiliation* refers to the attachment or identification they feel for a language whether or not they nominally belong to the social group customarily associated with it; and *language inheritance* refers to the ways in which individuals can be born into a language tradition that is prominent within the family and community setting whether or not they claim expertise in or affiliation to that language. In this scheme, language teachers need to ask whether the learner's relationship with each language thought to exist in that learner's repertoire is based on expertise, on inheritance, on affiliation, or on a combination.

We might expand on this as follows.

• *Language expertise.* What do teachers know about their pupils' ability in each of the posited languages? (Interestingly, although educators have become accustomed to classifying pupils according to stages or levels of putative competence in English [Hester, 1996], it is still not standard practice to attempt such an assessment in any rigorous way for their competence in languages other than English.)

   This question raises several other issues. For instance, what are the criteria for assessment? Are they based on any explicitly stated, and therefore contestable, language models or norms in all the languages involved?

• *Language affiliation.* Do teachers know anything about their pupils' sense of affiliation to any of the languages allegedly within their repertoire? How might such knowledge about their affective relationship with their languages be used in the classroom and the curriculum?

• *Language inheritance.* Does membership in an ethnic group mean an automatic language inheritance? In the light of our earlier discussion this assumption seems to be unsafe for some pupils. What are the consequences of an inaccurate assumption for curricular provision of community language teaching? Can educators rely on an abstract notion of the benefits of bilingualism when they are working with ethnic/linguistic minority pupils?

The potential value of these questions becomes clear if they are used to outline conventional TESOL assumptions and compare them with the kind of classroom intimated above.

Language expertise

The conventional TESOL assumption is that ethnic minority pupils are beginners or relative newcomers to English (or at any rate lack native-speaker expertise) but that they possess expertise in their home or community language (L1). A related assumption is that the ethnic majority pupil possesses native-speaker expertise in an undifferentiated English (i.e., no distinction is made between standard English and local vernacular Englishes).

   In contrast, it is difficult to assume that ethnic majority pupils faced with the complex urban realities sketched in the earlier sections possess expertise in English, especially standard English for academic purposes. A further complication is that many ethnic minority pupils disclaim expertise in their putative L1 (home/community) language (see M.T. and D.C. above). Minority pupils may also claim expertise in English—at least in the same kind of English possessed by their ethnic majority classroom peers.

Language affiliation

In attempting to adopt a positive approach to bilingualism, conventional contemporary TESOL practice tends not only to attribute expertise in the putative L1 to ethnic minority pupils but also to attribute a high degree of affiliation on the part of these ethnic minority pupils to their home and community languages. This tendency is reflected, for instance, in the standard recommendation that teachers maximise the use of linguistically familiar material to promote pupils' confidence and self-esteem. As one teacher puts it, "Well the Asians are taken care of with E2L. They get a lot of support and of course their culture is strong. They have a number of languages which they use. . . ." (Mac an Ghaill, 1988, p. 56). At the same time there is a tendency to assume White monolingual English speakers are automatically affiliated to standard

English. The urban realities cast doubt on these certainties. First, a significant number of ethnic minority adolescent pupils demonstrate a weak sense of affiliation to their supposed home/ community L1 (see D.C. and M.T. above). In addition, other ethnic minorities may claim affiliation to linguistic varieties that are supposed to be part of the natural inheritance of other ethnic groups (see P.M. above). At the same time a similar tendency is also visible amongst ethnic majority pupils (see, e.g., Hewitt, 1986; Rampton, 1995). And there is evidence that some White pupils have a weak affiliation with standard English and use nonstandard forms by choice (Hudson & Holmes, 1995).

Language inheritance

An underlying assumption in TESOL practice is that ethnic groups inherit (are born into) language traditions that transcend questions of the actual language use of individuals and collectives; at the same time TESOL practice often assumes that language inheritance is strictly endogamous. This view can be seen in instances when ethnic minority community languages are offered as study options but are only designed for putative L1 speakers. Once again, in the realities of urban multilingualism, a noticeable number of adolescents from both majority and minority ethnic groups do not show a strong allegiance to their supposed linguistic inheritance. Equally, many working-class White youngsters do not show an allegiance to what is supposed to be their linguistic inheritance (standard English). Many pupils of Asian descent may also claim a strong inheritance in relation to English (see A.T. above).

We do not want to suggest that the conventional assumptions are automatically invalid. Indeed some of these assumptions work well with some pupils. But clearly, it is vital to validate all such assumptions against the actualities of a linguistically and culturally diverse classroom.

Future development

We have attempted to identify the complexities of some of our urban classrooms. A period of open analysis, critical questioning, and working with new ideas in the classroom may lead to more responsive pedagogies. Current knowledge does not warrant the pronouncement of grand strategies or solutions. Certainly, the binary native-speaker-versus-other is increasingly redundant, and the development of more appropriate classroom approaches should be based on a sharper awareness of learners with different needs. But how to classify and organise such pedagogies is an issue that requires a lot more exploration and reflection. One such pedagogy would be readily recognisable to TESOL practitioners—one designed for the learner who is new to the English language and English-speaking cultural contexts.

However, beyond this, other forms of English language pedagogy might be better based on an assumption that most learners, albeit from different starting points, are unfamiliar with the deployment of standard English for academic purposes. This pedagogy might be accompanied by the development of context-sensitive and learning-oriented assessments to establish the degree of expertise an individual pupil possesses in understanding, speaking, reading, or writing any given language.

Finally, it is of the utmost importance that TESOL pedagogy explicitly recognise and address societal inequalities between ethnic and linguistic groups, inequalities that can indeed often lead pupils to respond ambiguously to questions about their linguistic expertise, affiliation, and inheritance. Like Cummins (1996), we are interested in creating a pedagogy that takes genuine account of learners' expertise and identities.

We hope we have shown the importance of developing more effective and more pupil-sensitive classroom and curriculum responses to multilingual urban contexts. Our current research explores ways of constructing such pedagogies, and we hope that this will be continued in the future, both by ourselves and others.

Notes

1   Throughout this article, for reasons of legislation and social context, we refer to TESOL in England specifically. Although there might be commonalities among the national TESOL practices within Britain as a whole, we do not claim that our descriptions and arguments are directly applicable to Scotland and Wales.
2   The term *bilingual pupil/learner* is widely used in England as a broad category to refer to pupils who are at various stages of learning English as a second or additional language for studying purposes and who have at least some knowledge and skills in another language or languages already.
3   For discussions of this issue in the Caribbean itself, see Devonish (1986) and Roberts (1988).
4   We emphasise that recognizing notions of hybridity does not in any sense ignore the very real ways in which certain ethnic minority groups suffer specific and systematic societal inequalities on the basis of fixed and ascribed ethnic identities.
5   These data were collected by Harris. Writing was elicited after a taught unit on language and power.
6   Approximately 200 languages (other than English) are spoken by pupils in England (School Curriculum and Assessment Authority, 1996). Most professional estimates suggest that approximately 10% of the total school population is bilingual, and the figure is increasing. The percentage of bilingual pupils in individual schools varies; in some urban schools the bilingual intake may be 85% (or above). Census information indicates that the number of people in undefined (other) and mixed ethnic categories has been increasing consistently in the past two decades (Owen, 1996).

References

Alladina, S. & Edwards, V. (1991). *Multilingualism in the English Isles* (Vol. 2). London: Longman.
Anderson, B. (1991). *Imagined communities*. London: Verso.
Bhabha, H. (1994). *The location of culture*. London: Routledge.
Cheshire, J., Edwards, V., & Whittle, P. (1993). Non-standard English and dialect levelling. In J. Milroy & L. Milroy (Eds.), *Real English: The grammar of English dialects in the English Isles* (pp. 53–96). London: Longman.
Cummins, J. (1996). *Negotiating identities: Education for empowerment in a diverse society*. Ontario: California Association for Bilingual Education.
Department of Education and Science. (1971). *The education of immigrants: Education survey 13*. London: Her Majesty's Stationery Office.
Department of Education and Science. (1995). *English in the National Curriculum*. London: Her Majesty's Stationery Office.
Devonish, H. (1986). *Language and liberation: Creole language politics in the Caribbean*. London: Karia Press.
Edwards, V. & Redfern, A. (1992). *The world in a classroom*. Clevedon, England: Multilingual Matters.
Garcia, O. (1996). Foreword. In C. Baker, *Foundation of bilingual education and bilingualism* (pp. vii–ix). Clevedon, England: Multilingual Matters.
Gilroy, P. (1987). *There ain't no Black in the Union Jack*. London: Routledge.
Hall, S. (1988). New ethnicities. In A. Rattansi & J. Donald (Eds.), *"Race," culture and difference* (pp. 252–259). London: Sage/Open University.
Hall, S. (1992). The question of cultural identity. In S. Hall, D. Held, & T. McGrew (Eds.), *Modernity and its futures* (pp. 274–316). Cambridge: Polity Press/Open University.
Hallan, V. (1994, Autumn). Whose ethnicity is it anyway? *Multicultural Teaching*, 14–15.
Harris, R. (1995). Disappearing language. In J. Mace (Ed.), *Literacy, language and community publishing* (pp. 118–144). Clevedon, England: Multilingual Matters.
Hester, H. (1996). The stages of English learning: The context. In *Invitational conference on teaching and learning English as an additional language* (pp. 182–187). London: School Curriculum and Assessment Authority. Summarized in *Teaching and learning English as an additional language: New perspectives* (SCAR Discussion Paper No. 5). (1996). London: School Curriculum and Assessment Authority.

Hewitt, R. (1986). *White Talk Black Talk. Inter-racial friendship and communication amongst adolescents*. Cambridge: Cambridge University Press.

Hewitt, R. (1991). Language, youth and the destabilisation of ethnicity. In C. Palmgren, K. Lorgren, & G. Bolin (Eds.), *Ethnicity and youth culture* (pp. 27–41). Stockholm, Sweden: Stockholm University.

Hewitt, R. (1995). The umbrella and the sewing machine: Trans-culturalism and the definition of surrealism. In A. Alund & R. Granqvist (Eds.), *Negotiating identities* (pp. 91–104). Amsterdam: Rodopi.

Hudson, R. & Holmes, J. (1995). *Children's use of spoken standard English*. London: School Curriculum and Assessment Authority.

Inner London Education Authority (ILEA). (1989). *Catalogue of languages: Spoken by inner London school pupils: RS 1262/89*. London: ILEA Research & Statistics.

Lawton, D. (1968). *Social class, language and education*. London: Routledge & Kegan Paul.

Leung, C. (1993). The coming crisis of ESL in the National Curriculum. *English Association for Applied Linguistics Newsletter, 45*, 27–32.

Leung, C. (1996). Content, context and language. In T. Cline & N. Frederickson (Eds.), *Curriculum related assessment, Cummins and bilingual children* (pp. 26–40). Clevedon, England: Multilingual Matters.

Leung, C., Harris, R., & Rampton, B. (1997). *The idealised native speaker, reified ethnicities and classroom realities: Contemporary issues in TESOL* (CALR Occasional Papers in Language and Urban Culture 2). London: Thames Valley University, Centre for Applied Linguistic Research.

Mac an Ghaill, M. (1988). *Young, gifted and black*. Milton Keynes, England: Open University Press.

Martin-Jones, M. (1989). Language education in the context of linguistic diversity: differing orientations in educational policy making in England. In J. Esling (Ed.), *Multicultural education policy: ESL in the 1990s* (pp. 36–58). Toronto, Canada: OISE Press.

Mercer, K. (1994). *Welcome to the jungle*. London: Routledge.

Owen, D. (1996). Size, structure and growth of the ethnic minority populations. In D. Coleman & J. Salt (Eds.), *Ethnicity in the 1991 census: Vol. 1. Demographic characteristics of the ethnic minority populations* (pp. 87–91). London: Her Majesty's Stationery Office.

Peach, C. (Ed.). (1996). *Ethnicity in the 1991 census* (Vol. 2). London: Her Majesty's Stationery Office.

Rampton, B. (1985). A critique of some educational attitudes to the English of British Asian schoolchildren, and their implications. In C. Brumfit, R. Ellis, & J. Levine (Eds.), *English as a second language in the UK* (pp. 187–198). Oxford: Pergamon Press.

Rampton, B. (1988). A non-educational view of ESL in Britain. *Journal of Multilingual and Multicultural Development, 9*, 503–527.

Rampton, B. (1990). Displacing the "native speaker": Expertise, affiliation and inheritance. *ELT Journal, 44*, 97–101.

Rampton, B. (1995). *Crossing: Language and ethnicity among adolescents*. London: Longman.

Rampton, B. (1996). Language crossing, new ethnicities and school. *English in Education, 30*(2), 14–26.

Rampton, B., Harris, R., & Leung, C. (1997). Multilingualism in England. *Annual Review of Applied Linguistics, 17*, 224–241.

Roberts, P. (1988). *West Indians and their language*. Cambridge: Cambridge University Press.

School Curriculum and Assessment Authority. (1996). *Teaching English as an additional language: A framework for policy*. London: Author.

Swann Report. (1985). *Education for all*. London: Her Majesty's Stationery Office.

Chapter 3

CHRISTINA HIGGINS

"OWNERSHIP" OF ENGLISH IN THE OUTER CIRCLE

An alternative to the NS-NNS dichotomy* (2003)

[...]

THE ACT OF LABELING SPEAKERS as belonging to the categories native speaker (NS) and nonnative speaker (NNS) implicitly underlies much of what TESOL professionals do. Rather than treating these as subjective categories, researchers have often applied them uncritically to the study of TESOL and English language learning despite concerns raised by researchers investigating phenomena associated with World Englishes. This study reports the results of research investigating the concept of *ownership* that derives from Norton's (1997) theoretical stance on ownership as legitimacy as a speaker and that is expressed through English speakers' *footing*, "the alignment we take up to ourselves and the others present as expressed in the way we manage the production or reception of an utterance" (Goffman, 1981, p. 128). Unlike Norton's critical ethnographic approach, however, the present study relies on conversational data recorded during an Acceptability Judgment Task (AJT). The analysis draws on conversation analytic (CA) methods to examine how speakers display their footing as legitimate speakers when discussing English sentences containing forms attested in both center and periphery varieties.

The problematic NS-NNS dichotomy

Scholars working on World Englishes issues raise questions about which criteria should determine who can be labeled a NS or a NNS because a single norm for standard English no longer exists, particularly at a global level (Brutt-Griffler & Samimy, 1999, 2001; Davies, 1991; Lin, 1999; Liu, 1999; Mufwene, 2001; Nayar, 1997; Pennycook, 1994, 2001; Wee, 2002; Widdowson, 1994). These researchers have critiqued the NS-NNS dichotomy for being more of a social construction than a linguistically based parameter and have asserted that speakers' own ideological stances toward their linguistic identities should be more significant than the label they are given by others. Other researchers have critiqued the dichotomy for dividing groups of speakers into *haves* and *have nots* from a top-down approach without taking the speakers' own perspectives into account. Firth and Wagner (1997) criticize research that only considers analyst-conceptions of NSs and NNSs to be relevant, and Davies (1991) argues that membership as a NS in a speech community is a matter of self-ascription. Instead of labeling speakers from an analyst-driven perspective, Davies (1991) suggests defining NSs as people who have a "special control over a language, insider knowledge about 'their' language" (p. 1). Brutt-Griffler and Samimy (2001) point out that self-ascribed linguistic identities are often not validated by others, and self-ascribed NSs are not recognized as such because the categories NS and NNS are often assigned on social characteristics rather than linguistic proficiency.

These researchers argue that it is important for TESOL professionals to understand the linguistic identities that English speakers hold because these identities have important practical implications. Given the ubiquity of English across the globe, it is likely that students who study in countries such as the United States, Canada, and England have developed orientations toward English that need to be addressed in the English language classroom. The categorization of English speakers from countries with a long history of English usage is of particular importance due to their increasing enrollment in institutions of higher education outside of their home countries. These students may view themselves as valid speakers of English and their placement in ESL classes as wrongly categorizing them (Nero, 1997); or, they may speak a variety that they view to be legitimate, albeit one that differs from the target variety of the classroom (Leung, Harris & Rampton, 1997).

In an effort to move beyond the NS-NNS dichotomy and the dominance of the linguistic norms for English associated with center countries, such as England and the United States, scholars have employed the concept of ownership to investigate speakers' ideological stances toward English. Widdowson (1994) and Chisanga and Kamwangamalu (1997) take the view that speakers in the postcolonial world may appropriate English at the grammatical level for their own contexts, thus owning the language by altering it to suit their own local purposes, divorced from the norms of the center. From this perspective, British or American English norms are no longer relevant to the speakers in the periphery nations. Taking a more critical perspective, Norton (1997; Peirce, 1995) argues that learners claim ownership of a language if they can access the material and symbolic resources associated with knowing the language. In her view, learners who view themselves as legitimate speakers of English can own English. Norton rejects the NS-NNS dichotomy for the ways in which it sets up barriers to success, particularly for those who speak a variety different from the standard English of a center nation such as England or the United States.

Nativeness in the outer circle of English

The *new Englishes paradigm* is a highly relevant framework with which to critically (re) examine the classification of English speakers around the globe. This paradigm examines the forms and functions of English varieties outside of traditionally native contexts, such as Australia, Canada, the United States, and Great Britain. This framework is rooted in the work of Kachru (1965, 1976, 1982, 1983, 1986, 1997) and has developed a large body of scholarship through journals such as *World Englishes* and in numerous edited volumes (Bailey & Görlach, 1982; Bamgbose, Banjo, & Thomas, 1995; Cheshire, 1991; Pride, 1982; Smith, 1981; Thumboo, 2001b). Within this paradigm, research has focused primarily on *institutionalized varieties of English* (IVEs), varieties that are used alongside other languages in countries previously colonized by Great Britain, such as Malaysia, Kenya, Singapore, Nigeria, and India:

> [IVEs] have a long history of acculturation in new cultural and geographical contexts;
> they have a large range of functions in the local educational, administrative, and legal

systems. The result of such uses is that such varieties have developed nativized discourse and style types and functionally determined sublanguages (registers), and are used as a linguistic vehicle for creative writing in various genres. We find such uses of English on almost every continent.

(Kachru, 1986, p. 19)

IVEs are spoken in what Kachru (1997) has labeled the *outer circle*, alternatively known as the second diaspora of English:

The Inner Circle represents the traditional bases of English, dominated by the "mother tongue" varieties of the language. In the Outer Circle, English has been institutionalized as an additional language . . . and the Expanding Circle includes the rest of the world. In this [Expanding] Circle, English is used as the primary foreign language.

(p. 214)

To account for the presence of speakers with varying degrees of proficiency within outer-circle countries, Kachru explains that within each society there exists a *cline of bilingualism*, that is, a range of variation in terms of the functions that speakers use English for and their proficiency in the language (Kachru, 1965).

Following Kachru's model, inner-circle speakers receive the label NSs, and expanding-circle speakers are typically regarded as NNSs; however, the classification of IVEs who reside in the outer circle is ambiguous at best. Although clear arguments have successfully shown that the Englishes they speak are distinct from *interlanguages* (ILs) in a number of ways (Kachru, 1997; Lowenberg, 1986; Sridhar & Sridhar, 1986), speakers of these varieties are still not characterized as NSs. Instead, these speakers are continually referred to as speakers of *non-native varieties* (Lowenberg, 1986), *institutionalized varieties* (Kachru, 1982), *second language varieties* (Prator, 1968), *indigenized varieties* (Moag & Moag, 1977), *local forms of English* (Strevens, 1992), and *associate languages* (Nayar, 1997).

Scholarship in the field of new Englishes has taken the very positive step of demonstrating that these varieties are not simply deficient versions of the inner-circle Englishes by illustrating the systematic and patterned ways in which these Englishes exhibit variation. However, what remains problematic is that, despite the documentation and acceptance of these linguistic innovations as the natural outcome of "the context of situation which is appropriate to the variety, its uses and users" (Kachru, 1983, p. 10), these new Englishes are still called *nonnative varieties* that follow *nonnative norms* (Bamgbose, 1998; Kachru, 1992a; Strevens, 1992; Thumboo, 2001a). Because it has become widely accepted that speakers in the outer circle have altered English by indigenizing and institutionalizing it, we should recognize that speakers of these Englishes are now following their own *native* (i.e., locally relevant) norms. The term native here does not refer to British or American varieties but to varieties such as Filipino, Malaysian, and Indian English. This proposal should not be confused with taking the view that speakers of the outer circle wish to sound like speakers from Australia, Great Britain, or North America. On the contrary, many studies have demonstrated that outer-circle speakers do not aspire to be like English speakers from the inner circle; in fact, they often consider speech that resembles *received pronunciation* (RP), traditionally considered the prestige dialect of British English, to be pretentious (Bamgbose, 1992; Kachru, 1976; Sey, 1973; Tay & Gupta, 1983). If one is to take a more critical perspective on the use of these terms, then there ought to be consideration of the possibility that some speakers in the outer circle are NSs in their own right (i.e., NSs of Singaporean English, Fijian English, Kenyan English, and so on). This view adopts a pluricentric understanding of English norms that is not based only on the inner-circle varieties.

In fact, it may be more helpful to avoid the use of the terms NS and NNS altogether in reference to English speakers because of the problematic assumption that (standard) inner-circle varieties are the only legitimate, and hence de facto, target varieties for outer-circle or expanding-circle speakers. Mufwene (2001) explains that the continued use of these two terms creates an unhelpful dichotomy among speakers and perpetuates the view that "only a minority of speakers around the world speak legitimate varieties, the rest speak illegitimate offspring of English" (p. 139). Even the terms inner circle and outer circle can be viewed as divisive. As Mufwene (2001) writes,

> the danger of subscribing to such a position lies in us linguists perpetuating biases similar to the distinction *inner circle* versus *outer circle*, which presents some varieties as peripheral or marginal, and in accepting distinctions which are social but not academic nor useful to understanding language evolution.
>
> (p. 139)

Ownership of English

The concept of ownership is seen as better suited to describe English speakers' proficiency because it avoids the overly static dichotomies that inner-outer circle, or NS-NNS, produce. Ownership, itself, is a construct that requires careful analysis because it is viewed as referring either to *indigenization* or *legitimacy*.

Ownership as indigenization

In research on IVEs, the term ownership has been used to refer to the ways in which speakers appropriate the English language for their own needs. For example, Chisanga and Kamwan-gamalu (1997) use this term to refer to the indigenization of English in South Africa by means of lexical borrowings, morpho-syntactic transfer, and semantic extension. Their study illus-trates the productive processes that exemplify the ways in which speakers have appropriated English for their own use, and it is representative of a long tradition of similar research, such as that by Kachru (1983), Lowenberg (1986), Platt, Weber, and Ho (1984), and Thumboo (2001b).

In his plenary address, entitled "The Ownership of English," Widdowson (1994) also used the term ownership to refer to the ways in which speakers appropriate English for their own use. He argues that NSs no longer have sole authority over which forms are grammatical because norms and standards are no longer only created by communities of speakers from mother-tongue contexts. He criticizes the application of exonormative standards to international varieties of English for measuring speakers' proficiency and describes indigenization as an alternative way of viewing mastery over the language. Widdowson (1994) states, "You are proficient in a language to the extent that you possess it, make it your own, bend it to your will, assert yourself through it rather than simply submit to the dictates of its form" (p. 384). The flexibility of the English language and the pluricentricity of norms have become the emphasis of this line of research; however, the issue of whether IVEs can or should be considered equivalent to native varieties of English, in terms of legitimacy, remains to be fully investigated or theorized.

Ownership as legitimacy

Norton (1997; Peirce, 1995) conceptualizes ownership as legitimacy within a broader framework that is useful for examining the complex linguistic identity of IVE speakers. She argues that the categorization of speakers into NSs and NNSs sets up a dichotomy that prevents learners from owning English because they are prevented from becoming legitimate speakers of it. Her study of immigrant women in Canada (Peirce, 1995) shows how the binary distinction between the language learner and the target language (TL) culture is problematic because a learner's *investment* in the TL is the product of the learner's social identity in relation to the social world. One of the participants in her study, Martina, developed investment in English due to her role as primary caregiver in her family. Though she initially relied on her children to translate for her because of her lack of proficiency, over time she invoked her identity as mother and wife to resist being marginalized by the TL community. Martina describes her experience of negotiating her rent with her landlord in a journal entry (Peirce, 1995):

> The first time I was very nervous and afraid to talk on the phone. . . . After ESL course when we moved and our landlords tried to persuade me that we have to pay for whole year, I got upset and I talked with him on the phone over one hour and I didn't think about the tenses rules. I had known that I couldn't give up. My children were very surprised when they heard me.
>
> (p. 22)

From this perspective, the learner's progress requires developing a relationship with the social world around her that involves a sense of legitimacy as a speaker of English. Viewing language as a form of *cultural capital* (Bourdieu, 1977), Norton writes, "If learners invest in a second language, they do so with the understanding that they will acquire a wider range of symbolic and material resources" (Peirce, 1995, p. 17). In other words, speakers' investment in English yields legitimacy for them because it allows them to participate more fully in their societies, equipped with all the necessary resources. In later work, Norton (1997) reveals how speakers' investment in the TL ultimately leads to ownership via a sense of the right to speak (i.e., legitimacy as a speaker): "If learners of English cannot claim ownership of a language, they might not consider themselves legitimate speakers of that language" (p. 422).

Norton developed her conceptualization of ownership to refer to second language acquisition among immigrants in Canada, but the issue of legitimacy she focuses on is also relevant for speakers from the outer circle. If these speakers are invested in their local varieties and view them as forms of symbolic capital, it follows that their standard (i.e., target) variety is a local variety, and, hence, that they view themselves as legitimate speakers of English. Of course, the concepts of legitimacy and ownership apply to all groups, whether in the inner, outer, or expanding circle. For example, researchers in Great Britain (Leung, Harris, & Rampton, 1997; Rampton, 1987, 1995) and the United States (Goldstein, 1987; Zuengler, 1989) have shown how speakers of nonstandard varieties, IL speakers, and IVE speakers orient themselves toward varieties of English that are not the standard, inner-circle variety for the purpose of expressing group solidarity or social identity. For all these groups, the determining factor in owning the English language is whether the speakers view the variety they use as being a legitimate variety in a social, political, and economic sense.

Though the issue of legitimacy is relevant for all groups of English speakers, the situation for IVE speakers is complicated by historical relations with the inner circle as the source of standard English. Many IVE speakers' ability to develop investment in the local variety of English is thwarted by the frequent problem of "linguistic schizophrenia" (Kachru, 1992a, p. 60), that is, the conflict of speaking a local, sometimes stigmatized, variety while simultaneously deferring to an inner-circle variety (typically the RP dialect of British English) as the standard variety. Consequently, the question of determining who speaks legitimate English hinges upon whether speakers view themselves as legitimate speakers of English vis-à-vis exonormative or endonormative standards.

Additionally, IVE speakers do not have equal access to the claim of ownership. Given the inequitable social, economic, and political histories of certain groups in colonial and postcolonial contexts, relatively few populations have achieved full access to English via English-medium schooling, the primary setting for acquisition of English (Kwan-Terry, 1991; Pennycook, 1994). In addition, governments may block claims to ownership. Wee (2002) illustrates a case in which legitimacy is withheld from speakers who claim English as their mother tongue. He explains that, despite claims by a growing number of Singaporeans of all races that English is their legitimate mother tongue and the primary or only language of the home, they are not recognized as NSs of English by the government. Instead, the Singaporean government prefers to assign NS status following ethnic lines instead of linguistic ones to preserve multiracial harmony in Singaporean society.

Legitimacy expressed through conversation

Norton's (1997; Peirce, 1995) conception of legitimacy is a personal, amorphous stance that is constructed and revealed through discourse; therefore, careful examination of language users' discourse should provide novel perspectives on legitimacy. In particular, three sets of constructs are useful for analysis of conversation. First, what is constructed through talk are the learners' *discourse identities*, which are shaped by their *situated identities.* According to Zimmerman (1998), "Discourse identities bring into play relevant components of conversational machinery, while situated identities deliver pertinent agendas, skills and relevant knowledge, allowing participants to accomplish various projects in an orderly and reproducible way" (p. 88). Zimmerman contrasts situated identities with *transportable identities*, which are characteristics such as gender or ethnicity that "travel with individuals across situations and are potentially relevant in and for any situation and in and for any spate of interaction" (p. 90). For the present study, however, I classified ownership as a feature of situated identity because legitimacy over English is not a static aspect of identity, as Peirce (1995) has shown.

Second, I analyzed the conversation for the way it demonstrates the speakers' footing, Goffman's (1981) term for the position or alignment an individual takes in uttering a given linguistic expression. For Goffman (1981), speakers may shift their footing from the *animator*, "the sounding box . . . the body engaged in acoustic activity," to the *author*, "someone who has selected the sentiments that are being expressed," to the *principal*, "someone whose position is established by the words that are spoken . . . a person active in some particular social identity or role, some special capacity as a member of a group, office, category, relationship, association, or whatever, some socially based source of self-identification" (p. 144).

Throughout the task used in the research, participants took on the discourse identities of recipients, as they were in the position to respond to the sentences they were presented with. They also took on discourse identities, such as speaker-recipient, questioner-answerer, and interrogator-interrogatee, when debating the acceptability of the sentences with one another. These shifts in discourse identities provided opportunities to see whether they aligned with one another as speakers with the situated identities of people holding legitimate authority over English.

The third set of concepts, *receptive roles*, provides further elaboration to the concept of footing. I used Scollon's (1998) receptive roles—*receptor*, *interpreter*, and *judge*—to identify the nature of the interactions because the participants were being asked to respond to utterances that had already been produced, in written format. Scollon's category of receptor parallels Goffman's (1981) animator, as this person receives the communication and does not evaluate it. The interpreter, the counterpart to the author, construes a meaning from the communication. Lastly, the judge evaluates and validates the communication, similar to the principal in Goffman's framework.

To investigate ownership of English through the concept of legitimacy, I compare the situated identities of speakers of outer-circle varieties of English to those of inner-circle varieties through the examination of three aspects of conversation that reveal receptor, interpreter, and judge footing.

The purpose of the study is to further explore Norton's (1997; Peirce, 1995) concept of ownership to see how speakers' talk enacts identities that carry legitimacy as English speakers. I chose CA methods to analyze talk recorded during the performance of an AJT containing 24 English sentences. Because Norton was interested in the relationship between her participants' English learning and their social positions as immigrants in Canada, she employed ethnographic methodology involving diaries, interviews, questionnaires, and observations. However, acknowledging the reality that many IVE speakers are reluctant to overtly claim ownership of English because of a lack of confidence in claiming their ownership, deference to inner-circle norms, or even governmental policy that labels them as NNSs, I avoided asking explicit questions that might trigger participants' metalinguistic judgments about their language use. Instead, I chose to rely on a close analysis of the talk that occurred during the AJT to provide a window into both inner- and outer-circle speakers' degrees of ownership toward English.

Method

Participants

A total of 16 speakers of English participated in this study who, on a geographic level, represented inner- and outer-circle countries. Each country was represented by two dyads. The outer circle was represented by participants from India, Malaysia, and Singapore who had been in the United States for less than 1 year and were enrolled in an advanced ESL composition course at the same university. The students from the outer-circle countries were placed in this course based on their scores on the Michigan Test of English Language Proficiency and an evaluation of their writing skills by ESL staff. The students from Malaysia and Singapore were of Chinese ethnicity, a factor that potentially distinguished them from their classmates of non-Chinese ethnicity, who shared the same home country but may not have shared the same degree of ownership of English due to a variety of historical factors that have led to advantaged access to English for many Chinese people in these two countries (Pennycook, 1994). Similarly, the Indian participants were all upper middle-class students who had benefited from private education, a tradition of higher education in their families, and regular exposure to English from a very young age.

The inner-circle participants were represented by two dyads of middle-class, White speakers of standard American English. All participants completed a questionnaire in which I asked them to list the languages they speak (see Table 3.1). The U.S. participants all characterized themselves as monolingual English speakers with limited proficiency in foreign languages, such as Spanish, German, and French. The questionnaire also asked the outer-circle participants,

Table 3.1 Linguistic repertoires of multilingual participants

Participant	Home country	Languages used	Participant's self-classification of English usage
Karthik	India	Tamil, Hindi, English	one of my languages as a multilingual speaker
Mina	India	English, Hindi, Sindhi, French	second language
Anand	India	English, Gujarati, Hindi	one of my languages as a multilingual speaker
Pradyuman	India	English, Hindi	one of my languages as a bilingual speaker
Mein-Yhee	Malaysia	English, Mandarin, Cantonese, Hakka, Malay	one of my languages as a multilingual speaker
Jasmine	Malaysia	Chinese, English, Japanese, Malay, Cantonese, Mandarin	one of my languages as a multilingual speaker
Stephanie	Malaysia	Mandarin, Malay, English	second language
Lucy	Malaysia	English, Malay, Cantonese	second language
Sook-Yin	Singapore	English, Mandarin, French	one of my languages as a bilingual speaker
Kenneth	Singapore	Chinese, English, Malay, Mandarin	one of my languages as a multilingual speaker
Tony	Singapore	Mandarin, Japanese, English	second language
Ee-Hong	Singapore	Malay, English, Mandarin	one of my languages as a multilingual speaker

Note. All names of participants are pseudonyms.

"How do you describe your use of English in your home country?" Their answers offer an initial understanding of their orientations toward English. Even though these speakers had all been classified as ESL students by the university they were attending, their self-classification showed differing views on this label.

Task

An AJT was chosen for the task so that participants would engage in conversations about the acceptability of English sentences. The purpose of using the AJT was not to see whether participants accepted specific forms, but to elicit and record talk that might contain within it their stances toward English. I intentionally paired participants who shared the same backgrounds because I felt that the imbalance in power due to the different degrees of legitimacy historically accorded to inner- and outer-circle varieties of English would have led to an atmosphere in which

Table 3.2 Acceptability judgment task sentences

Type and sentence	Country where attested
Neologism	
1. If a passenger on a preponed flight shows up at the time written on his ticket and finds that the plane has already left, he should be entitled to a refund.	India
2. I am sorry for the botheration I have caused you.	India, Malaysia, United Kingdom
3. The gloriosity of the sunset made us wish that we had our camera.	Invented
4. The perfectity of a new computer program can only be tested by running it.	Invented
Countability of nouns	
5. The school was able to buy new computer equipments for the students last year.	India, Malaysia, Philippines, Singapore
6. Many researches have shown that smoking cigarettes is dangerous.	Ghana, India, Malaysia, Singapore, United Kingdom
7. The children fell in the muds near the swamp behind the house.	Invented
8. I picked up a rice from the floor and threw it away.	Invented
Topic-comment structure	
9. English they have declared the official language of Kenya.	India, Nigeria
10. TV I don't usually watch because I have too much homework.	Malaysia
11. Outside the boys they like to play even if it is extremely cold.	Invented
12. For research papers, the students, they use computers to type them.	Invented
Tense/aspect	
13. She was having a headache and could not concentrate on the lecture.	India, Nigeria, Kenya
14. I have read this book yesterday.	India
15. Jones breaks the record for the highest number of invented goals per game this season.	Invented
16. Every time we go to the movies, my father bought popcorn for us.	Invented
Prepositions	
17. It is difficult for me to cope up with all the work that my boss gives me.	Malaysia, Singapore

continued

Table 3.2 Continued

Type and sentence	Country where attested
18. The student requested about an extension for her research paper because she was sick for five days.	India, Nigeria, South Africa
19. After you have read the instructions, please fill the form so that your request can be processed.	Invented
20. After the meeting, the managers discussed about the possibility of raising their invented employees' salaries by 10%.	Invented (possibly undergoing codification)
21. Although many students have studied English for more than five years, many of them have not mastered punctuation skills.	India, Kenya, Nigeria, Singapore, South Africa,
22. One of my instructor told me that when a person learns a language, he or she also learns the culture of that language.	Malaysia
23. In the presidential election last year, he won by substantial majority.	India, Malaysia, Singapore, United States, United Kingdom
24. Your daughter will attend the University of Wisconsin next year, isn't it?	India, Malaysia, Singapore, United Kingdom

Note. Except for the distractors, the first two sentences in each category are attested. The second two are invented based on productive morphological rules in English (neologisms and countability of nouns), misplacement of the topic in topic-comment structure, violation of punctual/nonpunctual distinction in tense and aspect, and unattested combinations of prepositions with verbs. Distractor sentences include variation in subject-verb agreement, articles, and tag question concord. The attested forms may occur in additional Englishes to those listed.

the outer-circle participants did not feel at ease to fully express themselves with inner-circle coparticipants. Pairing outer- and inner-circle speakers would have maintained the divide between the center and the periphery that sustains the lack of legitimacy of outer-circle Englishes because it would have placed the outer-circle speakers in the position of having to respond to the center in order to claim their legitimacy as English speakers. Pairing participants with similar backgrounds avoided the center-periphery orientation while still allowing for the potential outcome that the outer-circle dyads would produce exonormative standards through their talk, an outcome that would suggest that these speakers do not attribute much legitimacy to the local, indigenized varieties of their home countries.

The AJT sentences were presented only in written form to keep phonology from becoming a contributing factor to participants' evaluations of the nativeness of the English (cf. Smith, 1992). It should be noted that previous research has used AJTs to assess speakers' attitudes toward particular forms of local varieties of English (e.g., Sahgal & Agnihotri, 1985; Soo, 1991), but the goal of such research was to assess the acceptability of certain forms common to local Englishes. The 24 sentences I chose (see Table 3.2) for the AJT included grammatical and lexical forms used in descriptive research on IVE speakers (Cheshire, 1991; Kachru, 1992b; Platt, Weber, & Ho, 1984). I took 10 of the 24 sentences directly from attested grammatical varieties

Sample AJT Item

The children fell in the muds near the swamp behind the house.

OK   Not OK   Not Sure

Corrected Sentence: _____

How did you decide?   It sounds right/wrong   grammar rule   guess

Other method: _____

Figure 3.1 Sample AJT item

and manipulated another 10 to be ungrammatical by (a) intentionally pairing tense and aspect violations of syntax, (b) including lexical items that should violate morphological productivity principles in word formation, and (c) devising lexical items and topicalization structures that had not been attested. I used the remaining 4 sentences as distractors. I included varieties of English that speakers would and would not have likely encountered before so that they might discuss them differently depending on familiarity.

Participants from the same home country were asked to work together to evaluate the sentences and complete the AJT form. They were told that the purpose of the study was to better understand the ways in which people judge English sentences and were asked to circle on the form the strategy they had used to decide on their answer (see Figure 3.1).

The participants were left alone to complete the task while I recorded their discourse on an audiocassette. I also used a videocassette recorder as a back-up recording device and to identify which speaker was talking. Although nonverbal behaviors may well indicate another set of levels at which ownership can be examined, I limited my study to just the talk produced among participants. I set no time constraint because this factor might have limited discussion of sentences. I used CA methods (Pomerantz & Fehr, 1997; Sacks, Schegloff, & Jefferson, 1974) to transcribe the recorded discourse (for transcription conventions, see the Appendix).

Analysis

My analysis of the participants' situated identity relative to the AJT sentences was based on the language of the actions the participants took as they shifted their footing from receptor to interpreter to judge to evaluate the sentences. Throughout the analysis, I looked for recurrent patterns that would offer points of comparison on how dyads oriented to the acceptability of the sentences, following Goffman's (1981) advice that "linguistics provides us with the cues and markers through which such footings become manifest, helping us to find our way to a structural basis for analyzing them" (p. 157). Three linguistic patterns that emerged from the participants' talk reveal aspects of footing:

1. references to the speakers' own English usage
2. the use of human subject pronouns
3. modal usage

These linguistic features can be related to shifts in footing from the receptor to the interpreter to the judge, the entity whose position or beliefs are being applied to the utterance. They were therefore used to analyze participants' footing so that I could compare ownership between the inner- and outer-circle groups.

Results

For the sake of comparison, I used the discourse of one dyad from each country per example. The discourse showed the typical pattern that emerged wherein one member of the dyad would read the sentence aloud and the dyad would then discuss the sentence. Eventually, the dyads would come to an agreement so that they could complete the AJT form for each of the 24 sentences. Whether from the inner or outer circle, all dyads displayed similar linguistic cues and markers that indexed the authority they invoked to judge the sentences and, therefore, their degree of ownership over English.

Reference to own usage as a display of ownership

The most remarkable similarity in the discourse among all of the speakers is the references made to their own usage as the norm for deciding if a sentence was acceptable or not. This type of discourse reveals an orientation to English that self-ascribes the speakers as legitimate members of the group of speakers with authority over the language. Sometimes, the difference between what they reported as their own usage contradicted their reports of usage they had heard. The first example below is followed by the first turns of talk from a pair from each country. Each dyad's response to the lexical item *botheration* illustrates the similar ways in which the participants moved from being receptors (if they read the sentence aloud) to being interpreters (offering their understanding of the sentence), to being judges (when they determined whether the sentence was acceptable and then offered their basis for their judgment).

I am sorry for the botheration I have caused you. (AJT Sentence 18)

1. India (Dyad A)

1	M:	I think it's okay.
2	K:	Botheration?
3		I've <u>never</u> used that word. I've <u>heard</u> people use that word, but,
4	M:	I=
5	K:	=°botheration°
6	M:	I'm sorry for the botheration I have caused you. I hate to bother you, that's-
7	K:	I'm sorry for bothering you. Simple, easy,
8	M:	Ha ha.
9	K:	sweet.
10	M:	Yeah, that's simple, easy, sweet too but (.) um,
11	K:	This one I'm sorry for the botheration I've caused you. It sounds too long and cranky
12		to me.
13	M:	Ha ha. But I guess it's still correct.
14	K:	Yeah, I think, maybe it is. I've heard people use it. I never use it though.

Mina (M) and Karthik's (K) talk attests current usage of the archaic word *botheration*, a form that has been documented as occurring in India, though it is interesting to note that they disagree over whether it is a legitimate word. Karthik assumes the role of the interpreter in Lines

2 and 5 when he pronounces *botheration* with question intonation, and then again with low volume, revealing that the problem with the sentence is due to this lexical item. In Line 6, Mina illustrates her shift from receptor to interpreter and then to judge as she rewrites the utterance to meet her criteria for acceptability. In Lines 3, 11–12, and 14, Karthik documents his shift from receptor to judge, revealing the means by which he determines *botheration* to be ungrammatical. This excerpt reveals the range of standards among Indian speakers of English and also points to the ways in which these speakers rely on their own usage as a guide for what they consider to be correct English, despite what they have heard.

2.   Malaysia (Dyad A)

    1   M: [I'm sorry for the botheration-
    2   J: [I'm sorry for the botheration-
    3   M: ha ha ha- Is there such a word?
    4   J: I'm sorry for the for the (.) trouble I have caused you.
    5   M: Yeah, inconvenience, whatever, but not botheration.
    6   <misuse of word.>
    7   J: I'm sorry for the trouble I have caused you.
    8   M: Trouble, inconvenience, anything lah.

    In Excerpt 2, Mein-Yhee (M) and Jasmine (J) act as receptor in unison, and their simultaneous hitch right after their reading of *botheration* signals their shared orientation to the word as being problematic. Mein-Yhee's laughter in Line 3 points to her judgment of the word as unacceptable, and her question selects Jasmine as a capable judge because the question positions Jasmine as a knowing answerer. Jasmine's suggestion, "trouble," invokes the interpreter, and Mein-Yhee's turn in Lines 5 and 6 signal shared linguistic norms as the basis for finding *botheration* unacceptable and for revising the sentence.

3.   Singapore (Dyad A)

    1   S: I am sorry for the botheration I have caused you.
    2   K: No such thing as botheration. I'm sorry for the bother I have caused you. Um,
             °for
    3   the bother I've caused you,°
    4   S: >Trouble?<
    5   (1.0)
    6   [Certainly,
    7   K: [Yeah, I think it sounds better.

    Excerpt 3 shows strong confidence from Kenneth (K) that the sentence is not acceptable due to the fact that, for him, the word *botheration* does not exist. In Line 2, his footing can be interpreted as that of the judge, the source of authority for making the judgment, though his replacement of *botheration* to "bother" does not get taken up by Sook-Yin (S). Instead, like Mina, she suggests an alternative, "trouble," to signal her rejection of "bother" by enacting the role of author. Kenneth's agreement (Line 7) reveals a shared linguistic norm in regard to the final version of the sentence.

4.   USA (Dyad A)

    1   J: I am sorry for the bo<u>thera</u>tion I have cause you. (0.5) hh..
    2   (0.5)

3	P:	Hmm,
4	J:	Botheration is >NOT A WORD.< (0.5) I don't think.(0.5)
5	P:	[I don't think so either.
6	J:	[Well, it's not okay:
7	J:	I am sorry=
8	P:	=for the trouble.

Very similarly to the Singaporeans, the U.S. dyad in Excerpt 4 judge the sentence unacceptable because they reject it as part of their lexicon. Jill's (J) reading of the word combines her receptor role with the interpreter role as her stress midway through *botheration* marks it as being problematic. Line 4 is a clear statement of her view of the word, though it is interesting to see that she ameliorates her confidence with a quick mitigating statement, "I don't think." This excerpt offers evidence that standard English speakers of the inner circle are not necessarily the ones with the most authority or self-confidence in English; Jill's response in Line 4 and Paul's (P) in Line 5 both show more hedging than did the Singaporeans' or the Indians' responses.

The next example shows the ways in which the participants reacted when faced with an unattested neologism. Though all of the participants deemed it unacceptable, they shifted their footing to the role of the judge in ways that sometimes differed from the first example above. The dyads from India, Singapore, and Malaysia gave more reasons for their judgments than did the U.S. dyad, who were quicker to judge the word *gloriosity* as being unacceptable.

The gloriosity of the sunset made us wish that we had our camera. (AJT Sentence 20)

5. India (Dyad B)

1	A:	Gloriosity hh.=
2	P:	=Gloriosity hhh..
3	A:	Ooh, sounds, so hh..=
4	P:	The glorious, the glorious, uh
5		(1.0)
6	A:	I think gloriosity is wrong.
7	P:	It is. ha ha ha,
8	A:	It's just so wrong hh..
9	P:	I've never used that word (.) the gloriosity.
10	A:	I've never heard that word before-
11	P:	The glorious nature of the sunset [made us
12	A:	[I mean I've heard the
		word glorious but not
13		gloriosity. That sounds like too: (.) too glorious man. It just=
14	P:	=1 would just say the glorious sunset made us wish we had our camera. The
15		glorious sunset, you know.

The focus on the word *gloriosity* followed by a laughter token shows both speakers' orientations to the word as being problematic. Interestingly, the authority that the participants refer to comes from two different sources. Pradyuman (P) shifts his footing to that of the judge in his statement, "I've never used that word" (Line 9). Anand (A) judges the word based on what he has heard, so the authority is an entity potentially outside himself (Line 10). It is possible that he is somehow trying to bolster the authority behind the footing of Pradyuman's judge, but he does not refer to his own usage to do so.

6.   Malaysia (Dyad B)

1	L:	The gloriosity-
2	S:	I've not heard about that though.
3	L:	The gloria,
4	S:	No. The glorious- well:
5	L:	of sunset made us wish that we had our camera.
6		What is the root word of gloriosity? Gloria?
7	S:	Or the beauty of the sunset.
8	L:	Yeah, CAN. (0.5) better.
9	S:	I'm not sure but beauty would be better. Not just beauty, but
10	L:	Is there such a word? Is there such a word glorissity?
11	S:	I'm not sure, I'm not sure.
12	L:	But it [sounds wrong.
13	S:	[Could be wrong.

Similarly to Anand, Stephanie (S) relies on what she has heard as the basis for her judgment. She does not rely on her own usage, nor does Lucy (L). Instead, the young women seek an alternative word and display an uncertainty about the existence of *gloriosity* (Lines 9–13). This uncertainty indexes a lesser degree of ownership in this sequence of talk.

7.   Singapore (Dyad B)

1	T:	The \<glorious\> sunset made us wish that=
2	E:	=>No< no such gloriosity, right?
3	T:	Yeah.
4		(1.0)
5	E:	The glorious sunset made us wish that we had our cameras.

In Line 1, Tony's (T) drawn-out pronunciation of the word *gloriosity* points to the word as being problematic. Ee-Hong (E) orients to Tony's concern and asks Tony to draw on his own authority to judge the sentence. The question format of this judgment has the same degree of confidence as the Malaysians' judgment (Excerpt 6), but here, the Singaporean young men's discourse displays no doubt about whether the word is part of the English lexicon.

8.   USA (Dyad B)

1	S:	The gloriosity hh. of the sunset made us wish that we had our camera.
2		Okay, it's not a word. Not a word anyone would use.
3	C:	It's not a word but (.) do you want to say the glorious sunset made us wish that
4		we had a camera or?
5	S:	The glory of [the sunset.

Of interest in Excerpt 8 is Sally's (S) Line 2, where she says that *gloriosity* is "not a word anyone would use." By using the word *anyone*, her talk indexes her as the judge for the group of English speakers to which she belongs and on behalf of whom she speaks in making her judgment. Her use of *anyone* and the judgment that ensues legitimize Sally as a speaker with authority, a speaker with ownership of English. The U.S. dyad here agrees more quickly than the other dyads that the word is not acceptable and spends less time debating the acceptable word form.

One explanation for this difference is that the outer-circle speakers may have more experience with neologisms of this sort because they have lived in contexts in which they are likely to have encountered Englishes with a great deal of variance than the inner-circle U.S. speakers. In Singapore, Malaysia, and India, it is possible to encounter Englishes on a continuum, from pidgin varieties to acrolectal varieties, that mimic RP in every way but phonology. On the other hand, the middle-class, White U.S. speakers in the study are likely to be more limited in the varieties of English that they encounter, and, according to informal discussions with them after the study was carried out, the majority of speakers they interact with share very similar social and linguistic backgrounds.

Pronouns and co-occurring modals as displays of ownership

In many of the discussions about AJT items involving countability of nouns, speakers made judgments using the statement *you + can + say/use*, where they related their opinions to what is possible to say in English. Generic use of *you* became particularly revealing because, according to Goffman (1981), pronouns index the source of authority, or the judge role, in Scollon's terms. Goffman explains how pronouns are implicated in shifts in footing to the role of the principal: "Often this will mean that the individual speaks, explicitly or implicitly in the name of 'we,' not 'I' . . . the 'we' including more than the self" (p. 145). In these contexts, generic use of *you* that can be replaced by *one* indicates that the pronoun cannot exclude the addressee (Kitigawa & Lehrer, 1990). By using this type of generic *you*, the speakers in the dialogues below include their interlocutors as members of the group that can or cannot say particular utterances.

The use of *can* in these contexts expresses the idea that something is possible because certain characteristics or conditions exist; this type of *can* incorporates permission, possibility, and ability (Coates, 1983, p. 86). In the AJT discourse, sentences are deemed acceptable by the speakers based on the condition that they not violate the linguistic norms the speakers hold. Therefore, use of the recurrent syntactic frame *you + can + say/use* indexes ownership among speakers who use it in their judgments.

I picked up a rice from the floor and threw it away. (AJT Sentence 10)

9. India (Dyad A)

4	K:	Picked [up the rice from-
5	M:	[Picked up rice and threw it away.
6		That's grammar rule ha. (.) Not okay=
7	K:	=What do you have if you just have <one grain>?
8	M:	No [even if you have one grain its still rice.
9	K:	[Even if I know, I know.
10		Picked [up rice, yeah.
11	M:	[Yeah.
12	M:	Oh [not okay.
13	K:	[Not okay.
14	M:	You can't even say I picked up the rice from the floor and threw it away.
15		[It's wrong.
16	K:	[Yeah: can't, can't say that.

The use of *can* enacts the role of principal in Excerpt 9, as it indexes Mina (M) and Karthik (K) as people with authority over English who are able to assert what is possible to say in the language. They realize that the physical possibility of picking up one piece of rice exists (Line 7), but the sentence is not grammatical for them because it is not what an English speaker can say (Lines 14–16).

10. Malaysia (Dyad B)

1	S:	I pick up a ri:ce from the floor and threw it away –heh.
2		(0.5)
3		A rice. A grain of rice? Because rice is kind of like plural?
4	L:	Yeah, that's right if its-
5	S:	A grain of rice.
6	L:	Yeah.
7	S:	A grain.
8		(2.5)
9	L:	But who, a grain of rice ha ha,
10	S:	Sounds-
11	L:	-hh.. Usually ha ha a few rice.
12	S:	Yeah.
13	L:	Wait a minute. A grain of rice?
14	S:	It could be a grain, it could be uh: (.) I picked up a handful of rice, you know?

The Malaysian dyad's discourse above shows less conviction in terms of the modals or pronouns regarding the status of *a rice* (Line 1) than the Indians' discourse. However, Stephanie's (S) reception of the sentence with a sound stretch on *rice* reveals that she interprets the word as being problematic in some way, as does her repair of the troublesome word and Lucy's (L) agreement (Line 4). Interestingly, though, Stephanie's statement, "It could be a grain" (Line 14), evinces her knowledge of what is possible to say in English, and she offers this possibility by replacing *a rice* with "a handful of rice."

11. Singapore (Dyad A)

1	K:	Okay. I picked up-
2	S:	>A grain<.
3	K:	No, you can't pick up a rice.
4	S:	Yeah [a grain of rice,
5	K:	[A grain of rice, uh-huh.

When receiving the sentence in Line 1, Kenneth (K) shifts his footing from receptor to judge with his hitch and unfinished reading of the phrase *a grain*. Kenneth's statement, "you can't pick up a rice," makes use of the generic pronoun *you*, which can be understood as meaning *anyone*, thus indexing "any English speaker," in conjunction with "can't," indexing the role of the judge as he invokes his authority to evaluate the sentence. Sook-Yin's (S) agreement and the pair's simultaneous pronunciation of "a grain of rice" reveal a shared linguistic norm in regard to how to talk about rice.

12. USA (Dyad B)

1	C:	Ha ha. I picked up a rice from the floor and threw it away.
2		I guess you just say I picked up rice.
3		(0.5)

4		Would you say some rice?
5	S:	Or a _piece_ of rice.
6	C:	A piece?
7		(1.5)
8		What do you think they're saying?
9		(0.5)
10		I guess I would say (.) I picked up rice from the floor because (0.5) ri:ce can be
11		one grain or many grain (s).
12	S:	I would never say I picked up rice from the floor.
13		A little rice, or some rice or (0.3) a piece of rice
14		I would never just say rice.
15	C:	I pick, I can say I picked the rice up from the floor.
16	S:	But that's that would signify plural. Plurality though. This is a rice so they're
17		trying to use say singular.
18	C:	But there's no singular form of rice.
19	S:	Right, so you say a _piece_ of rice or a grain of rice. I picked up a _grain_ of rice from
20		the floor hh..
21	C:	Yeah, I understand what you saying but,
22	S:	So how do we want to correct it?

In Excerpt 12, Craig (C) offers a repair to _a rice_ with his statement, "I guess you just say I picked up some rice," though his use of "I guess" displays less confidence than the unmitigated statements made by the Indian or Singaporean dyads. A possible reason for his mitigating statement may be due to his dilemma over choosing "some rice" or "a piece/grain of rice," as the ensuing dialogue shows. This excerpt shows that these inner-circle speakers (from the same hometown) do not agree on how to correct the sentence, and they show this disagreement through use of pronouns and modals. In response to Sally's (S) statement, "I would never say just rice," Craig's Line 15 indexes him as a speaker with authority by using "I can say I picked the rice up from the floor." Craig and Sally both use "I" to clearly show that they feel comfortable judging the sentence, based on how they would speak. The discussion continues, but in the end, they decide to write down both of their corrected versions of the sentence, reflecting their differing linguistic norms for the ways to refer to _rice_.

The next example on the AJT is based on an attested form in many outer-circle countries. This example illustrates the number of methods that the participants employed to judge the sentence and demonstrates how all of these methods incorporate shifts from interpreter to judge. In addition, it nicely illustrates how, for some members of both the inner and outer circle, no single set of norms was definable as the source of authority.

She was having a headache and could not concentrate on the lecture. (AJT Sentence 13)

13. USA (Dyad A)

1	J:	She was having a headache and could not concentrate on the lecture.
2		(0.5)
3	P:	She was having a headache should be:,
4	J:	uh, I've never heard it put that way.
5		She had a headache.
6	P:	Having a headache, [could be:
7	J:	[She has a headache.

Excerpt 13 shows how one of the U.S. dyads relies upon the same methods for judging the sentence as several of the outer-circle dyads by referring to what they have heard, not what they would say themselves. Jill's (J) Line 4 is quite similar to statements made by Anand (Excerpt 5, Lines 10 and 12) and Stephanie (Excerpt 6, Line 2).

14. USA (Dyad B)

1	C:	She was having a headache and could not concentrate on the lecture.
2		(0.3)
3		That sounds okay.
4		(0.3)
5	S:	I would say she had a headache and couldn't concentrate on the lecture.
6	C:	That's getting really nitpicky. This is an understandable English sentence. I mean,
7		And it (.) doesn't (.) openly violate a lot of rules.
8	S:	I'll just write um: that's not right.
9	C:	A political statement by Miss S__K__.
10	S:	We:ll: I wouldn't make it.

Excerpt 14 shows how two U.S. speakers disagree over whether a sentence is acceptable and shows how they enact the role of judge quite differently. Craig (C) feels the sentence sounds acceptable, but Sally (S) is adamant that her own usage should be the guide.

Excerpts 15 and 16 show how members of the outer circle find the same sentence acceptable based on the way it sounds. They focus on the conjunction in the sentence instead of the verb.

15. India (Dyad A)

1	K:	She was having a headache (.) and so: could not concentrate on the lecture? Maybe?
2	M:	To me it sounds okay.
3	K	Sounds okay?
4	M:	She was having a headache and could not,
5	K:	Oh yeah.
6	M:	So and could not concentrate.
7		No, she could not concentrate on the lecture, because she was having a headache.
8	K:	It's just a different way of saying it though.

16. Singapore (Dyad B)

1	T:	Okay, she was having a headache and could not concentrate on the lecture.
2		(0.5)
3		Sounds right?
4		(0.5)
5	E:	Okay.
6	T:	She was having a headache, and hence, I think right sounds better.
7	E:	It doesn't matter hh.. It doesn't matter. It wouldn't matter to me,

Finally, Excerpt 17 shows that one of the Malaysian dyads deems both "was having a headache" and "had a headache" as acceptable. Their discourse reveals the possibility of multiple, coexisting linguistic norms for speakers.

17. Malaysia (Dyad A)

1	M:	She was having a headache and could not concentrate on the lecture.
2		(3.0)
3		think it's okay.
4		(3.0)
5	J:	Mm.(.) Or she had a headache and could not concentrate on the lecture. She was having,=
6	M:	=She was having a headache like say she was having a [headache
7	J:	[She was having a headache when
8		while in class, while a lecture, she had a headache and could not concentrate on the
9		lecture, hmm. [She was having a headache she was,
10	M:	[But is there anything wrong with this I mean we don't need to change if
11		that's that's not wrong, right?
12		(2.0)
13	J:	She had a headache, and [was-
14	M:	[Why do you think that she was having a headache is wrong?
15	J:	I didn't say it was wrong.
16	M:	Then it's ok↑ay. Hh..

Discussion

This study of speakers' orientations toward English norms questions the division between inner and outer circles because, in terms of ownership, members of both groups displayed similar indicators of authority over English. The ways in which speakers from both circles shifted roles from receptor to interpreter to judge followed noticeably similar paths as the speakers invoked their own usage or used the syntactic frame *you* + *can* + *say* to assume the role of judge in evaluating the sentences. Not all speakers invoked the same means to judge the sentences, however, and the various means by which they judged the sentences point to varying degrees of authority over English, even among inner-circle speakers. More often, though, the speakers from the outer circle displayed less certainty, or lesser degrees of ownership, than did the speakers from the inner circle.

This uncertainty among outer-circle speakers may be the result of their experience with multiple and conflicting norms for English. For example, it is surprising that the Singaporeans all rejected the use of "researches" or "equipments" as countable nouns when these particular forms have been attested multiple times in Singapore as well as in the United Kingdom (Lowenberg, 1986; Platt, Weber, & Ho, 1984). Their rejection of the forms may come from their exposure to American English norms, or else they may have acquired a heightened awareness of the features of Singaporean English, which are stigmatized in other regions of the world. In contrast to the outer-circle dyads, though, the discourse among the inner-circle pairs rarely showed doubt, a finding that indicates a great deal of self-confidence and a firm sense of legitimacy among the U.S. speakers that they are in an authoritative position from which to judge English. For both sets of dyads, the data show that speakers from the same countries may assume the role of judge with equal confidence, yet may still disagree with their partner, a finding that reflects the existence of different linguistic norms for all speakers.

This study is limited in its analysis of ownership because it only examines the situated linguistic identities expressed during an experimental task. The participants may orient to English very differently in other contexts, such as in an ESL class or in a conversation with a speaker from the inner circle. Furthermore, it is important to stress that the potential for ownership should not simply be applied to all IVE speakers because equal access to English is not present in outer-circle countries. Moreover, ownership is not meant to be a binary measure similar to the NS-NNS dichotomy or the inner–outer-circle division; speakers may have varying degrees of ownership because social factors, such as class, race, and access to education, act as gatekeeping devices. Even expanding-circle speakers from nations such as Korea or Brazil may have high degrees of ownership, particularly those who are educated in private, English-medium schools or those whose socioeconomic status affords them ownership of English. Conversely, it is important to acknowledge that the concept of ownership extends to speakers of nonstandard varieties in the inner circle, as they are often marginalized and perceived as speaking deficient, illegitimate varieties of English, a fact that often yields few opportunities for such speakers to feel as though they own English in any real sense.

Despite these limitations, this study suggests that IVE speakers who have not traditionally been considered on par with NSs of inner-circle varieties of English, or who might not overtly claim ownership in other contexts, may in fact orient toward English in very similar ways to speakers from the inner circle. With a better understanding of how speakers orient toward English, researchers will have a clearer starting point from which to understand language development among language learners. Furthermore, from a more practical point of view, English language professionals will benefit from knowing how their students orient toward English. If teachers are aware of which variety of English their students consider the TL to be and the degree of ownership the students display to that variety, they will better recognize students' language abilities and more fairly measure their linguistic achievements.

Appendix

Transcription conventions

(.)	micropause
(0.5)	half-second pause
[	talk in overlap
-	cut off
=	latched talk
:	sound stretch
hh..	out breath
↑	rise in pitch
CAPS	loud volume
XX	emphasis
.	falling contour
,	falling-rising contour
?	rising contour
°XX°	whispered
<XX>	slowly enunciated speech
>XX<	quickly enunciated speech
S__K__	talk omitted for anonymity

Note

* Some of the data presented in this study were collected originally for a paper presentation (Higgins, 1999). Another version of this paper was presented at another conference the following year (Higgins, 2000).

References

Bailey, R., & Görlach, M. (Eds). (1982). *English as a world language.* Ann Arbor: University of Michigan Press.

Bamgbose, A. (1992). Standard Nigerian English: Issues of identification. In B. B. Kachru (Ed.), *The other tongue* (2nd ed., pp. 148–161). Urbana: University of Illinois Press.

Bamgbose, A. (1998). Torn between the norms: Innovation in world Englishes. *World Englishes, 17,* 1–14.

Bamgbose, A., Banjo, A., & Thomas, A. (Eds.). (1995). *New Englishes: A West African perspective.* Ibadan, Nigeria: Mosuro Publishers for the British Council.

Bourdieu, P. (1977). The economics of linguistics exchanges. *Social Science Information, 16,* 645–668.

Brutt-Griffler, J., & Samimy, K. K. (1999). Revisiting the colonial in the postcolonial: Critical praxis for nonnative English-speaking teachers in a TESOL program. *TESOL Quarterly, 33,* 413–431.

Brutt-Griffler, J., & Samimy, K. K. (2001). Transcending the nativeness paradigm. *World Englishes, 20,* 99–106.

Cheshire, J. (Ed.). (1991). *English around the world: Sociolinguistic perspectives.* Cambridge: Cambridge University Press.

Chisanga, T., & Kamwangamalu, N. M. (1997). Owning the mother tongue: The English language in South Africa. *Journal of Multilingual and Multicultural Development, 18,* 89–99.

Coates, J. (1983). *The semantics of the modal auxiliaries.* London: Croomhelm.

Davies, A. (1991). *The native speaker in applied linguistics.* Edinburgh, Scotland: Edinburgh University Press.

Davies, A. (1996). Proficiency or the native speaker: What are we trying to achieve in ELT? In G. Book & B. Seidlhofer (Eds.), *Principle and practice in applied linguistics* (pp. 145–159). Oxford: Oxford University Press.

Firth, A., & Wagner, J. (1997). On discourse, communication, and (some) fundamental concepts in SLA research. *Modern Language Journal, 81,* 285–300.

Goffman, E. (1981). *Forms of talk.* Philadelphia: University of Pennsylvania Press.

Goldstein, L. (1987). Standard English: The only target for non-native speakers of English? *TESOL Quarterly, 21,* 417–436.

Higgins, C. (1999, September). *Grammaticality judgments and speakers of English from the outer circle.* Paper presented at the Second Language Research Forum, University of Minnesota, Minneapolis/St. Paul.

Higgins, C. (2000, April). *"Ownership" and global varieties of English: A conversation analytic study of linguistic identity.* Paper presented at the 14th Annual International Conference on Pragmatics and Language Learning, Parasession on Discourse and Grammar, University of Illinois at Champaign-Urbana.

Kachru, B. B. (1965). The Indianness in Indian English. *Word, 21,* 391–410.

Kachru, B. B. (1976). Models of English for the third world: White man's linguistic burden or language pragmatic? *TESOL Quarterly, 10,* 221–239.

Kachru, B. B. (Ed.). (1982). *The other tongue.* Urbana: University of Illinois Press.

Kachru, B. B. (1983). *The Indianization of English.* Delhi: Oxford University Press.

Kachru, B. B. (1986). *The alchemy of English.* Urbana: University of Illinois Press.

Kachru, B. B. (1992a). Models for non-native Englishes. In B. B. Kachru (Ed.), *The other tongue* (2nd ed., pp. 48–74). Urbana: University of Illinois Press.

Kachru, B. B. (Ed.). (1992b). *The other tongue* (2nd ed.). Urbana: University of Illinois Press.

Kachru, B. B. (1997). World Englishes 2000: Resources for research and teaching. In L. Smith (Ed.), *World Englishes 2000* (pp. 209–251). Honolulu: University of Hawaii Press.

Kitigawa, C., & Lehrer, A. (1990). Impersonal uses of personal pronouns. *Journal of Pragmatics, 14,* 739–759.

Kwan-Terry, A. (1991). The economics of language in Singapore: Students' use of extracurricular language lessons. *Journal of Asian Pacific Communication, 2,* 69–89.

Leung, C., Harris, R., & Rampton, B. (1997). The idealised native speaker, reified ethnicities, and classroom realities. *TESOL Quarterly, 31,* 543–559.

Lin, A. (1999). Doing-English-lessons in the reproduction or transformation of social worlds? *TESOL Quarterly, 33,* 393–412.

Liu, J. (1999). Non-native-English-speaking professionals in TESOL. *TESOL Quarterly, 33,* 85–102.

Lowenberg, P. (1986). Non-native varieties of English: Nativization, norms, and implications. *Studies in Second Language Acquisition, 8,* 1–18.

Moag, R., & Moag, L. (1977). The linguistic adaptions of the Fiji Indians. In V. Mishra (Ed.), *Rama's banishment: A centenary volume of the Fiji Indians* (pp. 112–138). Auckland, New Zealand: Heinemann.

Mufwene, S. (2001). New Englishes and norm setting: How critical is the native speaker in linguistics? In E. Thumboo (Ed.), *The three circles of English* (pp. 133–142). Singapore: UniPress.

Nayar, P. B. (1997). ESL/EFL dichotomy today: Language politics or pragmatics? *TESOL Quarterly, 31,* 9–37.

Nero, S.J. (1997). English is my native language . . . or so I believe. *TESOL Quarterly, 31,* 585–593.

Norton, B. (1997). Language, identity, and the ownership of English. *TESOL Quarterly, 31,* 409–429.

Peirce, B. N. (1995). Social identity, investment, and language learning. *TESOL Quarterly, 29,* 9–31.

Pennycook, A. (1994). *The cultural politics of English as an international language.* New York: Longman.

Pennycook, A. (2001). *Critical applied linguistics: A critical introduction.* Mahwah, NJ: Erlbaum.

Platt, J. T., Weber, H., & Ho, M. L. (1984). *The new Englishes.* London: Routledge & Kegan Paul.

Pomerantz, A., & Fehr, B.J. (1997). Conversation analysis: An approach to the study of social action as sense making practices. In T. Van Dijk (Ed.), *Discourse as social interaction* (pp. 64–91). London: Sage.

Prator, C. (1968). The British heresy in TESOL. In J. Fishman, C. A. Ferguson, & J. Das Gupta (Eds.), *Language problems in developing nations* (459–476). New York: Wiley.

Pride, J. B. (Ed.). (1982). *New Englishes.* Rowley, MA: Newbury House.

Rampton, B. (1987). Stylistic variability and not speaking "normal" English: Some post-Labovian approaches and their implications for the study of interlanguage. In R. Ellis (Ed.), *Second language acquisition in context* (pp. 47–58). Englewood Cliffs, NJ: Prentice Hall.

Rampton, B. (1995). *Crossing: Language and ethnicity among adolescents.* New York: Longman.

Sacks, H., Schegloff, E., & Jefferson, G. (1974). A simplest systematics for the organization of turn-taking in conversation. *Language, 50,* 696–735.

Sahgal, A., & Agnihotri, R. K. (1985). Syntax—the common bond. Acceptability of syntactic devices in Indian English. *English World-Wide, 6,* 117–129.

Scollon, R. (1998). *Mediated discourse as social interaction: A study of news discourse.* London: Longman.

Sey, K. A. (1973). *Ghanaian English: An exploratory survey.* London: Macmillan.

Soo, K. (1991). Malaysian English at the crossroads: Some sign-posts. *Journal of Multilingual and Multicultural Development, 11,* 199–214.

Smith, L. (Ed.). (1981). *English for cross-cultural communication.* London: Macmillan.

Smith, L. (1992). Spread of English and issues of intelligibility. In B. B. Kachru (Ed.), *The other tongue* (2nd ed., pp. 75–90). Urbana: University of Illinois Press.

Sridhar, K. K., & Sridhar, S. N. (1986). Bridging the paradigm gap: Second-language acquisition theory and indigenized varieties of English. *World Englishes, 5,* 3–14.

Strevens, P. (1992). English as an international language: Directions in the 1990s. In B. B. Kachru (Ed.), *The other tongue* (2nd ed., pp. 27–47). Urbana: University of Illinois Press.

Tay, M., & Gupta, A. F. (1983). Towards a description of standard Singapore English. In R. Noss (Ed.), *Varieties of English in Southeast Asia* (Series 11, pp. 173–189). Singapore: Southeast Asian Ministers of Education Organization Regional Language Centre.

Thumboo, E. (2001a). Foreword: After Kachru . . . . In E. Thumboo (Ed.), *The three circles of English* (pp. xiii–xv). Singapore: UniPress.

Thumboo, E. (Ed.). (2001b). *The three circles of English.* Singapore: UniPress.

Wee, L. (2002). When English is not a mother tongue: Linguistic ownership and the Eurasian community in Singapore. *Journal of Multilingual and Multicultural Development, 23,* 282–295.

Widdowson, H. G. (1994). The ownership of English. *TESOL Quarterly, 31,* 377–389.

Zimmerman, D. H. (1998). Discourse identities and social identities. In C. Antaki & S. Widdicombe (Eds.), *Identities in talk* (pp. 87–106). London: Sage.

Zuengler, J. (1989). Identity and IL development and use. *Applied Linguistics, 10,* 80–96.

Chapter 4

ENRIC LLURDA

NON-NATIVE SPEAKER TEACHERS AND ENGLISH AS AN INTERNATIONAL LANGUAGE (2004)

English as an international language

WITHOUT ANY DOUBT, the way English is perceived all over the world has recently undergone a great deal of change. In arenas devoted to multilingualism and to the preservation of the wealth and variety of languages in the world, criticism is commonly made of the aggressive expansion of English at the cost of other languages, which has prompted some scholars to use the labels 'killer language' (Pakir 1991; Mühlhäusler 1996) and 'tyrannosaurus rex' (Swales 1997) to refer to it. In less politically charged domains, linguists are also paying attention to the current situation of English as a global language (Crystal 1997) and developing models that help us speculate about its future evolution (Graddol 1997, 2001). Likewise, language researchers and educators are increasingly embracing the fact that English is spoken by more people as an L2 than as a mother tongue, and, consequently, they are taking on board the notion that English is no longer exclusively owned by the native-speaking communities but that its ownership is also shared by newly arrived members of the English-speaking community (i.e. non-native speakers), who therefore have a right to be heard in matters affecting the language (Widdowson 1994).

The powerful consequences of such a groundbreaking idea are still to be seen in full, but many changes are starting to take place in the areas of language teaching and language testing, as is clear from a recent study by Major et al. (2002), commissioned and funded by the ETS[1]. In that study, the authors compare results on the Test of Spoken English obtained by speakers of four different languages (English, Chinese, Japanese, and Spanish) on four different versions of the test: one in which the recorded passage was produced by native speakers of American English, and three more produced by speakers of each of the three other languages represented in the sample of test takers. Even though the results and the interpretations provided by the authors are far from conclusive, the potential implications of this study are profound. But even more significant is the fact that the study was commissioned in the first place, which indicates a growing acknowledgement of the existence of the huge number of non-native English speakers and the need to incorporate their voices into mainstream English language teaching and language testing.

Another indication of the increasing interest in the global expansion of English is the frequent use of the term World English in the literature, together with English as an International

Language (EIL) and English as a Lingua Franca (ELF), although with different degrees of consensus regarding the appropriateness of these terms (Eoyang 1999; Modiano 1999; Seidlhofer 2001). Eoyang, for instance, does not support the use of the term lingua franca, which he sees as being attached to the idea of an impure mixture of languages. As for the use of the term World English, Eoyang distinguishes among three different ways of being global: "through universality, widespread comprehensibility, and comprehensivity" (1999: 26). He comments further on this distinction and finally claims that "English is far from being a universal language" (ibid.), nor is it considered to be particularly widely comprehensible; therefore Eoyang concludes that it is the size of the language – that is, its comprehensivity – that earns it the right to be called World English. His claim is, however, marred by a discussion of the positive economic effects of the liberal approach which has traditionally been taken by English speakers (and more recently by Japanese speakers) to the incorporation of new vocabulary items from other languages. To such a claim, Edwards (2001: 11) responds by stating that "[l]anguages of 'wider communication' have no special linguistic capabilities to recommend them; they are simply the varieties of those who have power and prestige". Seidlhofer (2001), in contrast, shows a greater enthusiasm for the labeling of English as a lingua franca, and Modiano (1999) concentrates on the idea of EIL.

Brutt-Griffler (2002) has recently made an important contribution to understanding the development of World English, seeing it as the consequence of a process of macroacquisition by several speech communities in the world. Her view contradicts Phillipson's (1992) seminal work on linguistic imperialism, which blamed the colonial powers (for) extending the use of English worldwide. Brutt-Griffler looks at the spread of English from the point of view of the main characters in that process, which she refuses to consider as passive recipients of a colonial language but rather as active agents of appropriation of the language. Her interpretation of the reasons English became the preferred language at international levels is rooted in the desire by whole speech communities across the world to acquire the language as part of their struggle to be freed from their colonial burden. As great a paradox as it may appear, she quite reasonably argues that colonized people have used the colonizers' language as a fundamental tool in their quest for freedom. Brutt-Griffler's arguments are strongly based on Kachru's (1983, 1990) research on indigenized varieties of English, but she integrates Kachru's ideas into her comprehensive framework of language change as an expression of common language acquisition by whole speech communities – that is, macroacquisition – which does not lead to language extinction but to bilingualism.

Within this context, EIL is becoming established as the appropriate term to refer to most of the current uses of English worldwide, especially in those situations involving non-native speakers interacting in English both with native speakers and other non-native speakers. Although EIL as such is still far from being a coherent, concise language variety, some attempts are being made to establish what the basic traits of this variety are. Jenkins (2000) has taken up the ambitious task of describing the phonology of such an international variety of the language, and although her proposals do not enjoy the consensus of the entire linguistics community, they offer rich ideas that will stir debate and consequently further the establishment of EIL as a recognized variety. Another researcher who is also intensely devoted to the promotion of EIL is Seidlhofer, who is currently working on a corpus of English used as a lingua franca, the Vienna-Oxford ELF Corpus (Seidlhofer 2001), which should provide a basis for describing English as it is used by non-native speakers from different language backgrounds in international settings.

If we look more closely at the European Union, proposals are being made on the progressive establishment of a common lingua franca variety which some have already labeled Euro-English (James 2000; Jenkins et al. 2001). This variety would be used specifically in situations of international communication within the EU and would as such be different from English as it is spoken in the UK or in any other English-speaking country. This variety is emerging in spite of the lack of any official language planning or policy by EU institutions and regardless of the efforts, by different EU members to promote and protect their own national languages (Ammon 1994). In fact, this lack of a policy is giving way to a *de facto* establishment of English as the working language and most commonly used lingua franca within the EU (Ammon 1994; Ammon and McConnell 2002; Phillipson 2003).

Effects of EIL on language teaching

The transformation of English from being the language of a few powerful countries (i.e. the UK, USA) to becoming the international language it is today has brought with it many changes in the language teaching profession, which is trying to adapt to the new EIL environment and the new demands of its learners. Proposals are currently being made to move beyond the native speaker as the model in language teaching (Cook 1999, 2005) since, in the context of EIL, native speakers are only a part of the much larger group of speakers of the language. In fact, as Modiano (1999) argues, proficiency in speaking English is no longer determined by birth but by the capacity to use the language properly, a capacity that is shared by some – but not all – speakers, be they native or non-native.

Proposals aimed at incorporating new formulations of EIL into language teaching especially emphasise the need to draw on the previous knowledge of the language learner through exploiting their knowledge of their own language and culture. McKay (2000, 2003) proposes devoting time and attention in class to the learners' own culture as a means of empowering them and giving them the opportunity to share their own culture with other speakers of English. Likewise, Dendrinos (2001) claims that English lessons in English as a Foreign Language (EFL) contexts must endow students with the capacity to move freely from their L1 to the L2 and vice versa. She claims that learners of EIL will not be monolingual users of the newly acquired language, as they will have to act as interpreters or simply report in one language on information they will have processed in the other. Therefore, language classrooms must necessarily provide the conditions for them to practice these skills, rather than focussing on an artificially monolingual communicative setting. This is in line with the recent appreciation of L1 use and code-switching as a valuable pedagogical tool in the classroom (Auerbach 1993; Baiget et al. 1998; Cook 2005), and with Widdowson's claims that language authenticity goes beyond mere reproduction of native-speaker usage, as "the language that is authentic for native speaker users cannot possibly be authentic for learners" (1998: 711).

According to Kachru (1992: 362), "what is needed is a shift of two types: a paradigm shift in research and teaching, and an understanding of the sociolinguistic reality of the uses and users of English". Even the traditional notion of communicative competence has been called into question in the new environment of EIL (Alptekin 2002). Researchers on language teaching have moved from an emphasis on teaching learners the cultural aspects associated with the L2 as well as the pragmatic and discourse particularities of the native-speaker community (such as politeness in the UK or informality in American business English) to asking for a change in the formulation of communicative competence. In Alptekin's words:

> Only by producing instructional materials that emphasize diversity both within and across cultures can one perhaps avoid presenting English meanings in fragmented and trivialized ways, where communicative functions are conceived as simple speech

acts realized through specific structures, and where situational content generally portrays an idealized image of the English-speaking culture. It is perhaps time to rid the ELT field of its educational vision and practices based on a utopian notion of communicative competence involving idealized native speaker norms in both language and culture.

(Alptekin 2002: 60)

The role of non-native-speaker teachers in EIL teaching

The role of non-native speakers in language education has been appraised in such initiatives as the 1991 Statement on Non-Native Speakers of English and Hiring Practices and the constitution of The Non-Native English Speakers in TESOL (NNEST) Caucus in 1998.

Books such as Medgyes' (1994) and Braine's (1999) have greatly contributed to the interest in non-native speakers' positive role in the teaching of English as a second or foreign language. With the increasing establishment of English as the world lingua franca, non-native speakers will be in optimal positions to lead their students into the realm of EIL. Teachers of EIL should incorporate instructional materials and activities rooted in local as well as international contexts that are familiar and relevant to language learners' lives (Alptekin 2002). In addition – paraphrasing Kramsch (1997) – nonnative-speaker teachers are endowed with the privilege of bilingualism, as their experience of switching back and forth from their own language to the target one enhances their understanding of the demands of the learning situation. Non-native speakers have lived through the process of becoming bilingual and expressing themselves in different languages. English learners will become speakers of EIL, through which they will express their own selves in a multilingual world that uses English as the means of expression and as the instrument for interaction among people from disparate cultures. Non-native-speaker teachers are the ones who are inherently endowed with better expertise in guiding this process?[2]

Some critical voices have denounced the inequality derived from the dominance of English worldwide (e.g. Phillipson 1992) and have implicitly blamed language teachers (among whom non-native speakers are also included) for such an unfair promotion of one language at the expense of the others. However, as Rajagopalan (1999) quite rightly points out, ELT professionals in general, and non-native-speaker teachers in particular, should not feel ashamed of doing their job. Instead, they should make sure that a multicultural, critical perspective is maintained in the process of teaching and learning English. The issue is complex, as teachers may become unwitting instruments of dominant interests. It is true that power can be exercised both through coercion and through consent, and teachers may be consenting in maintaining the power inequality among languages simply by accepting established practices without question (Fairclough 1989).

Non-native-speaker teachers have been reported to have several advantages over native speakers, especially over those who are monolingual speakers of English. As Kramsch (1999: 34) puts it, "it is the teaching of ESL within an assimilationist ideology that has canonized (or beatified) the native speaker around the world", but an alternative is clearly possible. Most non-native-speaker teachers, in both ESL and EFL contexts, have an adequate level of language proficiency to perform their task. However, if we pause to reflect on the options that lie ahead of them in the new framework of EIL, rather than ESL or EFL, we will see that many teachers in EFL settings (particularly non-native speakers) do not seem to be very sensitive to the new perspectives that are opening up in front of them, and are still anchored in the old native-speaker dominated framework in which British or American norms have to be followed and native speakers are considered the ideal teachers.

In a study conducted with over 100 non-native EFL teachers working in primary and secondary schools in a mid-size city in Catalonia (Llurda and Huguet 2003), it was found that Catalan teachers still give greater value to the knowledge of the culture of Britain than to their own culture or that of other European countries. This is probably related to the fact that university departments in Spain (and most likely in many other European countries) are still devoting greater attention to traditional native-speaker cultures and literatures (i.e. British and American) than to those of other countries where English is also used (Llurda 2004). It may be argued that an English language class in a European country need not focus on the learners' culture, but as McKay (2000) convincingly argues, students may have to use English in order to explain their culture to foreigners, and therefore they need to be trained to do so. On the other hand, TESOL programs in North America tend to offer limited discussion space to issues directly affecting non-native speakers, and little attention is paid to the teaching of English in EFL contexts (Govardhan et al. 1999), even though about one third of students in their programs are non-native speakers, many of whom are probably going to go back to their countries of origin (Polio 1994; Liu 1999; Llurda 2005).

Until fairly recently, it was common in the literature to read the expression 'ambassador' to refer to the role of English language teachers. Teachers had to be the ambassadors of the 'English culture' in the classroom; that is, they had to teach the language and, side by side, introduce the social conventions, ideologies, and cultural expectations of the English-speaking community. Not much thought was given in such accounts to what the 'English-speaking community' was, or whether such a homogeneous community had ever existed. In Europe, the focus was on an idealized form of British culture, values, and society, heavily based on older stereotypes from Britain's imperial days. In other parts of the world, idealized visions of the 'English-speaking community' were either the same as in Europe or followed an equally idealized description of American culture and values. Thus, the language teacher had to be an ambassador of either British or American stereotypical values. Fortunately, this way of thinking is changing rapidly as language teaching theory gradually incorporates the consequences of accepting the globalness of English, and language teachers are no longer called on to act as ambassadors of the foreign culture. At best, they are identified as 'mediators' between the learners' source and target culture, a term that suggests the existence of a conflict. And, in fact, all language learning situations entail such a conflict. As Schumann (1978) pointed out, language learning is closely connected to the process of acculturation. The implication of this is that learning a new language means embracing a new culture, and such a process cannot happen without a certain amount of conflict. No matter how covert this conflict may be, the acquisition of a new language poses a threat to the existing linguistic status quo of the learners, and therefore to the very foundations of their own identity. Teachers are responsible for presenting the multifaceted reality in which the new language is used and for helping the learner express their own identity through this newly acquired voice. In this context, the way that code-switching is handled in the classroom will be of paramount importance, as it will greatly contribute to the learners becoming multicompetent speakers (Cook 1992).

Final remarks

Non-native speakers of English currently outnumber native speakers, so we can argue that there are more speakers of EIL than speakers of English as a native language. It's true that many different levels of proficiency may exist among those non-native speakers, and no serious counting has been undertaken to date regarding the actual number of proficient non-native English speakers. However, the vast majority of the many millions of non-native speakers of English are not conscious of being speakers of EIL. Rather, they perceive themselves as speakers – with a higher or lower degree of success, or 'corruption' – of a native variety of the language. I contend that the day non-native speakers of English become aware of their status as speakers of EIL, native-speaker control of the language will disappear, and non-native speakers will feel entitled to the authoritative use of a variety of the language that belongs to them. When that happens, native speakers will need to learn the conventions of EIL in order to communicate successfully with the larger community of English language speakers.

A somewhat different – but still valid – example can be found in what happened in Europe fifteen centuries ago when the Roman empire collapsed and the different communities all over Europe that had embraced the use of Latin continued to do so without paying respect to the original source of the language (i.e. Rome). Although their own varieties of Latin evolved, they managed to keep using Latin as a lingua franca for almost 1000 years. The parallel with EIL is that these countries did not mimic the evolution and changes that Latin was experiencing on the Italian peninsula. Instead, they kept to the international form of the language, which the people of the former heartland of the Roman empire also had to learn in order to communicate with their European neighbors. My point is that English has reached such a level of internationalization that local changes in the heartland should not be transferred to the international use of the language, and changes caused by the international nature of the language should be learned by members of the native-speaking communities. In other words, EIL must become a stabilized variety. The conditions for this are already in place. The political and military decline experienced by the Roman empire in the fifth century finds no match in the current situation of absolute control of the global political and military scene by the USA. Still, the linguistic situation is fairly comparable and may provide a good reference point for what would be a natural further step in the development of English as a world lingua franca.

Critics of the generalized use of English as a lingua franca in Europe are concerned about the loss of identity of the different peoples and cultures which characterize Europe and fear the permeation of American values into European life-styles. This is, of course, a highly political stance, as it attaches a negative value to Americanization, or Macdonaldization as some authors call it (Ritzer 1996). However, what opponents of the spread of English as a lingua franca in Europe fail to see is the fact that a language can be used separately from its original culture and ideology. In other words, accepting the language does not necessarily mean having to accept the dominant ideology of the country/ies the language comes from. An example of the possibility of detaching language and ideology can be found in the case of Basque nationalist groups. Even some radical supporters of an independent Basque nation frequently use Spanish as their language of communication. Quite often they simply lack the proficiency to use Basque comfortably. However, their ideology is as far away from the dominant Spanish ideology as it could be. The use of Spanish does not affect the outcome of their political discourse. Similarly, English can be used as a tool for linguistic unity without compromising cultural, historical, or ideological diversity. By doing so, minority cultures will find it easier to have their voice heard on the international stage. Otherwise, they will probably be condemned to cultural obscurity.

Notes

1   ETS is the agency responsible for the elaboration and implementation of – among others – the TOEFL (Test of English as a Foreign language) and the Test of Spoken English, which are required by most North American universities before accepting any non-native speaker into their programs.
2   In EFL contexts, this is also true of native speakers who have been long established in the local community and have learned its language.

References

Alptekin, C. (2002) Towards intercultural communicative competence in ELT. *ELT Journal* 56.1: 57–64.

Ammon, U. (1994) The present dominance of English in Europe. With an outlook on possible solutions to the European language problems. *Sociolinguistica* 8: 1–14.

—— and G. McConnell (2002) *English as an academic language in Europe.* Frankfurt: Peter Lang.

Auerbach, E.R. (1993) Reexamining English only in the ESL classroom. *TESOL Quarterly* 27.1: 9–2.

Baiget, E., J.M. Cots, M. Irún and E. Llurda (1998) El cambio de código en et aula de lengua extranjera: una perspectiva pragmática. In I. Vázquez and I. Guillén (eds), *Perspectivas pragmáticas en lingüística aplicada.* Zaragoza: ANUBAR. 275–84.

Braine, G. (ed.). (1999) *Non-native educators in English language teaching.* Mahwah, NJ: Lawrence Erlbaum Associates, Inc.

Brutt-Griffler, J. (2002) *World English. A study of its development.* Clevedon: Multilingual Matters.

Cook, V. (1992) Evidence for multicompetence. *Language Learning* 42.4: 557–91.

—— (1999) Going beyond the native speaker in language teaching. *TESOL Quarterly* 33.2: 185–209.

—— (2001) Using the first language in the classroom. *Canadian Modern Language Review* 57.3: 402–23.

—— (2005) Basing teaching on the L2 user. In E. Llurda (ed.), *Non-native language teachers: perceptions, challenges, and contributions to the profession* (pp. 47–62). New York: Springer.

Crystal, D. (1997) *English as a global language.* Cambridge University Press.

Dendrinos, B. (2001) The pedagogic discourse of EFL and the discursive construction of the NS's professional value. Paper presented at the International Conference on Non-Native Speaking Teachers in Foreign Language Teaching, Lleida, Catalonia, Spain.

Edwards, J. (2001) Languages and language learning in the face of World English. *ADFL Bulletin* 32.2: 10–15.

Eoyang, E. (1999) The worldliness of the English Language: a lingua franca past and future. *ADFL Bulletin* 31.1: 26–32.

Fairclough, N. (1989) *Language and power.* London: Longman.

Govardhan, A.K., B. Nayar and R. Sheorey (1999) Do U.S. MATESOL programs prepare students to teach abroad? *TESOL Quarterly* 33.1: 114–25.

Graddol, D. (1997) *The future of English?* London: British Council.

—— (2001) The future of English as a European language. *The European English Messenger* 10.2: 47–55.

James, A. (2000) English as a European lingua franca: current realities and existing dichotomies. In J. Cenoz and U. Jessner (eds), *English in Europe. The acquisition of a third language.* Clevedon: Multilingual Matters. 22–38.

Jenkins, J. (2000) *The phonology of English as an international language.* Oxford University Press.

—— , M. Modiano and B. Seidlhofer (2001) Euro-English. *English Today* 14.4: 13–19.

Kachru, B. (1983) *The indianization of English: the English language in India.* Oxford University Press.

—— (1990) *The alchemy of English. The spread, functions, and models of non-native Englishes.* Urbana: University of Illinois Press.

—— (1992) Teaching World English. In B. Kachru (ed.), *The other tongue. English across cultures* (2nd edition). Urbana: University of Illinois Press. 355–65.

Kramsch, C. (1997) The privilege of the nonnative speaker. *PMLA* 112.3: 359–69.

—— (1999) Response to Carmen Chaves Tesser and Eugene Eoyang. *ADFL Bulletin* 31.1: 33–5.

Liu, D. (1999) Training non-native TESOL students: challenges for TESOL teacher education in the West. In G. Braine (ed.), *Non-native educators in English language teaching.* Mahwah: Lawrence Erlbaum Associates. 197–210.

Llurda, E. (2004) 'Native/non-native speaker' discourses in foreign language university departments in Spain. In B. Dendrinos and B. Mitsikopoulou (eds), *Policies of linguistic pluralism and the teaching of languages in Europe* (pp. 237–43). Athens, Greece: University of Athens Publications.

—— (2005) Non-native TESOL students as seen by practicum supervisors. In E. Llurda (ed.), *Non-native language teachers: perceptions, challenges, and contributions to the profession* (pp. 131–54). New York: Springer.

—— and A. Huguet (2003) Self-awareness in NNS EFL primary and secondary school teachers. *Language Awareness* 12.3/4: 220–35.

Major, R.C., S.F. Fitzmaurice, F. Bunta and C. Balasubramanian (2002) The effects of nonnative accents on listening comprehension: implications for ESL assessment. *TESOL Quarterly* 36.2: 173–90.

McKay, S. (2000) Teaching English as an international language: implications for cultural materials in the classroom. *TESOL journal* 9.4: 7–11.

—— (2003) Toward an appropriate EIL pedagogy: re-examining common ELT assumptions. *International Journal of Applied Linguistics* 13.1: 1–22.

Medgyes, P. (1994) *The non-native teacher*. London: Macmillan.

Modiano, M. (1999) International English in the global village. *English Today* 15.2: 22–8.

Mühlhäusler, P. (1996) *Linguistic ecology. Language change and linguistic imperialism in the Pacific Rim*. London: Routledge.

Pakir, A. (1991) Contribution to workshop on endangered languages. International Conference on Austronesian Linguistics, Hawaii. [Quoted in Mühhäusler 1996.]

Phillipson, R. (1992) *Linguistic imperialism*. Oxford University Press.

—— (2003) *English-only Europe? Challenging language policy*. London: Routledge.

Polio, C. (1994) International students in North American MA TESOL programs. Paper presented at the 28th Annual TESOL Convention, Baltimore, MD.

Rajagopalan, K. (1999) Of EFL teachers, conscience, and cowardice. *ELT Journal* 53.3: 200–6.

Ritzer, G. (1996) *The McDonaldization of society* (Revised edition). London: Sage. [Quoted in D. Block and D. Cameron, *Globalization and language teaching*. London: Routledge.]

Schumann, J. (1978) The acculturation model for second language acquisition. In R.C. Gingras (ed.), *Second language acquisition and foreign language learning*. Washington, DC: Center for Applied Linguistics. 27–50.

Seidlhofer, B. (2001) Closing a conceptual gap: the case for a description of English as a lingua franca. *International Journal of Applied Linguistics* 11.2: 133–58.

Swales, J.M. (1997) English as tyrannosaurus rex. *World Englishes* 16.3: 373–82.

Widdowson, H.G. (1994) The ownership of English. *TESOL Quarterly* 28.2: 377–81.

—— (1998) Context, community, and authentic language. *TESOL Quarterly* 32.4: 705–16.

Chapter 5

VIVIAN COOK

THE NATURE OF THE L2 USER (2007)

THREE OF THE BASIC ISSUES raised by the multi-competence perspective for SLA research are:

(1) *Who are the L2 users?* Both as the possession of the individual and of the community, L1 and L2 are diverse and flexible, ranging from developing to relatively static to reducing. SLA research has to recognise the shifting flux of L1 and L2 systems.
(2) *What is the language that the L2 user knows?* Five meanings of 'language' are discussed: human representation system, institutional object, set of sentences, community and individual possession, concluding that the language systems of the individual and of the community need to be treated as a whole.
(3) *What is the community the L2 user belongs to?* L2 users belong to diverse communities of their own, both local and global. SLA research needs to explore the nature of these communities rather than assuming L2 users wish to be part of native monolingual communities.

[handwritten annotation: L2 not all the L2 users necess. want to be part a part of native monolingual communities.]

The nature of the second language user

The idea of linguistic multi-competence was first put forward in the early 1990s (Cook 1991). Recently it has been discussed in areas far outside its original remit – dynamic systems (De Bot, Lowie and Verspoor 2005), multilingualism (Herdina and Jessner 2002), macroacquisition of language by communities (Brutt-Griffler 2002), post-structuralist construction of identity (Golombek and Jordan 2005), lingua francas (Jenkins 2006), heritage languages (Valdés 2005) and cross-linguistic influence (Pavlenko and Jarvis 2006). This paper attempts to accommodate these developments within a multi-competence framework. Three questions will be tackled:

1   Who are the second language users?
2   What is the *language* they know?
3   What is the community they belong to?

Part of the same argument is expanded in more general terms in Cook (2009).

The classic view of second language acquisition (SLA) saw it as the learner creating an interlanguage by drawing on the first language (L1), second language (L2) and other factors (Selinker 1972). Initially the term multi-competence was devised as a convenient term for the knowledge of languages in one person's mind (Cook 1991), i.e. the L1 plus the interlanguage. This had the consequence of separating someone who knows two languages from the monolingual native speaker as a person in their own right: the relationship between the L1 and the interlanguage within one mind is different from that between the interlanguage in one mind and the L2 in another mind (which is actually a first language for the person involved). Hence the term *L2 user* became preferred over *L2 learner* and its variants as it conferred separate identity rather than dependent status: L2 learner implies the person is always learning, never getting there. The research that spins off from this conceptualisation of multi-competence has concerned itself with the relationships between the two language systems in one mind, particularly reverse transfer from L2 to L1 (Cook 2003) and with the relationships between the language systems and the rest of the L2 user's mind (Cook et al. 2006), visualised as an integration continuum between the two language systems (Cook 2003). A recent overview of multi-competence can be found in Cook (2008).

L2 ≠ L1 + interlanguage

Question 1. Who are the L2 users?

People accept the idea of the monolingual native speaker without much quibbling; they feel they know what they're talking about when they say *a native speaker of English* or *belonging to the English-speaking community*; they tend to believe that native speakers form a uniform community, even if daily experience should show them the contrary. The arguments against this idealisation will not be developed here as it has been a well-worn path in applied linguistics to reject Chomsky's definition of linguistic competence (Chomsky 1965) in favour of Hymesian communicative competence (Hymes 1972); nevertheless SLA research and language teaching have paid little attention to native speaker variation whether within or across individuals.

Defining the L2 user or the community of L2 users has proved far more problematic. The standard solution in SLA research is to speak only of the community of monolingual native speakers, whether of the L1 or the L2, as a monolithic whole. Almost invariably this leads to successful L2 users being seen as those who can pass as members of the monolingual native speaker community rather than having membership of a community of their own, a condition that very few would pass, seen in typical quotations like "Relative to native speaker's linguistic competence, learners' interlanguage is deficient by definition" (Kasper and Kellerman 1997: 5).

The aim here is to remind researchers that both the languages that the L2 users know and the communities they belong to are far from static. The classic SLA interlanguage model assumed clearly defined entities for L1 and L2; we all knew what these entities were; only interlanguage needed defining. But, as Dynamic Systems Theory insists (De Bot et al. 2005) and attrition studies have shown (Schmid et al. 2004), language is rarely if ever still. Communities too are variable and flexible, adapting and changing continuously through macro-acquisition (Brutt-Griffler 2002). This section raises some issues about the changing languages and communities of L2 users.

First language change

STATIC FIRST LANGUAGE

changing & unfixed nature of L1 & L2

The first language may be static or changing. An individual may be an adult with a so-called steady state of language knowledge, even if one accepts this is relative stasis rather than frozen. Only one's vocabulary is believed to change appreciably during adult life. Similarly the language of a community may have the appearance of a static standard form. The English language is spoken of as if it has now achieved a fixed final form that brooks no change and to which everything else has been prologue. There is also the language frozen in time of some emigrant groups: an Italian-American actor-director who was interviewed on Sicilian Television used an Old Sicilian dialect that had to be translated for a modern Sicilian audience (www.italiansrus.com/articles/subs/hyphenated_italians_part2.htm). For some purposes in some cases a first language is static, albeit in a highly idealised way. In most SLA research, stasis of the L1 is taken as the norm rather than seen as a moment when time stands still. The L1 is treated as fixed in the L2 user's mind and in the community they belong to.

DEVELOPING FIRST LANGUAGE

The individual may be a child developing their first language or, in the case of early bilinguals, first languages. Many L2 learners are not at an adult stage of development in their first language, particularly those in schools. The first language can also be developing in the L1 community, as in the case of creolisation where the group is inventing a new language from scratch. Like it or not, many, perhaps most, languages are developing in the individual and in the community. The L1 in many L2 users is not a constant object that SLA research can take for granted and in some cases is being created in the L1 community.

REDUCING FIRST LANGUAGE

Alternatively a first language may be reducing, declining in some way. Individuals appear to lose some aspects of their first language, whether through lack of everyday use, brain injury or the effects of normal aging. In terms of the community, languages too may reduce. At one extreme there is the emotive issue of language death; languages may lose their last speakers, say Dyirbal speakers in Australia (Schmidt 1985). The languages may be temporarily suppressed, like Min in Taiwan (Sandal et al. 2006) or Ulster Scots in Northern Ireland, now a recognised minority language in the European Union. It cannot be assumed that the first language in the L2 user's mind and L1 community is a constant.

The first language component of the multi-competence in the L2 user's mind is not then necessarily static but developing in the case of children or reducing in attrition. The individual's first language, taken for granted in SLA research, is complex and shifting. The L1 construct is an abstraction, a snapshot of a moving target. The same is true of language as the possession of a community. Notionally there may be a synchronic moment that isolates a state of a language from previous and future states – Modern English as spoken in 2006 – fleeting as this may be. The dynamic nature of the L1 community needs to be taken into account in SLA research.

Second language change

STATIC SECOND LANGUAGE

The static L2 user is an individual with a putatively constant L2 knowledge, someone using the second language as part of their repertoire for their own purposes, say Roger Federer being interviewed in English or a doctor in Spain treating a Japanese patient in English. That is to say ordinary people anywhere happening to use a language other than their first. The L2 user community may also be notionally static in that it involves a long-standing use of the two languages, such as the Polish/English community living in West London. For children it may be the micro-community of the bilingual family. This is distinct from the notion of *fossilisation*, with its negative connotations; people and communities reach a stable level of language for their purposes.

DEVELOPING SECOND LANGUAGE

The developing L2 user is the classic figure studied by SLA research the L2 learner, who forms the subject matter of the vast majority of SLA research and hardly needs enlarging on here. Communities also develop second languages in many ways. One case is the Italian learnt by Spanish-speaking migrant workers in German-speaking Switzerland, a logical if surprising solution to working together (Schmid 1994). While the change in the individual is taken for granted, the change in the community may also be relevant to multi-competence.

REDUCING SECOND LANGUAGE

L2 attrition also occurs in the individual. Many school learners retain rather little of their second language ten years later. Expats' children returning to their home country may rapidly lose their other language (Kanno 2000). While *attrition* is the usual term for this phenomenon, this involves a negative metaphor of invasion by the first language, which may well characterise some cases, not others, which are more driven by lack of use or other factors. In terms of L2 user communities, this reduction is most well-known as the familiar three-generation shift from first language to second language seen in many immigrant populations (Fishman 1991).

So the individual's language knowledge may be notionally static, developing or reducing. The L2 community similarly stays the same or changes in various ways. The second language in SLA research models is as much a label for a mass of varying attributes as the first language. Till now the specialist area of SLA research that has concerned itself with language change in general is attrition. But attrition as language change is not so much an extra area of study as an integral part of any SLA model. The ideal situation of the unvarying L1 and L2 is seldom found in individuals or communities and is an exceptional situation in SLA research rather than the norm.

To sum up this section, L2 users have a varied set of first languages and a varied set of second languages, whether static, developing or reducing. The habit of identifying the first language and second language as unchanging entities in SLA research belies their inherent variability and diversity. At some level it may indeed be necessary to reify the L1 and L2 into these highly abstract entities for our own research objectives but, like the Chomskyan definition of linguistic competence, we have to be careful not to throw the baby out with the bathwater. The classic interlanguage triad of L1, L2 and interlanguage ignored the variation within the constructs of L1 and L2. Multi-competence is a continually changing relationship between two or more language systems that are themselves constantly changing.

Question 2. What is the language the L2 user knows?

The other construct that forms part of the classic SLA model is language. The issue of what language the L2 user knows depends on the meaning given to the word *language*, barely debated in SLA research. Five meanings of the word *language* will be distinguished here, not intended as

Table 5.1 Meanings of *Language*

Lang1	a representation system known by human beings
Lang2	an abstract entity – *the English language*
Lang3	a set of sentences – everything that has or could be said
Lang4	the possession of a community
Lang5	knowledge in the mind of an individual

final definitions, but reflecting some of the broad meanings of *language* that are relevant to multi-competence. Table 5.1 summarises these five meanings for convenience.

Lang1 human representation system

At some level human beings differ from other creatures because they possess a systematic representation system. Exactly where the differences between human language and animal communication systems lie is as controversial as ever (Hauser et al. 2002; Gentner et al. 2006). Whether the function of human language is primarily for communication or for organising the contents of the mind is similarly a bone of contention. Nevertheless in one way or another a central meaning of *language* is as a defining property of human beings.

Lang2 abstract external entity

Language is also a countable noun in English, as in *the English language* or *the Chinese language*. There are discrete entities called *English* and *Chinese*, codified in the rules of a grammar book and the entries of a dictionary and sometimes controlled through an institution such as the French Academy. Often this sense refers to a prestige *standard* variety of the language spoken by a minority of people and jealously guarded against dialectal forms and historical shift, as witness the perpetual defence of standard English against the barbarians in middle-class newspapers. English in this sense is no concern of the person in the street but belongs to the cultivated elite living in the capital city of an ex-colonial power. Yet no single person actually knows a language in this sense – the Oxford English Dictionary has some 650 thousand entries of which no speaker of English knows more than a fraction. While the institutional object of language bears some relationship to what people know, it is more like that between the regulations for driving laid down in the UK Highway Code and an individual's behaviour driving to work in the morning. In some ways Lang2 represents the maximum that an idealised speaker of a standard variety of a language could possibly know, rather than the small amount that any actual individual knows or the variations in any individual's speech due to age, region, class and all the other sociolinguistic variables.

Lang3 a set of sentences

Lang3 'language' means a set of sentences – all the actual or potential sentences that could be said or written; a language is 'the totality of utterances that can be made in a speech-community' (Bloomfield 1926: 26). A language is the sum of all the sentences its speakers have said or, in

Chomskyan vein, could say. Language as a set of sentences is studied by corpus linguistics, whose task is to define the properties in a specific collections of texts, carefully chosen in advance. In this sense language is not an abstraction but a concrete object, made up of physical sounds, gestures or written symbols. Patterns can be extracted from these primary data, both by the linguist and the learner. But they remain patterns of data rather than systems of knowledge or behaviour.

Lang4 shared possession of a community

The Lang4 sense of language treats it as a social phenomenon, a shared cultural product – *the English-speaking world*, *native speakers of Chinese* etc. A language belongs to a particular human group and confers identity as a member of that group. It is tempting to equate the community with national boundaries – Japanese speakers tend to live in Japan – but language communities pay little attention to political borders – Chinese is used all over the world. Nor is it necessary to have a country to have a language – versions of Romani are spoken in most European countries by tens of thousands to hundreds of thousands of people. A language in the Lang4 sense is, broadly speaking, possessed by everybody who can understand each other, setting aside the difficulties over language versus dialect.

Lang5 mental knowledge system

The final Lang5 sense of *language* is as the mental possession of an individual – 'a language is a state of the faculty of language, an I-language, in technical usage' (Chomsky 2005: 2). Language is not only out there in the world but also inside the mind. A person who knows Lang5 English can connect the world outside to the concepts inside their minds in a particular way. The problem is how this sense corresponds to the abstract entity called English in the Lang2 sense or to the set of English sentences people encounter in the Lang3 sense. The mental knowledge of a grammatical rule is not the same as the rule in the Lang2 grammar book or the same as the patterns in a Lang3 set of sentences.

The other major quandary is the relationship between Lang5 mental knowledge and Lang3 set of sentences, usually phrased in terms of competence and performance. Discussions of linguistic competence usually point out: (a) studying the sentences produced in the past is looking at accidental creations rather than the potential sentences created by the mental language system; (b) many mental rules of grammar are not derivable from the properties of sets of sentence: the relationship between Lang3 and Lang5 is as murky as it has ever been. As is indeed the relationship between social Lang4 and mental Lang5, which continues to attract sniping from entrenched views on both sides, generative linguists insisting on the purity of their Lang5 accounts of competence, sociolinguists on the complex realities of Lang4 interaction between people. The Lang4 community and Lang5 mental senses are inextricably entwined: language is two-sided as being both individual knowledge and collective possession.

So people have *language* in the sense they speak a Lang1 human language, which apes and dolphins do not; they have some relationship with a Lang2 abstract entity called the English language, etc, which speakers of other languages do not; they produce a Lang3 set of sentences labelled English rather than French; they are members of a Lang4 community of English speakers that excludes, say, French speakers; and they have a mental Lang5 system of knowledge/processes, an English grammar, that differs from a mental grammar for French etc.

Language and multi-competence

Let us now try to relate these five senses of the word *language* to multi-competence.

Lang1 applied to multi-competence

Adding a second language, say Chinese, to the repertoire of an individual who speaks English makes no difference in the Lang1 sense of a human representation system: Chinese is another human language, another representation system. Occasionally SLA research claims that second languages are not learnt as languages at all but as some other type of knowledge (Clahsen and Muysken 1989). This would then put second languages in the same bracket as artificial computer languages like Prolog, which human beings can obviously learn and use but do not have the characteristics of human language. The Lang1 sense is only important for multi-competence if we deny second languages are human languages. Otherwise multi-competence is another manifestation of the human representation system that happens to have two languages – perhaps the normal version.

Lang2 applied to multi-competence

In the Lang2 sense of an institutional entity, multi-competence can be linked to two standard varieties of a language, say British RP in the L1 and Northern Chinese Mandarin in the L2. But the Lang5 knowledge of the second language in the L2 user's mind is as remote from the abstraction of Lang2 in the second language as in the first. If these two senses are not kept separate, language teaching and indeed SLA research may measure the L2 user against this Lang2 entity and find them wanting. Hardly surprising as these Lang2 entities do not represent the Lang5 linguistic competence of any individual. SLA research has tended to assume that the native speaker essentially has a perfect command of this abstract Lang2 entity and has compared this with the faltering steps of the L2 user (Cook 1979). If it is at all necessary to compare the languages of the monolingual native speaker and the L2 user, the same meaning of *language* needs to be used for both.

Lang3 applied to multi-competence

In the Lang3 sense, the second language is another set of sentences. The input that the L2 user has received can be seen as a Lang3 set of L2 sentences; but what about the L2 set that the L2 user produces? Weinreich (1953: 7) said that 'A structuralist theory of communication which distinguishes between speech and language . . . necessarily assumes that "every speech event belongs to a definite language"'; we know which sentences are L1, and which are L2. But code-switching research has shown that L2 users' sentences can in effect belong to both languages simultaneously. It is hard, if not impossible, to decide that some sentences of a L2 user belong to one language, some to another, without bringing in criteria from other senses of *language;* which sentences, say, use the word order of Lang2 English, which Lang2 Chinese?

There has been an increase in the use of L2 learner or user corpora such as the Seidlhofer (2002) and Granger (2003) projects, which will hopefully start producing results. But corpora-based studies that concentrate solely on the second language miss half the picture. One of the revelations of multi-competence research in the past few years has been the influence of the second language on the first (Cook 2003). A full account of the L2 user's actual and potential sentences means looking at everything and not assuming that the first language can be taken for granted as if it were identical to that of a monolingual. Duncan (1989) argued that bilingual speech therapy should be based on the child's first language as well as their second, i.e. on their multi-competence. The same applies to SLA research. For multi-competence the Lang3 starting point has to be the set of all sentences the L2 user produces, not just those arbitrarily assigned to a second language. This demands an analysis of the whole, not an arbitrary division of sentences into languages A and B. Studying the second language without the first is missing the unique feature of second language acquisition, namely the presence of the first language.

Lang4 applied to multi-competence

In the Lang4 sense *shared possession of a community*, much SLA research is crucially concerned with how people gain membership of a community along with the identity that comes with it, whether this community is in their present situation or their future plans, an abstract imagined community or a concrete reality. Language community and identity are basic to second language acquisition in terms both of the community the learners start out from and of the wider community they end up in.

But is there an L2 user community different from the monolingual native speaker community – a multi-competent community? Classic SLA research tacitly adopted this Chomskyan view of the homogenous monolingual community (Chomsky 1986: 17): L2 learners were assumed to want to belong to the community of native speakers; passing for a native speaker was a crucial test issue, which virtually all of them failed. Passing became a shibboleth for L2 research whether in discussions of the availability of Universal Grammar (Cook and Newson 2007) or of the age factor: 'Those studies cited for phonology have shown that some learners can achieve very high levels of native-like pronunciation in mostly constrained tasks but have yet to show that later learners can achieve the same level of phonology as native speakers in production' (de Keyser and Larson Hall 2005: 96): the only thing that proves L2 users have Universal Grammar or that they are affected by age is taken to be whether or not they speak like natives. The concept of the multi-competent community will be returned to in the next section.

Lang5 applied to multi-competence

The Lang5 mental sense of *language* means that the two languages are present in the same mind. In this broad sense all second language acquisition involves multi-competence. However, the two languages often seem to be regarded by researchers as sharing the same mind more or less by accident. We study the first language or we study the second; we compare how good people are at one language and how bad they are at the other, usually to the detriment of the second language. At some level, however, the multi-competent mind is a whole; the question is where, if at all, it divides into different languages, according to the possibilities in the integration continuum (Cook 2003), and how it keeps them separate when necessary (Lambert 1990). As with Lang3, looking at the mental system of the second language and excluding the first ignores the basic premise of multi-competence that two languages are involved.

The Lang5 second language in the L2 user's mind has as much and as little connection to the abstract entity of Lang2 as the first language. A Lang5 mental system within the speaker's mind is not an external Lang2 institutional entity. Nor is the Lang5 linguistic competence of individuals the same as their Lang3 performance even if once again there is a relationship of some type.

So what does it mean to say *an L2 learner of English* or *acquiring L2 English syntax* or *speaking L2 English*? In the SLA literature these have frequently collocated with words like *fail* and *lack of success*. The first three senses seem to have little connection with success: L2 users do not succeed at Lang1 human language because they have it already; they do not succeed in learning a Lang2 entity because nobody has done this or ever could; they do not produce a *better* or *worse* Lang3 set of sentences, but neutral patterns. Success may be a legitimate question to ask in terms of Lang4 and Lang5. For Lang4, L2 users are gaining membership of an L2-using community and we can ask whether they are succeeding or not; it is uninteresting to ask whether they succeed in passing as members of a monolingual native speaker community as this denies their distinct status, only applicable to those who wish to deny or disguise their origins, say spies and terrorists. Once we acknowledge the arbitrariness of calling the systems of the mind in the Lang5 mental sense by the name of Lang2 objects like English or Chinese, the language system in the L2 user's mind can be explored as holistic multi-competence, no longer counting languages.

Question 3. What is the community the L2 user belongs to?

We can now turn to the community that L2 users belong to. In language-related research language is assumed to be a crucial feature of one's identity as a member of a community: Pennycook (1994) says 'Anything we might want to call a language is not a pre-given system but a will to community'.

The overall issue is whether the language communities formed by L2 users are distinct from those of monolinguals; is multi-competence just for individuals or does it apply to communities as well? English has an international L2 user community of people across the world for which the native speaker community is virtually irrelevant; it is the interaction of academics, businessmen, tourists and others with each other and with non-native communities that matters. This section attempts to pin down some of the different communities to which L2 users may belong. These compartments are far from watertight and are obviously open-ended.

The community of minority language speakers communicating with the majority

Many people also have to speak a different language from their first language with the majority group in their setting, say resident Turks in Berlin using German for their everyday contacts with the German-speaking majority or Bengalis living in the East End of London. Their first language is spoken and used by an established resident community. Nevertheless most of them have to use the second language for dealing with the rest of the society around them. They constitute a multi-competent L2 user community as well as an L1 community. Their use of the second language makes them a member of a new community with an L1 for some purposes and an L2 for others, thus distinguishing them from the *pure monolingual community*. The second language is being used for practical purposes – the classic *second language situation*. The community is multi-competent in that two languages are in use for different purposes and with different people.

The community of minority language speakers communicating with other minority language speakers   In this situation they are use lingua franc English to communicate

Additionally most cities of the world now have, not just isolated groups of service language users, but also permanent communities of L2 users who use the majority language to mix with each other faute de mieux. London has speakers of 300 first languages, most of whom will be using English to talk to other people (Baker and Eversley 2000). The second language is functioning as a local lingua franca, sometimes with legal status, such as English as a national language of India. This language is not necessarily the language of the majority community in the country, as with Swahili in many African countries (770 thousand native speakers, 30 million lingua franca speakers) (Cordon 2005). The community is multi-competent in that many different L1s are interacting with a single L2.

The community of minority speakers (re)-acquiring the minority language

Another community of L2 users consists of people descended from a particular group learning the language of their historical origin – language maintenance or heritage. In Singapore, English has been the official first language in the schools for some time; children now attend classes in their mother tongues whether Mandarin, Tamil or Bahasa Malaysia. Language maintenance classes take place in most places, in London for Chinese and Polish for example. These people do not necessarily need the second language for practical everyday purposes so much as for identification with their roots. Multi-competence here then consists of adding an L2 as an extra identity rather than for everyday use.

The community of short-term visitors to a country

The language communities seen so far are geographically based in one location. But people also form mobile communities by going to countries where they have to speak another language: they are incomers for temporary or permanent stays. These short-term visitors include inter alias pilgrims to Mecca, migrant workers picking strawberries in Kent, and expats, the stereotype being tourists. Other groups may be more permanent, such as migrant workers, missionaries, prisoners, retirees and refugees. Visitors mostly have no real connection with the main society around them since they are not committed to permanent residence. Nor do they necessarily have any links to native speakers: 74% of tourism through English involves only L2 users (World Tourism Organisation, cited in Graddol 2006). Their uses for the second language reflect the purposes of their visit, ranging from the minimal use of some embassy staff to the maximal expertise that some British Colonial Officers had with local languages. Multi-competence consists then of a shared L2 added for a specific short-term reason to a variety of L1s.

The international professional community of L2 users

We have already alluded to the L2 user community that consists of people using a second language for diverse reasons around the globe with other people who are mostly not native speakers, whether through actual physical contact or through e-mails and telephones. English has become a Lingua Franca among many professions, for instance academics using English as the language for journals and conferences everywhere. Particular religions have expected believers to learn the language of their religious texts, whether Hebrew, Arabic, Latin, or, occasionally, English. Its speakers are members of communities that cross frontiers, whether professional or religious. In this case, the multi-competent speakers have many first languages but a single second language.

The micro community

People have often joked that the best way of learning a language is to marry someone who speaks it. Ingrid Piller (2002) has documented the successful use of language by couples who speak different first languages. The community here is micro – two people. Parents can decide to have a micro-community in which they use a language to their children they will not encounter outside the home, says George Saunders (1988) using German in Australia. But pairs of people can also decide to use a second language: Henry James used to converse with Joseph Conrad in French. The two languages have more or less equal status in this form of multi-competence, perhaps the only one that fits the maximal definition of bilingualism as equal ability in two languages.

The community of L2-educated students   *Language for instruction....*

Another community of L2 users seeks education through another language. On the one hand, in the Netherlands universities use English alongside Dutch. In reverse, some students go to another country to get their higher education, Zaireaas to Paris or Greeks to England. In other words, a second language is the vehicle for getting an education, more or less regardless of the native speakers (except in so far as they can profit by teaching *their* language). Multi-competence is building a particular L2 on to the L1 as an educational tool.

The community of students learning L2 in school   *they don't have to speak*

The most numerous group of second language learners is probably children based in countries where the language is not spoken, being taught another language within the educational system, nowadays in many cases from the age of two upwards. This is the classic foreign language situation whether French in England or Spanish in Japan. The traditional aim has been to allow the students to join one of the communities we have already described — future tourists or tourist workers, future international users etc. They do not form a community of use in the same sense as the others, perhaps the only group that can really be called learners rather than users since they have target communities to aim to belong to but are not members of an existing L2 community outside the classroom. But often the goal is simply to get through the hurdles set by the examination system: language is a school subject, taught and assessed like other subjects. Multi-competence here is adding an L2 as a school subject.

Once we give up the illusion that the L2 user is trying to become part of the native speaker community, there are many groups of people that they can join, of which we have seen some examples here. The L2 users' identities and goals are related to what they can achieve in these groups — by surviving in a country where their language is in the minority, by conducting business profitably through another language, by maintaining a happy marriage, and all the other aims that human beings may have to which language is relevant. The distinctive feature of second language acquisition is that people may become part of many different types of L2 user community, unlike the comparatively simple monolingual native speaker community. SLA research has to consider how to accommodate this variation rather than assuming that L2 users are peripheral members of a monolingual community.

Conclusions

At one level this paper is a plea to SLA research to make clear what it is talking about. The nature of the first language in the individual and the community needs to be spelled out for any piece of SLA research; neither the first language nor the second are by any means a given, whether static, developing or reducing. It is vital for any SLA research to make clear how the term *language* itself is being used. The L2-using community that the L2 users belong to, or want to belong to, needs careful consideration, rather than a knee-jerk reaction that the monolingual native speaker community is all.   *assume*

At another level this paper shows the difficulty in separating the two languages whether in the individual or the community. An individual or a community that know another language are not monolingual with an added language but some thing else. SLA research involves looking at both languages in the community or in the individual; their separation perpetuates a deficit model in which the L2 user lacks elements of language rather than possesses extra elements of language; seeing them as a whole tackles the true complexity of the mind that knows more than one language, getting away from separating languages and counting them to treating the L2 user as a whole within a community of their own.

References

Baker, P. and Eversley, J. 2000. *Multilingual Capital*. London: Battlebridge.

Bloomfield, L. 1926. "A set of postulates for the science of language". *Language* 2: 153–164. Reprinted in *Readings in Linguistics I*, M. Joos (ed.) 1957. Chicago: University of Chicago Press.

Brutt-Griffler, J. 2002. *World English: A Study of its Development*. Clevedon: Multilingual Matters.

Chomsky, N. 1965. *Aspects of the Theory of Syntax*. Cambridge, Mass.: MIT Press.

Chomsky, N. 1986. *Knowledge of Language: Its Nature, Origin and Use*. New York: Praeger.

Chomsky, N. 2005. "Three factors in language design". *Linguistic Inquiry* 36 (1): 1–22.

Clahsen, H. and Muysken, P. 1989. "The UG paradox in L2 acquisition". *Second Language Research* 5: 1–29.

Cook, V.J. 1979. "The English are only human". *English Language Teaching Journal* XXXIII (3): 163–167.

Cook, V.J. 1991. "The poverty-of-the-stimulus argument and multi-competence". *Second Language Research* 7 (2): 103–117.

Cook, V.J. (ed.) 2003. *Effects of the Second Language on the First*. Clevedon: Multilingual Matters.

Cook, V.J. 2008. "Multi-competence: black hole or wormhole?" In Han, Z-H., (ed.) *Facets of Second Language Process*. Clevedon: Multilingual Matters. 16–26.

Cook, V.J. 2009. "Language uses groups and language teaching". In Cook, V.J. and Li Wei (eds), *Contemporary Applied Linguistics*. Volume I: *Language Teaching and Learning* (pp. 54–74). London: Continuum.

Cook, V.J., Bassetti, B., Kasai, C., Sasaki, M. and Takahashi, J.A. 2006. "Do bilinguals have different concepts? The case of shape and material in Japanese L2 users of English". *International Journal of Bilingualism* 10, 2: 137–152.

Cook, V.J. and Newson, M. 2007. *Chomsky's Universal Grammar: An Introduction*. Oxford: Blackwell.

De Bot, K., Lowie, W. and Verspoor, M. 2005. *Second Language Acquisition: An Advanced Resource Book*. London: Routledge.

DeKeyser, R. and Larson Hall, J. 2005. "What does the critical period really mean?". In Kroll, J. and De Groot, A. (eds), *Handbook of Bilingualism*. Oxford: Oxford University Press. 88–108.

Duncan, D.M. 1989. *Working with Bilingual Language Disability*. London: Chapman and Hall.

Fishman, J. 1991. *Reversing Language Shift: Theoretical and Empirical Foundations of Assistance to Threatened Languages*. New York: Oxford University Press.

Gentner, T.Q., Fenn, K.M., Margoliash, D. and Nusbaum, H.C. 2006. "Recursive syntactic pattern learning by songbirds". *Nature* 440: 1204–1207.

Golombek, P. and Jordan, S.R. 2005. "Becoming 'black lambs' not 'parrots': a poststructuralist orientation to intelligibility and identity". *TESOL Quarterly* 39 (3): 513–533.

Gordon, R.G., Jr. (ed.) 2005. *Ethnologue: Languages of the World*; Fifteenth edition. Dallas, Tex.: SIL International. Online version: www.ethnologue.com/.

Graddol, D. 2006. *English Next*. London: the British Council. www.britishcouncil.org/files/documents/learning-research-english-next.pdf.

Granger, S. 2003. "The international corpus of learner English: a new resource for foreign language learning and teaching and second language acquisition research". *TESOL Quarterly* 37 (3): 538–545.

Hauser, M.D., Chomsky, N. and Fitch, T.M. 2002. "The faculty of language: what is it, who has it and how did it evolve". *Science* 298: 1569–1579.

Herdina, P. and Jessner, U. 2002. *A Dynamic Model of Multilingualism: Changing the Psycholinguistic Perspective*. Clevedon: Multilingual Matters.

Hymes, D. 1972. "Competence and performance in linguistic theory". In Huxley, R. and Ingram, E. (eds) *Language Acquisition: Models and Method*, New York: Academic Press. 3–23.

Jenkins, J. 2006. "Points of view and blind spots: ELF and SLA". *International Journal of Applied Linguistics* 16 (2): 137–162.

Kanno, Y. 2000. "Bilingualism and identity: The stories of Japanese returnees". *International Journal of Bilingual Education and Bilingualism* 3 (1): 1–18.

Kasper, G. and Kellerman, E. (eds) 1997. *Communication Strategies: Psycholinguistic and Sociolinguistic Perspectives.* London: Longman.

Lambert, W.E. (1990). "Persistent issues in bilingualism". In Harley, B., Allen, P., Cummins, J. and Swain, M. (eds), *The Development of Second Language Proficiency*. Cambridge: Cambridge University Press. 201–221.

Pavlenko, A. and Jarvis, S. 2006. *Cross Linguistic Influence.* Mahwah, NJ: Erlbaum.

Pennycook, A. 1994. *The Cultural Politics of English as an International Language.* Harlow: Longman.

Piller, I. 2002. "Passing for a native speaker: identity and success in second language learning". *Journal of Sociolinguistics* 6 (2): 179–206.

Sandal, T.L., Chao, W-Y. and Liang, C-H. 2006. "Language shift and accommodation across family generations in Taiwan". *Journal of Multilingual and Multicultural Development* 27 (2): 126–147.

Saunders, G. 1988. *Bilingual Children: From Birth to Teens.* Clevedon: Multilingual Matters.

Schmid, M., Köpke, B., Keijzer, M. and Weilemar, L. (eds) 2004. *First Language Attrition.* Amsterdam: John Benjamins.

Schmid, S. 1994. *L'italiano degli spagnoli. Interlingue di immigranti nella Svizzera tedesca.* Milano: Franco Angeli.

Schmidt, A. 1985. *Young People's Dyirbal: An Example of Language Death from Australia.* Cambridge: Cambridge University Press.

Seidlhofer, B. 2002. "Pedagogy and local learner corpora: working with learning-driven data". In Granger, S., Hung, J. and Petch-Tyson, S. (eds), *Computer Learner Corpora, Second Language Acquisition and Foreign Language Teaching.* Amsterdam: John Benjamins. 213–234.

Selinker, L. 1972. "Interlanguage". *International Review of Applied Linguistics* X (3): 209–231.

Valdés G. 2005. "Bilingualism, heritage language learners and SLA research: opportunities lost or seized?" *Modern Language Journal* 89 (iii): 410–426.

Weinreich, U. 1953. *Languages in Contact.* The Hague: Mouton.

NOTES FOR STUDENTS AND INSTRUCTORS

Study questions

1   By what criteria is the native speaker traditionally defined? According to Davies, what are the ways of coping with loss of identity as a native speaker?
2   Why do Leung, Harris and Rampton say that the notion of the native speaker is 'idealised'? What do the following concepts mean: language expertise, language affiliation, and language inheritance?
3   What are the key components of the concept of 'ownership', as Higgins used it with reference to world Englishes?
4   According to Llurda, what role have the so-called non-native-speaker teachers played in the gradual acceptance of English as an International Language?
5   What does the concept of *multicompetence* mean? How are the three questions that Cook raised – Who are the L2 users? What is the language they know? What is the community they belong to? – dealt with in *multicompetence*?

Study activities

1   Make a note of the people you interact with in a day. How many share the same first language with you? How many speak your first language as a second or additional language? Who amongst these people has changed their primary language of communication over the years and for what reason? Have you changed your primary language of communication? If yes, for what reason?
2   Find a couple of L2 speakers of any language and discuss with them the notions of *language expertise, language affiliation, language inheritance* and *ownership of language*. How do these concepts apply in each individual case?
3   Thinking of a L2 friend of yours, answer the three questions posed by Cook – Who is the L2 user? What is the language he or she knows? What is the community he or she belongs to? What evidence can you find of your friend to support the notion of *multicompetence*?

Further reading

Davies, Alan, 2003, *The Native Speaker: myth and reality*, Clevedon: Multilingual Matters, is an extended discussion of the various aspects of the notion of the native speaker and a critical evaluation.

Leung, Constant, 2009, 'Second language teacher professionalism' in J. Richards and A. Burns (eds), *Cambridge Guide to Second Language Teacher Education*, pp. 49–58, Cambridge: Cambridge University Press, extends the discussion of classroom realities in to professional development of the language teacher.

Harris, Roxy, 2006, *New Ethnicities and Language Use*, Basingstoke: Palgrave, focuses on the issue of ethnicity in a wider social context.

Rampton, Ben, 2006, *Language in Late Modernity: interaction in an urban school*, Cambridge: Cambridge University Press, further explores the realities of urban schools and critically analyses issues of social class, ethnicity and gender.

Higgins, Christina, 2009, *English as a Local Language: post-colonial identities and multilingual practices*, Clevedon: Multilingual Matters, is a synthesis of the author's work on the various facets of the global spread of English, hybridity theory and identity.

Llurda, Enric (ed.), 2005, *Non-native Language Teachers: perceptions, challenges and contributions to the profession*, New York: Springer, contains contributions from an international team of scholars on various dimensions of the non-native-speaker teacher.

Cook, Vivian, (ed.), 2002, *Portraits of the L2 User*, Clevedon: Multilingual Matters, describes a range of psychological and linguistic approaches to diverse topics about L2 users.

Cook, Vivian, (ed.), 2003, *The Effects of the Second Language on the First*, Clevedon: Multilingual Matters, examines changes in the first language of people who know a second language, thus seeing L2 users as people in their own right differing from the monolingual in both first and second languages.

PART II

Reconceptualizing language in language learning and practice

Introduction

JUST AS THEY HAVE CRITIQUED the concept of the native speaker, which often dominates the practice of language teaching and learning, applied linguists have raised questions about the notion of language in language teaching, language learning and language use. Although seldom explicitly articulated, the field of language teaching and learning does often assume that there is a model form of language that learners should follow. We can see it in the discussion of the use of the so-called authentic material in language teaching. While the model form may not necessarily be the standard variety of the target language, it is usually produced by the native speaker. It is very rarely mixed with elements of different languages or styles, containing plenty of hesitation, false starts, overlaps and interruptions as real conversational interactions typically are. The articles in this part of the Reader critically evaluate the notion of language from a number of different perspectives. The contexts in which the discussions are based include not only language teaching and learning but also language practices in broader social settings.

The first article in this part of the Reader, by Angel Lin, Wendy Wang, Nobuhiko Akamatsu and A. Mehdi Riazi, focuses on English in TESOL (Teaching English to Speakers of Other Languages). Using the authors' own autobiographical narratives, it illustrates how English is seen, learned and appropriated in different ways in diverse socio-cultural contexts, and how this local, socio-culturally situated knowledge can contribute to the knowledge of the discipline. They set themselves a challenging task of problematizing the discursive and institutional practices of Othering by deconstructing and destabilizing the dichotomy between native and non-native speakers of English and re-visioning the TESOL as teaching English for what they term as *glocalized* communication. The article is an interesting example of what the authors themselves describe as 'using the master's tools to deconstruct the master's house'.

Chapter 7 by Alastair Pennycook addresses the relationship between the call for authenticity, its relocalization in other contexts and the use of English. Using the global spread of hip-hop as an example, he examines the conflictual discourses of authenticity and locality, from those that insist that African American hip-hop is the only real variety and that all other forms are inauthentic deviations, to those that insist that to be authentic one needs to stick to one's 'own' cultural and linguistic traditions. The tension between a cultural dictate to keep it real and the processes that make this dependent on local contexts, languages, cultures and understandings of the real that Pennycook discusses finds its resonance in many different situations. We are reminded that the enthusiasm for authenticity is not restricted to English in English language teaching. The multiple realities of global hip-hop open up useful perspectives on the local and global use of languages.

In Chapter 8, Barbara Seidlhofer points out that the discussions about global English on the meta-level have not been accompanied by adequate empirical studies of the extensive contemporary use of English worldwide, namely English as a lingua franca. She argues that the lack of a descriptive reality precludes us from conceiving of speakers of lingua franca English as language users in their own right and thus makes it difficult to counteract the reproduction of native English dominance. To remedy the situation, Seidlhofer proposes a research agenda which accords lingua franca English a central place in description alongside English as a native language. A corpus project is described which constitutes a first step in this process. The article concludes with a consideration of the potentially very significant impact that the availability of an alternative model for the teaching of English as a lingua franca would have for pedagogy and teacher education.

Suresh Canagarajah continues with the focus on lingua franca English in Chapter 9 but locates it in the context of multilingual communities and language acquisition. Picking up the debates over the dichotomies of native versus non-native speaker, learner versus user, and interlanguage versus target language that persist in applied linguistics, Canagarajah argues that language learning and use succeed through performance strategies, situational resources, and social negotiations in fluid communicative contexts. Language proficiency is therefore practice-based, adaptive and emergent. Language acquisition needs to be reconceptualized as multimodal, multisensory, multilateral and multidimensional. This does not mean that the constructs such as form, cognition and the individual get ignored. But they are redefined as hybrid, fluid and situated in a more socially embedded, ecologically sensitive and interactionally open model.

While most of the articles that try to reconceptualize language in language learning and practice deal with the spoken form, Ken Hyland in Chapter 10 examines academic writing. As he points out, academic writing is not just about conveying an ideational content. It is also about the representation of self. Research has suggested that academic prose is not completely impersonal, but that writers gain credibility by projecting an identity invested with individual authority, displaying confidence in their evaluations and commitment to their ideas. One of the most visible manifestation of such an authorial identity is the use of the first personal pronouns and their corresponding determiners. But while the use of these forms are a powerful rhetorical strategy for emphasizing a contribution, many second language writers feel uncomfortable using them because of their connotations of authority. Hyland explores the notion of identity in L2 writing by examining the use of personal pronouns in sixty-four Hong Kong undergraduate theses, comparisons with a large corpus of research articles, and interviews with students and their supervisors. The study shows significant underuse of authorial reference by students and clear preferences for avoiding these forms in contexts that involved making arguments or claims.

Hyland argues that the individualistic identity implied in the use of *I* may be problematic for many L2 writers.

In reconceptualizing language in language learning and practice, applied linguists have made extensive use of corpus-based analytic techniques. Chapter 11 by Douglas Biber, Susan Conrad and Randi Reppen illustrates the range of issues in applied linguistics that the corpus linguistics approach can help to address. They identify two main strengths of the corpus-based approach: text corpora provide large databases of naturally-occurring discourse, enabling empirical analyses of the actual patterns of use in a language; and, when coupled with (semi-)automatic computational tools, the corpus-based approach enables analyses of a scope not otherwise feasible. The authors of the article demonstrate these strengths with respect to three areas of applied research: (1) English grammar; (2) lexicography; and (3) ESP and register variation. They argue for the importance of a variationist perspective, comparing the patterns of structure and use across registers and show how analysis of large corpora provides the empirical foundation for such a perspective. Their discussion raises two general points. First, the actual patterns of use in large text corpora often run counter to our expectations based on intuition. Second, corpus-based analyses show that even the notion of core grammar needs qualification, because investigation of the patterns of structure and use in large corpora reveals important, systematic differences across registers at all linguistic levels.

The last chapter in this part of the Reader is by Ronald Carter and Michael McCarthy. It is an example of the issues corpus-based analyses can address. Carter and McCarthy's concern in this article is the manifestation of creative language use in a range of discourses. Drawing data from the CANCODE corpus of everyday spoken English, they explore the extent to which everyday interaction displays literary and creative properties. They argue that different creative patterns of talk are produced for different purposes, and that ordinary, everyday language has its inherent creativity. Clines and continua best capture the different manifestations of creative language uses. Applications of such understandings to language learning and teaching, including the teaching of literature and culture, can benefit from closer scrutiny of corpus data.

Chapter 6

ANGEL LIN, WENDY WANG, NOBUHIKO AKAMATSU, AND A. MEHDI RIAZI

APPROPRIATING ENGLISH, EXPANDING IDENTITIES, AND RE-VISIONING THE FIELD

From TESOL to teaching English for globalized communication (TEGCOM) (2002)

English is now a heteroglossic language that has become pluralized. . . . We can point to the creative communicative strategies adopted by people from their own communities from way back in history to acquire and use English in their own terms.

(Canagarajah, 2000, pp. 130–131)

The world is not owned by English; English is owned by the world.

(Chap Yuen-ying;[1] Wang, 2001, p. 23; original in Chinese)

C AN ONE USE the "master's tools" to deconstruct the "master's house"? Writing in an appropriated[2] language from the "margins" or "periphery" of the academic field, while at the same time trying to destabilize the very dichotomies that saturate the language in which we write (e.g., "center-periphery"), we almost overly stretch the use of scare quotes, short of a better way of distancing our positions from the binary points of view embedded in the very language we use to write about these issues in applied linguistics. Our consciousness has been dichotomized by long-standing discursive practices of Othering (Kubota, 2001), and the hierarchy of forms of representation and knowledge in academia has long been constituted by the interests, desires, and ideologies of historically dominant groups (Richardson, 1997). Writing from the "margins" while simultaneously trying to overcome the "center-margins" dichotomy constitutes both an intellectual and discursive challenge.

It is with apprehension and yet determination that we set out to meet this challenge. We have been encouraged by the recent writings of scholars and researchers working in this area (Braine, 1999; Canagarajah, 1999a, 1999b, 2000; Graddol, 1999; Norton, 1997, 2000; Pennycook, 2000a, 2000b). We also explore different forms of representation and writing, as hitherto remote voices, attempting to negotiate identities and subject positions other than those traditionally constructed for us. Personal and biographical, yet sociological and political, our accounts are both reflexive and performative—we want to analyse our encounters and experiences with English in our own life trajectories just as we are constructing them and performing through them new voices, expanding identities, and alternative subject positions (Gee, Allen, & Clinton, 2001).

This article is divided into four main parts. In Part I, we describe an example of discursive and institutional processes of Othering—the dichotomizing, essentializing, and hierarchical-izing of "scientific" and "literary" writing genres in Western thought and academic traditions. In Part II, we critically analyse our own autobiographic narratives and use the collective story (Richardson, 1985, 1997) as a format to tell our stories of learning and teaching English in different sociocultural contexts. In Part III, we engage in discussions that aim at contributing to the disciplinary knowledge and discourse of teaching English to speakers of other languages (TESOL) and applied linguistics by illustrating both how English is seen, learned, and appro-priated in different ways in diverse sociocultural contexts, and how this local, socioculturally situated knowledge can contribute to the knowledge of the discipline. In Part IV, we problem-atize the discursive and institutional practices of Othering by deconstructing and destabilizing the dichotic categories of "native" and "non-native" speakers of English and propose a paradigm shift from doing TESOL to doing teaching English for glocalized[3] communication (TEGCOM).

Part I: Discursive and institutional processes of *othering:* dichotomizing, essentializing, and hierarchicalizing writing genres

> We are restrained and limited by the kinds of cultural stories available to us. Academics are given the "storyline" that "I" should be suppressed in their writing, that they should accept homogenization and adopt the all-knowing, all-powerful voice of the academy. But contemporary philosophical thought raises problems that exceed and undermine the academic storyline. We are always present in our texts, no matter how we try to suppress ourselves. . . . How, then, do we write ourselves into our texts with intellectual and spiritual integrity? How do we nurture our own voices, our own individualities, and at the same time lay claim to "knowing" something?
>
> (Richardson, 1997, p. 2)

It is interesting to read Richardson's (1997) analysis of 19th-century academic writing canons that were privileged by university and disciplinary institutions, with the power of these canons still being carried on into the 21st century. In Richardson's analysis of the historical separation of science and literature in academic institutions since the 17th century, we see an example of the processes of Othering, of dichotomizing, essentializing, and hierarchicalizing through discursive and institutional practices. Literary, metaphorical writing styles and scientific, "plain," factual writing styles have been constructed as dichotomous, essentialized categories, with the latter privileged and legitimated as the proper medium for the representation of truth and knowledge. However, "a plethora of disciplines—communications, linguistics, English criti-cism, anthropology, folklore, women's studies, as well as the sociology of knowledge, science, and culture—has been engaged in reconstructive analyses," showing that "literary devices appear in all writing, including scientific writing," and "all works use such rhetorical devices as metaphor, image, and narrative" (Richardson, 1997, p. 16).

In these analyses, we see the pervasive and continuous workings of processes of Othering, of the historical construction of essentialized, dichotomized notions and storylines of Self and Other, from the 17th century to the 19th century and to the present day. There is an intimate relation between these discursive and institutional practices of Othering and technologies of power (Foucault, 1972, 1980, 1988) that permeate not only the "master-primitive" colonial relations but also other forms of hierarchical social relations found in many societies: that is, man–woman, literate–illiterate, researcher–researched. As Canagarajah (1996) has shown, present day applied linguists' "objective" writing is but another example of how unequal power relations between the allegedly rational objective researcher (Self), who is constructed as capable of conducting meta-analysis and rational theorizing on the allegedly subjective researched (Other), who are often reported in ways that suggest that they are doing what they do without the ability to reflexively meta-analyse or theorize about what they do.

The previous discussion leads us to the consideration of the following important reflexive question: How should we position ourselves as we are writing this article and/or how do we get positioned by what we write and how we write about it; what kind of voice do we speak in? In positioning ourselves, we can draw on or choose from different cultural storylines available to us (Harre & van Langenhove, 1998). For instance, we can reproduce the pervasive storyline in academic disciplines, adopt (or borrow) the voice of the "objective" researcher, and write in a style that upholds the canons of scientific writing practices (Richardson, 1997). We can, alternatively, choose the other side of the coin, that is, discursively constructing an "authentic cultural voice" characterized by a literary, metaphorical, rhetorical style. In both cases, however, we would only be reproducing the dichotomizing and essentializing colonial storyline of Self and Other (with the "mainstream" being the Self and "us" being the Other). We therefore choose to evade this trap by deconstructing the dichotomous and essentialized storyline. We want to show that these dichotic, essentialized categories (i.e., "mainstream voice" and "indigenous, authentic cultural voice") cannot capture the complexities of the subject positions that we en-vision for ourselves—we are both "mainstream" and "indigenous," or we are neither "essentially mainstream" nor "essentially indigenous": To cross these dichotic boundaries, we draw on Richardson's (1997) hybridized genre, "the collective story," as a way of writing ourselves into the text—writing individual personal stories that have theoretical, sociological, and political implications. In the next section we introduce this genre and present our "collective story."

Part II: The collective story—where the personal and biographical and the sociological and political intersect

Richardson (1985) intertwines narrative writing with sociological analytic writing in a research-reporting genre that she calls "the collective story." The collective story "gives voice to those who are silenced or marginalized" and "displays an individual's story by narrativizing the experiences of the social category to which the individual belongs" (Richardson, 1997, p. 22). To Richardson, the collective story is not just about the protagonists' past but also about his or her future:

> Transformative possibilities of the collective story also exist at the sociocultural level. . . . By emotionally binding people together who have had the same experiences, . . . the collective story overcomes some of the isolation and alienation of contemporary life. It provides a sociological community, the linking of separate individuals into a shared consciousness. Once linked, the possibility for social action on behalf of the collective is present, and therewith, the possibility of societal transformation.
> (Richardson, 1997, p. 33)

Although Richardson emphasizes in the previous excerpt the similarity of experiences of "members" of a certain "social category" (identified according to certain similar conditions or experiences; e.g., cancer survivors, battered women), we want to emphasize the fluidity and nonessentialized nature of such social categories and how the rhetorical decisions made in the writing of the collective story contribute to the foregrounding of similarities of experiences, while de-emphasizing dissimilarities. On the one hand, we want to show in our collective story our uniqueness as individuals, each having a "unique trajectory that each person carves out in space and time" (Harre, 1998, p. 8). On the other hand, we want to show in our collective story how the "narrated experiences" of each of us are not isolated, idiosyncratic events, but "are linked to larger social structures, linking the personal to the public" and the biographical to the political (Richardson, 1997, p. 30). Those similarities of experiences and social conditions that each of us found ourselves in motivated our joining together to embark on the writing of this article in the first place. Resonating with Richardson's notion of using the collective story as a form of social action with transformative possibilities, we want to use our autobiographic narratives not only to report and interpret action, but also to shape future action, stressing "the prospective aspect of autobiographies" (Harre, 1998, p.143). Recent works in applied linguistics that drew on narrative analysis and autobiographical data (e.g., Kramsch & Lam, 1999; Lantolf & Pavlenko, 2001; Pavlenko, 1998, 2001; Young, 1999) as well as the endorsement of narrative and autobiographic research as legitimate approaches in recent research methodology discourses (e.g., Casey, 1995; Ellis & Bochner, 2000) have created in applied linguistics a much welcomed niche, an opening, a legitimate discursive space for us to explore ways of presenting our experiences with English as "English as a Foreign Language (EFL) learners" in different Asian contexts. In presenting these narrated experiences, we are also paving the way to create subject positions more complex than and alternative to those traditionally created for us in EFL learning and teaching discourses (e.g., the stereotype of the quiet, passive, Asian classroom learner of English).

Our collective story

The four authors of this article have learned and used English since childhood in different parts of Asia—Mainland China, colonial and postcolonial Hong Kong, Japan, and Iran, respectively. We crossed one another's pathways when we went to Canada to do our doctoral studies in English language education in the early 1990s. We parted upon graduation and each went into different career paths under different sociocultural and institutional structures. We decided to present our voices as language learners from different parts of the world to the "mainstream" audience by forming a panel, writing up our autobiographies of our experiences with English, and presenting them at the TESOL convention in 2001 (Lin, Wang, Akamatsu, & Riazi, 2001). Now we want to make deeper sense of what we have written by reflexively analysing our experiences, linking them to current discourses of language learning and identity and of local production of disciplinary knowledge in applied linguistics (e.g., Canagarajah, 2000; Leung, Harris, & Rampton, 1997; Norton, 1997, 2000; Toohey, 2000).

When we reflexively analyse our own autobiographies, we find a comparable storyline underlying our different stories. Due to limited space, we shall present excerpts from our narratives to illustrate the storyline, followed by a critical analysis to answer the following questions: Can we reposition ourselves by reimagining the storyline, and how can our stories contribute to the knowledge and discourse of the discipline?

Learning English in contexts where English is not a daily life language. First of all, the four learners were situated in a similar set of sociolinguistic conditions with respect to learning English. In their sociocultural contexts, English—not being a language for daily communication within their families or communities—was mainly encountered as an academic subject in school:

> How did I get interested in the English language in a non-English speaking country like China? My parents didn't speak a word of English. My first encounter with English was

when I was in the 3rd grade and English was a school subject. In the isolated China in the early 70s, many Chinese kids considered English to be too foreign and irrelevant to their lives; so there was lack of interest in the English subject.

(Excerpt from Wendy's story)

I grew up in a small town in Fars province, where English was not popular and was taught as a school subject only from grade seven. There weren't any private institutions to teach English either. Moreover, the socio-economic condition of families did not allow for a full-fledged schooling of their children, let alone for extra curricular subjects such as English. Therefore, chances for learning English in families or formal education were very low for us.

(Excerpt from Mehdi's story)

I grew up in a home and community where few had the linguistic resources to use English at all, and even if anyone had, she/he would find it extremely socially inappropriate (e.g., sounding pompous) to speak English. My chances for learning and using English hinged entirely on the school. However, I lived in a poor government-subsidized apartment building complex in the rural area in Hong Kong, where schools were mostly newly put up in the 1960s and they neither had adequate English resources (e.g., staff well-versed in spoken English) nor a well-established English-speaking culture.

(Excerpt from Angel's story)

I was good at math and science, and English was also my favorite subject. I felt that English was the easiest subject of all, in terms of getting good marks. . . . In my third year in junior high school (Grade 9), I decided to try to enter the most prestigious high school, which my brother attended. In spite of all my efforts, however, I failed the entrance examination for the high school and had to go to another school. I thought that my life was over. . . . I was unhappy about everything around me. . . . It was one of those days when I met Mr. Okuhara.

(Excerpt from Nobu's story)

Appropriating English to expand our horizons and identities. Given the situation that English is mainly learned as a school subject for academic grades, one will normally not expect the learner to have developed a high level of communicative competence in English. However, our stories illustrate how some teachers helped us appropriate English and engage in practices that expanded our horizons and identities. Those moments were experienced as self-transforming, culturally enriching, and also at times psychologically liberating (resonating with the emphasis of recent works on the intimate relationships between identity and language learning; e.g., Norton, 1997, 2000; Toohey, 2000). For instance, the hierarchical schooling system in Japan imposed a failure identity on Nobu when he failed to enter a prestigious high school; his meeting with a very special English tutor, Mr. Okuhara, had created a new, expanding identity for Nobu and had turned his life around—he wanted to become an English teacher, like Mr. Okuhara:

My first meeting with Mr. Okuhara was very brief; he just read through the textbook and reference books (i.e., grammar books) I was using in my high school and made a few comments on them. He then handed me another book to read. Boy, it was so difficult! There were a lot of words I didn't know, and some sentence structures were also complex. I could read only three pages or so in a week. . . . I studied English with

Mr. Okuhara for four years. In those four years, I read a variety of English books with him, such as autobiography, mystery, adventure, and philosophy. My reading ability in English improved so much and I learned many things from the English books. . . . However, it is the time I spent with him after each lesson that I appreciated more. He used to tell me about his youth and his teaching experiences . . . Mr. Okuhara was a very special person who influenced me most in my teenage. I realized that I would like to be an English teacher like Mr. Okuhara.

(Excerpt from Nobu's story)

Learning English in China in the 1970s should have also proved to be a lonely enterprise. However, there were two significant events in Wendy's early learning experience: (a) Wendy's parents wanted their daughter to take up the future identity of an interpreter, who would serve as a bridge between the Western world and their own world, and (b) Wendy's meeting with a special teacher, Mr. Qi, who had opened up a bilingual discursive space for her to feel secure enough to explore a new world and a new identity in English:

My parents passed on to me their beliefs and interest in the Western world. They strongly believed that the future of China was to be open to the Western world and English language is the key for communication. . . . My parents believed that I had language talent and could become an interpreter one day. So they seized the opportunity for me by signing me up for a language aptitude test when the Tianjin Foreign Languages School reopened the year after President Nixon's visit to China in 1972. I passed the language aptitude test and was admitted into an intensive English program in 1973. Getting into the English program changed the path of my life forever. . . .

I enjoyed practicing speaking English with peers and teachers. *All the teachers were fluent speakers of English, though not native, speakers.* The classes were small, with no more than 12 students in each class. I enjoyed going to English classes, particularly the English conversation class. *Our teacher, Mr. Qi, liked to code-switch between English and Chinese. This shaped the way we communicated with each other both in and out of class. In switching between the two languages, we learned to relate to each other and communicate in the world we created. The, use of both languages signified a sense of belonging to that world. . . . Chinese was the language to represent ourselves and English was the language we used to expand who we were and who we wanted to be.* To this end, *English became a language of dream and a language of freedom.*

(Excerpts from Wendy's story; italics added)

Likewise, English later became much more than a school subject to Angel. It became a tool for her to enrich and expand her sociocultural horizons, and a space for her to negotiate her "innermost self":

I had pen-pals from all over the world. . . . In my circle of girl-friends, having pen-pals had become a topic and practice of common interest and we would talk about our pen-pals and share our excitement about trading letters, postcards, photos, and small gifts with our pen-pals; we'd also show one another pictures of our pen-pals. . . . It's a spontaneous "community of practice" (Lave & Wenger, 1991) that had emerged from our own activities and interests. . . . I also started to write my own private diary in English every day about that time. . . . Although I had started off this habit mainly to improve my English, later on I found that I could write my diary faster in English than in Chinese . . . I felt that I could write my feelings freely when I wrote in English—less inhibition and reservation—I seemed to have found a tool that gave me more freedom to express my innermost fears, worries, anger, conflicts or excitement, hopes, expectations, likes and dislikes, as if this foreign language had opened up a new, personal space (a "third space," Bhabha, 1994) for me to more freely express all those difficult emotions and experiences (typical?) of an adolescent growing up, without feeling the sanctions of the adult world.

(Excerpts from Angel's story)

Mehdi's location in a tourist spot and his identity as one of the few tourist guides in the community gave him an impetus to learn English. Later, English came to be an important tool for him to acquire a socially upward, professional identity:

My first encounter with English language was in the form of facing foreign tourists coming to our historical town to visit the historical traces of the past dynasties. This created in me an impetus to learn English. . . . In grade seven, I had my first formal exposure to English language as a school subject. . . . Having finished my high school, I entered into a two-year college program in electronics. Students in this college were required to spend their first quarter totally learning English as all the textbooks were in English and even the language of instruction in some courses was also English. . . . This college program helped me a lot in changing my subject and field of study (from electronics to English) both in entering the field (English program) and later on in fulfilling the requirements of different levels of the English language program.

(Excerpt from Mehdi's story)

Anticlimax: Experiences of being positioned as an inferior copy of "The Master's Voice." Our storyline has so far been one of a successful journey of learning and mastering English for our own purposes. Two of the stories (Wendy's and Angel's), however, have an anticlimax, a difficult situation that destroyed most of their previously built-up confidence about themselves and their English. Positioned as an inferior (or "accented or not-competent" English speaker) by her Anglo classmates, Wendy was made to live with an *imposed Otherness.* She both missed and had to hide her bilingual, code-switching, confident, hybrid self (cf. Trinh, 1990) that she once enjoyed before going to Canada:

When I went to Canada in the late 1980s, I was a relatively fluent speaker of English. However, it didn't take me long to realize that my English was marked. All of a sudden my relationship with English changed. In China, being able to speak English was a plus; therefore I was + English. As a *non-native speaker* of English in Canada, the capitalized "I" automatically became a lower case and English became my problem . . . Soon after I started the MA program in English at York University, I felt numerous tensions building up around the language I thought I knew well. While I was proficient enough to function in the English-speaking environment as a graduate student, *I had the feeling that the person people saw and communicated with was not the person inside. The "me" shown through the English language was not the same "me" shown when I spoke Chinese or when I "messed up English with Chinese."* I started to experience a persona split. *I missed the old "me" with two languages in one person.* Now I felt like two people. The English *Me* was definitely much quieter, more reserved, and less confident to the point that my voice became so low that people couldn't hear what I was saying. I was constantly frustrated when people asked me "I am sorry, what did you say?" or "Pardon?" Each time I heard these, I became so self-conscious that I couldn't hear my own voice. It made me feel worse when I heard people say "Never mind!" I felt like an idiot, unable to comprehend what other people had said. All these instances made me wonder what was wrong with my English. Was my English that bad?

(Excerpt from Wendy's story; italics added)

Likewise, Angel was made to feel ashamed of her English:

English in my secondary school days was something I felt I mastered and owned. I felt competent and comfortable in it. It was not until my first year as an undergraduate English major in the University of Hong Kong that I was induced to feel ashamed about my own English—or made to feel that I hadn't really mastered it or owned it. Many of my fellow students at the university had mostly studied English literature in their secondary schools while I had only the slightest idea of what it was! (English Literature is not offered in the curriculum of most secondary schools, but it is offered in a small number of well-established prestigious schools in the urban area in HK). When I spoke in tutorial sessions, I noticed the difference between my Cantonese-accented English and the native-like fluent English that my classmates and the tutor spoke. It was, however, too late for me to pick up the native-like accent then.

(Excerpt from Angel's story)

Searching for resolution: Reclaiming and re-exercising ownership of English. Both Wendy and Angel constructed in the latter parts of their narratives a self that has reclaimed ownership of English through continuous education—gaining more linguistic as well as symbolic capital (Bourdieu, 1986):

Continuing education was my remedy for making up *what comes naturally to native speakers, the confidence to speak.* . . . not until I started teaching English as a second language with the Toronto Board of Education did I feel comfortable with English and myself. I no longer considered English as their language. It was mine. *It had to be mine before I could teach it to my students.*

(Excerpt from Wendy's story; italics added)

My life and career took a turn after my Master's degree and my residential years in the Robert Black College. I have acquired both the paper credentials and the actual linguistic and cultural resources to get and do the job of an English teacher. I had not (and have not) acquired a native-like English accent, but relatively speaking, my spoken English was more fluent and idiomatic than before the Robert Black College years. I no longer felt that I was an "impostor" (Bourdieu, 1991), or an "incompetent" teacher, an object of mockery by my middle-class students and colleagues. I seemed to have somehow managed to enter the elite group of English-conversant Chinese in Hong Kong.

(Excerpt from Angel's story)

It has to be pointed out that the resolution, which seemed to have come easily, was, in fact, just a temporary resolution. The feeling of having to prove oneself (and one's competence in English) is a recurrent one, and the struggle is one that continues, as both Wendy and Angel are reflecting on it now.

Helping our students. In the final part of the storyline, all four authors are engaged in the positioning of self as a helping teacher, as someone who wants to help learners like themselves to achieve what they have achieved in relation to English and to life in general:

> I strongly believe that helping learners relate to each other in the target language and develop the confidence to use the language as their own should be the primary objectives for second language teaching and learning.
>
> (Excerpt from Wendy's story)

> Whenever I hear my students express worries about their English proficiency, I also notice that they have had a very different relationship than that I have developed with English over the years. I am still trying to find ways to help them stop seeing English as only a subject, a barrier, a difficult task in their life, but as a friend who would open up new spaces, new challenges and new lands for them, both socioculturally and intellectually. . . . To me, this is a life-long research and practice question to embark on.
>
> (Excerpt from Angel's story)

> I'm not sure how much or if my students are satisfied with my classes, but I've been learning a lot from teaching here. For example, since I came here, I've been more able to put myself in my students' place and to improve my way of teaching. I've been not only teaching action research but also using it for my classes. . . . I'm beginning to feel that I can share what I've learned from my studies with my students and that I can learn from them.
>
> (Excerpt from Nobu's story)

> I try very hard to create a sense of self-confidence in my students and develop their potentialities. This, I understand, originates from my own experience as a learner. My students have come to know me as a caring teacher, an attribute that has occasionally received some criticisms on the part of my colleagues.
>
> (Excerpt from Mehdi's story)

Critical reflexive analysis of our collective story—Identities without guarantees. In writing our autobiographies to present at the 2001 TESOL Conference (Lin, Wang, Akamatsu, & Riazi, 2001), we have at times reproduced the dominant storylines of Self and Other and at other times attempted to put forward alternative subject positions for ourselves. Echoing Hall's (1996) notion of "Marxism without guarantees," we realize the limitations in trying to carve out new subject positions and identities using old discourses. For instance, while attempting to resist being positioned as an inferior copy of the "master's voice," we reproduced at times the dominant storyline and the essentialized and hierarchicalized categories of "native speakers" and "non-native speakers" (e.g., *"All the teachers were fluent speakers of English, though not native* speakers."—excerpt from Wendy's story). Can the subaltern really speak (Spivak, 1988)? Can we speak only through the "master's voice" or speak only as a "domesticated Other" (Spivak, 1988)? Is there any way of finding our voice, remaking our identities, reimagining our storylines, reworking the dominant discourses, and re-visioning the field?

The storyline of our collective story is a familiar one: "EFL learners" who aspire to master the English language, work extremely hard on it, have been helped by some special teachers or schools, have gained a considerable degree of success, have climbed up the socioeconomic ladder partially using this success with English, and have found a bilingual self both culturally enriching and psychologically liberating, as if finding a "third space" (Hall, 1996). Then the storyline of two of us (Angel as a colonial subject in pre-1997 British Hong Kong, and Wendy as a Chinese immigrant in Canada) gets an anticlimax, which is still a very familiar one. For instance, such an anticlimax is found in the storylines of biographies of former colonials such as Ghandi, who encountered experiences of being Othered as "coloured people" in South Africa despite his British education and fluent English (Ghandi, 1982). Yet, in producing our stories, it is as if we subconsciously wanted to reposition ourselves in a reimagined storyline found in idealized stories of cross-cultural encounters, that is, an encounter between equals, a peaceful friendship-building and mutually enriching meeting of different peoples and cultures on egalitarian footings of mutual curiosity and respect (e.g., as found in movies such as ET, versus movies or TV dramas such as *Aliens* or *The X-Files*).

Our reimagined storyline also says something else: We wanted to gain ownership of the cultural tool of English, to find our place and identity, to define who we are and what we shall become in a quest for expanded selves. Again, this is a familiar storyline—the quest for wider significance and expanded identities, socialness, and human mutuality, what Willis (1993) feels to be a quest that is part of the experiences of being human. Can our idealized, reimagined storyline be realized? Can we overcome those binary, essentialized, and hierarchical categories that saturate our language (e.g., "native vs. non-native speakers")? Can we appropriate those "first world" theories to understand and analyse "third world" experiences (Spivak, 1990) while at the same time trying to rework and destabilize those categories? And in what ways can our local stories and lived experiences contribute to the knowledge and discourse of the discipline? It is to a discussion of these issues that we shall turn in the next section.

Part III: Contribution of local knowledge to the discipline: sociocultural situatedness of English-language learning, teaching, and use

> Any episode of human action must occur in a specific cultural, historical, and institutional context, and this influences how such action is carried out.
>
> (Wertsch, 2000, p. 18)

Whereas many sociocultural and critical researchers have pointed to the sociocultural situatedness of language learning, teaching, and use (Canagarajah 1999b, 2000; Pennycook, 2000a, 2000b; Wertsch, 2000), mainstream TESOL methodologies are still mainly informed by studies and experiences situated in Anglo societies such as the United States, Canada, Australia, or Britain. This Anglo-centric knowledge base constitutes the canons of the discipline and often gets exported to periphery countries as pedagogical expertise to be followed by local education workers. Drawing on our own lived experiences in different sociocultural contexts, we shall discuss the value of local knowledge to the discipline with reference to the questions of (a) what counts as "good pedagogy" and (b) what motivates language learning?

What counts as "good pedagogy"?

Our local stories and lived experiences tell us that such a question should be rephrased as "What counts as good pedagogy *in specific sociocultural contexts?*" For instance, consider Mr. Qi's bilingual teaching strategy and Wendy and her peers' code-mixing and code-switching practices, which have helped them gain both confidence and fluency in using English for meaningful communication. These bilingual teaching and communicative practices are likely to be devalued or frowned upon under current Anglo-based orthodox pedagogies of the discipline, which have not had the benefit of gaining the socioculturally situated perspective that Wendy and her contemporaries had. Consider also Nobu's encounter with his mentor, Mr. Okuhara. The text reading and translation teaching method of Mr. Okuhara will hardly receive any commendation from current methodologies of the discipline. However, it was precisely Mr. Okuhara's teaching that had turned a little boy around and aroused in him great interest and motivation to learn English, and more importantly, to enter a new world and learn about that world through English.

We believe that the discipline needs to be informed and reshaped by much more such local stories as told by different learners, teachers, and researchers situated in different sociocultural contexts. Often found in the discipline are problematic implicit claims to context-free knowledge about English language teaching (ELT) methodologies. However, any relevant pedagogical knowledge has to be locally produced and negotiated in different sociocultural contexts (Canagarajah, 1999b, 2000; Holliday, 1994; Lin, 1999; Pennycook, 2000a, 2000b).

Investment in language learning: agency, ownership, and identity

From Wendy's reflection in the previous section and her autobiographic excerpts in Part II, we can see that the question of what fuels language learning is closely related to the learner's agency and identity making in appropriating English in her or his learning process (Norton, 1997, 2000). For instance, the bilingual discursive space that was creatively opened up by Mr. Qi and Wendy and her peers helped these Chinese students experiment with and expand their identities; they felt liberated to comment on current sensitive social and political issues in this bilingual space and identity position that they temporarily created and occupied for themselves. In Wendy's words, *"English became a language of dream and a language of freedom."* Furthermore, Wendy's aspired identity (as an interpreter) fueled her language learning efforts. Reflecting on the question of what fuels her language learning, Wendy writes,

> In analyzing my earlier experience as an English language learner, I have come to realize that imagination was an important source of my motivation. With a dream of becoming an interpreter that I inherited from my parents and took it as my own, learning the English language took on a personal meaning. English was no longer a simple school subject; it was a tool for me to realize my dream, to become who I wanted to be. The prospect of becoming an interpreter, a highly desired position in China, continued to fuel my motivation and got me through all the difficult times and obstacles.

In all of our lived stories, it appears that issues of agency, ownership, and identity are closely related to the learner's investment in English. For instance, in Mehdi's story, his dissatisfaction with the position and social identity as a "low-level electronic technician" led to his decision to invest in studying English. Using his good performance on the English section of the University Entrance Exam, he entered the university and became an English specialist. The decision to shift from the identity of a technician to the identity of a university English major and later an English expert kept his investment strong, despite severe hardships, such as having to work to provide for his family while at the same tune continuing with his university English studies.

In Nobu's story, the examination system seemed to have constructed a "failure identity" for him when he failed to enter the prestigious high school that his elder brother was attending.

He lost all interest in learning and studying. His subsequent important encounter with the English teacher, Mr. Okuhara, turned things around for him. Mr. Okuhara seemed to have validated in Nobu a sense of a worthwhile young man with great potential for learning the different kinds of knowledge in the world: philosophy, biography, adventure, history. All kinds of worthwhile readings were opened up to him through the supportive interactions with Mr. Okuhara, who provided a scaffolding (the L2-L1 annotation format) for Nobu to see his own potential and to develop a new sense of self. He was no longer that failure student, an identity constructed by the examination results; he was a young person being treated with respect and trust by a supportive teacher who was leading him into a whole new world of learning, mediated by Mr. Okuhara's text-reading and translating teaching method. He began to know who he was, and who he wanted to become: an English teacher like Mr. Okuhara himself—a new identity totally different from that failure identity imposed on him by the examination and schooling system. He knew where he was going and who he could become, and this led to his investment in his English learning.

In Angel's story, her investment in learning English was initially fueled by her desire to pass the examination, to achieve good results, and to please her parents. However, when she entered a community of practice in her circle of girlfriends, where it was trendy to write to overseas pen pals, her investment in English was fueled by her desire to enter into a new world with a new self in English; she felt that she could express her feelings more freely, as if in a third space, free from sanctions of the Chinese adult world. Her adolescent bonding with her pen pal, Gretchen, and her opening up of herself in English to her overseas pen pals led to a new sense of self for her—that English was not just a tool for getting rewards from adults; it was a tool for her to enter into different sociocultural groups, forming new friendships on an entirely different plane from her ordinary friendships.

All these stories witness the complex, intimate relationships among agency, ownership, identity, and investment in L2 learning. We can see how learning a language both shapes and is shaped by one's way of knowing, being, and behaving in a specific sociocultural context. This seems to touch on the same point suggested by Canagarajah (2000) when he discusses local agents' appropriation of English in specific contexts. In this regard, stories of language learners situated in different sociocultural contexts can make valuable contribution to the knowledge and discourse of the discipline. Much of conventional research seems to have been written by strangers who tend to simplify the worlds of their subjects, consciously or unconsciously. Personal stories (which are simultaneously sociological and political; see discussion in Parts I and II) told by the agents themselves unfold the complex and multidimensional nature of mastering and appropriating English in different sociocultural contexts. We believe it is time to re-vision the field and propose an alternative storyline and research program for the discipline.

Part IV: Re-visioning the field: from TESOL to teaching English for glocalized communication

> Rather than a coercive monologue by the industrialized world, contemporary international cultural relations appear more like a dialogue, albeit unbalanced in favor of industrialized countries, but a dialogue still. . . . "Glocalization," by accounting for both global and local factors, is a more appropriate conceptual framework to capture and accommodate international communication processes . . . the concept originated in Japanese agricultural and business practices of "global localization, a global outlook adapted to local conditions."
>
> (Kraidy, 2001, pp. 32–33)

In Part II of this article, we see that just as Wendy and Angel were beginning to feel that English had become part of their identities, they were confronted with processes of Othering, which made them feel like an "imposter" (Bourdieu, 1991), an illegitimate speaker of English, mainly because of their local "accent"—their voice not being heard as an "authentic English voice." It seems to be no accident that only Wendy and Angel's stories told of experiences of being Othered. Unlike Iran and Japan, Hong Kong was a British colony. As for Wendy's experiences in Canada, it is likely that the immigrant speaker can be subject to processes of subordination and Othering, a bit like subjects in colonies.[4]

The discourses in the applied linguistics and TESOL literature tend to classify people into "native English speakers" and "non-native English speakers." These categories also frequently appear in job advertisements for English teachers in Asian countries (e.g., "native English speakers preferred," "native English speakers only" found in the classified ads for English teachers in the *Korean Times*, February 10, 2001), and "native" and "non-native" categories of teachers receive different kinds of treatment and status in institutional structures (Canagarajah, 1999b; Lai, 1999; Oda, 1994, 1996; cf. Leung, Harris, & Rampton, 1997). These dichotic, essentialized categories are so pervasive in our consciousness that we even reproduce them in our own stories. Many learners of English in Asia themselves subscribe to the storyline that native English speakers are necessarily better English teachers than non-native English speakers. However, the world is increasingly witnessing "the decline of the native speaker," as Graddol (1999) puts it:

> First, . . . the proportion of the world's population speaking English as a first language is declining, and will continue to do so in the foreseeable future. Second, the international status of English is changing in profound ways: in the future it will be a language used mainly in multilingual contexts as a second language and for communication between non-native speakers. Third, the decline of the native speaker [*will* be explored] in terms of a changing ideological discourse about languages, linguistic competence, and identity.
>
> (p. 57)

Following in the footsteps of researchers doing important work in this area (e.g., Braine, 1999; Canagarajah, 1999a, 1999b; Graddol, 1999; Kubota, 2001), we continue with their work by attempting to further destabilize the "native speaker versus non-native speaker" categories and proposing to erase the boundaries. The approach we take is to problematize the colonial *Self–Other/Master–Friday* storyline underlying these categories.

If altering the discourse can lead to doing things differently (Erni, 1998), what difference will it make when we develop new ways of talking about English speakers and English voices by acknowledging the various, nonhierarchicalized ways of being an English speaker? As a step toward such reimagination and re-creation of discourses, we propose a paradigm shift from doing TESOL to doing TEGCOM. One rationale behind this proposal comes from the recognition that the name TESOL already assigns dichotic *Self–Other* subject positions to teacher and learner: It implicitly positions the Anglo teacher as *Self*, and positions the learner in a life trajectory of forever being the *Other*, and continuing the colonial storyline of Friday—the "slave boy" resigned to the destiny of forever trying to approximate the "master's language," but never legitimately recognized as having achieved it (de Certeau, 1974/1984, p. 155). Such a storyline precludes an alternative storyline such as that proposed in Part II previously.

If one is willing to shift her or his attention from the differential status of speakers (e.g., "native–non-native," "mainstream–minority," "first world-third world," etc.) to the mutual practice of communication itself (e.g., adopting an alternative storyline proposed previously in

Part II), then we see in the postmodern, glocalized world today that there are increasing, legitimate demands for cross-cultural communication to be construed and conducted as an endeavor of mutual efforts on egalitarian footings. The "communicative burden" in cross-cultural, cross-ethnic communication is increasingly conceived as something that should be shouldered more or less equally by all participants in communication, and not just the "non-native English speaker" (Goldstein, 2002; Lippi-Green, 1997). Both the name and discourses of TESOL assume that it is the "Other-language" speakers who need to be subjected to "pedagogical treatment" (de Certeau, 1974/1984, p.155)—to enable them to make themselves intelligible to "native English speakers." This lopsided storyline has its historical roots in the colonial era. However, in today's multipolar world, we can imagine a TEGCOM class in which all learners are monolingual "native English speakers" who need to be instructed in the ways of using English for cross-cultural communication (e.g., cross-cultural pragmatic skills and awareness) in specific sociocultural contexts (e.g., for conducting business in Japan, China, or Iran). If we can start to reimagine the storylines underlying TESOL and its discourses, we can perhaps rework and destabilize the hegemonic relations in different settings in the world.

Our lived experiences testify to the claim that it is when English learners have a sense of ownership of the language and are treated as legitimate English speakers, writers, and users that they will continue to invest in learning and using English, appropriating and mastering it for their own purposes in their specific contexts (see discussion in Part III). The answer to the question of whether an English speaker will serve as a good teacher or model is largely socioculturally situated (e.g., depending on the interactional practices that the teacher and her or his students cocreate in their specific sociocultural context) and cannot be determined (or even predicted) a priori based on the person's plus- or minus- "native speaker" status (see also discussion on what counts as good pedagogy in Part III). We, therefore, see these dichotic categories more as interested social constructions serving existing power structures (Foucault, 1980) in the TESOL field and industry than as innocuous academic terms with much theoretical or practical value.

Our proposal does not consist of merely renaming the field and erasing the previously mentioned dichotic boundaries. We are proposing a rethinking and re-visioning of the field from the perspective of sociocultural situatedness. Proposing TEGCOM means a fundamental change in conceptualizing the global and local divide in the discipline knowledge production and dissemination practices. Seeing English as a resource for glocalized communication where the global and local divide dissolves in the situated appropriation of a global means by local social actors for local purposes, a parallel decentering of the production of pedagogical knowledge in the discipline needs to happen. TESOL as a field guided by its instrumental rationality and modernist project of finding the most effective technology for teaching and learning English around the world has not concerned itself with the meta-analytical project of reflexively understanding its own implication in shaping the life chances, identities, and life trajectories of local people in different parts of the world. However, the "good" pedagogy cannot be found without taking socioculturally situated perspectives, and without engaging with issues of agency, identity, appropriation, and resistance of local social actors when they are confronted with the task of learning or using English in their specific local contexts. TEGCOM thus means a proposal of a paradigm change with implications for an alternative theoretical orientation and research program that put value on local situated knowledge.[5]

CODA

Writing this article has been a collective project. Wang first proposed using autobiographic narratives to analyse our English learning experiences and wrote a methodological review on autobiographic analysis. Although Lin wrote most of the theoretical parts, all the authors participated in writing the collective story and critical analysis of the narratives. Lin first went through the four autobiographies and suggested that a specific storyline seemed to be emerging from them (see Part II). All four authors then looked back at their stories to select the episodes that would exemplify the different parts of the storyline. In the process, both the storyline and the critical analysis were continuously revised through discussions. We want to stress that there is diversity of voices among ourselves even as we coconstruct the collective voice that we present in this article. Our bonding in this article is based on our highlighting of our similarities for the purpose of addressing this specific question: How we can reposition ourselves and make our remote voices heard in the discipline?

Can one use the "master's tools" to deconstruct the "master's house"? To the extent that we can rework, reimagine, and destabilize the various essentialized, dichotic, Self Other constructions and the Anglo-centric knowledge-production mechanisms that saturate and dominate our language and institutional practices, we may achieve a first step toward imagining and reimagining and ultimately realizing the world as a place where multiple voices situated in different local sociocultural contexts are heard, valued, and given a chance to contribute to the disciplinary knowledge and discourses of applied linguistics.

Notes

1   Chan Yuen-ying is Professor and Director of the Journalism and Media Studies Center at the University of Hong Kong.
2   *Appropriate* used as a verb means "taking something that belongs to others and making it one's own, using it for one's own purposes, and with one's own intentions." The appropriation of mediational means or cultural tools (e.g., language, discourse, literacy, social practice) by the child, learner, or newcomer in her or his process of learning and development is an important concept in Russian sociocultural theories of psychology and education (see Wertsch, 1998, 2000).
3   The term *glocal* and the process verb *glocalize* are formed by blending *global* and *local*. The idea has been modeled on Japanese *dochakuka* (deriving from dochuku "living on one's own land"), originally the agricultural principle of adapting one's farming techniques to local conditions, but also appropriated in Japanese business discourse to mean *global localization*, a global outlook adapted to local conditions (Robertson, 1995).
4   Regarding the possible gender differences on this issue among the authors, Nobu says "When I started my MA program in the USA, I had low expectations towards life in the USA (my first study abroad). I don't recall any specific incidents where I felt discriminated, but even if I had been discriminated, I would have taken it for granted because at that time I felt that I was not fully communicatively competent in English. (I should say that I did have good grammatical competence and academic thinking skills.) Maybe I had encountered such discriminatory occasions, with which Angel or Wendy would have felt annoyed, and I just didn't notice them. When I think back on my life in the USA, I was just hoping to acquire more knowledge of TESOL, to get an MA, and to come back to Japan. I didn't expect much. I fully accepted my identity as a foreign student from Japan, and therefore, maybe, I didn't care much about and paid little attention to my accent and the discrimination which my accent might have caused."
5   Due to limited space in this article, further delineation of the alternative theoretical orientation and research program proposed for TEGCOM will appear in a future article.

References

Bhabha, H. (1994). *The location of culture*. London: Routledge.
Bourdieu, P. (1986). The forms of capital. In J. G. Richardson (Ed.), *Handbook of theory and research for the sociology of education* (pp. 241–258). New York: Greenwood.
Bourdieu, P. (1991). *Language and symbolic power*. Cambridge, England: Cambridge University Press.
Braine, G. (Ed.). (1999). *Non-native educators in English language teaching*. Mahwah, NJ: Lawrence Erlbaum Associates, Inc.

Canagarajah, A. S. (1996). From critical research practice to critical research reporting. *TESOL Quarterly, 30*, 321–330.

Canagarajah, A. S. (1999a). Interrogating the "native speaker fallacy": Non-linguistic roots, non-pedagogical results. In G. Braine (Ed.), *Non-native educators in English language teaching* (pp. 77–92). Mahwah, NJ: Lawrence Erlbaum Associates, Inc.

Canagarajah, A. S. (1999b). *Resisting linguistic imperialism in English teaching.* Oxford, England: Oxford University Press.

Canagarajah, A. S. (2000). Negotiating ideologies through English: Strategies from the periphery. In T. Ricento (Ed.), *Ideology, politics and language policies: Focus on English* (pp. 121–132). Amsterdam: Benjamins.

Casey, K. (1995). The new research in education. In M. W. Apple (Ed.), *Review of research in education, 21* (pp. 211–253). Washington, DC: American Educational Research Association.

de Certeau, M. (1984). *The practice of everyday life.* (S. A. Rendall, Trans.). Berkeley, CA: University of California Press. (Original work published 1974.)

Ellis, C., & Bochner, A. (2000). Autoethnography, personal narrative, reflexivity: Researcher as subject. In N. K. Dennzin & Y.S. Lincoln (Eds.), *Handbook of qualitative research* (pp. 733–768). Thousand Oaks, CA: Sage.

Erni, J. N. (1998). Ambiguous elements: Rethinking the gender/sexuality matrix in an epidemic. In N. Roth, & K. Hogan (Eds.), *Gendered epidemic: Representations of women in the age of AIDS* (pp. 3–29). New York: Routledge.

Foucault, M. (1972). *The archeology of knowledge.* New York: Pantheon.

Foucault, M. (1980). Truth and power. In C. Gordon (Ed.), *Power/knowledge: Selected interviews and other writings, 1972–1977* (pp. 109–133). New York: Pantheon.

Foucault, M. (1988). The political technology of individuals. In L. H. Martin, H. Gutman, & P. H. Hutton (Eds.), *Technologies of the self: A seminar with Michel Foucault* (pp. 145–162). Amherst: The University of Massachusetts Press.

Gee, J. P., Allen, A.-R., & Clinton, K. (2001). Language, class, and identity: Teenagers fashioning themselves through language. *Linguistics and Education, 12*(2), 175–194.

Ghandi, M. K. (1982). *An autobiography or the story of my experiments with truth* (M. Desai, Trans.). Ahmedabad, India: Navajivan Publishing House.

Goldstein, T (2002). *Teaching and learning in a multilingual school: Academic and linguistic dilemmas.* Mahwah, NJ: Lawrence Erlbaum Associates, Inc.

Graddol, D. (1999). The decline of the native speaker. In D. Graddol & U. H. Meinhof (Eds.), *English in a changing world* (pp. 57–68). The AILA Review, 13, International Association of Applied Linguistics. Oxford, England: The English Book Centre.

Hall, S. (1996). The problem of ideology: Marxism without guarantees. In D. Moley & K.-H. Chen (Eds.), *Stuart Hall: Critical dialogues in cultural studies* (pp. 25–46). London: Routledge.

Harre, R, (1998). *The singular self: An introduction to the psychology of personhood.* London: Sage.

Harre, R., & van Langenhove, L. (1998). *Positioning theory: Moral contexts of intentional action.* Oxford, England: Blackwell.

Holliday, A. (1994). *Appropriate methodology and social context.* New York: Cambridge University Press.

Kraidy, M. M. (2001). From imperialism to glocalization: A theoretical framework for the information age. In B. Ebo (Ed.), *Cyberimperialism? Global relations in the new electronic frontier* (pp. 27–42). Westport, CT: Praeger.

Kramsch, C., & Lam, W. S. E. (1999). Textual identities: The importance of being non-native. In G. Braine (Ed.), *Non-native educators in English language teaching* (pp. 57–72). Mahwah, NJ: Lawrence Erlbaum Associates, Inc.

Kubota, R. (2001). Discursive construction of the images of U.S. classrooms. *TESOL Quarterly, 35*, 9–38.

Lai, M.-L. (1999). JET and NET: A comparison of native-speaking English teachers schemes in Japan and Hong Kong. *Language, Culture and Curriculum, 12*(3), 215–228.

Lantolf, J., & Pavlenko, A. (2001). (S)econd (L)anguage (A)ctivity Theory: Understanding second language learners as people. In M. Breen (Ed.), *Thought and actions in second language learning: Research on learner contributions.* London: Longman.

Lave, J., & Wenger, E. (1991). *Situated learning: Legitimate peripheral participation.* Cambridge, England: Cambridge University Press.

Leung, C., Harris, R., & Rampton, B. (1997). The idealized native speaker, reified ethnicities, and classroom realities. *TESOL Quarterly, 31*, 543–560.

Lin, A. M. Y. (1999). Doing-English-lessons in the reproduction or transformation of social worlds? *TESOL Quarterly, 33*, 393–412.

Lin, A. M. Y., Wang, W., Akamatsu, N., & Riazi, M. (2001, February). *Asian voices: Language learning, identity, and sociocultural positioning.* Paper presented at the TESOL Annual Convention, St. Louis, MU.

Lippi-Green, K. (1997). *English with an accent: Language, ideology, and discrimination in the United States.* London: Routledge.

Norton, B. (1997). Language, identity, and the ownership of English. *TESOL Quarterly, 31*, 409–429.

Norton, B. (2000). *Identity and language learning: Gender, ethnicity and educational change.* Harlow, Essex, England: Pearson Education Limited.

Oda, M. (1994). Against linguicism: A reply to Richard Marshall. *The Language Teacher, 18*(11), 39–40.

Oda, M. (1996, June). *Applied linguistics in Japan: The dominance of English in the discourse community.* Paper presented at the International Conference on Language Rights, Hong Kong Polytechnic University, Hong Kong.

Pavlenko, A. (1998). Second language learning by adults: Testimonies of bilingual writers. *Issues in Applied Linguistics, 9*(1), 3–19.

Pavlenko, A. (2001, September). In the world of the tradition, I was unimagined: Negotiation of identities in cross-cultural autobiographies. *International Journal of Bilingualism, 5*, 317–344.

Pennycook, A. (2000a). English, politics, ideology: From colonial celebration to postcolonial performativity. In T Ricento (Ed.), *Ideology, politics and language policies: Focus on English* (pp. 107–119). Amsterdam: Benjamins.

Pennycook, A. (2000b). Language, ideology and hindsight: Lessons from colonial language policies. In T. Ricento (Ed.), *Ideology; politics and language policies: Focus on English.* (pp. 49–65). Amsterdam: Benjamins.

Richardson, L. (1985). *The new other woman.* New York: Free Press.

Richardson, L. (1997). *Fields of play (Constructing an academic life).* New Brunswick, NJ: Rutgers University Press.

Robertson, R. (1995). Glocalization: Time—space and homogeneity—heterogeneity. In M. Featherstone, S. Lash, & R. Robertson (Eds.), *Global modernities* (pp. 25–44). London: Sage.

Spivak, G. C. (1988). Can the subaltern speak? In C. Nelson & L. Grossberg (Eds.), *Marxism and the interpretation of culture* (pp. 280–316). Urbana: University of Illinois Press.

Spivak, G. C. (1990). *The post-colonial critic.* New York: Routledge.

Toohey, K. (2000). *Learning English at school: Identity; social relations and classroom practice.* Clevedon, England: Multilingual Matters.

Trinh, T M.-H. (1990). Not you/like you: Post-colonial women and the interlocking questions of identity and difference. In G. Anzaldua (Ed.), *Making face, making soul* (pp. 371–375). San Francisco: Aunt Lute Foundation.

Wang, K. M. (2001, December 3–9). Embracing English; embracing the new century. *The International Chinese Newsweekly*, pp. 22–23.

Wertsch, J. V. (1998). *Mind as action.* New York: Oxford University Press.

Wertsch, J. V. (2000). Intersubjectivity and alterity in human communication. In N. Budwig, I. C. Uzgiris, & J. V. Wertsch (Eds.), *Communication: An arena for development* (pp. 17–31). Stamford, CT: Ablex.

Willis, P. E. (1993). Symbolic creativity. In A. Gray & J. McGuigan (Eds.), *Studying culture: An introductory reader* (pp. 206–216). London: Edward Arnold.

Young, R. (1999). Sociolinguistic approaches to SLA. *Annual Review of Applied Linguistics, 19*, 105–134.

Chapter 7

ALASTAIR PENNYCOOK

LANGUAGE, LOCALIZATION, AND THE REAL

Hip-hop and the global spread of authenticity (2007)

Introduction: Horizons of significance

LET US START WITH TWO fairly uncontroversial givens: Both English and hip-hop have spread across the world. The first is widely attested, although with equally widely divergent interpretations (Pennycook, 2003a), from Hanson's (1997) review of Crystal's (1997) book on English as a global language, which urges English speakers to relax because "English is streets ahead and fast drawing away from the rest of the chasing pack" (p. 22) to Phillipson's (1999) review of the same book, which warns us that this "celebration of the growth of English" is tied to "an uncritical endorsement of capitalism, its science and technology, a modernization ideology, monolingualism as a norm, ideological globalization and internationalization, trans-nationalization, the Americanization and homogenization of world culture, linguistic, culture and media imperialism" (p. 274); from a world Englishes perspective on "implications of pluri-centricity . . . the new and emerging norms of performance, and the bilingual's creativity as a manifestation of the contextual and formal hybridity of Englishes" (Kachru, 1997, p. 66) to a focus on how a particular community "appropriates English to dynamically negotiate meaning, identity, and status in contextually suitable and socially strategic ways, and in the process modifies the communicative and linguistic rules of English according to local cultural and ideological imperatives" (Canagarajah, 1999, p. 76).

The global spread of hip-hop is also widely attested, and likewise with a range of inter-pretations, from positions that suggest that hip-hop "is and always will be a culture of the African-American minority . . . an international language, a style that connects and defines the self-image of countless teenagers" (Bozza, 2003, p. 130) to Perry's (2004) contention that "Black American music, as a commercial American product, is exported globally. Its signifying creates a sub-altern voice in the midst of the imperialist exportation of culture" (p. 19); from Levy's (2001) description of hip-hop as "a global, post-industrial signifying practice, giving new parameters of meaning to otherwise locally or nationally diverse identities" (p. 134) to Mitchell's (2001) argument that "Hip-hop and rap cannot be viewed simply as an expression of African-American culture; it has become a vehicle for global youth affiliations and a tool for reworking local identity all over the world" (pp. 1–2). I will not attempt to unravel these different takes on language, culture and globalization here (for more discussion, see Pennycook, 2007), although I will largely be following the positions of Canagarajah (1999) and Mitchell (2001) to focus not so much on a vision of imperialistic spread as on the ways in which English and hip-hop become intertwined as local cultural and linguistic formations.

Localization inevitably involves complex relations of class, race, ethnicity, and language use. Although a local "Nederhop" movement of Dutch-language rap has emerged in Holland, for example, it features almost exclusively White Dutch youth. While this Nederhop movement can claim greater Dutch linguistic and cultural "authenticity," it also struggles against a more American/English oriented rap movement by non-White youth (largely of Surinamese origin), who can claim greater global authenticity in terms of the discourses of marginalization and racial identification within hip-hop (see Krims, 2000; Wermuth, 2001).

The hip-hop ideology of authenticity, of "keepin' it real," presents a particular challenge for any understanding of global spread. This take on the real is often derided as an obsession with a particular story about violence, drugs, and life in the hood, or with a belief that there is something essentially authentic in the description of brutal lifestyles. The implications of an emphasis on the real, however, need to be taken far more seriously than this. As Morgan (2005) suggests, "the hip-hop mantra 'keepin' it real' represents the quest for the coalescence and interface of ever-shifting art, politics, representation, performance and individual accountability that reflects all aspects of youth experience" (p. 211). Also in the U.S. context, as Perry (2004) argues, keeping it real has many different meanings from "celebrations of the social effects of urban decay and poverty" to "assertions of a paranoid vigilance in protecting one's dignity," from an "authenticating device responding to the removal of rap music from the organic relationship with the communities creating it" to "an explicitly ideological stand against selling one's soul to the devils of capitalism or assimilation" (p. 87).

This emphasis on being true to oneself might nevertheless be seen as the global spread of a particular individualist take on what counts as real. The notion of authenticity, however, can be understood not so much as an individualist obsession with the self but rather as a dialogical engagement with community. As Taylor (1991) argues, authenticity cannot be defined without relation to social contexts and "horizons of significance" (p. 39). Authenticity demands an account of matters beyond the self: "If authenticity is being true to ourselves, is recovering our own 'sentiment de l'existence'[1] then perhaps we can only achieve it integrally if we recognize that this sentiment connects us to a wider whole" (p. 91). The localization of horizons of significance pulls the ideology of keeping it real back toward local definitions of what matters. Alim's (2004) discussion of real talk, a hip-hop version of metalinguistic discourse on language and authenticity, captures the ways in which this is both creatively expressive yet discursively aware: "Not only is you expressin yoself freely (as in 'straight talk'), but you allegedly speakin the truth as you see it, understand it, and know it to be" (p. 86). The question, then, is what is real talk on the global stage?

As Androutsopoulos (2003) suggests, because "hip-hop is a globally dispersed network of everyday cultural practices which are productively appropriated in very different local contexts, it can be seen as paradigmatic of the dialectic of cultural globalization and localization" (p. 11).[2] One of the most fascinating elements of the global local relations in hip-hop, then, is what we might call *the global spread of authenticity*. Here is a perfect example of a tension between on the one hand the spread of a cultural dictate to adhere to certain principles of what it means to be authentic, and on the other, a process of localization that makes such an expression of staying true to oneself dependent on local contexts, languages, cultures, and understandings of the real. This tension opens up some significant issues for our understanding of language use and localization. Keeping it real in the global context is about defining the local horizons of significance while always understanding the relationship to a wider whole. How does rap undertake "the project of realism" (Krims, 2000, p. 70), real talk (Alim, 2004) in relation to language choice? Or how is the project of localism enacted? As I argue below, relocalized real talk is about redefining what it means to be local, about opening up new horizons of significance while challenging ortholinguistic practices and ideologies.

The project of localism: "They are trying to be Malay boys doing rap"

To use English in popular music is common, suggesting anything from an attempt to enter a wider market, to a belief that English is better suited to carry particular meanings or to perform particular genres. English-language popular music carries both images of modernity and possibilities of economic success. We might therefore be tempted to assume that the use of English is nothing but the creep of global homogenization. When we hear it being used, for example, by the vast majority of singers in the Eurovision song contest – a competition that might, by contrast, emphasize a multilingual and multicultural Europe, with varying styles of music and a range of national or regional languages putting European diversity on display – we may be very tempted to accept the visions of homogenization invoked by Phillipson (2003): "If inaction on language policy in Europe continues, at the national and supranational levels" he warns, "we may be heading for an American-English only Europe" (p. 192). As we shall see, however, the picture is surely more complex than this.

Alternatively, a more liberal interpretation suggests that English is for global communication, financial gain, and international identity, whereas local languages are for local audiences and identities. The vision of complementarity between English and local languages, whereby the former allows communication across boundaries, with the latter maintaining local identities and traditions, supports both the benefits of English as a global means of communication ("international intelligibility") and the importance of multilingualism ("historical identity"; see Crystal, 1997). As Hogben (1963) once proposed, English can serve people around the world as a universal second language "for informative communication across their own frontiers about issues of common interest to themselves and others" (p. 20), while other languages play a role as "a home tongue for love-making, religion, verse-craft, back chat and inexact topics in general" (p. 20). By relegating vernacular languages to only local expression, however, and by elevating English only to the role of international communication, such a view ignores the many complexities of local and global language use.

To use English lyrics may be to participate in a global subculture that is as opaque to many English users as lyrics in other languages. When Malaysian rappers Too Phat, for example, announce that "Hip hop be connectin' Kuala Lumpur with LB/Hip hop be rockin' up towns laced wit' LV/Ain't necessary to roll in ice rimmed M3's and be blingin'/Hip hop be bringin' together emcees,"[3] there are several things going on: On the one hand we have an image of global hip-hop connecting rappers (MCs) across the world, as well as the use of aspects of African American English and references to global fashion items; at the same time this is both a register that is obscure to many English speakers and a rejection of aspects of U.S. "bung" culture. Too Phat may be using a global language, but they are also using a particular register that is local, generational, cultural, and distinctive. They are both participating in and rejecting aspects of the global. This adoption of hip-hop amid rejection of parts of American culture has been widely noted. As Perullo and Fenn (2003) point out, for example, while the take-up of rap by Tanzanians initially involved wholesale adoption of American idioms, from clothes and names, to language and musical style, English-language Tanzanian hip-hop was soon distancing itself from various North American elements because "expression of themes such as violence and vulgar language was frowned upon by Tanzanians and considered disrespectful, while the topic of male/female relations was more appropriate and found in most Tanzanian music" (Perullo & Fenn, 2003, p. 27).

Senegalese rapper Faada Freddy of Daara J similarly notes that the hip-hop movement in Senegal was at first just imitating U.S. rap, "carry a gun, go down to the streets and try to show that you are someone that you can express yourself with violence." But eventually they realized that

> we should care more about our hunger problems . . . we live in a country where we have poverty, power, race . . . you know ethnic wars and stuff like that. So we couldn't afford to go like Americans, talking about "Bung Bling," calling our pretty women "Hoes" or stuff like that.
>
> (Interview, May 3, 2005)

As hip-hop developed in Senegal, they came to realize

> that rap music was about the reality and therefore we went back to our background and see that .. . OK . . . and not only rap music is a music that could help people . . . you know . . . solve their problems, but this music is ours! It is a part of our culture!
>
> (Interview, May 3, 2005)[4]

Lockard (1998) meanwhile notes a similar set of rejections elsewhere because the "profane bitterness, antisystemic radicalism, and overt sexual warfare" of some forms of rap, particularly from the United States, would be "considered excessive by most Southeast Asians" (p. 263). Singaporean producer and rap artist Shaheed explains, "We don't want to promote anything that is morally incorrect. That is my principle to me and to them. For me, if I find smoking and drinking is morally incorrect then I won't include it in my song" (Interview, December 13, 2003). Korean DJ Jun also talks of the move away from American hip-hop themes to deal with "the Korean problem": "It is like, every young Korean man has to join the army, so they are rapping about it" (Interview, November 2, 2003). Similar issues concern Joe Flizzow[5] of Too Phat:

> If suddenly I start rapping about pushing cocaine or rocking bung bung, then . . . that wouldn't be keeping it real, but what we rap about is related to stuff that is related to— that we go through. I mean we don't rap about violence. But we talk about issues that are relevant to the Malaysian scene.
>
> (Interview, December 12, 2003)

For many hip-hop artists, then, the first move toward localization is a rejection of aspects of rap from the United States and a turn toward overtly local themes. The penalties for not doing so can be, at the very least, mockery by one's peers. Australian rappers Two Up (2002) lay into local hip-hoppers trying to be American in the track "Why do I try so hard?": "Could someone tell me what's up with these try-hard homies?/Their caps are back to front but I think they're phonies." They are lambasted for their clothes and ways of walking: "The triple extra large pants so big they're saggin'/With the pimp limp their leg they be draggin';" for the places they hang out, the pretence at gangsterhood, and the imitation of all that is American: "The local shopping centre is the place you hang/Chillin' with your bitch and the rest of the gang/ Comparing knives, shooting dice and working on your plan/To become an Aussie version of the Wu-Tang Clan;" and above all for being young middle-class kids hanging around stores such as Grace Brothers (a department store in Sydney): "The gangs are gathered round the front of Grace Brothers/Some too young to drive, so they're waiting on their mothers/To come and pick them up and take them home/That's why they've got that flashy new mobile phone." To adhere too closely to an American version of hip-hop can evoke a derisive response.

If one part of localization is the insistence on local themes, it is also common for rap to develop in local languages. Daara J, cited above, are part of the complex Francophone circle of flow (see Pennycook, 2007) and use predominantly French and Wolof. Elsewhere, where the initial take-up may have been in English, this has often been followed by linguistic localization. In Tanzania, "swamp" soon developed: "Swahili became the more powerful language choice within the hip-hop scene because of a desire among youth to build a national hip-hop culture that promoted local rather than foreign values, ideas and language" (Perullo & Fenn, 2003, p. 33). In Tanzania's case, therefore, while hip-hoppers continued to adopt and adapt American styles and lyrics into their music and identity, the meanings of these appropriations changed as they were reembedded in Swarap with different cultural references, social concerns, and musical styles. As Bennett (2000) observes in the German context, "only when local rappers started to write and perform texts in the German language did their songs begin to work as an authentic form of communication with the audience" (p. 141). Discussing local language use in hip-hop in Zimbabwe, Italy, Greenland, and Aotearoa/New Zealand, Mitchell (2003) comments that "the rhizomic globalization of rap is not a simple instance of the appropriation of a U.S./African-American cultural form; rather, it is a linguistically, socially, and politically dynamic process which results in complex modes of indigenization and syncreticism" (pp. 14–15).

It might be tempting to conclude that the greater the use of English (or other metropolitan languages), the greater the identification with a global, commercial, imported version of rap, whereas the greater the use of local languages, the greater the identification with local politics, music, and culture. Such a formulation, however, misses several layers of complexity that need to be considered. In contexts where English is widely used, it may also already be seen as a local language. Malaysia is an obvious example here, and indeed the language shift in Malaysia appears, at least to some extent, to have been in the direction of English. Despite a ban on radio or television performances, 4U2C and KRU gained reasonably wide support in the 1990s with their Malay-language lyrics attacking pollution, the abandonment of children, alcoholism, and other significant but safe social concerns (Lockard, 1998). Since then, rappers such as Too Phat, using predominantly English, have come to the fore. As Pietro Felix, from their record label Positive Tone, explains,

> once KRU did it people started to go "oh OK it can be done in Malay also but look there is an English version. . . . This is cool and it is two Malay guys singing rap-they are not trying to be American, they are not trying to be Black, they are trying to be Malay boys doing rap." So everybody really took to them.
>
> (Interview, December 12, 2003)

This does not mean that all rap in Malaysia is moving toward English—local rap artists are using a range of languages, and Poetic Ammo's 1998 CD, *It's a Nice Day To Be Alive*, has tracks not only in English but also in Bahasa Malaysia (the national language), Tamil, and Cantonese— but it does suggest that the use of English or other languages engages a far more complex and dynamic set of concerns than are suggested by a dichotomy between the local and the global.

It is perhaps surprising that the multilingual codemixing so commonly found in Malaysia is not represented in Too Phat's separation of English and Malay. This is, however, more a product of official attitudes to language in Malaysia than of local language use. As reported in the Malaysian newspaper *Star* (2004), following a report that several tracks such as KRU's "Babe," Ruffedge's "Tipah Tertipu," and Too Phat's "Alhamdulillah" were to be taken off the air due to the Ministry of Information's proposed ban on Malay songs containing English words, the Deputy Minister, Datuk Zainuddin Maidin, was quoted as saying, "The ministry disallows Malay songs that incorporate English lyrics. We are following the guidelines given by Dewan Bahasa dan Pustaka (DBP) (the Agency for Language and Literature) which state that songs with inaccurate translations or improper language should be banned." The use of what is commonly called rojak English or rojak language[6] (referring to the mixed, salad-like makeup of multicultural Malaysia) has long been a point of contention. As the DBP director-general Datuk Abdul Aziz Deraman said, "Inappropriate usage of Bahasa Malaysia could corrupt the national language. The usage of rojak language could also lower the status of the national language and make the Malaysian race lose its identity and culture" ("In a twist over ban", 2004). As Pietro Felix of Positive Tone explained, using Malaysian English

> would count as slang. . . . Let's say you say something like—you start off with one verse in English and another verse in Malay, the song will get banned. You cannot have a bilingual song. . . . A lot of Malaysians use the word lah: "Come on lah," "let's go lah:' When we say something like that, they will ban that song because it is grammatically wrong.
>
> (Interview, December 12, 2003)

The use of one language or another therefore depends very much on the local configuration of culture, language, and politics. Although it might be assumed that to choose between Swahili and English in Tanzania, or Chichewa and English in Malawi, for example, is to choose between the local and the global, there is much more at stake here, including the history of language use and colonialism, commercial and aesthetic considerations, and local language ideologies (Perullo & Fenn, 2003). Although Malawi shares some similarities with Tanzania in its colonial past, the linguascape of Malawi is different. A less successfully imposed "national language," Chichewa struggles for ascendancy over other languages and English. A weaker economy and less-developed infrastructure, meanwhile, make recording in languages other than English more difficult, an important issue in a number of contexts where access to recording industry infrastructure is tied to other forms of linguistic, cultural, and economic capital. Although some Malawian rappers push the use of Chichewa for its greater accessibility to a wider audience, English has tended to dominate. Such questions push us to think beyond notions of "language choice" as if the issue were always one of deciding between discrete languages. As McCann and Ó Laoire (2003) argue, the "simplistic nature of the binary opposition" between Gaelic (personal, lyrical, authentic) and English (practical, plain, inauthentic) popular music in Ireland, constructs both a "reified view of 'tradition,'" thereby concealing important questions of social context and personal meaning" and "an either/or language choice between distinct alternative entities" (p. 234). Sinfree Makoni and I have argued (Makoni & Pennycook, 2005) that many such notions are based on the metadiscursive regimes that divided languages into separate and enumerable objects, overlooking the complex ways in which languages are interwoven and used.

Choice of languages also depends on particular identifications with English in relationship to a musical idiom. As Connell and Gibson (2003) observe, English music was popular in the former European Eastern Bloc countries, in part because of the political implications of listening to English/Western music. The use of English by rock groups in the DDR (East Germany), as in Russia and other communist states, was a highly political act (Larkey, 2003; Pennay, 2001). Although, as suggested above, the move from English to German allows for a more local form of expression, the use of English was initially an act of political critique rather than of commercial acquiescence. In a very different context, underground musicians in Indonesia "switched to Indonesian not out of a desire to 'indigenize' the music but with the aim of making their music resemble more closely underground music in the West, which they viewed as using everyday language to convey urgent and powerful messages to its listeners" (Wallach, 2003, p. 54).[7] In this context, then, the use of Indonesian is a form of translocal identification with the use of English elsewhere. If we wish to understand language choice, therefore, we cannot do so without an appreciation of local language ideologies. And as Woolard (2004) notes, "linguistic ideologies are never just about language, but rather also concern such fundamental social notions as community, nation, and humanity itself" (p. 58).

Embedded languages "the masses said, 'we can relate to this song'"

Understanding language use against the background of local cultural and political formations is also a question of taking their local embeddedness into account. The problem for understanding language use and choice has long been what Kroskrity describes as the "surgical removal of language from context" which "produced an amputated 'language' that was the preferred object of the language sciences for most of the twentieth century" (2000, p. 5). Music is of course crucial here. As Pietro Felix suggests, "Once Too Phat came out with one song called 'Anak Ayam' and . . . there was a layer of traditional music in the background. Everybody knows that song. So immediately the masses said 'we can relate to this song'" (Interview, December 12, 2003). As Joe Flizzow of Too Phat explains:

> Well I think the way we rap . . . we don't try to sound American, we just try to sound, well that is just how we sound, you know? But we do like Malaysian traditional instrumentations and elements of Malaysian music, so that is what makes us different, I would say, from other hip-hop.
>
> (Interview, December 12, 2003)

Malique explains further:

> It's not just the language, it's also the instruments involved . . . We're known for our fusion of traditional elements and we use old folk songs and we add a break beat to it and we rap on top of it . . . Like if you listen to a rap act rapping in a normal beat they would be like "oh, that's another rap act" right. But if you hear a rap like us on "Anak Ayam" you will be like "hey, how come they are rapping in English but the background is, you know, is Malay." So like something they can relate to. Like in Indonesia "Anak Ayam" was pretty big.
>
> (Interview, December 12, 2003)

From this perspective, it is not so much a local language, a local variety of English, or references to local contexts that place this track in its particular context, but rather the instantly recognizable melody in the background.

Another Malaysian group, Teh Tarik Crew, rejects the option of local instruments, however, suggesting that what makes their music Malaysian is, as Altimet puts it,

> the fact that it is made by us. You see when we were recording our first album a lot of people were telling us . . . we had great pressure to put in traditional elements. Like sounds, whatever. But we don't feel that it is necessary. You don't have to put in traditional sounds to sound Malaysian.
>
> (Interview, December 13, 2003)

For them, the use of traditional instruments is to buy into a somewhat stereotypical view of cultural identity. As they point out, if a European or North American band used samples of Asian music, it does not make them Asian. Localization, by contrast, is about talking about local conditions.[8] This raises some important questions for studies of localization of English. For too long, the focus on world Englishes has looked within languages—syntax, pronunciation, pragmatics—to find aspects of localization: A local English has emerged when it bears significant and regular differences from other varieties. Yet the discussion here raises other issues; language may become local by dint of background music or local themes. Localization may be as much about a language being in the world in particular ways as about changes to that language.

This position forces us to reconsider other ways in which we may think about localization. As Perullo and Fenn (2003) observe in the context of English use in Malawi, it is "radically recontextualised" as terms borrowed from African American English "take on new sets of meanings" based on Malawian interpretations of American inner-city gang life and "contemporary social experiences of Malawian youth" (p. 41). Once the mimetic use of language is seen as *enactment* rather than *copying*, the meanings of language use and choice lie "not in the semantic realm but in a participation-through-doing that is socially meaningful" (p. 45). Issues of language choice and style "constitute aspects of discursive and musical practice in Malawian rap culture that are conjoined via language ideologies and are not so easily separable in lived experience" (p. 46). It is this participation through doing, this enactment of language in different contexts that may render the apparent mimicry of English language hip-hop a site of difference. If we consider another of Too Phat's tracks, ("If I Die Tonight"),[9] we find first of all the kind of English localization that is the meat and drink of world Englishes: "If I die tonight, what would I do on my last day/I know I'd wake early in the morn' for crack of dawn's last pray/Then probably go for breakfast like I used to do/Fried kuey teow FAM and roti canai at Ruja's with my boo." Here, with its references to Muslim prayers at dawn and Malaysian Chinese and Indian food, we have a clear localization of English through references to local cultural elements.

Later on, however, as the lyrics move to other things to do on the last day, Malique suggests that he would "line up my shoes one by one/Start with Jordans and end with them Air Force Ones/Put a Post-it on the tongue of each one with the name of each dun/I think I know my homies and who would want which one." Here, with the consumerism, the Jordans, Post-its and homies, we are surely back in the global world of hip-hop fashion. Or are we? Can we in fact judge so easily what is local and global? Although we may be comfortable to say that fried *kuey teow* is a local reference (although even that, when we take into account other diasporas and travel, may not be so clear), can we assume that other references are not local? Or, put another way, when do Malique's Jordans become local? Once we take into account the localization that has already occurred previously, and once we consider enactment and recontextualization as localizing processes, it is far less clear whether we can take this as a global or a local reference, as English as a global language or English as a local language.

If, however, we take onboard the insights of a performative view of language (see Pennycook, 2003b, 2004, 2007), we can start to see such language use in productive rather than reflective terms. Instead of asking whether such a language use is local or not, we can see how it is rendered local in the doing. As Berger (2003) points out,

> While language choice in music may reflect prevailing language ideologies, that influence is often a two-way street; that is, rather than merely reproducing existing ideologies, singers, culture workers, and listeners may use music to actively think about, debate, or resist the ideologies at play in the social world around them.
>
> (pp. xiv–xv)

This is particularly true of musicians such as rap artists, whose focus on verbal skills performed in the public domain renders their language use a site of constant potential challenge. From a performative point of view, "history, tradition and identity are all performances, all the result of invested actors who position themselves vis-à-vis others in a complex and unfolding reality not of their own making" (Dimitriadis, 2001, p. 11). Rap in Libreville, Gabon, according to Auzanneau (2002) "is a space for the expression of cultures and identities under construction." Indeed,

> It is itself a space creating these identities and cultures, as well as codes and linguistic units that will ultimately be put into circulation beyond the songs. Rap thus reveals and participates in the unifying gregarity of the city's activities, and works with the city on the form, functions, and values of its languages.
>
> (p. 120)

From this point of view, what we are seeing here is the production of locality. When we talk of global English use, we are talking of the performance of new identities. Much of hip-hop challenges ortholinguistic practices and ideologies, relocating language in new ways, both reflecting and producing local language practices.

Conclusions: Xenoglossic becoming and new realities

It may be assumed that to use a language such as English is to be immediately engaged in exocentric cultural and ideological practices, whereas local languages are always about tradition and local culture. Once we look at this in the context of cultural practices such as those of hip-hop, it becomes clear that such a formulation is inadequate. Language use in any context is subject to the interpretation of those languages through local language ideologies. At issue, furthermore, is not so much a notion of language choice but rather an understanding of the complex relations between diverse languages and diverse realities. As Jacquemet (2005) puts it, we need to "examine communicative practices based on disorderly recombinations and language mixings occurring simultaneously in local and distant environments. In other words, it is time to conceptualize a linguistics of xenoglossic becoming, transidiomatic mixing, and communicative recombinations" (p. 274). From a performative point of view, language identities are performed in the doing rather than reflecting a prior set of fixed options.

The choices around moves into particular languages may be on pragmatic, aesthetic, or commercial grounds, but they are also political decisions to do with language, identity, and authenticity. Shusterman (2000) suggests that "the realities and truths which hip hop reveals are not the transcendental eternal verities of traditional philosophy, but rather mutable but coercive facts and patterns of the material, sociohistorical world" (p. 73). Hip-hop presents positions on language and reality. Global real talk, which, while easily glossed as keepin' it real, is better understood as a global ideology that is always pulled into local ways of being. By looking at authenticity in this way, we can understand the hip-hop ideology of keepin' it real as a discursively and culturally mediated mode of representing and producing the local. In his discussion of hip-hop in Brazil, Pardue (2004) suggests that hip-hoppers "view themselves as social agents who force the Brazilian public to be more inclusive about what constitutes knowledge and legitimate perspectives on reality" (p. 412). The language choices hip-hop artists make are similarly about viewing themselves as social agents who force the public to be more inclusive about what constitutes legitimate perspectives on language.

Notes

1   The feeling of existence or being. The term is from Jean-Jacques Rousseau.
2   My translation from the German.
3   Lyrics from "Just a lil' bit," featuring Warren G, from 360° (2002).
4   Interviews in this article were drawn from the Australian Research Council-funded project Postoccidental Englishes and Rap.
5   Too Phat are Malique Ibrahim (Mista Malique) and Johan Ishak (Joe Flizzow).
6   The Malay term *rojak*, meaning mixture or salad—typically a mix of pineapple, cucumber, tofu, and jicama in a *belacan* sauce—is used commonly to refer to the multicultural and multilingual mixture of Malaysian society.
7   Underground Indonesian rap artists Balcony and Homicide (2003) use both Indonesian and English in their lyrics.
8   It is interesting to note, however, that Teh Tarik Crew's name is derived from the popular Malay Teh Tarik ("pulled tea") served at local tea stalls, while Too Phat use the U.S. term *phat*.
9   "If I Die Tonight," featuring Liyana, 360° (2002). The track is a reference to, and includes a sample from, 2Pac's "If I Die 2Nite" (1998, rerelease, *Me Against the World*, Jive records).

Discography

Balcony & Homicide (2003). *Hymne penghitam langit dan prosa tanpa tuhan*. Harder Records: Bandung, Indonesia.
2Pac. *(1998). Me against the world*. Chicago, USA: Jive Records.
Poetic Ammo. (1998). *It's a nice day to be alive*. Kuala Lumpur, Malaysia: Positive Tone.
Too Phat. (2000). *Plan B*. Kuala Lumpur, Malaysia: Positive Tone.
Too Phat. (2002). *360°*. Kuala Lumpur, Malaysia: EMI.
Two Up. (2002). *Tastes like chicken*. Sydney, Australia: Village Idiot Records.

References

Alim, H. S. (2004). You know my steez: An ethnographic and sociolinguistic study of styleshifting in a Black American speech community (American Dialect Society Publication No. 89). Durham, NC: Duke University Press.
Androutsopoulos, J. (2003). Einleitung. In J. Androutsopoulos (Ed.), *HipHop: Globale Kultur – Locale Praktiken* [Hip hop: Global culture-local practices] (pp. 9–23). Bielefeld, Germany: Transcript Verlag.
Auzanneau, M. (2002). Rap in Libreville, Gabon: An urban sociolinguistic space. In A.-P. Durand (Ed.), *Black, blanc, beur: Rap music and hip-hop culture in the Francophone world* (pp. 106–123). Lanham, MD: Scarecrow Press.
Bennett, A. (2000). *Popular music and youth culture: Music, identity and place*. Basingstoke, UK: Palgrave.
Berger, H. (2003). Introduction: The politics and aesthetics of language choice and dialect in popular music. In H. Berger & M. Carroll (Eds.), *Global pop, local language*, (ix–xxvi). Jackson: University Press of Mississippi.

Bozza, A. (2003). *Whatever you say I am: The life and times of Eminem.* London: Bantam Press.

Canagarajah, S. (1999). *Resisting linguistic imperialism in English teaching.* Oxford, England: Oxford University Press.

Connell, J., & Gibson, C. (2003). *Sound tracks: Popular music, identity and place.* London: Routledge.

Crystal, D. (1997). *English as a global language.* Cambridge, England: Cambridge University Press.

Dimitriadis, G. (2001). *Performing identity/performing culture.* New York: Peter Lang.

Hanson, J. (1997). The mother of all tongues. [Review of the book *English as a global language.*] *Times Higher Education Supplement, 1288,* 22.

Hogben, L. (1963). *Essential world English.* London: Michael Joseph.

Jacquemet, M. (2005). Transidiomatic practices, language and power in the age of globalization. *Language & Communication, 25,* 257–277.

Kachru, B. (1997). World Englishes and English-using communities. *Annual Review of Applied Linguistics, 17,* 66–87.

Krims, A. (2000). *Rap music and the poetics of identity.* Cambridge, England: Cambridge University Press.

Kroskrity, P. (2000). Regimenting languages: Language ideological perspectives. In P. V. Kroskrity (Ed.), *Regimes of language: Ideologies, politics and identities* (pp. 1–34). Santa Fe, NM: School of American Research Press.

Larkey, E. (2003). Just for fun? Language choice in German popular music. In H. Berger & M. Carroll (Eds.), *Global pop, local language* (pp. 131–151). Jackson: University Press of Mississippi.

Levy, C. (2001). Rap in Bulgaria: Between fashion and reality. In T. Mitchell (Ed.), *Global noise: Rap and hip-hop outside the USA* (pp. 134–148). Middletown, CT: Wesleyan University Press.

Lockard, C. (1998). *Dance of life: Popular music and politics in Southeast Asia.* Honolulu: University of Hawaii Press.

Makoni, S., & Pennycook, A. (2005). Disinventing and (re)constituting languages. *Critical Inquiry in Language Studies, 2(3),* 137–156.

McCann, A., & Ó Laoire, L. (2003). "Raising one higher than the other": The hierarchy of tradition in representations of Gaelic- and English-language song in Ireland. In H. Berger & M. Carroll (Eds.), *Global pop, local language* (pp. 233–265). Jackson: University Press of Mississippi.

Mitchell, T. (2001). Introduction: Another root – Hip-hop outside the USA. In T. Mitchell (Ed.), *Global noise: Rap and hip-hop outside the USA* (pp. 1-38). Middletown, CT: Wesleyan University Press.

Mitchell, T. (2003). Doin' damage in my native language: The use of "resistance vernaculars" in hip hop in France, Italy, and Aotearoa/New Zealand. In H. Berger & M. Carroll (Eds.), *Global pop, local language* (pp. 3–17). Jackson: University Press of Mississippi.

Morgan, M. (2005). After. . .word! The philosophy of the hip-hop battle. In D. Darby & T. Shelby (Eds.), *Hip hop and philosophy: Rhyme 2 reason* (pp. 205–211). Chicago: Open Court.

Pardue, D. (2004). "Writing in the margins": Brazilian hip-hop as an educational project. *Anthropology and Education, 35,* 411–432.

Pennay, M. (2001). Rap in Germany: The birth of a genre. In T. Mitchell (Ed.), *Global noise: Rap and hip-hop outside the USA* (pp. 111–133). Middletown, CT: Wesleyan University Press.

Pennycook, A. (2003a). Beyond homogeny and heterogeny: English as a global and worldly language. In C. Mair (Ed.), *The cultural politics of English* (pp. 3–17). Amsterdam: Rodopi.

Pennycook, A. (2003b). Global Englishes, Rip Slyme and performativity. *Journal of Sociolinguistics, 7,* 513–533.

Pennycook, A. (2004). Performativity and language studies. *Critical Inquiry in Language Studies: An International Journal, 1(1),* 1–26.

Pennycook, A. (2007). *Global Englishes and transcultural flows.* London: Routledge.

Perullo, A., & Fenn, F. (2003). Language ideologies, choices, and practices in East African hip hop. In H. Berger & M. Carroll (Eds.), *Global pop, local language* (pp. 19–51). Jackson: University Press of Mississippi.

Perry, I. (2004). *Prophets of the hood: Politics and poetics in hip hop.* Durham, NC: Duke University Press.

Phillipson, R. (1999). Voice in global English: Unheard chords in Crystal loud and clear. [Review of the book *English as a global language.*] *Applied Linguistics, 20,* 265–276.

Phillipson, R. (2003). *English only Europe? Challenging language policy.* London: Routledge.

Shusterman, R. (2000). *Performing live: Aesthetic alternatives for the ends of art.* Ithaca, NY: Cornell University Press.

TheStarOnline. In a twist over ban on rojak songs. Retrieved April 25, 2004, from http://202.186.86.35/news/story.asp?file=2004/4/25/focus/7818109&news

Taylor, C. (1991). *The ethics of authenticity.* Cambridge, MA: Harvard University Press.

Wallach, J. (2003). "Goodbye my blind majesty": Music, language, and politics in the Indonesian underground. In H. Berger & M. Carroll (Eds.) *Global pop, local language* (pp. 53–86). Jackson: University Press of Mississippi.

Wermuth, M. (2001). Rap in the low countries: Global dichotomies on a national scale. In T. Mitchell (Ed.), *Global noise: Rap and hip-hop outside the USA* (pp. 149–170). Middletown, CT: Wesleyan University Press.

Woolard, K. (2004). Is the past a foreign country?: Time, language origins, and the nation in early modern Spain. *Journal of Linguistic Anthropology, 14*(1), 57–80.

Chapter 8

BARBARA SEIDLHOFER

CLOSING A CONCEPTUAL GAP

The case for a description of English as a lingua franca (2001)

[handwritten margin notes:] English lingua franca / the responsibility of teacher / problem of teaching? / How to teach / eng. lingua franca

Introduction

FUNDAMENTAL ISSUES to do with the global spread and use of English have, at long last, become an important focus of research in applied linguistics. The debate has been conducted particularly vigorously over the last decade, variously highlighting crucial cultural, ecological, socio–political and psychological issues. The realization that the majority of uses of English occur in contexts where it serves as a lingua franca, far removed from its native speakers' linguacultural norms and identities, has been an important leitmotif in this discussion.[1] And yet, the daily practices of most of the millions of teachers of English worldwide seem to remain untouched by this development: very few teachers 'on the ground' take part in this meta-level discussion, and most classroom language teaching *per se* has changed remarkably little considering how the discourse *about* it has. This is not surprising if we consider that what these teachers of English generally regard, for better or for worse, as their main knowledge base and point of reference, the target language as codified in grammars, dictionaries and textbooks, has not moved with the tide of applied linguistics research. This state of affairs has resulted in a conceptual gap in the discourse of ELT which, although it is giving rise to some misgivings and unease, has not been addressed directly and proactively. This paper attempts to take stock of this unsatisfactory situation and proposes a project that may constitute a radical but promising way forward.

A conceptual gap

[handwritten note: the responsibility of teacher : inform students the development]

Teaching English, which well into the heyday of communicative language teaching seemed a fairly straightforward activity, has become a much more complicated affair. Whereas language teachers used to be mainly educated about and preoccupied with various approaches to the description and instruction of the target language as such, we now find a much wider variety of concerns with the kind of socio-political and other issues referred to above demanding at least as much attention as the language proper. This has led to a broader conception of the profession, and to a discourse of ELT in which notions of 'correctness', 'norms', 'mistakes' and 'authority' seem to have given way to an ethos characterized by 'transformative pedagogy', 'learner-centredness', 'awareness' and '(self-)reflection' (cf. e.g. Pennycook 1999). In the discourse of language planning and education policy, monoculturalism, monolingualism, monomodels and monocentrism have been replaced by multiculturalism, multilingualism, polymodels and pluricentrism (cf. e.g. Bamgbose, Banjo & Thomas 1995; Bhatia 1997; Kachru 1992b; McArthur 1998; Smith & Forman 1997). European sociolinguists have expressed their concern about 'English only? in Europe' (Ammon, Mattheier & Nelde 1994) and second language acquisition research has taken its first significant steps 'beyond the native speaker' (Cook 1999).

The most important consequence of these developments for so-called non-native teachers of English, the majority of teachers of English worldwide, has probably been that the notion of native speakers' 'ownership of English' has been radically called into question (Widdowson 1994) and that a discussion has gathered momentum which highlights the potential special expertise 'non-native' teachers have on the grounds that they know the target language as a foreign language, share with their students the experience of what it is like to try and make it their own, often through the same first language/culture 'filter', and can represent relevant role models for learners (cf. e.g. Braine 1999; Brutt-Griffler & Samimy 1999; Kramsch 1998; Medgyes 1994; Rampton 1990; Seidlhofer 1999).[2]

The whole orientation of TEFL (teaching English as a foreign language), then, seems to have fundamentally shifted: from correctness to appropriateness, from parochial domesticity and exclusive native-speaker norms to global inclusiveness and egalitarian licence to speak in ways that meet diverse local needs.

Or has it?

My contention would be that while pedagogic ideas about teaching and learning on the one hand and sociolinguistic ideas about the sovereignty and prestige of indigenized varieties of English on the other may have changed quite dramatically, while the empire writes back and non-native teachers assert themselves, assumptions about the 'E' in TEFL have remained curiously unaffected by these momentous developments. In TEFL, what constitutes a valid target is still determined with virtually exclusive reference to native-speaker norms. True, at least the perception of what constitutes 'native speakers' is widening, but a question in urgent need of exploration is just what the 'English' is that is being taught and learnt in this emerging global era, how it squares with the socio-political and socioeconomic concerns discussed in the profession, and what its relevance is for the subject taught in classrooms all over the world.

That this issue has not really been on the agenda so far is borne out by the way 'English' is talked about in the relevant literature – the default referent, implicitly or explicitly, is ENL (English as a native language):

> . . . we suffer from an inferiority complex caused by glaring defects in our knowledge of *English*. We are in constant distress as we realize how little we know about *the language* we are supposed to teach.
>
> (Medgyes 1994: 40, emphases added)

> I believe in the fundamental value of a common language, as an amazing world resource which presents us with unprecedented possibilities for mutual understanding, and thus enables us to find fresh opportunities for international cooperation. In my ideal world, everyone would have fluent command of a single world language. I am already in the fortunate position of being a fluent user of *the language* which is most in contention for this role, and have cause to reflect every day on the benefits of having it at my disposal.
>
> (Crystal 1997: viii, emphasis added)

Consider what Medgyes and Crystal[3] are referring to by 'English' and 'the language'. Of course this depends on what they regard as 'a language', and there is, as Pennycook (1994: 26ff) also demonstrates, no definitive answer to this question. But I do take it to be a general consensus that what constitutes a language, and in particular 'English as a global language', is necessarily a discursive construct in need of deconstruction. The point I wish to make with reference to the above two extracts, then, is that <u>the fact that</u> these questions simply are not problematized throws readers back on the implicit, default referent, whether this is the one intended by the author or not. And this is one particular variety of English, namely that used by educated native speakers like Crystal himself. What he is 'a fluent speaker' of is English as a native language (ENL), and this variety is then bound to be understood to be 'the language in most contention' for the role of 'a single world language'. But of course like any natural language, this is full of conventions and markers of in-group membership such as characteristic pronunciations, specialized vocabulary and <u>idiomatic</u> phraseology, and references and allusions to shared experience and cultural background. And this is precisely the reason why educated 'non-native' speakers of it (such as Medgyes himself) are so resigned and defeatist about the 'glaring defects' in their knowledge of it: they cannot, by definition, be members of that native-speaker community, no matter how hard they try, no matter how long they study.

It seems clear, then, that every time we talk and write about 'English as a global language' we quite inevitably bring into play some rather fundamental issues. But the fact that they are fundamental has, so far at least, not meant that they get addressed explicitly. On the contrary, the general picture is one of lack of awareness. That this constitutes a really difficult problem is probably best illustrated with reference to writers whom nobody would suspect of native-speaker 'tunnel vision' and disregard for linguistic and cultural diversity. Phillipson and Skutnabb-Kangas (1999: 29) make various proposals for 'charting and countering Englishisation'. They suggest a number of research questions focusing on the role of English in Denmark, one of which is formulated and commented on like this:

> What is the significance of senior Danish politicians, who *use English with moderate proficiency*, inevitably creating false and unintended impressions when talking impromptu to the "world" press?
>   As an aside to this latter question, it should be mentioned that the four Danish exceptions to the Maastricht Treaty were hammered out at a summit in Edinburgh in 1991, at the close of which the Danish Foreign Minister referred to the "so-called Edinburgh agreement", implying that no real obligation had been entered into. When Salman Rushdie came to Denmark in 1996 to receive an EU literature prize – an event which was postponed because of a security scare – the Danish Prime Minister was asked by Rushdie whether the death threat was real or hypothetical, to which he replied that he did not have the "ability" to answer the question (a revelation that many Danish citizens might agree with, as the whole affair was mishandled). Are both errors due to mother-tongue transfer?
>
> (Phillipson & Skutnabb-Kangas 1999: 29f, emphases added)

This passage was rather painful to read for me, a 'non-native' user of English and language professional fairly conversant with some ENL varieties but mainly interested in English as a lingua franca (ELF), and coming as it did towards the end of an article which contained much I agreed with, it probably hit me with particular force. To start with, which 'English' is it that Danish politicians use with 'moderate proficiency'? As I read it, it is the same native speaker 'English' which Crystal and Medgyes are referring to, and which is simply assumed to be relevant in the context described. My contention would be that it is irrelevant. To take the example of *so-called*, it is true of course that ENL corpora and dictionaries based on them indicate that the 'attitudinally marked' use of this premodifier referred to by Phillipson and Skutnabb-Kangas is the more frequently attested one (though the other use is also attested). But native-speaker language use is not particularly relevant here: the Danish Foreign Minister is not a native speaker of English, and he was not speaking on behalf of ENL speakers, nor presumably exclusively to ENL speakers. He was using English as a lingua franca in the way he often has occasion to use it, with interlocutors who use it in the same way. And it is very likely indeed that such interlocutors would understand very well what he (presumably) meant by *so-called*, i.e. 'the agreement called the Edinburgh agreement', especially since many European languages have an analogous expression which can be used with the same two meanings (German *sogenannt*, Italian *cosiddetto*, etc.). Similarly, I would claim that *ability* in the second example would be perfectly intelligible to ELF interlocutors and only be perceived as odd if judged against ENL standards. To call these two formulations 'errors' is counterproductive at the very least, and evidence that ELF as a use in its own right, and ELF speakers as language users in their own right, have not yet entered peoples' consciousness, not even in the case of colleagues who have dedicated their working lives to protecting human language rights. Phillipson and Skutnabb-Kangas are well known as campaigners for linguistic equity and ecology, so we can be confident that what they say here is not due to an attitude of superiority; rather, I suggest it results from a general problem: a *conceptual gap* where English as a lingua franca should have pride of place. Lest my interpretation of Phillipson and Skutnabb-Kangas' view of 'English' should be perceived as overly critical, I ought to quote the endnote attached to the paragraph cited above:

> The Danes are, of course, not alone in having *problems with English*. In the latest communication, in four languages, from the follow-up group preparing the revision of the Draft Universal Declaration on Language Rights, the Catalan secretariat states that this key document is "in the way of being translated" (=in the course of) and that the scientific council is "pretending" to provide a forum for debate (=aiming at). It is unreasonable to expect that Danes, Catalans or other users of English as a second language use *English* supremely well. The dice are loaded against them, the conditions for communication are not symmetrical, and native speakers often seem to be unaware of this.
> (op.cit.: 33 fn 6; emphases added; glosses in parentheses are the original authors')

The point I am trying to make, then, is that it is highly problematic to discuss aspects of global English, however critically, while at the same time passing native speaker judgements as to what is appropriate usage in ELF contexts. The 'problems' which Danes, Catalans, etc have 'with English' may be problems in the eye of the native speaker beholder, i.e. problems if you take 'English' to be ENL. But 'English' does not simply transfer intact from one context to another – the 'E' in *English as a Native Language* is bound to be something very different from the 'E' in *English as a Lingua Franca*, and must be acknowledged as such. However, this difference is still waiting to be recognized, explored and acted upon in much applied linguistics, and particularly in mainstream English language teaching. Widdowson (1997) offers a conceptual framework for capturing two modes of thinking about 'the spread of English' which makes the fundamental differences between them quite clear:

> . . . I would argue that English as an international language is not *distributed*, as a set of established encoded forms, unchanged into different domains of use, but it is *spread* as

a virtual language. . . . When we talk about the spread of English, then, it is not that the conventionally coded forms and meanings are transmitted into different environments and different surroundings, and taken up and used by different groups of people. It is not a matter of the actual language being distributed but of the virtual language being spread and in the process being variously actualized. The distribution of the actual language implies adoption and conformity. The spread of the virtual language implies adaptation and nonconformity. The two processes are quite different. And they are likely to be in conflict. Distribution denies spread.

(Widdowson 1997: 139f)

It seems clear, then, that in order to capture the nature of lingua franca English we need to think of it as evolving out of spread, not distribution, and acknowledge the vital role and authority of ELF users as 'agents of language change' (Brutt-Griffler 1998: 387). There has as yet, however, been no large-scale, systematic effort to record what happens linguistically in this process. On the contrary, the general picture we get is that there is an established English being described more and more precisely in terms of native-speaker behaviour and then distributed. This not only does not recognize necessary diversity but acts against it: 'Distribution denies spread', as Widdowson puts it in the above quotation. This increasing precision in description is said to get closer and closer to the reality of native-speaker language use. But it is important to realize that native-speaker language use is just *one* kind of reality, and one of very doubtful relevance for lingua franca contexts. Moreover, as long as all the descriptive effort is geared to capturing L1 language use, the profession's attention is deflected from the increasingly urgent issues concerning the use of English as a lingua franca, and attitudes are reinforced which are antipathetic to ELF. However, I would argue that now that the right to descriptions in their own terms has finally been recognized for nativized varieties of English, it is high time that we granted the same right to ELF. My contention, then, is that we must overcome the (explicit or implicit) assumption that ELF could possibly be a globally distributed, franchised copy of ENL, and take on board the notion that it is being spread, developed independently, with a great deal of variation but enough stability to be viable for lingua franca communication. This assumption is of course one that has to be investigated empirically, but the point I wish to make here is that the need to do so has not even been acknowledged so far, and accordingly no comprehensive effort in this direction has been undertaken to date.

Conflicting tendencies

Talking about traditional TEFL aiming at 'distributing' English in its 'established encoded forms' is not to say, of course, that the description of 'E' in TEFL has not moved in the last decade or two – it has moved considerably, but in the other direction as it were, closer and closer to the home base: linguistic descriptions proper have been focusing on English as it is spoken and written as a first language.[4] Technological developments (allied, of course, with economic interests) have made it possible to sharpen that focus, so that we can now say with precision which speech acts prevail in calls to the British Telecom helpline (McEnery 2000) or which features of spoken English characterize casual conversations among friends and acquaintances in specific parts of the UK (Carter & McCarthy 1997), not to mention the precision with which written and spoken genres can now be profiled (cf. Biber 1988). The British component of the International Corpus of English is now completed; it is a corpus of a million words of spoken and written English, fully grammatically analysed, and its spoken part is 'the biggest collection of parsed spoken material anywhere' (ICE-GB website: www.ucl.ac.uk/english-usage/ice-gb/

index.htm). Such corpora make it possible to conduct extremely revealing, fine-grained analyses of, say, the rhetorical adverb *simply* in present-day British English (Aarts 1996), of synchronic and diachronic aspects of existential *there* (Breivik 1990) as well as studies of 'vague language' (Channell 1994) and 'patterns of lexis in text' (Hoey 1991).

The last quarter of the 20th century thus saw momentous developments and indeed a great enrichment of the study of L1 English, and the sheer scale and sophistication of corpus-based descriptions, e.g. drawing on the British National Corpus (cf. Aston & Burnard 1998), the Collins COBUILD Bank of English or the Longman-Lancaster Corpus, have revolutionized our thinking about what constitutes legitimate descriptions of any language. In terms of products for the general public, we now have entirely empirically-based reference works such as the *Longman Grammar of Spoken and Written English*, 'Grammar for the 21st century' [flyer] (Biber et al. 1999) or the *Collins COBUILD English Dictionary*, 'helping learners with *real* English' [cover]. But the scope of descriptions of 'the English language' has also widened dramatically: while until recently the only well-documented varieties of L1 English were British and North American, the International Corpus of English (ICE) encompasses over a dozen regional varieties including, for instance, Australia, East Africa, India, New Zealand and Singapore. ICE is described as 'the first large-scale effort to study the development of English as a world language' (ICE website: www.ucl.ac.uk/english-usage/ice/index.htm). But, again, it needs to be pointed out that this world language is defined in terms of speakers for whom English is 'either a majority first language . . . or an official additional language' (Greenbaum 1996: 3).[5] So although it is international and indeed global, it actually does not include a description of the use of English by the majority of its speakers, those who primarily learnt English as a lingua franca for communicating with other lingua franca speakers (cf. Graddol 1997).[6]

This state of affairs is reflected in the literature about teaching: there is a myriad of books and articles in the areas 'English as an international language' and 'intercultural communication'. Changes in the perception of the role of English in the world have significantly influenced current thinking about approaches to teaching (if not necessarily the teaching itself) and led to an increased socio-political and intercultural awareness (e.g. Abbott & Wingard 1981; Brumfit 1982; Byram & Fleming 1998; Canagarajah 1999; Gnutzmann 1999; Holliday 1994; Kramsch 1993; Kramsch & Sullivan 1996; McKay 2002; Quirk & Widdowson 1985; Smith 1981; Strevens 1980). However, as far as linguistic models as targets for learning are concerned, these usually do not figure as a focal concern, or matter for reflection, at all, and so, whether explicitly or implicitly, native-speaker models have largely remained unquestioned. This means that the *how* is changing, but linked to a *what* that is not. Certainly no linguistically radical proposals have been put forward which would match the thrust of the important innovations which have taken place in pedagogy. In short, no coherent and comprehensive lingua franca model has been proposed so far which does justice to these changes in terms of the actual language taught. This state of affairs allows the economic, social and symbolic power of 'native speaker English' to be reproduced (in the sense of Bourdieu & Passeron 1970) throughout ELT institutions and practices worldwide.[7]

The situation that presents itself, then, is oddly contradictory and paradoxical: on the one hand, we have a very lively and prolific field of research producing extralinguistic treatments of how 'English' is – depending on the specific researcher's domain of interest and ideological orientation – being variously spread, used, forced upon, or withheld from the world at large, coupled with assertions of local values and the importance of intercultural communication in pedagogy. On the other hand, the rapid development in computer technology has opened up hitherto undreamt-of possibilities in language description. The main research efforts in this area, however, are not expended on studying how English is actually used worldwide, but instead concentrate very much on English as a native language. We thus have an inverse relationship between perceived significance and relevance of 'English' in the world at large and linguistic description focusing on the 'ancestral home' of the language (Achebe 1975: 62).

The two contrary developments are interdependent and even reinforce one another: the more global the use of 'English' becomes, the greater the motivation, and of course the market, for descriptions of it, which, for historical and socioeconomic reasons, are largely provided by the 'Centre'. The more such products on offer, the more these are regarded, quite rightly, as promoting the dominance of (L1) English, and thus the more forceful the attempts in (or on behalf of) the 'Periphery' to resist 'linguistic imperialism' (cf. e.g. Canagarajah 1999; Phillipson 1992).

English as a lingua franca: the need for description

The intellectual battles which are being fought over issues rooted in ideological positions, commercial interests, ecological concerns and social identities go largely unnoticed by the largest group of users of 'English': those to whom 'English' serves on a daily basis as a lingua franca for conducting their affairs, more often than not entirely among so-called 'non-native' speakers of the language, with no native speakers present at all. These are people who have learned 'English' as an additional language, and to whom it serves as the most useful instrument (for reasons variously interrogated, lamented or celebrated in applied linguistics) for communication that cannot be conducted in the mother tongue, be it in business, casual conversation, science or politics – in conversation, in print, on television, or on the internet. Wherever such interactions take place and whatever the specific motivations and uses of English as an international lingua franca, the mismatch sketched in the last two paragraphs is quite striking: ELF speakers are usually not particularly preoccupied with the two prevailing research foci described above, viz. 'corpus-based description of native English' and 'linguistic imperialism'. They are not primarily concerned with emulating the way native speakers use their mother tongue within their own communities, nor with socio-psychological and ideological meta-level discussions. Instead, the central concerns for this domain are efficiency, relevance and economy in language learning and language use. In Kachru's words, 'the hunger for learning the language – with whatever degree of competence – is simply insatiable' (Kachru 1997: 69). This is one reason why fighting the (ab)use of 'English' for exerting power and domination via mainstream ELT is such an enormous task: people need and want to acquire the instrument 'English' whatever the ideological baggage that comes with it – a fact acknowledged, at least implicitly, even in Canagarajah's *Resisting Linguistic Imperialism in English Teaching* (e.g. 1999: 180f). Another reason of course is that it is not in the interest of those who are, for want of a feasible alternative, still widely perceived as the 'source' or 'owners' of the commodity 'English' to encourage a discussion about ethical questions and the suitability of the goods they have to offer. And as long as 'English' is kept in the conceptual straightjacket of ENL, it is difficult to see how change can be pursued proactively.

However, despite the fact that discussions of ethical issues are now available in the public domain, freely accessible and there to be taken up by anyone who chooses to, and although some scholars have been insisting for a long time that 'the unprecedented functional range and social penetration globally acquired by English demands fresh theoretical and descriptive perspectives' (Kachru 1996: 906), the suitability of the descriptive and pedagogic models we are operating with for the teaching and use of ELF has hardly been investigated at all. In what follows, I shall argue that it is both necessary and feasible to enquire into a suitable model for ELF, and offer suggestions as to how this might be done and what implications such an enquiry might have.

It would seem, then, that there is considerable scope, and hope, for large-scale, systematic research into how English is actually used as a lingua franca. However, the work actually published in this field is still extremely scarce, and very little descriptive research has been done that could serve as a potential basis for formulating a curriculum for the teaching of ELF. Having said this, a description of the phonology of English as an international language (Jenkins 2000) is now available, and important work on the pragmatics of 'non-native – non-native' communication in English has been, and is being, conducted (e.g. Firth 1996; Meierkord 1996; House 1999; Lesznyak 2002). James (2000) offers a rich conceptual discussion of the place of English in bi/multilingualism and makes reference to a project, currently in its pilot phase, entitled 'English as a *lingua franca* in the Alpine-Adriatic region'. He also sets out hypotheses as to what findings the future analysis of this use of English by speakers of German, Italian, Slovene and Friulian might yield. However, the shift in perspective from treating, in Kasper's words, 'non-nativeness as problem' to viewing 'non-nativeness as a resource' or 'non-nativeness as unattended' [because irrelevant] (Kasper 1997: 356f) is a recent one in both phonology and pragmatics, and certainly not subscribed to by a majority of scholars in these fields.

It would be beyond the scope of this article to try and summarize the intriguing findings of these studies, so some examples of the kinds of insight offered by them will have to suffice. Jenkins' work (e.g. 1998, 2000) centres around 'a pedagogical core of phonological intelligibility for speakers of EIL' (2000: 123) which she was able to propose after establishing which pronunciation features impeded mutual intelligibility in her empirical studies of what she terms 'interlanguage talk' among 'non-native' speakers of English. This procedure provided an empirical basis for her suggestion 'to scale down the phonological task for the majority of learners by . . . focusing pedagogic attention on those items which are essential in terms of intelligible pronunciation' (ibid.) and to prioritize features which constitute more relevant and more realistic learning targets for EIL speakers. These features constitute Jenkins' Lingua Franca Core. What I should like to emphasize in the present context is that Jenkins' Lingua Franca Core does not include, for instance, some sounds which are regarded, and taught, as 'particularly English' (and also as particularly difficult) ones by most learners and teachers, such as the phonemes /θ/ and /ð/ and the 'dark l' allophone, [ɫ]. That is to say that mastery of these sounds proved not to be crucial for mutual intelligibility and so various substitutions, such as /f, v/ or /s, z/ or /t, d/ for /θ, ð/ are permissible, and indeed also found in some native-speaker varieties.

While phonology is a fairly 'closed system' (although it does have fuzzy edges), pragmatics is a more open-ended affair, and accordingly findings in this area as regards ELF communication are different in nature and probably should not be expected to be 'conclusive' in the same way. As House indicates, the volume of research in ELF pragmatics undertaken so far is minimal: 'studies of intercultural communication in the scientific community have practically ignored ELF interactions' (1999: 74). But the findings which are beginning to emerge make it clear that there is a vast, complex and absolutely crucial area here waiting to be explored and exploited for ELF communication. Interestingly, while Jenkins emphasizes the feasibility of successful communication by means of a scaled-down phonological/phonetic repertoire, House takes a much more sceptical stance, as reflected in the subtitle of her (1999) paper[8] 'Interactions in English as lingua franca and the *myth* of mutual intelligibility' (emphasis added). Again, I can only give a glimpse of findings here, and further questions are raised by analyses carried out to date. At the most general level, an observation which has been made repeatedly is that ELF interactions often are consensus-oriented, cooperative and mutually supportive. For instance, a tendency has been noted to adopt a 'Let-it-Pass' principle, that is to say, interactants tend to gloss over utterances which cause difficulty rather than trying to sort them out explicitly, a phenomenon Firth (1996) terms 'the discursive accomplishment of normality' (cf. also Meierkord 1996; Wagner & Firth 1997). On the other hand, and this is what House is getting at in her subtitle, this 'let-it-pass' behaviour can also be interpreted as an indicator of interactants' mutual dis-attention, a 'palpable lack of mutual orientation', thus denying each other 'the most basic social alignment between speaker and hearer' (House 1999: 82). Interactants in the data analysed by her are shown to often act as initiators only, rather than as initiators and responsive recipients, and to lack 'pragmatic fluency' characterized by such features as smooth management of turn-taking and topic-changes as well as appropriate use of pragmatic routines such as gambits (in the sense of Edmondson & House 1981). It has to be pointed out, however, that only a limited repertoire of interaction, notably casual conversations and group discussions, has been analysed in this respect so far, so that it is conceivable that further research might show the present findings to be a function of the type and purpose of the interactions investigated. Indeed, the differences in the analyses available to date would seem to underline the need for a large corpus and a 'thick description' of the same data from various angles. At all events, whatever ways speakers use to interact by means of a lingua franca and how far they compensate for native-like conversational behaviour is a matter for further empirical enquiry.

There is also one large-scale project focusing on the written English produced by learners of 'English' coming from a great variety of first language backgrounds. This is the International Corpus of Learner English (ICLE for short; see e.g. the contributions to Granger 1998; Granger, Hung & Petch-Tyson 2002; Altenberg & Granger 2001; de Haan 1998; Petch-Tyson 2000, and more extensive studies based on this corpus, e.g. Lorenz 1999). However, the main thrust of this research enterprise is to identify characteristics of learner English from different L1 backgrounds, with the intention to facilitate comparisons between these foreign-language productions and native-speaker writing, and so to highlight the difficulties specific L1 groups have with native English in order to make it easier for those learners to conform to ENL if they so wish – hence the designation *'Learner* English'. There are also other, smaller and less structured *learner* corpora, notably those compiled by publishers big in ELT, such as the Cambridge Learners' Corpus and the Longman Learners' Corpus. While such projects are undoubtedly innovative and very useful in their own terms, they are obviously quite different from my own present concern. The main difference lies in the researchers' orientation towards the data and the purposes they intend the corpora to serve, namely as a sophisticated tool for analysing learner language so as to support them in their attempts to approximate to native (-like) English. However, it is conceivable that some of the data in learner corpora could also contribute to a better understanding of English as a lingua franca. For instance, what is frequently reported as 'overuse' or 'underuse' of certain expressions in learner language as compared to ENL (e.g. Chen 1998; Lorenz 1998) could also be regarded as a feature characterizing successful ELF use, or the 'deviations' from ENL norms reported in learner corpora research could be investigated to establish whether they can serve as pointers, or sensitizing devices, in the process of trying to profile ELF as a viable variety.

The difference in perspective between learner corpus research and my own is an important one, and essential for the main point I am trying to make in this paper. This difference can best be captured with reference to the notions of *learning strategies* vs. *communication strategies* (Bialystok 1990; Corder 1981: ch. 11; Faerch & Kasper 1983).[9] The students providing data for a learner corpus have been asked, usually in an instructional setting, to produce, say, an essay in 'English'. In the subsequent analysis, any observations about their language use are made in comparison with what native speakers would normally write (as reflected in an ENL reference corpus), for instance in terms of simplifying, replacing, overusing, underusing or avoiding certain features. Any 'deviations' from a native speaker norm are, then, to be seen as products of learning strategies: a constructive way of making do with the limited linguistic resources available at a particular stage of interlanguage. The important point to note is that the very same utterances can be regarded as communication strategies: evidence not of a linguistic deficit, but, if intelligible, of successful communication. In principle, then, the same data could be conceptualized as entirely different kinds of evidence. However, learner corpora were not devised with this objective in mind, and their suitability for contributing to a description of ELF would have to be examined with care.

Towards an ELF Corpus

So far I have been addressing what I see as an urgent (extralinguistic) need for a conceptualization of ELF. Clearly, however, more needs to be said about the (linguistic) feasibility of such an enquiry as well as its fit with current research paradigms. Of course, there have been various attempts in the past to do this, either as conceptually devised models of a reduced inventory as a first step, lightening the learning load as it were, from Ogden's Basic English, which was extremely influential in its time (e.g. Ogden 1930; see also Seidlhofer 2002) to Quirk's Nuclear English (1982) or as empirically derived suggestions based on manual vocabulary counts, the most famous of these being West's General Service List (1953).[10] None of these, however, fulfilled the combination of criteria that need to be met for a viable alternative to ENL in its own right, of which a very broad and substantial empirical base and a truly fresh approach in terms of independence from the dictates of ENL would seem to be the most important ones. The big opportunity which offers itself now is that it has become possible to take into account the considerable amount of conceptual work undertaken in the past and present while at the same time basing investigations on a large empirical foundation.

The feasibility of such a project is basically a question of methods and consequently has much to do with technology. But, as John Sinclair, the pioneer of corpus-based language description, so vividly demonstrates in his work, computational research on language has revolutionized language observation, analysis and description, in short, the whole research paradigm. And it is this, I would argue, which is waiting to be extended to research into ELF – needless to say, to complement ENL, not to replace it.

Let me suggest what it might mean to genuinely carry both the spirit and the technology of recent developments of language description over into the realm of ELF, to follow them through into a truly global view of English. Here is an extract from Sinclair's introduction to his book *Corpus, Concordance, Collocation* (1991), in which he writes about new ways of approaching language description with reference to native English. Readers are invited to engage in a thought experiment: simply imagine that what is being talked about is not native English, but English as a Lingua Franca:

> This book charts the emergence of a new view of language, and the technology associated with it. Over the last ten years, computers have been through several generations, and the analysis of language has developed out of all recognition.
>
> The big difference has been the availability of data. The tradition of linguistics has been limited to what a single individual could experience and remember . . . Starved of adequate data, linguistics languished – indeed it became almost totally introverted. It became fashionable to look inwards to the mind rather than outwards to society. Intuition was the key, and the similarity of language structure to various formal models was emphasised. The communicative role of language was hardly referred to.
>
> (Sinclair 1991: 1)

Taking the liberty to utilize this extract as an aid for reflection about, and from, an ELF perspective, it is fairly easy to see how 'the availability of data' would make 'the big difference' and allow us to focus on the 'communicative role' of ELF. When Sinclair talks about changing from looking 'inwards' to looking 'outwards' he is of course referring to introspection vs. observation, but assuming this point is well taken, an advocate of ELF might be forgiven for extending this extract to an analogy: this is that 'starved of adequate [ELF] data' the description of English 'became almost totally introverted', i.e. focusing on the use of native English only, and that it 'became fashionable to look inwards' into L1 English 'rather than outwards to society', for whom, seen on a global scale, 'English' means 'English as a Lingua Franca'.

In view of all this, it seemed desirable and timely to embark on the compilation of a corpus of English as a Lingua Franca. For the purposes of this corpus the term 'lingua franca' (cf. also Knapp & Meierkord 2002) is understood in the strict sense of the word, i.e. an additionally acquired language system that serves as a means of communication between speakers of different first languages, or a language by means of which the members of different speech communities can communicate with each other but which is not the native language of either – a language which has no native speakers. Malmkjær (1991) explains the term *lingua franca* in terms of pidginization:

> . . . if the members of two or more cultures which do not use the same language come into regular contact with each other over a prolonged period . . . it is probable that the resultant language contact will lead to the development of a pidgin language by means of which the members of the cultures can communicate with each other but which is not the native language of either speech community. A pidgin language is thus a lingua franca which has no native speakers, which is often influenced by languages spoken by people who travelled and colonized extensively . . . and by the languages of the people with whom they interacted repeatedly.
>
> (Malmkjær 1991: 81)

The point to be made, however, is that while 'a pidgin language is . . . a lingua franca', a lingua franca does not need to be reduced to a pidgin language, restricted in social role and linguistic resources, such as limited vocabulary and stylistic range, elaborated only through creolization when used as a mother tongue. Elaboration does not necessarily have to be tied to native speaker use. ELF is often used in what House (1999: 74) calls 'influential networks, i.e. global business, politics, science, technology and media discourse', and it is likely that an empirical investigation of ELF will show that a sophisticated and versatile form of language can develop which is *not* a native language.

The compilation of an ELF corpus is now in progress at the University of Vienna. In the current initial phase, this project is supported by Oxford University Press (and so called the *Vienna–Oxford ELF Corpus*). Since the intention is to capture a wide range of variation, a corpus of spoken ELF is the first target, at one remove from the stabilizing and standardizing influence of writing. Another important reason for concentrating on the spoken medium is that spoken interaction is overtly reciprocal, which means that not only production but also reception are captured, thus allowing for observations regarding the intelligibility of what interlocutors say. For the time being, the focus is on unscripted (though partly pre-structured), largely face-to-face communication among fairly fluent adult speakers from a wide range of first language backgrounds whose primary and secondary education and socialization did not take place in English. The speech events being captured include private and public dialogues, private and public group discussions and casual conversations, and one-to-one interviews. Ideally, speakers will be making use of ELF in a largely unselfconscious, instrumental (as opposed to identificatory) way – compare Hüllen's (1992) distinction between *Identifikationssprache* ('language of identification') and *Kommunikationssprache* ('language for communication'). At least for the first phase, it was decided to operate with a narrow definition of ELF talk. That is to say, an attempt is made to meet the following additional criteria: no native speakers should be involved in the interaction, and the interaction should not take place in an environment where the predominant language is 'English', such as an 'Inner Circle', ENL country. The size aimed for at the first stage is approximately half a million words (i.e. similar to the spoken part of ICE-GB), transcribed and annotated in a number of ways.[11]

It will thus become possible to take stock of how the speakers providing the data actually communicate through ELF, and to begin to build a characterization of how they use, or rather co-construct, 'English' to do so. As a first research focus, it seems desirable to complement the work already done on ELF phonology and pragmatics by concentrating on lexico-grammar and discourse, in an investigation of what (if anything), notwithstanding all the diversity, might emerge as common features of ELF use, irrespective of speakers' first languages and levels of proficiency. Questions investigated will include the following: What seem to be the most relied-upon and successfully employed grammatical constructions and lexical choices? Are there aspects which contribute especially to smooth communication? What are the factors which tend to lead to 'ripples' on the pragmatic surface, misunderstandings or even communication breakdown? Is the degree of approximation to a variety of L1 English always proportional to communicative success? Or are there commonly used constructions, lexical items and sound patterns which are ungrammatical in Standard L1 English but generally unproblematic in ELF communication? If so, can hypotheses be set up and tested concerning simplifications of L1 English which could constitute systematic features of ELF? The objective here, then, would be to establish something like an index of communicative redundancy, in the sense that many of the niceties of social behaviour associated with native-speaker models and identities might not be operable and certain native-speaker norms might be seen to be in suspense. Indeed, it may well be that situations occur in which 'unilateral' approximation to native speaker norms and expectations not shared in ELF interaction leads to communication problems, and that mutual accommodation[12] is found to have greater importance for communicative effectiveness than 'correctness' or idiomaticity in ENL terms. In conducting these investigations, the large body of work already available on (native) language variation and change, nativized varieties, pidginization and creolization as well as on simplification in language pedagogy will be invaluable.

Of course, it is early days yet and all these questions will have to be formulated and addressed with care and circumspection. Nevertheless, I should like to offer a brief example of the kind of enquiry I have in mind. Below is a dialogue between L1 speakers of German and French respectively. They have been asked to choose one picture out of several options which will best serve for a campaign for a charity:

Reto (L1 German) & Stephanie (L1 French)

1	R:	I think on the front xx on the front page should be a picture who-which
2		only makes p-people to er spend money, to the charity
3	S:	yes
4	R:	and I think er yeah maybe
5	S:	I think a picture with child
6	R:	Yeah, child are always good to
7	S:	Yes

8	-R:	to trap people spend money
9	S:	Yes. I think, erm, let me see, erm . . .
10	R:	I don't know . . . but maybe we should er choose a picture who gives the impression that this child needs needs the money or
11		
12	S:	So I think, then that's my, this one, no
13	R:	Yeah it's quite happy
14	S:	Yeah, she's happy er .. Maybe this one
15	R:	Yeah.
16	S:	He look very sad . . . and he has to carry heavier vase
17	R:	Mm, that's right.
18	S:	Too heavy for him, or . . .
19	R:	Hm hm
20	S:	But also this one, even if he's smiling
21	R:	Yeah, that's right . . . And maybe this one can show that the that the chari- er charity can really help
22		
23	S:	Uh huh
24	R:	and that the charity can er make a smile on a on a chil- on on a child's face
25		
26	S:	Yes
27	R:	Yeah I think this one would be
28	S:	A good one
29	R:	It would be good

. . .	*long pause*
-	*self-correction*
-R	*continuation*
xx	*unintelligible*

(Data including transcription provided by Jennifer Jenkins)[13]

It is obvious that the interactants are satisfied with their discussion: they agree on their criteria and negotiate a consensus, so in that sense we can regard this exchange as successful communication. The conversation also has a constructive, collaborative feel to it: in contrast to the data discussed in House (1999, see above), there is ample evidence of the interactants acting as responsive recipients as well as initiators: the *yes*'s and *yeah*'s tend to be genuine expressions of agreement, backchannelling is provided in the form of *Hm hm* and *Uh huh*, and there is even one instance of one speaker completing an utterance for her interlocutor (lines 27–28). But the point to be noted is that this communicative success comes about despite the fact that there is hardly a turn which is 'correct' or idiomatic by ENL standards. We find a wide range of oddities in terms of 'deviation' from ENL: the unintentionally comical phrase *a picture with child* in line 5 (though of course only comical for someone familiar with the ENL meaning of *with child*), idiosyncrasies such as *makes people to spend money* (line 2), *to trap people spend money* (line 8) and *make a smile on a child's face* (lines 24–25) and what would traditionally be called 'serious grammatical mistakes', such as missing third person *-s* in *He look very sad* (line 16), wrong relative pronoun in *a picture, who gives the impression* . . . (lines 10–11), missing indefinite article and unwarranted comparative in *he has to carry heavier vase* (line 16) as well as wrong preposition (or wrong verb) in *to spend money to the charity* (line 2).

Seen from the perspective of current mainstream ELT, this conversation contains many 'errors' which most teachers would certainly consider in need of correction and remediation. Despite all these, however, the exchange between Reto and Stephanie can be regarded as an instance of successful ELF communication. Of course this type of interaction relies heavily on shared context and has a limited potential for misunderstanding and conflict, and in many situations in which ELF is used such favourable conditions will not apply. But this caveat does not invalidate the observation that for the purpose at hand, the kind of English that is employed works, it serves the participants quite adequately for doing the job they have to do. The investigations I have carried out so far have confirmed that a great deal of ELF communication is conducted at roughly the level of Reto and Stephanie's proficiency, and that quite often it is features which are regarded as 'the most typically English', such as 3rd person -s, tags, phrasal verbs and idioms, which turn out to be non-essential for mutual understanding. This observation thus closely parallels Jenkins' finding that mastery of the sounds often perceived as 'particularly English', i.e. /θ/ and /ð/, is not crucial for ELF communication.

Of course, to most people who have experienced the use of English as a lingua franca all this might seem rather obvious: we all know intuitively that this is how it works. But this is exactly the point I wish to make: while we (wrongly) *think* we have (reliable) intuitions (the fallacy so effectively exposed by recent corpus linguistics), the problem is aggravated in the case of ELF because, by definition, there cannot even be any native speaker intuitions about ELF. So what we really have is *impressions* of ELF rather than *intuitions*. It would seem that this makes a broad empirical base on which to substantiate or indeed contradict these impressions particularly necessary.

In the teaching of English before the advent of computer-aided corpus linguistics, native speakers intuitively 'knew', but what they really said and wrote was not captured on a large scale, and hence was not accessible for description and close investigation and thus difficult to explain to learners, especially for teachers who had not grown up as speakers of the language they were teaching and thus could not even fall back on their native-speaker intuitions as the ultimate yardstick. In the case of ELF, nobody has grown up as a speaker of it. One could argue that this makes the need for an empirically based description even more urgent than in the case of ENL, where at least there are native speakers who can serve as informants, with all their limitations. So whereas the question usually asked about ENL by learners and teachers is '*can* one say that in English as a mother tongue?', it would not make sense to ask the same question about ELF. Rather, the only really useful analogous question about ELF would have to be an empirical one, namely '*has this been* said and understood in English as a lingua franca?' The Vienna-Oxford ELF corpus is intended as a first step towards addressing this question.

Conclusion

I would agree, then, with Sinclair's observation that 'the categories and methods we use to describe English are not appropriate to the new material. We shall need to overhaul our descriptive systems' (1985: 251). I would like to add, however, that this needs also to apply to ELF if we want to describe it: precisely the same arguments that Sinclair is making for the description of native-speaker language, for establishing the 'real English of native speakers', apply to the requirement of establishing the 'real English of ELF speakers'. However, the vast new technological apparatus now available has not been used for ELF, and the reality of ELF thus not been taken into account so far.

An important difference, of course, between corpus descriptions of ENL as opposed to ELF is that in the case of the former, corpus linguistics has been revising and indeed revolutionizing existing descriptions, and thus impacting significantly on reference materials such as dictionaries and grammars. In the case of ELF, however, the lack of a description has also meant that codification has been impossible to date. And here again an opportunity arises to build on the pioneering work which has been done on indigenized varieties of English, led by Braj Kachru (e.g. 1986, 1992a). Bamgbose (1998) argues very forcefully for codification of 'non-native varieties' as one of 'five internal factors . . . deciding on the status of an innovation' (p. 3):

> I use codification in the restricted sense of putting the innovation into a written form in a grammar, a lexical or pronouncing dictionary, course books or any other type of reference manual. . . . The importance, of codification is too obvious to be belaboured. . . . one of the major factors militating against the emergence of endonormative standards in non-native Englishes is precisely the dearth of codification. Obviously, once a usage or innovation enters the dictionary as correct and acceptable usage, its status as a regular form is assured,
>
> (p. 4)

What I propose, then, is to consider extending Bamgbose's claim to ELF and to explore the possibility of a codification of ELF with a conceivable ultimate objective of making it a feasible, acceptable and respected alternative to ENL in appropriate contexts of use. This is, of course, a long-term project and a huge and laborious task – an undertaking which must be carried out with extreme care, and which should not give rise to exaggerated expectations, let alone reckless premature commercial exploitation.

Once available, a description and codification of ELF use would constitute a new resource for the design of English instruction. The extent to which this resource is used would, of course, depend on a consideration of social, cultural and educational factors which necessarily bear upon language pedagogy. Even though its particular realisation is at the moment impossible to predict, it is easy to imagine the potentially huge implications this resource would carry for teacher education, curriculum design, textbooks and for how 'English' might be taught for lingua franca purposes where this is deemed desirable. For instance, as Jenkins so aptly puts it:

> There is really no justification for doggedly persisting in referring to an item as "an error" if the vast majority of the world's L2 English speakers produce and understand it. Instead, it is for L1 speakers to move their own receptive goal posts and adjust their own expectations as far as *international* (but not *intranational*) uses of English are concerned. . . . [This] also drastically simplifies the pedagogic task by removing from the syllabus many time-consuming items which are either unteachable or irrelevant for EIL.
>
> (Jenkins 2000: 160)

But as I have said, what exactly the relevance of such a description might be will have to be decided with reference to locally established pedagogic criteria: I would obviously not wish to claim that just because a description is available it should determine what is taught in specific settings or for specific purposes. But it does seem likely that the conceptualization of ELF as an alternative to ENL would open up an additional repertoire of options for appropriating 'English', of teaching the 'virtual language' (in the sense of Widdowson 1997 quoted above) or of using ELF as a possible first step for learners in building up a basis from which they can then pursue their own learning in directions (ELF or ENL) which it may be impossible, and unwise, to determine from the outset. In fact, uncoupling the language from its native speakers and probing into the nature of ELF for pedagogical purposes holds the exciting, if uncomfortable, prospect of bringing up for reappraisal just about *every* issue and tenet in language teaching which the profession has been traditionally concerned with.[14]

So how far any new findings will, or should, be acted upon is of course an open question. To be realistic, a linguistic innovation which goes against the grain of many people's tradition and etiquette is likely to meet with a great deal of resistance due to prejudice, market forces, vested interests, cultural sensibilities, aesthetic arguments and practical questions. But positive perspectives immediately arise as well: if recent important developments in applied linguistics on the meta-level are matched with an empirical basis for looking at the linguistic manifestations of ELF, this would help close the 'conceptual gap' I have discussed and provide us with a way of 'naming' ELF and making clear terminological distinctions.

There are also important advantages for ENL, and ENL speakers, in this: English as used by its native speakers has hitherto been faced with the impossible expectation that it should be 'all things to all people' and the inevitable failure in this has led to it (and its speakers) being subjected to accusations including those of contextual inappropriacy, cultural insensitivity and political imposition. At the same time, many native speakers of English feel that 'their language' is being abused and distorted through the diversity of its uses and users. If it becomes possible to call an instance of English use 'English as a lingua franca', analogous to, say, 'Nigerian English' and 'English English', this acts as a powerful signal that they are different 'territories' deserving mutual respect, and with their own 'legislation'. This would open up the possibility of engaging in 'code-switching' or at least 'concept-switching', and of an uninhibited acceptance of each use of 'English' in its own right – notably the appreciation of aesthetic and emotional aspects of literature, language play, rhetorical finesse, etc. Obviously, ENL would also remain intact as a target for learning in those circumstances where it is deemed appropriate. Most importantly perhaps, if ELF is conceptualized and accepted as a distinct manifestation of 'English' not tied to its native speakers, this opens up entirely new options for the way the world's majority of English teachers can perceive and define themselves: instead of being 'non-native' speakers and perennial learners of ENL, they can be competent and authoritative users of ELF. The 'native speaker teacher–non-native speaker teacher' dichotomy could then finally become obsolete in ELF settings, with the prospect of abolishing a counterproductive and divisive terminology which hinges on a negative particle, and which has bedevilled the profession for too long.

Notes

1   Cf. Gnutzmann 2000: 357: 'It has been estimated that about 80 per cent of verbal exchanges in which English is used as a second or foreign language do not involve native speakers of English (Beneke 1991)'. Crystal (1997: 54) gives the following estimates for speakers of English in terms of Kachru's 'concentric circles': Inner Circle [i.e. first language, e.g. USA, UK] 320–380 million, Outer Circle [i.e. additional language, e.g. India, Singapore] 150–300 million, Expanding Circle [i.e. foreign language, e.g. China, Russia] 100–1000 million.

2   For those who find it hard to believe that these developments are indeed quite recent, it might be interesting to have a look at papers which document interactions about the 'native–non-native' question, such as Akoha et al. (1991), which clearly show how new and strange challenges to 'native-speakerism' were only a decade ago, even to some applied linguists.

3   I hope it is clear that I am trying to make a general point here, not suggesting any conspirational intent on the part of Peter Medgyes and David Crystal – I picked the two quotations from hundreds which would have made exactly the same point. This was because their books are also thematically particularly appropriate for my concerns here, and declare it as their aim to contribute to open access and equity in this area.

4   But see below for corpora of 'learner English'.

5   'Its [ICE's] principal aim is to provide the resources for comparative studies of the English used in countries where it is either a majority first language . . . or an official additional language. In both language situations, English serves as a means of communication between those who live in these countries' (Greenbaum 1996: 3). 'Excluded from ICE is the English used in countries where it is not a medium for communication between natives of the country' (p. 4).

6   See also Kachru's criticism of the Cambridge International Dictionary of English for using the term 'inter-national' for referring to 'America, Britain and Australia' (1997: 70f.). The term 'international English' is usually not taken to include 'Expanding Circle' English (cf. e.g. Todd & Hancock 1986; Trudgill & Hannah 1995).

7   In an attempt to counteract this mechanism of (unwitting) reproduction, I will use inverted commas for any mention of 'English' when co- and context do not indicate which variety is being talked about (such as ENL, ELF or an indigenized 'Outer Circle' variety), as a reminder that any general reference to the denomination 'English' has to be regarded as provisional.

8   I focus on House (1999) here because this paper summarizes and discusses the state of the art in the pragmatics of ELF.

9   It has to be pointed out that the terminology in the literature about 'strategies' is far from unified, cf. the overview in Bialystok (1990).

10 Crystal (e.g. 1997: 136ff.) foresees the emergence of 'a new form of English – let us think of it as "World Standard Spoken English" (WSSE)'. He adds, though, that 'WSSE is still in its infancy. Indeed, it has hardly been born' and that it seems likely that the variety which will be 'most influential in the development of WSSE' is US English.

11 The texts are being transcribed orthographically and marked for speaker turns, pauses and overlaps, and provided with contextual notes and notes about para-linguistic features such as laughter. Part-of-speech tagging and syntactic parsing are to be added. A fairly basic system for marking for prosody is being worked out and piloted. It is currently not planned to provide a phonetic transcription of these texts, but it is hoped that sound files can be made available in the longer term.

12 Accommodation (in the sense of Giles & Coupland 1991) was found to be an important factor in Jenkins' (2000) study, and lack of it may have contributed to the impression of 'mutual dis-attention' House (1999: 82) got in the analysis of her data.

13 All the features of ELF interaction highlighted here have also been found in my own data, but I do not have any interactions as yet which entirely consist of such short turns as the present example, and therefore decided on the above extract as the most compact illustration available.

14 Kramsch (1999: 142) sounds a timely note of caution against a premature and naïve euphoria about 'global access': 'Global access to English, like global access to the Internet, facilitates communication, it does not necessarily facilitate understanding. In fact, it requires an additional effort in discursive reflexivity and linguistic circumspection to overcome the illusion of sameness created by the use of a common language. A pedagogy of English as a global language can capitalize on the outsideness of the local, non-native speaker to foster an understanding based not only on orate uses of language but on a critical reflection that can only be acquired through literacy'.

References

Aarts, B. (1996) The rhetorical adverb *simply* in present-day British English. In C. Percy, C. Meyer & I. Lancashire, *Synchronic corpus linguistics*. Amsterdam: Rodopi. 59–68.

Abbott, G. & P. Wingard (eds) (1981) *The teaching of English as an international language*. Glasgow & London: Collins.

Achebe, C. (1975) *Morning yet on creation day*. New York: Doubleday.

Akoha, J., Z. Ardo, J. Simpson, B. Seidlhofer & H.G. Widdowson (1991) Nationalism is an infantile disease. (Einstein) What about native-speakerism? *BAAL Newsletter* 39: 21–6.

Altenberg, B. & S. Granger (2001) The grammatical and lexical patterning of *make* in native and non-native student writing. *Applied Linguistics* 22.2: 173–94.

Ammon, U., K. Mattheier & P. Nelde (eds) (1994) *English only? In Europa / in Europe / en Europe*. *Sociolinguistica* 8. Tübingen: Niemeyer.

Aston, G. & L. Burnard (1998) *The BNC handbook*. Edinburgh University Press.

Bailey, R. & M. Görlach (eds) (1982) *English as a world language*. Ann Arbour, MI: University of Michigan Press.

Bamgbose, A. (1998) Torn between the norms: innovations in world Englishes. *World Englishes* 17.1: 1–14.

——— , A. Banjo & A. Thomas (eds) (1995) *New Englishes. A West African perspective.* Ibadan: Mosuro & The British Council.

Beneke, J. (1991) Englisch als lingua franca oder als Medium interkultureller Kommunikation. In R. Grebing, *Grenzenloses Sprachenlernen.* Berlin: Cornelsen. 54–66.

Bhatia, V. (1997) Introduction: genre analysis and world Englishes. *World Englishes* 16.3: 313–9.

Bialystok, E. (1990) *Communication strategies. A psychological analysis of second language use.* Oxford: Blackwell.

Biber, D. (1988) *Variation across speech and writing.* Cambridge University Press.

——— , S. Johansson, G. Leech, S. Conrad & E. Finegan (1999) *Longman Grammar of spoken and written English.* Harlow, Essex: Pearson.

Bourdieu, P. & J.-C. Passeron (1970) *Reproduction in education, culture and society.* Transl. R. Nice, London: Sage.

Braine, G. (ed.) (1999) *Non-native educators in English language teaching.* Mahwah, NJ: Erlbaum.

Breivik, L.-E. (1990) *Existential 'there': a synchronic and diachronic study* (2nd edition). Oslo: Novus.

Brumfit, C. (ed.) (1982) *English for international communication.* Oxford: Pergamon.

Brutt-Griffler, J. (1998) Conceptual questions in English as a world language. *World Englishes* 17.3: 381–92.

Brutt-Griffler, J. & K. Samimy (1999) Revisiting the colonial in the postcolonial: critical praxis for nonnative-English-speaking teachers in a TESOL program. *TESOL Quarterly* 33.3: 413–31.

Byram, M. & M. Fleming (eds) (1998) *Language learning in intercultural perspective.* Cambridge University Press.

Canagarajah, S. (1999) *Resisting linguistic imperialism in English teaching.* Oxford University Press.

Carter, R. &. M. McCarthy (1997) *Exploring spoken English.* Cambridge University Press.

Channell, J. (1994) *Vague language.* Oxford University Press.

Chen, H. (1998) Underuse, overuse, and misuse in Taiwanese EFL learner corpus. In S. Granger & J. Hung, *Proceedings of the First International Symposium on Computer Learner Corpora, Second Language Acquisition and Foreign Language Teaching.* The Chinese University of Hong Kong.

Cook, V. (1999) Going beyond the native speaker in language teaching. *TESOL Quarterly* 33.2: 185–209.

Corder, S.P. (1981) *Error analysis and interlanguage.* Oxford University Press.

Crystal, D. (1997) *English as a global language.* Cambridge University Press.

de Haan, P. (1998) How native-like are advanced learners of English? In A. Renouf, *Explorations in corpus linguistics.* Amsterdam: Rodopi. 55–65.

Edmondson, W. & J. House (1981) *Let's talk and talk about it. A pedagogical interactional grammar of English.* München: Urban & Schwarzenberg.

Faerch, C. & G. Kasper (1983) *Strategies in interlanguage communication.* London: Longman.

Firth, A. (1996) The discursive accomplishment of normality. On 'lingua franca' English and conversation analysis. *Journal of Pragmatics* 26.3: 237–59.

Giles, H. & N. Coupland (1991) *Language: contexts and consequences.* Milton Keynes: Open University Press.

Gnutzmann, C. (ed.) (1999) *Teaching and learning English as a global language.* Tübingen: Stauffenburg.

——— (2000) Lingua franca. In M. Byram, *The Routledge encyclopedia of language teaching and learning.* London: Routledge. 356–9.

Graddol, D. (1997) *The future of English?* London: British Council.

Granger, S. (ed.) (1998) *Learner English on computer.* London: Longman.

——— , J. Hung & S. Petch-Tyson (eds) (2002) *Computer learner corpora, second language acquisition and foreign language teaching.* Amsterdam: Benjamins.

Greenbaum, S. (ed.) (1996) *Comparing English worldwide. The international corpus of English.* Oxford: Clarendon.

Hoey, M. (1991) *Patterns of lexis in text.* Oxford: Oxford University Press.

Holliday, A. (1994) *Appropriate methodology and social context.* Cambridge University Press.

House, J. (1999) Misunderstanding in intercultural communication: interactions in English as a *lingua franca* and the myth of mutual intelligibility. In C. Gnutzmann, *Teaching and learning English as a global language.* Tübingen: Stauffenburg. 73–89.

Hüllen, W. (1992) Identifikationssprachen und Kommunikationssprachen. *Zeitschrift für Germanistische Linguistik* 20.3: 298–317.

James, A. (2000) English as a European lingua franca. Current realities and existing dichotomies. In J. Cenoz & U. Jessner, *English in Europe. The acquisition of a third language.* Clevedon: Multilingual Matters. 22–38.

Jenkins, J. (1998) Which pronunciation norms and models for English as an International Language? *ELT Journal* 52.2: 119–26.

——— (2000) *The phonology of English as an international language.* Oxford University Press.

Kachru, B. (1986) *The alchemy of English: the spread, functions and models of non-native Englishes.* Oxford: Pergamon. [Reprinted 1991, University of Illinois Press, Urbana, IL]

—— (ed.) (1992a) *The other tongue* (2nd edition). Urbana/Chicago: University of Illinois Press.

—— (1992b) Models for non-native Englishes. In B. Kachru, *The other tongue* (2nd edition). Urbana/Chicago: University of Illinois Press.

—— (1996) English as lingua franca. In H. Goebl, P. Nelde, Z. Stary & W. Wölck, *Kontaktlinguistik. Contact linguistics. Linguistique de contact.* Vol. 1. Berlin: De Gruyter. 906–13.

—— (1997) World Englishes and English-using communities. *Annual Review of Applied Linguistics* 17: 66–87. Cambridge University Press.

Kasper, G. (1997) Beyond reference. In G. Kasper & E. Kellerman, *Communication strategies: psycholinguistic and sociolinguistic perspectives.* London: Longman. 345–60.

Knapp, K. & C. Meierkord (eds) (2002) *Lingua franca communication.* Frankfurt/Main: Lang.

Kramsch, C. (1993) *Context and culture in language teaching.* Oxford University Press.

—— (1998) The privilege of the intercultural speaker. In M. Byram & M. Fleming, *Language learning in intercultural perspective.* Cambridge University Press. 16–31.

—— (1999) Global and local identities in the contact zone. In C. Gnutzmann, *Teaching and learning English as a global language.* Stauffenburg. 131–43.

—— & P. Sullivan (1996) Appropriate pedagogy. *ELT Journal* 50.3: 199–212.

Lesznyak, A. (2002) *Untersuchungen zu Besonderheiten der Kommunikation im Englischen als Lingua Franca.* Ph.D. Dissertation, Universität Hamburg.

Lorenz, G. (1998) Overstatement in advanced learners' writing: stylistic aspects of adjective intensification. In S. Granger, *Learner English on computer.* London: Longman. 53–66.

—— (1999) *Adjective intensification – learners versus native speakers. A corpus study of argumentative writing.* Amsterdam/Atlanta: Rodopi.

Malmkjær, K. (1991) *The linguistics encyclopedia.* London/New York: Routledge.

McArthur, T. (1998) *The English languages.* Cambridge University Press.

McEnery, T. (2000) Speakers, hearers and annotation – why it's difficult to do pragmatics with corpora. Paper given on 9 February, Institute of English Studies, University of London.

McKay, S. (2002) *Teaching English as an international language: rethinking goals and approaches.* Oxford University Press.

Medgyes, P. (1994) *The non-native teacher.* London: Macmillan.

Meierkord, C. (1996) *Englisch als Medium der interkulturellen Kommunikation. Untersuchungen zum non-native-/non-native speaker – Diskurs.* Frankfurt/Main: Lang.

Ogden, C. (1930) *Basic English. A general introduction with rules and grammar.* London: Kegan Paul.

Pennycook, A. (1994) *The cultural politics of English as an international language.* London: Longman.

—— (1999) Introduction: critical approaches to TESOL. *TESOL Quarterly* 33.3: 329–48.

Percy, C., C. Meyer & I. Lancashire (eds) (1996) *Synchronic corpus linguistics.* Amsterdam: Rodopi.

Petch-Tyson, S. (2000) Demonstrative expressions in argumentative discourse – a computer-based comparison of non-native and native English. In S. Botley & T. McEnery, *Corpus-based and computational approaches to discourse anaphora.* Amsterdam: Benjamins. 43–64.

Phillipson, R. (1992) *Linguistic imperialism.* Oxford University Press.

—— & T. Skutnabb-Kangas (1999) Englishisation: one dimension of globalisation. *AILA Review* 13: 19–36.

Rampton, B. (1990) Displacing the 'native speaker': expertise, affiliation and inheritance. *ELT Journal* 44.2: 97–101.

Quirk R. (1982) International communication and the concept of Nuclear English. In C. Brumfit, *English for international communication.* Oxford: Pergamon. 15–28.

—— & H.G. Widdowson (1985) (eds) *English in the world: teaching and learning the languages and literatures.* Cambridge University Press.

Seidlhofer, B. (1999) Double standards: teacher education in the Expanding Circle. *World Englishes* 18.2: 233–45.

—— (2002) The shape of things to come? Some basic questions. In K. Knapp & C. Meierkord, *Lingua franca communication.* Frankfurt/Main: Lang. 269–302.

Sinclair, J. (1985) Selected issues. In R. Quirk & H.G. Widdowson, *English in the world: teaching and learning the languages and literatures.* Cambridge University Press. 248–54.

—— (1991) *Corpus, concordance, collocation.* Oxford University Press.

Smith, L. (ed.) (1981) *English for cross-cultural communication.* London: Macmillan.

—— & M. Forman (eds) (1997) *World Englishes 2000*. Honolulu, Hawaii: College of Languages, Linguistics and Literature and the East-West Center.

Strevens, Peter. (1980) *Teaching English as an international language: from practice to principle*. Oxford: Pergamon Press.

Todd, L. & I. Hancock (1986) *International English usage*. London: Croom Helm.

Trudgill, P. & J. Hannah (1995) *International English: a guide to varieties of standard English* (3rd edition). London: Arnold.

Wagner, J. & A. Firth (1997) Communication strategies at work. In G. Kasper & E. Kellerman, *Communication strategies: psycholinguistic and sociolinguistic perspectives*. London: Longman. 323–44.

West, M. (1953) *A general service list of English words: with semantic frequencies and a supplementary word-list for the writing of popular science and technology*. London: Longmans.

Widdowson, H.G. (1994) The ownership of English. *TESOL Quarterly* 28.2: 377–89.

—— (1997) EIL, ESL, EFL: global issues and local interests. *World Englishes* 16.1: 135–46.

Chapter 9

SURESH CANAGARAJAH

LINGUA FRANCA ENGLISH, MULTILINGUAL COMMUNITIES, AND LANGUAGE ACQUISITION (2007)

The concept of language as a rigid, monolithic structure is false, even if it has proved to be a useful fiction in the development of linguistics. It is the kind of simplification that is necessary at a certain stage of a science, but which can now be replaced by more sophisticated models.

(Haugen, 1972, p. 325)

FIRTH AND WAGNER QUESTIONED some key dichotomies operative in second language acquisition (SLA) research in their 1997 article. Focusing mainly on the constructs *learner* versus *user*, *nonnative* versus *native* speaker (NNS vs. NS), and *interlanguage* versus *target language*, they contested the notions of deficiency imputed to the first construct in each pair. SLA[1] has generally worked with the assumption that learners are emulating the idealized competence of NSs, that they are handicapped in their capacity to communicate with the undeveloped language they possess, and that learning a language primarily constitutes mastering its grammar in specially designed pedagogical contexts.

1. Grammar versus pragmatics: Is one more primary in communication than the other, and are they in fact separable? Would pragmatic strategies enable one to communicate successfully irrespective of the level of grammatical proficiency? (House, 2003).
2. Determinism versus agency: Are learners at the mercy of grammar and discourse forms for communication, or do they shape language to suit their purposes? (Canagarajah, 2006a).
3. Individual versus community: Are language learning and use orchestrated primarily by the individual even when they occur through interaction? Or do communication and acquisition take place in collaboration with others, through active negotiation, as an intersubjective practice? (Block, 2003).
4. Purity versus hybridity: Are languages separated from each other, even at the most abstract level of grammatical form? And how do they associate with other symbol systems and modalities of communication? (Khubchandani, 1997; Makoni, 2002).
5. Fixity versus fluidity: What is the place of deviation, variation, and alteration in language, and can a system lack boundedness? Similarly, is acquisition linear, cumulative, unidirectional, and monodimensional? (Kramsch, 2002; Larsen-Freeman, 2002).

6. Cognition versus context: Do we formulate and store language norms detached from the situations and environment in which they are embedded? Is learning more effective when it takes place separately from the contexts where multiple languages, communicative modalities, and environmental influences are richly at play? (Atkinson, Churchill, Nishino, & Okada, 2007; Lantolf & Thorne, 2006).

7. Monolingual versus multilingual acquisition: Should we treat learning as taking place one language at a time, separately for each, in homogeneous environments? (Cook, 1999).

Firth and Wagner (1997) ushered in the questioning of the dichotomies, and we have gradually progressed to a position of model building, developing alternate theoretical paradigms that would integrate these constructs (see Zuengler & Miller, 2006, for a review). Although Firth and Wagner primarily sought parity between the constructs, we are now in a position not only to abandon the dichotomized orientation but also to synthesize the constructs on a radically different footing. Firth and Wagner ended their article with a broad call "to work towards the evolution of a holistic, bio-social SLA" (p. 296). We have hence/now constructed a range of specific models that elaborate and refine the biosocial paradigm (examples follow). Thus the first of the three requirements Firth and Wagner identified in order to redress the imbalance—in other words, an enhanced awareness of the contextual and interactional dimensions of language use—stands fulfilled. The other two requirements—in other words, an emic perspective and a broadened SLA database—are still to be realized. We need more insider studies from multi-lingual (especially non-Western) communities and data from outside the classroom to meet these requirements. Even in the case of theoretical awareness and model building, we do not have a consensus. Zuengler and Miller (2006) argued that the cognitive and social perspectives constitute "parallel worlds" in SLA studies (p. 35).

It is in this context that I present recent research related to lingua franca English (LFE)[2] as radically reconfiguring the new models of language usage and acquisition being constructed in our field. This emergent body of knowledge enables us to reappraise the constructs that were previously ignored or suppressed. To a considerable extent, LFE research presents data from contact situations in professional and everyday contexts outside the classroom, broadening the SLA database. Though we need more emic perspectives from non-Western communities, the studies by European scholars provide useful data from multilingual contexts. LFE research was available earlier, but it has developed to even more complex levels as the global currency of English has grown in relation to recent forms of postmodern globalization.[3] The new context, featuring transnational affiliations, diaspora communities, digital communication, fluid social boundaries, and the blurring of time-space distinctions has generated more information about atypical communicative contexts, encouraged studies on contact situations, and created an urgency to understand acquisition outside homogeneous communities.

Therefore, we now have new data and perspectives that were unavailable at the time of the initial debate. However, my argument here is not that SLA has to be revised only to accommodate the exceptional issues deriving from globalization and LFE.[4] These recent developments have only made us aware of some fundamental processes of language learning and usage relevant to diverse communities in different historical and geographical contexts. For example, we are now in a position to appreciate how language learning and usage have taken place in non-Western multilingual communities for centuries. The local knowledge of these periphery communities has been ignored in linguistic scholarship, as in many other fields in the academy.

Therefore, we should consider the critique, revision, and expansion of dominant constructs as a desirable process of knowledge construction. As Haugen (1972) noted, in the quotation in the epigraph, there is a place for enabling fictions at particular stages in scholarly inquiry.

However, in the light of new evidence, especially as social conditions themselves change and our inquiry becomes sharper, we have to deconstruct our earlier models and perhaps start anew. Globalization, multilingual contact, and LFE provide impetus for continuing this disciplinary rethinking with new urgency and addressing language processes and practices that have lain hidden all the time.

In this article, I first review studies on the acquisition and use of English as a contact language. Based on these research findings, I consider the implications for the dichotomized constructs in SLA. Then, I review the literature on communicative practices in non-Western communities, which confirms the practices informing LFE usage, suggesting the bases of the resources and skills multilinguals bring to language negotiation. The non-Western scholarship also raises additional complex questions about language use and acquisition that enable us to further advance our inquiry on SLA. As I move toward an alternate paradigm, I consider the reasons why such acquisition processes have not been addressed in the dominant SLA models. Examining the (structuralist) philosophical and (monolingual) social biases in knowledge construction, I move on to outline a new integration of the SLA constructs on a practice-based model that would better accommodate the communicative processes of multilinguals.

Acquiring and using lingua franca English

Graddol (1999) prophesied "in [the] future [English] will be a language used mainly in multilingual contexts as a second language and for communication between non-native speakers" (p. 57). This prediction is arguably already a reality. English is used most often as a contact language by speakers of other languages in the new contexts of transnational communication. Speakers of English as an additional language are greater in number than the traditionally understood NSs[5] who use English as their sole or primary language of communication. These developments have impressed upon us the need to understand the character of LFE, a variety that overshadows national dialects—the dominant ones such as British or American English and the recently nativized forms such as a Indian or Singaporean English—both in currency and significance (see Canagarajah, 2006b; Jenkins, 2006; and Seidlhofer, 2004, for the state of the art on LFE). How is this lingua franca,[6] a language so important for millions of global speakers, acquired and used?

LFE belongs to a virtual speech community. The speakers of LFE are not located in one geographical boundary. They inhabit and practice other languages and cultures in their own immediate localities. Despite this linguistic-cultural heterogeneity and spatial disconnect, they recognize LFE as a shared resource. They activate a mutually recognized set of attitudes, forms, and conventions that ensure successful communication in LFE when they find themselves interacting with each other. House (2003) appropriately called these *communities of imagination*, borrowing the well-known metaphor from Anderson (1984). It is unclear what constitutes the threshold level of English proficiency required to join this invisible community. Though some proficiency in English is certainly necessary, it is evident that even those individuals with a rudimentary knowledge can conduct successful communication while further developing their proficiency. This facility is no doubt attributable to the language awareness and practices developed in other contexts of communication with local languages. Multilingualism is at the heart of LFE's hybrid community identity and speaker proficiency.

A radical implication of this multilingualism is that all users of LFE have native competence of LFE, just as they have native competence in certain other languages and cultures. This characterization goes against our usual ways of using the concept of NS. Typically, one is an NS of only one language. However, this type of native competence (and insider status) in multiple languages is a well-known reality in many communities. LFE only makes this phenomenon more visible and global. An important implication is that unlike our treatment of those who are outsiders to British, American, or other national varieties of English, we cannot treat LFE speakers as incompetent. House (2003) put it this way: "a lingua franca speaker is not *per definitionem* not fully competent in the part of his or her linguistic knowledge under study" (p. 557). This assertion does not mean that LFE speakers do not develop their proficiency further—just as Anglo–American NSs still have to develop their proficiency in English. Perhaps we have to distinguish between competence and proficiency. Both LFE speakers and NSs have competence in their respective varieties, though there is no limit to the development of their proficiency through experience and time. The competence of LFE speakers is of course distinct. This competence for cross-language contact and hybrid codes derives from their multilingual life.

Because of the diversity at the heart of this communicative medium, LFE is intersubjectively constructed in each specific context of interaction. The form of this English is negotiated by each set of speakers for their purposes. The speakers are able to monitor each other's language proficiency to determine mutually the appropriate grammar, phonology, lexical range, and pragmatic conventions that would ensure intelligibility. Therefore, it is difficult to describe this language a priori. It cannot be characterized outside the specific interaction and speakers in a communicative context. Meierkord (2004) said that LFE "emerges out of and through interaction" and, for that reason, "it might well be that ELF never achieves a stable or even standardized form" (p. 129). In this sense, LFE does not exist as a system "out there." It is constantly brought into being in each context of communication.

Let us now unpack the implications of this negotiability for form. The form of LFE is variable.[7] Because the type of language is actively negotiated by the participants, what might be inappropriate or unintelligible in one interaction is perfectly understandable in another. This notion of form goes beyond the traditional understanding of variation as deriving from a common core of grammar or language norms. In other words, variation is at the heart of this system, not secondary to a more primary common system of uniform norms. Speakers understand the interlocutor's variants and proceed effectively with the communication, in turn using their own variants. As Gramkow Anderson (1993) put it "there is no consistency in form that goes beyond the participant level, i.e., each combination of interactants seems to negotiate and govern their own variety of lingua franca use in terms of proficiency level, use of code-mixing, degree of pidginization, etc." (p. 108).

To make matters more complicated, LFE's form is hybrid in nature. The language features words, grammatical patterns, and discourse conventions from diverse languages and English varieties that speakers bring to the interaction. Participants borrow from each other freely and adopt the other's language in their interaction with that participant. In her research on the syntactic character of LFE, Meierkord (2004) presented it as a heterogeneous form of English characterized by: (a) "overwhelming correspondence to the rules of L1 Englishes"; (b) "transfer phenomena, developmental patterns and nativised forms"; and (c) "simplification, regularisation and levelling processes" (p. 128).

Sampson and Zhao (2003) made an analogy between LFE and a pidgin language, based on data from multilingual sailors. They found the existence of Singaporean, Indian, and Phillipino Englishes, in addition to other languages, in the LFE of their participants. The sailors borrowed from the usage of each other to develop a hybrid language that is still shared and used smoothly for communication. Thus, LFE raises serious questions about the concept of language system. Is it possible to consider form as constituting an indeterminate, open, and fluid system?

How does such a fluid system facilitate harmonious communication? It is obvious that LFE speakers cannot depend on a preconstituted form for meaning. They activate complex pragmatic strategies that help them negotiate their variable form. It is amazing, therefore, that "misunderstandings are not frequent in ELF interactions," according to Seidlhofer (2004, p. 218). She went on to say that "when they do occur, they tend to be resolved either by topic change, or, less often, by overt negotiation using communication strategies such as rephrasing and repetition" (p. 218). A kind of suspension of expectations regarding norms seems to be in operation, and when forms from a different language or English variety surface, they do not interfere negatively. Planken (2005) described how this condition is achieved in intercultural business communication. She noted that the interlocutors do some preparatory work through opening comments to create a third space—a no-man's-land between their primary languages and cultures—to negotiate LFE on equal terms. Through reflexive comments on their own communicative practices, self-deprecating humor, and the evocation of their shared nonnativeness, they distance themselves from their own norms and activate flexible practices that facilitate communication.

As long as a certain threshold of understanding is obtained, interlocutors seem to adopt what Firth (1996) termed the *let it pass principle*, by which they overlook idiosyncracies. Part of these pragmatic resources are discourse strategies (at the suprasentential level) to accommodate local variants. Meierkord (2004) found that although individuals retain the characteristics of their own English varieties, they facilitate communication through syntactic strategies like segmentation (involving utterances that are shortened into clausal or phrasal segments that form the basic informational units) and regularization (involving the movement of focused information to the front of the utterance). These characteristics give the impression that LFE talk is "overtly consensus-oriented, cooperative and mutually supportive, and thus fairly robust" (Seidlhofer, 2004, p. 218).

If uniformity of form is not a requirement in LFE, more surprising is the finding that even the enabling pragmatic strategies do not have to be the same. House (2003) demonstrated how students of English from different countries bring pragmatic strategies valued in their own communities to facilitate communication with outsiders. These strategies are, paradoxically, culture-specific strategies that complement intercultural communication. For example, House found that "Asian participants employ topic management strategies in a striking way, recycling a specific topic regardless of where and how the discourse had developed at any particular point" (p. 567). This discourse of parallel monologues actually helps nonproficient English speakers because it enables them to focus on each move as if it were a fresh topic. In the three strategies House described, while the local cultural ways of interacting are alive in the English of Asians, they still serve to ensure intelligibility and communication with outsiders. This communication is possible because the other also brings his or her own strategies to negotiate these culture-specific conventions. Participants, then, "do their own thing," but still communicate with each other. Not uniformity, but alignment is more important for such communication. Each participant brings his or her own language resources to find a strategic fit with the participants and purpose of a context.

For communication to work across such radical differences, it is important that acquisition and use go hand in hand. As speakers use LFE, a lot of learning takes place: They monitor the form and conventions the other brings; they learn to ascribe meanings to their form and conventions; and they monitor their own form and convention to negotiate communication. Meeting different speakers from the vast, diffuse, and virtual community of LFE, one always has to learn a lot—and rapidly—as one decides which receptive and productive resources to adopt for a context. Furthermore, the lessons learnt in one encounter will help to constantly reconstruct the schema to monitor future communication of similar or different participants and contexts. In this sense, learning never stops in LFE. If there is no language use without learning, there is also no language learning outside of use. Because there is no a priori grammar, the variable language system has to be encountered in actual use. The contexts of intercultural global communication are unpredictable, and the mix of participants and purposes have to be encountered in real situations. Also, the strategies that enable negotiation are meaningless as knowledge or theory; they have to be constantly activated for their development. A language based on negotiation can be developed only through and in practice.

Implications for theorizing acquisition

Such a scenario of LFE communication complicates the dominant constructs of SLA and validates the questions raised by Firth and Wagner (1997). Because LFE is intersubjectively constructed in a situation- and participant-specific manner, it is difficult to elicit a baseline data to assess the proficiency of LFE speakers. LFE's form and conventions vary for different speakers and contexts. We have to judge proficiency, intelligibility, and communicative success in terms of each context and its participants. More importantly, we have to interpret the meaning and significance of the English used from the participants' own perspective, without imposing the researcher's standards or criteria invoked from elsewhere.

A related point here is that we have to rid ourselves of what Cook (1999) called the *comparative fallacy*. The haste to judge language performance using limited and unfair norms has affected much of what we have done so far in language learning.[8] The treatment of a putative NS of English as the norm is another manifestation of the comparative fallacy. The English of multilingual LFE speakers is not used in deference to the norms of prestige varieties such as British or American English. LFE speakers do not treat the speakers of these varieties as their frame of reference. House (2003) reminded us "the yardstick for measuring ELF speakers' performance should therefore rather be an 'expert in ELF use', a stable multilingual speaker under comparable sociocultural and historical conditions of use, and with comparable goals for interaction" (p. 573). This is a tongue-in-cheek statement, as we have seen that there is nothing stable about the multilingual speaker. Moreover, there is little that is comparable about LFE contexts or purposes of interaction, as each LFE interaction ushers in its own unique dynamics.

These realizations call into question the idea that the English of multilingual users is an interlanguage. Multilingual speakers are not moving toward someone else's target; they are constructing their own norms. It is meaningless to measure the distance of LFE speakers from the language of Anglo-American speakers as LFE has no relevance to their variety. Besides, we have to question the assumption in the interlanguage concept that there are gradations, a linear progression, and an endpoint to be achieved in language learning. We have seen that each LFE interaction is a unique context, raising its own challenges for negotiation. It may not be the case that one communicative act contributes to the other and so on, leading to a cumulative line of progression. Because the contexts are so variable and unpredictable, it is not possible to say that a target can be reached for perfect or competent LFE proficiency. (We may not be able to say that even for Anglo-American NSs of English.)

If at all, we can speak of achieving a type of language awareness and competence that can help handle diverse communicative situations. However, it is possible that multilinguals already come with this competence and do not wait for their interactions in English to develop that ability. Based on her findings of the creative and complex negotiation strategies of multilinguals, House (2003) argued "all these strategies seem to show that ELF users are competent enough to be able to monitor each others' moves at a high level of awareness" (p. 559). In this sense, their development of LFE proficiency has to be granted relatively greater agency, at least analogous to the agency attributed to the development in one's first language in certain generativist models. The LFE speaker comes with the competence—in many respects, more advanced than that of the child because of the years of multilingual practice enjoyed in their local communities—which is then honed through actual interactions. This development does not have to be marked by miscommunication or deficient usage, and should not be treated as such.

We realize, however, that the linguistic competence of an LFE speaker has to be defined more broadly and with greater complexity. The dominant orientation is to treat solely or mainly form as defining competence, with communicative competence given a secondary role. In LFE, form receives reduced significance; or, rather, form gets shaped according to the contexts and participants in an interaction. More important are a range of other skills, abilities, and awareness that enable multilingual speakers to negotiate grammar. In addition to grammatical competence, we have to give equal importance to: language awareness that enables speakers to make instantaneous inferences about the norms and conventions of their multilingual inter-locutors; strategic competence to negotiate interpersonal relationships effectively; and pragmatic competence to adopt communicative conventions that are appropriate for the interlocutor, purpose, and situation.[9]

The orientation to acquisition as a cognitive activity also needs clarification. We cannot focus on the activity and the content of the mind in understanding LFE proficiency. There is a con-siderable contribution from environmental and social domains. The rules, schema, and conven-tions developed by LFE users come loaded with significant social information. The variable and hybrid grammar of LFE cannot be acquired outside the contexts and social milieu that help select them and give meaning. If language has a cognitive habitation, such a cognition is shaped, enabled, and realized in social practice. In this respect, the distinction between competence and performance has to be revised. It can be argued that in the case of LFE, there is no meaning for form, grammar, or language ability outside the realm of practice. LFE is not a product located in the mind of the speaker; it is a form of social action.

In theorizing this complex social action, some scholars have begun to explore how successful communication depends on aligning the linguistic resources one brings to the social, situational, and affective dimensions operative in a context (see Kramsch, 2002). In other words, language learning involves an alignment of one's language resources to the needs of a situation, rather than reaching a target level of competence. Atkinson et al. (2007) defined alignment as "the means by which human actors *dynamically adapt to*—that is, flexibly depend on, integrate with, and construct—the ever-changing mind-body-world environments posited by sociocognitive theory. In other words, alignment takes place not just between human beings, but also between human beings and their social and physical environments" (p. 171, original emphasis). Atkinson and his collaborators went on to illustrate alignment through the English language learning interaction of a Japanese child and her tutor. What is more pertinent to this article (an issue the authors do not choose to develop) is the way both Japanese and English and, sometimes, coconstructed words and meanings of ambiguous linguistic identity are used as cues and effects of successful alignment to facilitate English language learning.

This notion of alignment makes us question another bias in SLA—language acquisition as an individual activity. It is clear that the individual's proficiency is shaped by collective and contextual factors. But there are other implications for assessing an individual's level of proficiency. As we saw, LFE makes sense only as an intersubjective construction, something achieved by two or more people, based on the strategies they bring to the interaction. We have to consider the collaborative nature of communication and linguistic negotiation in assessing the meaning and significance of an interaction.

From this perspective, the conduit model of meaning as information transfer (which informs SLA) has to be questioned. In LFE, meaning does not precede (and is not detachable from) the language in which it is communicated. House (2003) noted, "in ELF use, speakers must continuously work out a joint basis for their interactions, locally construing and intersubjectively ratifying meanings" (p. 559). Therefore, even an ungrammatical usage or inappropriate word choice can be socially functional. They can create a new meaning originally unintended by the speaker, or they may be negotiated by the participants and given new meanings. Participants negotiate the language effectively to ascribe meaning to everything. A radical implication of this assertion for assessing language proficiency is that error is also socially constructed. An error occurs when someone fails to ascribe meaning to a linguistic form used by another. In LFE, such cases rarely occur. Breakdown in LFE communication is possible only in rare cases of refusal to negotiate meanings—which is itself a form of communication as it conveys the participant's desire to cut off the conversation. Therefore, if there is a case of failed communication, we cannot blame an individual for lack of proficiency. This failed communication might be a divergence strategy (Giles, 1984). Those individuals who assess proficiency have to take into account such joint activity of participants in communication before rushing to rule something a mistake.

In relation to all these issues, we have to question whether researchers can study language acquisition by standing outside the interaction in question or, even worse, coming from outside the communities they study. Would they be imposing norms and meanings that do not matter to their participants? Given the intersubjective nature of LFE, how can researchers who do not participate in a specific communicative event claim to be privy to the norms and meanings operative for those involved? There is research documentation to suggest that in cases where speakers do not come from the LFE virtual community, sharing the basic communicative expectations, their interaction fails (House, 2003).

Ironically, the only cases of miscommunication House (2003) observed in her research were in the interactions of multilingual speakers with those individuals for whom English is native or sole language. This miscommunication in native-nonnative talk is easy to explain, as NSs would fail to negotiate, treating their norms as universally applicable. Would researchers be prone to similar misunderstanding, especially in cases where they are NSs, in addition to being outsiders to the interaction?

The intersubjective nature of communication makes us question the separation of the learner role from other social roles and identities. In traditional SLA research, a learner's language is not presumed to be functional (unless proven otherwise). The researcher's acts of othering, objectifying, patronizing, and judging further reduce the learner's social complexity. However, LFE users are always conscious of the social roles they play in their contexts of contact communication. We have to interpret their performance in terms of the purposes and roles that matter in that speech event. To further complicate theorization, LFE users do not remain with the rich and diverse identities they bring to the event; as we discussed earlier, they negotiate to modify and reconstruct new identities more amenable to the interaction. Therefore, to reduce the analysis to speaker-as-learner is to leave out many other features of communication that provide significance to the language data.

This recognition does not mean that other social identities may not subsume the learner identity or vice versa. We now know that in all language learning contexts, including academic venues, acquisition is a social process where subtle nonpedagogical meanings and identities are communicated. Even in classroom contexts, identities are multiple, conflictual, and changing (see Norton, 2000). Students convey other meanings and identities not prescribed in the lessons.

In my ethnography of classroom discourse, I show how students shuttle between identities of learner, friend, and in-group community member with their teachers, all the time conveying contextually relevant meanings, even as they gain communicative competence in code-switching (Canagarajah, 1999). They also find spaces for expressing resistant identities, deviating from the institutionally mandated roles and distancing themselves from messages of the hidden curriculum. Often even narrowly defined pedagogical exercises can be turned into richly purposive communication by students. Learners can subvert lessons that treat them as passive and mechanical through sarcasm, serving to prove themselves complex agents. Routine pedagogical exercises can be refrained to generate humour and play. These communicative acts and identities can imply complex proficiency. By the same token, interactions that are not framed as pedagogical (i.e., off-task, off-site activities) can be utilized for learning. These realizations make us question the assumption of learning as a conscious, controlled, predesigned, and predictable activity. We have to move toward conceiving of learning as often nonintentional, nonscripted, and nonlinear to understand LFE acquisition in everyday contexts.

As we consider acquisition as transcending the control of the individual and the scope of interpersonal relationships, we have to explore one's language development in relation to that of a whole community of speakers. When a language is being appropriated by a community to suit its own interests and values, developing unique grammars and conventions in the process, should we still assess the language of the individual in relation to NS norms? The term *macroacquisition* has been used to understand how a community appropriates another language and develops proficiency in endonormative terms (Brutt-Griffler, 2002). We have to develop ways to map the microacquisition of individuals with the macroacquisition of the communities of which they are a part. This process is not always isomorphic. In some ways, the individual has to align his or her learning to that of the community's norms; in other ways, he or she has to deviate from and resist the norms of the collective for the sake of voice and individuality. To make matters more complicated, while mapping the levels of alignment of the individual and the collective, we also have to realize that the language development of both is mobile and changing. In this sometimes asynchronous proficiency development in an unstable grammatical system, one needs creative strategies to make the appropriate alignment between one's language resources and the requirements of the context.

We can now appreciate how certain methodological constructs that were a cause of concern for Firth and Wagner (1997) are constitutive features of LFE. These features are the need to (a) consider meaning as negotiated and intersubjective; (b) treat form as shaped by participants for their own purposes in each communicative activity; (c) affirm learners as capable of exerting their agency to renegotiate and overcome errors; (d) integrate learning and use; (e) provide for nonlearner social identities in acquisition; (f) accommodate both purposive everyday communication and nonfunctional play as equally contributing to acquisition; (g) relate to language as practice; (h) treat cognition as situated and competence as performance; and (i) interpret the communication of novices in context without comparing it with NS norms or a target proficiency, or treating it as an interlanguage. The use of these methodological constructs is not optional, as Firth and Wagner seemed to allow, for different modes and cases of analysis. We cannot choose to either adopt or ignore them in the study of LFE acquisition and use. LFE is meaningless outside these conditions.

Language acquisition and use in multilingual communities

If multilingual speakers display such stupendous competence in acquiring and using a hybrid language like LFE, there is evidence that it comes from language socialization and awareness developed in their local communities. Higgins (2003) found in her group experiment that multilingual students were more successful in decoding the meaning of lexical and grammatical items from new Englishes than Anglo-American students. NSs had difficulties in such tasks as they did not bring skills and attitudes open to negotiation. The practices we observe in LFE users are common in other contexts of multilingual communication involving local languages.

Paradoxically, then, recent findings in LFE communicative practices help us appreciate language acquisition and use common to multilingual communities from precolonial times.

Though we do not have adequate scholarly descriptions of them in our field, these practices are not completely lost in these communities. We are beginning to see descriptions of such practices from Africa (Makoni, 2002), South America (de Souza, 2002), and the Polynesian Islands (Dorian, 2004), among others. They are striking in their differences from the dominant constructs in linguistics, and raise further questions that need exploration. I base the description of multilingual communication that follows on my own region of early socialization in South Asia, especially as it emerges through the perceptive discussion of Khubchandani (1997).[10]

Linguistic diversity is at the heart of multilingual communities. There is constant interaction between language groups, and they overlap, interpenetrate, and mesh in fascinating ways. Not only do people have multiple memberships, but they also hold in tension their affiliation with local and global language groups as the situation demands. Khubchandani (1997) used an indigenous metaphor, *Kshetra*, to capture this sense of community. *Kshetras* "can be visualized as a rainbow; here different dimensions interflow symbiotically into one another, responsive to differences of density as in an osmosis" (p. 84). Khubchandani called the unity that develops out of this diversity and continuity of affiliations a *superconsensus*.

Such individuals and communities are so radically multilingual that it is difficult to identify one's mother tongue or native language. People develop simultaneous childhood multi-lingualism, making it difficult to say which language comes first. As Kubhchandani (1997) pointed out, "identification through a particular language label is very much a matter of individual social awareness" (p. 173). Language identity is relative to the communities and languages one considers salient in different contexts. Therefore, the label is applied in a shifting and inconsistent manner.

Because of such intense contact, languages themselves are influenced by each other, losing their purity and separateness. Many local languages serve as contact languages, and develop features suitable for such purposes—that is, hybridity of grammar and variability of form. Khubchandani (1997) said "many Indian languages belonging to different families show parallel trends of development. . . [They] exhibit many phonological, grammatical and lexical similarities and are greatly susceptible to borrowing from the languages of contact" (p. 80). He went on to say that differences "between Punjabi and Hindi, Urdu and Hindi, Dogri and Punjabi, and Konkani and Marathi can be explained only through a pluralistic view of language" (p. 91). Though he did not elaborate, the pluralistic view of language would raise many enigmas for traditional linguistics: How do we classify and label languages when there is such mixing? How do we describe languages without treating them as self-contained systems? How do we define the system of a language without the autonomy, closure, and tightness that would preclude openness to other languages?

Such communities are so multilingual that in a specific speech situation one might see the mixing of diverse languages, literacies, and discourses. It might be difficult to categorize the interaction as belonging to a single language. Khubchandani (1997) explained "the edifice of linguistic plurality in the Indian subcontinent is traditionally based upon the *complementary* use of more than one language and more than one writing system for the same language in one 'space'" (p. 96; original emphasis). If social spaces feature complementary—not exclusive—use of languages, mixing of languages and literacies in each situation is the norm, not the exception. This communicative reality raises many questions for language acquisition: What kind of competence do people need to communicate in such contexts where different languages mix, mesh, and complement each other? How do people produce meaning out of this seeming chaos of multiple systems of communication?

It is clear that this linguistic pluralism has to be negotiated actively to construct meaning. In these communities, meaning and intelligibility are intersubjective. The participants in an inter-action produce meaning and accomplish their communicative objectives in relation to their purposes and interests. In this sense, meaning is socially constructed, not preexisting. Meaning does not reside in the language; it is produced in practice. As a result, "individuals in such societies acquire more *synergy* (i.e., putting forth one's own efforts) and serendipity (i.e., accepting the other on his or her own terms, being open to unexpectedness), and develop positive attitudes to variations in speech (to the extent of even appropriating deviations as the norm in the lingua franca), in the process of 'coming out' from their own language codes to a neutral ground" (Khubchandani, 1997, p. 94, original emphasis).

This description sounds similar to Firth's (1996) *let it pass principle* and Planken's (2005) *no-man's-land* where participants accommodate differences in language and conventions. Of course, it takes a lot of work to get to this point. *Synergy* captures the creative agency participants must exert in order to work jointly with the other participant to accomplish intersubjective meaning. *Serendipity* involves an attitudinal transformation. To accept deviations as the norm, one must display positive attitudes to variation and be open to unexpectedness. Participants have to be radically other entered. They have to be imaginative and alert to make on-the-spot decisions in relation to the forms and conventions employed by the other. It is clear that communication in multilingual communities involves a different mind-set and practices from the mind-set and practices in monolingual communities.

Implications for theorizing acquisition

How do local people develop proficiency in a form of communication that involves multiple communities and languages in contexts that can generate an unpredictable mix of forms and conventions? How is harmony achieved out of diversity, synchrony out of differences in form and conventions, alignment in discordant and unpredictable situations? Clearly, communication in contact situations is marked by enigmatic paradoxes.

Multilingual communication works because competence does not constitute a form of knowledge, but rather, encompasses interaction strategies. Khubchandani (1997) argued that the ability to communicate is not helped by explicit formulas such as formal grammars and dictionaries of words. For South Asians, "interpretation [is] dependent on the focus of communication 'field' and the degrees of individual's 'sensitivity' towards it" (p. 40). In other words, participants must engage with the social context, and responsively orchestrate the contextual cues for alignment. As we have already seen, meaning in language is not a product that can be prescribed objectively. Communication is intersubjective. Rather than knowledge of form, multilingual competence features an array of interactional strategies that can create meaning out of shifting contexts.

As Khubchandani (1997) explained, "communications in everyday life are based on the *synergic* relationship between the twin criteria: *(a) the reciprocity of language skills* among com-municators (spread over a speech spectrum comprising one or more languages, dialects, styles, etc.); and *(b) the mutuality of focus* (that is, sharing the relevance of the setting, commonly attributed to the attitudes, moods, or feelings of the participants)" (p. 49). What Khubchandani highlighted are skills and strategies. *Mutuality* and *reciprocity* indicate the ways participants align their moves and strategies in relation to their language resources. *Synergy* is the outcome of this alignment, when participants jointly invoke language resources and collaboratively build coherence. Multilingual competence is thus a mode of practice, not resident solely in cognition.

Furthermore, multilingual competence is open to unpredictability. In a sense, each context of communication poses a new and unpredictable mix of languages and conventions. As Khubchandani (1997) explained further, "it is often difficult to determine whether a particular discourse belongs to language A or B" (p. 93). Therefore, it is difficult to transfer the forms and conventions of one context to the next. In this sense, learning is nonlinear. It is for this reason that when SLA is able to theorize language use and acquisition as based on *directed effort* (something predictable, with learners armed with a stock of forms and strategies that can make them competent for successful communication), in the Indian community speech is "an effortless integral activity; discourse centres around the 'event' with the support of ad hoc 'expression' strategies" (p. 40). Local people realize that "the 'tradition inspired' standardized nuances of another language or culture" (p. 93) cannot help them communicate successfully in the mix of languages and dialects they encounter in each situation.

It appears as if all that speakers can do is to find a fit—an alignment—between the linguistic resources they bring and the context of communication. Thus, acquisition is not a cumulative process, but an ability to come up with diverse strategies for speech events that need to be addressed for their own sake. The mention of ad hoc strategies reminds us that competence is not predictability but alertness and impromptu fabrication of forms and conventions to establish alignment in each situation of communication. Thus, acquisition aims towards versatility and agility not mastery and control.[11]

In multilingual competence, grammar receives reduced significance. In contexts where deviation is the norm, multilinguals cannot rely on grammar or form. The linguistics system is a hybrid and variable one, even if it can be described a priori. To reduce further the importance of grammar, Khubchandani (1997) said that the speech process is "regarded as a non-autonomous device, communicating in symphony with other nonlinguistic devices; its full significance can be explicated only from the imperatives of context and communicative tasks" (p. 40). In other words, communication is multimodal. Meaning does not reside in language alone. Linguistic meaning is created in relation to diverse symbol systems (icons, space, color, gesture, or other representational systems) and modalities of communication (writing, sound, visuals, touch, and body), not to speak of diverse languages. If we need a grammar or rules for this mode of communication, it will be a grammar of multimodality—that is, it will contain rules that account for how language meshes with diverse symbol systems, modalities of communication, and ecological resources to create meaning. This orientation would set us on a different path of description from the structuralist tradition that proceeds further inwards into autonomous language to find the rules of linguistic meaning making.

This kind of expanded competence involves not just the rational faculty but other sensory dimensions as well. Kubhchandani (1997) evoked Hindu spiritual concepts to capture this idea: "ancient Indian grammarians talk about the *guna* (power, potency) of language when deliberating on the *dhvani* doctrine in Indian aesthetics. A message can convey meaning not merely through its intent in isolation (as indexed in the dictionary) but also in the context of identity (as when observing verbal protocol in a formal setting) or through its effect on the participants (as manipulated by observers)" (p. 52). It is *difficult* for nonparticipants observing an interaction in a detached manner to come up with a rationalist account for the success of communication. The meaning created by the participants, in relation to the dynamics governing that specific interaction, will not be available to outsiders. Because meaning is intersubjective, we have to accommodate the participants' physiological, biological, psychological, affective, and perceptual dimensions in meaningmaking. Khubchandani (1997) warned that "a seemingly incoherent manifestation in these societies can make sense, coalescing into a persuasive whole, almost in spite of disparate elements" (p. 94). A competence for such communication is therefore not only dependent on rational processes, but also involves other dimensions of human subjectivity, requiring a *multiscalar* mapping of acquisition (see Kramsch, 2002).

Such a competence is always in a state of becoming and, therefore, acquisition is emergent. There is no end point to learning, where one can say a person has mastered all the modalities and dimensions that shape communication in the diverse contact situations. First of all, there is no limit to the diversity, hybridity and variability that can characterize a language. Furthermore, each interaction, with its own set of participants, interests, and dynamics, features new requirements of form and convention. As a result, multilingual competence is treated as always evolving and creative. Khubchandani (1997) explained that the "total verbal repertoire is malleable, responsive to contextual expediencies resulting in uninhibited convergences between speech varieties with the contact pressures of pidginization, hybridization, code-switching and so on" (pp. 40–41). In other words, one's competence is based on the repertoire that grows as the contexts of interaction increase.

In this form of acquisition, therefore, it does not make sense to compare proficiency with baseline data (which would be hard to find as the interactions are so infinitely diverse and unpredictable). We cannot speak of a target to be achieved when the speaker would be perfectly competent for communication at various levels of ability in different contexts. It is also meaningless to speak of interlanguage because competence involves multiple languages with multilateral movement across each of them. A crucial difference here is that SLA accounts for multilingual competence one language at a time, when in reality, this type of competence is more than the sum of the parts, and constitutes a qualitatively different whole.

How does language competence develop out of variable forms, conventions, and modalities of communication? How is competence formed through shifting and unpredictable events? How is order created out of randomness? Can randomness facilitate rational processing and construct patterns of rules and formulae for communication? At the least, we have to think of competence as finding equilibrium between different modalities, hierarchies, and dimensions of communication. Applied linguists have started theorizing such a possibility through chaos-complexity theory (Larsen-Freeman, 2002), activity theory (Lantolf & Thorne, 2006), and phenomenology (Kramsch, 2002). In general, they treat competence as an adaptive response of finding equilibrium, rather than a cognitive mastery of rational control. In these orientations, cognition works in context, in situ. Competence is not applying mental rules to situations, but aligning one's resources with situational demands and shaping the environment to match the language resources one brings.

It is for these reasons that multilingual competence cannot rely solely on schools for its development. Because participants have to adopt communicative strategies relevant to each situation and one cannot predict the mix of languages and participants in each context, learning is more meaningful in actual contexts of language use and practice. It is not surprising that, in multilingual communities, language acquisition takes place most effectively in everyday contexts: "In heterogeneous plural environments, a child acquires language from everyday life situations where speech behavior is guided by implicit pressures based on close group, regional, supra-regional, and out group identities" (Khubchandani, 1997, p. 171). It is intriguing how multilingual acquisition has taken place successfully for centuries outside formal schooling in these communities. The multilingual speaker engages with the shifting and fluid situations in everyday life to learn strategies of negotiation and adaptation for meaning-making. Considerable personal appropriation of forms and conventions takes place as the speaker develops skills and awareness that contribute to his or her repertoire—a learning that is ongoing. In sum, acquisition is social practice, not separable mastery of knowledge, cognition, or form.

This description of multilingual competence and acquisition sounds similar in many respects to LFE competence and acquisition. In both, competence is situational, intersubjective, and pragmatic. In both, acquisition is adaptive, practice-based, and emergent. However, we also see some features of acquisition that emerge more distinctly from non-Western scholarship: Multilingual acquisition is nonlinear (i.e., multilateral), noncumulative (i.e., asynchronous), multimodal, multisensory, and, therefore, multidimensional. LFE scholars have to consider how their participants might be influenced by such characteristics as they continue their research. Yet, it is fascinating how two research traditions that are not in conversation with each other—and that relate to different geographical locations and historical periods—can come up with such similar descriptions of use and acquisition. If the established knowledge in SLA is not informed by the conditions that characterize language practices that are so pervasive among millions of people in the world, it is important to examine the rationale behind knowledge construction in our field.

Reconstructing disciplinary paradigms

It is now well recognized that the dominant constructs in SLA are founded on monolingual norms and practices. We are also beginning to see a realization among mainstream scholars that these constructs are misleading and distorting (see Dorian, 2004, for a discussion). McLaughlin (McLaughlin & Sall, 2001) recounted the belated recognition during her field work in Senegal that a local collaborator, whom she discounted as an informant of a language because he was associated with another language, was in fact a proficient insider with authoritative knowledge. Her unitary assumption of the NS did not let her accept her informant as having native proficiency in more than one language. Similarly, Makoni (2002) described how colonial practices of classifying and labeling languages distorted the hybrid reality of South African languages.

These limitations derive from the dominant assumptions of linguistics, informed by the modernist philosophical movement and intellectual culture in which they developed. To begin with, the field treats language as a thing in itself, as an objective, identifiable product. The field also gives importance to form, treating language as a tightly knit structure, neglecting other processes and practices that always accompany communication. Scholars have traced this development to Saussurean linguistics and the structuralist movement (Lantolf & Thorne, 2006). Other biases follow from this assumption. Khubchandani (1997) pointed out the inordinate emphasis on the temporal life of language, which motivates linguists to chart the linear stages by which imperfect forms develop to a stasis, at which point they become full-fledged forms. Inadequate attention is paid to the way in which various language forms and varieties are embedded in diverse environments, perfectly adequate in their own way for the functions at hand.

Therefore, Kubchandani (1997) called for a spatial orientation. Such an approach would also rectify the lack of attention to the ecological factors of language. We have to understand how language is meshed with other symbolic systems and embedded in specific environments, both shaping and being shaped by them. Mainstream linguistics also fails to give importance to attitudinal, psychological, and perceptual factors that mold the intersubjective processes of communication. This failing is partly due to the primacy of cognition and reason in communication within the mainstream paradigm. There is also a resulting lack of appreciation of the complexity of human communication, which is marked by indeterminacy, multimodality and heterogeneity. Mainstream linguistics prioritizes the homogeneity of community, competence, and language structure, treating it as the basic requirement that facilitates communication. Even when diversity is addressed, it is treated as a variation deriving from a common form or shared norms.

Critical scholars have discussed the motivations in promoting values based on homogeneity, uniformity, and autonomy in linguistic sciences. They have pointed out how there has been an ideological bias in European history toward unifying communities and identities around a single language (Singh, 1998), treating multilingualism as a problem (Ruiz, 1984), and establishing nationstates around the language of a dominant community (May, 2001). These values are informed by the social conditions and ideologies gaining dominance in Europe since the rise of the nationstate, the 17th-century enlightenment, and the French Revolution (Dorian, 2004; May, 2001). As Dorian (2004) reminded us, "monolingualism, now usually considered the unmarked condition by members of the dominant linguistic group in modern nation-states, was in all likelihood less prevalent before the rise of the nation-state gave special sanction to it" (p. 438). Pratt (1987) interpreted the imposition of homogeneity and uniformity in language and speech community as signifying the construction of *linguistic utopias* that serve partisan interests. Constructs based on monolingualism and homogeneity are well suited to communities that desire purity, exclusivity and domination. Acknowledging the heterogeneity of language and communication would force us to develop more democratic and egalitarian models of community and communication. Enabled by such historical processes as colonization and modernity linguistics has reproduced its underlying enlightenment values elsewhere and hindered the development of local language practices and knowledge.[12]

However, in the context of postmodern globalization, as all communities are becoming increasingly multilingual with the transnational flow of people, ideas, and things, scholars are beginning to question the dominant constructs in the field.[13] Even Western communities are beginning to acknowledge the diversity, hybridity and fluidity at the heart of language and identity. The struggle now is to find new metaphors and constructs that would capture multilingual communication. How do we practice a linguistics that treats human agency, diversity, indeterminacy, and multimodality as the norm? Because the constructs of modern linguistics are influenced by the modernist philosophical assumptions, some scholars are exploring alternate philosophical traditions to conceptualize these emerging realizations. Phenomenology (Kramsch, 2002), ecological models (Hornberger, 2003), chaos-complexity theory (Larsen-Freeman, 2002), sociocognitive theory (Atkinson et al., 2007), and Vygotskyan sociocultural theory (Lantolf & Thorne, 2006) are such attempts.

Scholars from postcolonial and non-Western communities are also beginning to represent their communicative practices in scholarly literature from the evidence they still find about them in their communities. This articulation is of course influenced by a worldview and culture that differ from modernity. As we saw in the previous section, Khubchandani (1997) resorted to Indian spirituality and philosophy to represent what he perceives as indigenous language practices. He uses metaphors like rainbow, symbiosis, osmosis, synergy, and serendipity to describe a multilingual reality that lacks a suitable language in mainstream linguistics. Though these less known publications of periphery scholars are full of insight, they still lack elaborate theorization to produce sophisticated alternative models.

There are other difficulties in working from untheorized local knowledge. One has to break the dominant hermeneutic molds offered by modernism in order to interpret this knowledge. Modernism has denigrated local knowledge, and has interpreted it negatively. Furthermore, local knowledge is not pure or whole, as dominant knowledge systems have appropriated it for their own interests and purposes. At any rate, we must not glorify non-Western traditions. The local can contain chauvinistic tendencies, especially because the onslaught of modernity has been forcing the local to retreat ever further into more recalcitrant positions, in a desperate attempt to maintain its independence. Also, although there are certain egalitarian practices at one level, inequalities in terms of caste, clan, and gender have to be negotiated at other levels of communication.[14]

My effort in this article is not to pit the views of non-Western scholars against emerging models in the West. My proposal is that the insights from non-Western communities should inform the current efforts for alternate theory building in our field. I provide an outline here of how a practice-based model would accommodate the realizations of LFE and multilingual competence. I see this orientation as accommodating the insights of the other model building activities referred to earlier, although going radically beyond the cognition-society or form-pragmatics, dichotomy to integrate them at the level of practice. Though this orientation is informed by the practices of everyday language use and acquisition in non-Western communities, it is also being theorized in the academy by models such as *communities of practice* (Lave & Wenger, 1991; Wenger, 1998) and *contact zones* (Pratt, 1991).[15]

This practice-based model is characterized by the following beliefs and assumptions:

1. What brings people together in communities is not what they share—language, discourse, or values—but *interests* to be accomplished.
2. These mutual interests would permit individuals to move in and out of multiple communities to accomplish their goals, without considering prior traits that are innate or that are exclusively shared with others.
3. This view would redefine communities as lacking boundedness and a center; they are, rather, contact zones where people from diverse backgrounds meet (Pratt, 1991).
4. What enables them to work together on their interests are negotiation practices they bring to various tasks (not common language, discourse, or values).
5. What enables them to develop expertise in the workings of each community is also practice—that is, engaging actively in purposive activities of that community (not accumulating knowledge and information theoretically without involvement), and acquiring a repertoire of strategies (not information, rules, or cognitive schemata).
6. Identities would then be based on affiliation and expertise rather than those ascribed by birth, family, race, or blood (Rampton, 1990).
7. Though language and discourse enable communication, they are shaped by the practice of diverse situations and participants. Form is reconstructed ceaselessly to suit the interests of the participants, in the manner of emergent grammar (Hopper, 1987).

The focus on practice does not mean that there is not a place for classroom learning. Pedagogy can be refashioned to accommodate the modes of communication and acquisition seen outside the classroom (see Canagarajah, 2005a, for a more elaborate pedagogical discussion). Rather than focusing on a single language or dialect as the target of learning, teachers have to develop in students a readiness to engage with a repertoire of codes in transnational contact situations. Although enabling students to join a new speech community was the objective of traditional pedagogy, we now have to train students to shuttle between communities by negotiating the relevant codes. To this end, we have to focus more on communicative strategies, rather than on forms of communication. Students would develop language awareness (to cope with the multiple languages and emergent grammars of contact situations), rather than focusing only on mastering the grammar rules of a single variety. In a context of plural forms and conventions, it is important for students to be sensitive to the relativity of norms. Therefore, students have to understand communication as performative, not just constitutive. That is, going beyond the notion of just constructing prefabricated meanings through words, they will consider shaping meaning in actual interactions and even reconstructing the rules and conventions to represent their interests, values, and identities. In other words, it is not what we know as much as the versatility with which we can do things with language that defines proficiency. Pedagogical movements such as learner strategy training and language awareness go some way toward facilitating such instructional strategies.

These changing pedagogical priorities suggest that assessment too must go through significant changes to evaluate one's ability to negotiate the complex communicative needs of multilingual and contact situations. As we realize that norms are heterogeneous, variable, changing, and, therefore, interactively established in each context, we have to move away from a reliance on discrete-item tests on formal grammatical competence and develop instruments that are more sensitive to performance and pragmatics. Assessment would focus on one's strategies of negotiation, situated performance, communicative repertoire, and language awareness. To this end, we must develop new instruments with imagination and creativity, as I have illustrated it elsewhere (Canagarajah, 2006c).

Conclusion

Although Firth and Wagner (1997) argued for rectifying the imbalance between the dichotomies that characterize SLA, we are now moving toward more radical options of reframing the constructs. The previously ignored or suppressed constructs are now becoming the basis for a new integration or synthesis. Language acquisition is based on performance strategies, purposive uses of the language, and interpersonal negotiations in fluid communicative contexts. The previously dominant constructs such as form, cognition, and the individual are not eradicated; they get redefined to adopt hybrid, variable, situational, and processual characteristics they did not have before. They are treated in a more socially embedded, interactionally open, and ecologically situated manner. The aim of this article is to integrate the dichotomies on the basis of practice, not to reverse the status of competing constructs. Thus, recent research on LFE communication and non-Western language practices enables us to move the questions raised by Firth and Wagner further along to another level.

Much against the position of some in the original debate that issues of acquisition are separate from broader issues of language communication (see Gass, 1998; Kasper, 1997; Long, 1997), we find that our definitions of language, communication, and communities shape our understanding of acquisition. There are both ideological and methodological implications behind the reexamination of SLA. To return to Haugen (1972), it is true that we work with simple and convenient models of language and acquisition at early stages of knowledge formation. However, models are also *interested*. That is, they are informed by specific social conditions and their dominant ideologies, and reflect the ends desired by dominant communities. As historical conditions change, and when we encounter new realities, brought to light partly by the critique of existing models, we must construct new paradigms informed by our new knowledge. It is time to revise, reformulate, and refine our models of acquisition for the more egalitarian context of transnational relations and multilingual communication.

Notes

1   Though I relate this discussion to the field of SLA, the article argues that the acquisition I have in mind goes beyond the first-second language distinction. Not only is language acquisition always multilingual, it also reveals processes that are similar for languages learnt earlier or later.

2   Other scholars (e.g., House, 2003; Seidlhofer, 2004) use the acronym ELF (English as a lingua franca). I have retained their acronym when I quote these scholars.

3   Perhaps Rampton (1997), among all the discussants, anticipated this development best as he outlined how globalization and diaspora life were transforming communication. Ironically, though Firth (1996) was one of the earliest researchers to initiate a study of LFE, he did not couch his argument on SLA in terms of this inquiry. In hindsight, it is possible to guess that it is Firth's LFE research that enabled Firth and Wagner (1997) to pose their questions with such force and foresight.

4   Note that there are lingua franca languages other than English. See McGroarty (2006) for a state of the art on diverse languages. The argument made in this article for the implications of LFE for language acquisition may apply to those lingua franca languages as well.

5   Though the construct of NS has been contested, I retain this term here for purposes of comparison with *multilingual speakers*. I am aware that many multilingual speakers will claim NS status in English.

6   House (2003) argued that LFE is indeed a full-fledged language, not a pidgin variety or register for special purposes: "ELF is neither a language for specific purposes nor a pidgin, because it is not a restricted code, but a language showing full linguistic and functional range" (p. 557). Note also that there are different orientations to LFE. Some scholars are on the quest to define LFE according to an identifiable grammatical and phonological system (see Jenkins, 2006; Seidlhofer, 2004)—see note 7. This article is informed by the alternate school that focuses on the pragmatic features that enable LFE communication (see House, 2003; Meierkord, 2004).

7   There is an attempt by some LFE scholars to identify the common aspects of phonological and grammatical form in LFE (see Jenkins, 2006; Seidlhofer, 2004) for pedagogical purposes. However, it is debated as to whether these items constitute the finite and invariable rules of LFE that might constitute a system or whether they are simply a list of typical and exemplary Features. From this perspective, it is also premature to say if LFE is teachable like other languages in a product-oriented and formalistic manner.

8   We have to distinguish the use of English in contact situations by multilinguals from interactions of second language speakers of English with speakers of a traditional national variety in a context where the frame of reference is a specific community (i.e., interacting with a speaker of American English in the United States; interacting with a speaker of Indian English in India). It is possible that the host community will use its norms to judge the effectiveness of speech, but, even here, multilinguals will tend to negotiate more equally (i.e., Indians would step out of their Indian English to negotiate the outsider's variety).

9   For a discussion of these competencies and their place in lingua franca communication, see Canagarajah (2006c).

10 The fact that I base this description on scholarship from non-Western scholars and communities does not imply that such features of multilingual communication have not existed in contexts of language contact in the West. It is simply that mainstream scholars have not adequately focused on them. Non-Western scholarship helps us discover the multilingual practices in the West.

11 For a theorization of communicative success as "seizing the moment and negotiating paradoxes," see Kramsch (2002, p. 25).

12 Postcolonial scholars see even more sinister motives in the way these constructs helped Europe establish its dominance over the communities it colonized in the 19th century. They point out that constructs like linguistic identity and speech community were put to use in lands like India to categorize people for purposes of taxation, administrative convenience, and political control (Mohan, 1992). In a very subtle way, these constructs have begun to shape social reality there with damaging results. Khubchandani (1997) observed "until as recently as four or five decades ago, one's language group was not generally considered as a very important criterion for sharply distinguishing oneself from others.. ... Following Independence, language consciousness has grown, and loyalties based on language-identity have acquired political salience" (p. 92). We can imagine how exclusive categories of identification can lead to ethnic and linguistic sectarianism. Furthermore, people have started perceiving themselves according to singular identities, lost their heterogeneity, and initiated conflicts and rivalries with members of what they perceive as alien language communities.

13 For a distinction between the social processes of modern and postmodern globalization, see Hall (1997) and Canagarajah (2005b).

14 For a detailed discussion of the difficulties in rediscovering local knowledge of non-Western communities in our profession, see Canagarajah (2005b).

15 House (2003) also believed that a model based on communities of practice would do justice to the realizations of LFE communication.

References

Anderson, B. (1984). *Imagined communities: Reflections on the origins and spread of nationalism*. London: Verso.

Atkinson, D., Churchill, E., Nishino, T., & Okada, H. (2007). Alignment and interaction in a sociocognitive approach in second language acquisition. *Modern Language Journal*, *91*, 169–188.

Block, D. (2003). *The social turn in second language acquisition*. Washington, DC: Georgetown University Press.

Brutt-Griffler, J. (2002). *World English: A study of its development*. Clevedon: Multilingual Matters.

Canagarajah, A. S. (1999). *Resisting linguistic imperialism in English teaching*. Oxford: Oxford University Press.

Canagarajah, A. S. (2005a). Introduction. In A. S. Canagarajah (Ed.), *Reclaiming the local in language policy and practice* (pp. xiii–xxx). Mahwah, NJ: Lawrence Erlbaum.

Canagarajah, A. S. (2005b). Reconstructing local knowledge, reconfiguring language studies. In A. S. Canagarajah (Ed.), *Reclaiming the local in language policy and practice* (pp. 3–24). Mahwah, NJ: Lawrence Erlbaum.

Canagarajah, A. S. (2006a). Toward a writing pedagogy of shuttling between languages: Learning from multilingual writers. *College English*, *68*, 589–604.

Canagarajah, A. S. (2006b). Negotiating the local in English as a lingua franca. *Annual Review of Applied Linguistics*, *26*, 197–218.

Canagarajah, A. S. (2006c). Changing communicative needs, revised assessment objectives: Testing English as an international language. *Language Assessment Quarterly*, *3*, 229–242.

Cook, V. (1999). Going beyond the native speaker in language teaching. *TESOL Quarterly*, *33*, 185–209.

de Souza, L. M. (2002). A case among cases, a world among worlds: The ecology of writing among the Kashinawa in Brazil. *Journal of Language, Identity, and Education*, *1*, 261–278.

Dorian, N. (2004). Minority and endangered languages. In T K. Bhatia & W. C. Ritchie (Eds.), *The handbook of bilingualism* (pp. 437–459). Oxford: Blackwell.

Firth, A. (1996). The discursive accomplishment of normality. On "lingua franca" English and conversation analysis. *Journal of Pragmatics*, *26*, 237–259.

Firth, A., & Wagner, J. (1997). On discourse, communication, and (some) fundamental concepts in SLA research. *Modern Language Journal*, *81*, 285–300.

Gass, S. (1998). Apples and oranges: Or, why apples are not orange and don't need to be. *Modern Language Journal*, *82*, 83–90.

Giles, H. (Ed). (1984). The dynamics of speech accommodation [Special Issue]. *International Journal of the Sociology of Language*, *46*.

Graddol, D. (1999). The decline of the native speaker. *AILA Review*, *13*, 57–68.

Gramkow Anderson, K. (1993). *Lingua franca discourse: An investigation of the use of English in an international business context*. Unpublished master's thesis, Aalborg University, Aalborg, Denmark.

Hall, S. (1997). The local and the global: Globalization and ethnicity. In A. D. King (Ed.), *Culture, globalization, and the world system* (pp. 19–40). Minneapolis: University of Minnesota Press.

Haugen, E. (1972). *The ecology of language*. In A. Dil (Ed). Stanford, CA: Stanford University Press.

Higgins, C. (2003). "Ownership" of English in the outer circle: An alternative to the NS/NNS dichotomy. *TESOL Quarterly*, *34*, 615–644.

Hopper, P. (1987). Emergent grammar. *Berkeley Linguistics Society*, *13*, 139–157.

Hornberger, N. H. (Ed.). (2003). *Continua of biliteracy: An ecological framework for educational policy, research, and practice*. Clevedon, UK: Multilingual Matters.

House, J. (2003). English as a lingua franca: A threat to multilingualism? *Journal of Sociolinguistics*, *7*, 556–578.

Jenkins, J. (2006). Current perspectives on teaching World Englishes and English as a lingua franca. *TESOL Quarterly*, *40*, 157–181.

Kasper, G. (1997). A stands for acquisition. *Modern Language Journal*, *81*, 307–312.

Khubchandani, L. M. (1997). *Revisualizing boundaries: A plurilingual ethos*. New Delhi, India: Sage.

Kramsch, C. (2002). Introduction: How can we tell the dancer from the dance? In C. Kramsch (Ed.), *Language acquisition and language socialization: Ecological perspectives* (pp. 1–30). London: Continuum.

Lantolf, J. P., & Thorne, S. F. (2006). *Sociocultural theory and the sociogenesis of second language development*. New York: Oxford University Press.

Larsen-Freeman, D. (2002). Language acquisition and language use from a chaos/complexity theory perspective. In C. Kramsch (Ed.), *Language acquisition and language socialization: Ecological perspectives* (pp. 33–46). London: Continuum.

Lave, J., & Wenger, E. (1991). *Situated learning: Legitimate peripheral participation*. Cambridge: Cambridge University Press.

Long, M. H. (1997). Construct validity in SLA research. *Modern Language Journal, 81*, 318–323.

Makoni, S. (2002). From misinvention to disinvention: An approach to multilingualism. In C. Smitherman, A. Spear, & A. Ball (Eds.), *Black linguistics: Language, society and politics in Africa and the Americas* (pp. 132–153). London: Routledge.

May, S. (2001). *Language and minority rights: Ethnicity, nationalism, and the politics of language.* London: Longman.

McLaughlin, E., & Sall, T. S. (2001). The give and take of fieldwork: Noun classes and other concerns in Fatick, Senegal. In P. A. Newman & M. Ratiff (Eds.), *Linguistic fieldwork* (pp. 189–210). Cambridge: Cambridge University Press.

McGroarty, M. (Ed.). (2006). Lingua franca languages [Special Issue]. *Annual Review of Applied Linguistics, 26.*

Meierkord, C. (2004). Syntactic variation in interactions across international Englishes. *English World-Wide, 25*, 109–132.

Mohan, K. (1992). Constructing religion and caste: Manipulating identities. *Social Science Research Journal, 1*, 1–12.

Norton, B. (2000). *Identity and language learning: Gender, ethnicity, and educational change.* Harlow, UK: Pearson.

Planken, B. (2005). Managing rapport in lingua franca sales negotiations: A comparison of professional and aspiring negotiators. *English for Specific Purposes, 24*, 381–400.

Pratt, M. L. (1987). Linguistic utopias. In N. Fabb, D. Attridge, A. Durant, & C. MacCabe (Eds.), *The linguistics of writing: Arguments between language and literature* (pp. 48–66). Manchester, UK: Manchester University Press.

Pratt, M. L. (1991). Arts of the contact zone. *Profession, 91*, 33–40.

Rampton, B. (1990). Displacing the Native Speaker: Expertise, affiliation, and inheritance. *ELT Journal, 44*, 97–101.

Rampton, B. (1997). Second language research in late modernity: A response to Firth and Wagner. *Modern Language Journal, 81*, 329–333.

Ruiz, R. (1984). Orientations to language planning. *NABE Journal, 8*, 15–34.

Sampson, H., & Zhao, M. (2003). Multilingual crews: Communication and the operation of ships. *World Englishes, 22*, 31–43.

Seidlhofer, B. (2004). Research perspectives on teaching English as a lingua franca. *Annual Review of Applied Linguistics, 24*, 209–239.

Singh, R. (Ed.). (1998). *The native speaker: Multilingual perspectives.* New Delhi, India: Sage.

Wenger, E. (1998). *Communities of practice: Learning, meaning, and identity.* Cambridge: Cambridge University Press.

Zuengler, J., & Miller, E. R. (2006). Cognitive and sociocultural perspectives: Two parallel SLA worlds? *TESOL Quarterly, 40*, 35–58.

Chapter 10

KEN HYLAND

AUTHORITY AND INVISIBILITY
Authorial identity in academic writing (2002)

1 Introduction

A **CENTRAL ELEMENT** of pragmatic competence is the ability of writers to construct a credible representation of themselves and their work, aligning themselves with the socially shaped identities of their communities. For those new to a particular social context this can pose a considerable challenge as they are likely to find that the discourses and practices of their disciplines support identities very different from those they bring with them (Barton and Hamilton, 1998; Bartholomae, 1986). These problems often place students at a rhetorical and interpersonal disadvantage, preventing them from communicating appropriate integrity and commitments, and undermining their relationship to readers. This socially denned rhetorical identity is accomplished through a range of rhetorical and interactive features, but most visibly in the use of first person pronouns and possessive determiners.

Surprisingly, given the conflicting advice and strong feelings it seems to generate, the role of first person has received relatively little empirical study. While it is clear that the conventions of personality are rhetorically constrained in academic writing, these constraints are uncertain, and the extent to which one can reasonably explicitly intrude into one's discourse, or assert one's personal involvement, remains a dilemma for novices and experienced writers alike. It is particularly problematic for students because they frequently feel positioned by the dominant disciplinary and institutional discourses they encounter in university studies, and the problem can be seriously compounded for NNSs whose rhetorical identities may be shaped by very different traditions of literacy.

In this paper, I explore the notion of writer identity as it is expressed through self-reference in the writing of L2 undergraduates at a Hong Kong university. The study examines the frequency and role of first person pronouns *I*, *we*, *me* and *us*, and the determiners *my* and *our* in 64 final year undergraduate reports, draws on comparisons with a large corpus of journal articles, and supplements these with interview data from students and their supervisors. My purpose is to examine how these students use and perceive self-reference and to explore possible explanations for their different communicative practices. I begin with a brief outline of the idea of discoursal identity (Ivanič, 1998) and the difficulties it can present for students, then go on to discuss first person uses in student writing.

2 Academic literacy and authorial identity

Academic writing, like all forms of communication, is an act of identity: it not only conveys disciplinary 'content' but also carries a representation of the writer. The notion of identity has only surfaced in writing research relatively recently, but it is increasingly seen as less a phenomenon of private experience than a desire for affiliation and recognition (Norton, 1997). This view emphasises that identity should be understood in terms of our networks of social relationships which bestow approval. They are constructed from the culturally available discourses which we draw on to communicate (Shotter and Gergen, 1989) and which provide us with ways of interpreting the world and representing ourselves that are tied to the practices and structures of social communities. In adopting the practices and discourses of a community we come, over time, to adopt its perspectives and interpretations, seeing the world in the same ways and taking on an identity as a member of that community. In sum, our discoursal choices align us with certain values and beliefs that support particular identities.

In other words, we do not simply report findings or express ideas in some neutral, context-free way, we employ the rhetorical resources accepted for the purpose of sharing meanings in a particular genre and social community. Writers have to select their words so that readers are drawn in, influenced and persuaded. Our use of these resources, and the choices we make from the alternatives they offer, signal who we are. The ways that writers represent themselves, and find themselves represented, by their rhetorical choices has been extensively discussed by Ivanič (Ivanič, 1998; Ivanič and Weldon, 1999) who argues that writers' identities are constructed in the 'possibilities for self-hood' available in the sociocultural contexts of writing. For Ivanič there are three aspects of identity interacting in writing which she calls the *'autobiographical self'*, influenced by the writer's life-history, the *'discoursal self'*, the image or 'voice' the writer projects in a text, and the *'authorial self'*, manifested in the extent to which a writer intrudes into a text and claims responsibility for its content. It is this third element of identity which I am concerned with in this paper, exploring the degree of authoritativeness writers are prepared to invest in their texts to personally get behind their statements.

This is most typically accomplished through a range of rhetorical and linguistic resources, variously called appraisal (Martin, 2000), evaluation (Hunston and Thompson, 2000), and stance (Hyland, 1999), which allow writers to take up positions and express judgments. Such strategies convey a range of cognitive and affective meanings and in so doing explicitly announce the writer and negotiate a rhetorical identity. One of the most obvious and important ways writers can represent themselves to readers however is to explicitly affirm their role in the discourse through first person pronouns (Hyland, 2001; Kuo, 1999; Tang and John, 1999). These writers point to the use of *I* as critical to meaning and credibility, helping to establish the commitment of writers to their words and setting up a relationship with their readers.

In addition to announcing the writer in the text, pronouns typically occur in thematic position in the clause. While the important focus of academic writing tends to be the events or concepts under discussion in the rheme, the choice of first position is very significant. The way a writer begins a clause not only foregrounds important information, firmly identifying the writer as the source of the associated statement, but also helps the writer control the social interaction in the text (e.g. Gosden, 1993). Consider the impact of such choices in these examples from single authors in my research article corpus:

(1) *I* agree with that, although *I* differ in the details as to the analysis of. . .

(Applied Linguistics)

I will show that a convincing reply is available to the minimalist.

(Philosophy)

We shall prove, however, that this is not the case.

(Physics)

The use of first person allows these writers to emphasise, and to seek agreement for, their own contributions. It leaves readers in no doubt where they stand and how their statements should be interpreted. First person then, is a powerful means by which writers express an identity by asserting their claim to speak as an authority, and this is a key element of successful academic writing.

3 Academic discourses and student positioning

It is important to recognise that while identities may be socially constructed through language, writers are not free to simply adopt any identities they choose. When we employ the discourses of a community, there is strong pressure to take on the identity of a member of that community. The term 'positioning' has been used to describe the process by which identities are produced by socially available discourses (Davies and Harré, 1990; Fairclough, 1995). This does not suggest however that people simply slot into pre-ordained social identities with ready-made sets of expected behaviours. There is always room for individual negotiation and manoeuvre as a result of the values and beliefs individuals bring with them from their home cultures. Discourses are not self-contained, monolithic entities which interlock snugly without overlap. Each of us is constantly influenced by a multitude of discourses which are situated in the groups in which we participate and which mediate our involvement in any one of them. Most importantly, much of our sense of who we are originates in our home cultures. The fact that we bring this sense of self to our acts of writing in the university can create an acute sense of dislocation and uncertainty.

Academic writing is a major site in which social positionings are constructed. The acquisition of disciplinary knowledge involves an encounter with a new and dominant literacy, even for L1 learners, and although undergraduates are not expected to enter a disciplinary community, they are assessed on their ability to engage in its specialised discourses (Belcher and Braine, 1995). Students have to develop the 'peculiar ways of knowing, selecting, evaluating, reporting, con-cluding and arguing that define the discourse of the community' (Bartholomae, 1986: 4). They must speak with authority, and to do this they must use another's voice and another's code, weakening their affiliations to their home culture and discourses to adopt the values and language of their disciplinary ones (Johns, 1997: 64). As a result, students often find their own experiences to be devalued and their literacy practices to be marginalised and regarded as failed attempts to approximate these dominant forms (e.g. Ivanič, 1998).

But while L1 undergraduates often experience a gulf between the identities they must adopt to participate in academic cultures and those of their home cultures, this can pose a much greater challenge for second language students whose identities as learners and writers are often embedded in very different epistemologies. The academy's emphasis on analysis and inter-pretation means that students must position themselves in relation to the material they discuss, finding a way to express their own contentions and arguments (Cadman, 1997). Writers are required to establish a stance towards their propositions, to get behind their words and stake out a position. Yet such an individualistic identity is problematic for students from cultures where the self is more collectively constructed (Ramanathan and Atkinson, 1999), representing an additional factor in acquiring an appropriate academic identity.

A further problem is that conventions of identity are notoriously uncertain. On one hand, impersonality is seen as a defining feature of expository writing as it embodies the positivist assumption that academic research is purely empirical and objective. Geertz (1988) calls this 'author-evacuated' prose, and many textbooks and style guides advise students to avoid personal intervention:

> To the scientist it is unimportant who observed the chemical reaction: only the observation itself is vital. Thus the active voice sentence is inappropriate. In this situation, passive voice and the omission of the agent of action are justified.
>
> (Gong and Dragga, 1995)

> Write your paper with a third person voice that avoids 'I believe' or 'It is my opinion'.
>
> (Lester, 1993: 144)

> The total paper is considered to be the work of the writer. You don't have to say 'I think' or 'My opinion is' in the paper. (. . .) Traditional formal writing does not use I or we in the body of the paper.
>
> (Spencer and Arbon, 1996: 26)

> In general, academic writing aims at being 'objective' in its expression of ideas, and thus tries to avoid specific reference to personal opinions. Your academic writing should imitate this style by eliminating first person pronouns . . . as far as possible.
>
> (Arnaudet and Barrett, 1984: 73)

However, other textbooks encourage writers to make their own voice clear through the first person:

> I herewith ask all young scientists to renounce the false modesty of previous generations of scientists. Do not be afraid to name the agent of the action in a sentence, even when it is 'I' or 'we'.
>
> (Day 1994: 166)

> . . . most of our recommendations are designed to help you maintain a scholarly and objective tone in your writing. This does not mean (and we have not said) that you should never use I or we in your writing. The use of I or we does not make a piece of writing informal.
>
> (Swales and Feak, 1994: 20).

> . . . the scientific attitude is not achieved by either the use or the avoidance of a particular pronoun. Rather, it is achieved through the qualities mentioned earlier: honesty, care in handling facts, dignity, and restraint in manner.
>
> (Mills and Water, 1986: 32–33)

To summarise, the absence of clear direction in their pedagogic texts, the positioning of institutionally authoritative discourses, and the preferred cultural practices for authorial concealment, mean that self-mention can be a considerable problem for L2 undergraduate writers. In this paper I will look at how both experts and L2 novices use first person and the impact this has on authorial identity.

4 Procedures and data

The study is based on an analysis of a corpus of 64 project reports (PR) written by final year Hong Kong undergraduates and interviews with students and their supervisors in eight fields selected to both represent a broad cross-section of academic practice and to facilitate my access to informants.

The final year report is the product of a directed research project typically spanning an entire year with credit for two courses. Students are assisted by a supervisor who, through regular individual consultations, approves their proposal, guides their research, and monitors their progress. The purposes of the projects are to enable students to apply theories and methods learned in their courses and demonstrate ability to effectively review literature, conduct research, analyse results and present findings. Reports are typically between 8000 and 13,000 words long and follow guidelines which reflect the research article formats of the particular discipline. They are assessed by two examiners in terms of how well students meet the objectives of the project and on the quality of the written work. This, then, is a high stakes genre for students and is by far the most substantial and sustained piece of writing that they will do in their undergraduate careers.

Reports were collected from biology (Bio), mechanical engineering (ME), information systems (IS), business studies (Bus), TESL, economics (Econ), public administration (PA), and social sciences (SS). These reports were scanned to produce an electronic corpus of 630,000 words after excluding appendices, reference lists, and text associated with tables. This corpus was then searched for the first person uses *I, me, my, we, us,* and *our,* using *WordPilot 2000,* a commercially available concordance programme. All cases were examined in context to ensure they were exclusive first person uses and to determine their pragmatic function. Several sweeps of the corpus suggested a broad categorisation scheme and detailed analysis helped to both validate these categories and allowed each instance to be classified as performing a particular function. A sample analysed by a colleague achieved an inter-rater agreement of 91%.

The results were then examined with reference to a large corpus of published research articles (RA) to explore areas of non-native like behaviour. The purpose of this exercise was not to evaluate learner performance or to suggest a deficit orientation to what L2 writers can achieve. Novice and professional writers are likely to differ considerably in their knowledge and understandings of appropriate academic conventions and practices, making direct comparisons unhelpful. The study of parallel corpora, however, can provide information about what different groups of language users actually *do.* They are useful because of what they tell us of different writers' linguistic and interactive schemata, in this case helping to throw light on student perceptions of academic conventions and how they seek to accommodate their own cultural practices. So, not only are the patterns of use in the 'expert' texts likely to contribute to supervisors' understandings of appropriacy and conventions of good disciplinary writing, they also provide the background by which we can understand learner practices.

The professional corpus comprised 240 research articles from ten leading journals in each of eight related disciplines, totalling 1.3 million words. A corpus twice as large as the student database was collected in order to strengthen observations about expert academic practices more generally, as opposed to those about a specific student population. The disciplines were selected to relate to the student fields as closely as possible and represented the main fields from which students were directed for their reading. The journals themselves were familiar to faculty and students alike and were regularly recommended to students in reading lists and by project supervisors. The journals were from biology (Bio) and physics (Phy) (sciences), mechanical (ME) and electronic engineering (EE) (engineering), applied linguistics (AL) (TESL), business studies

Table 10.1 Text corpora used in the study

Student reports	Texts	Words	Research articles	Texts	Words
Biology	8	53,200	Biology	30	143,500
Mechanical Eng.	8	101,700	Mechanical Eng.	30	114,700
Information Systems	8	45,500	Electronic Eng.	30	107,700
Business Studies	8	87,500	Marketing	30	214,900
Public and Social	8	134,600	Sociology	30	224,500
Administration			Philosophy	30	209,000
Social Studies	8	88,300	Applied Linguistics	30	211,400
TESL	8	78,100	Physics	30	97,300
Economics	8	39,400			
Overall	64	630,100		240	1,323,000

(Bus) (management and economics), and philosophy (Phil) and sociology (Soc) (public administration and social studies). The corpora are summarised in Table 10.1.

In addition to the text analyses, I interviewed one supervisor from each field (all English L1) and organised small focus groups of student writers (all Cantonese L1). Participants were asked to provide information about their own writing and their impressions of disciplinary practices. I used a semi-structured format consisting of a series of open-ended interview prompts. These began with detailed examinations of text extracts from subjects' and others' writing and included statements such as 'why do you think the writer uses *I* here?', 'what alternatives could she have used?', 'what impression do you get of the writer?', and so on. The aim here was to explore what participants believed writers had tried to achieve with specific choices. These discourse-based interviews then moved to more general observations of pronoun use: 'Do you use *I* in your writing?', 'Why/Why not?', 'Is it common in Chinese academic texts?', etc. In short, the prompts sought to elicit participants' understandings of the meanings and effectiveness of first person use, and to uncover their own discoursal practices.

4.1 Frequency of authorial self-mention

The results in Table 10.2 show that self-referential pronouns and determiners occurred about once every thousand words, or roughly 10 per student report. *I* was the most common author reference and first person singular pronouns comprised 60% of the total. Interestingly, plural forms were quite common in single-authored reports, and this was not entirely explained by the collaborative research on which these theses were often based.

The disciplinary variations only broadly correspond to preferences for self-reference in published texts (Hyland, 2001). Experienced writers select rhetorical options for projecting authority and engaging with readers that reflect the epistemological assumptions and social practices of their fields, with more explicit authorial involvement in the soft disciplines. Because the criteria of acceptability for interpretation are less clear-cut and variables less precisely measurable than in the hard fields, the writer's personal presence and authority is an important rhetorical resource for gaining approval for one's work (Hyland, 2000). This data however suggests that expert practices had little impact on student writing. This is perhaps because while students may have acquired some implicit understanding of disciplinary conventions through their reading, these variations are rarely spelt out for them.

Table 10.2 Frequency of author pronouns and determiners in student reports (per 10,000 words)

Discipline	Author	Total	I	Me	My	We	Us	Our
Information Systems	Individual	15.6	5.1	1.5	2.6	4.2	0.4	2.0
Economics	Individual	12.9	7.1	0.0	0.8	3.1	0.0	2.0
Business Studies	Multiple	12.2	0.2	0.1	0.1	7.7	0.5	3.6
Public and Social Administration	Individual	10.9	7.1	1.1	2.3	0.3	0.0	0.1
Social Sciences	Individual	8.9	2.5	1.0	2.3	1.5	0.3	1.4
TESL	Individual	8.3	3.7	1.0	2.6	0.5	0.0	0.5
Mechanical Eng.	Individual	8.6	2.5	0.1	1.9	2.9	0.4	0.9
Biology	Multiple	5.3	1.5	0.4	0.0	2.4	0.2	0.7
Overall		10.1	3.7	0.7	1.7	2.6	0.2	1.3

Table 10.3 Personal reference in research articles and student reports (per 10,000 words)

Field reference	Totals		Singular reference		Plural	
	Articles	Reports	Articles	Reports	Articles	Reports
Science and Engineering	32.7	9.4	0.1	4.9	30.6	4.5
Business and Professional	46.9	10.5	22.2	6.7	24.7	3.8
Overall	41.2	10.1	14.4	6.1	26.8	4.1

Turning to overall frequencies, comparison between the student and published texts shows that the professional writers were *four times* more likely to explicitly intervene with the first person, with figures higher for the soft disciplines than the hard ones. It is interesting to note that while we might intuitively predict agent-fronted active sentences to be easier to construct for L2 speakers, this imbalance suggests a considerable underuse of the author pronouns that facilitate this pattern. Table 10.3 gives an impression of this comparison by grouping the two genres by broad disciplinary foci.

4.2 *Discourse functions of authorial reference*

While frequency of occurrence is important in determining the scale of underuse, we can learn a lot more about authorial identity by exploring the rhetorical functions the first person is used to perform. The points at which writers choose to make themselves visible in their texts through self-reference have considerable rhetorical importance, indicating the kinds of commitments writers are willing to make and the information they are prepared to give about their beliefs as individuals. A typology of authorial roles implied in the use of first person pronouns has also been suggested by Tang and John (1999). While my categorisation recognises a similar cline of authority in the expression of authorial presence, it differs from theirs in excluding all generic

Table 10.4 Discourse functions of self-mention in student reports (%)

Function	Total		Bio	ME	IS	Econ	Bus	TESL	SS	PSA
	Raw	*%*								
Stating a goal/purpose	228	35	36	21	36	32	43	37	38	35
Explaining a procedure	199	31	32	29	37	31	27	34	32	32
Stating results/claims	103	16	29	19	9	26	13	14	13	18
Expressing self-benefits	58	9	11	8	18	0	11	3	11	8
Elaborating an argument	49	8	7	8	4	0	12	11	9	7
Totals	637									
Percentage		100	100	100	100	100	100	100	100	100

and inclusive uses of the first person and in focusing on the clear discoursal functions which accompany devices of self-reference. This has the advantages of more clearly highlighting only cases of self-mention and in avoiding the kinds of discoursal overlaps which occur when employing metaphorical labels such as "guide" and "architect". In this section I will elaborate this classification and identify the points at which writers choose to intrude most explicitly by using the first person.

Table 10.4 shows the distribution of author pronouns and determiners in the student corpus by their main functions. As can be seen, these were mainly to state a discoursal goal and explain a methodological approach while more argumentative functions, such as presenting and justifying claims, were more commonly expressed without direct reference to the author. These results can be compared with a detailed analysis of ten papers from each discipline from the research article corpus (Table 10.5). We can see here that the 'expert writers' were more willing to make a solid personal commitment to the most authorially powerful aspects of their texts, those which carried both the most risks and potentially gained them the most credit. Almost half the occurrences of self-mention were used to present arguments or claims, compared with only a quarter in the student texts, while the least frequent use in the research articles, stating a purpose, was the most common in the project reports, I discuss the student responses further below.

4.2.1 Expressing self-benefits

A number of writers included comments on what they had personally gained from the project and this category represents the least threatening function of authorial self-mention. This is a function which does not occur in the professional research texts but was included in several departmental rubrics to add a reflective dimension to the learning experience. This requires a personal statement, usually in the conclusion, where the writer can adopt a less threatening role than the originator of ideas or interpreter of results, presenting him or herself in a way which does not step beyond a familiar student identity.

(1) To conclude, this interview is very useful both in completing *our* final-year report and teaching *me* about how to do business in Hong Kong and China.

(PR: Bus)

Table 10.5 Discourse functions of self-mention in sample of 10 research articles (%)

Function	Total		Bio	Phy	EE	ME	Phil	Soc	AL	Mkg
	Raw	%								
Explaining a procedure	400	38	57	46	50	49	5	26	39	44
Stating results or claim	273	26	19	19	15	18	30	28	25	26
Elaborating an argument	220	21	15	17	20	14	41	20	25	19
Stating a goal/purpose	158	15	9	18	14	18	24	26	11	11
Expressing self-benefits	0	0	0	0	0	0	0	0	0	0
Totals	1051									
Percentage		100	100	100	100	100	100	100	100	100

After finishing the project, *I* found that Information System (IS) techniques can be applied to the real world. This helps *me* to be an IS professional in the future career.

(PR:IS)

This is a worth experience to *me* especially in last year of *my* tertiary study, *I* hope the success of the fatigue test program will become an educational tool for the student to know more about fatigue in the Mechanical laboratory.

(PR: ME)

4.2.2 Stating a purpose

In a third of all cases students used authorial pronouns to state their discoursal purposes in order to signal their intentions and provide an overt structure for their texts. This kind of framing helped clarify both the direction of the research and the schematic structure of the argument, but it also foregrounded a fairly low risk writer role, simply signposting readers through the text:

(2) In this section, *I* am going to describe the findings from *my* interviews with the students based on their experience of the lesson in which *I* used task-based grammar teaching approach.

(PR: TESL)

We are interested in the strategy of Coca-Cola when it started to open the China market.

(PR: Bus)

I hope to identify some genus- and species-specific sequences for PCR primer or DNA probe design for the detection of Salmonella spp.

(PR: Bio)

In this research, *we* deeply look at the elements in the demand for private cars.

(PR: Econ)

The high use of this function in the student texts contrasted with the research articles where only 15% of cases of self-reference were used for this purpose.

Although there is an overt intervention by writers here, the intervention is largely metadiscoursal, relating to facets of the text which make the organisation of the discourse explicit. Such functions carry little threat of criticism or rejection, being essentially either text-internal, working to organise the discourse for readers, or related to a research purpose formulated in consultation with a supervisor. Explicit author presence here therefore is relatively innocuous, commits the writer to little, and rarely shades into explicit claim-making. A number of students recognised this.

> 'I' is suitable for organising the report, we are just saying about the research not about the ideas. It is only about the intention of the research and this is OK. The supervisor already approved this.
>
> (Econ student)

> We are planning the essay here. This is not an important part so 'I' is OK to use.
>
> (PSA student)

4.2.3 Explaining a procedure

There is a similar metatextual dimension to describing the research procedures used and this also reflects a similarly low degree of personal exposure. This is the second most frequent use of authorial reference in the student corpus, although here there is less variation with the research articles. All the course guidelines stressed the importance of students clearly presenting their methodological approach, and this was also a feature of supervisors' comments. The ability to plan and carry out a viable and appropriate research methodology, demonstrating an ability to integrate and apply professional skills, surmount difficulties, and set out procedures, was seen as a crucial element of the report. Students recognised the importance of accomplishing this purpose and many were willing to detail their approach as a first-person account:

> (3) *I* have interviewed 10 teachers, there were 10 teachers from different primary and secondary schools in Hong Kong.
>
> (PR: TESL)

> In this project, *we* make use of the Hounsfield tensile testing machine to perform the test.
>
> (PR: Man Eng)

> In this study, *we* use the zebrafish, Danio rerio, as an indicator for this aquatic toxicity test because it is very sensitive to pollutants especially in the early life stage.
>
> (PR: Bio)

> *I* have collected the data of Hang Seng Index, Shanghai A, B-shares & Shenzhen A, B-shares indexes.
>
> (PR: Econ)

Taking responsibility for their methodological choices using the first person seemed to hold few terrors for these students, despite the admonishments of some textbooks concerning the anonymity of experimental replicability. This may be because they were comfortable with the conventions of a narrative schema which they largely adopted for accomplishing this purpose:

The method is very important. We have to be clear to describe it and show we can follow it from the beginning to the end. It is like a story, isn't it.

(Bio student)

I am not worried about writing 'we did this and then we did that'. This is the correct way to write the method section, step by step.

(TESL student)

My supervisor wants to see that I can use a suitable method and overcome the problems. I use 'I' when I describe this because I am just telling what I did. This is not a difficult part to write.

(IS student)

These students therefore used a first person textual rhetoric in recounting their procedures as it seemed a natural way of doing this. Human agents are integral to the meaning of research practices and students were confident enough to explicitly align themselves with the procedures they had performed. However, they seemed unaware that author prominence here might display disciplinary competence and emphasise the writer's unique role in making fine qualitative judgements. In expert genres this use of the first person can remind readers that personal choices have been made and that, in other hands, things could have been done differently, as can be seen in these research article examples.

(4) Considering the self-assembling structure like in Fig. 1, the largest force of SDA is required only for providing a beam being buckled. Therefore, *we defined* a threshold force and *examined* whether a SDA was capable of generating this force or not.

(RA: EE)

To test this hypothesis, *we determined* the flagellar RNA induction response to . . . .

(RA: Bio)

For this part of the analysis, *I noted* all statements in the body of the articles that referred to Iraq and Saudi Arabia together.

(RA: AL)

4.2.4 Elaborating an argument

This is a high-risk function where results contrast starkly between the two genres. Setting out a line of reasoning would seem to be a key purpose of academic writing but generally only the professional academics chose to stake their commitments to their arguments with the use of first person:

(7) *I think* it works something like this: suppose we start with a new, just-assembled ship S. . .

(RA: Phil)

It should be emphasized that when *we* used x instead of x^1 for calculation, *we* did not only mean the inaccuracy of the x pulse, which may happen frequently in experiments; more importantly *we* mean that the real damped spin system cannot stay at the inverted state for long.

(RA: Phy)

I am purposely associating these two examples.

(RA: Soc)

Most students sought to disguise their responsibility when elaborating arguments and giving opinions. Compared with the professional texts, very few student reports contained personal pronouns associated with explicit cognitive verbs such as *think*, *believe*, and *assume*. Moreover, they preferred not to express agreement, disagreement or interest in a position but to dip into the range of grammatical options which allowed them to avoid the potentially problematic role of writer-as-thinker, a role which carries accountability for the propositions expressed:

(8) Therefore, it is believed that motivating oneself is a way to get good school academic results.

(PR: TESL)

In addition, the contents should be flexible enough for the pupils to choose the. . .

(PR: IS)

Gender difference is predicted that males use more avoiding style while females use more accommodating style in managing intimate conflicts.

(PR: SS)

This does not suggest that the students did not have arguments or ideas, but only that they sought to create a distance from them, often failing to personally engage with their beliefs and their audience. The tutor comments in the previous section testify to the frustration readers often felt about this.

4.2.5 Stating results/claims

This is the most self-assertive, and consequently potentially the most face-threatening use of self-reference and, once again, it contrasts baldly with professional uses. In expert discourses, the explicitly persuasive use of self-mention is most clearly displayed by the fact that writers choose to announce their presence where they make a knowledge claim. At these points they are best able to explicitly foreground their distinctive contribution and commitment to a position. A close study of first person uses in the published corpus shows that in all disciplines writers used the first person to represent their unique role in constructing a plausible interpretation for a phenomenon, thereby establishing a personal authority based on confidence and command of their arguments. These examples from the articles illustrate how, by strongly linking themselves to their claims, writers can solicit recognition for both:

(5) *We have now discovered that* the Byr2 kinase catalytic domain can also bind to the regulatory domain of Byr2. *We have determined* the minimum binding domain for each of these interactions by characterizing the binding profile of a series of Byr2 deletion mutants.

(RA: Bio)

Likewise, *I have offered evidence that* some critical thinking practices may marginalize subcultural groups, such as women, within U.S. society itself.

(RA: AL)

In contrast to the research papers where this function comprised a quarter of all first person uses, this function accounted for just 16% of students uses and only eight students were prepared to firmly align themselves with their claims through use of a singular pronoun. Clearly the writer invests most by using an authorial reference for this purpose and is also most vulnerable to criticism. Pledging your personal conviction in your results with a first person commitment is a risky strategy, and often one that novice writers lacked the confidence to take. Rather than demarcating their own work from that originating elsewhere, these undergraduates preferred to downplay their personal role in making sense of their results, by removing themselves from their claims altogether:

(6) The experiment shows that the relationships between wear hardness and thickness can be found. From the result, the wear is directly proportional to the load and inversely proportional to the hardness; also, the hardness is inversely proportional to the thickness.

(PR: ME)

Moreover, the most important finding in the graph was that the 24h~LC50 of the cadmium chloride solution to zebrafish chlorinated embryos was 51.29.

(PR: Bio)

Overall, there are several interesting findings in this research. First, it has been found that the abnormal return of the Hang Seng Index Component Stocks trends to be negative during the pre-event period but positive in the post-event time.

(PR: Econ)

The results suggested that affectively most of the students preferred authentic materials and found them interesting and motivating to use. On the contrary, the results indicated that cognitively, students preferred to use textbook materials. Apart from the pedagogical value of textbook materials, it was found that authentic materials have greater potential in providing learners with opportunities to attain autonomy in learning.

(PR: TESL)

The students showed a clear preference for strategies of author invisibility when interpreting results, with the whole panoply of agentless passives, dummy 'it' subjects, and the attribution of interpretations to tables or experiments employed to disguise the writer's role. The interviews with students also showed that they were aware of the academic conventions which urge writers to strengthen the objectivity of their interpretations by masking their own voice, but they were also aware of the interpersonal consequences of projecting a prominent identity:

We have to be objective in reporting our results. I don't like to be definite because my idea may be wrong and not what my supervisor believes. He might have a different idea. I think it is better to be quiet and not use 'I' but just tell what the experiment shows.

(IS student)

Not quite sure about this. I don't want to assert, just write the result only. So I leave it out.

(SS student)

I don't want to make myself important. Of course it is my project and my result, but I am just ordinary student. Not an academic scholar with lots of knowledge and confident for myself.

(TESL student)

This reluctance to get behind their interpretations obviously does nothing to obscure the meanings the students are seeking to convey; most of these writers display the kind of competence in formal written English that would be expected of graduating students in similar contexts around the world. What is at issue here are differences in realisations of interpersonal meanings and expressions of self that can be traced to cultural and rhetorical variations between L2 learners and target academic practices. Several supervisors commented on these differences:

The project is not just about demonstrating research and presenting it in a scholarly way. It is a chance for them, maybe the only time they will get to do this, for them to explore something in real detail. We want them to really get involved and show us what they think. It is their project, a year's work, and it is important they leave no doubt about their own views.

(Economics supervisor)

I get a bit frustrated with this actually. Perhaps it's something cultural? We try and get the students to tell us what *they* did and what *they* think about what they find, to make a commitment to their research and their ideas. Often they don't do this though.

(Management supervisor)

Yes, I like to see students use the first person. Their own interpretations are important but often it is difficult to see what is theirs and what is lifted from sources. Maybe this is something to do with how they are taught to write essays at school. They hide themselves.

(TESL supervisor)

To summarise, these L2 writers not only chose to avoid self mention, but principally chose to avoid it at points where it involved making a commitment to an interpretation or claim. They generally sought to downplay their authorial identity by restricting their visibility to the more innocuous functions, such as guiding readers through the discourse.

4.3 Personal interactions: first person in acknowledgements

An interesting rhetorical contrast to the sporadic use of first person in the reports is their high frequency in acknowledgements, a function often considered peripheral to the main purpose of the report. Table 10.6 shows that the use of the first person held few fears for students in this genre and that recognising assistance constituted the major use of this form in most fields. The distinctions serve to more clearly highlight students' different practices and their perceptions of variations in the communicative risks involved.

Table 10.6 Self-mention in student report acknowledgements

	Total	Bio	ME	IS	Econ	Bus	TESL	SS	PSA
Raw figures	272	40	25	28	23	15	41	36	64
% of total uses	30	59	22	28	31	13	39	31	30

Virtually all the reports acknowledged assistance and students displayed a remarkable sophistication in their grasp of the shift in role relationships that this involved. Most commonly, students thanked supervisors, informants, lab staff, classmates, friends, and family, roughly in that order of frequency:

(8) *I* wish to special thanks City University Swimming Pool and Tai Po Jockey Club Swimming Pool, which provided the samples for swimming pool water analysis.
(PR: Bio)

I would like to thank *my* best friend, Mr. Pui Ming Mau, for his helpful discussion and support in the project.
(PR: TESL)

I hereby offer *my* deepest gratitude to my mother not only for her delicious dim-sum and midnight snacks, but also for her love and supports.
(PR: IS)

Thanks *my* mum and dad. If they did not bring *me* to this world, *I* cannot even start this project.
(PR: Bus)

Acknowledgements are obviously one of the most explicitly interactional genres of the academy, one whose communicative purpose virtually obliges writers to represent themselves and their views unreservedly. The authorial role of the first person still clearly positions the writer in relation to his or her statements, but this is a less threatening prospect in this section, as one of my informants suggested:

I like the acknowledgements. I can write for myself and say what I want. There is no need to write like the textbook.

This is one place, then, where writers are able to reveal an identity disentangled from the complex conventions of powerful academic discourse types. Here the authorial roles, individual and social purposes, and writer–reader relationships are radically different from the choices available in research genres. Essentially, the demands of the dissertation proper are relaxed and the writer is able to present him or herself in a way which corresponds more closely to a more familiar identity.

4.4 *Authority, subjectivity and cultural identity*

The rhetorical distribution of forms suggests that students consciously avoided the most authoritative functions and sought to deny ownership and responsibility for their views. There are several possible reasons why these students might choose to avoid self-mention in their reports: recommendations from style manuals, uncertainties about disciplinary conventions, culturally shaped epistemologies, culture-specific views of authority, conflicting teacher advice, or personal preferences. All these may play a part.

Some students saw the use of the first person as closely linked to a subjectivity which they considered inappropriate for academic discourse. Much conventional wisdom advocates objectivity and anonymity in academic writing and, in the absence of a strong English language culture outside Hong Kong classrooms, these novice L2 writers are largely dependent on their teachers for effective language patterns. While they gain an important sense of the rhetorical demands of their disciplines from articles and lectures, much of their understanding comes prior to university studies, from a crowded secondary school curriculum which can often provide only a fragmentary sense of the purpose and effect of particular forms. As a result, students often have rather rigid views about what is actually appropriate:

> In science we must be neutral and use the passive. It means that the research can be done by anybody else.
>
> (Bio student)

> In school we have to just put down the facts without personal ideas. We have to show the teacher that we understand the books. Now we must show that we follow the method to solve a problem. The steps. I think my supervisor is not interested in my idea but how I apply the theory.
>
> (Econ student)

> Our teachers always told us not to use 'I' in formal writing. 'I' is mainly for a personal letter I think.
>
> (SS student)

Attempts to avoid the personal responsibility that subjectivity entails may help account for the rather sporadic use of *we* in almost half of the single-authored student reports noted above. These examples are all from individual writers:

> (8) In chapter three, *we* have stated the lacking of strength on the current HOUNS-FIELD testing machine. *We* then set a series of objectives to strengthen the working ability of the HOUNSFIELD.
>
> (PR: ME)

> In *our* system, the Check Sum Algorithm provided by the Card Center will validate Credit Card Number by calculating the check sum of credit card number.
>
> (PR: IS)

> This is the first motivation to fuel *our* mind to write this research paper.
>
> (PR: Econ)

The reasons for this use are no doubt varied and complex. Several students mentioned the collaboratively conducted research which contributed to the individual reports, but underlying many responses was a clear desire to reduce attributions to self:

I use 'we' as I worked with my classmate on this project. Anyway, it is easier to say 'we' than 'I'. I just feel easier to use 'we'. The work is shared so I call it 'we'.

(PSA Student)

I think this is better than using 'I' in a science paper. I choose it carefully because my supervisor helps me a lot with this project so I don't want to say this is all my ideas.

(ME student)

This is a correct use, I think. I have seen it in books. I want to say what I did but I am not so confident to use 'I' all the time. 'We' is not so strong, isn't it?

(Bus student)

Many of these students seem uncomfortable with the subjectivity and assertiveness of the singular form and seek the rhetorical distance that the plural meaning allows, reducing their personal intrusion while not completely eliminating their presence from the text.

Most important, however, is the notion of authority. As I discussed earlier in this paper, academic literacy is a 'foreign culture' to students of all backgrounds, where they find their previous understandings of the world challenged, their old confidences questioned, and their ways of talking modified. For students struggling to gain control of their discipline and master its content, this can lead to a sense of powerlessness and uncertainty (Ivanič, 1998). In such circumstances it may be difficult for students to project an authoritative self. Respondents frequently said they wanted to dissociate themselves from the connotations of personal authority they believed the first person use carried:

I try to not use it. It is too strong. Too powerful. It means I am firm about my belief but often I am not sure. It is better to use passive sentence.

(Bio student)

I have seen 'we' and 'I' in academic papers but it is a good writer, isn't it. They have confidence to give their ideas clearly. Their own ideas.

(SS Student)

These students, therefore, tended to see self-reference as a marker of self-assurance and individuality which they did not feel when composing, preferring to take refuge in the anonymity of passive forms.

Part of their reluctance to stake out a firm authorial identity stemmed from the inequalities of power in the writer–reader relationship which many students experience when writing in the academy (Bizzell, 1992; Lemke, 1990). Genres signify certain roles and relationships as a result of their institutionally defined purposes, and these relationships are conspicuously unequal in the final year project report. This is a significant undergraduate genre and the judgments of reader-examiners can have a major impact on students' grades and futures. This, then, is not the best forum to declare an authoritatively independent self. But while this kind of institutional position-ing influences students' choices, it does not fully explain their obvious reluctance to take 'ownership' of their work. In fact, this reluctance of these students to take greater responsibility for their ideas contrasts markedly with Ivanič's (1998) British L1 students. These writers felt that the identities offered by academic writing negated their life experiences and believed that conformity to them actually *repressed* their opportunities for self-expression.

The Hong Kong learners, however, felt ambivalent about the discoursal identity implied in authorial commitment, and rejected the authority associated with first person choices:

> This is OK for scholars, but not our project. I think no one will use 'I' in his project.
>
> (Bio student)

> There is a conflict. My supervisor told me to give my interpretation, but I can't do this. I feel embarrassed to do it.
>
> (SS student)

> In Chinese we don't write like that. If I use 'I' it is not really me who thinks something. When I read it back I feel a different person wrote it.
>
> (Bus student)

Supervisors themselves were divided concerning students' use of the first person, but most encouraged students to stand behind their arguments:

> Yes, I have noticed it. Students often get into weird contortions to avoid using 'I'. I'm not sure why, but they can see from the readings we give them that they don't have to do this.
>
> (Info Systems supervisor)

> It is not just a question of content, getting the ideas or the findings down, but how they manage this. I get an impression of the writer when I read these reports, and often my impression is that they are trying to hide themselves. Maybe they don't know it is OK to use these.
>
> (Management supervisor)

> The rationale for the project is for students to try out things and give their views on them, their interpretations, but we get a lot of passives and they seem reluctant to really assert their views.
>
> (TESL supervisor)

Taking a stance and demonstrating confidence clearly implies that the writer is a distinctive, individual creator with a firm position and rights to ownership of his or her perspectives and text, but this kind of identity is not shared by all cultures. Scollon (1994: 34) suggests that academic writing 'is as much the construction of an authorial self as the presentation of fact', and that this notion of a rational, uniquely individual writer is a product of a culturally specific ideology. Both Ohta (1991) and Scollon (1994) suggest that the use of first person pronouns is largely unacceptable in the traditions of Asian cultures because of its association with individual rather than collective identity. Authorship in academic writing in English both carries a culturally constructed individualistic ideology and places the burden of responsibility for the truth of an assertion heavily on the shoulders of the writer. Such an identity both exposes the writer and reduces group solidarity, and as a result L2 students often view the use of *I* with misgivings.

Research in contrastive rhetoric has often produced conflicting findings, but the view that cultural differences can lead writers to employ different rhetorical and pragmatic discourse practices is now widely accepted (e.g. Connor, 1996). Some writers have attributed these differences to predominant patterns of social relationships within cultures, such as expectations concerning the extent of reader involvement (Clyne, 1987), or to interpersonal face considerations (Scollon and Scollon, 1995). Whatever motivates these differences however, culture shapes our communicative practices in significant ways, influencing our preferences for structuring information, the relationships we establish with our readers, and how far we want to personally appear in our texts. Students from western backgrounds may have a similar sense of being manipulated by the particular pragmatic conventions inscribed in academic discourses in English, but cultural norms are an additional complicating factor pressuring learners to abandon their familiar everyday conventions.

5 Conclusions

Self-mention constitutes a central pragmatic feature of academic discourse since it contributes not only to the writer's construction of a text, but also of a rhetorical self. The authorial pronoun is a significant means of promoting a competent scholarly identity and gaining acceptance for one's ideas, and while these students were sensitive to its rhetorical effects, they were reluctant to accept its clear connotations of authority and personal commitment. As a result they significantly underused authorial pronouns and determiners, downplayed their role in the research, and adopted a less clearly independent stance compared with expert writers.

The ways that writers choose to report their research and express their ideas obviously result from a variety of social and psychological factors. Most crucially, however, rhetorical identity is influenced by the writer's background and this becomes more intricate for students familiar with intellectual traditions which may be very different from those practised in English academic contexts. So, while Anglo-American academic conventions encourage a conscious exploitation of authorial identity to manage the reader's awareness of the author's role and viewpoint, L2 writers from other cultures may be reluctant to promote an individual self.

The message here for teachers is that we need to be aware of how academic conventions position students and be sensitive to the struggles of novice writers seeking to reconcile the discursive identities of their home and disciplinary cultures. This tentativeness and reluctance to display an authoritative persona among Asian writers may, in part, be a product of a culturally and socially constructed view of self which makes assertion difficult. It is equally possible however that native English speaking students experience similar problems when entering university. Teachers have an important consciousness raising task here to ensure students understand the rhetorical options available to them and the effects of manipulating these options for interactional purposes. With this rhetorical understanding our learners will be better able to gain control over their writing and meet the challenges of participating in academic genres in a second language.

References

Arnaudet, Martin, Barrett, Mary, 1984. Approaches to Academic Reading and Writing. Prentice Hall, Englewood Cliffs, NJ.
Bartholomae, David, 1986. Inventing the university. Journal of Basic Writing 5, 4–23.
Barton, David, Hamilton, Mary, 1998. Local Literacies. Routledge, London.
Belcher, Diane, Braine, George (Eds.), 1995. Academic Writing in a Second Language. Ablex, Norwood, NJ.
Bizzell, Patricia, 1992. Academic Discourse and Critical Consciousness. University of Pittsburgh Press, Pittsburgh.
Cadman, Kate, 1997. Thesis writing for international students: a question of identity? English for Specific Purposes 16 (1), 3–14.
Clyne, Michael, 1987. Cultural differences in the organisation of academic texts. Journal of Pragmatics 11, 211–247.

Connor, Ulla, 1990. Contrastive Rhetoric. Cambridge University Press, Cambridge.
Connor, Ulla, 1996. Contrastive Rhetoric: Cross-cultural Implications of Second-language Writing. Cambridge University Press, New York.
Davies, Bronwyn, Harre, Ron, 1990. Positioning: the discursive production of selves. Journal for the Theory of Social Behaviour 20, 43–63.
Day, Richard, 1994. How to Write and Publish a Scientific Paper. Oryx Press, Phoenix, AZ.
Fairclough, Norman, 1995. Critical Discourse Analysis. Longman, Harlow.
Geertz, Clifford, 1988. Words and Lives: The Anthropologist as Author. Stanford University Press, Palo Alto, CA.
Gong, Gwendolyn, Dragga, Sam, 1995. A Writer's Repertoire. Longman, New York.
Gosden, Hugh, 1993. Discourse functions of subject in scientific research articles. Applied Linguistics 14 (1), 56–75.
Hunston, Susan, Thompson, Geoffrey (Eds.), 2000. Evaluation in Text. Oxford University Press, Oxford.
Hyland, Ken, 1999. Disciplinary discourses: writer stance in research articles. In: Candlin, C.N., Hyland, K. (Eds.), Writing: Texts, Processes and Practices. Longman, London, pp. 99–121.
Hyland, Ken, 2001. Disciplinary Discourses: Social Interactions in Academic Writing. Longman, London.
Hyland, Ken, 2001. Humble servants of the discipline? Self mention in research articles. English for Specific Purposes 20 (3), 207–226.
Ivanič, Roz, 1998. Writing and Identity: The Discoursal Construction of Identity in Academic Writing. Benjamins, Amsterdam.
Ivanič, Roz, Weldon, Sue, 1999. Researching the writer-reader relationship. In: Candlin, C.N., Hyland, K. (Eds.), Writing: Texts, Processes and Practices. Longman, London, pp. 168–192.
Johns, Ann, 1997. Text, Role and Context. Cambridge University Press, Cambridge.
Kuo, Chih-Hua, 1999. The use of personal pronouns: role relationships in scientific journal articles. English for Specific Purposes 18 (2), 121–138.
Lemke, Jay, 1990. Talking Science: Language, Learning and Values. Ablex, Norwood, NJ.
Lester, James, D., 1993. Writing Research Papers, seventh ed. Harper Collins, New York.
Martin, James, R., 2000. Analysing genre: functional parameters. In: Christie, F., Martin, J.R. (Eds.), Genre and Institutions. Continuum, London.
Mills, Gordon, Water, John, A., 1986. Technical Writing, fifth ed. Harcourt Brace Jovanovich, Fort Worth, TX.
Norton, Bonny, 1997. Language, identity and the ownership of English. TESOL Quarterly 31, 409–429.
Ohta, Amy Snyder, 1991. Evidentiality and politeness in Japanese. Issues in Applied Linguistics 2 (2), 183–210.
Ramanathan, Vai, Atkinson, Dwight, 1999. Individualism, academic writing and ESL writers. Journal of Second Language Writing 8, 45–75.
Scollon, Ron, 1994. As a matter of fact: the changing ideology of authorship and responsibility in discourse. World Englishes 13, 34–46.
Scollon, Ron, Scollon, Suzanne, 1994. Intercultural Communication. Blackwell, Oxford.
Shotter, John, Gergen, Kenneth, 1989. Texts of Identity. Sage, Newbury Park, CA.
Spencer, Carolyn, Arbon, Beverly, 1996. Foundations of Writing: Developing Research and Academic Writing Skills. National Textbook Co, Lincolnwood, IL.
Swales, John, Feak, Christine, 1994. Academic Writing for Graduate Students: Essential Tasks and Skills. University of Michigan Press, Ann Arbor, MI.
Tang, Ramona, Suganthi, John, 1999. The 'I' in identity: exploring writer identity in student academic writing through the first person pronoun. English for Specific Purposes 18, S23–S39.

Chapter 11

DOUGLAS BIBER, SUSAN CONRAD, AND RANDI REPPEN

CORPUS-BASED APPROACHES TO ISSUES IN APPLIED LINGUISTICS (1994)

1 Introduction

BY UTILIZING LARGE, DIVERSE CORPORA in conjunction with computational and quantitative tools, corpus-based analyses have provided new insights into many areas of language structure and use. For example, numerous studies describing the formal variants and functions of particular grammatical constructions have been based on analysis of large text corpora (see the bibliography compiled by Altenberg (1991), containing approximately 650 references to studies based on corpora). Book-length treatments of this kind include Tottie's (1991) analysis of negation in English, Mair's (1990) analysis of infinitival complement clauses, and Meyer's (1992) study of apposition.

There are two major advantages to the use of text corpora for linguistic analysis:

1. They provide a large empirical database of natural discourse, so that analyses are based on naturally-occurring structures and patterns of use rather than intuitions and perceptions, which often do not accurately represent actual use.
2. They enable analyses of a scope not feasible otherwise, allowing researchers to address issues that were previously intractable. This is particularly true of computer-based text corpora,[1] which can be analyzed using (semi-)automatic techniques. Such analyses can examine much more language data than otherwise possible, including more texts, longer texts, a wider range of variation (texts from different language varieties), a wider range of linguistic characteristics, and the systematic co-occurrence patterns among linguistic features. In addition to quantitative analyses previously not possible, corpus-based approaches thus allow investigation of issues such as register variation and the discourse factors influencing the choice among structurally related variants (e.g. adverb placement, or active versus passive constructions).

It turns out that these characteristics are as advantageous for studies in applied linguistics as they are for studies in descriptive linguistics. Much of the work in applied linguistics builds upon the findings of theoretical research to make concrete recommendations concerning language-related practice in real-world domains. Unfortunately, if the underlying theoretical research lacks an adequate empirical basis, applications of the research are correspondingly flawed. An alternative approach is to directly study the patterns of language structure and use as they exist in real-world domains, so that applied recommendations are based on a solid empirical foundation. Corpus-based analyses are particularly well-suited to research purposes of this kind.

The present paper illustrates the use of the corpus-based approach to address applied issues in three areas: (1) English grammar, (2) lexicography, and (3) ESP and register variation. Each section illustrates a corpus-based analysis with data from commonly available corpora (e.g. the Longman/Lancaster, LOB (Lancaster–Oslo/Bergen), and London–Lund corpora; see Appendix for a description of these and other commonly used corpora). The analyses in each area show that, as linguists, we often have strongly held intuitions, but those intuitions frequently prove to be incorrect when they are tested empirically against the actual patterns of use in large text corpora.

Another important insight from corpus-based research is the realization that few linguistic descriptions are adequate for a language as a whole. That is, languages are not homogeneous in their linguistic characteristics. Rather, empirical analyses of large corpora show repeatedly that there are important, systematic differences among registers at all linguistic levels. Although the section on ESP and register variation addresses these issues directly, the sections on grammar and lexicography also highlight differences of this kind, showing how corpus-based analyses enable identification and interpretation of the salient linguistic characteristics within and among the range of registers in a language.

2 Grammatical issues

Materials used in the teaching of grammar have commonly been based on intuition–that is, native speakers' judgments of what is grammatical and which structures are frequently used. Because materials exhibit widespread agreement on many aspects of English grammar instruction, it might be assumed that they provide an accurate portrayal of language use and represent the most effective pedagogic practices. For example, a quick survey of ESL/EFL grammars shows that there is remarkable agreement concerning the core topics of English grammar: most of these books cover the same set of topics, have similar organizations, and give the same relative priority to different topics.

Consensus does not necessarily reflect validity, however. A corpus approach, because it is empirically based, allows us to test assumptions about language use against patterns found in naturally occurring discourse and then to review our pedagogical practices in light of this information. In fact, corpus-based research shows that the actual patterns of function and use in English often differ radically from prior expectations. This section illustrates findings of this type with respect to the teaching of postnominal modification in English, showing that some relatively common linguistic constructions are overlooked in pedagogic grammars, while some relatively rare constructions receive considerable attention.

Table 11.1 summarizes the treatment given to postnominal modifiers in four popular ESL/EFL grammar textbooks (full details are given in the references). There are many structural options for postnominal modification in English:

A.   Head noun + relative clause

    1. the artist who stands out most prominently
    2. the substance from which committees are formed
    3. the little frowning smile *she used*

B. Head noun + participial clause

    4. the transient current resulting from switching operations
    5. any vessel owned by the plaintiffs

C. Head noun + prepositional phrase

    6. talks on the protectorate's future
    7. his seat at the breakfast table
    8. a meeting *of labour MPs*

D. Head noun + infinitival clause

    9. the person *to see*

E. Apposition (head noun + noun phrase)

    10. Sir Roy's chief aide, *Mr. Julius Greenfield*
    11. the bargedwellers, creatures neither of firm land nor water

F. Head noun + adjective phrase

    12. an artist popular in the 60's.

Table 11.1 summarizes the number of pages devoted to the first three of these modifier types: relative clauses, participial clauses, and prepositional phrases.[2] This table also summarizes the treatment given to prepositional phrases functioning as verb modifiers (e.g. I went [to the store]).

As Table 11.1 shows, these grammars are similar in the relative emphasis that they place on the different kinds of postnominal modification. Relative clauses are clearly regarded as a central construction and receive extensive discussion in all four grammars. In contrast, participial clauses tend to be regarded as a kind of reduced relative clause and receive little discussion in their own right. Prepositional phrases as postnominal modifiers receive the least attention: they are given little discussion in Murphy and Altman (1989) and Cake and Rogerson (1986), and they are essentially ignored in Danielson and Porter (1990) and Azar (1981).

Table 11.2 shows that the actual patterns of use in three written registers are quite different from the emphases in these pedagogical grammars. In editorials, relative clauses are slightly more

Table 11.1 Summary of the number of pages devoted to three types of postnominal modifiers (versus prepositions used as verb modifiers) in popular ESL/EFL grammars

Pages devoted to:	Relative clauses	Prep. phrases as noun modifiers	Participial clauses as noun modifiers	Prepositions + prep. phrases as verb modifiers
Grammars				
Murphy and Altman (1989)	10	2	2	33
Danielson and Porter (1990)	11	1?	1?	13
Azar (1981)	17	1?	3	20
Cake and Rogerson (1986)	22	1	3	5

? marks a minimal treatment of the given construction – usually one or two example sentences with no explicit discussion

Table 11.2 Frequencies of different types of postnominal modifiers (per 1,000 words) in three registers *

	Editorials	Fiction	Letters
Number of texts	**27**	**29**	**6**
that rel. clauses restrictive	1.8	0.7	0.5
WH rel. clauses restrictive	5.4	2.1	1.1
WH rel. clauses non-restrictive	1.9	2.2	0.3
Rel. clauses with no rel. pronoun	0.1	0.1	0.2
Participial postnominal modifiers (past and present)	4.9	1.8	0.2
Prepositional phrases as noun modifiers	38.2	15.2	16.8
Prepositional phrases as verb modifiers	44.1	56.2	45.8

* Based on the LOB Corpus + a private corpus of letters; total number of words = c. 115,000

common than participial clauses, although both constructions occur with only moderate frequencies. In contrast, prepositional phrases as noun modifiers are far more common than either of these other constructions. Fiction and letters show similar patterns, although the overall frequency of postnominal modifiers is much lower than in editorials. There are few relative clauses or participial clauses in fiction, and almost none of these features occur in personal letters. In contrast, there are moderate but notable numbers of prepositional phrases as postnominal modifiers in both fiction and letters. Text Sample 1 illustrates the extensive use of prepositional phrases as noun modifiers in a passage from a popular magazine. Of the seven bracketed postnominal modifiers (with head nouns in boldface), six are prepositional phrases:

Text Sample 1. Magazine article.

On standard issue **maps** (of Manhattan], **Ninety-sixth Street** [on the Upper East Side] is shown slightly thicker than **the lines** [representing neighboring streets], to signify that **traffic** [on it] runs both east and west. There is **no hint** [of a border] [on these maps], no intimation that Ninety-sixth Street marks a division [between two dramatically different worlds].

The use of prepositional phrases as postnominal modifiers is not restricted to specialized English registers; rather, Table 11.2 shows that even in popular written registers, prepositional phrases are considerably more common as postnominal modifiers than either relative clauses or participial clauses.[3] The grammatical priorities of pedagogical grammars simply do not match the actual patterns of use in this area. Further, it is not accurate to argue that prepositional phrases as noun modifiers are an easy construction that requires little attention. In fact, from a cross-linguistic perspective, this is a marked construction. While it is typical for languages to employ a range of phrases to mark various case relations to verbs, it is unusual to find these same kinds of phrases functioning as nominal modifiers. Thus, in addition to being extremely common in English, prepositional phrases as noun modifiers are likely to be troublesome for L2 students.

There are two general implications of these analyses. First, while beginning L2 students need to master certain core grammatical constructions, they are not necessarily the ones that have been traditionally emphasized in pedagogic grammars. That is, most textbooks focus exclusively on concerns of difficulty and teachability to decide which grammatical constructions to emphasize and how to sequence the presentation of topics. However, an equally important consideration is whether beginning students will ever need to produce or comprehend the construction in question outside the language classroom, and if so, how frequently that need will arise. In some cases, features disregarded by introductory textbooks are considerably more common in natural English discourse than other features regarded as having core pedagogical status. While we recognize the importance of considerations such as difficulty and teachability for pedagogic practice, we regard the actual patterns of use as an equally important consideration. Although some common features may be difficult for students to acquire, mastery of these features is important if students are to comprehend and use language outside the language classroom.

The second implication of these findings is that an ESP approach will often be the most effective one for teaching intermediate and advanced students. That is, the markedly different patterns of linguistic form and function that occur across registers indicate that there is no single set of linguistic features that should be emphasized for all students, once they have mastered the rudiments of English grammar. Rather, it is important to teach the linguistic characteristics and functions of particular target registers, so that students will be able to control the language structures they encounter in actual discourse and to adjust their language use appropriately for different registers.

Numerous similar examples could be given for other areas of English grammar. The point here is not to criticize these four grammars or pedagogical grammars in general; rather, these analyses are presented to show the importance of a corpus-based perspective. That is, corpus-based research sheds new light on some of our most basic assumptions about English grammar, and as a result it offers the possibility of more effective and appropriate pedagogical applications.[4]

3 Lexicographic issues

Similar to the patterns for grammatical features, corpus-based lexicographic research has shown that words and word senses have quite different distributions across registers – and that our intuitions about a word often do not match the actual patterns of use. Sinclair (1991) illustrates this latter point through an analysis of the word *back*. Most dictionaries list the human body part as the first meaning of *back*, and many people identify this as the core meaning. From analysis of the COBUILD Corpus, however, this meaning is seen to be relatively rare. Rather, the adverbial sense meaning 'in, to, or towards the original starting point, place or condition', which is not usually given prominence in dictionary listings, is the most common usage (Sinclair 1991:112).

It further turns out, however, that a corpus can give even more information about lexical use by adopting a register perspective. For example, analysis of the use of the word *back* in two registers from the Longman/Lancaster Corpus reveals important differences. In social science texts, the word *back* is by far most commonly used in an adverbial sense (e.g. *went back*, *came back*), supporting Sinclair's general conclusions. In fiction, though, the body part meaning (e.g. *my back*) is much more common than in social science (15.9 times per million words in social science versus 104.5 times per million words in fiction).

The distribution of words and word senses across registers can be further illustrated by an analysis of adjectives marking 'certainty'. Table 11.3 compares the distributions of *certain*, *sure*, and *definite* across two text corpora: the Longman/Lancaster Corpus, representing written texts from ten major topical domains (e.g. natural science, social science, fiction), and the London–Lund Corpus, representing spoken texts collected in a range of situational settings (e.g. face-to-face conversations, interviews, sports broadcasts, sermons).

All counts given in the table are normalized to frequencies per 1 million words of text. In the Longman/Lancaster Corpus, *certain* and *sure* occur with roughly the same frequency (259

Table 11.3 Comparison of normalized frequencies (per 1 million words of text) of three
CERTAINTY adjectives*

	Frequency counts per 1 million words of:		
	certain	sure	definite
Longman/Lancaster Corpus (written texts)	259.0	234.0	34.9
London–Lund Corpus (spoken texts)	292.5	426.9	19.4

* Based on the Longman/Lancaster English Language Corpus (written texts; sample = c. 11,000,000 words) and London–Lund Corpus (spoken texts; c. 500,000 words)

versus 234 times per million words), but *sure* occurs much more frequently than *certain* in the London–Lund Corpus (427 versus 292 times per million words). Compared to the other two words, *definite* is rare in both corpora.

Table 11.4 shows, however, that the overall frequencies given in Table 11.3 are misleading, because consideration of a corpus as a homogeneous whole hides important differences among registers. Thus, *certain* is actually much more frequent than *sure* in social science texts (359 versus 74 times per million words), and even *definite* is more frequent than *sure* in this register (114 versus 74 times per million words). In contrast, the exact opposite distribution is found in fiction: *sure* is much more frequent than *certain* (353 versus 179 times per million words), and *definite* is quite rare (occurring only 11 times per million words).

Word distributions are not in themselves very useful for lexicographic research because they do not necessarily correspond to differences among the major word senses. However, large text corpora can be analyzed using other tools that provide lexicographers with important new insights into word meanings. First, concordances are commonly generated from computer-based corpora, to provide an exhaustive listing of the use of a word in its textual contexts. For example, Table 11.5 presents a small portion of the concordance listing for *certain* in the Longman/Lancaster Corpus.

Concordances are an important aid to lexicographers in identifying the various senses of a given word, and they represent a major advance over the manual sorting of citation index cards (still practiced in some lexicographic organizations). Since manual techniques depend on the skill and coverage of human readers, there is no assurance that all major senses of a word will be represented; further, manual techniques provide no reliable basis for assessing the relative frequency of different word uses. In contrast, concordances based on large corpora can provide too much information, so that lexicographers are overwhelmed by the amount of data. For

Table 11.4 Comparison of normalized frequencies (per 1 million words of text) of three
CERTAINTY adjectives in two specific text categories*

	Frequency counts per 1 million words of:		
	certain	sure	definite
Social Science	358.7	73.8	114.2
Fiction	178.5	353.1	10.8

* From the Longman/Lancaster Corpus: Social Science (sample size = c. 1,900,000 words) and Fiction (sample size = c. 4,000,000 words)

Table 11.5 Sample concordance listings for certain from the Longman/Lancaster Corpus

---

1.
to boys. For both are treated in the same way up to
    a *certain* age.
Discrimination does begin fairly early, however, despite the staunch refusal

2.
much about the physical-material aspect of the matter. Let us now turn
    to *certain* non-material
aspects. There can be no doubt that the idea of

3.
this statement. We, or rather our hunting ape ancestors, became infantile
    in *certain* ways
but not in others. The rates of development of our

4.
by gross national product. Perhaps it cannot be measured at all except
    for *certain* symptoms
of loss. However, this is not the place to go

5.
to the ambient temperatures required by farm livestock. There
    are *certain* fundamental
differences between ruminant animals and pigs and poultry which makes

6.
the following positions. Considering the way the human eye is constructed, it
    is *certain* that
it will never see the galloping horse as it

7.
She had been thinking about it ever since she'd heard, and she
    was *certain* he
hadn't killed his wife, but she wondered if he had

---

example, the concordance for *certain* extracted from a 10-million word sample of the Longman/Lancaster Corpus contains approximately 3,000 entries. Simply identifying the major patterns in a database of this size is a daunting task; to group different uses accurately and rank them in order of importance is not really feasible without the use of additional tools.

One such tool is to automatically sort concordance lines according to their different collocational patterns.[5] Entries can be sorted according to their collocates on both the left and the right. For example, the entries in Table 11.5 illustrate several of the common left collocates for *certain*: *a certain, to certain, in certain, for certain, there are certain, it is certain, he/she is/was certain*. It can be seen even from this very short list that *certain* has several different major senses. Table 11.6 summarizes these major collocational patterns, giving an overview of the use of *certain* in the Social Science and Fiction text categories from the Longman/Lancaster Corpus. This table presents the average frequency (per 100,000 words) of different collocational pairs in texts from each of the two registers. Collocations with preceding words are given in the top half of the table, while the bottom half presents the major collocations with following words. Those collocations that are significantly more frequent in Social Science are marked by a single *, while those that are significantly more frequent in Fiction are marked by a double **.

Table 11.6 Comparison of average frequencies of collocations for certain in two text categories of the Longman/Lancaster English Language Corpus: Social Science and Fiction[†]

	Average freq. of certain in Social Science	*Average freq. of certain in Fiction*	
Collocations with preceding words			
a+	10.0	7.3	
in+	3.7 *	0.3	
of+	3.2 *	0.3	
to+	2.0 *	0.4	
.+	1.5 *	0.5	
for+	1.5 *	0.4	
that+	1.3 *	0.1	
,+	1.2 *	0.3	
under+	1.0 *	0.04	
there BE+	0.7 *	0.3	
it BE+	0.4	0.1	***
you/he/she/they BE +	2.5	6.4 **	***
I/we BE +	0.0	0.5 **	***
quite+	0.1	0.5	***
Collocations with following words			
+ *kind(s)*	1.4 *	0.05	
+ *amount(s)*	1.2	0.8	
+ *aspect(s)*	1.2 *	0.06	
+ *extent*	1.0	0.1	
+ *type(s)*	0.9 *	0.04	
+ *that*	1.2	1.2 ***	

* Collocations significantly more common in social science (p < .05)
** Collocations significantly more common in fiction (p < .05)
*** Collocations that mark 'certainty'

[†] Counts are normalized per 100,000 words of text. Averages are based on 42 Social Science texts and 84 Fiction texts, representing approximately 6 million words of text. ANOVAs were used to determine statistical significance.

The corpus-based analysis summarized in Table 11.6 highlights two important observations about the use of *certain*. First, we again see marked differences between intuition and actual language use when we compare this information to native speaker intuition. An informal survey found that native speakers most commonly associate *certain* with the condition of certainty. In contrast, Table 11.6 shows that this is a rare use of *certain*. Only five of the collocational pairs listed in the table mark 'certainty'; these are identified by triple asterisks (e.g. *it is certain*, *she/he/they is/are certain*, *I am certain*). In contrast, *certain* is much more commonly used to mark a referent as named but not clearly described or known, as in *a certain kind*, *in certain types*, *to a certain extent*, *there are certain aspects*. The concordance entries 1–5 in Table 11.5 illustrate this use of *certain*.

The second observation from Table 11.6 is that the two major senses of *certain* are not at all uniformly distributed across registers. Rather, *certain* marking certainty is significantly more common in Fiction than in Social Science, while most occurrences of *certain* in Social Science mark referents as named but not clearly described (and thus in some sense *not* certain!).

More sophisticated computational and statistical tools could be used to analyze finer patterns; however, even at this level it is clear that corpus-based investigation leads to findings useful to lexicography but not otherwise possible. For example, when senses of a word are ordered in a dictionary entry, several factors may be considered, including historical development, clarity of meaning, and concreteness. Findings of corpus-based research make it possible also to consider the frequency of different word senses across various registers. Such information is now being incorporated in corpus-based dictionary projects, used for applications in language learning, and for automated computational processing of text.

4 Issues in ESP and register analysis

Within applied linguistics, numerous studies of particular registers have been carried out by researchers in ESP and EAP. This perspective could be summarized as the general view that there are important and systematic differences among text varieties at all linguistic levels, and that any global characterizations of 'General English' should be regarded with caution. Researchers in ESP/EAP further emphasize the implications of this view for language pedagogy: that teachers of advanced students should focus on the English of particular varieties, in naturally-occurring discourse, rather than 'general' patterns that are culled from linguists' intuitions and do not accurately reflect the grammar of any variety. Johns and Dudley-Evans (1991) and Johns (1991) survey previous research in ESP/EAP, while Swales (1990) provides a book-length treatment focusing primarily on the research article in English.

In fact, there are several other subdisciplines that focus on the linguistic analysis of text varieties and the differences among varieties. Within descriptive and socio-linguistics, there is a long tradition of research on 'registers', 'genres', and 'styles', dating from the work of Ferguson, Halliday, Leech, Crystal, and others in the early 1960s. More recently, sociolinguistics and functional linguistics such as Chafe, Heath, Ochs, Romaine, Schiffrin, and Tannen have made important contributions in this area; recent edited collections within this tradition include Ghadessy (1988) and Biber and Finegan (1994b).

Within computational linguistics, research on 'sublanguages' deals with many of the same issues, with the ultimate goal of automatically processing texts from particular varieties with a high degree of accuracy (see Kittredge and Lehrberger 1982; Grishman and Kittredge 1986). Finally, there has been considerable research focusing on student composition (see the survey in Hillocks 1986), as well as a number of rhetorical studies of particular genres (e.g. Bazerman 1988).

Unfortunately, researchers in these subdisciplines rarely acknowledge the existence of one another, let alone build upon a collective research tradition. This is perhaps most surprising for work done in applied linguistics and descriptive linguistics, since these areas share many of the same research techniques and goals. Researchers in descriptive linguistics rarely cite publications in even the major applied journals (such as *TESOL Quarterly* or *Applied Linguistics*), while researchers in ESP/EAP seem equally unaware of the major descriptive/theoretical or discourse journals (e.g. *Language*, *Linguistics*, *Language in Society*, *Discourse Processes*, and *Text*). Publications in less accessible outlets are even less likely to be used across subdisciplines. However, there is extensive overlap among these subfields, and important studies within each of them could be profitably informing on-going research efforts. Atkinson and Biber (1994) survey research studies in all of these subdisciplines under the general rubric of 'register' studies.[6]

Research in these subdisciplines tends to be empirical, based on analysis of some collection of texts. These studies typically focus on the description of particular linguistic features in particular text varieties. In addition to these research goals, however, a corpus-based approach enables a variationist perspective. Using computational (semi-)automatic techniques to analyze large text corpora, it is possible to investigate the patterns of variation across a large number of registers, with respect to a wide range of relevant linguistic characteristics. Such analyses provide an important foundation for work in ESP in that they characterize particular registers relative to the range of other registers, and they help to demonstrate the extent of the linguistic differences across registers (and thereby the need for proficiency in particular registers).

This approach is illustrated here using Biber's multi-dimensional (MD) analysis (e.g. Biber 1988, 1992). Studies in this framework have shown that there are systematic patterns of variation among registers; that these patterns can be analyzed in terms of underlying 'dimensions' of variation; and that it is necessary to recognize the existence of a multidimensional space in order to capture the overall relations among registers. Each dimension comprises a set of linguistic features that co-occur frequently in texts.

The dimensions are identified from a quantitative analysis of the distribution of linguistic features in a sample of 481 texts (c. 960,000 words) from the LOB and London–Lund corpora. There is space for only a brief methodological overview here; interested readers are referred to Biber (1988, especially Chapters 4–5) for a more detailed presentation.

First, the texts in these corpora were automatically analyzed for 67 linguistic features representing several major grammatical and functional characteristics, such as prepositional phrases, nominal forms, lexical classes (e.g. hedges, emphatics), and dependent clauses. Second, the frequency of each linguistic feature in each text was counted, and all counts were normalized to their occurrence per 1,000 words of text. Third, a factor analysis was run to identify the co-occurrence patterns among linguistic features, that is, the 'dimensions'. Fourth, dimension scores were computed for each text, so that texts and registers could be compared with respect to each dimension. Finally, the dimensions were interpreted functionally, based on the assumption that linguistic features co-occur in texts because they share underlying communicative functions. Similarly the patterns of variation among registers were interpreted from both linguistic and functional perspectives.

Six major dimensions are identified and interpreted in Biber (1988, especially Chapters 6–7). Each comprises a distinct set of co-occurring linguistic features; each defines a different set of similarities and differences among spoken and written registers; and each has distinct functional underpinnings. To illustrate, Table 11.7 presents the defining linguistic features for two of the dimensions: 'Involved versus Informational Production' (Dimension 1) and 'Non-Abstract versus Abstract Style' (Dimension 5).[7] Figure 11.1 presents the differences among ten spoken and written registers (including four subregisters from medical prose) within this two-dimensional space.[8]

The register characterizations on Figure 11.1 reflect different relative frequencies of the linguistic features comprising Dimensions 1 and 5, listed in Table 11.7. For example, medical research articles and scientific prose have the largest negative scores on Dimension 1 (scores between –18 and –25 on the vertical axis); these scores represent very frequent occurrences of nouns, long words, prepositions, etc. (the negative features on Dimension 1), together with markedly infrequent occurrences of private verbs, that-deletions, contractions, etc. (the positive features on Dimension 1). Medical and scientific prose also have the largest negative scores on Dimension 5 (scores between –5 and –9 on the horizontal axis); these scores reflect very frequent occurrences of conjuncts, agentless passives, past participial adverbial clauses, by-passives, etc. (the negative features on Dimension 5). At the other extreme, conversations have the largest

Table 11.7 Summary of the linguistic features grouped on Dimensions 1 and 5

DIMENSION 1		DIMENSION 5	
'Involved Production'		**'Non-Abstract Style'**	
Private verbs	.96	[No positive features]	
that-deletion	.91		
Contractions	.90	'Abstract Style'	
Present tense verbs	.86	Conjuncts	−.48
2nd person pronouns	.86	Agentless passives	−.43
DO as pro-verb	.82	Past participial adv. clauses	−.42
Analytic negation	.78		
Demonstrative pronouns	.76	BY-passives	−.41
		Past participial postnominal clauses	−.40
General emphatics	.74		
1st person pronouns	.74	Other adverbial subordinators	−.39
Pronoun IT	.71		
BE as main verb	.71		
Causative subordination	.66		
Indefinite pronouns	.62		
General hedges	.58		
Sentence relatives	.55		
WH-questions	.52		
Possibility modals	.50		
Non-phrasal coordination	.48		
WH-clauses	.47		
Final prepositions	.43		
'Informational Production'			
Nouns	−.80		
Word length	−.58		
Prepositions	−.54		
Type/token ratio	−.54		
Attributive adjs.	−.47		

positive score on Dimension 1, reflecting very frequent occurrence of the positive features on that dimension (private verbs, contractions, etc.) together with markedly few occurrences of the negative features (nouns, long words, etc.). Conversations also have the largest positive score on Dimension 5, reflecting the near complete absence of conjuncts, agentless passives, etc.

As can be seen from Figure 11.1, these ten registers are strikingly different in their linguistic characteristics, even within this two-dimensional space. This figure graphically illustrates the need for ESP/EAP approaches. For example, it shows that scientific prose and medical prose are quite different from the other eight registers in being extremely informational (Dimension 1) and abstract/passive in style (Dimension 5). It further shows that there are systematic but much smaller differences among the four subregisters within medical research articles; for example, Methods sections are marked as the most informational and abstract type of prose considered here (see Biber and Finegan 1994a).

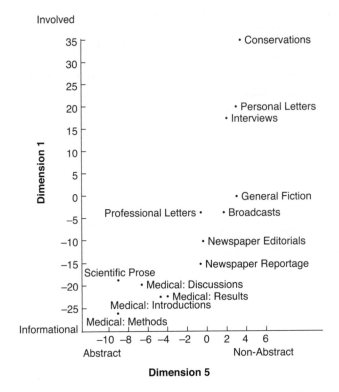

Figure 11.1 Linguistic characterization of ten spoken and written registers with respect to Dimension 1: 'Involved versus Informational Production', and Dimension 5: 'Non-Abstract versus Abstract Style'

At the other extreme, conversation is marked as being extremely involved and non-passive/non-abstract in its linguistic characteristics. Personal letters and interviews have similar characteristics, but the characterizations are not nearly as extreme as in conversations.[9]

When all six dimensions are considered, the differences among registers are even more notable. These patterns show that there is no single register that can be identified as 'general English', and that advanced instruction based on our intuitions about 'general' or 'core' English is not likely to provide adequate exposure to the actual linguistic patterns found in the target registers that students must use on a regular basis.

5 Conclusion

In a paper of this size, it is possible to survey only a few of the many applied research issues that are amenable to corpus-based investigations. There are numerous other areas that can be addressed from this perspective.

One such area concerns language acquisition and learning. Currently we are using the corpus-based approach to explore a number of L1 and L2 acquisition issues, including the development of discourse competence and register awareness, and a comparison of spoken and written registers produced by children. Other research on child language acquisition has also utilized the CHILDES database, which is among the most extensive text collections focusing on a particular research area (MacWhinney 1991).

A corpus-based approach also gives new perspectives on areas that have been previously investigated. For example, at Northern Arizona University, several corpus-based dissertation projects of this type are currently in progress: by Reppen, to investigate the development of writing skills in elementary school, across a number of genres and by students from different demographic backgrounds; by White, to investigate the linguistic characteristics of job interviews, comparing the discourse produced in different job situations, by interviewees from different backgrounds, including successful versus unsuccessful candidates; by Burges, to investigate the linguistic characteristics of written business communication (especially public memos), describing how social relations in the workplace are established and maintained by surface linguistic features; by Conrad, to investigate linguistic differences among professional journals, textbooks, and student writing across several academic disciplines. Although there have been previous studies on all these topics, the corpus-based approach facilitates investigations of a wider scope, enabling macroscopic analyses of the inter-relations among several different parameters of variation.

A corpus-based approach is also well suited for discourse comparisons cross-linguistically. For example, Lux and Grabe (1991) describe two corpus-based analyses of this kind: comparing newspaper editorials in English and Brazilian Portuguese, and comparing university student writing in Ecuadorian Spanish and English. Biber (1995) compares the dimensions of variation underlying the range of spoken and written registers in English, Nukulaelae Tuvaluan, Korean, and Somali. In addition, a corpus-based approach can be used in diachronic studies. Biber and Finegan (1989, 1992) analyze the development of several written registers over four centuries, while Atkinson (1992) presents a detailed investigation of the development of medical texts.

Finally, there are a number of social issues that could be investigated from a corpus perspective. To date, most descriptions of social variation have focused on individual linguistic characteristics (e.g. different phonetic realizations of a vowel or consonant) across a relatively restricted range of language use. However, corpus-based analyses could be used to identify the patterns of co-occurring linguistic features underlying dialect variation, and to describe and compare complete dialects (defined by social class, education, gender, etc.). Such analyses could further include comparison of the range of spoken and written registers within each dialect, with the eventual goal of an integrated account of dialect and register variation in a language (cf. Finegan and Biber 1994).

This paper has illustrated some of the techniques that are available to the applied linguist through the use of corpus-based approaches and has highlighted some of the pedagogical applications of corpus-based findings to date. Because corpus-based research examines a large amount of naturally-occurring language, it is particularly useful for comparing our intuitions against actual patterns of language use and for analyzing complex issues, such as the range of register variation in English. Given the explosion in the availability of on-line corpora and computational research tools, analyses and applications of corpus-based work should become increasingly common over the coming years.

Appendix

Commonly used corpora

The three best known text corpora of English are the Brown Corpus, LOB (Lancaster–Oslo/Bergen) Corpus, and London–Lund Corpus. The Standard Corpus of Present-Day Edited

American English, known as the Brown Corpus, was compiled by Francis and Kucera (1964/ 1979) at Brown University in the early 1960s. This corpus contains 1,000,000 words of written, edited American English published in 1961; the corpus comprises 500 text samples, each 2,000 words long, taken from 15 different text categories (e.g. press reportage, editorials, academic prose, general fiction). The Lancaster–Oslo/Bergen (LOB) corpus is a collection of British English texts with a parallel size and structure to the Brown Corpus (Johansson, Leech, and Goodluck 1978). The London–Lund Corpus is based on the spoken texts collected as part of the Survey of English Usage (Svartvik and Quirk 1980); it comprises 87 text samples, each at least 5,000 words long, representing several major speech situations (e.g. face-to-face and telephone conversations, radio broadcasts, interviews, public speeches).

More recent corpora

Other more recently compiled text corpora are considerably larger. The Longman/Lancaster English Language Corpus (Summers 1991) comprises c. 30 million words of text structured around ten major topic-based categories (e.g. applied science, arts, fiction). The British National Corpus – which is currently being compiled by Oxford University Press, Longman Group, W & R Chambers, the British Library, and the Universities of Oxford and Lancaster – will have 100 million words sampled from a wide range of spoken and written registers (including c. 10 million words from spoken registers). Other corpus projects have chosen to emphasize the overall size over the design. For example, the COBUILD project, which was one of the earliest teams to use a very large corpus (Sinclair 1987), and the Data Collection Initiative, sponsored by the Association of Computational Linguistics, both focus on the rapid collection and exploitation of on-line textual data. These text collections are over 100 million words in size and constantly growing, using readily available materials with less concern for their register categories. Taylor, Leech, and Fligelstone (1991) provide a useful survey of the English machine-readable corpora that were available in 1989.

One of the most pressing research needs at present is for the development and analysis of spoken corpora. To date, the London–Lund Corpus has been the main computer-based corpus of spoken texts available for public use. This corpus has provided a tremendous resource for empirical analysis of spoken language, but it is also restricted in several respects: by present-day standards, the corpus is relatively small (c. 500,000 words), it includes only British English, and a large number of the speakers are in academic professions. The British National Corpus will provide a much larger and more diverse sample of spoken British English (c. 10 million words of natural spoken texts, collected in a wide range of situations from a demographically representative range of speakers). A research project currently underway at the University of California, Santa Barbara, is building the first computer-based corpus of spoken American English intended for public distribution. Corpus-based research on spoken American English is thus lagging far behind research on British English, making this an important area for future investigations.

Diachronic corpora

The Helsinki Diachronic Corpus of English (Kytö 1991) and the ARCHER corpus (Biber et al. 1994) are designed to cover the development of English registers over several historical periods. The Helsinki Corpus covers the periods from Old English up to Early Modern English, while the ARCHER corpus includes texts from 1650 to the present.

Notes

1   In descriptive, socio-, and anthropological linguistics, there has been a relatively long history of studies using collections of natural texts that are not based on computers.

2   The other three types of postnominal modification – infinitival clauses, apposition, and adjectival phrases – generally receive minimal treatment in pedagogical grammars, although apposition is quite common in some registers.

3   Findings of this type are even more important for an ESP/EAP perspective. Academic prose is one of the few English registers that shows a widespread use of relative clause constructions although prepositional phrases are still more common.

4   Although textbooks for students typically do not include functional, corpus-based information, certain materials for teachers already do. Celce-Murcia and Larsen-Freeman (1983) includes numerous functional descriptions based on corpus analysis, distinguishing among the various uses of a construction and highlighting the most important functions. Celce-Murcia (1990) further discusses the importance of discourse analysis for grammar instruction.

5   In addition, there are a number of statistical tools that have been developed to measure the degree of association between a target word and other words in the context (see Church, Gale, Hanks, and Hindle 1991; Bindi, Calzolari, Monachini, and Pirrelli 1991).

6   Biber (1994) argues that attempts to make discrete distinctions between 'registers', 'genres', 'styles', and other text varieties are not useful, because there is a continuous space of variation among situationally-defined varieties. The term 'register' is proposed as a general cover term for situationally-defined text varieties at any level of generality; the term 'text type' for linguistically-defined varieties. This study further attempts to develop a framework to specify the level of generality of registers, enabling assessment of the extent to which any two registers are comparable.

7   The polarity of Dimension 5 has been reversed to aid in the comparison to Dimension 1.

8   Texts for the four medical subregisters are taken from the ARCHER Corpus (see Biber, Finegan, Atkinson, Beck, Burges, and Burges 1994).

9   These analyses show that there are marked linguistic differences among registers. However, since registers are defined situationally rather than on a linguistic basis, they are not equally coherent in their linguistic characteristics. A complete description of a register should include a linguistic characterization of typical texts (the mean scores, as in Figure 11.1), analysis of the range of variability within a register, analysis of any distinct subregisters, and analysis of the variation within texts from a register (cf. the investigations in Biber 1988, Chapter 8). A complementary perspective is to analyze *linguistically* well-defined text categories, or 'text types'. Registers and text types represent two alternative approaches to linguistic variation: Registers are defined on the basis of their situations and purposes, but they can be compared with respect to their linguistic characteristics; text types are defined on linguistic grounds, but the types can be interpreted functionally. Given a text type perspective, linguistically distinct texts within a register would be taken to represent different types, while linguistically similar texts from different registers would represent a single text type (cf. Biber 1989).

References

Altenberg, B. 1991. 'A bibliography of publications relating to English computer corpora' in S. Johansson and A-B. Stenström (eds) 1991: *English Computer Corpora: Selected Papers and Research Guide*. New York: Mouton.

Atkinson, D. 1992. 'The evolution of medical research writing from 1735 to 1985: The case of the *Edinburgh Medical Journal*'. *Applied Linguistics* 13:337–74.

Atkinson, D. and D. Biber. 1994. 'Register: A review of empirical research' in D. Biber and E. Finegan (eds) 1994b: *Sociolinguistic Perspectives on Register*. New York: Oxford University Press.

Azar, B. S. 1981. *Understanding and Using English Grammar*. Englewood Cliffs, NJ: Prentice-Hall.

Bazerman, C. 1988. *Shaping Written Knowledge*. Madison: University of Wisconsin Press.

Biber, D. 1988. *Variation Across Speech and Writing*. Cambridge: Cambridge University Press.

Biber, D. 1989. 'A Typology of English Texts'. *Linguistics* 27: 3–43.

Biber, D. 1992. 'On the complexity of discourse complexity: A multidimensional analysis'. *Discourse Processes* 15: 133–63.

Biber, D. 1994. 'An analytical framework for register studies' in D. Biber and E. Finegan (eds) 1994: *Sociolinguistic Perspectives on Register*. New York: Oxford University Press.

Biber, D. 1995. *Dimensions of Register Variation: A Cross-linguistic Comparison*. Cambridge: Cambridge University Press.

Biber, D. and E. Finegan. 1989. 'Drift and the evolution of English style: A history of three genres'. *Language* 65: 487–517.

Biber, D. and E. Finegan. 1992. 'The linguistic evolution of five written and speech-based English genres from the 17th to the 20th centuries' in M. Rissanen *et al.* (eds) 1992: *History of Englishes: New Methods and Interpretations in Historical Linguistics*. Berlin: Mouton.

Biber, D. and E. Finegan. 1994a. 'Intra-textual variation within medical research articles' in N. Oostdijk and P. de Haan (eds) 1994: *Corpus-based Research into Language*. Amsterdam: Rodopi.

Biber, D. and E. Finegan (eds). 1994b. *Sociolinguistic Perspectives on Register*. New York: Oxford University Press.

Biber, D., E. Finegan, D. Atkinson, A. Beck, D. Burges, and J. Burges. 1994. 'The design and analysis of the ARCHER Corpus: A progress report' in M. Kytö, M. Rissanen, and S. Wright (eds) 1994: *Corpora Across the Centuries*. Amsterdam: Rodopi.

Bindi, R., N. Calzolari, M. Monachini, and V. Pirrelli. 1991. 'Lexical knowledge acquisition from textual corpora: A multivariate statistic approach as an integration to traditional methodologies' in *Proceedings of the Seventh Annual Conference of the UW Centre for the New OED and Text Research*. Oxford, England.

Cake, C. and H. D. Rogerson. 1986. *Gaining Ground: Intermediate Grammar Text*. Cambridge, MA: Newbury House.

Celce-Murcia, M. 1990. 'Discourse analysis and grammar instruction'. *Annual Review of Applied Linguistics* 11:135–51.

Celce-Murcia, M. and D. Larsen-Freeman. 1983. *The Grammar Book: An ESL/EFL Teacher's Course*. New York: Newbury House.

Church, K., W. Gale, P. Hanks, and D. Hindle. 1991. 'Using Statistics in Lexical Analysis' in U. Zernik (ed.) 1991: *Lexical Acquisition: Exploiting On-line Resources to Build a Lexicon*. Hillsdale, NJ: Lawrence Erlbaum.

Danielson, D. and P. Porter. 1990. *Using English: Your Second Language*. Englewood Cliffs, NJ: Prentice-Hall.

Finegan, E. and D. Biber. 1993. 'Register and social dialect variation: An integrated approach' in D. Biber and E. Finegan (eds) 1994b: *Sociolinguistic Perspectives on Register*. New York: Oxford University Press.

Francis, W. N. and H. Kucera. 1964/1979. *Manual of Information to Accompany a Standard Corpus of Present-Day Edited American English, for Use with Digital Computers*. Department of Linguistics, Brown University.

Ghadessy, M. (ed.). 1988. *Registers of Written English: Situational Factors and Linguistic Features*. London: Pinter.

Grishman, R. and R. Kittredge (eds) 1986. *Analyzing Language in Restricted Domains: Sublanguage Description and Processing*. Hillsdale, NJ: Lawrence Erlbaum.

Hillocks, G. 1986. *Research on Written Composition*. Urbana, IL: ERIC Clearinghouse on Reading and Communication Skills.

Johansson, S., G.N. Leech, and H. Goodluck. 1978. *Manual of Information to Accompany the Lancaster–Oslo/Bergen Corpus of British English, for Use with Digital Computers*. Department of English, University of Oslo.

Johns, A. M. 1991. 'English for Specific Purposes (ESP): Its history and contributions' in M. Celce-Murcia (ed.) 1991: *Teaching English as a Second or Foreign Language*. New York: Newbury House.

Johns, A. M. and T. Dudley-Evans. 1991. 'English for Specific Purposes: International in scope, specific in purpose.' *TESOL Quarterly* 25: 297–314.

Kittredge, R. and J. Lehrberger (eds) 1982. *Sublanguage: Studies of Language in Restricted Semantic Domains*. Berlin: De Gruyter.

Kytö, M. 1991. *Manual to the Diachronic Part of the Helsinki Corpus of English Texts: Coding Conventions and Lists of Source Texts*. Helsinki: University of Helsinki.

Lux, P. and W. Grabe. 1991. 'Multivariate approaches to contrastive rhetoric'. *Lenguas Modernas* 18: 133–60.

MacWhinney, B. 1991. *The CHILDES Project: Tools for Analyzing Talk*. Hillsdale, NJ: Lawrence Erlbaum Associates.

Mair, C. 1990. *Infinitival Complement Clauses in English: A Study of Syntax in Discourse*. Cambridge: Cambridge University Press.

Meyer, C. F. 1992. *Apposition in Contemporary English*. Cambridge: Cambridge University Press.

Murphy, R. and R. Altman. 1989. *Grammar in Use: Reference and Practice for Intermediate Students of English*. Cambridge: Cambridge University Press.

Sinclair, J. (ed.). 1987. *Looking Up*. London: Collins.

Sinclair, J. 1991. *Corpus, Concordance, Collocation*. Oxford: Oxford University Press.

Summers, D. 1991. *Longman/Lancaster English Language Corpus: Criteria and Design*. Technical Report, Longman.

Svartvik, J. and R. Quirk (eds). 1980. *A Corpus of English Conversation*. Lund Studies in English 56. Lund: CWK Gleerup.

Swales, J. M. 1990. *Genre Analysis: English in Academic and Research Settings.* Cambridge: Cambridge University Press.

Taylor, L., G. Leech, and S. Fligelstone. 1991. 'A survey of English machine-readable corpora' in S. Johansson and A-B. Stenström (eds) 1991: *English Computer Corpora: Selected Papers and Research Guide*. Berlin: Mouton.

Tottie, G. 1991. *Negation in English Speech and Writing: A Study in Variation*. San Diego: Academic Press.

Chapter 12

RONALD CARTER AND
MICHAEL McCARTHY

TALKING, CREATING
Interactional language, creativity and context (2004)

WHEN CREATIVE USES OF SPOKEN LANGUAGE have been investigated, the main examples have been restricted to particular contexts such as narrative and related story-telling genres. This paper reports on an initial investigation using the 5 million word CANCODE corpus of everyday spoken English and discusses a range of social contexts in which creative uses of language are manifested. A main conclusion reached is that creative language use often signposts the nature of interpersonal relationships, plays an important role in the construction of identities and is more likely to emerge in social contexts marked by non-institutionalized, symmetrical, and informal talk. The paper also argues that different creative patterns of talk are produced for different purposes, that clines and continua best capture such distinctions and that applications of such understandings to language learning and teaching, including the teaching of literature and culture, can benefit from closer scrutiny of such data.

1 Introduction

The analysis of creative language has been seen mainly in terms of distinctions between literary and non-literary language, with analysis, following in the tradition of Russian formalist aesthetic theory, highlighting the extent to which 'literary' language foregrounds attention by deviating from expected patterns and promoting new, schema-refreshing ways of seeing the familiar and everyday. Traditional discussion in the field of stylistics (Short 1996; Widdowson 1992) has largely followed such theoretical precepts but has recently been extended to include non-canonical texts such as advertising copy, newspaper headlines, and jokes, with an emphasis on the centrality of language play in a range of everyday discourses and on the breaking down of divisions between literary and non-literary language (Alexander 1997; Carter and McRae 1996; Chiaro 1992; Cook 1994, 1996, 2000; Crystal 1998; Kramsch and Kramsch 2000). In these traditions, however, applications to the analysis of everyday spoken interaction have been limited.

Work in cognitive psychology and linguistics has further developed insights into the common nature of creative language with representative authors such as Lakoff and Turner (1989), Lakoff and Johnson (1999), Turner (1991), Sweetser (1990), and Gibbs (1994, 1999) arguing that familiar figures of speech such as metaphor, irony, and hyperbole are natural and normal components of language, and that the human mind should thus be seen as essentially non-literal in its figurations of the world. The ubiquitous nature of metaphor has led to arguments that thought itself is structured metaphorically (Cameron 1999; Cameron and Low 1999). With some notable exceptions (for example, Candlin *et al.* 2000; Cameron 1999; Eggins and Slade 1997; Goddard 1996; Kuiper 1996; Kuiper and Haggo 1984; Ragan 2000; Mertz 1989), the data produced in such accounts have, however, been almost exclusively confined to written texts, the data have been examined along mainly formalist lines and, crucially, researchers have not paid systematic attention to the contextual conditions of its production.

However, other traditions have focused much more extensively on the poetics of talk. Traditions of research in ethnopoetics and in anthropological and cross-cultural studies of verbal art have embraced culturally-specific, contextually-sensitive accounts of verbal aesthetics (e.g. Friedrich 1979, 1986; Hanks 1996; Hill 1985; Hymes 1996; Mannheim 1986; Rubin 1995; Tedlock 1975, 1977). Tannen (1989) underlines that features such as figures of speech, imagery, and repetition, normally only analyzed in conventional 'literary' forms, are ubiquitous in conversation. Most studies within this tradition have focused on the relatively restricted genre of stories and of narrative and dramatic performance as manifested in more monologic discourse styles. Studies which have explored the artistry of everyday exchanges and interactions (e.g. Tannen 1989; Norrick 1993, 2000, 2001) have been largely confined to the genre of narrative or to restricted social contexts such as dinner-party or family conversations. None the less, detailed attention is given in these studies to spoken creativity and to contextual conditions. Such studies also eschew formalist definitions of linguistic creativity, preferring more functional and contextualized accounts. It is a tradition of investigation with which we align ourselves.

2 Organizing the research

2.1 What is linguistic creativity in this research? Basic frameworks, definitions and questions

In previous papers (Adolphs and Carter 2003; Carter 1999; Carter and McCarthy 1995b; McCarthy 1998b) we have begun to explore the pervasiveness of creative language use in a corpus of everyday spoken English (the CANCODE corpus, see 2.2). Research so far on the CANCODE corpus has identified key features such as verbal repetition as well as a wide range of 'figures of speech' such as metaphor, simile, metonymy, idiom, slang expressions, proverbs, hyperbole. We are learning, however, that it is not possible to define creativity in wholly formalist ways, that is, by identifying particular forms in the corpus, not least because in spoken interaction what counts as creative use varies.

The purposes for creative language in common everyday speech can include: offering some new way of seeing the content of the message; making humorous remarks; underlining what is communicated; expressing a particular attitude, including negative and adversarial attitudes; making the speaker's identity more manifest; playing with language form to entertain others; ending one bit of talk and starting another; or simply oiling the wheels of the conversation (as well as several of these functions and purposes simultaneously).

Another reason for avoiding formalist definitions is that some uses of language may be felt to be creative by one participant in a dialogue but not necessarily by others and may sometimes not even be noticed by the producer(s) of utterances. For example, in some contexts figures of speech pass unnoticed as normal, routine, even pre-formulated units; in other cases, the same figures of speech are drawn to the attention of speakers. And even so-called 'dead' metaphors or cliches can be put to effective creative use in the dynamics of dialogue. Thus, in our definition, creativity almost always depends for its functions on the intentions and interpretations of the participants. We also recognize that most established definitions of linguistic creativity imply change and normally involve a single producer who brings about 'novel' changes to the language or to forms of language in ways which are innovative and schema-refreshing. There are several such uses in our data but the main focus in this paper is on creative uses of language as they occur in interpersonal exchanges, in specific contexts of interaction and through the dialogic effects of the individual encounter.

The following examples from a conversational extract to be discussed below (1. Sunday afternoon) illustrate some of the above mentioned features.

1. ⟨S 02⟩   [Laughs] cos you come home
    ⟨S 03⟩   I come home
    ⟨S 02⟩   You come home to us

2. ⟨S 03⟩   Sunday is a really nice day I think
    ⟨S 02⟩   It certainly is
    ⟨S 03⟩   It's a really nice relaxing day

3. ⟨S 03⟩   I reckon it looks better like that
    ⟨S 02⟩   And it was another bit as well, another dangly bit
    ⟨S 03⟩   What, attached to
    ⟨S 02⟩   The top bit
    ⟨S 03⟩   That one
    ⟨S 02⟩   Yeah. So it was even
    ⟨S 03⟩   Mobile earrings
    ⟨S 01⟩   I like it like that. It looks better like that

An immediately striking creative use occurs in 3 in the word *mobile* which is metaphorically linked with the word 'earrings'. There is a pun on the meaning of 'mobile' (with its semantics of movement) and the fixture of a *mobile* – meaning either a brightly coloured dangling object which is normally placed over a child's bed or cot to provide distraction or entertainment, or else which is a piece of moving art. And a piece of metaphoric word play at this point in the unfolding discourse prompts, as we shall see in the commentary below, further play with figures of speech. This usage is a more conventional instance of linguistic creativity involving changes in, to, and with the language. However, we propose a further and complementary definition which also takes fuller account of functions in context and which acknowledges that to recognize linguistic creativity much depends on how language is used by speakers in relation to local contextual purposes and, especially, interpersonal interactions with language.

Repetition is a good example of speakers 'talking, creating'. Repetition works as a more subtle token of a *relationship*, not just between utterances or turns but between speakers, the main purpose often being to co-construct interpersonal convergence and to creatively adapt to the other speaker(s). According to Tannen (1989), repetition is a key component in the poetics of talk:

Repetition is a resource by which conversationalists together create a discourse, a relationship, and a world. It is the central linguistic meaning-making strategy, a limitless resource for individual creativity and interpersonal involvement.

(Tannen, 1989: ch 3)

For example, the above extracts, 1–3, mainly involve repetition across speaking turns. But the repetition is not simply an echo of the previous speaker. The forms include both verbatim phrasal and clausal repetition and repetition with variation (for example, the addition of the word 'relaxing' in extract 2). The patterning with variation includes both lexical and grammatical repetition (the repetition of the word *bit* or *like* – in its different grammatical realizations as verb and preposition—as well as repetition of the deictic determiner *that* in extract 3), pronominal repetition with variation (extract 1), and phonological repetition with variation (for example, *bit/better* in extract 3). Repetition is evident here in varied linguistic ways but the main creative functions are in the dialogic building of relationships and of accord between the speakers.

This account of linguistic creativity is different from creativity as defined by Chomsky who sees it as a fundamental species-specific capacity for generating an infinite number of rule-governed language choices which are for the most part new to both speaker and listener and yet are readily understood by both. In Chomsky's definition (1964: 7) the creative capacity also extends to the ability to construct a context in which an interpretation of the language can be made, even if the language is not formed according to the rules governing that language. We share in particular Chomsky's stress on the creative capacity of the receiver of a message (1964: 9) but argue that, because his view is limited to the problems of handling invented sentences, it does not account for the speaker's capacity to handle stretches of text or naturally-occurring, contextually variable sequences of speaking turns in which patterns of language can form and reform dynamically and organically over stretches of discourse, and emerge through the joint conditions of production.

In a sense, of course, and except for the most routinely formulaic or inattentive turns, almost all conversational exchanges are creatively co-produced. As Sacks (1984) argues, ordinary talk has to be achieved and it is a human, social, and creative accomplishment which is far from being 'ordinary'. One aim in this paper is to attempt to underline this point but we also hope to go beyond Sacks' insights to explore more fully not only what is linguistically creative in everyday interactions but also begin to identify contexts in which creative language use may be less evident. We argue in particular that creative language choices compel recognition of the social contexts of their production: principally, the construction and maintenance of inter-personal relations and social identities. Our main research aim in this paper then is to explore what kinds of functions linguistic creativity has in different speech genres, social contexts, and types of interaction and then draw some conclusions concerning such language functions and contexts, mainly in relation to language study and teaching.

2.2 Generic organization and speech genres in CANCODE[1]

The data collected and transcribed for the CANCODE corpus are classified along two main axes according to CONTEXT-TYPE and INTERACTION TYPE. Context-type reflects the interpersonal relationships that hold between speakers, embracing both dyadic and multi-party conversations and in all cases it is the relationship between speakers – that is, the ways in which they communicate at this level – which qualifies data for inclusion in the category, and not simply the particular environment in which the audio-recording is made. Four broad types are identified along a cline from *transactional*, *professional socializing*, to *intimate*. The 'transactional' is the most public and often involves contexts in which there is no previous relationship established between the speakers. In the 'professional' category the speakers are not necessarily peers but they do share either a profession or a regular place of work. 'Socializing' typically involves contexts such as sports clubs and pubs, as well as recreational and other group meetings. An 'intimate' context-type is normally a private, cohabiting relationship where speakers can be assumed to be

Table 12.1 CANCODE text types and typical situations in which they might be found

Context-type	Interaction-type		
	Information-provision	Collaborative idea	Collaborative task
Transactional	commentary by museum guide	chatting with hairdresser	choosing and buying a television
Professional	oral report at group meeting	planning meeting at place of work	colleagues window-dressing
Socialising	telling jokes to friends	reminiscing with friends	friends cooking together
Intimate	partner relating the story of a film seen	siblings discussing their childhood	couple decorating a room

linguistically most 'off-guard'. Although there are points of overlap between categories, the relationship categories do represent, albeit roughly, a cline of 'public' to 'private' speech, with the 'transactional' and 'intimate' categories respectively at each end of the cline. The 'professional' category is more public than the 'socializing' category, which in turn is more public than 'intimate'.

Along the axis of INTERACTION TYPE, distinctions are made between data that are predominantly collaborative and those that are non-collaborative and, further, for the collaborative type, those which are task-oriented and those which are not. In non-collaborative texts one speaker dominates significantly, supported by back-channelling from the other speaker(s). Typically, the dominant speaker in these texts relates an event, tells a joke, gives instructions, explanations, or professional presentations. On one level, of course, these exchanges are also collaborative; on another level they resemble a unilinear transfer of information. The blanket term adopted for such an interaction type is *information provision*.

The two other interaction types represent more collaborative and dialogic speech encounters. *Collaborative idea* involves the interactive sharing of thoughts, opinions, and attitudes, while the category of *collaborative task* is reserved for task-oriented communication. Also included in this category are the exchange of goods and the discussion of an entity that is referred to during the exchange, such as a catalogue or a computer screen. Overall, texts have proved more difficult to categorize in terms of interaction type due to the problem of embedding. Category membership is thus allocated according to the activity that is dominant in each conversation. A significantly more detailed account of the CANCODE corpus and its design may be found in McCarthy (1998a) where the dangers inherent in reifying the categories are also fully acknowledged.

Combining the two axes provides a matrix of twelve text types as can be seen in Table 12.1, which also suggests some situations in which the text types might be found.

In subsequent analyses of data in this paper there will be constant reference back to the context- and interaction-types described here.

2.3 *Organizing the data: a brief note*

The data for this paper were collected by random searching of the corpus cells using standard software tools. Although ten extracts (varying between 500 and 800 words) were searched in each cell, the overall approach is qualitative rather than quantitative, not least because, in the current stages of automatic retrieval of language, manifestations of linguistic creativity are not easily identifiable by quantitative means. The overall approach to the data is to use it to exemplify categories rather than to undertake a quantitative survey of the corpus. Thus the corpus has to be 'read' like a transcribed, living soap opera, in a series of representative extracts. In short, a methodology which combines the fine-tooth comb of conversation analysis with the immediate availability of the large number of contextually controlled samples which the corpus offers seems to be the only way forward in the current state of corpus technology.

3 Analysing the data

The contextual nature of different types of creative language can be illustrated by the following extract from the CANCODE corpus, extracts from which have already been discussed above. Note that, in all subsequent extracts from CANCODE, line/turn numbers are used for identification and, with the exception of the first extract which has already been highlighted above, the main words, phrases and other units of language highlighted for subsequent commentary are italicized.

1 SUNDAY AFTERNOON

[Contextual information: extract from a conversation involving three Art College students. The students are all female, are the same age (between 20 and 21) and share a house in Wales. Two of the students [⟨S 01? and ⟨S 03?] are from the south-west of England and one [⟨S 02?] is from South Wales. They are having tea at home on a Sunday. The main CANCODE speech genre involved in the Sunday afternoon extract is 'socializing/collaborative idea'].

1	⟨S 03⟩	I like Sunday nights for some reason, [laughs] I don't know why.
2	⟨S 02⟩	[laughs] Cos you come home.
3	⟨S 03⟩	I come home+
4	⟨S 02⟩	You come home to us.
5	⟨S 03⟩	+and pig out.
6	⟨S 02⟩	Yeah yeah.
7	⟨S 03⟩	Sunday is a really nice day I think.
8	⟨S 02⟩	It certainly is.
9	⟨S 03⟩	It's a really nice relaxing day.
10	⟨S 02⟩	It's an earring.
11	⟨S 03⟩	Oh lovely oh lovely.
12	⟨S 02⟩	It's fallen apart a bit. But
13	⟨S 03⟩	It looks quite nice like that actually. I like that. I bet, is that supposed to be straight?
14	⟨S 02⟩	Yeah.
15	⟨S 03⟩	I reckon it looks better like that.
16	⟨S 02⟩	And it was another bit as well. Was another dangly bit.
17	⟨S 03⟩	What..attached to+
18	⟨S 02⟩	The top bit.
19	⟨S 03⟩	+that one.
20	⟨S 02⟩	Yeah. So it was even.
21	⟨S 03⟩	Mobile earrings.
22	⟨S 01⟩	I like it like that. It looks better like that.

23 ⟨S 02⟩   Oh what did I see. What did I see. Stained glass. There w=, I went to a craft fair.
24 ⟨S 03⟩   Mm.
25 ⟨S 02⟩   C=, erm in Bristol. And erm, I know, [laughs] I went to a craft fair in Bristol and
              they had erm this stained glass stall and it was all mobiles made out of stained glass.
26 ⟨S 03⟩   Oh wow.
27 ⟨S 02⟩   And they were superb they were. And the mirrors with all different colours, like
              going round in the colour colour wheel. But all different size bits of coloured glass
              on it.
28 ⟨S 03⟩   Oh wow.
29 ⟨S 02⟩   It was superb. Massive.

As observed by Goffman (1981) and Tannen (1989) in relation to their data, the extensive repetition here is used in particular to create an affective convergence and a commonality of viewpoint. In fact, there is also a more cumulative effect and conditions are established in which speakers grow to feel they occupy shared worlds and viewpoints, in which the risks attendant on using figures of speech creatively are reduced and in which intimacy and convergence are actively co-produced. These relationship-reinforcing shared worlds and viewpoints are created in a number of ways: for example, by means of supportive minimal and non-minimal backchannelling e.g. *Oh lovely, oh, lovely; yeah, yeah* (11.6, 11, 14); by means of specifically reinforcing interpersonal grammatical forms such as tails (McCarthy and Carter 1997) . . . *They were superb, they were* (1.27) and tags; *They do, don't they*; and by means of affective exclamatives *oh wow* (1.28). The exchanges are also impregnated with vague and hedged language forms (for example, *fallen apart a bit, the top bit, I reckon, for some reason, I don't know why*), and a range of evaluative and attitudinal expressions (often juxtaposed with much laughter) which further support and creatively adapt to the informality, intimacy, and solidarity established.

Repetition can have, however, more than a simply reinforcing and convergence-creating function. For example, in an earlier phase of this exchange two of the girls deliberately take on parodic voices by mimicking low-prestige accents and concerns, in the process indirectly co-producing an ironic, humorous reflection on their own needs. The repetitions here draw attention to the effects produced.

⟨S 02⟩   Well they* would go smashing with a cup of tea wouldn't they.
⟨S 01⟩   Oh they would.
⟨S 01⟩   [In mock Cockney accent] Cup of tea and a fag.
⟨S 03⟩   [In mock Cockney accent] Cup of tea and a fag missus. [Reverts to normal accent]
              We're gonna have to move the table I think.
[* reference to a type of cake being offered by one of the girls]

The chorus-like repetition by speaker 3 of speaker 1's parody and her addition of *missus* underlines the collaborative nature of the humour. The girls membership themselves temporarily as 'working-class cockney women', such a self-categorization and its precise occasion of utterance being among the key elements in the creation of identities in talk emphasized by Antaki and Widdicombe (1998). Other figures of speech here are also more directly interpersonal, for example the similes inviting comparison; in this case, a perceived likeness between stained glass mobiles seen at a local craft fair and a colour wheel (11.25–28). There is also a case for seeing some of the formality switches (for example, *pig out*, 1.5) as constituting ironic-comic reversals of the kind not uncommonly connected with humorous creative effects (Norrick 1993;

Clift 1999). Sometimes the effect of these features is playfully to provide for humour and entertainment; but such patterns also generate innovative ways of seeing things and convey the speaker's own more personalized representation of events. So this example shows creation of convergence; creative use of speech; creative adaptation of the use of expressions; and creation of identity. The following sections show the range of ways linguistic creativity can be used and consider the ways this seems to happen in particular sample contexts.

3.1 Contextualizing the data further: lifeguards and journalists

Two more examples, *lifeguards* and *journalists*, are from contrasting contexts. The first example involves two lifeguards who have taken a break from their duties at a swimming pool. In such circumstances it is of course difficult to know whether the lifeguards are operating in a professional capacity or are sufficiently disengaged from their professional roles for the genre of talk to correspond more closely to a friendly socializing encounter (see Eggins and Slade 1997, for many such examples). Such blurrings of category are inevitable and a blurring of categories may in fact provide a more accurate portrayal of a notion such as 'workplace talk' than monolithic categorizations of professional or task-oriented discourse. It is decided in this paper to retain the term *professional* for the context, since the location, uniforms, and roles occupied by the participants are closer to the professional than to the nonprofessional socializing axis. Small talk and casual conversation of varying types is endemic in professional settings, as the papers in Coupland (2000) demonstrate. In this *lifeguards* example the speakers are engaged in the genre of 'professional/collaborative idea'.

2 Lifeguards

[Contextual information: lifeguards in an office, chatting in-between taking entrance fees from customers. ⟨S 01⟩ lifeguard: male (32); ⟨S 02⟩ lifeguard: male (31). The speakers are discussing possible reading matter for a forthcoming holiday]

1 ⟨S 01⟩ The thing about hard-backs is if you take a hard-back on the beach *pages don't blow up*. Some pages are bound and if you take a paper-back on the beach *all the bleeding glue melts*.
2 ⟨S 02⟩ Oh.
3 ⟨S 01⟩ You end up *pages all over the place*.
4 ⟨S 02⟩ That might do there and all cos it's like about ninety to hundred degrees at the moment there.
5 ⟨S 01⟩ Yeah.
6 ⟨S 02⟩ So.
7 ⟨S 01⟩ It's er. I was in, I was in, reading F H M on the sunlounger *happy as hell*. Not very hot. Pages open. Mm. The next thing you know this page came in my hand and all glue that holds the pages had melted and there were pages *blowing all over the place*. *Not a happy hamster*.
8 ⟨S 02⟩ [laughs] Not a happy one. I've gotta take something and there's like a good book-shop er in Manchester airport. So you get there early enough anyway. So.
9 ⟨S 01⟩ Mm.
10 ⟨S 02⟩ Straight down to W H Smith's and er see what books I can get.
11 ⟨S 01⟩ Mm.

12 ⟨S 02⟩   I'm not gonna like leave it 'til we get there cos they'd be like you know. *Separate*
             Tales of Doctor Duck or sommat

13 [laughter]
    ⟨S 01⟩   I were taking, I bought Marvin Gaye's biography and taking that and erm what's the
             other one. Phil Lynott you know *him out of Thin Lizzie?*

14 ⟨S 02⟩   Yeah.
15 ⟨S 01⟩   Him [unintelligible] +
16 ⟨S 02⟩   [unintelligible]
17 ⟨S 01⟩   +died of drugs and er+
18 ⟨S 02⟩   Yeah.
19 ⟨S 01⟩   +his erm, he married *Leslie Crowther's, Crowther's daughter* didn't he?
20 ⟨S 02⟩   Yeah.
21 ⟨S 01⟩   I'll have a look through them two. Something about like biographies I find them
             more interesting than than fiction. Fiction's all right innit.

22 ⟨S 02⟩   I like some of Yeah.
23 ⟨S 01⟩   When you're reading something you know that somebody's done+
24 ⟨S 02⟩   Made up.
25 ⟨S 01⟩   +or been through that+
26 ⟨S 02⟩   Yeah.
27 ⟨S 01⟩   +or experienced like it's it makes it a little bit more interesting.
28 ⟨S 02⟩   See I like er last time, well not last time but a couple of times before I went to er
             Tenerife wit t'ex-missus like.

29 ⟨S 01⟩   Mhm.
30 ⟨S 02⟩   Er I took er a book on on the Holocaust at er, well no like.
31 ⟨S 01⟩   *A bit of light reading.*
32 ⟨S 02⟩   Well yeah. *A bit of light reading.*

The lifeguards' discourse is especially marked by a mutuality within which both participants strive to align knowledge and viewpoint, establishing intertextual co-reference and reinforcing shared knowledge. For example: . . . *he married Leslie Crowther's daughter* (1.19), *didn't he; . . . you know him out of Thin Lizzie* (1.13) [Leslie Crowther is a well-known British TV personality; Thin Lizzie were a famous pop group of the 1970s]. In particular, the mutuality is achieved by: overt agreement by means of simple acknowledgement (*yeah*); supportive back-channelling (*Mm*); acceptance of propositions by repetition (for example: the repetition of the phrase *all over the place* when discussing the dangers of soft-back books in high temperatures or the parallels of *a bit of light reading* 11.31–32). Such mutuality is assumed from the earliest stages of this exchange. From the beginning metaphors are in evidence (*the pages don't blow up, all the bleeding glue melts* 11.1–2) and the lifeguards appear to feel sufficiently at ease with one other. Having further creatively aligned and re-aligned their mutual knowledge, feelings, and attitudes, co-productivity leads organically into more conventionally recognized creative language choices: deliberate hyperbole (*all the glue had melted; pages blowing all over the place*); extravagant similes (*happy as hell; They'd be like you know Separate Tales of Doctor Duck*) (1.12); understatements (*not a happy hamster; a bit of light reading*) (11.7 and 32). Nearly all of these formulations result in laughter or further elaboration. The term *involvement* used by Tannen does not wholly capture the extent to which shared feelings and attitudes are mutually constructed as a frame or 'platform' for creative verbal play which is then in its turn further co-produced. From a Vygotskian perspective, we have something akin to the development of a collective mind, enacting itself in distinctly social space (Vygotsky 1978; Emerson 1983).

In both extracts so far, we may also discern evidence of 'footing shifts', after Goffman (1979, 1981). Goffman (1981) describes footing as 'alignment, or set, or stance, or posture, or projected self' (p.128); changes in the alignment establishes new 'frames' in which the talk is interpreted. Turn construction and placement can signal shifts in footing and render a conversational frame more visible. Shifts are often marked by discourse markers, and in the two extracts, markers such as *the thing about X is . . .* , *the next thing you know, . . .* , *like, you know,* suggest that new conversational frames are projected in which evaluation or stance of some kind is to be creatively displayed.

The next example involves radio journalists.

3 Radio journalists

[Contextual information: radio journalists on a local radio station are engaged in a meeting, the main purpose of which is to decide which stories to programme. The context is professional, (even though the relationships are clearly sufficiently familiar to suggest that the context could be marked as socializing). And the nature of the interaction (predominantly collaborative task) also shifts in a dynamic way as goals change so that parts of the talk are clearly more relational than transactional and in some stretches of the discourse the contours are closer to collaborative idea. The dominant paradigm is, however, 'professional/collaborative task'. ⟨S 01⟩ radio producer: male (40s) ⟨S 02⟩ journalist: female (20s); ⟨S 03⟩ journalist: female (20s); ⟨S 04⟩ journalist: male (40s); ⟨S 05⟩ journalist: female (20s) (These people don't appear on the transcript: ⟨S 06⟩ journalist: male (30s); ⟨S 07⟩ radio engineer: male (30s); ⟨S 08⟩ news editor: male (40s)).]

 1 ⟨S 01⟩   Erm. This isn't really any= anybody's patch but you might want to do it tomorrow. Bea=Beatrix Potter's diary is going on sale at Phillips in London tomorrow and apparently we talked about this last week it tells of her unhappy life in the Lake District. Which is a complete, everybody thought.
 2 ⟨S 05⟩   Oh I thought she was happy as a sandboy.
 3 ⟨S 04⟩   *All the bleeding tourists going round her house she didn't like.*
 4 [laughter]
 5 ⟨S 01⟩   Yeah.
 6 ⟨S 02⟩   No it's not her unhappy life in the Lake District.
 7 ⟨S 05⟩   *It's all them mice wasn't it.* [laughs]
 8 ⟨S 02⟩   It was her happy life in London cos she lived in Kensington didn't she?
 9 ⟨S 01⟩   Oh is it.
10 ⟨S 02⟩   Yeah. She lived in Kensington and that was how she spent her childhood. Trapped by the city and+
11 ⟨S 01⟩   Oh that's+
12 ⟨S 02⟩   +retreated into a+
13 ⟨S 01⟩   +that's boring isn't it.
14 ⟨S 02⟩   +pet pet
15 ⟨S 04⟩   No it's not such a good story+
16 ⟨S 01⟩   Yeah.
17 ⟨S 04⟩   +now is it.
18 ⟨S 01⟩   No. [laughs]
19 ⟨S 03⟩   Oh well. I'm not gonna bother with that.
20 ⟨S 01⟩   [laughs]

21 ⟨S 02⟩   Sorry. I mean I di=
22 ⟨S 05⟩   Who did that?
23 ⟨S 02⟩   I was reading a piece erm
24 ⟨S 05⟩   That's good.
25 ⟨S 02⟩   Beatrix Potter did that. [laughs]
26 ⟨S 01⟩   Right.
27 [laughter]. . . . .
28 [laughter]
29 ⟨S 04⟩   Erm.
30 ⟨S 01⟩   What's this Mafeking relieved? Erm.
31 [laughter]
32 ⟨S 01⟩   Erm+
33 ⟨S 03⟩   [unintelligible]
34 ⟨S 01⟩   +Earl of Derby officially opening Liverpool airport's upgraded passenger facilities.
35 ⟨S 03⟩   Ooh yeah. We'll have that one.
36 ⟨S 01⟩   Erm tomorrow evening apparently. Half past six. If these prospects are for the right
            day.
37 ⟨S 02⟩   Never heard of this guy. The Earl of Derby.
38 ⟨S 03⟩   Derbyshire versus [unintelligible].
39 ⟨S 05⟩   Earl of Derby.
40 ⟨S 04⟩   You've never heard of the Earl of Derby?
41 ⟨S 02⟩   No. Never fe=, *I wouldn't know him if I fell over him.*
42 ⟨S 01⟩   Erm+
43 ⟨S 05⟩   *Drunk as a lord.*
44 ⟨S 02⟩   [laughs]
45 ⟨S 01⟩   +and that is about, Oh erm Jason this might erm be interesting for you. Tomorrow
            eleven P M tomorrow is the deadline for an unclaimed lottery p= prize of nearly a
            hundred and ten thousand pounds. And they reckon the ticket was bought in
            Wirral.
46 ⟨S 03⟩   Really.
47 ⟨S 02⟩   Oh.
48 ⟨S 03⟩   *Oh it was me.*

In the 'radio journalists' discourse a mutuality is achieved not dissimilar to that in the 'lifeguards' talk above. Even though the discourse is multi-party rather than two-party, there is clear evidence that information is provided in a listener-sensitive way and that efforts are made to achieve shared knowledge, to align perspectives and to establish agreement on the preferred action for the group as they decide on which stories are to run later that day. Footing shifts are evident again (e.g. . . ., oh, . . ., what's this . . .?), suggesting participants' sensitivity to the conversational frame. Overall, though, in this example mutuality is less collectively achieved than pre-established. There is less effort invested in aligning attitudes or in reinforcing points of view. Indeed, in this extract there is an altogether greater sense of ritual, perhaps resulting in part from the generic stability of such (presumably daily) professional meetings. The familiarity of the genre matches the familiarity of the participants with one another and with their own roles. An ambience is thus created in which roles can be more overtly performed. As shown below, linguistic creativity is relatively dense in this extract. It is co-produced but there is an altogether less marked sense of it emerging steadily and organically from the relationships between the participants in a particular encounter.

The differences between the two genres in the two examples may be important. The lifeguards' talk is predominantly professional collaborative idea (with 'socializing' tendencies); the journalists talk is predominantly professional collaborative task (with tendencies towards 'socializing' and 'collaborative ideas'). The task-directed nature of their activity influences the contours of their talk; there is greater emphasis on transactional content and less emphasis on interpersonal relations. And the work-related setting is also a factor in inhibiting too overt a creative co-production of mutuality. Although acknowledgements (*yeah*), laughter and back-channelling are present, such features are generally less active. Creative uses of language include:

- *Irony*. For example, in reply to an earlier question concerning the visit of the Housing minister, one of the journalists replies humorously *I just dropped him off. That was w= why I was late*. A question concerning the winning of a large lottery prize elicits another playful piece of fiction from another of the team: *Oh, it was me* (1.48). There are ironic functions here in the mock 'withholding' of news in a 'newsroom'.
- *Imaginative play with shared knowledge*. This results in a creation of impossible, fictional worlds. For example, in the case of the discussion of the (now dead) British writer of fiction for children, Beatrix Potter, one of the journalists imaginatively projects a situation in which tourists visit the writer's house even though it is known that the house was not established as a tourist attraction until after her death. *All the bleeding tourists going round her house she didn't like* (1.3). A similarly creative play with intertextual reference makes real and embeds in the current discourse the fictional mice which inhabit Beatrix Potter's stories (*It's all them mice wasn't it.* (1.7)). The fictional mice are assumed to be real mice which make her life in her house in London unhappy.
- *Puns and wordplay*. For example, with reference to the Earl of Derby as a possible source for a story, one of the speakers quips *I wouldn't know him if I fell over him* (1.41) which elicits a punning play with the institutionalized simile *Drunk as a lord* (1.43).[2]

The journalists' discourse includes more banter and wordplay as a creative complement to the tasks in hand, serving almost as an element which undercuts the seriousness of the tasks in hand in the meeting. Overall, the creativity is directed more towards a topic or topics. It is more ideational than affective or interpersonal; it is more concerned to play with ideas rather than feelings or attitudes, though never, of course exclusively. The creativity is co-produced but altogether more staged. It achieves shared values and degrees of interpersonality but the discourse is constructed through individual performances, more overt display of the self (the *dramatis personae* in the humorous episodes projected in lines 41 and 48 are the two speakers themselves) and the formation of individual and group identities. The journalists' use of the first person reference in positioning themselves within the humorous episodes may be seen as an example of what Harré (1988: 166), arguing the constructionist view, refers to as using pronouns to 'locate acts of speaking at locations in a social world'.

Different types of interaction and context are thus helpful in accounting for the varied and complex ways in which creativity is achieved and in identifying grounds and motivations for creativity. However, although linguistic creativity is common in a range of spoken discourses, there is none the less a danger that creative language use might be thought equally to impregnate all the above cells in the CANCODE generic framework. In fact, as we have begun to argue, no cell in the matrix can be excluded but tendencies, at least on the evidence of these limited samples, are stronger in some contexts and in some types of interaction than in others.

3.2 *Further classifying and contextualizing the data: credit security controllers and DIY*

In the following extract, the participants are concluding a meeting concerned with credit control. It is not possible to cite the full version of the extract because it runs to several minutes of recording. Although repetitions and supportive backchannels occur during this time, the transcript reveals no other features of creative language use in over ten minutes of exchanges. The generic context is that of 'professional/transactional information provision' and the extract here occurs when the meeting is coming to a close.

4 Credit security controllers

[Contextual information. The primary purpose of the meeting is an examination of the legal particulars of documents relating to Credit Security. The extract here is taken from the end of the meeting: ⟨S01⟩ field officer: male (30s); ⟨S 02⟩ field officer: male (40); ⟨S 03⟩ manager: male (55)]

1   ⟨S 03⟩   But the release now of savings is going to be an issue all right isn't it.
2   ⟨S 02⟩   Yeah.
3   ⟨S 01⟩   Yes.
4   ⟨S 02⟩   How is it approved. And can the board delegate that authority to somebody. To to release erm can, yeah that's right. Can the board delegate it?
5   ⟨S 03⟩   Well I [unintelligible] Well my reading of that would say that that is quite specific.
6   ⟨S 02⟩   Yeah.
7   ⟨S 03⟩   You don't know whether there's provision for the appointment of loans officers and credit officers and all this kind of.
8   ⟨S 02⟩   Mm.
9   ⟨S 03⟩   I wouldn't. There doesn't seem to be anything there except to say that the board must approve this.
10 ⟨S 02⟩   But but in accordance with the registered rules.
11 ⟨S 03⟩   [unintelligible]
12 ⟨S 02⟩   That's the only pos=, so it's, the question is thirty two three B. What's the inter=, can that, can the board delegate its authority under that section Geoff.
13 ⟨S 01⟩   Yeah.
14 ⟨S 02⟩   Thirty two three B.
15 ⟨S 03⟩   Or I wonder is that a limit according to the registered rules. Monitoring of it.
16 ⟨S 01⟩   [unintelligible]
17 ⟨S 03⟩   [whistles]
18 ⟨S 02⟩   I know.
19 ⟨S 01⟩   I used to [unintelligible].
20 ⟨S 03⟩   [unintelligible]
21 [laughter]
22 ⟨S 01⟩   *I used to think I was a pair of curtains but then I pulled myself together.*
23 [laughter]
24 ⟨S 01⟩   *I used to think I was being ignored but nobody still talks to me.*
25 ⟨S 02⟩   [laughs]
26 ⟨S 01⟩   Cowardly [unintelligible] this morning. What was in the tea? It's that s=, it's that bloody *foreign coffee* [laughs] that's what is it.

27 ⟨S 03⟩ *Foreign coffee?*
28 ⟨S 01⟩ That's that *foreign coffee* [unintelligible].

After such a long period of time in which documents are pored over and during which time the main purpose of the exchanges has been to transmit or obtain information, the speakers take a holiday from information transfer and joke and banter their way through to the end of the formal proceedings of the meeting (11.19–28; note the whistle, which suggests a different conversational frame has been or is being established). The business done, it seems, they are free to play with words and the labels for what is in their immediate environment. The context and interaction type have restricted opportunities for such engagements. An increase in creativity coincides for all the speakers with points of release from institutional identities in which information transfer is the main requisite. In short, they creatively re-cast themselves through the shift in language and conversational frame.

The next example, *DIY*, involves a group of friends discussing home improvements. [The term *DIY* (Do It Yourself) refers to activities, usually connected with home improvements]. The genre here is 'intimate collaborative idea'.

5. DIY

[Contextual information: ⟨S 01⟩ secretary: female (31); ⟨S 02⟩ scientist: female (31); ⟨S 03⟩ unemployed: female (28); ⟨S 04⟩ production chemist: male (29). Speakers 03 and 04 are partners]

1 ⟨S 03⟩ I mean *there's not room enough for two people in my kitchen*. You're still *brushing up against each other* all the time. It's quite stressful when you're cooking.
2 [unintelligible]
3 ⟨S 01⟩ [unintelligible] making square pastry or something like that.
4 ⟨S 03⟩ [unintelligible] knock through into that shed. But it's still, I th=, I still think it's a good idea *it's too much like hard work*.
5 ⟨S 02⟩ Mm.
6 ⟨S 03⟩ I could just see if we're gonna do *a great big massive thing* like that *it'll be years* before we get any semblance of any decent kitchen.
7 ⟨S 04⟩ The thing to do is, when you g=, when you start making money is pay someone to do it.
8 ⟨S 03⟩ Yeah.
9 ⟨S 01⟩ Some things I think are definitely worth paying someone to do.
10 ⟨S 03⟩ *Abso-bloody-lutely.*
11 [unintelligible]
12 ⟨S 01⟩ [unintelligible] house-keeper.
13 [laughter]
14 [unintelligible]
15 ⟨S 04⟩ Yeah.
16 ⟨S 03⟩ Bloody too right.
17 ⟨S 02⟩ I would as well.
18 ⟨S 01⟩ That's the first I'd get.
19 [laughter]
20 ⟨S 02⟩ Me too. I would. Especially if I lived with Tom.
21 ⟨S 03⟩ He's not untidy is he?

22 ⟨S 02⟩   Oh God. *He lives in total chaos.*
23 ⟨S 03⟩   Well I do really.
24 ⟨S 02⟩   *I've been on a campaign to sort him out.*

We began with a prototypical example of densely recurring repetitive patterning (Extract 1: *Sunday afternoon*) in which symmetries of feeling provided a basis for a marked instance of metaphoric word play. In this example (Extract 5) language choices are made to underscore more critical and adversarial attitudes and the absence of echoic repetition across speaking turns appears to reinforce this. The extract also involves a cluster of specific figures of speech (a term, ironically, only rarely analysed with reference to speech); for example, metaphor, idioms, puns, slang, proverbs, hyperbole all cluster within a relatively short stretch of dialogue. Metaphorical expressions such as the reference to being on a 'campaign' to sort out a boyfriend or 'brushing up' against somebody in a small kitchen coexist with hyperbolic expressions (*in total chaos; great big massive thing; it'll be years . . .*) and deliberately counterfactual statements (*there's not room enough for two people in my kitchen* 1.1), wordplay by infixing (*abso-bloody-lutely*, which also suggests a footing shift to a less serious mode of evaluation), deliberate underplaying by simile (*it's too much like hard work* 1.4). The analysis here further underlines how creative language is often related to the expression of emotion and affect. But it also exposes the extent to which language analysis, founded in the past century mainly on ideational, truth-conditional, and decontextualized referential approaches, needs to take fuller account of the relationship between creative language use in dialogue and the expression of emotion and identity-display. The creative language certainly serves here a more affectively divergent purpose. We acknowledge, however, that even here the two speakers seem largely to concur and that in our data there are few examples of speakers breaking generic boundaries or overtly resisting norms in order to express rebellion, to underline a negative stance or to conflict with what is expected. Such elements form an important component of creativity (see also note 4 below); but in our corpus creative language use is largely convergent.

4 Creativity clines: mapping language and social context

The examples analyzed above illustrate points on a creativity cline or continuum and how those points along the clines are organically related to particular social contexts and relationships. The most creative language features, our initial research suggests, cluster, both in stretches or bursts and reciprocally and interactively as well as being particularly salient at both topic- and transaction-boundaries and in the interpersonal management of discourse evidenced in footing shifts, etc. There are two main levels of 'creative' interactions: first, presentational uses of figures of speech, open displays of metaphoric invention, punning, uses of idioms, and departures from expected idiomatic formulations; second, less immediately identifiable, maybe even semi-conscious repetition: parallelisms, echoes, and related matchings which regularly result in expressions of affective convergence, in implicit signals of intimacy and symmetries of feeling. This is not to say, of course, that a museum guide does not invest creatively in ensuring that a flow of information or a set of responses to questions is interactionally appropriate. But linguistic creativity is less likely to occur in those contexts which involve uni-directional information provision or in those contexts of professional interaction in which the main purpose is trans-actional or where relations between participants in a particular context may be more asymmetrical. The more intimate the discourse and the more participants are involved in sharing experiences and ideas ('collaborative ideas' discourses, in particular), the more they may feel prompted to creative language use.

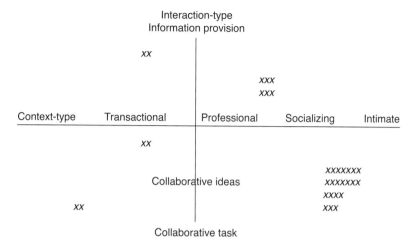

Figure 12.1 Creative language use in relation to context and interaction

[NB Hatching illustrates points along continua of context and interaction at which creative language use is most likely to be densest. Thus, the more hatching there is, the more likely it is that creative language occurs in such contexts]

Following Adolphs and Carter (2003), Figure 12.1 attempts a provisional mapping of the CANCODE categories of speech genres with the kinds of evidence of creativity found in the different speech genres in the corpus.[3] The categories are not wholly water-tight, of course. For example, there is much linguistic creativity in the more formal, 'professional task' encounter of the radio journalists above (which in any case contains an embedding of more 'socializing' and 'collaborative ideas' contexts). As we continue to investigate such data, we acknowledge too that we are interpreting the data as outsiders, ascribing to participants particular intentions, assigning to stretches of language particular functions and framing accounts of effects and of emotional contours which may not accord with the value systems of participants. However, though subject to ongoing evaluation, the categories do operationalize different varieties and clines of creative talk within a broader semiotic of spoken discourse.

5 Applications and conclusions

Discussions of creativity in relation to language teaching and learning have tended to focus on issues of learners' own creativity in relation to language learning processes. For example, research by Tarone and Broner (2001) underlines the relationship between language play and problem-solving capacities of learners on- and off-task. The research presented in this paper points in parallel directions but argues for a greater focus on language and for awareness of language in extended stretches of discourse covering a range of genres. Applications from this focus are many and varied. For example, the teaching of literature in a variety of cultural contexts may be better informed by understandings of the creative character of everyday language, supporting attempts by some practitioners (see Carter and McRae 1996; Carter and McCarthy 1995b; Cook 2000, especially part 3) to establish continuities between literary and everyday language and establish stronger bridges between language and literature teaching. Appreciation of literary and broader cultural variation can also be supported by reference to what learners already understand and can do in much everyday interaction.

But it is not only in the teaching of literature where the value of exposure to the more open-ended and creative aspects of language may be exploited. One criticism of notional-functional and task-based approaches to language teaching and learning is their tendency towards focusing on the transfer of information, with the danger that language use comes to be seen only as utilitarian and transactional. While learners undoubtedly have survival needs, and while a language such as English has indeed become a utilitarian object for many of its world-wide users, learners in many contexts around the world pass relatively quickly from purely utilitarian motivations towards goals associated with expressing their social and cultural selves (Widdowson 2000) and seek that kind of liberation of expression which they enjoy in their first language. In these respects methodologies which build on I (illustration) I (interaction) I (induction) structures, as illustrated in Carter and McCarthy (1995a), may help learners better to internalize and appreciate relationships between creative patterns of language, interpersonal purposes and contexts which can foster both literary appreciation and greater language understanding. Aston (1988) nicely refers to 'learning comity' (the book's title) as a desirable response to the transactional bias of contemporary language pedagogy, and much of his argumentation centres round bridging 'interactional' gaps (and the development of interactional competence tasks), as opposed to the transactional information gaps so beloved of communicative pedagogy.

For example, classroom research could be undertaken to evaluate activities in which learners explore by interaction and induction the effects produced by sequences of the kind found in 'extract 1: Sunday afternoon' above. Initial 'noticing' tasks could include questions directed to the setting for the conversation, the relationships between the speakers and the topics discussed. Observations then in turn lead to analysis and discussion of particular features of language use such as repetition, the use of the word 'mobile', the different forms of echoing across speaking turns and of how this awareness of patterning (further supported by interaction gap filling tasks) then relates to 'rules' of interpersonal language use.

The overall aim is to raise consciousness and to assess learners' awareness of how meanings and relationships can be creatively co-constructed. Although the main aim is the development of receptive skills, with increasing exposure to more examples learners may also feel encouraged to play with words and to re-form patterns, developing in the process a fuller interactional competence. And, of course, there is no reason why such tasks cannot also be embedded within more transactional contexts (since, as we have seen, such uses of language occur across context and interaction-types) and conclusions drawn for classroom practice. Similar examples could form a key component in research agendas.

Researching the 'poetry' of spoken discourse also requires attention to materials development which fosters reflection on different types of discourse, the relationship between interpersonal language and different socio-cultural contexts and the ways in which verbal art and language play are manifested in different cultures (Brumfit 1985; Kramsch and Sullivan 1996). 'Learning' such creativity in behaviourist terms is not the goal but much language teaching is concerned with helping the learner to present him-/herself in their desired way in the target language, and the work of sociolinguists and sociologists of language which underlines how speakers construct and position themselves in social space by their rhetorical actions, utilizing the lexico-grammatical resources of the language (see Harré 1985, for example, on 'situational rhetorics'), may be substantiated in the observation and analysis of everyday language. Such research is clearly relevant to the learner's engagement with the resources and meaning potential of the target language.

We do, of course, accept that the learner can only be an outside observer of the real-time contexts frozen in time and space on the bland and anodyne surface of the paper transcript or the equally displaced audiotape. However, much the same pertains to any typical text brought into the classroom by the teacher or the course materials writer: learners may only rarely experience themselves as the true addressees of the texts they are asked to digest, but learners in the main can re-contextualize for themselves a wide range of presented texts. Many of them do it on a daily basis when watching TV soap operas; it is not for nothing we referred earlier to reading the corpus like a soap opera. Raw corpus material may need some editing to make it suitable for local contexts and classrooms, but, again, we would not wish to be precious and to say that the transcript must remain inviolate at all costs; experienced teachers are good at editing texts to remove off-putting or distracting elements while retaining targeted elements for pedagogy. The challenges of interpretation of conversations embedded in contexts and cultures are similar to those of the interpretation of literary texts, and pedagogy has never shied away from the literary challenge. Kramsch (1993) constantly reminds us that the learner is someone struggling not just with lexico-grammar and pronunciation, but with moving from one cultural context (the classroom) to another (the target culture), in search of that third place in between, where a transformed identity is forged.

Further research can include both descriptive and pedagogical paradigms as well as interactions between these paradigms. For example, further language description might focus on the following: the importance of building in studies of prosody (Couper-Kuhlen 1996; Günthner 1999); more effective theorizations of affect and emotional responses in language use, initially, following Miall (1988), in respect of particular figures of speech; fuller studies in relation to problem-posing and problem-solving practices in the work-place, not least in the areas of HIV and psychotherapeutic counselling where creative language choices can create paradigm shifts in awareness and perception and in the relationship between professional and patient (Candlin *et al.* 2000; Garbutt 1996; Ragan 2000); more contextually-appropriate theories of value, especially aesthetic value (Armstrong 2001); further cross-lingual and cross-mode studies, building on data such as the Nottingham email/IRC corpus[4] but also looking more closely at the subtle creative relationships between the 'creative' and the 'critical' (Rampton 1995; Boxer and Cortes-Conde 1997); improved corpus search methodologies for creative language use in discourse, including searching on core words, core structures of repetition, key transcription encodings such as [laughs/laughter] and key (seemingly counter-intuitive) triggers of creativity such as the word *literally* as it signals word play; taking fuller research cognizance of the different ways in which creativity is contextually shaped in and through language use in different cultures (Chu 1970; Fabb 1997: chs 9 and 10; Lubart 1999; Mar'i and Karayanni 1983; Hanks 1996). And the descriptive insights gained can then be further researched in relation to contexts of teaching and learning as outlined above.

Our preliminary research into spoken discourse in a range of generic varieties underlines the extent and significance of creativity in a range of encounters and for a range of functions. It reveals an interplay of complex patterns and choices relative to particular speech genres and particular social contexts. Initial research indicates the need to take fuller account of a variety of functions involving speakers in particular contexts of interaction. As a linguistic phenomenon creativity is probabilistic, that is, it is more likely to occur in intimate and collaborative dialogic conditions. It involves both senders and receivers in its formation and does not exist wholly as aesthetic presentation; it is typically co-produced and regularly clusters in and is emergent from particular interpersonal and affective exchanges. Creative language use is an everyday, demotic phenomenon. It is not a capacity of special people but a special capacity of all people. As Harris (1980 and elsewhere) has consistently argued, it shows speakers, and, we would argue, language learners as language makers and not simply as language users.[5]

Appendix

Notes on transcription

Transcription convention for	Symbol	Explanation
Speaker codes	⟨S 01⟩, ⟨S 02⟩, etc.	Each speaker is numbered ⟨S 01⟩, ⟨S 02⟩, etc.
Extralinguistic information	[ ]	This includes things like laughter, coughing and inaudible speech on the tape.
Interrupted sentence	+	These instances are marked by a + at the point of where one speaker's utterance is interrupted and are followed by another + when the speaker resumes his or her utterance: ⟨S 01⟩ I think I would like+ ⟨S 02⟩ Right. ⟨S 03⟩ + to teach. These interruptions may overlap with the previous speaker's utterance or occupy an individual turn after which the interrupted speaker resumes his or her turn. Or: these interruptions occupy turns by themselves and do not overlap with the utterance that has been interrupted.
Back-channel	( )	Back-channel items tend to overlap with the turn of the current speaker and are therefore inserted into his or her utterance, e.g.: ⟨S 01⟩ I think I would like ((S 02⟩ Right) to teach.
Unfinished words	=	Speakers not only change their course in mid-sentence but also in the middle of individual words which has been marked as follows: ⟨S 01⟩ I wouldn't ha=, I wouldn't have thought so.
Punctuation	. ? ,	A full stop or question mark is used to mark the end of a sentence (depending on intonation). 'Sentences' are anything that is felt to be a complete utterance, such as: ⟨S 01⟩ What did you think of the film? ⟨S 02⟩ Lovely. 'Lovely' is considered as a sentence here. Unfinished sentences are not followed by a full stop. A comma indicates that the speaker has recast what he/she was saying, e.g.: ⟨S 01⟩ I bet, is that supposed to be straight? These include false starts.

Notes

1   CANCODE stands for 'Cambridge and Nottingham Corpus of Discourse in English'. The corpus was developed at the University of Nottingham, UK between 1994 and 2001, and was funded by Cambridge University Press, with whom sole copyright resides. The corpus conversations were recorded in a wide variety of mostly informal settings across the islands of Britain and Ireland, then transcribed and stored in computer-readable form. The corpus is designed with a particular aim of relating grammatical and lexical choice to variation in discourse context and is used in conjunction with a range of lexicographic, grammar, and vocabulary teaching projects (Carter and McCarthy 1995a; Carter, Hughes and McCarthy, 2000). In spite of trends to ever larger, multi-million-word corpora and associated quantitative analysis, in the case of CANCODE the main global aim has been to construct a corpus which is contextually and interactively differentiated and which can allow more qualitative investigation. The data have been especially carefully collected with reference to a range of different speech genres and social contexts. In all cases, to safeguard against possible misinterpretation by the analyst, information on speaker relationships is provided in the majority of cases by the person contributing the data to the corpus. An assessment of speakers' own goals remains central to the analysis.

2   Puns are a particular feature of demotic creativity: 'In studying the ludic element in culture, literary and everyday, I should logically also posit a similar element in those who receive and respond to wordplay: that is, all of us. Punning is a free-for-all available to every-one, common property; it is a democratic trope. It is the stock-in-trade of the low comedian and the most sophisticated wordsmith: James Joyce and Max Miller . . . It is and always has been'. (Redfern 1984: 175)

3   Further extracts from CANCODE data can be found in Carter and McCarthy (1997).

4   The significance of the relationship between creative communication and more intimate speech genres is further evidenced in a sub-corpus of emails and IRC (Internet Relay Chat) data collected in Nottingham as a supplement to the CANCODE corpus. Several thousand emails and several hours of IRC data (Fung 2001; Gillen and Goddard 2000) on a variety of topics are being collected in order to examine the continua between planned and unplanned discourse, the interpenetration of spoken discourse features into written text (Baron 2000; Cherny 1999) as well as the creativity manifest in these more informal, mixed-mode forms of communication (Crystal 2001). The research follows studies of bland multi-lingual crossings of the kind documented by Rampton (1995) where a key argument is that these creative combinations are not merely ornamental but encode purposeful functions in the expression of identity and the construction of shared worlds, including worlds which seek to exclude others or to adopt an adversarial stance to others (see also Bauman and Briggs 1990).

5   Harris's work (e.g. Harris 1980, 1998) has implications too for our initial point of departure on this paper. The past emphasis on creativity in written texts and certain kinds of performed spoken texts (e.g. folk narratives) occurs at the expense of banal, everyday conversation, but Harris's notion of 'integrational' linguistics sees both spoken and written texts as co-existing as 'species of situated communicative action' (Fleming 1995: 94). The work of William Hanks is similarly suggestive for future developments of the research reported in this paper, in particular for his view of the 'contextually saturated' nature of language (Hanks 1996: esp. ch. 7).

References

Adolphs, A. and R. A. Carter. 2003. 'Creativity and a corpus of spoken English' in S. Goodman, T. Lillis, J. Maybin, and N. Mercer (eds): *Language, Literacy and Education: A Reader*. Trentham Books: Stoke-on Trent, pp. 247–62.

Alexander, R. 1997. *Aspects of Verbal Humour in English*. Tübingen: G. Narr.

Antaki, C. and S. Widdicombe. 1998. 'Identity as an achievement and as a tool' in C. Antaki and S. Widdicombe (eds): *Identities in Talk*. London: Sage Publications, pp. 1–14.

Armstrong, I. 2001. *The Radical Aesthetic*. Oxford: Blackwell.

Aston, G. 1988. *Learning Comity*. Bologna: Editrice CLUEB.

Baron, N. 2000. *Alphabet to Email: How Written English Evolved and Where it's Heading*. London: Routledge.

Bauman, R. and C. L. Briggs. 1990. 'Poetics and performance as critical perspectives on language and social life', *Annual Review of Anthropology* 19: 59–88.

Boxer, D. and F. Cortes-Conde. 1997. 'From bonding to biting: conversational joking and identity display', *Journal of Pragmatics* 27: 275–94.

Brumfit, C. J. 1985. 'Creativity and constraint in the language classroom' in R. Quirk and H. G. Widdowson (eds): *English in the World: Teaching and Learning the Language and Literatures*. Cambridge: Cambridge University Press, pp. 148–57.

Cameron, L. 1999. 'Identifying and describing metaphor in spoken discourse data' in L. Cameron and G. Low (eds): *Researching and Applying Metaphor*. Cambridge: Cambridge University Press, pp. 105–33.

Cameron, L. and G. Low. (eds) 1999. *Researching and Applying Metaphor*. Cambridge: Cambridge University Press.

Candlin, C., A. Lin and T. W. Lo. 2000. 'The social significance of voices and verbal play: exploring group membership and identity in the discourses of Hong Kong youth' in Research Report, *The Discourse of Adolescents in Hong Kong*, Centre for Language Education and Communication Research, City University of Hong Kong.

Carter, R. A. 1999. 'Common language: corpus, creativity and cognition'. *Language and Literature* 8/3: 195–216.

Carter, R. A. and M. J. McCarthy. 1995a. 'Grammar and the spoken language', *Applied Linguistics* 16/2: 141–58.

Carter, R. A. and M. J. McCarthy. 1995b. 'Discourse and creativity: Bridging the gap between language and literature' in G. Cook and B. Seidlhofer (eds). *Principle and Practice in Applied Linguistics*. Oxford: Oxford University Press, pp. 303–23.

Carter, R. A. and M. J. McCarthy. 1997. *Exploring Spoken English*. Cambridge: Cambridge University Press.

Carter, R. A. and J. McRae. (eds) 1996. *Literature and the Learner: Creative Classroom Practice*. Harlow: Longman/Pearson Education.

Carter, R. A., R. Hughes and M. J. McCarthy. 2000. *Exploring Grammar in Context*. Cambridge: Cambridge University Press.

Cherny, L. 1999. *Conversation and Community: Chat in a Virtual World*. Stanford: CSLI Publications.

Chiaro, D. 1992. *The Language of Jokes: Analysing Verbal Play*. London: Routledge.

Chomsky, N. 1964. *Current Issues in Linguistic Theory*. Mouton: The Hague.

Chu, Y.-K. 1970. 'Oriental views of creativity' in A. Angoff and B. Shapiro (eds): *Psi Factors in Creativity*. New York: Parapsychology Foundation, pp. 35–50.

Clift, R. 1999. 'Irony in conversation'. *Language in Society* 28: 523–53.

Cook, G. 1994. *Discourse and Literature: The Interplay of Form and Mind*. Oxford: Oxford University Press.

Cook, G. 1996. 'Language play in English' in J. Maybin and N. Mercer (eds): *Using English: From Conversation to Canon*. London: Routledge, pp. 198–234.

Cook, G. 2000. *Language Play, Language Learning*. Oxford: Oxford University Press.

Couper-Kuhlen, E. 1996. 'The prosody of repetition: on quoting and mimicry' in E. Couper-Kuhlen and M. Selting (eds): *Prosody in Conversation: International Studies*, Cambridge: Cambridge University Press, pp. 366–405.

Coupland, J. (ed.) 2000. *Small Talk*. London: Longman.

Crystal, D. 1998. *Language Play*. Harmondsworth: Penguin.

Crystal, D. 2001. *Language and the Internet*. Cambridge: Cambridge University Press.

Eggins, S. and D. Slade. 1997. *Analysing Casual Conversation*. London: Cassell.

Emerson, C. 1983. 'The outer world and inner speech: Bakhtin, Vygotsky and the internalization of language', *Critical Inquiry* 10/2: 245–64.

Fabb, N. 1997. *Linguistics and Literature*. Oxford: Blackwell.

Fleming, D. 1995. 'The search for an integrational account of language: Roy Harris and conversation analysis', *Language Sciences* 17/1: 73–98.

Friedrich, P. 1979. 'Poetic language and the imagination: A reformulation of the Sapir Hypothesis' in *Language, Context and the Imagination. Essays by Paul Friedrich*. Stanford, CA: Stanford University Press, pp. 441–512.

Friedrich, P. 1986. *The Language Parallax: Linguistic Relativism and Poetic Indeterminacy*. Austin: University of Texas Press.

Fung, L. 2001. 'E-chat and new Englishes'. Mimeo. School of English Studies, University of Nottingham.

Garbutt, M. 1996. Figure Talk: Reported speech and thought in the discourse of psychotherapy. Unpublished Ph.D. thesis. Department of Linguistics, Macquarie University, Sydney.

Gibbs, R. W. 1994. *The Poetics of Mind: Figurative Thought, Language and Understanding*. Cambridge: Cambridge University Press.

Gibbs, R. W. 1999. 'Researching metaphor' in L. Cameron and G. Low (eds): *Researching and Applying Metaphor*, Cambridge: Cambridge University Press, pp. 29–47.

Gillen, J. and A. Goddard. 2000. ' "Is there anybody out there?": Creative language play and "literariness" in internet relay chat (IRC)'. Mimeo. Centre for Language and Communication, Manchester Metropolitan University.

Goddard, A. 1996. 'Tall stories: The metaphorical nature of everyday talk', *English in Education*, 30/2: 4–12.

Goffman, E. 1979. 'Footing', *Semiotica* 25: 1–29.

Goffman, E. 1981. *Forms of Talk*. Oxford: Blackwell.

Gordon, D. 1983. 'Hospital slang for patients: Crocks, gomers, gorks and others', *Language in Society*, 12: 173–85.

Günthner, S. 1999. 'Polyphony and the "layering of voices" in reported dialogues: An analysis of the use of prosodic devices in everyday reported speech', *Journal of Pragmatics*, 31: 685–708.

Hanks, W. F. 1996. *Language and Communicative Practices*. Boulder, CO: Westview Press.

Harré, R. 1985. 'Situational rhetoric and self-presentation' in J. Forgas (ed.): *Language and Social Situations*. New York: Springer Verlag, pp. 175–86.

Harré, R. 1988. 'Accountability within a social order: the role of pronouns' in C. Antaki (ed.): *Analysing Everyday Explanation*. London: Sage Publications, pp. 156–67.

Harris, R. 1980. *The Language Makers*. London: Duckworth.

Harris, R. 1998. *Introduction to Integrational Linguistics*. Oxford: Pergamon.

Hill, J. 1985. 'The grammar of consciousness and the consciousness of grammar', *American Ethnologist* 12: 725–37.

Hymes, D. 1996. *Ethnography, Linguistics, Narrative Inequality: Toward an Understanding of Voice*. New York: Taylor and Francis.

Kramsch, C. 1993. *Context and Culture in Language Teaching*. Oxford: Oxford University Press.

Kramsch, C. and O. Kramsch. 2000. 'The avatars of literature in language study', *The Modern Language Journal* 84/iv: 553–73.

Kramsch, C. and P. Sullivan. 1996. 'Appropriate pedagogy', *English Language Teaching Journal* 50/3, 199–213.

Kuiper, K. 1996. *Smooth Talkers: The Linguistic Performance of Auctioneers and Sportscasters*. Mahwah, NJ: Lawrence Erlbaum Associates.

Kuiper, K. and D. Haggo. 1984. 'Livestock auctions, oral poetry, and ordinary language', *Language in Society* 13: 205–34.

Lakoff, G. and M. Johnson. 1999. *Philosophy in the Flesh: The Embodied Mind and its Challenge to Western Thought*. New York: Basic Books.

Lakoff, G. and M. Turner. 1989. *More Than Cool Reason: A Field Guide to Poetic Metaphor*. Chicago: Chicago University Press.

Lubart, T. I. 1999. 'Creativity across cultures' in R. J. Sternberg (ed.): *Handbook of Creativity*. Cambridge: Cambridge University Press, pp. 339–50.

Mannheim, B. 1986. 'Popular song and popular grammar, poetry and metalanguage', *Word* 37: 45–74.

Mar'i, S. K. and M. Karayanni. 1983. 'Creativity in Arab culture: Two decades of research', *Journal of Creative Behaviour* 16/4: pp. 227–38.

McCarthy, M. J. 1998a. *Spoken Language and Applied Linguistics*. Cambridge: Cambridge University Press.

McCarthy, M. J. 1998b. 'Talking their heads off: the everyday conversation of everyday people', *SELL* 10: 107–28.

McCarthy, M. J. and R. A. Carter. 1997. 'Grammar, tails and affect: Constructing expressive choices in discourse', *Text* 17/3: 205–29.

Mertz, E. 1989. 'Sociolinguistic creativity: Cape Breton's Gaelic linguistic tip' in N. Dorian (ed.): *Investigating Adolescence*. Cambridge: Cambridge University Press, pp. 103–16.

Miall, D. S. 1988. 'Metaphor and affect: The problem of creative thought', *Metaphor and Symbolic Activity* 2/2: 81–96.

Norrick, N. 1993. *Conversational Joking: Humor in Everyday Talk*. Bloomington: Indiana University Press.

Norrick, N. 2000. *Conversational Narrative*. Amsterdam: John Benjamins.

Norrick, N. 2001. 'Poetics and conversation', *Connotations* 10/2–3: 241–67.

Ragan, S. L. 2000. 'Sociable talk in women's health care contexts: two forms of non-medical talk' in J. Coupland (ed.): *Small Talk*. Harlow: Longman, pp. 269–87.

Rampton, B. 1995. *Crossing: Language and Ethnicity Among Adolescents*. Harlow: Longman.

Redfern, W. 1984. *Puns*. Oxford: Blackwell.

Rubin, D. C. 1995. *Memory in Oral Traditions: The Cognitive Psychology of Epics, Ballads and Counting-Out Rhymes*. Oxford and New York: Oxford University Press.

Sacks, H. 1984. 'On doing "being ordinary"', in J. M. Atkinson and J. Heritage (eds): *Structures of Social Action: Studies in Conversational Analysis*. Cambridge: Cambridge University Press, pp. 413–29.

Short, M. H. 1996. *Exploring the Language of Poetry, Prose and Drama*. Harlow: Longman.

Sweetser, E. 1990. *From Etymology to Pragmatics: The Mind-Body Metaphor in Semantic Structure and Semantic Change*. Cambridge: Cambridge University Press.

Tarnnen, D. 1989. *Talking Voices: Repetition, Dialogue and Imagery in Conversational Discourse*. Cambridge: Cambridge University Press.

Tarone, E. and M. Broner. 2001. 'Is it fun? Language play in a fifth grade Spanish immersion classroom,' *Modern Language Journal* 85/3: 363–79.

Tedlock, D. 1975. 'Learning to listen: oral history as poetry', *Boundary* 2/3: 707–26.

Tedlock, D. 1977. 'Toward an oral poetics', *New Literary History* 8/3: 507–19.

Turner, M. 1991. *Reading Minds: The Study of English in the Age of Cognitive Science*. Princeton: Princeton University Press.

Vygotsky, L. 1978. *Mind in Society: The Development of Higher Psychological Processes*. Cambridge, MA: Harvard University Press.

Widdowson, H. G. 1992. *Practical Stylistics*. Oxford: Oxford University Press.

Widdowson, H. G. 2000. 'On the limitations of linguistics applied', *Applied Linguistics* 21/1: 3–25.

NOTES FOR STUDENTS AND INSTRUCTORS

Study questions

1 According to Lin, Wang, Akamatsu and Riazi, what contributions can 'local knowledge' make to English language teaching?
2 What do the following concepts mean: globalization, localization, glocalization?
3 What does the concept *authenticity* mean in the context of language teaching and in African American hip-hop as described by Pennycook?
4 Why is it important to have a detailed and systematic description of lingua franca English, in Seidlhofer's view? In what way can corpus linguistics help?
5 What are the key differences between the practice-based model of language acquisition, as discussed by Canagarajah, and the other linguistic form or cognitive process oriented models?
6 What are the reasons for the apparent under-use of authorial reference by ESL students in L2 writing, according to Hyland?
7 In what way does corpus-based analysis go against our intuitions of language use and the notion of core grammar?
8 What does *creativity clines* mean in Carter and McCarthy's terms? How does the concept relate to language use in social contexts and relationships?

Study activities

1 Have you been taught a second language by a non-native-speaker teacher? If yes, do you feel that having a non-native-speaker teacher helped or hindered your learning? In what way? What positive contribution do you think 'local knowledge' can make to the teaching and learning of foreign languages?
2 Can you find examples similar to African American hip-hop where a specific cultural form has been transplanted to a different context? How does the notion of *authenticity* apply in these examples? Is *glocalisation* a useful concept for studying these examples?

3   Record a brief conversation with friends, say 10 minutes. Listen to the recording carefully and list all the false starts, repetition, incomplete sentences, and mispronunications, as well as the creative use of language, e.g. a joke, invention of a new phrase, mimicking and exaggeration of accent. Find an example of a conversational exchange in a language teaching textbook. Does it contain any of the features you find in your recording of the conversation with friends? What implications does it have for language teaching and learning?

Further reading

Lin, Angel M. Y. (ed.), 2006, *Problematizing Identity: everyday struggles in language, culture and education*, Mahwah, NJ: Lawrence Erlbaum, is a collection of articles that aims to explore how social inequality is being reproduced in language and education.

Lin, Angel M. Y., and Martin, Peter (eds), 2005, *Decolonisation, Globalization: language-in-education policy and practice*, Clevedon: Multilingual Matters, surveys language-in-education policies and practices in different parts of the world, in the context of decolonisation and globalization.

Pennycook, Alastair, 2007, *Global Englishes and Transcultural Flows*, Oxford: Routledge, is an extended discussion of the author's analysis of hip-hop and looks at how global Englishes, transcultural flows and pedagogy are interconnected in ways that oblige us to rethink language and culture within the contemporary world.

Pennycook, Alastair, 2010, *Language as a Local Practice*, Oxford: Routledge, addresses the questions of language, locality and practice as a way of moving forward in our understanding of how language operates as an integrated social and spatial activity.

Seidlhofer, Barbara, Breiteneder, Angelika, and Pitzl, Marie-Luise, 2006, English as a lingua franca in Europe: Challenges for applied linguistics, *Annual Review of Applied Linguistics*, 26: 3–34, provides an overview of empirical research into English as a lingua franca (ELF) in the European context. It highlights some of the challenges that the emergence of ELF poses for various areas of applied linguistics.

Facchinetti, Roberta, Crystal, David, and Seidlhofer, Barbara (eds), 2010, *From International to Local English – and Back Again*, Bern: Peter Lang, addresses the issues of internationalisation and localisation of the English language.

Canagarajah, Suresh, 2002, *A Geopolitics of Academic Writing*, Pittsburgh: University of Pittsburgh Press, argues for an understanding of divergent rhetorical structures and writing practices so that knowledge construction in the academy can be pluralized.

Canagarajah, Suresh, 2002, *Critical Academic Writing and Multilingual Students*, Ann Arbor: University of Michigan Press, is a book for teachers on how to accommodate the dialects and discourses of nonnative students.

Canagarajah, Suresh (ed.), 2005, *Reclaiming the Local in Language Policies and Practices*, Mahwah, New Jersey: Lawrence Erlbaum, is a collection of essays which aims to emphasize *the local* in theorizing about language policies and practices in applied linguistics.

Hyland, Ken, 2004, *Disciplinary Discourses: social interactions in academic writing*, Ann Arbor: The University of Michigan Press, explores the cultures of academic communities, considering how academics use language to organise their professional lives, carry out intellectual tasks and reach agreement on what will count as knowledge.

Hyland, Ken, 2005, *Metadiscourse: exploring interaction in writing*, London: Continuum, examines the linguistic expressions which refer to the evolving text and to the writer and imagined reader of that text, i.e. metadiscourse.

Hyland, Ken, 2009, *Academic Discourse*, London: Continuum, explores the nature and importance of academic discourses in the modern world, offering a description of the conventions of spoken and written academic discourse and the ways these conventions construct both knowledge and disciplinary communities.

Biber, Douglas, Conrad, Susan, and Reppen, Randi, 1998, *Corpus Linguistics: investigating language structure and use*, Cambridge: Cambridge University Press, is an introduction to the field of corpus linguistics.

Conrad, Susan, and Biber, Douglas (eds), 2001, *Variation in English: multi-dimensional studies*, London: Longman, is a collection of studies that shows how corpus-based analysis can reveal variations in English in a systematic way.

Biber, Dourglas, Connor, Ulla, and Upton, Thomas, 2007, *Discourse On the Move: using corpus analysis to describe discourse structure*, Amsterdam: John Benjamins, is an exploration of how corpus-based methods can be used for the description of discourse organization through case studies of particular genres: fundraising letters, biology/biochemistry research articles, and university classroom teaching.

Biber, Douglas, and Conrad, Susan, 2009, *Register, Genre, and Style*, Cambridge: Cambridge University Press, introduces the methodological techniques for describing and analysing register, genre and style.

O'Keeffe, Anne, McCarthy, Michael, and Carter, Ronald, 2007, *From Corpus to Classroom: language use and language teaching*, Cambridge: Cambridge University Press, summarises recent work in corpus research, focusing particularly on spoken data. It is based on analysis of corpora such as CANCODE and Cambridge International Corpus, and written with particular reference to the development of corpus-informed pedagogy.

Carter, Ronald, 2004, *Language and Creativity: the art of common talk*, Oxford: Routledge, analyzes naturally-occurring spoken language to reveal that ordinary people in everyday speech contexts demonstrate creative capacities for sensitivity to their contexts.

McCarthy, Michael, and Carter, Ronald, 1993, *Language as Discourse: perspectives for language teaching*, Harlow: Longman, describes the discoursal properties of language and demonstrates what insights this approach can offer to the student and teacher of language.

McCarthy, Michael, 1998, *Spoken Language and Applied Linguistics*, Cambridge: Cambridge University Press, argues for putting spoken language right at the centre of the syllabus. It brings together a number of separate studies by the author, based on the CANCODE spoken corpus, and weaves them together to illustrate the central role the study of spoken language can play in applied linguistics.

Other publications of interest include:

Widdowson, Henry, 1998, Context, community and authentic language, *TESOL Quarterly*, 32, 4: 705–716, which addresses the issue of authenticity of the language used in teaching and in real-life situations.

Widdowson, Henry, 2004, *Text, Context, Pretext: critical issues in discourse analysis*, Oxford: Blackwell, is a synthesis of the author's extensive work on discourse analysis and language in education.

On World Englishes, the following may be of interest:

Bolton, Kingsley, and Kachru, Braj (eds), 2005, *World Englishes*, 6 volumes, London: Routledge.

Crystal, David, 2003, *English as a Global Language*, Cambridge: Cambridge University Press.

Jenkins, Jennifer, 2009, *World Englishes: A resource book for students*, Oxford: Routledge.

Kirkpatrick, Andy, 2007, *World Englishes: implications for international communication and English language teaching*, Cambridge: Cambridge University Press.

Mesthrie, Rajend, and Bhatt, Rakesh, 2008, *World Englishes: the study of new linguistic varieties*, Cambridge: Cambridge University Press.

Kachru, Braj, Kachru, Yamuna, and Nelson, Cecil, 2009, *Handbook of World Englishes*, Oxford: Blackwell.

PART III

Critical issues in applied linguistics

Introduction

As has been discussed in the General Introduction, applied linguistics has gone from linguistics applied to a field of critical enquiry with its own identity. Research in applied linguistics has raised a number of fundamental questions that the social sciences generally are also concerned with. Issues such as structure, agency, subjectivity power and ideology have all been addressed by applied linguists. In two areas, applied linguistics seems to have made particularly significant contributions, namely, identity in language learning and language practices, and communicative competence. This part of the Reader selects six articles that demonstrate the applied linguistics' perspectives on these two topics.

In the first article of this part, Bonny Peirce Norton argues that second language acquisition (SLA) theorists have struggled to conceptualize the relationship between the language learner and the social world because they have not developed a comprehensive theory of social identity that integrates the language learner and the language learning context. She also maintains that SLA theorists have not adequately addressed how relationships of power affect interaction between language learners and target language speakers. Using data collected in Canada from diaries, questionnaires, individual and group interviews, and home visits, Norton illustrates how and under what conditions the immigrant women in her study created, responded to, and sometimes resisted opportunities to speak English. She argues that current conceptions of the individual in SLA theory need to be reconceptualized. She draws on the post-structuralist conception of social identity as multiple, a site of struggle and subject to change to explain the findings from her study. Further, she argues for a conception of investment rather than motivation to capture the complex relationship of language learners to the target language and their sometimes ambivalent desire to speak it. The notion of investment conceives of the language learner, not as a historical and uni-dimensional one, but as having a complex social history and multiple desires. The article includes a discussion of the implications of the study for classroom teaching and current theories of communicative competence.

David Block, in Chapter 14, offers a further theoretical account of identity in applied linguistics. In particular, he reflects on the post-structuralist theory of identity that appears to be dominating the current discourse on this issue. The post-structuralist approach tends to regard identity in contemporary society as unstable, fragmented, ongoing and discursively constructed. Block explores how such an approach may be problematic for applied linguistics. He considers an alternative that uses psychoanalysis to investigate the subconscious deeper inner workings of the mind and how they might impact on one's sense of self and identity. Yet, having attempted to apply this alternative approach to his own data on second language learner identities, Block concludes that 'identity making is negotiated between the informant and the researcher and is not something that the latter must dig out of the former' (p. 259). It is important therefore to reconcile structure and agency on the one hand and the inner life of the individual and what Bourdieu calls *habitat* on the other.

Among the key components of identity are gender, class and race. Chapter 15 by Ryuko Kubota addresses them with specific reference to second language writing. The chapter first summarizes the constructivist and post-structuralist approaches to gender discussed in second language learning. It then applies these approaches to issues of gender, class and race in second language writing as well as the interrelations among them. Recent discussions on gender and language have problematized fixed understandings of the gender binary in relation to language use. They have explored how gendered use of language is socially and discursively constructed and how gender, language, power and discourse are related to each other in dynamic and transformative ways. It is suggested that new approaches to gender, class and race be dialectic in that they should both explore differences between social categories in a non-essentialist way and expose discourse and power relations that are embodied in these differences. Kubota outlines an agenda for future research on gender, class and race in second language writing which incorporates these approaches.

The next three articles discuss the concept of *communicative competence* from different perspectives. The term communicative competence was coined by the American anthropological linguist Dell Hymes in reaction against the perceived inadequacy of Chomsky's distinction between *competence* and *performance*. It refers to a language user's grammatical knowledge of syntax, morphology, phonology, etc., as well as social knowledge about how and when to use linguistic structures appropriately. It has had a fundamental influence on applied linguistics and provided the theoretical motivation for the communicative approach to language teaching. In Chapter 16, Constant Leung acknowledges the positive impact of the concept of communicative competence in English language in shifting the focus of language teaching from a grammatical rule-based pedagogy to the communicative, which emphasizes the social context and social rules of use. However, as Leung points out, the transfer of this concept from research to language teaching has produced abstracted contexts and idealized social rules of use based on (English language) native-speakerness. Drawing on research evidence from the fields of World Englishes, English as a lingua franca and second language acquisition, Leung argues that it is imperative for English language teaching (ELT) to take notice of real-world social, cultural and language developments in contemporary conditions and to re-engage with a set of reformulated ethnographic sensitivities and sensibilities.

In Chapter 18, Claire Kramsch and Anne Whiteside investigate the communicative competence of multilingual individuals in a multicultural setting. Drawing on the complexity theory and interactional sociolinguistics, the authors explore how an ecological approach to language data can illuminate aspects of linguistic practices in multilingual environments. Particular attention is given to the components of a competence in multilingual encounters that has not been sufficiently taken into consideration by applied linguists. They call it 'symbolic competence', 'the ability not only to approximate or appropriate for oneself someone else's language, but to shape the very context in which the language is learned and used' (p. 310).

The last article in this Part of the Reader is by Deborah Cameron. She examines the discourse on communication skills which has informed the teaching of spoken language to a variety of learners. She argues that what is emerging is a global ideology of 'effective communication', instantiated not in the use of any particular language, but rather in particular genres and styles of speaking. The favoured genres and styles may be assumed without adopting the code they are associated with. This, Cameron suggests, is not unlike the kind of liberal multilingualism, much in vogue among new global capitalists, which holds that we are all the same under the skin. On the surface there are still many different languages, but under the banner of effective communication, all become vehicles of the expression of similar values and the enactment of similar subjectivities.

Critical discussions of key concepts such as identity and competence, as illustrated by the articles in this Part of the Reader, both help to raise the awareness among language teaching professionals of the broader social issues in applied linguistics research and have a significant impact on policy and practice.

Chapter 13

BONNY NORTON PEIRCE

SOCIAL IDENTITY, INVESTMENT, AND LANGUAGE LEARNING (1995)

Everybody working with me is Canadian. When I started to work there, they couldn't understand that it might be difficult for me to understand everything and know about everything what it's normal for them. To explain it more clearly I can write an example, which happened few days ago. The girl [Gail] which is working with me pointed at the man and said:

"Do you see him?"—I said

"Yes, Why?"

"Don't you know him?"

"No. I don't know him."

"How come you don't know him. Don't you watch TV. That's Bart Simpson."

It made me feel so bad and I didn't answer her nothing. Until now I don't know why this person was important.

Eva, February 8, 1991[1]

No researcher today would dispute that language learning results from participation in communicative events. Despite any claims to the contrary, however, the nature of this learning remains undefined.

Savignon, 1991, p. 271

H OW WOULD SECOND LANGUAGE ACQUISITION (SLA) theorists conceptualize the relationship between Eva, an immigrant language learner, and Gail, an anglophone Canadian, both of whom are located in the same North American workplace in the 1990s? Because they have struggled to conceptualize the relationship between the individual language learner and larger social processes, a question such as this poses a problem for SLA theorists. In general, many SLA theorists have drawn artificial distinctions between the language learner and the language learning context. On the one hand, *the individual is* described with respect to a host of affective variables such as his/her motivation to learn a second language. Krashen (1981, 1982), for example, has hypothesized that *comprehensible input* in the presence of a low *affective filter is* the major causal variable in SLA. In Krashen's view, this affective filter comprises the learner's motivation, self-confidence, and anxiety state—all of which are variables that pertain to the individual rather than the social context. Furthermore, the personality of the individual has been described unidimensionally as introverted or extroverted, inhibited or uninhibited, field dependent or field independent.[2] With reference to these theories, Eva might be described as someone who is unmotivated with a high affective filter; perhaps an introverted personality who is unable to interact appropriately with her interlocutors. Or she might be portrayed as a poor language learner who has not developed sociolinguistic competence.

Other theories of SLA focus on social rather than individual variables in language learning. The *social* frequently refers to group differences between the language learner group and the target language group (Schumann, 1976). In this view, where there is congruence between the second language group and the target language group, what Schumann (1976) terms *social distance* between them is considered to be minimal, in turn facilitating the acculturation of the second language group into the target language group and enhanced language learning. Where there is great social distance between two groups, little acculturation is considered to take place, and the theory predicts that members of the second language group will not become proficient speakers of the target language. Supporters of the Acculturation Model of SLA (Schumann, 1978) might argue that despite the fact that Eva and Gail are in contact, there is great social distance between them because there is little congruence between Eva's culture and that of Gail. For this reason, Eva might struggle to interact successfully with members of the target language community.

Because of the dichotomous distinctions between the language learner and the social world, there are disagreements in the literature on the way affective variables interact with the larger social context. For example, although Krashen regards motivation as a variable independent of social context, Spolsky (1989) regards the two as inextricably intertwined. Although Krashen draws distinctions between self-confidence, motivation, and anxiety, Clement, Gardner, and Smythe (quoted in Spolsky, 1989) consider motivation and anxiety as a subset of self-confidence. Although Krashen considers self-confidence as an intrinsic characteristic of the language learner, Gardner (1985) argues that self-confidence arises from positive experiences in the context of the second language: "Self-confidence . . . develops as a result of positive experiences in the context of the second language and serves to motivate individuals to learn the second language" (p. 54).

Such disagreements in the SLA literature should not be dismissed, as Gardner (1989) dismisses them, as "more superficial than real" (p. 137). I suggest that this confusion arises because artificial distinctions are drawn between the individual and the social, which lead to arbitrary mapping of particular factors on either the individual or the social, with little rigorous justification. In the field of SLA, theorists have not adequately addressed why it is that a learner may sometimes be motivated, extroverted, and confident and sometimes unmotivated, introverted, and anxious; why in one place there may be social distance between a specific group of language learners and the target language community, whereas in another place the social distance may be minimal; why a learner can sometimes speak and other times remains silent. Although muted, there is an uneasy recognition by some theorists that current theory about the relationship between the language learner and the social world is problematic. Scovel (1978), for example, has found that research on foreign language anxiety suffers from several ambiguities, and Gardner and MacIntyre (1993) remain unconvinced of the relationship between "personality variables" (p. 9) and language achievement.

The central argument of this paper is that SLA theorists have not developed a comprehensive theory of social identity that integrates the language learner and the language learning context. Furthermore, they have not questioned how relations of power in the social world affect social interaction between second language learners and target language speakers. Although many SLA theorists (Ellis, 1985; Krashen, 1981; Schumann, 1978; Spolsky, 1989; Stern, 1983) recognize that language learners do not live in idealized, homogeneous communities but in complex, heterogeneous ones, such heterogeneity has been framed uncritically. Theories of the good language learner have been developed on the premise that language learners can choose under what conditions they will interact with members of the target language community and that the language learner's access to the target language community is a function of the learner's motivation. Thus Gardner and MacIntyre (1992), for example, argue that "the major characteristic of the informal context is that it is voluntary. Individuals can either participate or not in informal acquisition contexts" (p. 213). SLA theorists have not adequately explored how inequitable relations of power limit the opportunities L2 learners have to practice the target language outside the classroom. In addition, many have assumed that learners can be defined unproblematically as motivated or unmotivated, introverted or extroverted, inhibited or uninhibited, without considering that such affective factors are frequently socially constructed in inequitable relations of power, changing over time and space, and possibly coexisting in contradictory ways in a single individual.

Drawing on a recent study (Peirce, 1993) as well as my reading in social theory, I will propose a theory of social identity that I hope will contribute to debates on second language learning. This theory of social identity, informed by my data, assumes that power relations play a crucial role in social interactions between language learners and target language speakers. In March 1991, for example, when I asked Eva why the communication breakdown between her and Gail had taken place, Eva indicated she had felt humiliated at the time. She said that she could not respond to Gail because she had been positioned as a "strange woman." What had made Eva feel strange? When I analyzed Eva's data more closely, I realized that Gail's questions to Eva were in fact rhetorical. Gail did not expect, or possibly even desire a response from Eva: "How come you don't know him. Don't you watch TV. That's Bart Simpson." It was Gail and not Eva who could determine the grounds on which interaction could proceed; it was Gail and not Eva who had the power to bring closure to the conversation. If, as Savignon (1991) argues, language learning results from participation in communicative events, it is important to investigate how power relations are implicated in the nature of this learning.

I therefore take the position that notions of the individual and the language learner's personality in SLA theory need to be reconceptualized in ways that will problematize dichotomous distinctions between the language learner and the language learning context. I argue that SLA theory needs to develop a conception of the language learner as having a complex social identity that must be understood with reference to larger, and frequently inequitable social structures which are reproduced in day-to-day social interaction. In taking this position, I foreground the role of language as constitutive of and constituted by a language learner's social identity. It is through language that a person negotiates a sense of self within and across different sites at different points in time, and it is through language that a person gains access to—or is denied access to—powerful social networks that give learners the opportunity to speak (Heller, 1987). Thus language is not conceived of as a neutral medium of communication but is understood with reference to its social meaning. I support these arguments with findings from a longitudinal case study of the language learning experiences of a group of immigrant women in Canada (Peirce, 1993).

The study: immigrant women as language learners

From January to June 1990 I helped teach a 6-month ESL course to a group of recent immigrants at Ontario College in Newtown, Canada.[3] After the course was complete, I invited the learners to participate in a longitudinal case study of their language learning experiences in Canada.

Five women agreed to participate in the study: Mai from Vietnam, Eva and Katarina from Poland, Martina from Czechoslovakia, and Felicia from Peru. My research questions were divided into two parts:

Part I

How are the opportunities for immigrant women in Canada to practice ESL socially structured outside the classroom? How do immigrant women respond to and act upon these social structures to create, use, or resist opportunities to practice English? To what extent should their actions be understood with reference to their investment in English and their changing social identities across time and space?

Part II

How can an enhanced understanding of natural language learning and social identity inform SLA theory, in general, as well as ESL pedagogy for immigrant women in Canada? (Peirce, 1993, p. 18)

The study lasted 12 months—from January to December 1991. A major source of data collection was a diary study: From January to June 1991, the participants kept records of their interactions with anglophone Canadians and used diaries to reflect on their language learning experiences in the home, workplace, and community. During the course of the study, we met on a regular basis to share some of the entries the women had made in their diaries and to discuss their insights and concerns. I also drew a substantial amount of data from two detailed questionnaires I administered before and after the study, as well as personal and group interviews, and home visits.

One of the assumptions on which I based my research questions was that practice in the target language is a necessary condition of second language learning. As Spolsky (1989) argues, extensive exposure to the target language, in relevant kinds and amounts, and the opportunity to practice the target language are essential for second language learning: Learning cannot proceed without exposure and practice. These conditions, furthermore, are graded: The more exposure and practice, the more proficient the learner will become. Spolsky (1989) argues that the language learner can have exposure to and practice in the target language in two qualitatively different settings: The natural or informal environment of the target language community or the formal environment of the classroom. The focus of my research was on the natural language learning experiences of the women in their homes, workplaces, and communities.

The theory: social identity, investment, and the right to speak

Social identity as multiple, a site of struggle, and changing over time

In examining the relationship between the language learners in my study and the social worlds in which they lived, I drew in particular on Weedon's (1987) conception of social identity or subjectivity. Feminist poststructuralism, like much postmodern educational theory (Cherry-holmes, 1988; Giroux, 1988; Simon, 1992), explores how prevailing power relations between individuals, groups, and communities affect the life chances of individuals at a given time and place. Weedon's work, however, is distinguished from that of other postmodern theorists in the rigorous and comprehensive way in which her work links individual experience and social power in a theory of subjectivity. Weedon (1987) defines subjectivity as "the conscious and unconscious thoughts and emotions of the individual, her sense of herself and her ways of understanding her relation to the world" (p. 32). Furthermore, like other poststructuralist theorists who inform her work (Derrida, Lacan, Kristeva, Althusser, and Foucault), Weedon does not neglect the central role of language in her analysis of the relationship between the individual and the social: "Language is the place where actual and possible forms of social organization and their likely social and political consequences are defined and contested. Yet it is also the place where our sense of ourselves, our subjectivity, is constructed" (p. 21).

Three defining characteristics of subjectivity, as outlined by Weedon, are particularly important for understanding my data: the multiple nature of the subject; subjectivity as a site of struggle; and subjectivity as changing over time. First, Weedon (1987) argues, the terms *subject* and *subjectivity* signify a different conception of the individual from that associated with humanist conceptions of the individual dominant in Western philosophy. Whereas humanist conceptions of the individual—and most definitions of the individual in SLA research—presuppose that every person has an essential, unique, fixed, and coherent core (introvert/extrovert; motivated/unmotivated; field dependent/field independent), poststructuralism depicts the individual as diverse, contradictory, and dynamic; multiple rather than unitary, decentered rather than centered. By way of example (and at the risk of oversimplification) a humanist might be attracted by a book with the title *How to Discover Your True Self.* A poststructuralist, on the other hand, might prefer a book titled *It's OK to Live with Contradictions.*

Second, the conception of social identity as a site of struggle is an extension of the position that social identity is multiple and contradictory. Subjectivity is produced in a variety of social sites, all of which are structured by relations of power in which the person takes up different subject positions—teacher, mother, manager, critic—some positions of which may be in conflict with others. In addition, the subject is not conceived of as passive; he/she is conceived of as both subject of and subject to relations of power within a particular site, community, and society: The subject has human agency. Thus the subject positions that a person takes up within a particular discourse are open to argument: Although a person may be positioned in a particular way within a given discourse, the person might resist the subject position or even set up a counterdiscourse which positions the person in a powerful rather than marginalized subject position. Third, in arguing that subjectivity is multiple, contradictory, and a site of struggle, feminist poststructuralism highlights the changing quality of a person's social identity. As Weedon (1987) argues, "the political significance of decentering the subject and abandoning the belief in essential subjectivity is that it opens up subjectivity to change" (p. 33). This is a crucial point for second language educators in that it opens up possibilities for educational intervention.

I will demonstrate below that although it might be tempting to argue that Eva was essentially an introverted language learner, the data which follows provides convincing evidence that Eva's social identity was not fixed; it was a site of struggle and changed dramatically over time—as did her interactions with anglophone Canadians. At the time of the Bart Simpson exchange, however, Gail was in a powerful subject position and Eva did not actively resist being positioned as "strange." Because of the construction of Eva's social identity in Canada as immigrant, the social meaning of Gail's words to her were understood by Eva in this context. Had Eva been, for example, an anglophone Canadian who endorsed public rather than commercial television, she could have set up a counterdiscourse to Gail's utterance, challenging Gail's interest in popular culture. However, because of the unequal relations of power between Gail and Eva at that point in time, it was Gail who was subject *of* the discourse on Bart Simpson; Eva remained subject *to* this discourse. Thus while Eva had been offered the opportunity to engage in social interaction, to "practice" her English, her subject position within the larger discourse of which she and Gail were a part undermined this opportunity: "It made me feel so bad and I didn't answer her nothing." This discourse must be understood not only in relation to the words that were said, but in relationship to larger structures within the workplace, and Canadian society at large, in which immigrant language learners often struggle for acceptance in Canadian society.

From motivation to investment

A logical extension of reconceptualizing notions of the individual in SLA theory is the need to problematize the concept of motivation. In the field of second language learning, the concept of motivation is drawn primarily from the field of social psychology, where attempts have been made to quantify a learner's commitment to learning the target language. The work of Gardner and Lambert (1972) and Gardner (1985) has been particularly influential in introducing the notions of *instrumental* and *integrative* motivation into the field of SLA. In their work, instrumental motivation references the desire that language learners have to learn a second language for utilitarian purposes, such as employment, whereas integrative motivation references the desire to learn a language to integrate successfully with the target language community.

Such conceptions of motivation, which are dominant in the field of SLA, do not capture the complex relationship between relations of power, identity, and language learning that I have been investigating in my study of immigrant women. In my view, the conception of investment rather than motivation more accurately signals the socially and historically constructed relationship of the women to the target language and their sometimes ambivalent desire to learn and practice it. My conception of investment has been informed by my reading in social theory, although I have not as yet found a comprehensive discussion of the term in these contexts. It is best understood with reference to the economic metaphors that Bourdieu (1977) uses in his work—in particular the notion of cultural capital. Bourdieu and Passeron (1977) use the term cultural capital to reference the knowledge and modes of thought that characterize different classes and groups in relation to specific sets of social forms. They argue that some forms of cultural capital have a higher exchange value than others in a given social context. I take the position that if learners invest in a second language, they do so with the understanding that they will acquire a wider range of symbolic and material resources,[4] which will in turn increase the value of their cultural capital. Learners will expect or hope to have a good return on that investment—a return that will give them access to hitherto unattainable resources. Furthermore, drawing on Ogbu (1978), I take the position that this return on investment must be seen as commensurate with the effort expended on learning the second language.

It is important to note that the notion of investment I am advocating is not equivalent to instrumental motivation. The conception of instrumental motivation generally presupposes a unitary, fixed, and ahistorical language learner who desires access to material resources that are the privilege of target language speakers. In this view, motivation is a property of the language learner—a fixed personality trait. The notion of investment, on the other hand, attempts to capture the relationship of the language learner to the changing social world. It conceives of the language learner as having a complex social identity and multiple desires. The notion presupposes that when language learners speak, they are not only exchanging information with target language speakers but they are constantly organizing and reorganizing a sense of who they are and how they relate to the social world. Thus an investment in the target language is also an investment in a learner's own social identity, an identity which is constantly changing across time and space.

Communicative competence and the right to speak

Given the position that communication and social interaction are implicated in the construction of a language learner's social identity, my research on immigrant women in Canada develops questions I have raised in earlier research (Peirce, 1989) about the way Hymes' (1971) views on communicative competence have been taken up by many theorists in the field of second language learning over the past 15 years. I have argued (Peirce, 1989) that although it is important for language learners to understand the rules of use of the target language, it is equally important for them to explore whose interests these rules serve. What is considered appropriate usage is not self-evident but must be understood with reference to relations of power between interlocutors. I take the position that theories of communicative competence in the field of second language learning should extend beyond an understanding of the appropriate rules of use in a particular society, to include an understanding of the way rules of use are socially and historically constructed to support the interests of a dominant group within a given society. Drawing on Bourdieu (1977), I argue in this paper that the definition of competence should include an awareness of the right to speak—what Bourdieu calls "the power to impose reception" (p. 75). His position is that the linguist takes for granted the conditions for the establishment of communication: that those who speak regard those who listen as worthy to listen and that those who listen regard those who speak as worthy to speak. However, as Bourdieu argues, it is precisely such assumptions that must be called into question.

The analysis: identity, investment, and language learning

Although the findings from my study are extensive (Peirce, 1993), I wish to highlight data that address the question, How can an enhanced understanding of natural language learning and social identity inform SLA theory? First, I will address how the notion of investment helps explain the contradictions between the women's motivation to learn English and their sometimes ambivalent desire to speak it. Second, I highlight data from two of the participants—Martina and Eva—to analyze the relationship between investment, social identity, and language learning.

Investment and social identity

All the participants in the study were highly motivated to learn English. They all took extra courses to learn English; they all participated in the diary study; they all wished to have more social contact with anglophone Canadians; and all of them, except Martina, indicated that they felt comfortable speaking English to friends or people they knew well. It is significant, however, that all the women felt uncomfortable talking to people in whom they had a particular symbolic or material investment. Eva, who came to Canada for "economical advantage,"[5] and was eager to work with anglophones, practice her English and get better jobs, was silenced when the customers in her workplace made comments about her accent. Mai, who came to Canada for her life in the future and depended on the wishes of management for her job security and financial independence, was most uncomfortable speaking to her boss. Katarina, who came to Canada to escape a communist and atheistic system, and had a great affective investment in her status as a professional, felt most uncomfortable talking to her teacher, the doctor, and other anglophone professionals. Martina, who had given up a surveyor's job to come to Canada "for the children," was frustrated and uncomfortable when she could not defend her family's rights in the public world. Felicia, who had come to Canada to escape "terrorism," and had great affective investment in her Peruvian identity, felt most uncomfortable speaking English in front of Peruvians who speak English fluently.

The concept of motivation as currently taken up in the SLA literature conceives of the language learner as having a unified, coherent identity which organizes the type and intensity of a language learner's motivation. The data indicate that motivation is a much more complex matter than hitherto conceived. Despite being highly motivated, there were particular social conditions under which the women in my study were most uncomfortable and unlikely to speak (see also Auerbach & McGrail, 1991; Cumming & Gill, 1992; Goldstein, 1991; Peirce, Harper, & Burnaby, 1993; Rockhill, 1987). The data suggest that a language learner's motivation to speak is mediated by investments that may conflict with the desire to speak. Paradoxically, perhaps, the decision to remain silent or the decision to speak may both constitute forms of resistance to inequitable social forces. For example, although Felicia resisted speaking English in front of strangers because she did not want to be identified as an immigrant in Canada, other immigrant language learners are anxious to speak English for the express purpose of resisting unscrupulous social practices. For example, in his Toronto-based study of Spanish-speaking immigrants, Klassen (1987) found that some language learners wanted to learn English as a means of defence in their daily lives. An understanding of motivation should therefore be mediated by an understanding of learners' investments in the target language—investments that are closely connected to the ongoing production of a language learner's social identity. This position will be defended more comprehensively in the following discussion of Martina and Eva's experiences of learning English in Canada. In the following discussion, I demonstrate how the conception of social identity as multiple, a site of struggle, and subject to change helps to explain the conditions under which Martina and Eva spoke or remained silent.

Martina: Social identity as multiple and a site of struggle

Martina was born in Czechoslovakia in 1952. She came to Canada in March 1989 when she was 37 years old, with her husband Petr and their three children (Jana 17, Elsbet 14, Milos 11 at the time). She came to Canada for a "better life for children." Neither she nor her husband knew any English before they came to Canada, but her children had received some English language training in Austria where the family had spent 19 months waiting for Canadian visas. Although Martina had a professional degree as a surveyor, she worked as a "cook help" at a restaurant, Fast Foods, before she started the ESL course in January 1990.

Initially, Martina was dependent on her children to perform the public and domestic tasks of settling into a new country. When Martina went looking for a job, she took her eldest daughter with her, even though her daughter would become distressed because nobody wanted to employ her mother. When Martina wanted to help serve customers at Fast Foods, she asked her daughters to tell her what words to use. As Martina's English improved, she took on more of the parental tasks in the home. Many of Martina's diary entries describe the way that she used English to perform a wide variety of tasks in the home and community. It was Martina rather than her husband Petr who did most of the organization in the family, like finding accommodation, organizing telephones, buying appliances, finding schools for the children. Martina also helped her husband to perform public tasks in English. When Petr was laid off work, he relied on Martina to help him get unemployment insurance and he asked Martina to help him prepare for his plumber's certificate by translating the preparation book from English to Czech.

I wish to argue that Martina's investment in English was largely structured by an identity as primary caregiver in the family. It was important that she learn English so that she could take over the parental tasks of the home from her children. The very reason why Martina and Petr came to Canada was to find a "better life for children." Martina was anxious not to jeopardize the children's future by having them take on more public and domestic tasks than were absolutely necessary. Furthermore, because Martina had the responsibility for dealing with the public world, she was also anxious to understand the Canadian way of life—how things get done in Canadian society.

The poststructuralist view that social identity is nonunitary and contradictory helps to explain how Martina responded to and created opportunities to practice English. To illustrate this point, I will address some of the multiple sites of Martina's identity formation: She was an immigrant, a mother, a language learner, a worker, a wife. As a socially constructed immigrant woman (Ng, 1987; Boyd, 1992), Martina never felt comfortable speaking. Despite the fact that Martina showed remarkable resourcefulness and progress in her language learning, she frequently referred to herself as "stupid" and "inferior" because she could not speak English fluently. As she wrote in December 1991:

1. I feel uncomfortable using English in the group of people whose English language is their mother tongue because they speak fluently without any problems and I feel inferior.

Significantly, however, despite feelings of inferiority and shame, despite what could be described as a high affective filter, Martina refused to be silenced. I suggest that the reasons why Martina refused to be silenced were because her social identity as a mother and primary caregiver in the home led her to challenge what she understood to be appropriate rules of use governing interactions between anglophone Canadians and immigrant language learners. The multiple sites of identity formation explain the surprises in Martina's data—occasions when Martina would speak despite the fact that she was not a "legitimate speaker" (Bourdieu, 1977, p. 650) in the particular discourse. To mention only two occasions: First, Martina surprised her children (and no doubt her landlord and herself) by entering into a long conversation with her landlord on the phone in which she insisted that her family had not broken their lease agreement. In her diary of March 8, 1991, she wrote:

2. The first time I was very nervous and afraid to talk on the phone. When the phone rang, everybody in my family was busy, and my daughter had to answer it. After ESL course when we moved and our landlords tried to persuade me that we have to pay for whole year, I got upset and I talked with him on the phone over one hour and I didn't think about the tenses rules. I had known that I couldn't give up. My children were very surprised when they heard me.

Second, Martina surprised customers at Fast Foods (who looked at her strangely) and co-workers (who were surprised, but said nothing) by taking the initiative to serve the customers while the other workers were playing a video game in the manager's office. Consider the following entry from her diary on March 7, 1991.

3. My experiences with young Canadians were very bad, maybe I didn't have fortune. Usually I worked only with my manager, but when was P.A. day or some holidays for students, the manager stayed in his office and I worked with some students. Very often I worked with two sisters Jennifer (12 years) and Vicky (15 years) and the assistant manager who was at a cash [register]. These two girls loved talking but not with me. Even though I was very busy, they talked with young customers and laughed and sometime looked at me. I didn't know, if they laughed at me or not. When we didn't have any customers, they went to the manager office and tried to

help the manager with "wheel of fortune" on the computer. Later when some customers came in and I called these girls, they went but they made faces. I felt bad and I wanted to avoid this situation. In the evening I asked my daughter what I have to tell the customer. She answered me "May I help you" then "pardon" and "something else." When I tried first time to talk to two customers alone, they looked at me strangely, but I didn't give up. I gave them everything they wanted and then I went looking for the girls and I told them as usually only "cash." They were surprised but they didn't say anything.

I suggest that Martina's perseverance with speaking ("I couldn't give up," "I didn't give up") and her courage to resist marginalization intersect with her social identity as a mother in two ways. First, as a primary caregiver, she could not rely on her husband to deal with the public world and defend the family's rights against unscrupulous social practices. Martina had to do this herself, regardless of her command of the English tense system, the strange looks she received from her interlocutors, and her feelings of inferiority. Second, Martina drew on her symbolic resources as a mother to reframe the power relations between herself and her co-workers. Thus, instead of conceding to their power as legitimate speakers of English, she reframed their relationship as a domestic one in which, as children they had no authority over her, as a parent: Consider the following extract taken from an interview with Martina on March 17, 1991:

4. In restaurant was working a lot of children, but the children always thought that I am—I don't know—maybe some broom or something. They always said "Go and clean the living room." And I was washing the dishes and they didn't do nothing. They talked to each other and they thought that I had to do everything. And I said "No." The girl is only 12 years old. She is younger than my son. I said "No, you are doing nothing. You can go and clean the tables or something."

Martina's social identity was a site of struggle. By setting up a counterdiscourse in her workplace and resisting the subject position immigrant woman in favor of the subject position mother, Martina claimed the right to speak. It is precisely this ability to claim the right to speak that I suggest should be an integral part of an expanded notion of communicative competence.

Eva: Social identity as changing over time

Eva was born in Poland in 1967 and came to Canada as a refugee in 1989 when she was 22 years old. She immigrated because she wanted "economical advantage." Eva had finished high school and worked as a bartender before she left Poland. She chose to come to Canada because it is one of the few industrialized countries that encourages immigration. She came alone, with no family or friends, but did know one person in Newtown before she arrived. Before Eva came to Canada, she spent 2 years in Italy where she became fluent in Italian. She knew no English before she arrived in Canada.

When Eva arrived in Newtown, she found employment at what she calls "The Italian store" which is situated in the heart of an established Italian neighborhood in Newtown. Eva herself lived in this neigfhborhood, as do many recent immigrants to Newtown. Eva was given the job at the Italian store because she was a fluent speaker of Italian. Eva was happy at the Italian store but was concerned because she wanted to learn English and had little opportunity to practice English while working in this store. After she finished the ESL course in June 1990, she began looking for another job in earnest, at a place where she could become a more proficient speaker of English. She found employment at a restaurant in Newtown called Munchies, where she was the only employee who could not speak English fluently. Eva was a fulltime employee whose main job was to clean the store and prepare the food for cooking.

The conception of social identity as subject to change helps explain the way Eva over time responded to and created opportunities to practice English in her workplace. The central point I wish to make here is that it was only over time that Eva's conception of herself as an immigrant—an "illegitimate" speaker of English—changed to a conception of herself as a multicultural citizen with the power to impose reception. When Eva first started working at Munchies, she did not think it was appropriate for her to approach her co-workers and attempt to engage them in conversation. As she said in an interview on March 7, 1991,

5. When I see that I have to do everything and nobody cares about me because—then how can I talk to them? I hear they doesn't care about me and I don't feel to go and smile and talk to them.

Note that Eva does not complete a crucial part of her sentence. "Nobody cares about me because?" The data suggest that nobody acknowledged Eva because she had the subject position immigrant in the workplace: As Eva put it, she was someone who was not fluent in English; she was "not Canadian," she was "stupid," she had "the worst type of work" in the store. To speak under such conditions would have constituted what Bourdieu (1977) calls *heretical usage* (p. 672). Eva accepted the subject position immigrant; she accepted that she was not a legitimate speaker of English and that she could not command reception of her interlocutors. As she herself said, when she first arrived in Canada, she assumed that if people treated her with disrespect, it was because of her own limitations. She conceded to these rules of use in her workplace, rules that Eva herself accepted described as normal. As she said in an interview on January 23, 1991,

6. I think because when I didn't talk to them, and they didn't ask me, maybe they think I'm just like—because I had to do the worst type of work there. It's normal.

As Eva's sense of who she was, and how she related to the social world began to change, she started to challenge her subject position in the workplace as an illegitimate speaker of English. An extract from an interview on January 23, 1991, indicates how Eva claimed spaces in conversations with co-workers. Her purpose was to introduce her own history and experiences into the workplace in the hope that her symbolic resources would be validated. This surprised her co-workers.

7. (*B* refers to Bonny and *E* refers to Eva.)

    B: You were saying Eva that you are starting to speak to other people? The other people who work [at Munchies]?
    E: Ya. Because before?
    B: Is everybody there Canadian?
    E: Ya. Because there everybody is Canadian and they would speak to each other, not to me—because—I always was like—they sent me off to do something else. I felt bad. Now it's still the same but I have to do something. I try to speak.
    B: How are you doing that?

E: For example, we have a half-hour break. Sometimes—I try to speak. For example, they talk about Canada, what they like here, the places which they like?

B: Like to visit? Vacations?

E: Ya. Then I started to talk to them about how life is in Europe. Then they started to ask me some questions. But it's still hard because I cannot explain to them how things, like

B: How do you actually find an opportunity in the conversation to say something. Like, if they're talking to each other, do you stop them?

E: No.

B: You wait for a quiet—Then what do you say?

E: No. I don't wait for when they are completely quiet, but when it's the moment I can say something about what they are talking about.

B: When you started doing that, were they surprised?

E: A little bit.

As Eva continued to develop what I have called an identity as a multicultural citizen, she developed with it an awareness of her right to speak. If people treated her with disrespect, it was their problem and not her problem. Thus when, after a year's experience in the workplace, a male customer said to her in February 1992,[6] "Are you putting on this accent so that you can get more tips?" Eva had been angry, rather than ashamed; she had spoken out, rather than been silenced. When she said to him, "I wish I did not have this accent because then I would not have to listen to such comments," she was claiming the right to speak as a multicultural citizen of Canada. Over time, then, Eva's communicative competence developed to include an awareness of how to challenge and transform social practices of marginalization.

The implications: classroom-based social research

Although it is beyond the scope of this article to offer a comprehensive analysis of ways in which my research might inform second language teaching, I take in good faith Savignon's (1991) comment that communicative language teaching looks to further language acquisition research to inform its development. I have argued thus far that SLA theorists have struggled to define the nature of language learning because they have drawn artificial distinctions between the individual language learner and larger, frequently inequitable social structures. I have drawn on Martina and Eva's data to argue that the individual language learner is not ahistorical and unidimensional but has a complex and sometimes contradictory social identity, changing across time and space. I have drawn on my data to argue that motivation is not a fixed personality trait but must be understood with reference to social relations of power that create the possibilities for language learners to speak. I have suggested that even when learners have a high affective filter, it is their investment in the target language that will lead them to speak. This investment, in turn, must be understood in relation to the multiple, changing, and contradictory identities of language learners.

An important implication of my study is that the second language teacher needs to help language learners claim the right to speak outside the classroom. To this end, the lived experiences and social identities of language learners need to be incorporated into the formal second language curriculum. The data indicates, however, that students' social identities are complex, multiple, and subject to change. What kind of pedagogy, then, might help learners claim the right to speak? Drawing on insights from my research project in general and the diary study in particular (see Peirce, 1994), as well as a wide range of classroom research (e.g., Auerbach, 1989; Cummins, 1994; Heath, 1983, 1993; Heller & Barker, 1988; Morgan, 1992; Stein & Janks, 1992; Stein & Pierce, 1995), I suggest that what I call *classroom-based social research* might engage the social identities of students in ways that will improve their language learning outside the classroom and help them claim the right to speak. It may help students understand how opportunities to speak are socially structured and how they might create possibilities for social interaction with target language speakers. Furthermore, it may help language teachers gain insight into the way their students' progress in language learning intersects with their investments in the target language.

I define classroom-based social research (CBSR) as collaborative research that is carried out by language learners in their local communities with the active guidance and support of the language teacher. In many ways, language learners become ethnographers in their local communities. Like the students in Heath's (1983) study, learners will develop their oral and literacy skills by collapsing the boundaries between their classrooms and their communities. Adult immigrants, however, differ from native-born students in that they do not have easy access to the linguistic codes or cultural practices of their local communities. The emphasis on CBSR, therefore, is to focus precisely on these aspects of social life, with a view to enhancing language learning and social interaction. As will be discussed below, a crucial component of CBSR is the use of the written word for reflection and analysis. As Ngo (1994) has convincingly argued from her personal experience of immigration, writing can build bridges not only across geographic space but across historical time:

> Through my writing I found myself again after a long time of being lost. I learned who I was in the past, who I was then, and who I wanted to be in the future. There I finally found freedom in writing. I flew in the sky with my pencil and notebook.

CBSR might include the following objectives and methodologies.

Objective 1: Investigative opportunities to interact with target language speakers

Learners can be encouraged to investigate systematically what opportunities they have to interact with target language speakers, whether in the home, the workplace, or the community. To this end, they might make use of observation charts or logbooks.

Objective 2: Reflect critically on engagement with target language speakers

Learners can be encouraged to reflect critically on their engagement with target language speakers. That is, learners might investigate the conditions under which they interact with target language speakers; how and why such interactions take place; and what results follow from such interaction. This might help learners develop insight into the way in which opportunities to speak are socially structured and how social relations of power are implicated in the process of social interaction. As a result, they may learn to transform social practices of marginalization.

Objective 3: Reflect on observations in diaries or journals

Learners can be encouraged to reflect on their observations in diaries or journals. This will create opportunities for learners to write about issues in which they have a particular investment, and in so doing, develop their talents as writers. Specifically, learners could use their diaries to examine critically any communication breakdowns that may have occurred with target language speakers. These diaries could be written in the target language and collected regularly by the teacher. The diaries might give the language teacher access to information about the students' opportunities to practice the target language outside the classroom, their investments in the target language, and their changing social identities. The teacher could help students critically reflect on findings from their research and make suggestions for further research, reflection, and action where necessary.

Objective 4: Pay attention to and record unusual events

Learners could be encouraged to pay particular attention to those moments when an occurrence, action, or event, surprises them or strikes them as unusual. By recording their surprises in the data collection process, the learners may become conscious of differences between social practices in their native countries and those in the target language community. Given the subject position student researcher rather than language learner or immigrant, learners may be able to critically engage their histories and their experiences from a position of strength rather than a position of weakness. With this enhanced awareness, learners may also be able to use the language teacher as an important resource for further learning.

Objective 5: Compare data with fellow students and researchers

Students could use the data they have collected as material for their language classrooms, to be compared with the findings of their fellow students and researchers. In comparing their data with other learners, the students will have an investment in the presentations that their fellow students make and a meaningful exchange of information may ensue. Students may begin to see one another as part of a social network in which their symbolic resources can be produced, validated, and exchanged. The teacher may also be able to use this information to structure classroom activities and develop classroom materials that will help learners claim the right to speak outside the classroom. Drawing on Heath (1993), the teacher could make use of drama to help students develop confidence in interacting with target language speakers. Furthermore, the teacher may be able to guide classroom discussion from a description of the findings of the research, to a consideration of what the research might indicate about broader social processes in the society. In this way, the teacher could help students interrogate their relationship to these larger social processes, understand how feelings of inadequacy are frequently socially constructed, and find spaces for the enhancement of human possibility.

In sum, second language theorists, teachers, and students cannot take for granted that those who speak regard those who listen as worthy to listen, and that those who listen regard those who speak as worthy to speak.

Notes

1 Quoted in Peirce, 1993, p. 197. Eva explained that the man her co-worker pointed to had a "Bart Simpson" t-shirt on. Spelling mistakes in the original have been corrected.
2 See Brown (1987) for an overview of the literature on personality variables and language learning.
3 The names of places and participants have been changed·to protect the identities of participants.
4 By *symbolic resources* I refer to such resources as language, education, and friendship, whereas I use the term *material resources* to include capital goods, real estate, and money.
5 The only alterations that have been made to the written contributions of the participants are spelling corrections.

6   Although the diary study was officially over by February 1992, I continued to maintain contact with the participants.

References

Auerbach, E. R. (1989). Toward a social-contextual approach to family literacy. *Harvard Educational Review*, *59*, 165–181.

Auerbach, E., & McGrail, L. (1991). Rosa's challenge: Connecting classroom and community contexts. In S. Benesch (Ed.), *ESL in America: Myths and possibilities* (pp. 96–111). Portsmouth, NH: Heinemann.

Bourdieu, P. (1977). The economics of linguistic exchanges. *Social Science Information*, *16*, 645–668.

Bourdieu, P., & Passeron J. (1977). *Reproduction in education, society, and culture*. Beverley Hills, CA: Sage Publications.

Boyd, M. (1992). Immigrant women: Language, socio-economic inequalities, and policy issues. In B. Burnaby & A. Cumming (Eds.), *Socio-political aspects of ESL in Canada* (pp. 141–159). Toronto, Canada: OISE Press.

Brown, H. D. (1987). *Principles of language learning and teaching*. Englewood Cliffs, NJ: Prentice Hall.

Cherryholmes, C. (1988). *Power and criticism: Poststructuralist investigations in education*. New York: Teachers College Press.

Cumming, A. & Gill, J. (1991). Motivation or accessibility? Factors permitting Indo-Canadian women to pursue ESL literacy instruction. In B. Burnaby & A. Cumming (Eds.), *Socio-political aspects of ESL education in Canada* (pp. 241–252). Toronto, Canada: OISE Press.

Cummins, J. (1994). Knowledge, power, and identity in teaching English as a second language. In F. Genesee (Ed.), *Educating second language children: The whole child, the whole curriculum, the whole community* (pp. 33–58). Cambridge: Cambridge University Press.

Ellis, Rod. (1985). *Understanding second language acquisition*. Oxford: Oxford University Press.

Gardner, R. C. (1985). *Social psychology and second language learning. The role of attitudes and motivation*. London: Edward Arnold.

Gardner, R. C. (1989). Attitudes and motivation. *Annual Review of Applied Linguistics, 1988*, *9*, 135–148.

Gardner, R. C., & Lambert, W. C. (1972). *Attitudes and motivation in second language learning*. Rowley, MA: Newbury House.

Gardner, R. C., & MacIntyre, P. D. (1992). A student's contributions to second-language learning. Part I: Cognitive variables. *Language Teaching*, *25*, 211–220.

Gardner, R. C., & MacIntyre, P. D. (1993). A student's contributions to second-language learning. Part II: Affective variables. *Language Teaching*, *26*, 1–11.

Giroux, H. A. (1988). *Schooling and the struggle for public life: Critical pedagogy in the modern age*. Minneapolis: University of Minnesota Press.

Goldstein, T. (1991). *Immigrants in the multicultural/multilingual workplace: Ways of communicating and experience at work*. Unpublished doctoral dissertation, Ontario Institute for Studies in Education/University of Toronto, Canada.

Heath, S. B. (1983). *Ways with words: Language, life, and work in communities and classrooms*. Cambridge: Cambridge University Press.

Heath, S. B. (1993). Inner city life through drama: Imagining the language classroom. *TESOL Quarterly*, *27*, 177–192.

Heller, M. (1987). The role of language in the formation of ethnic identity. In J. Phinney & M. Rotheram (Eds.), *Children's ethnic socialization* (pp. 180–200). Newbury Park, CA: Sage.

Heller, M., & Barker, G. (1988). Conversational strategies and contexts for talk: Learning activities for Franco-Ontarian minority schools. *Anthropology and Education Quarterly*, *19*, 20–46.

Hymes, D. (1971). On communicative competence. In C. J. Brumfit & K. Johnson (Eds.), *The communicative approach to language teaching* (pp. 5–26). Oxford: Oxford University Press.

Klassen, C. (1987). *Language and literacy learning: The adult immigrant's account*. Unpublished master's thesis, Ontario Institute for Studies in Education/University of Toronto, Canada.

Krashen, S. (1981). *Second language acquisition and second language learning*. Oxford: Pergamon.

Krashen, S. (1982). *Principles and practice in second language acquisition*. Oxford: Pergamon.

Morgan, B. (1992). Teaching the Gulf War in an ESL classroom. *TESOL Journal*, *2*, 13–17.

Ng, R. (1987). Immigrant women in Canada: A socially constructed category. *Resources for Feminist Research/Documentation sur la recherche feministe*, *16*, 13–15.

Ngo, H. (1994, March). *From learner to teacher: Language minority teachers speak out*. Paper presented at the 28th Annual TESOL Convention, Baltimore, Maryland.

Ogbu, J. (1978). *Minority education and caste: The American system in cross-cultural perspective.* New York: Academic Press.

Peirce, B. N. (1989). Toward a pedagogy of possibility in the teaching of English internationally: People's English in South Africa. *TESOL Quarterly, 23,* 401–420.

Peirce, B. N. (1993). *Language learning, social identity, and immigrant women.* Unpublished doctoral dissertation. Ontario Institute for Studies in Education/University of Toronto, Canada.

Peirce, B. N. (1994). Using diaries in second language research and teaching. *English Quarterly, 26,* 22–29.

Peirce, B. N., Harper, H., & Burnaby, B. (1993). Workplace ESL at Levi Strauss: "Dropouts" speak out. *TESL Canada Journal, 10,* 9–30.

Rockhill, K. (1987). Literacy as threat/desire: Longing to be SOMEBODY. In J. Gaskill & A. McLaren (Eds.), *Women and education: A Canadian perspective* (pp. 315–331). Calgary, Canada: Detselig Enterprises.

Savignon, S. (1991). Communicative language teaching: State of the art. *TESOL Quarterly, 25,* 261–278.

Schumann, J. (1976). Social distance as a factor in second language acquisition. *Language Learning, 26,* 135–143.

Schumann, J. (1978). The acculturation model for second-language acquisition. In R. C. Gringas, (Ed.), *Second language acquisition and foreign language teaching* (pp. 27–50). Washington, DC: Center for Applied Linguistics.

Scovel, T. (1978). The effect of affect on foreign language learning: A review of the anxiety research. *Language Learning, 28,* 129–142.

Simon, R. (1992). *Teaching against the grain: Texts for a pedagogy of possibility.* New York: Bergin & Garvey.

Spolsky, B. (1989). *Conditions for second language learning.* Oxford: Oxford University Press.

Stein, P., & Janks, H. (1992). The process syllabus: A case study. *Perspectives in Education, 13,* 93–105.

Stein, P., & Peirce, B. N. (1995). Why the Monkeys Passage bombed: Tests, genres, and teaching. *Harvard Educational Review, 65* (1): 50–65.

Stern, H. H. (1983). *Fundamental concepts of language teaching.* Oxford: Oxford University Press.

Weedon, C. (1987). *Feminist practice and poststructuralist theory.* London: Blackwell.

Chapter 14

DAVID BLOCK

IDENTITY IN APPLIED
LINGUISTICS (2006)

Introduction

THERE HAS BEEN A VERITABLE EXPLOSION in recent years as regards the number of researchers in the social sciences who are putting identity at the centre of their work, prompting Bauman to observe that identity is 'today's talk of the town and the most commonly played game in town' (Bauman 2001: 16). Social theorists and sociologists, such as Stuart Hall, Anthony Giddens, Manuel Castells, Chris Weedon and Bauman himself, have all contributed to the development of a general poststructuralist/constructivist take on identity, situated at the forefront of discussions of the current state of late modern/postmodern societies. This poststructuralist approach to identity supersedes structuralist approaches, which seek to establish universal laws of psychology or social structure to explain individuals' fixed identities. Specifically, as Smart (1999) notes, poststructuralism is about a 'critical concern' with issues, such as:

> (i) the crisis of representation and associated instability of meaning; (ii) the absence of secure foundations for knowledge; (iii) the analytic centrality of language, discourses and texts; and (iv) the inappropriateness of the Enlightenment assumption of the rational autonomous subject and a counter, contrasting concentration on the ways in which individuals are constituted as subjects.
>
> (Smart 1999: 38)

Importantly, poststructuralists reject anything that smacks of essentialism, defined by Mary Bucholtz as follows:

> Essentialism is the position that the attributes and behavior of socially defined groups can be determined and explained by reference to cultural and/or biological characteristics believed to be inherent to the group. As an ideology, essentialism rests on two assumptions: (1) that groups can be clearly delimited; and (2) that group members are more or less alike.
>
> (Bucholtz 2003: 400)

What I have written thus far refers to the social sciences in general, but it also rings true for applied linguistics, where poststructuralism seems to be the default epistemological stance for sociolinguists and second language learning researchers who focus on identity as a key construct in their work. Though I agree in principle with this poststructuralist approach to identity, a perverse scepticism inside me makes me think that in a relatively uncritically manner, too many researchers are signing up to a kind of official protocol, based above all on the work of social theorists such as Castells, Giddens, Hall and Weedon, whereby it is taken as axiomatic that identity is unstable, fragmented, ongoing, discursively constructed and so on.

This paper, then, is a short reflection on this poststructuralist take on identity: what it is, a critique of it and what the critique means to me. I begin with a definition of the post structuralist approach to identity and then consider a well articulated critique of this approach by Bendle (2002). I explore how the poststructuralist approach to identity might be problematic, in particular in how it marginalizes the traditional interests of psychologists in the self. I then move to examine the example of one second language learning researcher, Granger (2004), who has attempted to bring the self into second language learning research by drawing on work in psychoanalysis. I also consider how her approach might be applied to some of my own data, before concluding with some thoughts on this work and how seriously I should take Bendle's critique.

Poststructuralist identity

First and foremost, poststructuralists see identity not as something fixed for life, but as an ongoing lifelong project in which individuals constantly attempt to maintain a sense of balance, what Giddens (1991) has called 'ontological security', that is the possession of '"answers" to fundamental questions which all human life in some way addresses' (Giddens 1991: 47). This ongoing search for ontological security takes place at the crossroads of the past, present and future, as in their day-to-day interactions with their environments, individuals are constantly reconciling their current sense of self and their accumulated past, with a view to dealing with what awaits them in the future. This process is necessarily conflictive in nature: metaphorically, it involves a dialectic whereby often-contradictory forces must be synthesized. It is not, therefore, about the simple accumulation of experiences and knowledge.

The outcome of the conflictive struggle for ontological security is not generally neat and tidy, and it often leads to feelings of ambivalence. Ambivalence emerges from the uncertainty of feeling a part of activities or collectives of individuals and feeling apart from them (Bauman 1991). It involves the conflicting feelings of love and hate and it is the simultaneous affirmation and negation of such feelings. For Anthony Elliot, 'the *ambivalence* of identity . . . [is] the tension between self and other, desire and lack, life and death, consciousness and unconsciousness' (Elliot 1996: 8). Papastergiadis (2000) relates ambivalence to the notions of 'nearness' and 'farness' put forward by Simmel (1950) in his discussion of the 'stranger', that is the state of being intimate with one's surroundings while remaining, metaphorically, outside them.

Ambivalence is thus the natural state of human beings who are forced by their individual life trajectories to make choices where choices are not always easy to make and to develop syntheses. However, this process of synthesizing is not a simple half-and-half proposition whereby the individual becomes half of what he/she was and half of what he/she has been exposed to. Rather, the result is emergent in that it arises in a not-altogether predictable way and it cannot be reduced to the constituent parts which make it up. It occupies a 'third place' (Bhabha 1994; Hall 1996), which results from the 'negotiation of difference . . . within which . . . elements encounter and transform each other' (Papastergiadis 2000: 170).

This mention of negotiation of difference and the idea that individuals strive for a coherent life narrative, seeking to resolve conflicts and assuage their ambivalent feelings, raises the issue of the extent to which identity is a self-conscious, reflexive project of individual agency, created and maintained by individuals. Surely, in the work of some authors, there is perhaps too much talk about individuals making choices, in other words, an overemphasis on individual agency. Giddens, for example, has suggested that even in the most extreme of life conditions, there is some space for individual choice and the 'reflexive constitution of self-identity' (Giddens 1991: 86). Elsewhere, the cultural anthropologist, Mathews (2000), argues that identities are not entities into which one is 'raised'; rather, one 'assumes' an identity and then works on it. Identity is thus seen to develop in what Mathew's (2000) calls the *cultural supermarket*: just as the modern supermarket offers foods from all over the world, in all shapes and sizes, so the international media and advanced technology together make available to individuals around the world a range of identities to be assumed. However, the cultural supermarket is not a completely free market where any self-identity under the sun can be assumed; nor is it a reality in an equal way for all of the inhabitants of this planet. In the former case, there are social structures within which individuals exist (be these state governments, peer groups or educational systems) which constrain the amount and scope of choice available to individuals. In the latter case, there are individuals living within social structures that do not allow them to make as many choices (e.g. societies where the roles of men and women are circumscribed by tradition).

Discussing language and minority rights, May (2001) argues that much of the work around the concept of hybridity and third places is 'overstatement' and '[i]f taken to an extreme, for example, all choices become possible; a position represented by the methodological individualism of rational choice theory' (May 2001: 39). In making his criticism, May echoes the views of social theorists such as Layder (1997) who defend the notion that social constructs such as ethnic affiliation, while not fixed for life, do nevertheless provide a grounding for much of one's day-to-day activity. What May writes is also in line with current discussions on the role of consciousness in the construction of subjectivities in cultural anthropology, where authors such as Ortner take the following stance:

> At the individual level, I will assume that, with Giddens, that actors are always at least partially 'knowing subjects', that they have some degree of reflexivity about themselves and their desires, and that they have some 'penetration' into the ways in which they are formed by circumstances. They are, in short, conscious in the conventional psycho-logical sense, something that needs to be emphasized as a complement to, though not a replacement of, Bourdieu's insistence on the inaccessibility to actors of the underlying logic of their practices. . . . I will be addressing subjectivity in the more psychological sense, in terms of inner feelings, desires, anxieties, intentions and so on, of individuals, but at other times I will be focusing on large scale cultural formations.
>
> (Ortner 2005: 34)

Despite his concern about the limits of agency, May accepts a degree of instability in social constructs such as ethnicity in the form of ongoing negotiation (as argued by Papastergiadis), but, in agreement with Layder and Ortner, he does not want to throw away all notions of structure which condition lives. May explains his position as follows:

> Negotiation is a key element here to the ongoing construction of ethnicity, but there are limits to it. Individual and collective choices are circumscribed by the ethnic

categories available at any given time and place. These categories are, in turn, socially and politically defined and have varying degrees of advantage or stigma attached to them. . . . Moreover, the range of choices available to particular individuals and groups varies widely.

(May 2001: 40)

I agree with May that it is probably wrong to take concepts such as hybridity, third places and choice to the extreme of arguing that social phenomena such as ethnic affiliation cease to have any meaning. Indeed, I see parallels to his views in current discussion and debates about gender (e.g. Alsop *et al* 2002; Eckert and McConnell-Ginet 2003), where there is disagreement about whether or not poststructuralism, associated with arguments against fixed and 'essentialized' notions of femininity and masculinity, offers a way forward, or simply serves to drain debate of any foundation from which to argue. As authors such as Spivak (1999) have observed, there may be strategic reasons for engaging in essentialized community politics. However, such strategic activity takes place at the level of *praxis*, that is in people's day-to-day activities, and while essentializing group and cultural traits and practices might work at this level as a tool to get things done, it does not seem a good strategy to adopt when working as a researcher, trying to construct understandings and explanations of observed phenomena. Working as a researcher, I think that hybridity and third places work far better than essentialized notions of identity when it comes to making sense of the cases of individuals who have moved between and among qualitatively different sociocultural contexts.

One way to take on board May's concerns about abandoning structure in favour of agency is to frame identity work in terms of individual participation in 'communities of practice' (e.g. Lave and Wenger 1991; Eckert and McConnell-Ginet 1992; Wenger 1998). Eckert and McConnell-Ginet define a community of practice as 'an aggregate of people who come together around mutual engagement in an endeavour' (Eckert and McConnell-Ginet 1992: 464). Emerging from this mutual engagement in an endeavour are '[w]ays of doing things, ways of thinking, ways of talking, beliefs, values, power relations – in short practices . . .' (Eckert and McConnell-Ginet 1992: 464). Such a framework starts with the assumption that learning is situated 'in the context of our lived experience of participation in the world . . . [and] is a fundamentally social phenomenon, reflecting our own deeply social nature as human beings capable of knowing . . .' (Wenger 1998: 3). There is also the belief that the relationship between social participation and communities of practice is crucial. Social participation refers 'not just to local events of engagement in certain activities with certain people, but to a more encompassing process of being active participants in the *practices* of social communities and constructing *identities* in relationship to these communities' (Wenger 1998: 3). Communities of practice correspond to the different subject positions people adopt on a moment-to-moment and day-to-day basis, and indeed throughout their lifetimes, depending on who they are with: family, colleagues at work, social groups at schools and so on.

Reference to communities of practice and individual participation relates directly back to the idea that identity is an emergent process, taking place at the crossroads of structure and agency. This means that while identity is conditioned by social interaction and social structure, it at the same time conditions social interaction and social structure. It is, in short, constitutive of and constituted by the social environment. This is the two-way action of 'structuration theory', as outlined by Giddens (1984). Giddens rejects the structuralist approach to social phenomena whereby the actions of individuals are determined by structures; however, at the same time, he does not want to account for human activity by solely depending on agency. Thus, for Giddens, individuals do not develop their sense of self, working exclusively from the inside out or from the outside in; rather, their environments provide conditions and impose constraints whilst they act on that same environment, continuously altering and recreating it.[1]

Structuration theory and other poststructuralist models of identity share the view of identity as process as opposed to essentialized fixed product. One consequence of this view is that very term 'identity' might well be seen as too static in its nominal form. Thus, some authors (e.g. Hall 1995) prefer to use 'identification' in an attempt to capture this processual angle. Elsewhere, Weedon (1997) does not even mention 'identity' in her discussion of post-structuralist constructions of the self. Weedon rejects '[h]umanist discourses [that] presuppose an essence at the heart of the individual which is unique, fixed and coherent'. Instead, she refers to 'subjectivities', which she defines as 'the conscious and unconscious thoughts and emotions of the individual, her sense of herself and her ways of understanding her relation in the world'. (Weedon 1997: 32). Finally, for authors such as Harré, identity is about the constant and ongoing positioning of individuals in interactions with others. The key concept of 'positioning' is defined as 'the discursive process whereby people are located in conversations as observably and subjectively coherent participants in jointly produced storylines' (Davies and Harré 1999: 37). This plurality of terms notwithstanding, 'identity' is still the most often-used term, as witness by its appearance in recent book titles by Pavlenko and Blackledge (2004), Joseph (2004), Block (2006; 2007), and Benwell and Stokoe (2006).

Finally, theorists and researchers adopting a generally poststructuralist approach to identity have tended to emphasize one or more social variables which include ethnicity, race, nationality, gender, social class and language, all glossed in Table 14.1 below. This table, however, requires several qualifications and clarifications. First, all of the identities listed and glossed in the table are about positionings by others and self-positionings, about ascriptions from without and affiliations from within, what Blommaert (2005) calls 'ascribed' and 'achieved' (or 'inhabited') identities. The different identity types are, therefore, co-constructed and furthermore, simultaneously individual and collective in nature. Secondly, although I list and gloss these different identity types separately, I in no way wish to suggest that they stand independent of one

Table 14.1 Individual/collective identity types (based on Block 2006: 37)

Ascription/affiliation	Based on
Ethnic	A sense of a shared history, descent, belief systems, practices, language and religion, all associated with a cultural group
Racial	Biological/genetic make-up, i.e. racial phenotype (NB: Often conflated with ethnicity)
National	A sense of a shared history, descent, belief systems, practices, language and religion associated with a nation state
Gendered	Nature and degree of conformity to socially-constructed notions of femininities and masculinities
Social Class	Associated with income level, occupation, education and symbolic behaviour
Language	The relationship between one's sense of self and different means of communication: language, a dialect or sociolect. Could be understood in terms of Leung *et al*'s (1997) *inheritance*, *affiliation* and *expertise*

another in the larger general identity of a person. As I explain elsewhere (Block 2006, forthcoming), when discussing race, ethnicity, nationality, gender, social class and language, it is indeed difficult to discuss one type of identity without mentioning others. Thus, masculinities and femininities must be understood in terms of language positioning (Eckert and McConnnell-Ginet 2003); race and ethnicity are interrelated in many people's minds (Pilkington 2003); language and social class are tightly linked (e.g. Eckert 2000); and so on. Thirdly and finally, there obviously are other angles on identity not listed or glossed. For example, in recent years, there has been a growing attention to sexual identity (e.g. Cameron and Kulic 2003) and given the recent rise in high profile religious activity in the world (e.g. Christian fundamentalism in the US, Islamic fundamentalism in Iran), religious identity promises to become key area of inquiry in coming years (e.g. Modood 2005).

To conclude this discussion, a poststructuralist approach to identity frames identity as socially constructed, a self-conscious, ongoing narrative an individual performs, interprets and projects in dress, bodily movements, actions and language. All of this occurs in the company of others – either face-to-face or electronically mediated – with whom to varying degrees the individual shares beliefs and motives and activities and practices. Identity is about negotiating new subject positions at the crossroads of the past, present and future. The individual is shaped by his/her sociohistory but also shapes his/her sociohistory as life goes on. The entire process is conflictive as opposed to harmonious. The individual often feels ambivalence and there are unequal power relations to deal with, around the different educational resources and assets, that is, social capital, possessed by participants.

As I have made clear thus far, it is my view that this approach to identity has become dominant among theorists and researchers interested in how individuals 'do' themselves in different social contexts: a casual perusal of recent works in sociology and anthropology journals, research monographs, edited collections and texts bears this claim out. However, with so many social scientists adopting this poststructuralist framework, some voices have begun to emerge critiquing the foundation on which the research boom is based. One such voice is Bendle (2002), to whom I now turn.

Bendle's critique

Bendle (2002) discusses the rise of identity as a key concept in the social sciences and how its current dominance in the social sciences is problematic. Bendle begins with the notion that both theorists and the focus of their enquires change over time, citing several reasons why the focus on the self, in particular, has come about. First, there is the late nineteenth and early twentieth century psychology and psychiatry, with the likes of William James and Sigmund Freud at the forefront. For the first time, theorists put the self at the centre of research, as something worthy of empirical study, requiring expert knowledge. Secondly, Bendle notes that during the nineteenth and twentieth centuries there was a slow process of secularization in Europe. This secularization led to a greater valuing of life on earth and self-fulfilment via worldly activity as opposed to other-worldly activity (i.e. religion). A third reason for the rise of identity relates to certain human rights advances in the advanced industrialized nations, particularly in the twentieth century. These advances took place concurrently with the rise of secularism and this is no accident, as the latter phenomenon meant the eroding of traditional institutions blocking social mobility, be this across social class, ethnic or gender lines. Finally, as was observed above, social scientists themselves have changed the way they see the world. According to Bendle, there has been movement from a structuralist preoccupation with stability, function and structure to a priming of individual agency, a movement from fixed, essentialised notions of race, ethnicity, gender and so on, to a poststructuralist, constructivist perspective which sees these categories as more fluid and unstable.

For Bendle, the rise of identity as a key concept in so much recent and current work in the social sciences is 'indicative of [a] crisis', which manifests itself in two ways. On the one hand, there is now a widespread belief, and even an assumption among many social scientists, that the formation, maintenance and projection of identity has changed in recent years. This is most of all the case in the post-industrial and industrialized world where decisions about what is important to study are made. This realization that identity is something worthy of study has, in turn, led to a notable increase in the amount of research aimed at investigating it. However, more research has led to a second way in which the rise of identity is indicative of crisis, namely, it has shown how ill-prepared so many researchers have been for the new reality to which they have turned their attention. In other words, identity as a concept is often under-theorized and therefore unable to work as a framework for the target of study. Of course a big problem is how identity has come to be framed as an ongoing process as opposed to a single set product. Bendle wonders how social scientists can see it as so important yet so ungraspable. He writes:

> There is an inherent contradiction between a valuing of identity as something so fundamental that it is crucial to personal well-being and collective action, and a theorization of 'identity' that sees it as something constructed, fluid, multiple, impermanent and fragmentary. The contemporary crisis of identity thus expresses itself as both a crisis of society, and a crisis of theory. The crisis of identity involves a crisis of 'identity'.
>
> (Bendle 2002: 1–2)

This crisis of identity is more pronounced in sociology, in particular among those who examine globalizing forces and flows related to the movement of peoples, money and culture around the world. And the crisis arises no doubt because of the newness of the ontology which has become the focus. However, the crisis also results from having borrowed the concept of identity from an already established field, which many would see as its rightful home: psychiatry. Bendle constructs an effective deconstruction of the work of Giddens and Castells, two of the better known globalization and identity theorists in recent years. He makes the point that they have, in effect, superficialized identity, focusing on surface malleability and change in the self in response to an ever more complex set of stimuli served up by the environment. And, he notes that they have not explained '[u]pon what psychological substrate such a transient construction rests and how it mobilizes the energies that are observably necessary to maintain an integrated personality in dynamic conditions of social change' (Bendle 2002: 8).

Bendle argues that there is need to move from 'surface' models of analysis put forth by so many today to more 'depth' models and from overly optimistic and romanticized approaches to more pessimistic and 'dark' ones. For Bendle such a move means looking more carefully at ego psychology and so called 'left' psychoanalytic theories of identity. This should be done in the name of balance and the healthy consideration that there just might be an inner core self, not entirely stable and surely conflicted, which acts as a constraint on human development. There is, therefore, more to the fluid and fragmented identity than a response to the environment. In addition, the notions of multiple identities and fragmentation, so important to poststructuralists and constructivists, would be seen by psychoanalysts as something to be treated. While the former seem to put conflict out there as something that can be resolved, the latter see conflict as evasively retiring into the inner recesses of the mind.

For Bendle, Giddens is one of the few general poststructuralist/constructivist theorists who try to engage with psychoanalysis. In Giddens' 1991 book there are references to Freud, Lacan and others. Unfortunately, Bendle thinks that Giddens has either not fully understood the work of these authors, and therefore has misrepresented it, or that he simply has not been able to convey his understandings to readers in a coherent fashion. While Giddens brings in terminology such as 'ontological security' and 'existential anxiety', he soon takes the more optimistic tack that human beings manage to adapt to social change around them leaving to the side the inner self of paranoia, schizophrenia, false self, disorder and so on. He therefore does not address how all of these inner-self phenomena might hold individuals back and act as a check on their self-realization, self-identity projects. Indeed, the very term self-identity seems to be at the crossroads of psychological and sociologically informed versions of who people are. However, Giddens, and many, many others who hold similar views on identity, have systematically failed to address the psychological while emphasizing the social.

Applied linguistics and identity

What is a trend in the social sciences generally comes to be a trend in applied linguistics, and the interest in poststructuralist approaches to identity has been no exception. In the past six years alone (2000-present), there have been at least ten monographs, textbooks and collections, published in English, which highlight identity and draw on this protocol. These publications include: Norton's (2000) study of immigrant women in Canada; Toohey's (2000) study of the relationship between the communication activities of language minority children in primary education in Canada and their socialization processes; Pavlenko *et al*'s (2001) edited collection on language learning and gender; Schechter and Bayley's (2002) study of the language practices and language affiliations of Mexican American families in the US; Hall's (2002) textbook on culture and research; Bayley and Schechter's (2003) collection of papers on language socialization and multilingualism; Kanno's (2003) study of the life stories of Japanese returnees; Miller's (2003) account of the language and socialization processes of immigrant children in Australia; Pavlenko and Blackledge's (2004) collection of papers on the negotiation of identities in different language, cultural and political contexts; and Block's (2006) discussion of multilingual identities in London.

The last publication cited above shows how in my own work, I have also accepted the post structuralist take on identity. However, I cannot help but wonder if many authors (myself included) are perhaps signing up to it in a relatively uncritical manner. I also wonder if, as Mervyn Bendle argues, these authors are to varying degrees guilty of adopting a model of identity which is 'radically under-theorised and incapable of bearing the analytical load that the contemporary situation requires' (Bendle 2002: 1). In particular, I wonder what has happened to the psychological self in the publications that I read.

Granger, psychoanalysis and second language learning

Granger is one applied linguist who has at least to some extent taken up Bendle's call for a more psychologically informed approach to identity.[2] Focusing on the phenomenon of silence in second language learning, she laments that it has traditionally been seen either as a sign that language learners do not comprehend or as a period during which they gather the linguistic knowledge necessary to be able to speak. For Granger, such interpretations of silence ignore a third possibility, namely that silence is a part of an internal identity struggle as individuals sort out feelings of loss (of the L1) and anxiety at the prospects of an uncertain future in a new language. She draws on Freudian psychology and Lacanian psychoanalytic theory (primarily via Fink 1995) and develops a theory of identity that seems to be, at first glance, somewhat in line with what Bendle has in mind.

Granger mines Freudian and Lacanian psychoanalysis for concepts which she then uses to make sense of two databases: published memoirs written by individuals who have experienced language and culture border crossing in their lifetimes and diary studies of language learners, produced by applied linguists. She discusses the ego as 'a kind of overseeing intermediary, negotiating relations between internal and external worlds' (Granger 2004: 42), where the medium of this negotiation is language. There is talk of anxiety, conflict, projection and avoidance, all of which arise in relation to experiences of destabilization and loss. Parallels are drawn between what the infant experiences and what child, adolescent and adult L2 learners experience. Above all, ambivalence and liminality (i.e. existing at the threshold) are the emotional and physical metaphors, respectively, that arise from destabilization and the loss of the 'love object', in this case what Granger calls 'the first language self'. The latter is 'the self that could make itself known, to the world and to itself, in its first language' (Granger 2004: 56). Thus, in Granger there is a discourse of psychoanalysis which the author aims to draw on in her attempt to make sense of silence in second language learning. However, what I note in her database, and the subsequent analysis of it, is that she is dealing less with silenced learners than with conflicted learners. I now turn to an example of how she 'psychoanalyses' a particular case.

In a seminal and oft cited article, Bailey (1983) reviews diary studies carried out during the late 1970s by nine language teachers/applied linguists (including Bailey herself) and two 'non teachers'. Bailey focuses on two key constructs – competitiveness and anxiety – charting how they manifest themselves in diary entries. In one example, Walsleben (1976) describes her experience of learning Farsi as a foreign language. In her account there is open conflict between the diarist and the teacher and this leads to Walsleben eventually to give up the learning of Farsi. One point of conflict with the teacher is the practice of administering frequent vocabulary tests to students unprepared to take them and who view them as a waste of time. Walsieben tells the story of how on one particular day, matters came to a head:

> After the break (the teacher) announced that he would give the vocabulary test, 'If that's OK.' Shirley stated again her difficulty in studying uncontextualized words for a vocabulary tests, and (the teacher) explained that he nonetheless felt that it was a justifiable way of building up our vocabularies. When he repeated that he was going to give the test and he looked at me when he said, 'If that's okay.' I responded tersely, 'You're the professor, but in my opinion it's a poor use of time: That was the proverbial last straw. For the next hour and a half the whole class was embroiled in a very emotional exchange of opinions dealing with what the class was and was not, what it could and should be, who would let whom do what.
>
> (Bailey 1983: 87 [Walsleben 1976: 34–35])

As Bailey puts it, in this case it seems that the diarist is not competing with her classmates; rather, she 'is struggling with the instructor for control of her language learning experience' (Bailey 1983: 87). A week after the blow-up with the teacher, Walsleben dropped out of the class.

For Granger, Walsleben's experience might be seen as a struggle with the teacher for control of her language learning, as Bailey suggests; however, there is another way, based in psychoanalysis, of framing Walsleben's experience. According to this line of analysis, Walsleben is involved in a struggle between the inside and outside, between Freud's' 'I should like to eat this' and 'I should like to spit it out' (Freud 1925: 439). Granger sums up Walsleben's state and that of other diarists in Bailey's survey who mention conflicts with their teachers as follows:

> This conflict between 'taking in' a second language and rejecting it is rooted in the ambivalence of the learner's desire both to learn and to refuse learning that accompanies learning's perpetual state of emergency . . . It is articulated . . . in frequent analogies that the diarists make between the relationships of teachers and students and those of aprons and children. These analogies also call to mind once again the Freudian concept of family romance . . . entailing, in part, motives of sibling rivalry, among which is a sense in which the child may imagine herself as the product of a clandestine love affair between her mother and a man other than her actual father, or alternatively as the only 'legitimate' child among her siblings.
>
> (Granger 2004: 99)

The kind of ambivalence described by Granger, revisiting Walsleben, can also be found among students participating in research I carried out over ten years ago, as I now explain.

The case of Silvia

The small database I will examine here is a part of a larger case study I developed over ten years ago in Barcelona, around a highly motivated upper intermediate level learner of English named Silvia.[3] I interviewed Silvia on a more or less weekly basis over a ten-week course she was attending. My interest at the time was in what she would cite as salient in her lessons and how she would evaluate these salient items. Examining the data now, I would say that Silvia adopted different subject positions as she provided accounts of her lessons. For example, there was one ongoing narrative which involved Silvia's relationships with her fellow students. Another involved her contesting the way the teacher corrected her written work. Here I will look at two excerpts, produced in two different interviews which relate to Silvia's construction of relationship with her teacher. The interviews originally took place in Spanish, but here I present English translations. I have used a simplified form of transcription to aid readability.

In excerpt 1, Silvia (S) is talking to me (D) about her relationship with her teacher, a topic that she herself had brought up:

S: The only thing is that sometimes I think that teachers, because they speak English and you don't, they are above you. And this infuriates me, actually because . . . I don't know, but you get this feeling a little and I've mentioned it to other people and they've told me I'm right. I mean it's not just my thing, I'm not going to have any kind of inferiority complex.

D: What? That I have something you don't have?

S: That I don't have and it's costing me a lot to have it and for this reason [they] look down on [you].

D: I've never thought about that. But don't you think that it's also mixed up with the power relation that might exist between teacher and student?

S: Yes, of course, there is always a power relation between the teacher and the student. At times, it has bothered me.

D: It's the feeling that the person . . . yeah, I understand.

S: And you say: 'Well who do you think you are? You're just a teacher'. It's true. You might know a lot of English but I know a lot of other things.

(Silvia, 2 June 1993)

On the surface, the important thing in this exchange is how Silvia, a well-educated upper-middle class woman, announces that there are things that she does not have to take from someone who is 'just a teacher'. She expresses certain resentment at the power inherent in the position of teacher and she does not accept the fact that the classroom situation puts her in a less powerful position, albeit for only four hours a week. And all of this, because the teacher has English, the object of her desire and efforts.

From the kind of psychoanalytic perspective that Granger has adopted, this exchange is chock-full of significance. There is the latterly mentioned object of desire – English – and how teachers flaunt the linguistic knowledge that the student is spending time and paying money to acquire. However, there is perhaps a degree of displacement going on here: is it English or the teacher herself that Silvia desires? There is also deciding how to interpret the end of intervention 1, when Silvia empathically declares that she is 'not going to have any kind of inferiority complex'. This denial might well be seen as a de-projection of how she feels, that is, a statement meaning the opposite of what it appears to mean.

Two weeks later, after the final lesson, Silvia surprised me with an interesting statement about her relationship with teachers, which in a way seemed less than congruent with her remarks about teachers being 'just teachers':

> I like talking to teachers. I don't know why, but I like it a lot. And besides, we went to the bar and had a glass of *cava*. But of course since we had never gone to the bar with her, you never get to know her very well. So we were asking her where she was from and how she had ended up here and everything. I don't know, you situate people more when you know a little about their past because if not . . .
>
> (Silvia, 16 June 1993)

Here Silvia celebrates how she finally was able to talk to her teacher away from the pressures of the course. She confesses that she likes talking to teachers. However, following Granger's psychoanalytical methodology, what sense can one make of Silvia's comments?

Taking the two excerpts together, there seems to be a parallel structure at work here. For Granger, there is a 'conflict between "taking in" [a teacher] and rejecting [her] [which] is rooted in the ambivalence of the learner's desire both to [align with the teacher] and to refuse [aligning with the teacher]'. Taking into account that Silvia in effect has studied several different languages in her lifetime and that at the time of the study she was in the middle of two years of uninterrupted enrolment, the psychoanalyst would likely wonder about the object of her desire: As I queried previously, is it the language or contact with teachers?

The short answer to this question is: I do not know. Here, I am engaging with psychoanalysis in an attempt to make sense of Silvia's words. However, I should make clear that I do not see myself as a competent psychoanalyst of learner accounts of their language learning experiences. Indeed, I am concerned that I might be seen to be trivializing theoretical frameworks, taken up on the spur of the moment by a researcher wishing to vary his approach to data. Surely, taking up the subject position of psychoanalyst requires more of the individual than having read a couple of books about Lacan.

There is also the issue of how data match up with claims made by the researchers about the inner lives of informants In Granger (2004), I think that revisiting Bailey's data is problematic for two reasons: first, because Granger is working with data collected by diarists/researchers with other purposes in mind, and secondly, because she only has access to a small part of the total database. As Fink (1997) notes, good psychoanalysis involves sustained contact between a trained psychoanalyst and an individual positioned as 'patient' and not the kind of secondary analysis that Granger has carried out.

So, where does all of this leave us as regards the poststructuralist approach to identity and Bendle's critique? I attempt an answer to this question in the final section.

Conclusion

On the one hand, I find Bendle's comments and suggestions about the poststructuralist approach to identity thought provoking. I can easily see his point about the inherent contradiction in valuing identity as such an important construct while saying that it is 'something constructed, fluid, multiple, impermanent and fragmentary'. In addition, my poststructuralist tendencies notwithstanding, I have always had niggling doubts about the apparent lack of any core self in publications that I read. Is there nothing stable deep inside, behind the different subject positions? However, taking on board Bendle's arguments puts me in a difficult situation: I still need to reconcile structure and agency – the ongoing problem par *excellence* for poststructuralists – but I also need to be attentive to the subconscious deeper inner workings of the mind and how they might impact on one's sense of self and identity. The question is: Can one take all of this on? Bendle seems to think that researchers and theorists can do so, and indeed are duty bound to do so, writing that 'an adequate response requires that critical and uncompromising analysis be conducted at the interface of sociology with the key underlying models of identity derived from constructionism, psychoanalysis and psychology' (Bendle 2002: 17). However, I am not so sure about this proposal for at least three good reasons.

First, there is the simple but basic rule of thumb that the right analysis for the questions being asked is always one carried out by a researcher knowledgeable and competent enough to ask and answer these questions. Perhaps psychoanalysis is not for social scientists who are interested in developing understandings of the identity work done by people living what Bauman (2005) has called 'liquid lives'. Liquid lives are lives in the fast lane, where 'the conditions under which . . . [people] act change faster than it takes the ways of acting to consolidate into habits and routines' (Bauman 2005: 1). When researching the fast and furious world that Bauman describes, the right analytical framework may well be something that Bendle would find 'superficial'. In my recent research on migration (Block 2006), it has seemed far more appropriate to focus on the hurly burly of today's globalized world than the inner drives and desires of my informants.

Secondly, a move to include psychoanalysis in identity research might also be inappropriate if psychoanalysis is considered to be about praxis, an applied activity, as opposed to theory, a speculating activity (Fink 1997). In this case, a psychoanalytical framework might offer an effective way of making patients feel better about themselves, but it might not offer the best possible framework for understanding observed phenomena. There are obvious parallels here to what I said earlier in this paper about the possible benefits of essentializing ethnic identities. Research epistemologies are often very different from practical epistemologies.

Thirdly and finally, I note that as an analytical tool, psychoanalysis can be intrusive to those being studied. What I mean is that it focuses exclusively on individuals and their very personal inner lives. Thus a perusal of some of the publications cited previously in the discussion of identity in applied linguistics (e.g. Norton 2000; Kanno 2003; Block 2006) shows how these researchers are far less intrusive. In a sense, identity making is negotiated between the informant and the researcher and is not something that the latter must dig out of the former.

Notes

1   Not everyone would agree with my view that Giddens sees a strong role for social structure in his work. See Layder (1997) for a critical view.
2   This is not to say that Granger is the only applied linguist ever to mention language learning and psychology in the same breath: Guiora *et al* (1972) carried out research around concepts like 'language ego' some 35 years ago. However, she is the only recent book-length analysis based on psychoanalysis that I have been able to find.
3   The case of Silvia is dealt with in a very different manner in Block (2000), where she is assigned the name 'GJ'.

References

Alsop, R., Fitzsimons, A. and Lennon, K. (2002), *Theorizing Gender*. Cambridge: Polity.
Bailey, K. (1983), 'Competitiveness and anxiety in adult second language learning: looking at and through the diary studies', in H. Seliger and M. Long (eds), *Classroom-oriented Research in Second Language Acquisition*. Rowley, MA: Newbury House, pp. 67–103.
Bauman, Z. (1991), *Modernity and Ambivalence*. Cambridge: Polity.
Bauman, Z. (2001), *Community*. Cambridge: Polity.
Bauman, Z. (2005), *Liquid Life*. Cambridge: Polity.
Bayley, R. and Schechter, S. R. (eds) (2003), *Language Socialization in Bilingual and Multilingual Societies*. Clevedon, UK: Multilingual Matters.
Bendle, M. (2002), 'The crisis of "identity" in high modernity', *British Journal of Sociology*, 53 (1), 1–18.
Benwell, B. and Stokoe, E. (2006), *Discourse and Identity*. Edinburgh: Edinburgh University Press.
Bhabha, H. (1994), *The Location of Culture*. London: Routledge.
Block, D. (2006), *Multilingual Identities in a Global City: London Stories*. London: Palgrave.
Block, D. (2007), *Second Language Identities*. London: Continuum.
Blommaert, J. (2005), *Discourse*. Cambridge: Cambridge University Press.
Bucholtz, M. (2003), 'Sociolinguistic nostalgia and the authentication of identity', *Journal of Sociolinguistics*, 7, (3): 398–416.
Cameron, D. and Kulic, D. (2003), *Language and Sexuality*. Cambridge: Cambridge University Press.
Davies, B. and Harré, R. (1999), 'Positioning and personhood', in R. Harré and L. van Langenhove (eds), *Positioning Theory*. London: Sage, pp. 32–52.
Eckert, P. (2000), *Language Variation as Social Practice*. Oxford: Blackwell.
Eckert, P. and McConnell-Ginet, S. (1992), 'Think practically and look locally: language and gender as community-based practice', *Annual Review of Anthropology*, 21: 461–90.
Eckert. P. and McConnell-Ginet, S. (2003), *Language and Gender*. Cambridge: Cambridge University Press.
Elliot, A. (1996), *Subject to Ourselves: Social Theory, Psychoanalysis and Postmodernity*. Cambridge: Polity.
Fink, B. (1995), *The Lacanian Subject: Between Language and Jouissance*. Princeton, NJ: Princeton University Press.
Fink, B. (1997), *A Clinical Introduction to Lacanian Psychoanalysis: Theory and Technique*. Cambridge, MA: Harvard University Press.
Freud, S. (1925), 'Negation', in *The Penguin Freud Library*, Vol. 11. London: Penguin, pp. 435–42.
Giddens, A. (1984), *The Constitution of Society: Outline of the Theory of Structuration*. Cambridge: Polity.
Giddens, A. (1991), *Modernity and Self-Identity: Self and Society in the Late Modern Age*. Cambridge: Polity.
Granger, C. (2004), *Silence in Second Language Learning. A Psychoanalytic Reading*. Clevedon: Multilingual Matters.
Guiora, A., Beit-Hallahini, B., Brannon, R., Dull, C. and Scovel, T. (1972), 'The effects of experimentally induced changes in ego states on pronunciation ability in a second language: an exploratory study', *Comprehensive Psychiatry*, 13, 421–8.
Hall, J. K. (2002), *Teaching and Researching Language and Culture*. London: Longman.
Hall, S. (1995), 'Fantasy, identity and politics', in E. Carter, J. Donald and J. Squires (eds), *Cultural Remix: Theories of Politics and the Popular*. London: Lawrence and Wishart, pp. 63–9.
Hall, S. (1996), 'The question of cultural identity', in S. Hall, D. Held, D. Hubert and K. Thompson (eds), *Modernity: An Introduction to Modern Societies*. Oxford: Oxford University Press.
Joseph, J. (2004), *Language and Identity*. London: Palgrave.
Kanno, Y. (2003), *Negotiating Bilingual and Bicultural Identities*. Clevedon: Multilingual Matters.

Lave, J. and Wenger, E. (1991), *Situated Learning: Legitimate Peripheral Participation*. Cambridge: Cambridge University Press.

Layder, D. (1997), *Modern Social Theory: Key Debates and New Directions*. London: Routledge.

Leung, C., Harris, R. and Rampton, B. (1997), 'The idealised native speaker, reified ethnicities and classroom realities', *TESOL Quarterly*, 31 (3), 543–60.

Mathews, G. (2000), *Global Culture/Individual Identity: Searching for a Home in the Cultural Supermarket*. London: Routledge.

May, S. (2001), *Language and Minority Rights*. London: Longman.

Miller, J. (2003), *Audible Differences: ESL and Social Identity in Schools*. Clevedon, UK: Multilingual Matters.

Modood, T. (2005), *Multicultural Politics: Racism, Ethnicity and Muslims in Britain*. Edinburgh: Edinburgh University Press.

Norton, B. (2000), *Identity in Language Learning: Gender, Ethnicity and Educational Change*. London: Longman.

Ortner, S. (2005), 'Subjectivity and cultural critique', *Anthological Theory*, 5 (1), 31–52.

Papastergiadis, N. (2000), *The Turbulence of Migration*. Cambridge: Polity.

Pavlenko, A. and Blackledge, A. (eds) (2004), *Negotiation of Identities in Multilingual Settings*. Clevedon, UK: Multilingual Matters.

Pavlenko, A., Blackledge, A., Piller, I. and Teutsch-Dwyer, M. (eds) (2001), *Multilingualism, Second Language Learning, and Gender*. New York: Mouton De Gruyter.

Pilkington, A. (2003), *Racial Disadvantage and Ethnic Diversity in Britain*. London: Palgrave.

Schechter, S. and Bayley, R. (2002), *Language as Cultural Practice : Mexicanos en et norte*. Mahwah, NJ: Lawrence Erlbaum.

Simmel, G. (1950), 'The Stranger', in K. Wolff (ed.), *The Sociology of Georg Simmel*. Glencoe, Ill: Free Press, pp. 401–8.

Smart, B. (1999), *Facing Modernity*. London: Sage.

Spivak, G. (1999), *A Critique of Postcolonial Reason: Toward a History of the Vanishing Present*. Cambridge, MA: Harvard University Press.

Toohey, K. (2000), *Learning English at School*. Clevedon, UK: Multilingual Matters.

Walsleben, M. (1976), 'Cognitive and affective factors influencing a learner of Persian (Farsi) including a journal of second language acquisition'. Unpublished manuscript, University of California, Los Angeles.

Weedon, C. (1997), *Feminist Practice and Poststructuralist Theory* (2nd edn). Oxford: Blackwell.

Wenger, E. (1998), *Communities of Practice*. Cambridge: Cambridge University Press.

Chapter 15

RYUKO KUBOTA

NEW APPROACHES TO GENDER, CLASS, AND RACE IN SECOND LANGUAGE WRITING (2003)

Introduction

EVERY LANGUAGE LEARNER has certain attributes of gender, class, and race. Bilingual writers engage in writing in their first and second languages with their multiple and shifting gender, class, and racial identities, although their identities may not be consciously realized. In larger educational contexts, these categories often significantly and contentiously influence various decisions with regard to such issues as how to develop or choose curriculum and materials, the content and presentation of classroom instruction, and the recruitment of students, teachers, or administrators.

Nonetheless, analysis of widely available publication titles in second language writing, as well as in the larger field of second language research, indicate that these categories have not been given major or explicit attention. The lack of attention to gender, class, and race in the general field of second language research is evident in some of the introductory books on second language acquisition. These books often categorize these issues under learner variables, but do not typically give them as much attention as the other variables. Larsen-Freeman and Long (1991), for instance, has a section on factors influencing differential success among second language learners, in which they mention age, aptitude, social–psychological factors including motivation and attitudes, personality, cognitive style, hemisphere specialization, and learning strategies. Of race, class, and gender, only gender is mentioned as one of "other factors." Another introductory book on second language acquisition by Gass and Selinker (2001) discusses the above listed factors as "non-language influences" but makes no mention of race, class, or gender. Yet, second language researchers interested in sociocultural approaches to understanding second language acquisition and learning increasingly do pay attention to these issues. Mitchell and Myles (1998, p. 20) state:

> [I]nterest in the learner as a social being leads to concern with a range of socially constructed elements in the learner's identity, and their relationship with learning—so *class*, *ethnicity*, and *gender* make their appearance as potentially significant for L2 learning research.

(Italics in the original)

Similarly, commenting on critical approaches to qualitative research, Peirce (1995) suggests that one of the assumptions underlying these approaches is that inequalities in terms of gender, race, class, ethnicity, and sexual orientation produce and are produced by asymmetrical power relations in society. As second language researchers and practitioners become more attuned to sociopolitical aspects of language learning, issues of race, class, and gender, as well as the interconnectedness of these three categories, inevitably become an integral focus of inquiry.

Among the three categories, gender seems to have been explored more extensively than the other two. Although the number of publications is still small, interest in gender has indeed been observed recently in the field of second language writing (Belcher, 1997, 2001; Johnson, 1992; Pavlenko, 2001a) as well as in composition studies in general (i.e., Jarratt & Worsham, 1998; Micciche, 2001; Phelps & Emig, 1995; Ritchie & Boardman, 1999). Vandrick (1994) speculates that the alignment between L1 composition studies and gender issues is facilitated through the field of literature, which is influenced by feminist theories, and a large number of women instructors in college composition classes, which is the case in the field of ESL as well. In the larger field of second language education/acquisition and bilingualism, an increased focus on gender is evidenced by several extensive reviews of studies on gender and language (Ehrlich, 1997; Pavlenko, 2001b; Sunderland, 2000). One of the common issues raised in these review articles is the limitation of a fixed view of gender and language as well as the male/female gender dichotomy created in the investigation of how men and women learn and use a second language in bilingual or multilingual settings. Moving beyond this one-to-one relationship between gender and language as well as the binary view of gender as a fixed set of opposite biological traits, constructivist and poststructuralist approaches explore how gender differences and gender identities are constructed in social relations and discourses (i.e., uses of language unified by common assumptions). Such alternative views allow one to understand gender, manifested in language use and language learning, as a social construct that is dynamic and always shifting.

This paper synthesizes some key concepts that have emerged in recent discussions on gender in the larger fields of bilingualism and second language acquisition and education and applies these concepts to exploring issues of gender, class, and race in second language writing research. Critiques of binaries and essentialism in various forms constitute an important part of post-process approaches which attempt to uncover power, politics, and ideologies underlying various social relations (see Atkinson's introduction to this issue). Although gender, class, and race are separate categories, constructivist and poststructuralist approaches to gender and language provide a general conceptual framework that can be useful in exploring issues of race and class as well as the mutually constitutive nature of these three concepts. Given the wide range of topics to cover in this paper, the focus here is not to provide a comprehensive review of literature in relation to these three topics, but to survey some key concepts and use them to explore some future directions for second language writing research.

Before moving to the main discussion, it is necessary to point out that the intersection between second language writing and second language acquisition is not entirely clear because of their divergent foci. Carson (2001) argues that while second language writing primarily has a pragmatic concern for learner performance at a discourse level, much of second language acquisition has a focus on competence on the morphosyntactic level. Likewise, a complete congruence between bilingualism and second language writing may be untenable. Bilingualism research often uses psycholinguistic or sociological inquiry to study how people manipulate two languages orally, although there is a recent scholarly interest in autobiographical writing about the author's own development of biliteracy or bilingualism (Belcher & Connor, 2001; Pavlenko, 2001a). Although research on second language acquisition or bilingualism may not be directly applicable to second language writing, the general processes and factors involved in second language acquisition and bilingual development obviously underlie writing in a second language and thus these two areas influence each other in terms of research inquiry (Silva, Leki, & Carson, 1997). Indeed, both second language acquisition and teaching and learning second language writing are parallel issues, as Carson (2001) illustrates. Although one common thread in second language acquisition and second language writing seems to be relatively light attention to gender, class, and race in general, recent research has given increasing attention to issues of gender. The following section provides a brief overview of discussions on gender in the fields of second language education/acquisition and bilingualism.

Gender in second language research

Issues of gender in the research fields of second and foreign language education, second language acquisition, and bilingualism have been synthesized in some recent review articles. Reviewing studies on language and gender in the broader field of second and foreign language education, Sunderland (2000) synthesizes a large number of publications with a wide range of topics, including language learning ability, motivation/investment, teacher perceptions, learning styles and strategies, classroom interaction, teaching materials, testing, learner identities, masculinities, and pedagogies. The body of work demonstrates a wide range of scholarly focus and commitment from a straightforward data-based approach that investigates gender differences to critical explorations of gender biases and asymmetrical power relations. One problem raised by Sunderland is the male/female binary seen in the "gender differences" approach to language use, which has reinforced the fixed notion of female deficit and male dominance or superiority in language use. Sunderland states that much of the work on gender and language has seen gender mostly as a binary category, even though there have been new theorizations of gender with a focus on various alternative concepts such as multiple and fluid identities, social and linguistic construction ("becoming" rather than "being"), individual agency, gender identity as constituted through "performativity" (i.e., repeated performance of gendered norm) rather than as reflecting essentialized categories of masculinity and femininity (Butler, 1990). According to Sunderland, this binary overlooks gender intragroup differences and intergroup overlap, the context of the local meaning, and the possibility of gender being shaped by language use, rather than the other way around. This observation moves gender differences beyond the fixed and universal relationship between gender and language.

The limitation of fixed notions of gender difference in SLA research is also addressed by Ehrlich (1997), who recommends focusing on social and linguistic constructions of gender. Along with Sunderland (2000), Ehrlich argues that the focus on male/female difference tends to exaggerate and overgeneralize the difference, create a fixed and static notion of gender differences in language-related behaviors, and ignore the social, cultural and situational contexts in which language is acquired and used. According to Ehrlich, current trends in language and gender research focus on the constructivist notion that "language use constructs gender difference as a social category" (p. 424) and that "individuals construct or produce themselves as women or men by habitually engaging in social practices that are associated with culturally and community-defined notions of masculinity and femininity" (p. 436). Contrasting with the fixed view of male/female dichotomy in language use, this paradigm views users of language as being able to participate in a social practice that challenges the normative construction of gender.

The social construction of gender difference in language use is further elaborated in feminist poststructuralist approaches to gender and language in bilingual/multilingual contexts (Pavlenko, 2001b). In theorizing about the relationship between bilingualism and gender based on a review of a large number of studies, Pavlenko (2001b) discusses several assumptions of feminist poststructuralist approaches to the study of language and gender. These assumptions conceptualize gender or the meaning of gender as a system of social relations rather than an individual trait, as socially and culturally constructed, as dynamic and subject to change, and as always context dependent. Thus, there is no one-to-one relation between gender and language but rather there are multiple relations and meanings. In other words, "there are no linguistic behaviors, styles, or practices that can be universally associated with a particular gender group" (p. 126). Another feminist poststructuralist assumption is that gender asymmetries are constructed and negotiated in discourses; that is, gender identities with a hierarchy of power embodied in them are produced, reinforced, or challenged in discourses or in uses of language that reflect normative or counter-hegemonic conceptions of gender.

The above overview of different approaches to gender and language reflect in part various approaches to conceptualizing gender difference in the field of feminism. A summary of different approaches to gender difference in feminism presented by Weedon (1999) is useful here. The view that women's language is inferior to men's and that men's language use is the norm corresponds with a traditional view of gender difference. The approach that explores gender difference in gender-specific language use by focusing on same-sex interactions parallels the "equal-but-different" argument that critiques the traditional view as well as the liberal feminist view that advocates gender equality in the public sphere. As seen below, however, this position does not sufficiently challenge deep-rooted patriarchy or normative notions of femininity and masculinity. An attempt to move beyond the difference approach and give positive meanings to women's language use, as briefly mentioned later (i.e., Belcher, 1997; Tannen, 1998) parallels radical feminism that aims to decolonize women's bodies and minds and to affirm women's unique identities. Finally, the notion of social and discursive construction of gendered language reflects postmodern approaches to feminism.

As in feminism, different approaches to exploring gender difference in language use are contested. Just as Sunderland (2000) provided a critique of the "gender differences approach," Pavlenko (2001b) recognizes the limitations of the traditional approaches to gender and language which these poststructuralist approaches attempt to overcome. These limitations consist of a "deficit" or "dominance" framework, which views women as innately inferior or oppressed language users, and a "difference" paradigm that correlates linguistic variables with the sex of the language user. In a similar vein, Wareing (1994) argues that the "dominance" approach has revealed unequal gender relations of power by examining cross-gender conversations, whereas the difference approach has explored gender-specific communicative norms by examining same-sex interactions. The difference paradigm, in particular, is embedded in various inquiries in social sciences which emphasize neutrality. As Cameron (1992) demonstrates, linguistic inquiries since Saussurean structuralism have focused on binary oppositions ranging from linguistic concepts (e.g., *langue versus parole*) to linguistic elements (e.g., minimal pairs). However, despite the scientific and neutral tone behind the "differences approach," there is an implicit assumption that male language use is the norm. Thus, although the differences and deficit approaches have shed light on the relations among gender, language, and power, both of them are likely to support the argument that women should alter their speech styles instead of challenging the male dominance manifested in language use (Wareing, 1994).

The above discussion shows that the concept of "difference" is indeed contentious and political. An emphasis on difference often leads to "essentialism," or adherence to the pure essence or uniqueness of a certain group, giving a fixed identity to the group. However, these criticisms of difference do not necessarily reject scholarly investigations of differences. As poststructuralism critiques fixed differences, it also rejects fixing the meaning of essentialism (Fuss, 1989). In other words, essentialism or emphasis on difference does not always have negative consequences; it can be appropriated in a counter-hegemonic way by the marginalized to create a positive meaning for their unified identity. It is thus necessary to understand the strategic creation or exploitation of differences for the purpose of either legitimating or opposing existing relations of power. This requires researchers to become aware of the political and strategic meanings of differences endorsed or challenged by research.

In summary, recent studies on language and gender in the broader fields of second and foreign language education, second language acquisition, and bilingualism caution against creating a male/female dichotomy in relation to various issues in language learning and language use. Such a binary fixes a certain set of traits as male/female and falls into a deterministic view that ultimately legitimates the superiority of men's use of language, even if the stance is against male dominance. Moreover, the binary leaves no room for individual agency that allows men and women to choose linguistic forms and behaviors in particular social contexts, individual creativity, and possible transformation of the normative categories often assigned to women and men. At the same time, it is necessary to acknowledge the strategic use of difference that can create oppositional voices or identities for marginalized groups. Alternative views suggest that the relationship between language and gender is formed through social practice and in discourse and that it is always dynamic and shifting. The ways men and women learn and use a language are not determined by their gender but constructed, negotiated, and transformed through social practices informed by particular social settings, relations of power, and discourses (those on gender role, expectations, etc.).

Connection to class and race

The above review of discussions on language and gender research provides a useful tool for exploring issues of race and class as well. Rather than viewing race and class as fixed categories that determine the use and learning of a second language among particular racial or socio-economic groups, poststructuralist and constructivist approaches allow one to explore how race and class get constructed by social practices and discourses and how people with certain racial and socioeconomic status get positioned or position themselves in learning and using a language. One good example of racial and gender identity construction in acquiring a second language is a study by Ibrahim (1999). Ibrahim demonstrated how French-speaking continental African immigrant high school boys in Canada "become black" through identifying themselves with Black American pop culture, such as rap (especially gangsta rap) and hip-hop, and learning Black English as a second language. Conversely, immigrant girls from Africa had an ambivalent relationship with rap because they viewed it as sexist. Although they also learned English through music, it was a different kind of black pop music that was softer and contained mostly romantic themes. This example cogently shows that race and racial identity are not fixed but shifting and that language learning is also part of this process of racial identity construction.

The example presented by Ibrahim (1999) also demonstrates how gender and race are intertwined. The review articles on language and gender that I have referred to (i.e., Ehrlich, 1997; Pavlenko, 2001b; Sunderland, 2000) also underscore the interconnectedness of gender with other social categories such as class, race, ethnicity, culture, sexuality, and age. Many of the other works cited in this paper demonstrate interrelations among these categories, confirming that "ethnicity, gender and class are not experienced as a series of discrete background variables, but are all, in complex and interconnected ways, implicated in the construction of identity and the possibilities of speech" (Norton, 2000, p. 13) and writing.

The overview I have presented thus far provides several implications for studies in second language writing. First, any differences approach, whether it is related to gender, class, or race, needs to be conducted and interpreted with caution. Such an approach could (re)produce a fixed binary between male and female, middle-class and working-class, or white people and those of color, reinforcing a fixed knowledge of how and what a certain group of people write in a second language. As mentioned, this does not necessarily indicate that any research that focuses on gender, class, or racial differences is unnecessary or inappropriate; quite the opposite, these differences need to be unpacked in relation to power and discourse. However, this kind of research requires recognition and critical scrutiny of the politics of difference behind it. It is necessary to understand how research can shape and fix the dominant knowledge of dichotomized differences as neutral truths or how research can reveal different meanings in these categories. As Wareing (1994) suggests, research can seek dialectic frameworks that both investigate gender differences and critique dominance/subordination relations so that a positive new orientation is created for what has so far been the language of the marginalized.

Applying this dialectic approach, the following section explores possible research directions for second language writing, particularly in ESL and EFL. It will explore questions that investigate racial, class, and gender differences as well as issues of power in relation to these differences. The aim here is to suggest research possibilities that could stimulate further dialogue rather than to provide an exhaustive list of research topics. Although my exploration is divided into the three categories, they are interconnected as emphasized thus far.

Application to second language writing

Gender

By applying an approach that both explores differences and scrutinizes the power and politics behind them, second language writing research may explore gender differences in how men and women or boys and girls write differently in L2 with respect to process and product. These differences, however, should not be conceptualized as fixed traits, but as phenomena contingent on context and power. The question of gender differences can be explored in various contexts, such as instructional settings, testing, cyberspace, and publishing. Other foci can be categorized in many different ways, but one way is to use the conventional categories of process and product. Research on gender difference in the writing process may examine topic choice, planning, writing, peer editing, and revising, whereas a focus on product may explore word choice, syntax, discourse organization, audience awareness, and so on. The research design could be quantitative or qualitative or both.

Among only a handful of studies with explicit attention to gender in the field of second language writing, Johnson (1992) investigated how ESL women writers adjust complimenting strategies according to the gender of the addressee in writing peer-reviews. This research complements another study of peer reviews which found that women L1 writers used positive evaluation, intensifiers, and personal referencing more frequently than men and that the gender of the addressee played a significant role in choosing these strategies (Johnson & Roen, 1992). Based on the data obtained from women L1 writers in the same study, Johnson (1992) investigated how women L2 writers, compared to the L1 writers, varied these strategies according to the gender of the addressee. The study found that while women L1 writers used more positive evaluations, intensifiers, personal references, and closing compliments to female addressees than to male addressees, women L2 writers did not vary their strategies either to the same degree or in the same ways as the L1 writers did.

The results pose an interesting question with regard to ESL writers' conformity to the norms. Referring to another study that found a tendency among both male and female native-

English-speaking student writers to rate papers with female-linked complimenting strategies as less effective (Roen & Johnson, 1992), Johnson (1992) argues that to conform to the L1 norm in this case might negatively position women L2 writers in the rhetoric that is perceived as less powerful and effective. The poor quality of female-linked strategies perceived by L1 students is related to the underlying premise in the "dominance" and "differences" approaches discussed earlier. That is, female use of language is not only different from that of the male counterpart but also inferior. Here, women L2 writers are in a double bind; while acquiring the gendered norm may force them into an inferior position in cross-gender situations, not acquiring the socially appropriate norm may prevent them from becoming legitimate participants in same-gender situations. One solution for L2 writers suggested by Johnson (1992) is to make their own informed choice through raising their awareness of how men and women L1 writers use different strategies and how these strategies are valued in society. Yet the multiple and dynamic nature of meanings in relation to gendered language use, which has been discussed earlier, poses slightly different kinds of questions: How do writers come to have particular perceptions about the effectiveness of gendered strategies? Are female-oriented complimenting strategies necessarily less effective in different-sex interactions? How and why do men and women choose particular gendered complimenting strategies? How can women L2 writers strategically position themselves in the gender hierarchy to achieve their goals?

The study by Johnson (1992) clearly shows that research on gender difference in second language writing cannot escape issues of power and equity, requiring investigation on whether a certain gendered characteristic in L2 writing, if any, is valued or devalued by gatekeepers, including learners (in peer-editing situations), teachers, composition raters, peer-reviewers or editors (in publishing). This question investigates how power and privilege in relation to gender are manifested in L2 writing, leading to the question of how existing relations of power can be transformed. Another dimension of power and politics is the reader's response to "gendership" in writing. Haswell and Haswell (1995) demonstrated how readers were influenced by various preconceptions such as gender bias and gender blindness in responding to two "cross-dressed" L1 texts, each written by a female and a male undergraduate student in a college English composition class (i.e., a male-sounding text written by a woman and a female-sounding text written by a man). This study raises the issue of the positionality of the writer in gendered discourse, multiple possibilities for the author's gendership, and readers' negotiation of meaning influenced by gender ideologies. A written text indeed constitutes a site of struggle where meaning is constructed through negotiation between author subjectivities and reader expectations. In L2 situations, a similar study would yield a more complicated relation between the author and the audience, because gender expectations might differ across cultures, as the study by Johnson (1992) implies.

A related area of inquiry is the relationship between second language writing and identity construction. Recent discussions on voice in second language writing, as seen in the *Journal of Second Language Writing* (Belcher & Hirvela, 2001), have revealed the social, rather than the purely individual or autonomous, nature of writing. That is, writing is a social activity in which writers align themselves in acceptable discourses to express themselves by reinventing ideas and linguistic expressions created by others (e.g., Prior, 2001). In this view, writers' identities are socially constructed and writers position themselves in social identities available to members of the discourse community (Clark & Ivanič, 1997; Ivanič, 1998). Just as the meaning of gender is multiple and shifting, writers' gender identities are plural, complex, and dynamic, as illustrated by a study of immigrant women's identities and their investment in learning English in Canada as shown through their diaries and interviews (Norton, 2000).

Given that gender constitutes part of a writer's multiple identities, investigating how the development of second language writing reflects, affects, or constructs gender identity would provide important insights. For instance, it has been pointed out that the argumentative and adversarial language often used in academic and political discourses reflects masculinity (Belcher, 1997; Tannen, 1998) and may conflict with some women writers' identities, causing discomfort, struggle, or dilemma. Examining the struggle experienced by women writers would encourage a critical reevaluation of male dominance in communication and explore new linguistic possi-bilities by addressing how teachers and learners can create and advocate new ways of writing that are congruent with L2 women learners' identities. Furthermore, as in feminism, women teachers and learners must work together across racial and class boundaries. It is necessary to explore how second language women writers can form solidarity with women L1 writers in the creation of new linguistic possibilities.

Another slightly different inquiry into identity in writing is the ways in which male or female writers describe their second language learning experiences. In analyzing published memoirs of personal cross-cultural autobiographies, Pavlenko (2001a) showed that while male authors tended to downplay issues of gender and viewed language learning as an individual achievement, female writers tended to emphasize the recreation of their new identities in another language through fostering friendship and connectivity with others. This new genre of study raises the question of how these published memoirs, which are circulated widely among the general public, both reflect and reproduce dominant views of cross-cultural gender differences. More research is needed to investigate how discourses on gender, culture, and language evident in these published works influence L2 student writers who try to cross cultural and linguistic boundaries.

Class

The gap between the rich and the poor has increased dramatically in the 1980s and early 1990s in the United States (U.S. Census Bureau, 2001) and is growing globally as well (BBC Online, 2001). This implies that both local and global socioeconomic disparities exist among second language writers. Furthermore, this suggests that social class should not be considered only in terms of the measures traditionally used to define it—i.e., income and occupation within a particular nation-state—but in terms of social and economic divisions between the center and the periphery on a global scale as well. For instance, economic disparity between center and periphery scholars who write for publication (Canagarajah, 1996) can be an important topic of inquiry.

In the larger fields of literacy and composition studies, the ways class influences people's learning experiences in mainstream educational settings have been addressed as one of the topics of inquiry. For instance, Heath (1983) studied the ways in which children and adults in a white working-class community and in a black working-class community, only a few miles apart in the southeastern United States, participated in oral and written communication in different ways compared to middle-class townspeople. Rose (1989) describes his own struggle to make it through the US educational system as a son of working-class immigrants, as well as the challenges faced by students in remedial writing classes, many of whom were from bilingual, bicultural, and working-class backgrounds. Both of these works illustrate varied "Discourses" (Gee, 1996) in conflict, demonstrating a mismatch between the social and linguistic conventions that these students acquired through social practices in their families, communities, and churches, and expected ways of thinking and using language in schools and colleges. These examples also show how class is intertwined with other categories of inquiry, as mentioned thus far.

YUKO KUBOTA

...tudies provide the field of second language writing with a set of questions that are ... to the research agenda on gender, although identification of one's class is obviously more complex than in the case of gender. It is necessary to avoid assigning a rigid socioeconomic label to an individual or a group of second language writers because class involves multiple layers of defining factors. Nonetheless, one possible issue to explore is how L2 writers with different socioeconomic status write differently in L2 with respect to process and product. Again, the contexts can be instructional setting, testing, cyberspace, and publishing. The topics of inquiry for process and product would parallel the gender issues. The research design could also be quantitative or qualitative. At the political and ideological level, equity issues also need to be addressed here. For instance, one might investigate whether certain socioeconomic groups' characteristics in L2 writing are valued or devalued by gatekeepers, including learners, teachers, composition raters, peer-reviewers, or editors. Other questions include: How are power and privilege in relation to class manifested in L2 writing and how can the relations of power be transformed?

As in gender, the writer's social class is linked to the writer's identity. Thus, one might investigate how the development of second language writing skills reflects, affects, or constructs a writer's class identity. As in issues of gender, the process of aligning oneself within the available discourses constructed by and for the economically dominant group is likely to cause discomfort, struggle, or dilemma for writers from a lower socioeconomic background. Again, the examination of the struggles experienced by these writers would prompt critiques of the dominant discourse and promote political action for creating new possibilities. With the development of critical pedagogies, there will probably be a greater interest in the creation of counter-hegemonic identities in education for racial, ethnic, linguistic, and socioeconomic minority students. This interest would encourage exploration of the ways in which teachers and learners can create and advocate new ways of writing that affirm class identity in mainstream society.

There is, however, a cautionary view; socioeconomic status may not exactly be comparable to race or gender. Soliday (1999) points out that while it is possible to affirm positive identities for racial minorities and women or to critique these groups' forced assimilation into the dominant discourse, academic communities do not usually celebrate lower-class students' inability to buy a computer or textbooks nor do we say that gaining economic resources is assimilationist. Although working class identities are often valued and celebrated in non-academic discourses, they do not have a privileged status in academic communities. This view suggests a greater need to critically examine social and educational policies imposed on the have-nots, as observed in college basic skills requirements which, despite good intentions, further prevent class mobility for students who struggle to be successful students between job and family responsibilities.

Race

In the above discussions of both gender and class, the first topic for inquiry I introduced had to do with gender or class difference in writing process and product. It is possible to ask a similar question about race: i.e., how do L2 writers with different racial backgrounds write differently in term of process and product? This question, however, sounds unclear. First of all, what does "L2 writers with different racial backgrounds" mean? If "race" is defined in a sociological sense as a "category of people that is set apart from others because of socially-defined physical characteristics" (Thompson & Hickey, 1994; p. 231), "racial groups" can be East Asians, South Asians, Blacks, Caucasians, American Indians, and so on. If the category is expanded to include ethnicity, and an ethnic group is defined as "a category of people set apart from others because of distinctive social and cultural characteristics, such as ancestry, language, religion, customs, and lifestyles" (Thompson & Hickey, 1994; p. 232), "racial groups" become synonymous to groups of people divided by their language background such as Chinese, Korean, Japanese, Vietnamese, Thai, German, Finnish, etc. In fact, a racial/ethnic background is often related to a linguistic background and a focus on ethnic rather than broader racial groups seems to provide more meaningful inquiry into L2 writing. Thus, in the following discussion, "race" will be interpreted as not just a biological category but a notion that encompasses language and culture. The question then becomes: How do L2 writers with different linguistic or cultural backgrounds write differently in term of process and product?

This question, however, has been addressed quite extensively in second language writing research. Contrastive rhetoric, for instance, has investigated rhetorical conventions of different languages (cf. Connor, 1996), while other studies have focused on how ESL learners with different cultural and linguistic backgrounds approach writing tasks differently (Carson & Nelson, 1994, 1996). What then would a new approach to race in second language writing look like?

Before exploring answers to that question, it would be useful to critically review the conventional approach to race (or culture and language) in educational or psychological research. Research interest in racial (cultural or linguistic) difference has generated genetic explanations of human behaviors. For instance, the racial difference in academic achievement was investigated in the 1960s (Jensen, 1969) and again in the 1990s in *The Bell Curve: Intelligence and Class Structure in American Life* (Herrnstein & Murray, 1994). Paralleling the deficit view of female or working-class language use, such research endorsed deficit theories, which define certain types of genetic (racial) heritage as deficits, while treating a certain type (i.e., white) as the norm. This line of research has a racist tone and was inherited by cultural deficit theories, which implied that under-achievement of minority students is related to their socioeconomically, culturally, and linguistically impoverished environments (cf. Ovando & Collier, 1998). It is important to note that cultural explanations of achievement differences may reflect "cultural racism"—a contemporary form of racism that usually negates overt forms of racism and instead disguises itself by describing group differences in cultural terms (May, 1999; Van Dijk, 1993). This critical review suggests that deficit theories—genetic or cultural—may underlie the traditional approach to contrastive rhetoric, which focuses on deviation from the Standard American Schooled English norm (Kaplan, 2001).

As discussed earlier, finding rhetorical or linguistic differences among different racial, ethnic, and language groups in itself is unproblematic. As in the case of gender, the danger is in wittingly or unwittingly creating fixed and static knowledge about how these different groups write in their first and second languages and legitimating a certain hierarchy of power for different languages or ethnic varieties of a language. The politics behind the creation of differences should be exposed and investigated. Thus, contrary to the "deficit" or "assimilationist" approach, an alternative approach to race/ethnicity in L2 writing can use the concept of race/ethnicity for an oppositional, liberatory, and transformative aim. Echoing critical multiculturalism, whiteness studies, and postcolonial critique, a new approach could focus on the deconstruction of the norm as well as the binary images of racial, ethnic, or cultural difference between how white middle-class writers write in English and how Others write in their languages. It can also explore the possibility of giving a positive value to under-privileged cultural (racialized) rhetoric. For instance, Comfort (2001) documented African American graduate students' desire to fully participate in white academic discourse while maintaining their own values, perspectives, and expressions. The same issue certainly applies to second language writers from different racial backgrounds. In order for the academy to become open to diverse ethnic/racial conventions of writing, instructors need to begin changing the ways they interact with texts.

A new alternative approach to culture/ethnicity/race in second language writing may investigate such questions as: How are the norm and binary difference of cultural (racialized) rhetorical forms discursively constructed in relation to power and privilege? How are students' identities in regard to cultural (racialized) rhetoric constructed by competing discourses of race, culture, and language? How can second language learners and non-native teachers join in solidarity to transform the norm and create new linguistic possibilities? The new approach requires the mobilization of non-native researchers of color pursuing a new rhetorical space in English and white researchers committed to not only "studying down" but also "studying up" the power hierarchy (Roman, 1993).

Conclusion

This paper has explored some possible future research agendas for second language writing with regard to race, gender, and class. It is important to reiterate that these categories often overlap, requiring examination of their interrelationships. A study by Casanave (1992), for instance, describes the painful socialization process in the graduate school experience of a young English-dominant bilingual woman from a Puerto Rican working-class family in New York. As a doctoral student of sociology, she was forced to position herself in a positivistic discourse promoted by white middle-class European and American male academics, which disabled her from sharing her academic experience with her family and friends. This example demonstrates a clash between one's racial, class, and gender identities and the acquisition of an academic discourse. Research attention should be paid to the interconnectedness of these categories.

Race, class, gender and other issues related to equity will perhaps gain popularity as a research topic in the future. While writing on these assigned topics as a non-native Asian woman, I dream of a future discussion forum in our field—a panel that includes several papers on gender, class, and race presented by white and non-white male and female researchers. It is my hope that both men and women from diverse racial, cultural and socioeconomic backgrounds will actively participate in the critical investigation of these topics.

References

BBC Online. (2001). World inequality. Retrieved October 18, 2002, from http://news.bbc.co.uk/hi/english/business/newsid_1442000/1442073.stm

Belcher, D. (1997). An argument for nonadversarial argumentation: On the relevance of the feminist critique of academic discourse to L2. *Second Language Writing*, 6, 1–21.

Belcher, D. (2001). Does second language writing theory have gender? In T. Silva & P. K. Matsuda (Eds.), *On second language writing* (pp. 59–71). Mahwah, NJ: Lawrence Erlbaum.

Belcher, D., & Connor, U. (Eds.). (2001). *Reflections on multiliterate lives.* Clevedon: Multilingual Matters.

Belcher, D., & Hirvela, A. (2001). Special issue on voice. *Journal of Second Language Writing*, 10, 1–2.

Butler, J. (1990). *Gender trouble: Feminism and the subversion of identity.* New York: Routledge.

Cameron, D. (1992). *The feminist critique of language* (2nd ed.). London: Routledge.

Canagarajah, A. S. (1996). Non-discursive requirements in academic publishing, material resources of periphery scholars, and the politics of knowledge production. *Written Communication*, 48, 435–472.

Carson, J. (2001). Second language writing and second language acquisition. In T. Silva & P. K. Matsuda (Eds.), *On second language writing* (pp. 191–199). Mahwah, NJ: Lawrence Erlbaum.

Carson, J. G., & Nelson, G. L. (1994). Writing groups: Cross-cultural issues. *Journal of Second Language Writing*, 3, 17–30.

Carson, J. G., & Nelson, G. L. (1996). Chinese students' perceptions of ESL peer response group interaction. *Journal of Second Language Writing*, 5, 1–19.

Casanave, C. (1992). Cultural diversity and socialization: A case study of a Hispanic woman in a doctoral program in sociology. In D. E. Murray (Ed.), *Diversity as resource: Redefining cultural literacy* (pp. 148–182). Alexandria, VA: TESOL.

Clark, R., & Ivanič, R. (1997). *The politics of writing*. London: Routledge.

Comfort, J. R. (2001). African-American women's rhetorics and the culture of Eurocentric scholarly discourse. In C. G. Panetta (Ed.), *Contrastive rhetoric revisited and redefined* (pp. 91–104). Mahwah, NJ: Lawrence Erlbaum.

Connor, U. (1996). *Contrastive rhetoric: Cross-cultural implications of second-language writing*. New York: Cambridge University Press.

Ehrlich, S. (1997). Gender as social practice: Implications for second language acquisition. *Studies in Second Language Acquisition, 19*, 421–446.

Fuss, D. (1989). *Essentially speaking: Feminism, nature & difference*. New York/London: Routledge.

Gass, S., & Selinker, L. (2001). *Second language acquisition: An introductory course* (2nd ed.). Mahwah, NJ: Lawrence Erlbaum.

Gee, J. P. (1996). *Social linguistics and literacies: Ideology in discourses* (2nd ed.). London: Taylor & Francis.

Haswell, J., & Haswell, R. H. (1995). Gendership and the miswriting of students. *College Composition and Communication, 46*, 223–254.

Heath, S. B. (1983). *Ways with words: Language, life, and work in communities and classrooms*. Cambridge: Cambridge University Press.

Herrnstein, R. J., & Murray, C. (1994). *The bell curve: Intelligence and class structure in American life*. New York: The Free Press.

Ibrahim, A. (1999). Becoming Black: Rap and hip-hop, race, gender, identity and the politics of ESL learning. *TESOL Quarterly, 33*, 349–369.

Ivanič, R. (1998). *Writing and identity: The discoursal construction of identity in academic writing*. Amsterdam: John Benjamins.

Jarratt, S. C, & Worsham, L. (Eds.). (1998). *Feminism and composition studies: In other words*. New York: The Modern Language Association of America.

Jensen, A. (1969). How much can we boost IQ and scholastic achievement? *Harvard Educational Review, 39*, 1–123.

Johnson, D. M. (1992). Interpersonal involvement in discourse: Gender variation in L2 writers' complimenting strategies. *Journal of Second Language Writing, 1*, 195–215.

Johnson, D. M., & Roen, D. H. (1992). Complimenting and involvement in peer review: Gender variation. *Language in Society, 21*, 27–57.

Kaplan, R. B. (2001). Foreword: What in the world is contrastive rhetoric? In C. G. Panetta (Ed.), *Contrastive rhetoric revisited and redefined* (pp. vii–xx). Mahwah, NJ: Lawrence Erlbaum.

Larsen-Freeman, D., & Long, M. (1991). *An introduction to second language acquisition research*. London/New York: Longman.

May, S. (1999). Critical multiculturalism and cultural difference: Avoiding essentialism. In S. May (Ed.), *Critical multiculturalism: Rethinking multicultural and antiracist education* (pp. 11–41). London: Falmer Press.

Micciche, L. R. (2001). Contrastive rhetoric and the possibility of feminism. In C. G. Panetta (Ed.), *Contrastive rhetoric revisited and redefined* (pp. 79–89). Mahwah, NJ: Lawrence Erlbaum.

Mitchell, R., & Myles, F. (1998). *Second language learning theories*. London: Arnold.

Norton, B. (2000). *Identity and language learning: Gender, ethnicity and educational change*. Harlow, Essex: Pearson Education Limited.

Ovando, C. J., & Collier, V. P. (1998). *Bilingual and ESL classrooms: Teaching in multicultural contexts* (2nd ed.). New York: McGraw Hill.

Pavlenko, A. (2001a). Language learning memoirs as a gendered genre. *Applied Linguistics, 22*(2), 213–240.

Pavlenko, A. (2001b). Bilingualism, gender, and ideology. *The International Journal of Bilingualism, 5*(2), 117–151.

Peirce, B. N. (1995). The theory of methodology in qualitative research. *TESOL Quarterly, 29*, 569–616.

Phelps, L. W., & Emig, J. (Eds.). (1995). *Feminine principles and women's experience in American composition and rhetoric*. Pittsburgh, PA: University of Pittsburgh Press.

Prior, P. (2001). Voices in text, mind, and society: Sociohistoric accounts of discourse acquisition and use. *Journal of Second Language Writing, 10*, 55–81.

Ritchie, J., & Boardman, K. (1999). Feminism in composition: Inclusion, metonymy, and disruption. *College Composition and Communication, 50*, 585–606.

Roen, D. H., & Johnson, D. M. (1992). Perceiving the effectiveness of written discourse through gender lenses: The contribution of complimenting. *Written Communication*, *9*, 435–464.

Roman, L. G. (1993). White is a color!: White defensiveness, postmodernism, and anti-racist pedagogy. In C. McCarthy & W. Cricklow (Eds.), *Race, identity, and representation in education* (pp. 71–88). New York: Routledge.

Rose, M. (1989). *Lives on the boundary: The struggles and achievements of America's underprepared.* New York: The Free Press.

Silva, T., Leki, I., & Carson, J. (1997). Broadening the perspective of mainstream composition studies: Some thoughts from disciplinary margins. *Written Communication*, *14*, 398–428.

Soliday, M. (1999). Symposium: English 1999 Class dismissed. *College English*, *61*, 731–741.

Sunderland, J. (2000). Issues of language and gender in second and foreign language education. *Language Teaching*, *33*, 203–223.

Tannen, D. (1998). *The argument culture: Moving from debate to dialogue.* New York: Random House.

Thompson, W. E., & Hickey, J. V. (1994). *Society in focus: An Introduction to sociology.* New York: HarperCollins College Publishers.

U.S. Census Bureau. (2001). Historical income data. Retrieved October 18, 2002, from www.census.gov/hhes/income/histinc/histinctb.html.

Van Dijk, T. A. (1993). *Elite discourse and racism.* Newbury Park, CA: Sage.

Vandrick, S. (1994). Feminist pedagogy and ESL. *College ESL*, *4*, 69–92.

Wareing, S. (1994). Gender differences in language use. In J. Sunderland (Ed.), *Exploring gender: Questions and implications for English language education* (pp. 34–38). New York: Prentice Hall International English Language Teaching.

Weedon, C. (1999). *Feminism, theory and the politics of difference.* Oxford: Blackwell.

Chapter 16

CONSTANT LEUNG

CONVIVIAL COMMUNICATION

Recontextualizing communicative competence (2005)

Introduction

THE ACTIVITY OF ENGLISH LANGUAGE TEACHING (ELT) aimed at speakers of different languages has been the subject of critical self-examination by various practitioners, theorists and researchers for some time now. From Phillipson's (1992) critique of ELT as a form of post-WWII neo-colonialism and Pennycook's (1994) notion of English as a "global commodity" to Canagarajah's (1999) critique of the indiscriminate exporting of metropolitan based teaching methodologies to other educational environments and Brumfit's (2001: 117) reflexively-posed contention that ". . . it is not clear exactly what it is that one is saying in talking about somebody as a second language user", many of the educational and intellectual assumptions and certainties that appeared to have underpinned much of ELT as a transnationalized enterprise in the 1970s and early 1980s have been challenged.

The English language, both as a set of linguistic resources and as a medium for communication, has witnessed profound developments in the last few decades. It is used by huge numbers of diverse speakers in varieties of ways that could not have been envisaged in the 1960s and 1970s. It will be argued here that the concept of communicative competence, which has provided the intellectual anchor for the various versions of Communicative Language Teaching (CLT) that appear in a vast array of ELT teacher training and teaching materials, is itself in need of examination and possibly recasting. *Inter alia*, the thorny and complex issues of language authority and norms in the conceptualization of English language teaching will be examined. The central aim of this article is to attempt to make a move towards a more sentient re-articulation of the concept of communicative competence in English as a second or additional language in contemporary conditions. Throughout this conceptual discussion my main interest is in what Widdowson (1989) refers to as "language knowledge", or more precisely, the epistemological nature of language and sociocultural knowledge implicated in the concept of communicative competence. Perhaps it should be emphasized that the arguments and comments made here are primarily concerned with conceptual issues and not with the views and practices of any particular group/s of teachers.

I will first revisit some of the seminal texts produced in the formative period of development of the concept of 'communicative competence'. The constituent parts of this concept will be examined with a view to foregrounding the explicit and implicit assumptions about language knowledge and language authority. After this the focus will shift to relevant works in areas such as English as a lingua franca (ELF), World Englishes, and critical SLA theory. The main reason for traversing these vast domains of enquiries is to extract arguments and perspectives which will suggest directions for updating and re-orienting the concept of communicative competence. In the final sections I will suggest a reframed ethnographic orientation that is capable of making connections with emergent sensibilities in diverse contexts of English language learning, teaching and use.

The term 'English as a second language' (ESL) is conventionally used to refer to a context of use and/or learning where English is adopted as the medium of communication for at least some public or government functions (e.g. English in India and for some minority-language communities in countries such as the USA and the UK), and the term 'English as a foreign language' (EFL) is used where English is not used/learned for public functions. While these terms are still quite useful short-hand labels, recent developments in the use of English in different contexts have made these terms increasingly difficult to apply, as will be made obvious later. For the future, terms such as 'English as an additional language' (EAL) and "English *for* Speakers of Other Languages" (Widdowson 2004: 363, original italics) are probably preferable because they are less weighed down with history, and because they signal the possibility of defining English from the standpoint of the users/learners. However, here I will continue to use the established terms ESL and EFL where they are consistent with and appropriate to the points being made.

Communicative competence

In the English-language applied linguistics literature, the emergence of the concept of communicative competence was generally associated with a break with an overly grammar-based paradigm for language studies. The works of Austin (1962), Halliday (1973, 1975), Halliday, McIntosh and Streuens (1964) and many others in the 1960s and early 1970s in the fields of language studies and language teaching had paved the way for a paradigm shift. Hymes' (1972, 1977, 1994) ethnographically-oriented exploration of and elaboration on communicative competence – itself a critique of Chomsky's (1965) highly abstracted notion of competence – serves in many ways as a clarion call for language educators to pay attention to social rules of use, a dimension of language use "without which the rules of grammar would be useless", as Hymes (1972: 278) says in an oft-quoted remark. (See also Campbell and Wales 1970; for a discussion, see Howatt with Widdowson 2004: 326–37.) This inclusion of the 'social' makes it necessary to engage with questions of context of communication and aspects of culture when working towards an integrated theory of language in use. In this connection, Hymes (1972: 281) suggests that four empirical questions must be raised:

1) Whether (and to what degree) something is formally *possible*;
2) Whether (and to what degree) something is *feasible* in virtue of the means of implementation available;
3) Whether (and to what degree) something is *appropriate* (adequate, happy, successful) in relation to a context in which it is used and evaluated;
4) Whether (and to what degree) something is in fact done, actually *performed*, and what its doing entails.

[emphasis in original]

I will return to some of the implications of these questions for ELT later. For now it is sufficient to note that in this attempt to formulate the concept of communicative competence, the constituent parts are context-sensitive, and they are to be described and ascertained empirically through observation and research. For instance, in relation to language as a code, Hymes (1977: 4) has this to say:

> one cannot take a linguistic form, a given code, or even speech itself, as a limiting frame of reference. One must take as context a community, or network of persons, investigating its communicative activities as a whole, so that any use of channel and code takes its place as part of the resources upon which the members draw.

And later, slightly recast:

> [Ethnography of communication] would approach language neither as an abstracted form nor as an abstract correlate of a community, but as situated in the flux and pattern of communicative events. It would study communicative form and function in integral relation to each other.
>
> (Hymes 1994: 12)

There is little doubt that this socio-culturally alert concept of communicative competence has had a profound influence on ELT. Indeed the term Communicative Language Teaching (CLT) was coined around this period in the mid-1970s to mark a major shift in curriculum and pedagogic approaches.[1] The following statements from two popular ELT teacher education books bear witness to this point:

> in the early 1970s, a 'sociolinguistic revolution' took place, where the emphasis given in linguistics to grammar was replaced by an interest in 'language in use' . . . The sociolinguistic revolution had a great effect on language teaching . . . [It] was responsible for the development of a type of syllabus which aimed to cater for the teaching of language in use – of communicative competence.
>
> (Johnson 2001: 182–3)

> The communicative movement in ELT . . . has, as one of its bases, a concept of what it means to know a language and to be able to put that knowledge to use in communicating with people in a variety of settings and situations. One of the earliest terms of this concept was *communicative competence* . . .
>
> (Hedge 2000: 44–5; italics in original)

The recontextualization[2] of the concept of communicative competence for second and foreign language teaching can be seen to have been significantly represented by the theoretical work of Canale and Swain in the 1980s. Building on the works of Hymes and others, they produced a series of articles which can be regarded as a reference point for the formation of the concept of communicative competence in second and foreign language pedagogy (see Canale 1983, 1984; Canale and Swain 1980a,b).[3] In these early 1980s articles Canale and Swain suggest that communicative competence comprises four areas of knowledge and skills:

1) *Grammatical competence.* This competence is concerned with "knowledge of lexical items and of rules of morphology, syntax, sentence-grammar semantics, and phonology" (Canale and

Swain 1980a: 29). This type of knowledge and skill will allow the learner to understand and produce accurately the literal meaning of utterances.

2) *Sociolinguistic competence.* This competence, broadly speaking, deals with what Hymes (1972, 1974) would call the rules of use:

> [it] addresses the extent to which utterances are produced and understood appropriately in different sociolinguistic contexts depending on contextual factors such as status of participants, purposes of the interaction, and norms or conventions of interaction . . . Appropriateness of utterances refers to . . . appropriateness of meaning and appropriateness of meaning concerns the extent to which particular communicative functions (e.g. commanding, complaining and inviting), attitudes (including politeness and formality) and ideas are judged to be proper in a given situation.
>
> (Canale 1983: 7)

I take this last point to include what Hymes means by "whether (and to what degree) something is in fact done", in other words, probabilistic rules of occurrence concerning whether something is "sayable" in a given context.

3) *Discourse competence.* This competence is concerned with what Halliday and Hasan (1976) would refer to as cohesion and Widdowson (1978) as coherence. It deals with the knowledge and skill required to combine grammatical forms and meanings to produce different types of unified spoken or written texts, e.g. oral and written narratives, business reports and so on:

> Unity of a text is achieved through cohesion in form and coherence in meaning. Cohesion deals with how utterances are linked structurally and facilitates interpretation of a text. For example, the use of cohesion devices such as pronouns, synonyms . . . Coherence refers to the relationship among the different meanings in a text, where these meanings may be literal meanings, communicative functions and attitudes.
>
> (Canale 1983: 9)

4) *Strategic competence.* This type of competence refers to:

> mastery of verbal and non-verbal communication strategies that may be called into action for two main reasons: (a) to compensate for breakdowns in communication due to limiting conditions in actual communication (e.g. momentary inability to recall an idea or grammatical form) or due to insufficient competence in one or more of the other areas above; and (b) to enhance the effectiveness of communication (e.g. deliberately slow and soft speech for rhetorical effect).
>
> (Canale 1983: 11)

Communicative competence, in this formulation, represented a considerable broadening of the conceptual base of second language curriculum and pedagogy. The attempt to embrace social, discoursal and interactional dimensions in language teaching was both challenging and stimulating. Although there were different interpretations within the professional and academic research community at the time and in subsequent years – see e.g. Brumfit (1984) for a collection of views and Bachman (1990) for an expanded model of communicative competence – it would not be an exaggeration to say that the theoretical framework presented by Canale and Swain very quickly acquired, as Brown (2000) points out, the status of a central doctrine for ELT, which in various manifestations in applied linguistics and ELT teacher education handbooks and manuals has persisted to this day.

Recontextualization

The transfer of Hymes' ideas to ELT has involved some recontextualization of the original meanings. From the point of view of this discussion, it is important to note that in the recontextualization process, Hymes' research oriented ideas have gone through an epistemic transformation: from empirically oriented questions to an idealized pedagogic doctrine. As Dubin (1989: 174) observes:

> it is apparent that over time there has been a shift away from an agenda for finding out what is happening in a community regarding language use to a set of statements about what an idealized curriculum for L2 learning/acquisition should entail . . . [The concept of communicative competence] has moved away from being a societally-grounded theory in terms of describing and dealing with actual events and practices of communication which take place within particular cultures.

This conversion of research concerns to a pedagogic doctrine was a collective, cumulative and, in all probability, a non-conscious process. In many ways the process of recontextualization unavoidably implicates some sort of transformation of the original because the different fields of intellectual activity and enquiry involved have different priorities and concerns. In this case language teaching professionals (including linguists *qua* language educators) are not necessarily interested in ethnographic research accounts of how communication is accomplished in different settings; they are more directly concerned with what information or content should be included in the curriculum and how such content should be worked on in the classroom. Once the questions raised by Hymes were incorporated into a conceptual framework, curriculum discussions had to attend to guidelines for developing teaching and learning content and activities. The need to specify what is to be taught and learned inevitably turns research questions, which allow the possibility of both instability in existing knowledge and emergence of new knowledge, into pedagogic guidelines and principles which have to assume a degree of stability, transparency and certainty in existing knowledge. This is, of course, not a zero-sum game; it is a matter of degree. For instance, in Canale and Swain's 1980 article the pedagogising of grammatical competence, sociolinguistic competence and strategic competence is presented in terms of what is to be selected and included in the curriculum from the existing stocks of knowledge. The discussion is not couched in terms of whether we have such knowledge or whether our existing knowledge is relevant, adequate and/or appropriate. On the issue of discourse competence the authors are less certain but nevertheless suggest that

> [u]ntil more clear-cut theoretical statements about rules of discourse emerge, it is perhaps most useful to think of these rules in terms of the cohesion (i.e. grammatical links) and coherence (i.e. appropriate combination of communicative functions) of groups of utterance.
>
> (Canale and Swain 1980a: 30)

The process of recontextualization of the concept of communicative competence can be seen quite clearly in the discussions of curriculum or syllabus development. For instance, in a discussion on the development of a communicative syllabus, Yalden (1983: 86–7) suggests that the designer has to determine some aspects of the syllabus components:

The components [of a communicative syllabus] could be listed as follows:

1. as detailed a consideration as possible of the *purposes* for which the learners wish to acquire the target language;
2. some idea of the *setting* in which they will want to use the target language. . .
3. the socially defined *role* the learner will assume in the target language, as well as their interlocutors . . .
4. the communicative *events* in which the learners will participate . . .

[emphasis in original]

The purposes, settings, roles and events were sometimes established by carrying out student needs surveys. Such surveys and analyses are not generally interested in the type of information and data discussed by Hymes, i.e. how communication is performed and what patterns of meaning-making and meaning-taking occur in specific contexts. Curriculum developers are concerned with working out students' projected communication purposes and contexts, e.g. learning English as a school subject or learning to use English in an English-speaking work environment. The general idea here is that once the students' purposes and contexts of use are established, curriculum/syllabus designers can draw on their knowledge of language teaching/ learning (i.e. theory and technical know-how) and language use (i.e. the 'what' and the 'how') to specify the teaching programme with respect to the various parts of the overall competence to be taught.[4] The language content is thus built on idealized typifications of what native speakers may say and do in specified contexts.

In ELT teacher training materials the process of recontextualization is also visible. In an early discussion on the principles of CLT, Morrow (1981: 60–1) advised the teacher to:

- focus on enabling students to learn "how to do something" and avoid concentrating on formal knowledge such as the past tense for its own sake – ". . . the starting point (and end point) of every lesson should be an operation of some kind which the student might actually want to perform in a foreign language. In reading, this might be understanding a set of instructions . . .";
- promote an ability to handle language use in the spoken and written modes as whole texts, above "the sentence level" in "real" time with "real language in real situations" [the notion of "real" here refers to simulated forms of actual communication as represented by classroom activities];
- encourage active use of language in the classroom and "replicate as far as possible the processes of communication, so that practice of the forms of the target language can take place within a communicative framework".

Twenty years later, Brown's (2001: 43) characterisation of CLT includes the following:

- a focus on "the components (grammatical, discourse, functional, sociolinguistic, and strategic) of communicative competence";

- the use of language teaching techniques and student tasks "to engage learners in the pragmatic, authentic, functional use of language for meaningful purposes";
- the positioning of the teacher as "a facilitator and guide . . . Students are therefore encouraged to construct meaning through genuine linguistics interaction with others".

More recently, McDonough and Shaw (2003: 21) list the implications of the cumulative discussions on the communicative approach in the past thirty years that have "helped to form the kinds of teaching materials we work with and our attitudes to managing our classrooms". These include a concern for

- the "meaning potential" (pragmatic meaning in the context of use) and function/s of language as well as for language form/s when designing classroom work;
- appropriacy of language "alongside accuracy" in given contexts;
- use of language "beyond the sentence level".

There is a certain commonality in the way CLT is described in the popular ELT teacher training texts cited above. The common concerns are: pragmatic language meaning in context (sociolinguistic competence), knowledge and use of language above the sentence level in spoken and written discourse (discourse competence), and active language use in learning activities (strategic competence). These can be seen as an attempt to extract what is useful in the original Canale and Swain formulation of communicative competence for practical purposes in ELT. But this kind of operationalization of the concept of communicative competence does not fit comfortably with what was initially proposed by Hymes. The Hymesian ethnographic project advocated the need to investigate and understand language use in specific social and cultural contexts. In this perspective, as Grillo, Pratt and Street (1987: 274) observe,

> [t]here can be no a priori universalism. There may be universal forms of speech and language, but these need to be discovered by research in specific cultures and comparison between cultures. Only fieldwork, only ethnography, will suffice to tell.[5]

It is therefore somewhat ironic to see that a kind of scaled-down universalism, i.e. the language and communication inventory drawn up on the basis of teachers' and materials writers' knowledge of what is likely to be said, returns in an educational guise.[6] The social now resides in the pedagogic projections of the expert knower, the expert teacher. The immediate question is: what has made this expert-generated universalism possible?

Language knowledge and language authority: the native speaker perspective

In addition to the point made by Dubin (see earlier quote on p. 279), one may add that the "idealized curriculum for L2 learning" was often built on the perspective of an imagined or idealized native speaker of English. It may well be that a native speaker's language knowledge has been seen as a convenient source of ethnographic insight. The persistent over-use of the concept of native speaker as a pedagogic reference point has been discussed and critiqued over the years (e.g. Cook 2002; Rampton 1990; Widdowson 2003: ch. 4). But the native speaker has proved to be a remarkably resilient concept, and it is still part of the bedrock of transnationalized ELT. Perhaps this is not surprising, because we can see traces of the native speaker in the Canale and Swain's influential early discussions. In a passage on sociocultural rules, the authors suggest that ". . . it is not clear that native speakers of the second language [English] expect second language learners at the early stages of a programme . . . to have mastered sociocultural rules bearing on appropriateness" (Canale and Swain 1980: 12). In another passage on the probabilistic rules of occurrence it is stated that "[k]nowledge of what a native speaker is likely to say in a given context is to us a crucial component of second language learners' competence to understand second language communication and to express themselves in a native-like way . . ." (ibid.: 16). In a discussion on scoring student responses in a French as a second language assessment project, Canale (1984: 116) recommends the following:

> Appropriateness. The concern here is the extent to which both the information and form of information are socially appropriate and natural/authentic (e.g. appropriate degree of politeness and formality, most likely form of message that native speakers use) depending on contextual variables such as topic, role of participant, setting and purpose.

The durability of the norming effect of the concept of the native speaker can be found in an emergent field of study where one might have expected a degree of built-in resistance. One of the pedagogic issues in the field of English as an international language (EIL) or English as a lingua franca (ELF) is: what kind of English should be adopted as the model or norm for teaching? Even in this newly created intellectual space where the notions of norms and standards could be discussed and critiqued more freely (in theory), the controlling hand of the abstracted and idealized (English) native speaker is easily felt. For instance, in a reasoned argument about the need for an EIL corpus, Prodromou (2003: 11), having asked rhetorically "On what data can we base alternative models for teaching EIL?", describes his own work in this way:

> My own corpus differs from previous work on non-native speech in focusing on natural, spontaneous speech produced by *proficient* non-native users of English as a foreign language. The data I will describe consists exclusively of naturally occurring conversation by highly accomplished users of EIL.
>
> [emphasis in original]

It seems clear in this case that tacit judgements have been made with some unspecified native-speaker norms in mind. How else could one identify "*proficient* non-native users" when an EIL model apparently does not yet exist? The pervasive influence of native-speakerness seems to have drifted onto centre stage, perhaps without the scriptwriter noticing. In a discussion on what teachers should know when they teach EIL, Sifakis (2004: 239) draws a distinction between communication-bound issues (the means with which interlocutors accomplish "cross-cultural comprehensibility") and normbound issues (e.g. English grammar and pronunciation) which, in the author's view, should adhere to native speaker "codification and standardness". Again, the native speaker's right of entry is untrammelled. (I will return to the significance of EIL/ELF as a field of enquiry later.)

The process of drawing up curriculum specifications has in effect treated Hymes' research questions as some sort of metaphoric *pro forma* headings under which details of what and how language is used are supplied. These details are selected and supplied on the basis of a combination of informed expertise attained through professional training and professional work such as student needs surveys (which could be carried out by native and nonnative speakers alike) and a native speaker's experience and/or intuition on matters of grammaticality and socio-cultural practices in language use. Judgement-making remarks such as *We'd say "I'm very well, thank you" when people ask you how you are, we wouldn't reply by saying "Good", and We wouldn't say* "*the tree is ill*" are examples of this kind of claim to native-speaker authority. Of the two claims to authority, professional expertise and native-speakerness, it is quite clear that in the professional world of ELT the second is generally regarded as more preferable and more valuable. For example, as part of a policy to improve the quality of English teaching in schools, there is now a Native-speaking English Teachers (NET) scheme in Hong Kong. The Assistant Language Teacher (ALT) scheme in Japan waives the professional ELT qualification requirement if the applicants are from English-speaking countries.[7] (For a further discussion see McKay 2003: 8–13.) But what is the basis of this native-speaker authority, and what does this approach to authority in English leave out of the account?

The appeal to native-speakerness as a source of language expertise and authority is grounded in an observation that people tend to generally know their first/native language better than any other language/s they may speak in terms of pronunciation, vocabulary, grammar patterns and rules of use. There is also an implicitly posited link between one's first/native language and one's tacit knowledge of what is grammatically allowable, whether or not it is actually said. In addition to this, Davies (2003: 110) observes that native speakers, *inter alia*, "can decide what is now in use", and "[have] more awareness of . . . context" which can assist the interpretation of intended meaning.

At the level of broad generalisation, these observations seem to be consistent with common experience. But these broad generalisations do not yield the context-derived descriptive information needed for curriculum development, if Hymes' notion of communicative competence were to be at the heart of such enterprises. The problem lies in the tendency to assume that there is an almost hard-wired relationship between the status of being a native speaker of a language and a complete knowledge of and about that language (see Leung, Harris and Rampton 1997; Rampton 1990) and that all native speakers share the same knowledge. If we ask the question *How much grammar does a native speaker of English know and how much of this knowledge can s/he use?*, it becomes obvious that one cannot really answer this question without shifting the terms of reference by saying *It depends on which native speaker/s and in what context*. In other words, the abstract construct of the native speaker ceases to be useful as soon as we try to extract descriptive details from it.

Of course the opposite would be true if we were to ask *How much and what sort of grammar does John the journalist need to know?* Here we have, at least in principle, a question that allows empirical investigation. In fact, with respect to the four components of communicative competence discussed earlier, the notion of the native speaker as a heuristic-cum-descriptive device would only make sense if we specify individual/s or group/s of native speakers and the contexts of language use. So the written discourse competence required of journalists working for tabloids, as opposed to those who work in television, can in principle be described empirically. Thus, in so far as one may wish to refer to native speakers as a reference point for a specific curriculum, they have to be specified in terms of a whole range of attributes such as social/community position, context and modality of language use, gender, age and so on. So while there are clearly native speakers of English (as there are native speakers of other languages), there isn't a universal model of native speakers' use of language. This is in fact a key reason behind the points made by Hymes in the early 1970s.

A related problem is the abstracted concept of English (as a language) in the formulation of 'the native speaker of English'. Of the four sub-components of communicative competence discussed earlier, the domain of grammaticality seems to be the least complexified by social and cultural factors.[8] But even here the conferred straight-forwardness isn't quite as secure as it might seem at first glance. Consider the following expression: *We're goin' cinema*. Most middle-aged and middle-class native speakers of southern 'standard' English in Britain (not necessarily living in southern England) would probably find *We're goin' cinema* ungrammatical; but the Ø-*to* form of expression of motion or direction is commonly used by London youths, particularly in everyday informal conversations. The differences in respect of locality, age and social background point to the need to recognize the importance of language varieties (of the same language). As Davies (2003: 34) observes: "grammaticality is not language-based but variety-based . . . even structurally related varieties of one language cannot have exactly the same grammar". So there isn't a unified and bounded phenomenon called English, except in the sense of English being a set of codified lexical and grammatical resources which can be exploited and used for speech and writing or, as Widdowson (2003: 51) calls it, "a virtual language".

What is important here is that the notion of language variety has strong social and cultural associations. In the field of ELT, the 'native speaker' variety presented is generally the standard English used (or putatively used) by a minority group of "self-elected elite" (Widdowson 2003: 37) of education and language-teaching professionals. While it is possible to list some of the lexical, syntactic and semantic differences between the standard varieties and the non-standard varieties of English (for examples, see Jenkins 2003: 64–71), it is not possible to produce a Hymesian-minded second language curriculum with just a code-oriented account of linguistic features of a particular native speaker variety. As Canale and Swain's formulation of communicative competence makes amply clear, knowledge of a linguistic code is just one of the components of overall competence. The social and cultural dimensions are in many ways at the heart of the concept of communicative competence. The operative word here is *appropriate* or *appropriateness*.

In the original Hymes schema appropriateness in language use is primarily an empirical issue; one has to go out, as it were, and find data to show what appropriateness is in different settings and with different participants. Some generalizations may be developed through detailed observation and analysis of actual social interaction. In this way accounts of generalizable patterns of language use in certain social contexts, e.g. ways and means of presenting a request by a socially powerful person, can be built up.

In the recontextualization process, however, appropriateness has turned into a pedagogic space where specific forms of language use are selected and projected as being appropriate according to some normative assumptions of language practice set in an imagined social exchange. For instance, on the topic of good manners, students are advised that

> Americans sometimes find it difficult to accept the more formal Japanese manners. They prefer to be casual and more informal, as illustrated by the universal 'Have a nice day!' American waiters have a one-word imperative 'Enjoy!' The British, of course, are cool and reserved. The great topic of conversation between strangers in Britain is the weather – unemotional and impersonal . . .
>
> (Soars and Soars 1996: 41)

The problem with this kind of projection is threefold. First, such an exercise in script-writing necessarily demands "a fundamental idealization of a culturally homogeneous speech community" (Levinson 1983: 25), the existence of which is in itself debatable. The difficulty here is that building up a curriculum on the basis of such idealized projections may turn out to be no more than working with teacher intuition – no doubt a useful resource but not a source of generalizable non-trivial observation.

Second, while it may be possible to introspectively develop an account of how some native speakers may go about using language in supposedly appropriate ways, it is far from the case that members of any real native speaking community would always use the same agreed set of rules in actual engagement. Fairclough (1992: 34) observes that "[i]n no actual speech community do all members always behave in accordance with a shared sense of which language varieties are appropriate for which contexts and purpose". We can extend this observation beyond language variety to say that members of a native-speaker community do not necessarily adhere to some shared rules of use with respect to co-operation, directness, explicitness, politeness and other considerations in all instances of social interaction. Nonobservance of these rules is the stuff of life.

Third, if the projection of social norms were to be seen as anything other than probabilistic guidelines, then the kind of invented description supplied by Soars and Soars would actually be a form of prescription. At best, the pedagogic value of such prescription is likely to be short-lived because novice speakers of English may soon learn to abandon prescribed social routines and language expressions since in real-life encounters their use value is limited. At worst, a strong and insistent form of this kind of prescriptivism may serve to mislead students as to what constitutes appropriateness among speakers of English.

Furthermore, the notion of appropriateness is often invested with a good deal of pragmatic power. There is an assumed correspondence between appropriate language use in accordance with shared social rules and felicitous communication outcome, and vice versa. In reality, flouting of the social rules may be communicatively effective:

> in general, if there is some communicative convention C that one does in context Y, then suppose instead one does B in Y, or does A but in context Z, one will not normally be taken to have simply violated the conventions C and produced nonsense. Rather, one will generally be taken to have exploited the conventions in order to communicate some further pertinent message.
>
> (Levinson 1983: 26)

In English-speaking communities around the world, the cultural and literary notions of irony, sarcasm and indeed humour would not exist if everyone always behaved "appropriately". It may well be the case that some learners of English are not in a position to exploit such cultural resources in their second language. But one has to be at least cautious about how much weight one should give to such projected and idealized descriptions and prescriptions of appropriateness in a pedagogic language model.

Views from other perspectives

We have now seen that the concept of communicative competence, as it was formulated some thirty or so years ago, has gathered up a package of theoretical and epistemic assumptions and social values in the recontextualization process. These assumptions and values have permeated the ELT profession through textbooks, examination and test syllabuses, teaching manuals and teacher training materials which, in their turn, have influenced curriculum specification, teaching practice and learning experience. Critics of the status quo have argued for the need to reconceptualize ELT (see e.g. McKay 2003; Pennycook 2000). One way of making a contribution to this process of (self-)critical examination is to look at some recent developments in adjacent fields of enquiry to see what, if any, relevant insights can be found, particularly with respect to the primacy of native-speakerness and the associated notion of (standard) English in the concept of communicative competence. Developments in at least three fields of enquiry can throw some light on this discussion.

Englishes in the world

It is estimated that there are between 320–380 million native speakers of English and between 300–500 million ESL speakers in countries such as India, the Philippines and Nigeria where English has been institutionalized (e.g. a medium of the legal or education system). In addition to the ESL speakers, it is estimated that there are about 500–1000 million people around the world who use English for a variety of purposes and for whom English is neither their native/first nor their second language; in more traditional terms these would be regarded as EFL speakers (Crystal 2003; for a discussion on the these estimates and categories see Jenkins 2003: section A, and Graddol and Meinhof 1999). These numbers are interesting in that they point to the fact that native speakers of English are a minority in the English-using world, and they provide a backdrop against which we can begin to appreciate the nature and scale of language preference, displacement and shift involving English.

There is now a considerable literature on the existence of national or regional varieties of English which are non-native varieties, e.g. Indian English, Nigerian English, Malay English, Singapore English and so on. Historically these varieties tend to be found in parts of the world where contact with English had been established as part of earlier colonization, in other words the 'outer circle' in Kachru's (1985, 1992) well-known three-circle division of the world in terms of the statuses and functions of the English language. According to Kachru, these Englishes are used for public communication in their 'home' societies and can be characterized in a number of ways:

> (a) they have an extended range of uses in the sociolinguistic context of a nation; (b) they have an extended range of register and style range; (c) a process of nativization of the registers and styles has taken place, both in formal and in contextual terms; and (d) a body of nativized English literature has developed . . .
>
> (Kachru 1992: 55)

Even a quick glance at the literature in this field would suggest that fundamental questions such as *Who owns English?* and *What do these new varieties comprise?* are being addressed theoretically and empirically (see e.g. Chisanga and Kamwangamalu 1997; Davies 1991, 2002; Jenkins 2003: section B; Kachru 1992; Wee 2002; Widdowson 1994). The salience of these discussions for us is that they have highlighted the need to pay attention to the existence of different ways of knowing and using English as a set of linguistic resources. In one sense the phenomenon of nativization is neither new nor recent; the existence of Australian English, Scottish English and so on has long been acknowledged. But accounts of regional Englishes have pointed to the increasing pace and intensity in the diversification of form and use and, as a correlate, the spread of nativization of English in different places, for instance:

- phonological reductions, e.g. seven-vowel contrasts in Hong Kong English as opposed to eleven in British RP (Hung 2002);
- lexical and syntactic additions and extensions, e.g. *lobola* for the property or money brought by a bridegroom to the bride's parents[9] and *is it?* as a universal tag question indicating speaker interest without reference to gender, number or person in the preceding turn in Southern African English (Chisanga and Kamwangamalu 1997);
- genre hybridisation, e.g. the blending of traditional mantras such as "family and God" with the contemporary discourse of "individual effort and market forces" in Malaysian advertisements (Hashim 2002).

These and other similar observations tell us that there are structural, semantic and discourse innovations in the ways English is understood and used. Epistemologically the term 'nativization' neatly returns us to the ethnographic concerns with the local, which was one of the original inspirations for the conceptualization of communicative competence. In a world where students of English are not necessarily learning it to interact with native speakers of English, as McKay (2003) observes, there are sound pedagogic and practical reasons to pay attention to the existence of different varieties of English as a key curriculum and classroom teaching consideration.[10]

English as a lingua franca

English is often referred to as a global language. It is the preferred language for international political, business and professional communication, even in contexts where alternative (and politically powerful) local languages are available (Phillipson 2004). In these communications or interactions, all (or practically all) participants are non-native speakers of English. In this sense English is used as a lingua franca (ELF).[11] The occurrence and use of ELF signal a language-contact situation where, without the community-wide moment-by-moment monitoring and control by native speakers, English is potentially amenable to development and change, or as Seidlhofer (2004: 212) argues more decisively, "ELF has taken on a life of its own, independent to a considerable degree of the norms established by its native users". Sociolinguistically it is important to note that many of these interactions tend to occur in what House (1999) refers to as "influential frameworks", e.g. multilateral business meetings involving multinational corporations, European Union policy meetings, and international academic/professional conferences; in other words, the use of ELF can be and is often associated with high status and elite situations and users.

Research in ELF is beginning to produce descriptions of some of its linguistic and pragmatic features and to explore these observed features theoretically. Jenkins (2000, 2002, 2003) has developed a phonological lingua franca core that shows that accurate production of some consonant sounds, vowel length and the placing of tonic stress appears to be important for intelligibility. For instance, substituting the vowel /a:/ with /ɜ:/ (e.g. *bath* vs. *birth*) is reported to cause difficulties for interlocutors (Jenkins 2002: 88). Other phonological features appear to be much more tolerant, as it were, of variations from native-speaker pronunciation, and these include consonant sounds such as /ð/ and /θ/, and the absence of the use of weak forms (ibid.). Seidlhofer (2004) suggests that the various ongoing projects studying different aspects of lexico-grammar of ELF, including the Vienna-Oxford International Corpus of English (VOICE), are beginning to show that some features, such as the dropping of the third-person present-tense -s, do not appear to hinder communication, whereas the use of idiomatic speech can cause intelligibility problems for interlocutors.

Work on the pragmatics of ELF to date suggests that this is likely to be an area of considerable complexity. House (1999), for instance, reports that in her data for a group of German-, Dutch- and Hungarian-speaking students engaged in a game, there was little evidence of the participants undertaking explicit repairs when misunderstanding occurred, and there was much evidence of very short turns and parallel talk. Firth (1996) reports a 'let-it-pass' principle in ELF business talk in that participants appear to be prepared to tolerate ambiguity and not to seek reformulations or negotiation of meaning. Meierkord (2002) observes that in ELF face-to-face talk, participants may not deploy their first language communicative norms in relation to turn length, pausing and overlapping speech; she also finds evidence that there is some kind of construction of 'third culture' or 'interculture' when participants in ELF talk use laughter as a substitute for back-channel verbal signals such as *really?* The complexity shown by the work in ELF pragmatics is a good indication of the diverse contexts in which ELF is being used as a recognisable variety/ies. In so far as pragmatics is an aspect of language use which is particularly susceptible to the influences of local cultural practices and local norms of engagement generated by participants, these diverse findings can be seen to reflect that ELF is developing "a life of its own". Indeed the capacity to accommodate and incorporate change is a hallmark of a global language. As Bruthiaux (2003: 21) observes:

> a language with global ambitions [must] be amenable to unplanned change, a process unlikely to take place freely if the language is strongly associated with a single dominant culture with powerful centralizing and standardizing tendencies.

In different ways, the research in this area is pointing to the need for ELF to be treated as sui *generis*. It also alerts us to the need to recognize emergent varieties of English.

The 'social' in second language acquisition: widening perspectives

The tendency to interpret 'communicativeness' in terms of active use of functionally oriented language by students in simulated classroom tasks has been supported by what might be referred to as the mainstream research paradigm for the past thirty years or so. A good deal of SLA research during that time has framed the notion of the 'social' in terms of teaching and learning. Block (2003: 26–30) characterizes this as the Input-Interaction-Output model. The general principle is that language acquisition involves (a) purposeful and active language use which creates the opportunity for the learner to make sense of the target language (input and interaction) and (b) production or rehearsal of language in classroom tasks (output). (For detailed discussions, see e.g. Dulay, Burt and Krashen 1982; Crookes and Gass 1993a,b; Krashen 1982, 1985; Nunan 1991; Skehan 1998; Swain 1985, 1995.) In this perspective the notion of the social is tacitly understood in terms of social interaction in the context of pedagogic activities. It is argued that interaction offers learners an opportunity to use and work out meaning even when the actual language forms encountered may be beyond their current level of linguistic competence. In general, then, the idea of communicating with others is often seen as a pedagogic device and 'communication' as a bounded phenomenon of language-learning activity. One of the consequences of this is that the social dimension – the dynamic and co-constructed processes of actual communication – has been narrowly rendered into a form of guided social practice to be learned by students in the CLT teacher training literature, as we saw earlier.

This classroom-bound pedagogising of the 'social' has led to what Pavlenko (2002: 280) refers to as a "reductionist, static and homogenous view of culture" and, one might add, language practices (recall the earlier example of the alleged characteristic of Americans being informal or the British being impersonal). Such reductionist and static idealizations are at best partial representations of social reality. There is no one fixed way of greeting people, any more than there is one way of talking to a bank clerk or an airline worker. So, even if we were to assume ideal learning conditions and perfect learner capacity to take advantage of classroom input and practice, we would still be working with a partial representation of what the 'social' is.

Another aspect of the narrowing of the 'social' is the projection of social interaction as a freely engaged, untrammelled and decontextualized human activity in classrooms everywhere. The assumption seems to be that teacher–designed learning activities can engender uninhibited social interaction in the classroom. The reality is, of course, quite different. Social interaction between teachers and students, and among students themselves, is unavoidably influenced by participants' perception of their role and interest in context, participant power differentials, localized social practices and cultural values, and a whole host of other contingent matters, as many teachers would readily testify (Leung, Harris and Rampton 2004; Morita 2004). Furthermore, the Input-Interaction-Output model of SLA cannot account for what goes on outside the classroom, where language learners can encounter even more complex contexts and rules of social interaction. Norton's (2000) study of a group of immigrant women in Canada shows that the opportunity to speak English can be tied up with one's social position. For instance Eva, one of the participants in Norton's study, found her fellow workers had little interest in engaging in conversation with her when she was regarded as an outsider and when she was assigned menial low-grade jobs. In some situations, as Pavlenko (2002: 287) puts it, "some target language speakers may simply refuse to interact with L2 users". In another study, Gordon (2004) shows that in a particular US community, gendered division of domestic responsibilities has created opportunities for immigrant Laotian women to come in contact with their children's schools and social services. In turn, these encounters create the opportunities for the women to develop a knowledge of the genres of English appropriate for dealing with these institutions (an opportunity their husbands have not encountered in their manual jobs). The point here is that the 'social' is far more complex than what is normally projected in CLT teaching literature. And any attempt at understanding, describing and teaching what is socially appropriate and feasible language must look beyond the designed interaction stipulated by the learning task and beyond the classroom.

Re-engaging the social: convivial communication

This discussion has been, by and large, conceptually oriented, and it would seem that there is much re-orienting to be done at the heart of the concept of communicative competence. The interpretations and operationalization of the concept of communicative competence over the past thirty years or so, as evidenced by the mainstream of ELT literature, have psychologized and reified the social dimension. This is not a debate about the importance of individual psychological and cognitive processes in learning, about which there is no question. But if the concept of communicative competence is to serve ELT in the world today in the spirit of empirical receptivity in which it was conceived, then we need to recast some of the possibly unwitting epistemic and pedagogic assumptions. In this connection the three essential qualities in an ethnographer's experience described by Roberts et al. (2001: 93) are germane to this discussion:

> Epistemological relativity . . . involves recognizing one's own assumptions about knowledge, and how it is legitimised in one's own society, so as to be able to view the knowledge of other societies with a more open mind . . . Reflexivity . . . refers to the ability to reflect critically on the way in which one's own cultural background and standpoint influence one's view of other cultures . . . Critical consciousness . . . views ethnography not simply as a convenient tool for studying and research but as itself a product of particular dominant societies at a particular period.

At first sight such ethnographic sensitivities and sensibilities are not relevant to ELT. The ELT profession does not require its practitioners to become ethnographers. But by the nature of their professional work, ELT practitioners often find themselves at the interfaces of cultures and languages where professional judgements and evaluation (e.g. good/bad, acceptable/not acceptable and so on) are made. It is in these moments of professional decision-making that ethnographic sensitivities are potentially helpful. Epistemological relativity, for an ELT professional, means that one accepts that there are infinite ways of using language and that differences do not automatically call for judgmental evaluation. The notion of reflexivity can be interpreted to mean a preparedness to interrogate the ethno-cultural and sociolinguistic basis of one's own judgements on one's own and others' preferred language forms and ways of using language. Critical consciousness calls for an alertness about the culturally specific ways of describing and analysing both language and language teaching and learning in primarily English-speaking countries. These three sensitivities are germane to the whole spectrum of pedagogic issues in ELT – from lexical choices to discourse pragmatics, and from definitions of a good language learner to teacher–student relationships – and if adopted they would potentially enable the ELT professional to re-engage with the socially dynamic uses of English and to continuously re-work the contextualized meaning of the concept of communicative competence.

This is not a call for "anything goes", nor is it an endorsement of abdication of a teacher's professional responsibility to teach language forms and language use. Under contemporary conditions, it seems absolutely necessary for the concept of communicative competence to attend to both the standard and local Englishes, and to tune in to both established and emergent forms and norms of use. Through the adoption of different sets of intellectual sensitivities and sensibilities, such as the ones suggested by Roberts et al. (2001), we can begin to de-reify culture-, context- and time-bound notions of linguistic correctness, social and cultural appropriateness, real-life feasibility and possibility in a convivial mood. In the light of what we now know in terms of World Englishes and ELF, it is quite clear that, from the point of view of curriculum conceptualization, the unquestioned and routine adoption of a particular native-speaker variety of English and a particular set of idealized social rules of use is no longer educationally satisfactory or desirable. It may well be that, for instance, General American (pronunciation) and formal North American registers are appropriate as pedagogic reference points for an academic English programme in a US college, but they may not be suitable for a similar programme in Singapore or India. The pedagogic language model for any English-teaching programme should be related to its goals in context. An idealized native-speaker model should not be an automatic first choice. As Widdowson (2004: 361) argues:

> one objection to insisting on conformity to native-speaker norms is that to do so sets goals for learners which are both unrealistic and unnecessary . . . It also has ideological implications . . . it can also be seen as the authoritarian imposition of socio-cultural values which makes learners subservient and prevents them from appropriating the language as an expression of their identity.

The objectification and reification of curriculum knowledge largely based on native-speaker idealizations and the reduction of the social to mean classroom interaction have effectively insulated the concept of communicative competence from the developments in English and the myriad ways in which it is now understood and used in different contexts. Theoretically as well as pedagogically, there is every reason to reconnect with the social world if the concept of communicative competence is to mean anything more than a textbook simulacrum of Englishes in the world.

Notes

1   It is not suggested here that prior to the advent of communicative competence and CLT all ELT classroom teaching and materials were entirely grammar-based. The shift is more in terms of intellectual orientation and professional discourse. See also Savignon (2005) for a view on the formative period of CLT.

2   I am using the term 'recontextualization' in a sense that echoes Bernstein's (1996: 116-18) usage: the selective appropriation and transfer of knowledge from one field to another.

3   Some of Canale and Swain's work on communicative competence during this period often focused on French as an L2 in the Canadian context.

4   It is not suggested here that all curriculum writers shared an identical schema. See Piepho (1981) for an example of a more student-oriented stance within a communicative approach.

5   For a discussion of the methodological-cum-theoretical trajectory of this perspective, see Rampton (1998).

6   Gumperz ([1981] 1997: 40) sounded an early note of caution when he stated that "[m]any sociolinguistic studies of communicative competence, in fact, aim at little more than statements of regularities that describe the occurrence of utterances or verbal strategies isolated by traditional methods of analysis in relation to types of speakers, audiences, settings and situations. This leads to a highly particularistic notion of competence . . .".

7   For details of the NET scheme see www.emb.gov.hk/index.aspx?nodeid=1286andlangno=l, and for details of the ALT scheme see www.mofa.go.jp/j info/visit/jet/position.html.

8   This can, of course, be traced back to an over-interpretation of Chomsky's (1965: ch. 1; 1986: chs. 1 and 2) concept of idealized native speaker and Pinker's (1994: ch. 3) idea of 'mentalese'.

9   Lexical additions drawing on a local language can be found in other nativized 'native speaker' varieties of English, e.g. billabong in Australian English.

10   A practical example of attempting to work with local language practices and language norms can be found in Brown and Lumley (1998). This is an account of a local development of an English language proficiency test for teachers of English in Indonesia in which the authors attempt to operationalize communicative competence in terms of contextualized local English language use and cultural norms.

11   The most widely accepted interpretation among ELF researchers is that ELF interaction includes native speakers but that they do not include native speakers in their data collection, while a small minority do not include native speakers in ELF in any respect (Jenkins, personal communication, March 2005). My pedagogic focus here allows a more inclusive approach, if for no other reason than a pragmatic one that native-speaking English teachers often find themselves in ELF situations in places such as Hong Kong where all other participants are L1 speakers of other languages and where local ELF norms operate.

References

Austin, J.L. (1962) *How to do things with words.* London: Clarendon Press.

Bachman, L. (1990) *Fundamental considerations in language testing.* Oxford University Press.

Bernstein, B. (1996) *Pedagogy, symbolic control and identity.* London: Taylor and Francis.

Block, D. (2003) *The social turn in second language acquisition.* Edinburgh University Press.

Brown, A. and T. Lumley (1998) Linguistic and cultural norms in language testing: a case study. *Melbourne Papers in Language Testing* 7.1: 80–96.

Brown, H.D. (2000) *Principles of language learning and teaching* (4th edition). White Plains, N.Y.: Pearson Education (Longman).

—— (2001) *Teaching by principles: an interactive approach to language pedagogy* (2nd edition). White Plains, N.Y: Pearson Education.

Brumfit, C. (ed.) (1984) *General English syllabus design.* Oxford: Pergamon Press, in association with the British Council.

—— (2001) *Individual freedom in language teaching.* Oxford University Press.

Bruthiaux, P. (2003) Contexts and trends for English as a global language. In H. Tonkins and T. Reagan (eds), *Language in the twenty-first century.* Amsterdam: John Benjamins. 9–22.

Campbell, R. and R. Wales (1970) The study of language acquisition. In J. Lyons (ed.), *New horizons in linguistics.* Harmondsworth, UK: Penguin Books. 242–60.

Canagarajah, A.S. (1999) *Resisting linguistic imperialism in English teaching.* Oxford University Press.

Canale, M. (1983) From communicative competence to language pedagogy. In J. Richards and J. Schmidt (eds), *Language and communication.* London: Longman. 2–27.

—— (1984) A communicative approach to language proficiency assessment in a minority setting. In C. Rivera (ed.), *Communicative competence approaches to language proficiency assessment: research and application.* Clevedon: Multilingual Matters. 107–22.

—— and M. Swain (1980a) Theoretical bases of communicative approaches to second language teaching and testing. *Applied Linguistics* 1.1: 1–47.

—— and M. Swain (1980b) *A domain description for core FSL: communication skills.* Ontario: Ministry of Education.

Chisanga, T. and N. Kamwangamalu (1997) Owning the other tongue: the English language in Southern Africa. *Journal of Multilingual and Multicultural Development* 18.2: 89–99.

Chomsky, N. (1965) *Aspects of the theory of syntax.* Cambridge, MA: MIT Press.

Cook, V. (2002) Language teaching methodology and the L2 user perspective. In V. Cook (ed.), *Portraits of the L2 user.* Clevedon: Multilingual Matters. 327–43.

Crookes, G. and S.M. Gass (eds) (1993a) *Tasks and language learning.* Clevedon: Multilingual Matters.

—— and S.M. Gass (eds) (1993b) *Tasks in a pedagogical context: integrating theory and practice.* Clevedon: Multilingual Matters.

Crystal, D. (2003) *English as a global language* (2nd edition). Cambridge University Press.

Davies, A. (1991) *The native speaker in applied linguistics.* Edinburgh University Press.

—— (2002) Whose English? Choosing a model for our language tests. Plenary paper given at the International Conference on Language Testing and Language Teaching (CET), Shanghai, September.

—— (2003) *The native speaker: myth and reality*, Clevedon: Multilingual Matters.

Dubin, F. (1989) Situating literacy within traditions of communicative competence. *Applied Linguistics* 10.2: 171–81.

Dulay, H., M. Burt and S. Krashen (1982) *Language two.* New York: Oxford University Press.

Fairclough, N. (1992) The appropriacy of 'appropriateness'. In N. Fairclough (ed.), *Critical language awareness.* London: Longman. 33–56.

Firth, A. (1996) The discursive accomplishment of normality. On lingua franca English and conversation analysis. *Journal of Pragmatics* 26: 237–59.

Gordon, D. (2004) 'I'm tired. You clean and cook.' Shifting gender identities and second language socialisation. *TESOL Quarterly* 38.3: 437–57.

Graddol, D. and U. Meinhof (eds) (1999) *English in a changing world [AILA Review 13].* Oxford: Catchline.

Grillo, R.D., J. Pratt and B.V. Street (1987) Anthropology, linguistics and language. In J. Lyons (ed.), *New horizons in linguistics 2.* London: Penguin. 268–95.

Gumperz, J.J. ([1981] 1997) Communicative competence. In N. Coupland and A. Jaworski (eds), *Sociolinguistics: a reader and coursebook.* New York: Palgrave. 39–48.

Halliday, M.A.K. (1973) *Explorations in the functions of language.* London: Edward Arnold.

—— (1975) *Learning how to mean: explorations in the development of language.* London: Edward Arnold.

—— and R. Hasan (1976) *Cohesion in English.* London: Longman.

—— , A. McIntosh and P. Streuens (1964) *The linguistic sciences and language teaching.* London: Longman.

Hashim, A. (2002) Culture and identity in the English discourses of Malaysians. In A. Kirkpatrick (ed.), *Englishes in Asia: communication, identity, power and education.* Melbourne: Language Australia. 75–94.

Hedge, T. (2000) *Teaching and learning in the language classroom.* Oxford University Press.

House, J. (1999) Misunderstanding in intercultural communication: interactions in English as a lingua franca and the myth of mutual intelligibility. In C. Gnutzmann (ed.), *Teaching and learning English as a global language.* Tübingen: Stauffenburg. 73–89.

Howatt, A.P.R., with H.G. Widdowson (2004) *A history of English language teaching.* Oxford University Press.

Hung, T. (2002) Languages in contact: Hong Kong English phonology and the influence of Cantonese. In A. Kirkpatrick (ed.), *Englishes in Asia: communication, identity, power and education.* Melbourne: Language Australia. 191–200.

Hymes, D. (1972) On communicative competence. In J.B. Pride and J. Holmes (eds), *Sociolinguistics.* London: Penguin.

—— (1974) *Foundations in sociolinguistics: an ethnographic approach.* Philadelphia: Centre for Curriculum Development.

—— (1977) *Foundations in sociolinguistics: an ethnographic approach.* London: Tavistock Publications.

—— (1994) Towards ethnographies of communication. In J. Maybin (ed.), *Language and literacy in social practice.* Clevedon: Multilingual Matters, in association with the Open University. 11–22.

Jenkins, J. (2000) *The phonology of English as an International Language: new models, new norms new goals.* Oxford University Press.

—— (2002) Pronunciation goals for EAL: by default or by design? In C. Leung (ed.), *Language and additional/second language issues for school education.* Watford: National Association for Language Development in the Curriculum. 59–68.

—— (2003) *World Englishes: a resource book for students.* London: Routledge.

Johnson, K. (2001) *An introduction to foreign language learning and teaching.* Harlow, UK: Pearson (Longman).

Kachru, B.B. (1985) Standards, codification and sociolinguistic realism: the English language in the outer circle. In R. Quirk and H.G. Widdowson (eds), *English in the world: teaching and learning the language and literatures.* Cambridge University Press. 11–30.

—— (1992) Models for non-native Englishes. In B.B. Kachru (ed.), *The other tongue: English across cultures.* Chicago: University of Illinois Press. 48–74.

Krashen, S. (1982) *Principles and practice in second language acquisition.* Oxford: Pergamon.

—— (1985) *The input hypothesis.* New York: Longman.

Leung, C., R. Harris and B. Rampton (1997) The idealised native speaker, reified ethnicities, and classroom realities. *TESOL Quarterly* 31.3: 543–60.

——, R. Harris and B. Rampton (2004) Living with inelegance in qualitative research on task-based learning. In K. Toohey and B. Norton (eds), *Critical pedagogies and language learning.* Cambridge University Press. 242–67.

Levinson, S.C. (1983) *Pragmatics.* Cambridge University Press.

McDonough, J. and C. Shaw (2003) *Materials and methods in ELT: a teacher's guide* (2nd edition). Oxford: Blackwell.

McKay, S.L. (2003) Toward an appropriate EIL pedagogy: re-examining common ELT assumptions. *International Journal of Applied Linguistics* 13.1: 1–22.

Meierkord, C. (2002) 'Language stripped bare' or 'linguistic masala'? Culture in lingua franca conversation. In K. Knapp and C. Meierkord (eds), *Lingua franca communication.* Frankfurt am Main: Peter Lang. 109–33.

Morita, N. (2004) Negotiating participation and identity in second language academic communities. *TESOL Quarterly* 38.4: 573–603.

Morrow, K. (1981) Principles of communicative methodology. In K. Johnson and K. Morrow (eds), *Communication in the classroom.* Harlow, UK: Longman. 59–66.

Norton, B. (2000) *Identity and language learning: gender, ethnicity and educational change.* Harlow, UK/New York: Longman.

Nunan, D. (1991) Communicative tasks and the language curriculum. *TESOL Quarterly* 25.2: 279–95.

Pavlenko, A. (2002) Poststructuralist approaches to the study of social factors in second language learning and use. In V. Cook (ed.), *Portraits of the L2 user.* Clevedon: Multilingual Matters. 277–302.

Pennycook, A. (1994) *The cultural politics of English as an international language.* London: Longman.

—— (2000) The social politics and the cultural politics of language classrooms. In J.K. Hall and W.G. Eggington (eds), *The sociopolitics of English language teaching.* Clevedon: Multilingual Matters. 89–103.

Phillipson, R. (1992) *Linguistic imperialism.* Oxford University Press.

—— (2004) Figuring out the Englishisation of Europe. Plenary Address given at the British Association of Applied Linguistics Annual Meeting, London, September.

Piepho, H.-E. (1981) Establishing objectives in the teaching of English. In C.N. Candlin (ed.), *The communicative teaching of English: principles and an exercise typology.* Harlow, UK: Longman. 8–23.

Pinker, S. (1994) *The language instinct: the new science of language and mind.* London: Penguin.

Prodromou, L. (2003) In search of the successful user of English. *Modern English Teacher* 112.2: 5–14.

Rampton, B. (1998) Speech community. In J. Blommaert and C. Bulcaen (eds), *Handbook of pragmatics.* Amsterdam: John Benjamins. 1–33.

—— (1990) Displacing the 'native speaker': expertise, affiliation, and inheritance. *ELT Journal* 44.2: 97–101.

Roberts, C., M. Byram, A. Barro, S. Jordan and B. Street (2001) *Language learners as ethnographers.* Clevedon: Multilingual Matters.

Savignon, S. (2005) Communicative language teaching: strategies and goals. In E. Hinkel (ed.), *Handbook of research in second language teaching and learning.* Mahwah, NJ: Lawrence Erlbaum. 635–51.

Seidlhofer, B. (2004) Research perspectives on teaching English as a lingua franca. *Annual Review of Applied Linguistics* 24: 209–39.

Sifakis, N.C. (2004) Teaching EIL – teaching international or intercultural English? What teachers should know. *System* 32.2: 237–50.

Skehan, P. (1998) *A cognitive approach to language learning.* Oxford University Press.

Soars, L. and J. Soars (1996) *New headway (intermediate)*. Oxford University Press.

Swain, M. (1985) Communicative competence: some roles of comprehensible input and comprehensible output in its development. In S. Gass and C. Madden (eds), *Input in second language acquisition*. Rowley, MA: Newbury House. 235–56.

—— (1995) Three functions of output in second language learning. In G. Cook and B. Seidlhofer (eds), *Principle and practice in applied linguistics: studies in honour of H.G. Widdowson*. Oxford University Press. 125–44.

Wee, L. (2002) When English is not a mother tongue: linguistic ownership and the Eurasian community in Singapore. *Journal of Multilingual and Multicultural Development* 23.4: 282–95.

Widdowson, H.G. (1978) *Learning language as communication*. Oxford University Press.

—— (1989) Knowledge of language and ability for use. *Applied Linguistics* 10.2: 128–37.

—— (1994) The ownership of English. *TESOL Quarterly* 28.2: 377–89.

—— (2003) *Defining issues in English language teaching*. Oxford University Press.

—— (2004) A perspective on recent trends. In A.P.R. Howatt and H.G. Widdowson (eds), *A history of English language teaching*. Oxford University Press. 353–72.

Yalden, J. (1983) *The communicative syllabus: evolution, design and implementation*. Oxford: Pergamon.

Chapter 17

CLAIRE KRAMSCH AND ANNE WHITESIDE

LANGUAGE ECOLOGY IN MULTILINGUAL SETTINGS

Towards a theory of symbolic competence (2008)

1 Introduction

WHEN DIANE LARSEN-FREEMAN gave her groundbreaking talk on chaos theory and SLA at the Second Language Research Forum (Larsen-Freeman 1997), few language teachers imagined how chaos/complexity science could possibly be relevant to their daily task of having to teach grammatical forms and functions, communicative strategies and cultural knowledge in language classrooms. Yet complexity theory was soon picked up by American and Dutch educators interested in language ecology (van Lier 2000, 2004; Kramsch 2002; Leather and van Dam 2002); it was connected with the work that had long been going on in Europe in ecolinguistics (Haugen 1972; Fill and Mühlhäusler 2001; Steffensen 2007), and was brought to bear on the way the teaching of foreign languages and cultures was being conceptualized (Larsen-Freeman 2003; van Lier 2004; Risager 2006; Kramsch and Steffensen 2007).

Ten years later, the increasingly multilingual and multicultural nature of global exchanges is raising questions about the traditionally monolingual and monocultural nature of language education, and its modernist orientation. The prototypical communicative exchange, used by researchers to explore the processes of second language acquisition, and by teachers (and textbooks) to teach communicative or intercultural competence in a foreign language, usually includes two or three interlocutors, who all conduct the interaction in the same standard target language, all agree on what the purpose of the exchange is and what constitutes a culturally appropriate topic of conversation, all have equal speaking rights and opportunities. But, as recent work in pragmatics and sociolinguistics has shown (e.g. Rampton 1995; Johnstone 1996; Blommaert 2005; Coupland 2007), in multidialectal and multilingual settings the reality can be quite different, especially in our late modern times.

In the many places around the world where multiple languages are used to conduct the business of everyday life, language users have to navigate much less predictable exchanges in which the interlocutors use a variety of different languages and dialects for various identification purposes, and exercise symbolic power in various ways to get heard and respected (Rampton 1998, 1999). They have to mediate complex encounters among interlocutors with different language capacities and cultural imaginations, who have different social and political memories, and who don't necessarily share a common understanding of the social reality they are living in (Blommaert 2005). This presents a double challenge. For researchers, the lack of a shared understanding, due to global migrations and deterritorialized living conditions in late modern societies, poses a problem because much of applied linguistic data only make sense on the basis of a shared understanding of reality between the researcher and a given speech community. For language teachers, it complicates the teaching of what has been traditionally called "communicative competence." For, in such environments, as we shall see below, successful communication comes less from knowing which communication strategy to pull off at which point in the interaction than it does from choosing which speech style to speak with whom, about what, and for what effect.

This paper draws on insights from complexity theory and post-modern sociolinguistics to explore how an ecological approach to language data can illuminate aspects of language use in multilingual settings. We first present transcripts of exchanges taking place among multilingual individuals. We then examine what various contextually-oriented approaches to discourse can reveal about these multilingual interactions. We extend these analyses by drawing on insights from complexity theory and recent work in interactional sociolinguistics. We finally outline the components of a language competence in multilingual encounters that has not been sufficiently taken into consideration by applied linguists and that we call "symbolic competence."

2 An example of language ecology in practice

We first turn to data collected by Anne Whiteside (AW) as part of her research on Maya-speaking immigrants from Yucatan, Mexico, now living in San Francisco, California (Whiteside 2006). Attempting to understand their patterns of language use and the reasoning behind them, Whiteside spent over two years working closely with four local Yucatecans, following them in their daily lives, helping to organize community events, and exchanging English, Spanish, and computer literacy lessons for lessons in Maya.

There are now an estimated 25,000 Yucatecans living in the greater San Francisco Bay area, and some 50–80,000 in California, many of whom left Yucatan over the last decade (INDEMAYA 2005). Like an increasing number of migrants crossing the Mexico/California border, many arrive without legal papers (Passell et al. 2004; Passell 2005), lured by service sector jobs that have replaced entry-level manufacturing jobs in California's post-industrial economy. Their situation is typical of workers in a global economy that knows no national borders, no standard national languages, and thrives on the informal economic and social margins of national institutions.

Whiteside found that since many work two and three jobs, and with long-term residence uncertain because of undocumented status, learning English often takes a back seat. Her informants worked in restaurants where as many as eight languages were routinely spoken, with English, if spoken, as the highly accented lingua franca. Spanish use was common, linking Yucatecans with other marginalized Spanish-speaking workers and allowing undocumented individuals to blend with Latino legal residents and citizens. Yet informants also complained of discriminatory treatment by speakers of other varieties of Spanish, and noted a tendency of fellow immigrants to disguise their Yucatecan accents. English provided an escape from such distinctions. And English is seen as portable capital, motivating some to learn it to teach future migrants back in Yucatan. By contrast, Maya can be a social liability, and speakers described a sense of "shame" speaking Maya in public, inhibited by racialized colonial discourse and stereotypes linking Maya with poverty and ignorance (Güemez Pineda 2006). Maya was used predominantly at home and among work teams, where it provided a safe code in which to vent about oppressive conditions.

Whiteside collected data between January 2004 and June 2005, using participant observation, videotapes, interviews, and a language and literacy survey of 170 Yucatec Maya adults.[1] The data presented below are taken from 12 multilingual conversations she recorded in stores located in a predominantly Spanish-speaking neighborhood. The speakers in these conversations are Yucatecans Bela Chan and Don Francisco Canche (DF) (pseudonyms), some local merchants, and the researcher. These conversations were transcribed and analyzed using conversation analysis, looking in particular at preferred and dispreferred responses, repairs, evaluations, alignments, and indexicalities. It was in the course of these analyses that the need for a more ecological approach to the data emerged, which might link the microanalysis of the conversational data to the broader ecological context.

In the first set of data we discuss here, Don Francisco, 49, who runs an informal restaurant out of his apartment, is taking the researcher through his neighborhood as he shops for food. He has agreed to help her research project since she has been teaching him to read in Spanish, which he never learned. As DF chaperones AW around, he is regularly interrupted by greetings in Maya and Spanish from fellow townspeople, now San Francisco neighbors, who know his status as a successful farmer in Yucatan. To local merchants DF is a preferred customer, one who makes frequent trips to supply his busy restaurant and who spends a lot of money. On this occasion he is stopping in to check out supplies and place orders, eager to show the researcher his routines and to demonstrate the Maya the merchants are learning. We next present the data with brief descriptions, followed by more detailed analyses in sections 3 and 4.

At the Vietnamese grocery

The first excerpt occurs in a grocery story with Vietnamese writing on its awning. The Vietnamese owner, whom DF introduces as Juan, has been speaking to DF in English, who answers him in Spanish. Juan is busy loading meat from the freezer into the display case, and this exchange comes at the end of a short conversation about the meat DF needs.

EXCERPT 1

1	Juan:	how much *panza* you want?	(tripe)
2	DF:	*voy a comprar cinco libras*	I'm going to buy 5 lb
		de panza mañana	of tripe tomorrow.
3	Juan:	OK *mañana*	
4	DF:	/\ma' alob.	good
5	Juan:	_/OK!	
6	DF:	\/Dios bo dik	thanks
7	Juan:	_/bo dik	
8	DF:	_/saama	tomorrow
9	Juan:	@@,	
10		@@	
11		_saama	
12	DF:	ah	

"Juan," who has adopted a Spanish name for his Spanish-speaking customers, and has demonstrated his understanding of DF's Spanish earlier in the conversation, uses mixed utterances in

#1 and #3. DF closes in Maya (#4) to which Juan answers in English, but DF persists in Maya (#6). Juan echoes him (#7), but his laugh in #9,10 marks an affective change. Juan's final "saama" (#11) indexes a willingness to let the customer have his way. We give a more extensive analysis of this excerpt in section 4.2.

At the Chinese grocery

The next five excerpts take place in a Chinese-run grocery store, where DF has stopped to find out how much *masa* (corn-flour dough) his son had picked up earlier in the day. DF, who is four foot ten, makes an odd pair with AW, Anglo-American and five foot nine.

EXCERPT 2

1	DF:	((TO BUTCHER IN MAYA))	
2	Butcher:	si si si	
3	DF:	((TO CLERK)) buenas . . .	
4		*vengo <?> mi maestra*	I'm with my teacher
5	AW:	<LO HI LO>	
6		teacher	
7	Clerk:	OH [@]	
8	DF:	[ah]	
9		*es mi maestra*	She's my teacher
10		ah	
11		*eh-nomás, este, pasé a preguntar/*	I just uh came to ask
12		*la masa que agarró mi hijo*	the masa that my son
13		*ochenta y ahora/*	took, 80 and now
		. . .	
22	Clerk	*si bien.*	yes good.
23		*le toco masa acá ahora*	he'll take masa here now

DF first speaks with the butcher, a fellow Yucatecan, in Maya, then turns to the clerk in Spanish, introducing AW as "*mi maestra*." He then asks about the order in #11–13.

The clerk answers him in broken Spanish (*Si bien. le toco masa acá ahora*) which can be glossed as "OK good, he'll come and get the masa here now." In Excerpt 3, DF explains why he sent his son instead of coming himself to pick up the order.

EXCERPT 3

31	DF:	*estamos de paseo con la= maestra*	we're out walking with the teacher
32		*por eso yo no /\vine*	that's why I didn't come
33	Clerk:	ah/	
34	DF:	.si\	
35		ah	
36	Clerk:	((to AW)) my Spanish is really limited	
37		but I try to understand him	
38		@[@@@@]	
39	AW:	[that's	
40		good]	
41	DF:	[si ah ha]	

In #36, the clerk addresses AW in English, aligning herself with the English speaker, now referring to DF in the third person, and laughs. AW evaluates this positively, as does DF. In the intervening lines, the clerk tries to explain to AW her routine with DF, but her English is not much clearer than her Spanish: "the masa I always send it there, he always pick it up there already." In Excerpt 4, DF turns to an older woman—possibly the clerk's relative—who is sorting beans.

EXCERPT 4

74	DF:	*mucho trabajo.*	a lot of work.
75	Older lady:	ah @@@	
76	DF:	*eso es el* ticher.	this is the teacher.
77	Clerk:	((TO OLDER LADY: IN CHINESE))	
78	Older lady:	hi @@@	
79	AW:	hi	
80	Clerk:	((TO DF)) *mañana* when you come	
		[I give you no *español*]..	
81	Older lady:	[@@@@@]	
82	Clerk	[[*solo* English]]	
83	DF:	[[@@@]]	
84		NO,<@ no@>.	
85	Clerk:	Jose, tomorrow when you come in I don't	
		speak Spanish with you any	
86		more.	
87	DF:	[@@@@]	
88	AW:	[no, no, I'm]not teaching him English.	
89		I'm teaching him to read and writing in	
		Spanish.	
90		I'm not teaching him English.	
91	Clerk:	oh, oh,	
92		read and write Span-[ish.]	
93	AW	[yah,] read and write Span-ish	
94	Clerk:	that's good 'cause he like he not even	
		recognize the numbers	

The older woman laughs in response to DF's Spanish, but he persists, introducing AW as "*el ticher,*" a mixed utterance that the clerk translates into Chinese for her. The Clerk then addresses DF as "Jose," threatening to use only English with him. DF responds with a laugh (#87). In #88, AW jumps in, correcting what she perceives as an erroneous assumption on the part of the clerk that she is teaching DF English, which the clerk is enforcing by addressing him in English. Her statement suggests that DF, who spends most of his time in his Spanish- and Maya-dominant restaurant and apartment building, has made learning Spanish literacy, not English, his priority. AW's emphatic "no no" can also be seen as an attempt to save DF's face, which has been threatened by the clerk's scolding tone, and by her use of a stereotypical name not DF's own. AW's repetition in #90 can be interpreted as "teacher talk" to the NNS clerk, and her adoption of the prosody of the clerk's English in #93 as "foreigner talk." The clerk realigns herself with the revised teaching agenda in #91, noting that DF cannot read numbers. After a few other remarks the conversation returns to this topic. We shall return to this excerpt at greater length in section 4.2.

EXCERPT 5

107	AW:	we're going to learn to read the numbers	
108		((TO DF)) *dice que vamos a aprender a leer los numeros para que*	
109		[*puedas . . .*]	she says we're going to learn numbers so that you can . . .
110	DF:	[hm]	
111	Clerk:	[that's the] most important part first:	
112		one, two three four five six seven eight nine ten.	
113	AW:	that's right	
114		yah	
115		where did YOU learn English?	
116	Clerk:	America	
117	AW:	[oh=]	
118	Clerk:	[many] years ago	
119		<HI you know I start from beginning	
120		I start from one, two three four five. HI>	
121		I never know it in my life because my mother come	
122		when I come in 19 uh 80	
123		I still went to ESL program	
124		I still learn	
125		that's why he [can too]	
126	AW:	yah]	
127		yah yah	
128	Clerk:	((to DF)) when me *aquí*	when I (was) here
129		twenty years early	twenty years ago
130		*nada* speak English	I spoke no English
131	DF:	*nada*	none
132	Clerk:	*nada*	none
133		*todo* English *aquí*	everything/all English here
134	DF:	ah	

In #108, AW translates for DF, acknowledging that DF may not understand her exchange with the clerk, but the clerk persists in English, taking an authoritative stance, "that's the most important part first." As the *maestra*, and English expert, AW then asserts her own authority to approve of this priority, but then turns the topic (#115) to the clerk's status as English learner. The clerk takes this opportunity to launch into a 'can-do' story that draws on the immigrant frame "pulling-yourself-up-by-your-own-bootstraps." Her story ends with a moral ("that's why he can too") that draws a parallel between her and DF. However, by referring to him in the third person in his presence and talking "over" him in a code he doesn't understand, the clerk distances herself from DF. Considering that he is her preferred customer, this move can be taken as an affront.

The clerk then turns to address DF in #128 in a mixture of broken English and broken Spanish or "foreigner English" that further positions her in the English speaking camp ("*todo* English *aquí*").

EXCERPT 6

135	Clerk:	learn first	
136		ABCD	
137		*todo aquí*	everything here
138	DF:	*ah, entiendes Maya,*	*ah,* you understand Maya
139		*año más*	(one) more year
140		*ah*	
141		*entiendes Maya*	
142	AW:	a lot of people speak Maya here, huh?	
143	Clerk:	yeah	
144	AW:	you're learning some Maya?	
145	Clerk:	uh:: not much	
146		Latinos is <LO??LO>	
147	DF:	*ahí esta?*	that's it?
148		*eh= en la tarde/[y=/]*	In the afternoon and
149	Clerk:	[OK]	
150	DF:	*bueno, (?)*	Good.
151		*nos vemos*	See you.
152	Clerk:	OK	
153		good to see you.	

In #138, DF counters her suggestion that he "learn first ABCD" by predicting that a year from now the clerk will be speaking Maya. Given the recent influx of Maya-speaking clientele in the neighborhood, DF suggests that her customers, not the all-English melting pot, will prevail through their buying power. We return to this interaction in section 4.2.

At the Vietnamese butcher

In the next two excerpts, AW and Bela Chan, both women in their 50s, are out pricing meat in anticipation of an upcoming fiesta, for a typical Yucatecan pork dish, *cochinita pibil.* Raised in a Maya-speaking family, Bela stopped using Maya after being ridiculed for being "country," code for backward/Indian, and has trouble speaking it. With a Maya and a Chinese grandmother, an Afro Honduran and a Spanish grandfather, all of whom spoke Maya, Bela has roots in four continents. After 15 years in San Francisco, Bela has made little headway in English, which she uses neither in the Spanish-dominant neighborhood where she lives nor at the Spanish Baptist church she attends. In the Yucatan, she held a managerial position in a Korean-run garment factory or *maquiladora;* by contrast she has worked "on her knees" in the USA, a consequence she attributes to her undocumented status.

This butcher shop is advertised with a sign in Vietnamese; its customers speak English, Spanish, and several Asian languages, presumably including Vietnamese. The two Asian-looking butchers, whom we call Butcher A and Butcher B, both use some Spanish, although Butcher B is more proficient. The butchers stand behind a tall rectangular case full of meat, making fairly transparent what's going on. Bela, who is under five feet tall, is hard to see from that height; AW, at five foot nine, is closer to them. Yet Bela doesn't strain to make herself heard or understood: the implication is that if the butchers want a sale they will do what it takes to understand her. The whole interaction, 51 turns of talk, involves 27 instances of code-switching, during which everyone speaks everyone else's language, with the exception of side-play between butchers in their L1.

Prior to the following exchange. Butcher B tells them the price in Spanish ($1.97 a lb) and they negotiate the amount needed, with Butcher A tactfully repairing Bela's ambiguous "fifti pound" ("One five or five-0 you want?"). Having established the quantity, they negotiate the price:

EXCERPT 7

60	Butcher A:	<you need two leg . . . 20 pound each>	
61		so I order two.	
62	AW:	((TO BELA))	
63		<HI *pregúntele si es más barato* HI>	ask if its cheaper
64	Bela:	*¿si?*	yes?
65	Butcher A:	oh	
66		*¿habla español?*	you speak Spanish?
67	Bela:	*es más barato*	it's cheaper
68		uh huh	
69	Butcher A:	oh ((SPEAKS TO OTHER BUTCHER IN WHAT SEEMS TO BE CHINESE)).	
70		<he said OK>	
71	Butcher B:	*uno cincuenta y nueve la libra*	$1.59 a pound
72	AW:	*uno cincuenta y nueve si compramos más?* . . . (3) if we buy more?	
73		ok. (??)	
74	Butcher B:	*¿quiere?*	you want it?
75	AW:	*ah..*	
76		[*vamos a*]	we will . . .
77	Bela:	[next week]	
78	AW:	[[*vamos a..*]]	we will . . .
79	Bela:	[[next week]]	
80	Butcher A:	[ok]	
81	Bela:	[next week]	
82	Butcher A:	*¿cuándo quiere?*	when do you want?
83		next week *¿cuándo?*	when?
84		*¿que día?*	what day?
85	AW:	ah, *todavía estamos pensando* <LO *verdad* Lo> thinking, right?	we're still
86	Butcher A:	[ok]	
87	Bela:	[*ya*]	
88	Butcher B:	*si bueno*	OK good

AW's side play to Bela in Spanish in #63, to which the butchers respond with side play in Chinese (#69), is a common haggling strategy, the team huddle before the play. Butcher B comes back in #71 with a reduced price ($1.59) after which he asks for a commitment. This is followed by hedging in Spanish and English, at which point Butcher A in #82 switches to Spanish, in which he is far from fluent, aligning himself with AW and Bela's sideplay in Spanish. As they close the encounter in the next excerpt, Butcher A presents them with a Spanish name.

EXCERPT 8

95	Bela:	What's your name?	
96	Butcher B:	Felipe	
97	Bela:	Felipe (.)	
98		/\OK Felipe	
99	Butcher A:	*Felipe sabe español muy bien*	Felipe knows good Spanish
100	Butcher B:	this one with my name	
		((LEANING OVER THE COUNTER TO GIVE BELA A CARD))	
101	Bela:	@@[@@]	
102	AW:	[thank you]	

Bela responds to Butcher B's introduction (#97) by repeating his name. The rising–falling tone in her next turn (#98) indexes surprise/acceptance at the butcher's Spanish name, which she follows in #101 with a laughter of recognition. Bela is no stranger to Asians who adapt themselves to new linguistic and cultural contexts: her Chinese-born grandmother spoke Maya, and the Korean factory owners she worked for in Yucatan spoke Spanish and English. In an interview with AW, Bela expressed impatience with fellow townspeople in the USA who pretend to be from other parts of Mexico. She is clearly aware of how this game of masks is played to strategic advantage in such multicultural contexts.

3 Contextually oriented data analyses

How can we analyze these data? Several approaches in applied linguistics take a situated, contextualized view of language use in social settings, in particular conversational analysis and mediated communication studies. We consider each in turn. As we shall argue, what becomes salient in these interactions is how problematic the traditional notions of context have become in a global environment.

3.1 Conversation analysis

First we turn to conversation analysis (CA). Both in its "pure" and in its "applied" form,[2] the branch of the sociology of language called conversation analysis provides an epistemological way of looking at what the participants in these encounters are doing. "Pure" CA, represented by such foundational work as Sacks *et al.* (1974), Sacks (1992), Schegloff (2007), and inspired by ethnomethodology (Garfinkel 1967), revolutionized the study of talk in interaction by rigorously confining its analysis to observable phenomena and the organization of sequences of turns-at-talk. Its strictly emic perspective has encouraged researchers to do close readings of conversational phenomena. It does not ask: what did the participants have in mind, or what larger forces prompted them to say what they said? But, rather: what do speakers orient to in their turn-by-turn contributions to the ongoing exchange? What normative expectations and assumptions inform and underpin the production of their conversational sequences (Schegloff 2007), their membership categorization devices (Sacks 1992)?

In Excerpt 1, for example, by showing the unfolding of an unproblematic closing routine consisting of three adjacency pairs: good/OK, thanks/thanks, tomorrow/tomorrow, CA can show evidence of the familiar accomplishment of the expected leave-taking between merchant and customer. In Excerpt 8, the identification routine in which Bela's turn "What's your name?" elicits Butcher A's turn "Felipe" is expected to set up an enviromnent that will facilitate future transactions. Bela's repetition of the name Felipe momentarily flouts that expectation, as it offers a dispreferred response to the previous Q/A pair: "What's your name?"—"Felipe." Of course, Bela's surprise only makes sense to us because we share her expectation that a Chinese butcher should bear a Chinese name, not a Spanish one. In Excerpt 2, CA would find it significant that DF categorizes AW as "mi maestra" while AW categorizes herself as "teacher," and that DF, in Excerpt 4, picks up on AW's self-categorization by referring to her as "el ticher." Inferences could be drawn as to the kind of social structure these two participants are constructing through these categorization devices. The strength of CA as an epistemological approach rather than a mere tool of analysis lies in its constructionist view of the social world that emphasizes participants' local, situated, ethnographic understanding of social reality. The analyst's membership knowledge of this reality is crucial for the analysis. For, while the participants themselves might not be able to verbalize their orientation to this or that aspect of the interaction, the analyst, can recognize and interpret it based on his/her shared understanding of the social world.

While pure CA has dealt mostly with monolingual, symmetrical exchanges between native speakers in everyday life, it has been adopted and expanded by researchers in the broader field of microethnography and discourse analysis (DA), with varying degrees of adherence to ethnomethodological analytical principles. CA has been applied to the analysis of bilingual and multilingual interactions in cross-cultural settings (e.g. Moerman 1988; Gafaranga 2005; Torras 2005) and to second/foreign/lingua franca talk (e.g. Firth 1996; van Dam 2002). In particular it has informed analyses of the social symbolic meanings of code-switching, both the "on the spot observable" and the "in the head" meanings (Zentella 1997). The literature on the application of CA to bi/multilingual interaction and language alternation is extensive (see, e.g., Auer 1984, 1998; Richards and Seedhouse 2005; Wei 2005) and it varies in its tolerance to interpretations that go beyond what is strictly demonstrably relevant to the participants themselves.

The distinction between pure and applied CA has become somewhat blurred as applied CA has overlapped with much of DA. As Wooffitt (2005) puts it: "Whereas in CA the analytic focus is on people's own sense-making practices as they are revealed in the turn by turn unfolding of interaction" (2005: 84), in DA "the action orientation of language is located at a broader level, on the wider interpersonal or social functions served by a passage of talk" (2005: 80). Our data cannot be understood without factoring in the broader societal language ideologies at work in the participants' choice of this or that code, their exercise of this or that symbolic power.[3] CA is not intrinsically incompatible with the analysis of power relations and other macro-phenomena like ideology, history, and cultural values, but rather than assume that social inter-action merely reflects preexisting power relationships, it shows how "the sequential structures out of which the differential distributions of resources emerge are not a natural but an *oriented to* feature of the interaction" (Hutchby 1999: 90 cited in Wooffitt 2005: 194). In other words CA can serve as a reality-check for DA. For example, at the Vietnamese butcher in Excerpts 7 and 8, CA can show how Bela's economic power gets interactionally generated through her words as well as through her silences and how these are taken up by the butchers and the researcher in the store. However, neither CA nor DA can deal with the multiple levels of the global context itself, which is not restricted to a Vietnamese store in San Francisco but now includes the reenactment of practices carried out in Yucatan or ventriloquated words by a Chinese clerk mouthing Anglo prejudice.

3.2 *Mediated communication analysis*

Mediated discourse or sociocultural communication studies (e.g. Wertsch 1990; Scollon and Scollon 2001; van Lier 2004) focus less on the individuals than on the mediated action itself as a kind of social symbolic action. For example, in Excerpt 7, the accomplishment of the interaction is *mediated* through gestures like cutting, pointing, etc. and artifacts such as the tall rectangular meat case, the short stature of the customer, and the multiple languages used in the sideplays and the main track exchanges of butchers and customers. The relationships between the participants and their environment, or *affordances*, are seized upon and constructed as "opportunities for or inhibition of action" (van Lier 2004: 4), as when butcher A overhears Bela and AW's sideplay in Spanish and seizes this opportunity to switch from English to Spanish, negotiate a lower price with his colleague in Chinese, and have Butcher B return to the customer in Spanish. This exchange is also a good illustration of this approach's notion of *activity*, grounded in physical, social, and symbolic affordances, among which language plays an important part as "a system of relations" (van Lier 2004: 5). In the encounters above, the participants are vying not only for economic goods and services but for symbolic power and recognition. We can see this particularly well in the dialectic between two opposite perceptions of DF in Excerpt 5: that of a lazy, reluctant learner of English presented by the Chinese clerk and that of an eager learner of Spanish literacy presented by AW. DF himself resolves this tension by reaching for a synthesis—a third identity, namely that of a proud and well-respected speaker of Maya who, moreover, casts himself as a teacher of his native language to non-native merchants in his neighborhood. But this dialectic itself is perhaps too neat; it does not account for the unstable play of perceptions and counterperceptions between a Chinese clerk who recognizes her former self in the Yucatec migrant and the Maya speaker who styles himself as the successful resident that the Chinese clerk has become.

The approaches discussed above: conversation and discourse analysis, and the study of mediated communication provide a useful basis for understanding what is going on in our data. However, they presuppose a social reality bound by the usual constraints of time and space. Globalization has disrupted this social reality. The protagonists in these exchanges are physically and emotionally living on several axes of space and time that are embodied in their daily practices. Erickson (2004) makes the distinction between *kronos*, that is, "the quantitative aspect of time, time as continuous and thus as measurable"; and *kairos*, the subjective time of "tactical appropriateness, of shifting priorities and objects of attention from one qualitatively differing moment to the next" (2004: 6). The use of multiple codes in the data at hand and the exploitation of their various subjective resonances by the participants require taking into account not only the measurable communicative time of turns-at-talk within an activity, but the subjective, embodied time of cultural memory (Damasio 1999; Gibbs 2006). The Yucatecans in these encounters may be objectively present in a store in San Francisco, but their bodies carry subjective traces of their experiences living in Yucatan, crossing the border, learning to negotiate the vicissitudes of daily life as undocumented residents of the Bay Area. On certain streets they may move discretely, like stage crew executing a scene change, but among people they trust, speaking Maya, they become lead actors. The Maya language is for them embodied memory that, while located in individual bodies, resurrects a collective memory of group practices in the present. DF's voice speaking Maya with a fellow Yucatecan recreates the Yucatan in San Francisco. Without the notion of subjective time, it is difficult to understand the importance DF attaches to teaching Maya to so many of the merchants in his neighborhood or to explain Bela's dispreferred response in Excerpt 8—two aspects to which we return in section 4.2. In the following we propose an ecological approach that combines insights from complexity theory and postmodern thought in sociolinguistics.

4 Ecologically oriented analysis

4.1 Aspects of complex dynamic systems

Dynamic systems theory, also called complexity theory (Byrne 1997; Larsen-Freeman 1997; Cilliers 1998; Larsen-Freeman and Cameron 2008; Mason 2008; Peters 2008) is, when taken to its logical conclusions, a late modernist theory that hails more from Bakhtin's dialogism (Bakhtin 1981) than Marxist dialectics. Dialogism, the principle behind Bakhtin's existentialist philosophy of the relativity of self and other, and of the openness of time, shares with complexity theory and with postmodern sociolinguistics some basic tenets that can be summarized as follows:

1   *Relativity of Self and Other.* In complex dynamic systems like human relations, both the self and the other are intrinsically pluralistic, and possibly in conflict with themselves and with one another. Because the I is not unitary, but multiple, it contains in part the other and vice-versa; it can observe itself both subjectively from the inside and objectively through the eyes of the other. Hence the frequency of stylization, parody, double-voicing in the discourse of everyday life observed by sociolinguists like Rampton (1995) and others. The researcher is part of this subjective/objective observation game. His/her categories of observation and their relevance for the researcher are themselves relative to his/her subject position and to the perspective of the participants.

2   *Timescales.* A dynamic systems theoretical model of language shows that the meanings expressed through language operate on multiple timescales, with unpredictable, often unintended, outcomes and multiple levels of truth and fantasy, reality and fiction. Our memories are not in the past but live on as present realities in our bodies to be both experienced and observed (Hofstadter 2007). Blommaert (2005) refers to this phenomenon as "layered simultaneity." "We have to conceive of discourse as subject to *layered simultaneity*. It occurs in a real-time, synchronic event, but it is simultaneously encapsulated in several layers of historicity, some of which are within the grasp of the participants while others remain invisible but are nevertheless present" (2005: 130). Simultaneity does not necessarily mean congruence. Blommaert notes that the participants in verbal exchanges might speak from positions on different scales of historicity, thus creating "multiple and contradictory temporalities" that may lead to different intertextual references and to communicative tensions (2005: 128), such as we have in Excerpt 5.

3   *Emergentism.* Complexity theory has in common with postmodern sociolinguistic theory the notion that any use of language, be it learning a language or using it to haggle, assert yourself, or exercise power does not derive from structures in the head—beliefs, rules, concepts and schemata—but are new adaptations that emerge from the seamless dynamic of timescales. As Blommaert writes: "Meaning emerges as the result of creating semiotic simultaneity" (2005: 126).

4   *Unfinalizability.* Complexity theory does not seek dialectical unity, or bounded analyses of discrete events, but on the contrary open-endedness and unfinalizability. It counts under "participants" not only the flesh and blood interlocutors in verbal exchanges, but also the remembered and the imagined, the stylized and the projected, and the objects of identification (Hofstadter 2007). Similarly, sociolinguists have problematized the notion of bounded speech communities and focused our attention on open-ended, "deterritorialized" (Rampton 1998) communicative practices rather than on the "territorial boundedness" posited by the "one language—one culture assumption" (Blommaert 2005: 216).

5 *Fractals.* Complexity theory, like postmodern sociolinguistics, is concerned with patterns of activities and events which are self-similar at different levels of scales, that is, which are fractal figures for larger or smaller patterns. In the encounters above, stereotypical names like *Jose* or *Felipe* are fractals of a whole Hispanic culture, Maya greetings and leave takings are fractals of a Maya culture, and the stigmatization of Maya speakers as poor Indians in Yucatan is refracted in the stigmatization of Maya speakers as illegal immigrants by the US immigration authorities.

In the following analysis we draw on a complexity theory of language learning, as proposed by Larsen-Freeman (1997) and Larsen-Freeman and Cameron (2008: 115–161) and a sociolinguistic theory of language use as proposed recently by Blommaert (2005) to suggest an ecological reading of the data at hand.

4.2 An ecological analysis of the data

An ecological perspective on the data can build on the other analytic approaches, and view the unfolding events as the enactment, re-enactment, or even stylized enactment of past language practices, the replay of cultural memory, and the rehearsal of potential identities.

THE ECOLOGY OF MULTILINGUAL SPACES

By performing English, Maya, Spanish, or Chinese, rather than only learning or using these languages, the protagonists in these data signal to each other which symbolic world they identify with at the time of utterance. In the Vietnamese store in Excerpt 1, DF's and Juan's little *pas de deux* around the use of English, Spanish, and Maya indexes the various ways in which the protagonists wish to position themselves in the ongoing discourse. At the end of a transaction in which Juan has been speaking a mix of English and Spanish, and DF has been speaking exclusively Spanish, Juan and DF take leave—Juan in English, DF in Maya. Taking leave is always a delicate part of any verbal exchange as it has to sum up the exchange, make plans for future exchanges, and perform a recognizable and acceptable leave-taking routine. But in multilingual exchanges like this one, it is doubly delicate, as language choice can always become foregrounded. Since Juan had addressed DF in English and had been responded to in Spanish, Juan's OK in line 3 can be seen to be oriented not only toward the content of DF's utterance, but toward the language that DF chose to speak in. A gloss of this "OK" might be "I agree to sell you 5 lb of tripe tomorrow" but also "I agree to respond to you in Spanish" or "I acknowledge the legitimacy of Spanish in my store."

In #4, DF suddenly switches to Maya. Because the store is located in a predominantly Spanish speaking area of San Francisco, DF's efforts to get Juan and other merchants to respond to him in Maya has been a form of public resistance to a Spanish colonial discourse which holds Maya in low esteem among Mexicans.[4] Here, a Vietnamese clerk serves as an unwitting catalyst for DF's efforts to provide a place for himself between the polarity Spanish–English that divides much of California today. Whereas speaking Maya can be a social millstone in Yucatan and marks speakers as belonging to a recent wave of migrants with dubious immigration status, in some neighborhoods of San Francisco Maya can be made to yield a different social capital vis-à-vis third ethnic groups, that is, immigrants who are neither Mexicans nor Anglos, DF's use of Maya gives him a prestige of distinction vis-à-vis Mexicans, Spanish gives him a distinction on a par with Anglos.

be applied
What whether only English policies should

Juan's laughter in #9–10 is both amused and slightly embarrassed at having to produce Maya sounds in front of the Anglo visitor. In the usual hierarchy of codes in this Hispanic neighborhood, English and Spanish would be the two unmarked codes, followed perhaps by Vietnamese as the storeowner's language, but Maya is definitely marked. However, it has, in this case, acquired some historical presence due to DF's repeated efforts to teach the local merchants some Maya, so we can interpret Juan's chuckle as a sign that he is both willing to respect DF's language and ambivalent about his own legitimacy as a Maya speaker. It is worth noting that DF does not administer his little Maya lesson in all stores. In the Chinese store, for example, he uses Spanish throughout even when admonishing the clerk that her ability to understand Maya is improving (Excerpt 6, #138–141).

The Chinese clerk in Excerpts 2–6 also plays with the languages available in her store. She alternately speaks Chinese with her old relative, Spanish with putative "Mexicans" like DF, and English with Anglos like AW. These three languages index respectively: her ethnic or cultural identity as a Chinese, the accommodating role that she wants to assume and cultivate with Spanish-speaking customers, and the public voice she feels appropriate to adopt with Anglos. But she clearly uses these languages to align herself symbolically with the shifting centers of power in her store. For her in these data, Chinese is the language of intimacy with fellow customers, family, and friends; Spanish is the useful service language of local transactions, but it also indexes for her the stigma of non-assimilated immigrants; English is her public transactional language but she can also use it as a way of distancing herself from Mexican newcomers.

Viewing these exchanges as dynamic complex systems enables us to see the various languages used by the participants as part of a more diversified linguistic landscape with various hierarchies of social respectability among codes, and added layers of foregrounding of the code itself rather than just the message. To the multiplicity of languages we must add their subjective resonances in the speakers' embodied memories.

THE ECOLOGY OF EMBODIED TIME

It is important to note that the protagonists' choice of language is not dictated by some pre-existing and permanent value assigned to each of these languages, rather, the meaning of these choices emerges from the subjective perceptions of shifting power dynamics within the interaction. It draws on multiple timescales of experience, for example, at the Chinese grocery, the clerk's memories of learning English in America (Excerpt 5 #118 ff), DF's reminders of past Maya lessons with the clerk and his prediction of her future progress (Excerpt 6, #138–141), and, as mentioned in the previous section, reenactments of similar transactions between DF and the Yucatecan butcher in their native Yucatan (Excerpt 2, #1). This last timescale is particularly important for an understanding of the social prestige accorded to DF in this neighborhood of San Francisco. His weekly tours of the grocers and butchers recreate the network of Maya-speaking connections he had in his hometown. They also show that social capital varies greatly at different scales, so that in Yucatan, DF can be a wealthy respected merchant, while at the Mexican national level he may be perceived as poor, Indian, and illiterate. The connections between these different timescales bolster the invisible symbolic power of his undocumented presence in the United States. They cast a halo around his words that cannot be captured by looking only at the utterances produced in the present. For example, DF's broad smile and assertive posture when he turns to the Chinese clerk in Excerpt 2 #3 and proclaims "buenas . . .," carry evidence of the self-assuredness displayed a minute ago by a successful merchant chatting with his fellow Yucatecan in their common language.

The conflation of timescales can be further exacerbated by imprecise tense markers in the various grammars used by the participants. For example, between Excerpts 2 and 3 in an exchange not presented here, DF asks the Chinese clerk about the remainder of the 80 lb of masa that he ordered earlier. But because Maya has no verb tense morphology, DF's use of tense markers in Spanish is intermittent (DF: *ochenta llevo ahora* = I take 80 now). Chinese does not have any verb tense morphology either, so the clerk, who tries to clarify things by responding in Spanish: *aquí treinte* (here thirty) does not help matters by using *aqui* (here) instead of *ahora* (now). When DF then answers: *mas al rato* (later), the temporal confusion is extreme. Will he or will he not take the 80 lb of corn flour? Will he do it now or later? This can only be disambiguated through reference to their prior arrangements. It seems to suggest that the transaction might be in fact the reenactment of an exchange that took place earlier and is now being performed again for the benefit of the guest of honor, the researcher herself, who is being "toured around" (cf. #31 "*estamos de paseo con la* = *maestra*"). If that interpretation is correct, then the analysis has to take the words not as the spontaneous productions typical of natural conversations, but as a reflective replay for the benefit of a third party, a staging of sorts. Of course, this staging or styling serves also to nurture the human and commercial relations DF is keen on keeping up with the merchants in his neighborhood.[5]

Besides the conflation of timescales in the performing bodies of these social actors, we notice another aspect of embodied time. Spanish, Maya, English, Chinese, all acquire a subjective overlay of Mexican-ness, Maya-ness, etc. that makes uttering Spanish or Maya words more than the sum of their grammars or of the communicative roles they perform. Beyond haggling over the price of meat, the protagonists in these exchanges are performing not only themselves, but their cultures, their families, their countries of origin or the mythic and emotional memories that these historical realities have become. They are not just performing "being Maya," they are maintaining alive an idealized or "de-territorialized" kind of Maya-ness that transcends geographic boundaries and awaits to be reterritorialized in the subject positionings of individual speakers (Rampton 1998). Each of their utterances is less the performance of a language than the enactment of a performative speech act that creates the very reality it purportedly refers to (Pennycook 2007: ch. 4). As Blommaert notes: "The performance of identity is not a matter of articulating *one* identity, but of the mobilization of a whole *repertoire* of identity features converted into complex and subtle moment-to-moment speaking positions" (2005: 232).

A good example of this is given at the Vietnamese butcher shop. As we described in section 2, Bela's linguistic abilities include: conversational Spanish, limited English, and passive knowledge of Maya. At the end of the transactional encounter with the two Chinese butchers in Spanish (Excerpt 8), Bela asks Butcher B in English (#95) what his name is, presumably for future reference if she decides to buy meat in this store, since he is the one who earlier gave her—in Spanish—a good price. The reason for her switch to English is not immediately clear, but it makes the butcher's response all the more striking. Like Juan, the Vietnamese grocer in Excerpt 1, this Chinese butcher has taken on a Spanish name for his Spanish-speaking customers. Bela's choice of a dispreferred response to his name in #97—"Felipe (.)," a simple reiteration of the name rather than a vocative—draws attention to the name itself and what it connotes about the Mexican-ness of a Chinese butcher. Who says that a Chinese butcher cannot make himself into a Mexican butcher, since indeed, as the other Chinese butcher says: "*Felipe sabe español muy bien*," glossed as: "Since he speaks Spanish well, he is entitled to give himself a Spanish name" or "Felipe is not just any name he gives himself, it means that he also knows Spanish well." With "/\OK Felipe" Bela accepts "Felipe's" unexpected Hispanic identity. Hoping that these two customers come back, and offering a personal contact as incentive, Butcher B hands Bela his card, adding in English "This one with my name." At the end of this exchange, the two butchers, who both know English, Chinese, and Spanish, make sure they cover all their bases with this elusive, multilingual customer: Butcher A addresses her in Spanish in #99, Butcher B in English in #100. If we take Butcher B's adopted identity for the linguistic construction that it is, then we have to admit that in the multilingual and multicultural environment of immigrant communities, the symbolic dimension of interactions is as significant as their pragmatic one.

5 Symbolic competence

An ecological analysis of these data reveals a much greater degree of symbolic action than is usually accounted for in applied linguistics. Social actors in multilingual settings seem to activate more than a communicative competence that would enable them to communicate accurately, effectively, and appropriately with one another. They seem to display a particularly acute ability to play with various linguistic codes and with the various spatial and temporal resonances of these codes. We call this competence "symbolic competence."

Symbolic competence is the ability not only to approximate or appropriate for oneself someone else's language, but to shape the very context in which the language is learned and used. Such an ability is reminiscent of Bourdieu's notion of *sens pratique*, exercised by a habitus that structures the very field it is structured by in a quest for symbolic survival (Bourdieu 1997/2000: 150). Here, however, we are dealing with a multilingual *sens pratique* that multiplies the possibilities of meaning offered by the various codes in presence. In today's global and migratory world, distinction might not come so much from the ownership of one social or linguistic patrimony (e.g. Mexican or Chinese culture, English language) as much as it comes from the ability to play a game of distinction on the margins of established patrimonies. Because it depends on the other players in the game, we should talk of a "distributed" symbolic competence, that operates in four different ways.

5.1 Subjectivity or subject-positioning

Different languages position their speakers in different symbolic spaces (see, e.g., Weedon 1987). In the data above, speakers take on subject positions regarding the symbolic power of this versus that language, the respective social values of Maya, Chinese, Spanish, and English. In Excerpt 7, for example, Bela is linguistically at a disadvantage in English but she is commercially at an advantage, because she is the one who has the purchasing power. Because she is perceived as a powerful customer, the butchers and the clerk will go along with whatever language she wants to speak: English at first when she looks like she prefers English; then Spanish in #66ff, when she is overheard speaking Spanish to AW. In turn Bela's ambiguity serves to play one language against the other and, after the price has been brought down, to gain time until next week. This could be seen as strategic competence on Bela's part, but strategic competence has been conceived up to now as an individual compensatory tactic (Canale and Swain 1980: 30), whereas the symbolic competence apparent here is a distributed competence that emerges from playing the game.

Subject positioning has to do less with the calculations of rational actors than with multilinguals' heightened awareness of the embodied nature of language and the sedimented emotions associated with the use of a given language. In Excerpt 2, the pleasure that the butcher and Don Francisco experience at using with each other the language of their common village in Yucatan is still visible in DF's self-assured demeanor when he turns around and switches to Spanish in #3. The clerk's volubility in English in Excerpt 5 indexes her pleasure at being able to converse in English with the researcher, something she cannot do with DF in Spanish. And AW's switch to Spanish in Excerpt 5 #108 aligns her emotionally with DF, who may have felt affronted by the clerk's use of English.

5.2 Historicity or an understanding of the cultural memories evoked by symbolic systems   *for example*   *Chen Mo, dragon*

Throughout the data presented here, we have been confronted with the cultural memories carried by words, gestures, body postures, and scripts taken from a different timescale in a different place and reterritorialized in a Californian grocery store. We have noticed the timescale of Yucatan irrupting in the timescale of San Francisco, but there are other examples. During a visit to another Vietnamese grocery, AW and the clerk engaged in a comparative account of the ancient history of the Maya in Mexico versus the ancient history of the Chinese in Vietnam (Kramsch and Whiteside 2007). Neither the clerk nor the researcher were really teaching each other a history lesson; rather, each was lending weight to her words by performing ritualized utterances about the ancient nature of Maya and Chinese civilizations—an exchange of social symbolic power that put both parties on an equal footing. The utterances in these exchanges sounded formulaic because they were what Pierre Nora calls *lieux de mémoire*, realms or archetypes of social memory (1997: 3031). Any utterance or turn-at-talk can become a *lieu de mémoire*, formed by the sedimented representations of a people. Whether these representations are accurate or not, historically attested or only imagined, they are actually remembered by individual members and serve as valid historical models. As Blommaert writes: "The synchronicity of discourse is an illusion that masks the densely layered historicity of discourse" (2005: 131). Indeed, symbolic competence is the ability to perform and construct various historicities in dialogue with others.

5.3 Performativity or the capacity to perform and create alternative realities

Within an ecological perspective of human exchanges, utterances not only perform some role or meaning, but they bring about that which they utter, that is, they are performatives. We have seen how the utterances of the protagonists in our data recreate environments from other scales of space and time, produce fractals of patterns from one timescale to another. Multilingual environments can elicit complex relationships between speech acts and their perlocutionary effects. Take for example Excerpt 4. The clerk clearly devalues DF by ignoring that his utterance: "eso es el ticher" (#76) names the researcher as "the teacher," and by taking on herself the teacher role (#80). She puts down his Spanish by embedding it in her English: "*Mañana* when you come I give you *no español, solo* English," then calling him "Jose" in #85. The cartoon-like foreigner talk is not lost on the older lady and on DF himself who bursts out laughing. But we understand that it was an insult and not just a joke from its perlocutionary effect on AW. Her immediate overlapping response in English in #88 ("No no I'm not teaching him English") seeks to cancel the potential perlocutionary effect of the insult by resignifying the ESL issue into a Spanish literacy issue ("I'm not teaching him English. I'm teaching him to read and write in Spanish")—a symbolic move that reestablishes DF at par with the clerk: in the same manner as the clerk learned English, DF is now learning Spanish literacy.[6] Such a move exploits the time lag, materialized here by the general laughter in #81–87, between the illocutionary force of the clerk's derogatory utterance and its perlocutionary effect on DF, and reconfigures the whole environment. The actors in the Chinese grocery store are quick to adapt to the alternative configuration introduced by AW in #88 and DF regains the symbolic space that was his at the onset of the exchange. Thus a third aspect of symbolic competence is the capacity to use the various codes to create alternative realities and reframe the balance of symbolic power.

5.4 Reframing

Finally, the data highlight the importance of reframing as a powerful means of changing the context. In Excerpt 6, DF reframes the face threatening situation defused by AW's intervention into one that reestablishes his legitimacy. For the Chinese clerk, legitimacy as an immigrant comes from having learned English, knowing how to count in English and the English alphabet. For DF, legitimacy comes from having money and clout from the old country, and influence in the neighborhood, even though he is illiterate. In Excerpt 4, by resignifying the clerk's insult into an erroneous statement of fact (#88), AW reframed her relationship with DF (#88–90) from an ESL teacher to a Spanish literacy maestra. In turn, DF reframes his relationship with the clerk: at first it was the clerk who in #80 constructed for herself a "teacher" role to "Jose" the pupil. In Excerpt 6 #138–141, DF suddenly turns the tables as the Maya "teacher." His insistence that she will end up understanding Maya is less a statement about her than about him contesting and reframing the view that "*todo* English *aquí*." Maya, he suggests, will be an increasing part of this world, as will Spanish. And, indeed, he gives leave in Spanish (#150–151), while the clerk closes the conversation in English (#152–153).

Symbolic competence could thus be defined as the ability to shape the multilingual game in which one invests—the ability to manipulate the conventional categories and societal norms of truthfulness, legitimacy, seriousness, originality—and to reframe human thought and action. We have seen that this kind of competence is multiply distributed and that it emerges through the interaction of multiple codes and their subjective resonances. It is true that symbolic competence is not reserved to multilingual actors in multilingual encounters. Analyzing exchanges between monolingual speakers of English, Gumperz (1982) found that the meaning of utterances there too lie not only in the way participants orient themselves to the ongoing exchange, but in the way they implicitly ventriloquate or even parody prior utterances and thereby create affordances in ways that are favorable to them. Multilingual encounters increase the contact surfaces among symbolic systems and thus the potential for creating multiple meanings and identities. In the late modern stance offered by an ecological perspective, symbolic competence is both semiotic awareness (van Lier 2004), and the ability to actively manipulate and shape one's environment on multiple scales of time and space. Symbolic competence in our view adds a qualitative metalayer to all the uses of language studied by applied linguists, one that makes language variation, choice, and style central to the language learning enterprise.

Conclusion

An ecological analysis of multilingual interactions enables us to see interactions in multilingual environments as complex dynamic systems where the usual axes of space and time are reordered along the lines of various historicities and subjectivities among the participants. While the global economy has deterritorialized and dehistoricized the spaces of human encounters, participants find a way of reterritorializing and rehistoricizing them in their moment-by-moment utterances. Our analysis of their interactions has revealed the importance of taking into account embodied perceptions, portable cultural memories, and the power that comes from resignifying the illocutionary force of performatives. In environments where the boundaries of the distant and the proximal, the past and the present, the real and the imagined have become blurred, when names have become arbitrary, and signifiers are no longer transparent, multilingual exchanges require us to position ourselves as researchers in much more multidimensional ways than is usually done in applied linguistics.

For language learners and educators, symbolic competence is not yet another skill that language users need to master, nor is it a mere component of communicative competence. Rather, it is a mindset that can create "relationships of possibility" or affordances (van Lier 2004: 105), but only if the individual learns to see him/herself through his/her own embodied history and subjectivity and through the history and subjectivity of others. Our symbolic survival is contingent on framing reality in the way required by the moment, and on being able to enter the game with both full involvement and full detachment. In this sense, the notion of symbolic competence is a late modern way of conceiving of both communicative and intercultural competence in multilingual settings.

Appendix: Transcription conventions based on Dubois (2006)

Boundary Tone/Closure

Terminative	.		
Continuative	,		
Truncated intonation unit	-		
Appeal	?		

Vocalisms

Breath (in)	(H)
Laugh	@

Manner

Manner/quality	<MISC.
Voice tone	<VOX>

Metatranscription

Unintelligible	(??)
Comment	((WORDS))
Overlap	[ ]

Tone shifts

Rising tone	/
Falling tone	\
Low to high tone	_/
High-low-high	V

Notes

1 The interviews were conducted with the four focal participants and with 13 non-Yucatecan service professionals working with this population.
2 The distinction between 'pure' and 'applied' conversation analysis was made by ten Have (1999: 8) to distinguish between a focus on specific interactional situations and how interactants orient to these situations and their requirements (pure CA) on the one hand, and a focus on the larger institutional arrangements as they pertain to the organization of interaction (applied CA) on the other hand. We apply this distinction to the two strands of CA we find in the literature today: the strictly local and the more ethnographically contextual.
3 Indeed, the study of talk in interaction has been associated with late modernist theories of structure–agency dialectic (Giddens 1991) and the construction of intersubjectivity and identity (Antaki and Widdicombe 1998).
4 This interpretation follows from Whiteside's general observation that the Maya speakers in this study tend to refrain from using Maya in non-Maya speaking contexts. DF's deliberate flouting of this general practice must be seen as an act of defiance.
5 Rampton (1995) has convincingly shown on the language practices of multilingual adolescents in British schools the interpersonal effects of 'styling', i.e. performing a language or language variety other than one's own for placating, teasing, mocking, or playful purposes (see also Goffman 1959). Coupland (2007) points out that stylization, like staging, is a form of multi-voiced utterance originally theorized by Mikhail Bakhtin (1981).
6 What is perhaps at issue here is AW's attempt to deflect another possible threat to DF's face, a future-oriented one since, if DF is mistakenly perceived as receiving English lessons and then subsequently

perceived as not making progress, he will be in danger of losing face as one who, in spite of instruction, is incapable of making progress in English. We thank an anonymous reader for this very plausible interpretation.

References

Antaki, C. and S. Widdicombe (eds). 1998. *Identities in Talk*. London: Sage.

Auer, P. 1984. *Bilingual Conversation*. Amsterdam: John Benjamins.

Auer, P. 1998. *Code-switching in Conversation: Language, Interaction, and Identity*. London: Routledge.

Bakhtin, M. M. 1981. *The Dialogic Imagination*, ed. M. Holquist, transl. C. Emerson and M. Holquist. Austin, TX: University of Texas Press.

Blommaert, J. 2005. *Discourse*. Cambridge: Cambridge University Press.

Bourdieu, P. 1997/2000. *Pascalian Meditations*, transl. R. Nice. Stanford: Stanford University Press.

Byrne, D. 1997. 'Complexity theory and social research.' Social Research Update. Quarterly by the Department of Sociology, University of Surrey, Guildford, UK. www.soc.surrey.ac.uk/sru/SRU18.html.

Canale, M. and M. Swain. 1980. 'Theoretical bases of communicative approaches to second language teaching and testing,' *Applied Linguistics* 1: 1–47.

Cilliers, P. 1998. *Complexity and Postmodernism: Understanding Complex Systems*. London: Routledge.

Coupland, N. 2007. *Style. Language Variation and Identity*. Cambridge: Cambridge University Press.

Damasio, A. 1999. *The Feeling of What Happens. Body and Emotion in the Making of Consciousness*. New York: Harcourt.

DuBois, J. W. 2006. *Basic Symbols for Discourse Transcription*. Retrieved 15 December 2006 from www.linguistics.ucsb.edu/projects/transcription/representing.

Erickson, F. 2004. *Talk and Social Theory*. Cambridge: Polity Press.

Fill, A. and P. Mühlhäusler (eds). 2001. *The Ecolinguistics Reader. Language, Ecology and Environment*. London: Continuum.

Firth, A. 1996. 'The discursive accomplishment of normality: On 'lingua franca' English and conversation analysis,' *Journal of Pragmatics* 26: 237–59.

Gafaranga, J. 2005. 'Demythologising language alternation studies: Conversational structure vs. social structure in bilingual interaction,' *Journal of Pragmatics* 37: 281–300.

Garfinkel, H. 1967. *Studies in Ethnomethodology*. New York: Prentice-Hall.

Gibbs, R. 2006. *Embodiment and Cognitive Science*. Cambridge: Cambridge University Press.

Giddens, A. 1991. *Modernity and Self-Identity*. Stanford: Stanford University Press.

Goffman, E. 1959. *The Presentation of Self in Everyday Life*. New York: Anchor Books.

Güemez Pineda, M. 2006. *Language, Culture and Indigenous Rights in Rural Yucatan*. Paper presented at the Mayab Bejlae: Yucatan Today. 21–23 April 2006. Kroeber Hall, University of California Berkeley.

Gumperz, J. J. 1982. *Discourse Strategies*. Cambridge: Cambridge University Press.

Haugen, E. 1972. *The Ecology of Language: Essays by Einar Haugen*, ed. A. S. Dil. Stanford: Stanford University Press.

Hofstadter, D. 2007. *I Am a Strange Loop*. New York: Basic Books.

INDEMAYA (Instituto para el Desarrollo de la Cultura Maya del Estado de Yucatán). 2005. *Diagnóstico de Migración y Políticas Publicas en el Estado de Yucatán: Síntesis Diagnóstica*. INDEMAYA, Instituto Nacional de Antropologia e Historia.

Johnstone, B. 1996. *The Linguistic Individual: Self-expression in Language and Linguistics*. Oxford: Oxford University Press.

Kramsch, C. (ed.). 2002. *Language Acquisition and Language Socialization. Ecological Perspectives*. London: Continuum.

Kramsch, C. and A. Whiteside. 2007. 'Three fundamental concepts in SLA and their relevance in multilingual contexts'. *Modern Language Journal Focus Issue* 91: 905–20.

Kramsch, C. and S. V. Steffensen. 2007. 'Ecological perspectives on second language acquisition and socialization' in N. Hornberger and P. Duff (eds): *Encyclopedia of Language and Education Vol. 8. Language and Socialization*. Heidelberg: Springer Verlag.

Larsen-Freeman, D. 1997. 'Chaos/complexity science and second language acquisition,' *Applied Linguistics* 18(2): 141–65.

Larsen-Freeman, D. 2003. *Teaching Language: From Grammar to Grammaring*. Boston: Heinle/Thomson.

Larsen-Freeman, D. and L. Cameron. 2008. *Complex Systems and Applied Linguistics*. Oxford: Oxford University Press.

Leather, J. and J. van Dam (eds). 2002. *Ecology of Language Acquisition*. Dordrecht: Kluwer Academic.

Mason, M. 2008. 'What is complexity theory and what are its implications for educational change?' *Educational Philosophy and Theory* 40 (1): 35–49.

Moerman, M. 1988. *Talking Culture. Ethnography and Conversation Analysis*. Philadelphia: University of Pennsylvania Press.

Nora, P. 1997. *Les lieux de mémoire*. Paris: Gallimard.

Passell, J. S. 2005. Unauthorized Migrants: Numbers and Characteristics. Retrieved 10 November 2005 from http://pewhispanic.org/reports/report.php?ReportID=46.

Passell, J. S., C. Randall, and M. E. Fix. 2004. Undocumented Immigrants: Facts and Figures. Retrieved 15 July 2005 from www.urban.org/url.cfm?ID=1000587.

Pennycook, A. 2007. *Global Englishes and Transcultural Flows*. London: Routledge.

Peters, M. A. 2008. 'Editorial: Complexity and knowledge systems,' *Special Issue. Educational Philosophy and Theory* 40(1): 1–3.

Rampton, B. 1995. *Crossing*. London: Longman.

Rampton, B. 1998. 'Speech community,' in J. Verschueren, J. O. Ostman, J. Blommaert and C.Bulcaen (eds): *Handbook of Pragmatics*. Amsterdam: John Benjamins, pp. 1–34.

Rampton, B. (ed.). 1999. 'Styling the other,' *Special issue. Journal of Sociolinguistics* 3(4).

Richards, K. and P. Seedhouse (eds). 2005. *Applying Conversation Analysis*. Houndmills, Basingstoke: Palgrave Macmillan.

Risager, K. 2006. *Language and Culture. Global Flows and Local Complexity*. Clevedon, UK: Multilingual Matters.

Sacks, H. 1992. *Lectures on Conversation*. Vols 1 and 2, ed. G. Jefferson, intro. E. A. Schegloff. Oxford: Blackwell.

Sacks, H., E. A. Schegloff, and G. Jefferson. 1974. 'A simplest systematics for the organization of turn-taking for conversation,' *Language* 50: 696–735.

Schegloff, E. A. 2007. *Sequence Organization in Interaction: A Primer in Conversation Analysis, Vol. I*, Cambridge: Cambridge University Press.

Scollon, R. and S. Scollon. 2001. *Intercultural Communication*. 2nd edn. Oxford: Blackwell.

Steffensen, S. V. 2007. 'Language, ecology and society: An introduction to dialectical linguistics,' in J. C. Bang and J. Door. *Language, Ecology and Society—A Dialectical Approach,* eds S.V. Steffensen and J. Nash. London: Continuum.

Ten Have, P. 1999. *Doing Conversation Analysis. A Practical Guide*. London: Sage.

Torras, M. C. 2005. 'Social identity and language choice in bilingual service talk' in K. Richards and P. Seedhouse (eds): *Applying Conversation Analysis*. Houndmills, Basingstoke: Palgrave Macmillan, pp. 107–23.

van Dam, J. 2002. 'Ritual, face, and play in a first English lesson: Bootstrapping a classroom culture' in C. Kramsch (ed.): *Language Acquisition and Language Socialization. Ecological Perspectives*. London: Continuum, pp. 238–65.

van Lier, L. 2000. 'From input to affordance: Social-interactive learning from an ecological perspective' in J. P. Lantolf (ed.): *Sociocultural Theory and Second Language Learning*. Oxford: Oxford University Press, pp. 245–60.

van Lier, L. 2004. *The Ecology and Semiotics of Language Learning. A Sociocultural Perspective*. Dordrecht: Kluwer Academic.

Weedon, C. 1987. *Feminist Practice and Post-structuralist Theory*. Oxford: Blackwell.

Wei, L. (ed.) 2005. 'Conversational Code-switching,' *Special Issue. Journal of Pragmatics* 37(3).

Wertsch, J. 1990. *Voices of the Mind: A Sociocultural approach to Mediated Action*. London: Harvester Wheatsheaf.

Whiteside, A. 2006. *'We are the explorers': Transnational Yucatec Maya-speakers negotiating multilingual California*. Unpubl. PhD dissertation, University of California, Berkeley.

Wooffitt, R. 2005. *Conversation Analysis and Discourse Analysis. A Comparative and Critical Introduction*. London: Sage.

Zentella, A. C. 1997. *Growing Up Bilingual*. Oxford: Blackwell.

Chapter 18

DEBORAH CAMERON

GLOBALIZATION AND THE TEACHING OF 'COMMUNICATION SKILLS' (2002)

I think it's essential for us to be able – in this global community and as the global community becomes even smaller through the Internet and through all kinds of electronics – that we are able to communicate. . . . It is essential that there be a uniform way of talking, for the economy, for national communications, for exchange of politics and even on the level of individual couples being able to communicate. . . . And there are rules for that.

(Judith Kuriansky, psychologist and therapist, speaking on the BBC World Service, August 1999)

THE EPIGRAPH TO THIS CHAPTER reproduces some remarks made by a well-known American expert on communication in response to my own arguments about the effects of globalization on language and language-use.[1] At the time of our encounter I was finishing a book about the contemporary obsession with 'communication skills' and 'communication problems' (Cameron 2000). One of my conclusions was that globalization had given new legitimacy, and a new twist, to the long-lived idea that linguistic diversity is a problem, while linguistic uniformity is a desirable ideal. My interlocutor did not dispute the factual part of this argument, but she did take issue with my negative attitude to the developments I had identified. What I regarded as a regrettable curtailment of linguistic diversity, she celebrated as progress towards increased global harmony and mutual understanding.

The argument which the two of us conducted in the last months of the twentieth century is not, in its general outlines, new. On the contrary, what Umberto Eco (1995) labels 'the search for the perfect language' – typically conceived in universal or global terms, and representing a mythical unity among the peoples of the world – has inspired arguments for at least two millennia. In the nineteenth century, the quest for linguistic unity was pursued through the creation of international auxiliary languages like Esperanto and Volapük. In the twentieth century argument came to centre on the desirability or otherwise of using English as a global lingua franca. That debate continues (see also Kubota, 2002 and Wallace, 2002). But it is not what was at issue in the disagreement between Dr Kuriansky and myself.

When she asserted the need for 'a uniform way of talking' in the global community, she did not mean that the people of the world should abandon their native tongues and agree to communicate in one language, be it English, Mandarin or Esperanto. Nor was she making a plea for standard English to replace every other dialect. When she said 'there are rules', she was not talking about rules of grammatical correctness, but rather about norms for relating to other people through talk. She went on to give some concrete examples of these norms. Speaking directly is better than speaking indirectly. Speaking positively is better than criticizing. Negotiating is better than arguing. Sharing your feelings is better than being silent and withdrawn.

Dr Kuriansky maintained that norms of this sort are applicable across languages, dialects, cultures and contexts. Where a community departs from them, the result will be problematic. Thus she claimed (citing her professional experience of working with Japanese organizations) that the existence of multiple levels of formality in Japanese is not just a problem for foreigners trying to communicate with Japanese, but an obstacle to good communication among Japanese themselves. When another participant in the discussion, a former Buddhist monk from Tibet, explained that he spent a certain period of each day in total silence, 'listening to what is within', Dr Kuriansky responded that meditation can be an aid to good communication; it helps to clarify thoughts and feelings so they can later be shared more fully and honestly with others. (The Tibetan shared with me later that he felt she had missed the point.)

What, it might be asked, does this have to do with the theme of globalization and language teaching? The short answer, on which I will elaborate below, is that in the rise of experts like Dr Kuriansky (most of them not trained in linguistics or language teaching, but in psychology, therapy or counselling), in their public utterances and in their activities as consultants to various organizations, I believe we are witnessing the consolidation of a new and powerful discourse on language and communication, which has significant implications both for language teaching and for discussions of its politics.

'Communication' and the international politics of language

In recent years, critical discussions of the international politics of language and language teaching have often been framed in terms of the concept of 'linguistic imperialism' (cf. Phillipson 1992; Pennycook 1994; Canagarajah 1999). I have no intention of arguing that this concept is no longer relevant or useful, for clearly the phenomena it encompasses are still very much with us. However, I do want to suggest that there are other, newer phenomena which are less well accounted for in the conceptual framework of linguistic imperialism. For instance, the views on language and communication expressed by Dr Kuriansky are undoubtedly ethnocentric – they display intolerance of cultural difference and presuppose the superiority of the expert's own cultural/ linguistic norms. But this ethnocentrism does not take the form of linguistic imperialism as that term is ordinarily understood; i.e. promoting one language over others. Instead it involves promoting particular interactional norms, genres and speech-styles *across* languages, on the grounds that they are maximally 'effective' for purposes of 'communication'. Ryuko Kubota (2002) provides another example in her account of some recent changes in the practices of Japanese schools. Genres such as 'debate', and 'logical' styles of prose writing, have been imported from Western educational traditions with the intention of remedying alleged deficiencies in Japanese habits of thought and expression. However, there is no question of displacing Japanese itself as the medium for speech and writing. Rather students are expected to master new and supposedly 'better' ways of expressing themselves in Japanese.

What is imposed in cases like the one Kubota mentions is not someone else's language, but someone else's definition of what is acceptable or desirable in your own. I would argue that it is important to distinguish between this and more traditional forms of linguistic imperialism, not only because the effects are different, but also and perhaps more importantly because the underlying attitude to language and culture is different. In particular, it is (on the surface, at least) more inclined to view diversity in positive terms, as a natural and valuable aspect of human experience. This idea of diversity as enriching, however, tends not to be pushed to the point where it might threaten the very notion of a (universal or fundamentally shared) 'human experience' (see also Kramsch and Thorne, 2002). Instead, the potential threat is neutralized in a rhetoric of 'unity in diversity'. This has become a favoured trope of the new capitalism, well illustrated by advertisements for transnational clothing retailers like Benetton and Gap, which pointedly feature models with a range of skin colours, all dressed in the same jeans and sweaters. Here the differences we conventionally think of as 'deep' (e.g. racial or ethnic identity) are portrayed as superficial; the young people in the poster are part of a global community defined not by ancestry but by preferred styles of clothing.

Discourse on the subject of 'global communication' contains analogous tendencies and similar contradictions. Rather than propose a wholesale levelling of difference through the adoption of a single global language, it has elaborated a version of 'unity in diversity', according to which the existence of different languages is not in itself a problem; problems arise only to the extent that these languages embody different or incommensurable worldviews. It is those 'deeper' differences that need to be levelled if global communication is to be effective. Hence the recommendation that, for instance, Japanese students should learn to write Japanese in accordance with Western norms of 'logic', or that Japanese businesspeople should adopt more 'direct' or 'informal' ways of interacting among themselves. On the surface, this approach preserves linguistic diversity, but at a deeper level the effect is to make every language into a vehicle for the affirmation of similar values and beliefs, and for the enactment by speakers of similar social identities and roles. Language becomes a global product available in different local flavours.

I have been focusing on the ways in which the new rhetoric of global communication *differs* from older discourses of linguistic imperialism, but there are also continuities. The dissemination of 'global' communicative norms and genres, like the dissemination of international languages, involves a one-way flow of expert knowledge from dominant to subaltern cultures. (I use the terms 'dominant' and 'subaltern' here in preference to the more familiar 'centre' and 'periphery' because globalization arguably calls into question the applicability of the latter terms as they are usually defined. Any detailed discussion of that issue, however, is beyond the scope of this chapter.) As will no doubt be evident from my listing of the communicative norms adduced by Judith Kuriansky, the ideal of 'good' or 'effective' communication bears a non-coincidental resemblance to the preferred speech-habits of educated middle-class and predominantly white people brought up in the USA. (Beyond that, the ideal reflects the principles governing a specific communicational activity, therapy, which is not confined to the USA but is particularly culturally salient there.) I know of no case in which the communicative norms of a non-Western, or indeed non-Anglophone society have been exported by expert consultants. Finns do not run workshops for British businesses on the virtues of talking less; Japanese are not invited to instruct Americans in speaking indirectly. The discourse of 'global' communication is not a case of postmodern 'hybridity' or 'fusion'.

The relevance of the foregoing discussion to language *teaching* can be seen if we ask how the dissemination of 'global' norms for 'effective' communication is actually accomplished. The process of dissemination does not depend exclusively on the activities of experts like Judith

Kuriansky who produce texts for both professional and lay audiences, speak publicly via the media and provide consultancy services to organizations. At ground level, dissemination is accomplished through instruction and training in particular linguistic practices. Forms of instruction and training which aim to develop 'communication skills', typically defined in terms of the discourse outlined above, are increasingly common in all kinds of contemporary institutions, ranging from elementary schools to multinational corporations.

Here it might be objected that these forms of instruction are quite different from what is usually meant or implied by 'language teaching', and certainly from the kind of language teaching with which this book is mainly concerned, namely the teaching of foreign or second languages. Communication skills training is not necessarily directed at second language learners specifically: many or most recipients are either native monolingual or highly proficient bilingual speakers of the language in which (and through which) they are learning to 'communicate'. On the other hand, there are forms of instruction, many of them in the category of language teaching for specific purposes or for business, which incorporate concerns like 'negotiation', 'meeting skills', 'presentation skills', etc., into programmes aimed at particular groups of L2 learners such as managers in multinational companies. In future it seems probable that a communication skills element will be incorporated into L2 teaching for less elite occupational groups, for instance those who work or aspire to work in the internationalized service sector (as Monica Heller remarks (2002), many entry-level service jobs in tourism, travel, leisure and hospitality demand foreign language competence). In sum, just as I have already argued that globalization poses a challenge to prevailing ideas about 'linguistic imperialism', perhaps it also demands that we revisit our assumptions about the nature and scope of 'language teaching'.

But to bring out the full force of this argument it is necessary to place the notion of 'communication skills' in a broader context than I have done so far. An illuminating analysis of 'communication skills' and the associated instructional practices must take account of how 'skills' are in general defined and what place they occupy in contemporary discourse on teaching and learning. It is also important to look closely at what 'communication' means in that discourse, and how it has come to be categorized as a 'skill'. Below, I will suggest that current understandings of 'skills', of 'communication' and of the relationship between them are themselves products of globalization: they are related on one hand to changes in the organization of work driven by intensified economic competition, and on the other to changing conceptions of knowledge in the wake of the information revolution.

Communication, 'skills' and the 'new work order'

'Communication' is among the keywords of the global age, just as it was a keyword, though with a different set of meanings, in the age of the industrial revolution (Williams 1983: 72–3). In contemporary usage we hear and read frequent references to '[information and] communication technologies (ICTs)' and '[mass] communications media', both of which, of course, are implicated in the processes of globalization. Global markets depend on the rapid information flows made possible by ICTs, while media corporations (like Disney and News International) are powerful players in those markets, whose products also contribute to globalization at the cultural level. When the word 'communication' collocates with 'skills', however, the reference is rarely if ever to computers, the Internet or satellite TV. Rather it is usually to the oldest, least technologized and least mediated of all communication channels: spoken interaction, or talk.

In support of this claim we might note that in surveys undertaken to assess which skills are needed to maximize employability, employers almost invariably distinguish 'communication *depends to IT*

sales

skills' from 'literacy' and 'ICT skills'. Furthermore, they consistently rate the 'communication skills' displayed by recruits to the workforce as *more important* than their literacy skills or their facility with ICTs – and also, in many cases, as less satisfactory. A survey reported in *People Management* in November 1997, for example, found that 'Oral communication was cited [by employers] as the most important soft skill but was perceived to be sorely lacking in recruits coming straight from further or higher education. While 91 per cent of respondents believed that this was an essential skill, only 32 per cent said it was present among this group'.

pressed
President

The obvious question here is why oral communication should be the object of so much concern. Why are key actors in the new economy – including politicians and policymakers as well as employees and other representatives of the commercial world – so preoccupied with something that used to be thought of as a mundane activity requiring little in the way of special 'skill', namely interacting with others via the medium of spoken language? The answer lies in what Gee *et al.* (1996) have called 'the new work order'. Although there is debate about the exact nature and extent of change, it is widely agreed that during the 1980s and 1990s there were important shifts in the conceptualization and the experience of work, reflecting the emergence of a deregulated, hyper-competitive, post-industrial, globalized economy. The resulting 'new work order' makes new demands on workers; Gee *et al.* are among a number of commentators (see also Fairclough 1992, and contributors to Cope and Kalantzis 2000) who draw attention to the specifically linguistic aspects of those demands.

It is true, of course, that linguistic abilities were an important factor in labour market stratification long before the current, global phase of capitalism. Individuals have long been, and still are, denied access to certain kinds of work because of their inability to read and write, or to use a standard language rather than a non-standard dialect, or to speak the dominant language of a multilingual society. But whereas the industrial economy required large numbers of manual workers, who were colloquially referred to as 'hands' and whose language skills were seen as largely irrelevant, the new capitalism is different. For one thing it is dominated by forms of work in which language-using is an integral part of almost every worker's function. In his influential text *The Work of Nations*, former USA Labor Secretary Robert Reich (1992) suggested that the traditional 'manual/non-manual' distinction was in the process of being superseded by a new division of labour, in which an elite class of 'symbolic analysts' – creative professionals skilled in the manipulation of words, numbers, images and digital bits – would dominate a much larger and less privileged group of workers providing routine services, either 'in person' or behind the scenes. While the work done by these service providers is not necessarily any more creative or demanding than traditional manual work, it does put more pressure on literacy skills (since service work often requires extensive data inputting and record keeping) and more generally, interpersonal communication skills (being pleasant and attentive to customers and clients in face-to-face talk or on the telephone). The implication, at least in those economically advanced societies where manufacturing industries are in decline while the service and creative industries are expanding rapidly, is that individuals will need a relatively high level of linguistic skill if they are to participate in waged labour at all.

Because of these developments there has been a marked 'skilling up' of talk at work. In the rhetoric and practice of many institutions; talking has been promoted from a taken-for-granted social accomplishment of all normal humans to a complex task requiring special effort to master. At the same time, mastery of this task is expected of workers across the occupational and social spectrum. Consider, for instance, part of the 'person specification' for a job in the UK's National Health Service (taken from *The Medical Monitor*, 1994). The ideal recruit is defined as someone who can, *inter alia*:

- demonstrate sound interpersonal relationships and an awareness of the individual clients' psychological and emotional needs;
- understand the need for effective verbal and non-verbal communication;
- support clients and relatives in the care environment by demonstrating empathy and understanding.

One might suppose that this advertisement is aimed at members of one of the 'caring professions' – perhaps the hospital is seeking a medical social worker or a clinical psychologist. In fact, the job on offer is that of a hospital orderly: in other words, a cleaner. There is, of course, nothing new or surprising in the assumption that hospital cleaners will talk to patients. But specifications like the one just quoted change what was previously understood as an informal, 'natural' and, in this context, incidental activity into a formalized professional responsibility. And this formalization of workers' responsibility to 'communicate' not only changes the status of the activity denoted by 'communication', it also implies that there are standards for the performance of that activity. Communication becomes not just something workers are required to do, but something they are expected to be, or become, *good at*. What counts as 'good' is defined by the institution: in the hospital case, for instance, the specification suggests that a cleaner must have particular conversational abilities (e.g. 'demonstrating empathy and understanding') and be able to give a quasi-theoretical account of why these abilities are important ('understand the need for effective verbal and nonverbal communication'). Defining what kinds of talk employees must be able to produce in a given workplace context (e.g. 'demonstrating empathy') makes it possible to consider designing instructional programmes in which those ways of talking are explicitly taught.

The practice of instructing people in speaking and listening is also gaining ground in educational institutions, not least because of politicians' and policymakers' concern that education should prepare students to meet the needs of the new economy. As I have noted already, employers who are asked to specify their needs consistently stress that what matters to them is not the specialist subject knowledge new recruits bring with them from education, but transferable or 'key' skills – among which oral communication skills are ranked as particularly important. Discussing the educational consequences of the 'enterprise culture' promoted by Margaret Thatcher's administration in Britain during the 1980s, Norman Fairclough notes 'a general shift towards seeing knowledge operationally, in terms of competence . . . and towards seeing education as training in skills' (1995: 239). In retrospect, Thatcherite 'enterprise culture' can be seen as part of the early stages of globalization; as that process has advanced, the emphasis placed on skills has become even more marked. There has been a move towards incorporating skills more explicitly into the educational curriculum, especially in post-compulsory education (in the UK this means education after the age of 16). For example, students following advanced level academic courses which qualify them for university entrance will in future be required to produce a portfolio demonstrating competence in communication (both oral and written), application of number and the use of ICTs. National Vocational Qualifications (NVQs), for which instruction is partly workplace-based and partly college-based, also include communication as one 'area of competence' in which students are assessed.

Yet it would be wrong to suggest that the present preoccupation with communication skills is solely a reflex of recent and ongoing changes in the economic sphere, or that instruction in oral communication is a purely vocational enterprise aimed at increasing the employability of entrants to the labour market. On the contrary, it may be argued that in its attitudes to communication, the new capitalism has followed rather than led, borrowing many of its ideas and techniques from what could loosely be called 'self-improvement culture'. That culture is also the locus for a good deal of informal (non-institutional) instruction in oral communication skills, undertaken by individuals voluntarily and for personal rather than professional reasons. Contemporary attitudes to 'communication' – and contemporary approaches to teaching it – cannot be fully understood without reference to the culture of self-improvement.

Communication and the culture of self-improvement

What I am calling 'self-improvement culture' comprises a range of practices and text-types focusing on the individual and her or his relationships with others, and particularly on the problems of modern personal life. Among the most accessible expressions of this culture are self-help and popular psychology books, and broadcast talk shows of the 'confessional' type where people talk about their experiences, problems and feelings, sometimes receiving advice from an expert (a therapist, counsellor or psychologist). Large numbers of people are at least occasional consumers of this kind of material, and it is so ubiquitous in contemporary popular culture that it is difficult for anyone to remain entirely unfamiliar with it. More active forms of self-improvement include taking a course in something like assertiveness training or positive thinking, transactional analysis or neurolinguistic programming, being 'in therapy', or participating in groups with a quasi-therapeutic purpose, such as one of the twelve-step programmes of the 'recovery' movement (e.g. Alcoholics Anonymous). Commentators on the culture of self-improvement usually date its emergence as a salient phenomenon to the late 1960s and 1970s, and while some self-improvement activities have apparently declined since then (e.g. being in therapy for reasons of personal growth rather than clinical need); others (e.g. reading popular psychology books) have flourished and grown.

All the forms of self-improvement mentioned above place considerable emphasis on 'communication' (not surprisingly, since after all their roots are in therapy – the so-called 'talking cure'). Being able to 'communicate' – that is, talk openly and honestly about one's experiences and feelings, while listening non-judgementally to the talk of other people about *their* experiences and feelings – is held to be the key to solving problems and improving relationships with significant others. Many self-improvement activities not only emphasize this point in general terms, they also teach or model particular ways of 'communicating'. Assertiveness training for example teaches how to communicate 'honestly and directly' (e.g. by performing speech acts like refusals on record without mitigation); transactional analysis teaches trainees how to spot 'crossed' messages; twelve-step programmes model a particular narrative structure for presenting one's life experience (the story that begins 'I'm X and I'm an alcoholic').

Self-improvement practices concerned with 'communication' have had a direct and significant influence on the thinking and practice of the new capitalism. 'Therapeutic' approaches, particularly assertiveness training and transactional analysis, are widely used in workplace training. This is a good example of what Norman Fairclough calls 'the technologization of discourse' (Fairclough 1992), whereby communication techniques elaborated for a particular purpose are taken out of their original context and used for a quite different purpose. In the culture of self-improvement, people learn techniques for creating rapport for use in intimate personal relationships. In the business context these same techniques may be taught, but they will be used to *simulate* intimacy with customers to encourage them to buy, and then to return. Advocates of teaching oral communication skills in schools often refer approvingly to the idea that the same skills can be applied in many domains – they are not merely vocational skills, but 'life skills'. In the words of one advocate, 'all children benefit from learning skills that will make them better friends, better life-partners, better employees and better human beings' (Phillips 1998: 7).

The idea that communication skills training is capable of producing 'better human beings' can be linked with an argument put forward by the social theorist Anthony Giddens in his book *Modernity and Self-Identity* (1991). Giddens suggests that in 'late modern' societies – those which are furthest from 'traditional' or pre-modern ways of life – the individual self has become 'a reflexive project' – something the individual has to 'work on' rather than being able to take for granted. In traditional societies, people expect their own lives to follow a similar course to those of their parents; but in late modern societies the pace and extent of social change means that the experience of older generations does not provide a model for their children. Instead of being able to fit their experiences into a pre-existing social narrative, late modern individuals have to construct their own story. Hence the popularity of therapy and quasi-therapeutic activities which offer guidance on how to do this. Giddens also points out that in a highly mobile and individualistic culture where people no longer spend their whole lives in the same close-knit communities, the formation of intimate relationships presents particular challenges. In a world of strangers, people do not know who you are until you tell them. This, Giddens suggests, is another reason why late modern cultures place such emphasis on 'communication skills', and most especially, on the skills of self-expression and mutual self-disclosure.

Current concerns about 'communication' (in the sense of 'spoken interaction') are underpinned by a complex set of factors. New ideas about the nature of work and the demands it places on workers, recent trends towards skill-based or competence-led curricula in education, and therapeutic notions of the self as a reflexive project requiring work to perfect, all contribute to the increasing sense that speaking and listening, long taken for granted as things everyone could do 'naturally' without special help, are in need of more explicit and systematic attention. At this point, then, we must turn to the question of what form that attention actually takes – what is taught under the heading of communication skills, how it is taught, and what problems are raised by the enterprise.

Teaching talk in L1 – a curious enterprise?

Earlier in this chapter I pointed out that communication skills training is often aimed at L1 users rather than L2 learners. The examples I studied, some of which I will refer to here, were all designed on the assumption that trainees would be adults with native or native-like fluency in English. But this points to a striking peculiarity of oral communication skills training: it casts a group of people who would normally be considered fully competent linguistically and communicatively (adult native speakers) as needing expert assistance with an activity they have been performing since early childhood (interacting verbally with others). This is a case of what Giddens (1991) describes as the incursion of 'expert systems' into areas where previously people's ability to do things was acquired informally through observation and direct experience. Among Giddens's own examples is 'parenting', an activity (raising children) which now supports a huge expert literature and a cadre of specialist professionals, whereas not long ago knowledge about it was largely experiential and transmitted informally from older to younger generations (especially from mothers to daughters). The growth of expert systems in any domain tends to promote the attitude that knowledge acquired without expert support is somehow insufficient to meet contemporary standards (parenting is, again, a good example of this tendency). In the sphere of 'communication', the increasing salience of expert knowledge leads to native speakers being treated, for some purposes at least, almost as though they were second language learners. There are, of course, much older traditions of instruction in spoken first language-use for specific purposes: classical rhetoric, for example, which prepared citizens of ancient Greece and Rome to participate in political and legal discourse; or more recently, the training given to lawyers in courtroom advocacy, ministers of religion in preaching, politicians in public oratory and therapists in non-directive counselling techniques. These forms of spoken discourse were and still are viewed as appropriate objects for formal instruction because they are part of the arcane knowledge of a particular profession: their conventions are unlikely to have been picked up in the course of everyday experience. But the kind of instruction in communication skills which I am concerned with here focuses on much more ordinary kinds of spoken interaction, and often on what might be considered quite basic and elementary aspects of communicative competence.

Consider, for instance, the fairly widespread practice (especially in workplace training) of teaching 'listening skills'. In the workplaces whose training I looked at (shops, supermarkets and call centres), listening was an object of considerable concern.[2] Many of the managers and trainers I talked to, as well as the authors of widely used training materials, believed that many people had great difficulty with listening because they had never been instructed in the relevant skills. In the words of one organization which required all employees to undergo training in what it called 'expanded listening', 'as important as listening is, it's the one communication skill we're never really taught'. Several organizations' training materials that I looked at stated that 'most people listen at a 25% level of efficiency' — though it was not made clear either how this statistic was arrived at or what it actually means. One organization had adopted a 'four-stage model' of listening — 'hearing, understanding, interpreting, responding' — and trainees were required to work through these stages in response to a prompt, by verbalizing each in turn. Communication trainers used various other classroom activities to promote better listening comprehension. For example, at one call centre whose training programme informants described to me, trainees worked in pairs, taking it in turn to read out a set of increasingly complicated instructions which their partner then had to repeat back accurately from memory.

As well as the ability to decode and retain information accurately, training in listening also covers the ability to demonstrate to an interlocutor that you are listening to them and understanding what they say. This is a particular concern in the context of telephone service, since the absence of visual cues makes it more important to demonstrate listening verbally; but I encountered the same concern in workplaces like supermarkets where contact between staff and customers is face-to-face. Training addresses the issue by explicitly teaching strategies like using minimal responses, asking clarification questions, paraphrasing and making checks to confirm you have understood the customer correctly. Here for instance is a listening skills checklist taken from a training manual used with call centre employees.

- Demonstrate that you are actively listening by your responses and your interest — make listening noises, e.g. *yes, I see, fine, I'm making notes.*
- Use your questioning skills to control the conversation at the same time enabling clients to communicate their messages logically.
- Ask specific questions.
- Use statements to clarify and give information.
- Paraphrase or repeat back your understanding of the client's requirements.
- Summarize to control the conversation and clarify the final position.
- Limit your own talking — you cannot talk and listen at the same time.

Some points on this list are expanded on elsewhere in the manual. The instruction 'use your questioning skills to control the conversation' refers back to an earlier unit describing different types of questions in English and their functions — yes/no questions, WH questions, disjunct either/or questions, tag questions, hypothetical questions. The idea is that different question forms will produce different kinds of answers from the customer. When the trainer has gone through the checklist, trainees are typically given a practice task, such as role-playing a phone call or an encounter with the customer, in which they try to use the recommended strategies.

The kind of instruction just described is based on the assumption that trainees are not already competent listeners, and moreover that this is the case because they have never previously been *taught* how to listen. From a linguist's perspective this is a strange assumption. It overlooks the possibility that most people are never taught to listen in their first language because they do not need to be: listening is a 'skill' extensively practised by hearing humans from infancy, and normal levels of exposure to spoken language input are sufficient to develop competence in it. No doubt some people on some occasions listen poorly, but this is more likely to reflect boredom or lack of motivation than some deep-seated deficiency in their ability to take in and interpret utterances produced by others. It is very unlikely that L1 users' problems with listening comprehension resemble, either in degree or in kind, the problems experienced by L2 learners whose knowledge of the target language is limited.

Nevertheless, the approaches used by trainers to develop communication skills might well remind us of approaches commonly used with second language learners. The activities described above include, for instance, structured listening comprehension tasks where the input becomes progressively more complex, and the provision of lists of forms that can be used for the same communicative function — asking a question, say — followed by a role-play exercise in which trainees practise using the various alternatives appropriately. The strategies taught under the heading of 'active listening' (such as paraphrasing, asking clarification questions and making confirmation checks) are examples of what the SLA literature calls 'negotiation for meaning': language teachers as well as communication trainers devise tasks which encourage the use of these strategies. Examining communication training materials, I was often struck by the resemblance they bore to a certain kind of foreign language teaching text. Some language textbooks contain units of work on topics like 'travelling' and 'going to the doctor': the unit starts with a fictional dialogue set in a railway station or a doctor's surgery, it introduces new vocabulary relevant to the topic, and then focuses on useful grammatical structures — in the travel case, for instance, time and place expressions useful for discussing your itinerary. Workplace communication training manuals, not dissimilarly, often contain units on topics like 'dealing with complaints' which include exemplary made-up dialogues and sections explaining which words, grammatical constructions and politeness formulae are appropriate in this particular communicative situation.

I am not suggesting that there are no differences between communication training manuals and language textbooks. But the resemblances which arguably do exist between them underline the point that communication training addressed to L1 users tends to assume a remarkably low level of communicative competence, the ability to make linguistic choices based on judgements of contextual appropriateness. There is also an assumption that the relevant choices need to be drawn explicitly to the speaker's attention, which implies that conscious knowledge *about* different language forms is necessary to ensure that the speaker in practice makes the 'appropriate' choice. Again, this is a curious assumption. How many adult speakers really need to be reminded that on the phone it is important to demonstrate attention using minimal responses — let alone have the relevant responses ('yes', 'OK', 'I see', etc.) modelled for them to practise? Who needs to be told that statements are used for giving information whereas questions are more appropriate for eliciting it? I was not surprised to find, in interviews with communication trainees, that many were critical of some parts of their training on the grounds that these just 'stated the obvious' and were to that extent a waste of time.

But wasting trainees' time on low-level skills is not the only or the most serious problem raised by communication skills training. At this point we must return to the more broadly *ideological* implications of what is taught under the heading of 'good' or 'effective' communication.

Effective communication – effective for who and for what?

Any kind of language instruction depends on selecting and codifying (systematically writing down in the form of rules) the particular linguistic norms that will be transmitted to learners; deciding what kind of grammar or pronunciation will be adopted as a model, or what style and level of formality will be presented as the norm. Language-teaching, then, especially when carried out on a relatively large scale, both requires and contributes to the process of language standardization, which may be defined in the terms of Milroy and Milroy (1998: 47) as 'the suppression of optional variability'.

The teaching of 'communication skills', just like grammar teaching or elocution teaching, clearly has normative and standardizing effects. In at least some workplaces, one explicit goal of communication training is to reduce or even eliminate variation in people's ways of interacting. Just as many organizations insist that their employees wear a uniform or observe a strict dress code, so an increasing number insist that employees subordinate their own linguistic personae to a centrally-designed corporate linguistic persona. Speech, like appearance, is treated as act aspect of 'branding', and in order to ensure that customers get a consistent experience of the brand, employees are required to deliver standard verbal routines in an approved style; at the extreme, they may have to follow a script specifying the correct form of words exhaustively.

The normative/standardizing impulse can also take less obviously coercive forms, however. Recall, for instance, the person specification I quoted earlier, stating that applicants for the job of a hospital cleaner should be able to 'demonstrate empathy and understanding'. This statement, like many other statements of the same kind (for instance the criteria used to assess communication skills in examinations like Britain's NVQs), represents a value judgement, on the basis of which a norm is constructed: it defines 'demonstrating empathy' as an aspect of good communication. There are many other communicative abilities to which the specification could have referred, but does not (e.g. 'be able to tell a joke' or 'be capable of defending yourself in an argument'). By implication, these abilities are not valued in the same way as 'demonstrating empathy'. As more and more organizations (businesses, hospitals, schools and colleges, public examination boards, etc.) institute programmes of instruction and assessment for spoken communication, and as this in turn obliges them to codify its norms, it is likely that an increasing consensus will emerge about what constitutes 'effective communication'.

This consensus will not be socially, culturally or ideologically neutral. Just as in the case of grammar or pronunciation, a standard for 'effective communication' is always in practice based on habits and values which are not cultural universals, but are specific to a particular cultural milieu. And just as in the case of grammar and pronunciation, the effect of institutionalizing some people's preferred practices as norms will be to define large numbers of other people as inadequate or 'substandard' communicators.

The potential for ethnocentrism here is particularly obvious. Much expert discourse about interpersonal communication is produced by psychologists, therapists and counsellors; though this kind of expertise is by now widely diffused, its roots are in Western modernity with its rational, goal-oriented and individualistic outlook. Many of the communicative strategies which are most enthusiastically advocated by experts in this tradition, such as speaking directly (the key recommendation of assertiveness training) and engaging in open self-disclosure, are problematic in cultures whose notions of personhood and modes of social organization diverge markedly from the Western/Anglo mode. Ethnographers and sociolinguists have documented the very considerable variation that exists in cultural attitudes to, say, reticence versus verbosity, what levels of directness or of verbal aggression are considered normal or tolerable, how and in what circumstances emotion may be expressed or personal information disclosed, how parents should relate to children, and so on.[3] But many experts continue to give the impression that they regard['] their own norms as universal desiderata – the standard for 'effective communication' rather than one possible, culturally and contextually specific version of it.

As multinational corporations and Western consultants extend their sphere of influence, there is every reason to think that particular, and basically American (US), norms of interaction are being exported to other parts of the world, even when no attempt is made to export the English language itself. In Hungary, for example, since the end of the communist era there has been an influx of Western business organizations, and controversy has been caused by the insistence of some of these multinationals that customers be addressed (in Hungarian) using the informal, egalitarian style which is the norm in most Western companies, though this flouts local expectations and well-established rules of Hungarian usage.[4] In Western Europe, small examples of American service-speak overlaying native conventions are routinely observable. British servers now say 'How may I help you?' when in the past they said 'Can I help you?'; French market traders end transactions by wishing *you bonne journée.* (On the other hand, an initiative whereby Scottish supermarket customers were greeted at the entrance by a staff-member who handed them a basket and exhorted them to 'enjoy your shopping experience' had to be abandoned because of the ridicule it occasioned.)

It may well be objected that the above examples, involving formulaic routines in service contexts, are trivial; I do not dispute it. What is not trivial, however, is the ideology of communication, of which these globalized politeness formulas are only the most superficial expressions: 'it is essential that there be a uniform way of talking . . . and there are rules for that'. If, as this chapter has suggested, 'communication' is emerging as the supreme value of language teaching, for first language users as well as second language learners, then it is crucial for language teaching professionals to engage with questions about what kinds of communication are valuable. Such questions are just as significant, politically speaking, as questions about which actual languages) should serve as means of communication in a globalized world.

Notes

1 Dr Kuriansky is a clinical psychologist and therapist, who is also known to a large audience in the LISA as 'Dr Judy', broadcaster and author of several popular advice texts.
2 Throughout this chapter I follow a general policy of not naming, or giving details about, the organizations whose training materials and practices I examined. No organization whose permission I sought agreed to the use of its real name in published work, on the grounds that this might compromise commercial interests. In addition, some materials were obtained and examined without the knowledge of anyone who had the authority to grant or withhold permission. In these cases I have placed my obligation to protect my informants above my obligation to reveal my sources for the benefit of other scholars.
3 A good selection of classic ethnographic work on these topics may be found in Bauman and Sherzer (1974) (includes contributions on silence and directness); Brown and Levinson (1987) (politeness across cultures); Lutz and Abu-Lughod (1980) (the expression of emotion across cultures); Schieffelin and Ochs (1986) (carer-child interaction across cultures).
4 Thanks to Erika Sólyom for information on this topic.

References

Bauman, R. and Sherzer, J. (eds) (1974) *Exploration in the Ethnography of Speaking*, Cambridge: Cambridge University Press.

Brown, P. and Levinson, S. (1987) *Politeness: some universals in language use*, Cambridge: Cambridge University Press.

Cameron, D. (2000) *Good to Talk? Living and Working in a Communication Culture*, London: Sage.

Canagarajah, A. S. (1999) *Resisting Linguistic Imperialism in English Teaching*, Oxford: Oxford University Press.

Cope B. and Kalantzis, M. (eds) *Multiliteracies: literacy learning and the design of social futures*, London: Routledge.

Eco, U. (1995) *The Search for the Perfect Language*, trans. J. Fentress, Oxford: Blackwell.

Fairclough, N. (1992) *Discourse and Social Change*, Cambridge: Polity Press.

—— (1995) *Critical Discourse Analysis*, London: Longman.

Gee, J. P., Hull, G. and Lankshear, C. (1996) *The New Work Order: behind the language of the new capitalism*, Boulder, CO: Westview Press.

Giddens, A. (1991) *Modernity and Self-Identity: self and society in the late modern age*, Cambridge: Polity.

Heller, M. (2002) Globalization and the commodification of bilingualism in Canada. In David Block and Deborah Cameron (eds) *Globalization and Language Teaching*. London: Routledge, pp. 47–63.

Kramsch, C. and Thorne, S. L. (2002) Foreign languge learning as global communicative practice. In David Block and Deborah Cameron (eds) *Globalisation and Language Teaching*. London: Routledge, pp. 83–100.

Kubota, R (2002). The impact of globalization on language teaching in Japan. In David Block and Deborah Cameron (eds) *Globalisation and Language Teaching*. London: Routledge, pp. 13–28.

Lutz, C. and Abu-Lughod, L. (eds) (1980) *Language and the Politics of Emotion*, Cambridge: Cambridge University Press.

Milroy, J. and Milroy, L. (1998) *Authority in Language* (third edition), London: Routledge.

Pennycook, A. (1994) *The Cultural Politics of English as an International Language*, London: Longman.

Philips, A. (1998) *Communication: a key skill for education*, London: BT Forum.

Phillipson, R. (1992) *Linguistic Imperialim*, Oxford: Oxford University Press.

Reich, R. (1992) *The Work of Nations*, New York: Vintage.

Schieffelin, B. and Ochs, E. (1986) *Language Socialization Across Cultures*, Cambridge: Cambridge University Press.

Wallace , C. (2002) Local literacies and global literacy. In David Block and Deborah Cameron (eds) *Globalisation and Language Teaching*. London: Routledge, pp. 101–114.

Williams, R. (1983) *Keywords: a vocabulary of culture and society*, London: Fontana.

NOTES FOR STUDENTS AND INSTRUCTORS

Study questions

1 What does *investment* mean in Norton's terms? In what way is it different from *motivation*?
2 According to Block, how might the post-structuralist approach to identity be problematic? What is the difference between identity and identification?
3 In what way has the transfer of the concept of communicative competence from research to language teaching produced 'abstracted contexts and idealized social rules of use', as suggested by Leung?
4 How are the three identity components – gender, class and race – that are discussed by Kubota related to each other? What are the alternative approaches to these identity issues in applied linguistics?
5 What is Symbolic Competence? How does it differ from Communicative Competence?
6 Why does Cameron call effective communication a 'global ideology'? What are the manifestations of this ideology in the context of workplace communication and language teaching and learning?

Study activities

1 Interview some language learners and ask them how they would identify themselves. What are the salient factors they mention in their self-identification, e.g. age, gender, country or place of origin, ethnicity, education level, socio-economic class, occupation, social networks? Discuss with them how identity affects their language learning. Can you notice any specific language behaviour that can be interpreted as an act of identity?
2 Explore the issue of literacy in your own country, culture or community. To what extent is the level of literacy related to gender and socio-economic class?
3 Find a multilingual speaker and observe his or her use of languages in different contexts. Which of the three concepts – communicative competence, multicompetence, symbolic competence – best account for the speaker's multilingual practice?

Further reading

Norton, Bonny, 2000, *Identity and Language Learning: gender, ethnicity and educational change*, Harlow: Longman, looks at how changing identities of the learner affect the process of learning a second language, and considers how language teachers can address the complex histories of language learners by integrating research, theory, and classroom practice.

Norton, Bonny, and Toohey, Kelleen (eds) 2004, *Critical Pedagogies and Language Learning*, Cambridge: Cambridge University Press, addresses such topics as critical multiculturalism, gender and language learning, and popular culture. The contributors examine the meaning of creating equitable and critical instructional practices, by exploring diverse representations of knowledge. In addition, recommendations are made for further research, teacher education and critical testing.

Norton, Bonny, and Pavlenko, Aneta (eds), 2004, *Gender and English Language Learners*, Alexandria, VA: TESOL Publications, is a collection of studies focusing on the issue of gender in English language teaching.

Block, David, 2003, *The Social Turn in Second Language Acquisition*, Edinburgh: Edinburgh University Press, argues for the need for SLA researchers to widen the research agenda by adopting a more multi-disciplinary and socially informed perspective.

Block, David, 2007, *Second Language Identities*, London: Continuum, examines how identity is an issue in different second-language-learning contexts.

Block, David, 2006, *Multilingual Identities in a Global City: London stories*, Basingstoke: Palgrave, is an in-depth study of the linguistic, national, ethnic, social class and gendered identities of individuals living in London at the beginning of the twenty-first century.

Kubota, Ryuko, 2004, The politics of cultural difference in second language education. *Critical Inquiry in Language Studies*, 1 (1), 21–39, critically examines how different social categories are implicated in second language education.

Lin, Angel, Grant, Rachel, Kubota, Ryuko, Motha, Suhanthie, Sachs, Gertrude Tinker, Vandrick, Stephanie and Wong, Shelly, (2004), Women faculty of color in TESOL: Theorizing our lived experiences. *TESOL Quarterly*, 38 (3), 487–504, focuses on the issues of race and gender.

Kubota, Ryuko and Lin, Angel (eds), 2006, Race and TESOL. *TESOL Quarterly*, 40, (3), is a special issue on gender in English language teaching.

Leung, Constant (ed.), 2002, *Language and Additional/Second Language Issues for School Education: a reader for teachers,* Watford: National Association for Language Development in the Curriculum (NALDIC), provides guidelines to teachers on the issues of diversity and competence in language teaching.

Leung, Constant and Creese, Angela (eds), 2010, *English as an Additional Language: approaches to teaching linguistic minority students*, London: Naldic/Sage, is a resource book for teachers working with English as an additional language students on the issues of communication and participation in language learning.

Kramsch, Claire (ed.), 2002, *Language Acquisition and Language Socialization: ecological perspectives continuum*, brings together well-known scholars in two relatively distinct fields – language acquisition and language socialization – to describe language development from a relational perspective.

Kramsch, Claire, 2009, *The Multilingual Subject*, Oxford: Oxford University Press, explores the subjective aspects of the language learning experience, and looks at the relationship between symbolic form and the development of a multilingual subjectivity; links with memory, emotion, and the imagination; and the implications for language teaching pedagogy.

Cameron, Deborah, 2000, *Good to Talk? Living and Working in a Communication Culture,* London: Sage, is an attempt to look critically at what lies behind the upsurge of concern about talk in our workplaces, classrooms and private lives, and places these developments in historical context and relates their forms to the broader economic and social changes associated with globalization.

Block, David and Cameron, Deborah, (eds) 2001, *Globalization and Language Teaching,* Oxford: Routledge, considers the issues globalization raises for second language learning and teaching in an economy where the linguistic skills of workers is becoming increasingly important.

Other publications of interest include:

Pavlenko, Aneta, Blackledge, Adrian, Piller, Ingrid and Teutsch-Dwyer, Marya, 2001, *Multilingualism, Second Language Learning and Gender.* Berlin: Mouton de Gruyter.

Edwards, John, 2009, *Language and Identity.* Cambridge: Cambridge University Press.

Riley, Philip, 2007, *Language, Culture and Identity.* London: Continuum.

Omoniyi, Tope and White, Goodith (eds), 2006, *Sociolinguistics of Identity*. London: Continuum.
Fought, Carmen, 2006, *Language and Ethnicity*. Cambridge: Cambridge University Press.
Fishman, Joshua and Garcia, Ofelia (eds), 2010, *Handbook of Language and Ethnic Identity: Disciplinary and Regional Perspectives*. Oxford: Oxford University Press.

PART IV

Applied linguistics in a changing world

Introduction

APPLIED LINGUISTICS IS OFTEN DESCRIBED as a problem-solving approach to real-world problems of language and communication. In the General Introduction, I raised the question of what problems can applied linguistics actually help to solve. The articles in this Part of the Reader showcase some of the examples of applied linguistics at work.

John Flowerdew in Chapter 19 presents a case study of an English-as-a-second-language-speaking scholar from Hong Kong and his experience in publishing a scholarly article in an international refereed journal on his return from doctoral study in the United States. While addressing the practical question of what it means to be a non-anglophone researcher seeking international publication in English but living and researching in a non-anglophone country, Flowerdew also raises the critical issues of *discourse community* and *learning as participation*. He applies elements of the social constructivist theory to interpret the difficulties the writer experiences. He also considers the role that TESOL may play in addressing these difficulties.

Tim McNamara in Chapter 20 deals with language assessment as social practice. He argues that a growing awareness of the fundamentally social character of language assessment challenges us to rethink our priorities and responsibilities in language testing research. This awareness has been brought about by the treatment of the social character of educational assessment in Samuel Messick's (1989) influential work on validity, and by the intellectual changes triggered by postmodernism, where models of individual consciousness have been reinterpreted in the light of socially motivated critiques. McNamara concludes by arguing that the institutional character of assessment often means that the needs of learners are not well served by much language assessment theory and practice, and calls for a re-examination of our research priorities.

The article by Patricia Duff, Ping Wong and Margaret Early in Chapter 21 was first published in *The Canadian Modern Language Review* and reprinted in *The Modern Language Journal* as an article exchange between the two publications. The criteria for the exchange include relevance to international readers and likelihood to provoke scholarly discussion among readers. In the article, Duff, Wong and Early present a qualitative study of an English as a second language program for immigrant men and women in Western Canada seeking to become long-term resident care aides or home support workers. They examine the linguistic and social processes at work in the education and integration of immigrant ESL speakers into the work-force and the broader community; the issues participants in such programs face; and the insights that can be gleaned for understanding language socialization in this context. They pay particular attention to the contrast observed in one such program between the focus on medical and general English language proficiency, as well as nursing skills, and the actual communication require-ments within institutions with large numbers of staff and patients who do not speak English, and who, in the case of the elderly, may also face communication difficulties associated with ageing, illness and disability. Implications for future research and curriculum development are discussed.

Chapter 22 by Nancy Hornberger examines language policies in multilingual societies. She argues that the one language–one nation ideology of language policy and national identity is no longer the only available one worldwide, if it ever was. Multilingual language policies, which recognize ethnic and linguistic pluralism as resources for nation-building, are increasingly in evidence. These policies, many of which envision implementation through bilingual intercultural education, open up new worlds of possibility for oppressed indigenous and immigrant languages and their speakers, transforming former homogenizing and assimilationist policy discourses into discourses about diversity and emancipation. Hornberger uses the metaphor of ecology of language to explore the ideologies underlying multilingual language policies, and the continua of a/the biliteracy framework as ecological heuristic for situating the challenges faced in implementing them. Specifically, she considers community and classroom challenges inherent in implementing these new ideologies, as they are evident in two nations which introduced transformative policies in the early 1990s: post-apartheid South Africa's new Constitution of 1993 and Bolivia's National Education Reform of 1994. She also discusses the implications for multilingual language policies in the United States and elsewhere.

Chapter 23 by Christina Schaffner demonstrates how the disciplines of Translation Studies (TS) and Political Discourse Analysis (PDA) can benefit from closer cooperation between each other. Political discourse very often relies on translation. Schaffner begins the article by presenting examples of actual translations of political texts, commenting on them from the point of view of TS. These examples concern the political effects caused by specific translation solutions; the processes by which information is transferred via translation to another culture; and the structure and function of equally valid texts in their respective cultures. She then outlines the scope for interdisciplinary cooperation between PDA and TS. This is illustrated with reference to an awareness of the product features, multilingual texts, process analysis, and the politics of translation.

In Chapter 24, Janet Maybin and Joan Swann examine the issue of creativity in everyday language use. Applied linguists have argued that creativity is not only a property of especially skilled and gifted language users, but is pervasive in routine everyday practice. They have investigated literariness, language play and humour as examples of linguistic creativity. Such a broad approach has led to a more general refocusing within applied linguistics on language users as creative designers of meaning. Building on the existing work on linguistic creativity, Maybin and Swann call for a more dynamic model which can address the dialogical nature of everyday creativity, its socio-historical dimensions and processes of contextualization. In order to suggest how such a model could be developed, the authors draw on Russian socio-historical conceptions of the evaluative function of language as a social sign and bring together the applied linguistic research with work from linguistic anthropology on contextualization, framing and reflexivity within performance. They argue that while linguistic anthropologists have focused mainly on traditional oral art, the framing and critical potential of performance is also keyed by more fleeting uses of poetic language in everyday interaction. Using four contrasting examples of data, Maybin and Swann suggest how an integrated analytical framework might be developed which addresses textual, contextual and critical dimensions of creativity.

Chapter 25 by Aneta Pavlenko won the 2009 TESOL award for distinguished research. It presents a case study of a police interrogation of a speaker of English as a second language. Pavlenko shows that the high linguistic and conceptual complexity of police cautions, such as the Miranda warnings – warnings that are required to be given by police in the United States to criminal suspects before they are interrogated, to inform them about their constitutional rights – complicates the understanding of these texts even by English-as-a-second-language speakers with a high level of interactional competence. She argues that the US criminal justice system should accommodate speakers of English at all proficiency levels by adopting a bilingual standard, that is, by offering the Miranda warnings in English and in a standardized translation into the speaker's native language. She further argues that common legal terms, concepts and texts need to find a place in the adult English as a second language curriculum.

The final chapter in this Part by Guy Cook, Matt Reed and Alison Twiner examines the discourse of organic food promotion and the convergence of commercial and political discourses. As the organic food market has grown, campaigners and independent producers have faced the dilemma of how far they should promote their cause using standard marketing language. Cook, Reed and Twiner report on a research project which combined corpus analysis, interviews and focus group discussions to investigate the discourse of organic food promotion in Britain, the thinking behind it, and how people react to it. They found growing convergence across the sector. Whether produced by supermarkets, small politically committed producers, or environmentalist campaign groups, the language used tends to be poetic, vague, dialogic, narrative and emotive, with an emphasis upon bucolic imagery and consumer self-interest. Text producers assume that consumer attitudes can be easily manipulated by such an approach. Their focus group data however suggest both a critical resistance to marketing language in general, and that attitudes to food may be less amenable to manipulation through standard promotional techniques than is commonly assumed. Their findings contribute not only to an understanding of food politics and persuasive discourse more generally, but also to the development of a discourse analytic methodology which integrates textual analysis with an investigation of sender and receiver perceptions.

References

Messick, Samuel, 1989, Validity. In R.L. Linn (ed.), *Educational measurement* (third edition). New York: Macmillan, 13–103.

Chapter 19

JOHN FLOWERDEW

DISCOURSE COMMUNITY, LEGITIMATE PERIPHERAL PARTICIPATION AND THE NONNATIVE-ENGLISH-SPEAKING SCHOLAR (2000)

WITH THE EVER-INCREASING TREND towards international scholarly publication in English, an important question that has not been much addressed in the literature is the particular challenges to achieving publication that are presented to scholars whose L1 is not English. These nonnative-English-speaking scholars, it can be argued—other things being equal—are at a disadvantage vis-à-vis their native-English-speaking peers when it comes to writing up the results of their research for publication. There is a considerable literature on the role of TESOL in the preparation of students for graduate-level academic writing (see, e.g., Allison, Cooley, Lewkowicz, & Nunan, 1988, for a review), and manuals are available to assist in the writing of research papers (e.g., Swales & Feak, 1994; Weissberg & Buker, 1990). However, little, if any, attention has been paid to the potential role of TESOL in helping nonnative-speaking scholars after they have finished their academic study and are seeking to develop their academic careers. A few studies have touched on the problems experienced by such people, for example, Gosden's (1995, 1996) research into the publishing practices of young Japanese academics. In addition, within the field of TESOL, a number of recently published first-person accounts of the apprenticeship into scholarly writing offer advice to others drawn from the personal experience of their narrators (Connor, 1999; Li, 1999). Although these accounts offer some recommendations for TESOL, the field needs to learn more about the particular difficulties of nonnative-speaking scholars before a comprehensive agenda for helping them can be developed. There is a need, therefore, for more case studies of individual writers from different disciplines, countries, and sociocultural and linguistic backgrounds before TESOL can identify appropriate ways to help these people with their language problems.

Research in academic literacy has increasingly come to emphasise the importance of discourse communities in shaping the generic competence of young scholars (Bartholomae, 1985; Bizzell, 1982a, 1982b; Dias, 1994). Authors such as Swales (1990), Berkenkotter and Huckin (1995), Belcher (1994), Casanave (1995), and Dudley-Evans (1991) have investigated how novice scholars are inducted into their disciplinary discourse communities through various forms of apprenticeship. The notion of *discourse community* is relevant in the study of academic literacy because it stresses the participatory, negotiable nature of learning and the fact that learning is not always based on overt teaching. Most of the empirical case studies of academic literacy development based on the notion of discourse community have been concerned with native speakers (NSs), although Swales (1990) and Casanave (1995) are notable for their focus on nonnative speakers (NNSs).

Swales (1990) presented three cases of nonnative-speaking scholars developing their scholarly writing skills at the University of Michigan in the United States. Of the three, one planned to return to an academic career in her home country, Egypt. Swales's account of this scholar ended with her impending return. As Swales stated, however, "if [the subject's] story is going to contribute to what we know about being a non-anglophone researcher in the Third World the case study needs to continue" (p. 208). Unfortunately, to my knowledge, nobody has taken up the story of Swales's subject following her return to Egypt. Building on the pioneering work of Swales, however, this article presents a case study of another nonnative-speaking scholar and his experience of writing and publishing an article after his return home from doctoral study in the United States.

Because this research is basically ethnographic in nature, it does not begin with a pre-established set of research questions; rather, the key issues are developed out of the data. As the ethnographic account will make clear, these key issues include the importance of knowing the rules of the publishing "game," the mediated nature of the publication process, the importance of adapting content to fit the expectations of the journal, the problem of distinguishing the dividing line between content and form, and the problems of geographical isolation. The article argues that the concepts of *discourse community* and *legitimate peripheral participation* are important in understanding these issues involved in the process of NNSs' scholarly apprenticeship.

Theoretical background

Discourse communities

A discourse community is a group of people who share a set of social conventions that is directed towards some purpose (Swales, 1990). Casanave (1995) traces the concept to Kuhn (1970), who characterises it as consisting of the practitioners of a scientific speciality who share language, beliefs, and practices. Members are able to function as scientists, according to Kuhn, because they share "similar educations and professional initiations," because they have "absorbed the same technical literature and drawn many of the same lessons from it," because they share goals and professional judgments, and because their communication is "full" (cited in Casanave, 1995, p. 87). Swales lists six criteria for defining a discourse community: (a) common goals, (b) participatory mechanisms, (c) information exchange, (d) community-specific genres, (e) a highly specialized terminology, and (f) a high general level of expertise. To acquire membership in a discourse community, an individual has to learn the conventions that underpin Swales's six criteria. This is normally done by some form of formal or informal apprenticeship—Kuhn's *professional initiations*. Thus Bizzell (1982a, 1982b) and Bartholomae (1985) argue that students entering academic disciplines must learn the genres and conventions that are commonly employed by members of the disciplinary discourse community. As Berkenkotter and Huckin (1995) point out, students must also learn what Bazerman (1980, 1985) calls the *conversations of the discipline*, the issues and problems that are current at any one time. Such issues and problems are developed through study and collaboration on research projects with experienced practising scholars. In recent work, drawing on Bazerman (1988), among others, Prior (1998) has warned of some of the dangers of existing views of discourse communities, suggesting that the latter are not as homogeneous and closed as previously implied but are dynamic, open, subject to change, and made up of many subgroups, both large and small.

By means of fine-grained, *thick* descriptions (Geertz, 1973), researchers such as Myers (1985), Berkenkotter, Huckin, and Akerman (1988), Berkenkotter and Huckin (1993, 1995), and Prior (1998) have demonstrated how this process of gaining entry into the community and maintaining membership occurs. At the same time they have considered what factors are beneficial or otherwise in acquiring and maintaining the appropriate generic conventions.

As one example of such research, Myers (1985) conducted a study that showed how scientific texts are the products of a discourse community of researchers and not just of individuals. By comparing successive versions of proposals written by two biologists for research funding, Myers showed how, in writing and rewriting, these scientists both responded to and developed a disciplinary consensus.

As another example, in their study of a graduate student's writing development and his acquisition of discipline-specific text conventions, Berkenkotter and Huckin (1995) demonstrated how these conventions were linked to the learning of the research methodology employed by the disciplinary community. To achieve success in his writing, the student gradually abandoned the articulate but informal style he brought with him when he entered the programme, in favour of the more formal register that was required by the disciplinary community. Access to and acceptance by the disciplinary community are thus dependent upon the learning of the beliefs, values, and conventions that characterise that community.

In a further study, Berkenkotter and Huckin (1995, chapters 3, 4) turn their attention to an experienced scholar, demonstrating how an established expert also needed to observe the conventions of the chosen discourse community if she wanted to maintain her position by having her work published. The biologist involved in this study submitted an article to a journal whose introduction was considered by the reviewers to be lacking in the conventional literature review. It was only when the writer positioned her study in her introduction within the context of related scientific activity in the field that the paper was accepted for publication. Berkenkotter and Huckin thus show how experienced scholars who have already published widely may also need to continue to reflect the beliefs, values, and conventions of the target discourse community in order to maintain their position.

Prior (1998), based on ethnographic case studies, has further emphasised the "mediated" (p. 22) nature of academic writing, that is, how literary products do not emanate from a single author but are jointly constructed by various parties in addition to the actual writer, as he or she reads, discusses, revises collaboratively, and so on.

Legitimate peripheral participation

As the above examples show, the sort of knowledge that is required in order to be accepted by the discourse community in scholarly writing is not usually acquired in the formal setting of a classroom. Such learning is what Lave and Wenger (1991) refer to as *legitimate peripheral participation*—*legitimate*, because anyone is potentially a member of what Lave and Wenger call the *community of practice*, or discourse community; *peripheral*, because participants are not central but are on the margins of the activity in question; and *participation*, because learners are acquiring the knowledge through their involvement with it. Knowledge is thus a process, not a product. It is only valid when activated within the discourse community As Lave and Wenger put it, knowledge is acquired through "centripetal participation in the learning curriculum of the ambient community" (p. 100).

As the example of Berkenkotter and Huckin's (1995) experienced biologist demonstrates, such learning is also ongoing; even experienced scholars need to continually negotiate their position as members of the disciplinary community as that position is ratified by acceptance of their writing for publication. Bazerman's (1980, 1985) *conversations of the discipline* are ongoing; to maintain membership of the discourse community, therefore, scholars need to engage in continual legitimate peripheral participation. Learning is not a onetime process but continues throughout the life of a scholar.

One way of conceptualising graduate education is as the facilitation of legitimate peripheral participation for young scholars. Arguably, graduate students learn as much through the various opportunities for peripheral participation they are exposed to—working as members of research teams, interacting with their academic supervisors (who may act as mentors), submitting papers for publication, and communicating with journal editors and reviewers—as they do in the more formal, taught part of their courses, if not more than they do there. When doctoral graduates, having finished their studies, leave their prestigious research universities to take up positions in other, perhaps more isolated and less privileged institutions, the opportunities for peripheral participation are reduced. Writing about students within the United States, Geertz has labeled this phenomenon the *exile from paradise* syndrome (cited in Swales, 1990, p. 207). Emphasising the even greater plight of graduates who leave the United States, Swales maintains that the term *exile* in Geertz's formulation would be even more appropriate for NNSs returning to their home countries than for the U.S. graduates Geertz had in mind. The intellectual dislocation that accompanies such a return for NNSs is extreme.

Although legitimate peripheral participation and the related notion of discourse community are important, this does not mean that there is no place at all for formal training. As Lave (1998, p. 250) notes, instruction is not to be avoided. Rather, classroom time can be seen as an opportunity for facilitating and reflecting upon legitimate peripheral participation as opposed to an opportunity for the transmission of knowledge. I will return to this point in my conclusion.

The study

Purpose and context

The purpose of the study reported here was to examine the process a recently returned nonnative-English-speaking doctoral graduate went through in attempting to publish an academic paper in an international refereed journal in English. The study was carried out within the broader framework of a research project conducted over several years that sought to develop an understanding of the perceptions, problems, and strategies of Hong Kong Cantonese L1 academics in writing for publication in international refereed journals in English. The project was carried out by means of a quantitative survey of Cantonese L1 academics (Flowerdew, 1999d), interviews with Cantonese L1 academics (Flowerdew, 1999b), interviews with journal editors (Flowerdew, 1999a), a study of editorial correspondence conducted between journal editors and referees and Cantonese L1 contributors (Flowerdew & Dudley-Evans, 1999), and studies of the written work of Cantonese L1 academics (Flowerdew, 1999c).

Method

The method used in this investigation was, broadly speaking, ethnographic, with a single case study format. In order to examine the issue from a number of different perspectives and achieve an element of triangulation, I used several sources of data for the study. The central focal point of the analysis and point of orientation of the other sources were the various drafts and the final version of a paper published in the *XYZ Journal* (a pseudonym). The author of this paper was a young Hong Kong scholar, referred to here as Oliver (a pseudonym), who had recently returned from doctoral study in the United States. His field of study was mass communication. Other data sources were my in-depth interviews and e-mail communication with Oliver; correspondence between Oliver and the journal editor, reviewers, and the in-house editor who worked on the paper; field notes and a report written by an NS in Hong Kong who provided editorial assistance to Oliver; participant verification (Ball, 1988) of the final report by Oliver; my discussions throughout the case study with the research assistant/local editor (hereafter LE); and a written account produced by the LE.

The case study was conducted in Hong Kong over several months during 1998. As part of the full-scale project described above, the LE helped with data collection and analysis. He made himself available to provide editorial assistance to Hong Kong Cantonese L1 academics in return for their agreement to serve as possible subjects for a case study. Oliver was one of those people who agreed to participate in this exchange. In return for editorial assistance, Oliver provided various drafts and final versions of academic papers he had written and was interviewed on a number of occasions by both the LE and myself. He also provided copies of correspondence he had conducted with editors in connection with papers he had submitted for possible publication. A preliminary analysis of the articles and correspondence provided by Oliver suggested that a manageable case study could be conducted by focussing on just one article, which was an empirical public opinion survey study relating to Hong Kong's political transition from British to Chinese sovereignty.

Participant

Educational background. As indicated in interviews, Oliver had considerable exposure to English throughout his life. His first contact with the language was at kindergarten, when he was 3–4 years old. Following kindergarten, he went to an English-medium elementary school. After that he moved to an English-medium secondary school that was staffed primarily by Irish Jesuit priests. His undergraduate education was at a Hong Kong university that has a bilingual policy of teaching in Chinese or English. On graduation, he worked for a time. Later, for his MA and PhD, he moved to a major research university in the United States, where he had very little contact with non-English speakers either inside the university or outside, where he had friends in the local community living for 2 years with an American family. Oliver said that he considered both Chinese and English as his mother tongue.

It was clear from Oliver's account of his experiences in the United States that he had benefited greatly from the opportunities for legitimate peripheral participation provided in his PhD programme. In his courses he would work in small groups of five to six students, and every paper they produced was looked at thoroughly by a faculty member. Oliver described his advisor as a particularly important "mentor," who helped him "not just academically but personally" (I, author, December 15, 1998).[1] He worked with his advisor as both a teaching and research assistant. "I have to work at least 10 hours for my boss," Oliver told me in an interview, "and basically most of the stuff was his research—maybe I collect the data and make the first draft of the article for him and this is not course work." While working with Oliver, the advisor would correct his writing and tell him what his problems were. When asked in the same interview if he still kept in touch with his advisor and other mentors, Oliver answered, "definitely," adding that he was still collaborating with his advisor on papers and that he regularly sent articles to both his former advisor and a faculty member in political science. Prior to participating in this study, Oliver had published a number of international refereed articles, some as a single author and some coauthored with his advisor.

Attitude towards writing for publication in English. In line with the majority of Hong Kong scholars (Flowerdew, 1999d) and indeed scholars worldwide, it was very important for Oliver to publish in English. Academic tenure and promotion in Hong Kong are dependent upon publication in international refereed journals. Oliver did write in Chinese, but only if he was commissioned to do so. Publication in international journals (in English) is more important for career progression than publication in Chinese language journals, which are usually not refereed:

> I don't like to write in Chinese but not because I hate Chinese but simply the Chinese journals are not recognized—the English article will count more than the Chinese one.
>   (I, author, December 15, 1998)

In addition, because his research training had been in English, Oliver found it easier to write in that language: "I am used to writing in English journals, so it is more difficult to switch to Chinese" (I, author, December 15, 1998).

When asked how he had learned to write for publication in English, Oliver stated that he had learned "style and organization" (I, author, December 15, 1998) through research methods and graduate courses in the United States. The following statement regarding the difficulty some NNSs have in academic writing shows Oliver's awareness of the importance of writing in the appropriate academic register:

> I do want to say that some people after many years do not know how to write. They think with a very different perspective. I think it may be cultural. It simply doesn't fit the mentality of the Western reviewers, and every time I review their articles I have to change quite a bit, a large portion of the paper to bring more sense, to make it acceptable to the Western journals.
>   (I, author, December 15, 1998)

Oliver believed that it was difficult for Hong Kong scholars like him to publish in international journals:

> I think Hong Kong scholars to be published in international journals is real hard. I think first of all it's the language problem. I think the journal editors' first impression of your manuscript they discover that it is not written by a native speaker—no matter how brilliant your idea, they will have the tendency to reject.
>   (I, author, December 15, 1998)

In particular, Oliver took exception to journal reviewers who specifically identified him as an NNS:

> What makes me feel bad is I get letters from the reviewer, and in the first two sentences it will say this is definitely not written by a native speaker[2]—they shouldn't point this out as part of the main criteria for rejecting the article.
>   (I, author, December 15, 1998)

In addition to the language problem, however, Oliver experienced difficulties related to his isolation from the mainstream—Geertz's (1973) *exile from paradise* syndrome, Bazerman's (1980, 1985) *conversations of the discipline*, and Lave and Wenger's (1991) *legitimate peripheral participation*:

There is the language problem, but there is more than that. Hong Kong scholars submitting to the States are suffering from a lack of common dialogue from the mainstream. What I mean, when I was in the US, although I am a NNS, I don't feel the problem. I speak every day with them certain topics, but when I leave the States I lose that ability to link the hot topic, voice the politically correct voice. I should use this kind of subtle cross-cultural academic dialogue. It's also influencing the NNSs the non-American European scholars etc. who have to submit to these journals. . . . the less dialogue, the less good work you can produce in the mainstream journals. It is a circular spiral process . . . yes, being connected to the leading edge, and the further you get away the more you're not sure what's going on anymore . . . .

(I, author, December 15, 1998)

Although Oliver separates the isolation problem from the language problem in this statement, with his introductory "There is the language problem, but there is more than that," as his ensuing description of the difficulties of isolation reveals, this too is deeply linguistic. His multiple references to "dialogue," "topic," and "voice" in describing the problem of isolation make this very clear.

The importance of communication is again highlighted in the following response to a question about whether Oliver suffered difficulties in maintaining contact with the mainstream:

Well, definitely, when I was there [the United States] I could fly to the cities quite easily and maybe talk to them [other researchers], maybe even on a single paper, and I could go to local conferences, and at these conferences we discussed our papers, and I mean thoroughly. Now we can still communicate on e-mail, but it's not as deep as direct conversation.

(I, LE, March 31, 1998)

Oliver's attempt to publish his article

Context

At the time the study was conducted, Oliver had been working for a short time as an assistant professor at a Hong Kong university. This period was a particularly hectic one for Oliver. He was preparing for his PhD dissertation defence, which would take place in several months back in the United States, and his academic appointment would be up for renewal shortly. In order to have a good chance of renewal, Oliver needed to demonstrate that he had been successful in research and teaching. His research performance would be evaluated on the basis of how successful he had been in obtaining grant funding and in publishing in international refereed journals. His teaching would be evaluated on the basis of a teaching portfolio he would have to prepare, which would incorporate descriptions of the courses he had taught and the results of student and peer evaluation. At the same time as he was trying to publish the article that is the focus of this study, Oliver was undergoing a similar process with various other articles, most, although not all, of which were based on material in his recently completed PhD dissertation. This publication activity was in addition to starting up new research projects and developing and teaching new courses.

Article submission and revision

The process Oliver went through in writing and publishing his article is mapped out in the following chronology. The data for this analysis were collected jointly by the LE and myself.

November 1, 1996: Original draft completed. The original draft was worked on during the summer of 1996, although notes and data collection actually stretched back over a period of almost 4 years.

May 1997: Conference paper delivered at international conference in North America. Oliver indicated that he received little useful feedback on the paper at this conference (I, LE, March 31, 1998).

June–September 1997: Paper submitted to various journals. The journal selected for the initial submission of the paper was the premier first-tier journal in Oliver's primary academic area. Oliver received a rejection notice and believed that even with revisions the paper would not be published in this journal. He was anxious to establish an academic publishing record during 1997–1998 in order to prepare for reappointment. The second submission was to what Oliver described as a "third-tier" journal (I, LE, March 31, 1998). Here the response was that the paper, with revisions, would be considered. However, the publishing opportunities for the period 1997–1998 were already filled, and the editor said that he did not want to make Oliver wait (I, LE, March 31, 1998). He accordingly recommended that Oliver submit his paper to *XYZ Journal,* which was in fact more prestigious, being considered as first tier by both Oliver and a number of academics in the discipline who were consulted. This journal, however, was devoted primarily not to Oliver's main field of interest but to a related area, being more concerned with area studies than with mass communication. Nevertheless, Oliver took the advice of the editor and submitted his paper to *XYZ Journal.*

September 4, 1997: XYZ Journal gives a positive response. This time Oliver considered the journal's response to be positive. First, the single referee's report that accompanied the editor's letter, although pointing out defects in the paper (including "second language mistakes that interfere with clarity and obscure meaning"; FN, LE, April 18, 1998) was encouraging. The reviewer described Oliver's paper as "valuable" and stated that "both the data and the argument [of the paper] contribute significantly to a deepened understanding of [X] ." On the basis of these positive comments, the reviewer urged the editor to publish Oliver's article, stating that even though *XYZ Journal* had already recently devoted a special edition to the topic of Oliver's article, "I encourage you to publish this thought provoking article later in the year."

Following the reviewer's advice, the editor held out the possibility of publication of a suitably revised resubmission:

> On the basis of an encouraging referee report, I write to tell you that we will be happy to review a revised version of the manuscript and give you a rapid response. Though we reserve final judgment until we receive the final version, we are prepared to encourage you to address the issues set forth here in the review.
>
> (L, journal editor, September 4, 1997)

As what appeared to be a further inducement, the editor also stated, "Moreover, as we have gone through a transition of leadership here at *XYZ Journal,* this is one of the few manuscripts where we have encouraged revision." In spite of this apparent encouragement to submit a revised version, in her closing paragraph the editor rather enigmatically suggested that Oliver might nevertheless want to consider other journals:

> You will note that the referee suggested some other journals for publication. I think there is great merit in considering them and suggest you think carefully about submitting this manuscript to them. We shall understand here.

September 12, 1997: Oliver informs **XYZ Journal** *of his intention to submit a revised version.*

October 1997: Manuscript edited and resubmitted. Oliver engaged the services of an L1 writer (the LE) to edit the manuscript. The LE understood that Oliver expected him to be able to edit the manuscript independently, and the LE felt that the edit would be somewhat superficial and, further, that in order for the paper to be published, the editing needed to go beyond "surface" features of grammar and lexis to tackle the overall organization and "flow" of the paper (FN, LE, April 3, 1998). Oliver and the LE discussed some of these issues after the manuscript had initially been edited, but the LE noted that Oliver was only able or willing to give him about half the time he actually needed. For his part, Oliver was expecting the LE to do two things: see if there was anything that someone not in the field might not understand and make some grammatical or stylistic changes.

November 4, 1997: **XYZ Journal** *responds to the resubmission.* In her letter of response, the journal editor indicated that the paper had been reviewed by the same reviewer as the original submission. The message was to proceed. However, the editor reported that the reviewer indicated that "an immense editing job had to be done" and that acceptance was conditional upon Oliver's ability "to undertake the editing or arrange for the editing to be done by someone else following the examples presented to you." Five pages of actual editing were included by way of example. The editor further indicated that the journal was "making an effort to reduce the time spent in editing manuscripts." In addition, she hardened her approach by ending the letter with a reiteration of the suggestion in her previous letter that Oliver consider submission to publications that were in her opinion more directly related to Oliver's field and that "may have the capacity to undertake the extensive editing we have shown you."

November 12, 1997: Oliver informs **XYZ Journal** *of his intention to make a further resubmission.*

January 1, 1998: Reedited manuscript submitted. Having completed the reediting, the LE was dissatisfied with this process as he again felt that Oliver did not have enough time to direct the edit and that the cumulative effect of the various edits may have obscured the original text to some extent. He felt that a final, coordinated edit would have smoothed the flow of the manuscript.

March 5, 1998: Letter of acceptance received and publishing agreement signed.

April 8, 1998: E-mail correspondence begins. For the first time, the journal editor contacted Oliver directly by e-mail, clearly in preparation for the further editing that was to come. Over the following month, in effect, the in-house editor needed to become familiar with the content of the paper and did so by asking a huge number of questions (45) regarding details in the paper. In addition, in spite of the earlier warning from the editor that the journal could not do the "immense editing job" that the article required, portions of the paper were rewritten by the journal's in-house editor and submitted for Oliver's consideration and clarification.

May 5, 1998: Copy editing completed. The in-house editor e-mailed Oliver to say that he would be returning the manuscript (by fax) for further editing. He also stated that this would delay publication of the paper and that "We are sorry for the abrupt change of schedule but we all want the article to be as good as it can be." The in-house editor did an aggressive job, cutting the paper from 43 pages to 29. Entire paragraphs were removed, and virtually every sentence was rewritten.

May 1998: Editing completed by Oliver and manuscript resubmitted. Oliver was flexible enough to accept most of the changes made by the in-house editor. However, he had to negotiate several areas that to him represented factual errors, inaccuracies, or outright falsehoods.

June 1998: Paper published in XYZ **Journal.**

The role of the LE

The LE had considerable research experience, having worked for many years in the research office of a North American government agency. As an editor, the LE felt he was constricted by his own lack of disciplinary knowledge, on the one hand, and by the limited role assigned to him by Oliver, on the other. In his account of the editing experience, the LE wrote, "Essentially the directions were simply to 'edit what you can'" (R, LE, December 2, 1998). To do justice to the paper, however, the LE felt he needed lengthy discussion with Oliver to find out exactly what he was trying to say:

> Very quickly into the edit it became apparent that there would be some difficulty in dealing with those requirements that went beyond the English portion of the edit. The structure and thematic consistency needed attention but seemed to be outside the edit mandate.

Oliver, however, did not envisage such consultation as part of the editing process. He expected the LE to be able to work independently and revise the paper appropriately on his own. Consequently, the LE reported, "As the editor I had to determine what was ethical and reasonable under the circumstances" (R, LE, December 2, 1998). The LE accordingly limited his editing largely to what might be termed surface features of grammar, lexis, and paragraph coherence.

For the LE, the role of the reviewer was much more critical to the paper than his own editing:

> It was the considerable expertise of the . . . reviewer which was responsible for the positive response initially given to the paper. His/her ability to look beyond the language and beyond the structural and thematic problems was crucial to the life of the paper and this may not have been the case given a reviewer with less ability/vision.
> (R, LE, December 2, 1998)

Paradoxically, the LE felt that his own contribution might have been greater had the paper initially been rejected. Oliver would then have had "no choice but to provide the impetus for a more carefully directed rewrite" (R, LE, December 2, 1998). As it was, after editing the LE and Oliver set aside some time for discussion, but even this was problematic, as office space was shared, students interrupted constantly, and one meeting even had to be held in the staff restaurant. The LE estimated that a good exchange of views would have required several hours but that he and Oliver spent only about half of the necessary time on this task. The LE further stated,

> One of the things that was clear about this paper was that it would have benefited from a further edit after the author had made the necessary changes and before it was resubmitted. The reasons for this are that the number of edits that were done acted to obscure the text to some extent. In other words the flow of the paper could not be adjusted until the edits were completed and the reader was able to "see" a clean copy. Much, but not all, of the second edit could have been avoided if this process had been followed.
>
> (R, LE, December 2, 1998)

During the second edit, in fact, the LE felt that there was more opportunity to work on the overall clarity of the paper—that is, "to effect thematic changes and improve upon the continuity of the paper." In this respect the second edit done by the LE was more satisfactory.

The LE's overall evaluation of the editorial process from the point of view of Oliver was as follows:

> In the end, I have to believe that for the author the entire process must have been extremely stressful. Finding a suitable L1 editor, dealing with the subsequent edits and contending with the vagaries regarding content, as well as having to address the editorial demands of the journal editor and the reviewers all represent L2 challenges which seem far beyond those experienced by L1 scholars.
>
> (R, LE, December 2, 1998)

The role of the journal editor, the reviewer, and the in-house editor

Journal editor: The journal editor's role in the publication process for Oliver's paper is somewhat ambiguous. In her first letter, as stated in the chronology above, she invited a resubmission but encouraged Oliver to submit his manuscript to another journal. One possible interpretation of this is that although she herself was not that enthusiastic about the paper, on the basis of the reviewer's recommendation she felt obliged to at least offer resubmission.

In her second letter, on the recommendation of the same reviewer, she again signaled that Oliver could proceed. But she also again expressed her reservations—in emphasizing the immense editing job that was required, in suggesting that Oliver obtain assistance in editing his manuscript, in stating that the journal was trying to cut down on time spent editing, and in reiterating her suggestion that Oliver consider submitting his paper elsewhere (to a journal with better facilities for editing his manuscript).

Reviewer: As noted by the LE, the reviewer's role was crucial: He or she was able to envision the final paper based upon the initial submission, which was by no means clear either to the LE or to me.

In-house editor: The role of the journal's in-house editor went far beyond what would normally be expected of a copy editor. He changed not only surface stylistic features but also—in making drastic cuts—the whole organization of the manuscript. Oliver described the job the in-house editor did as "a huge edit" and as "the most difficult" of all the editing processes he had gone through (FN, LE, June 15, 1998). He described the changes as primarily two types: linguistic-stylistic and organizational-structural. He attributed the organizational-structural changes to disciplinary factors. The journal was primarily focussed on area studies, whereas Oliver saw himself more closely affiliated to mass communication. The extensive cuts, then, were mainly in the methodology section. Oliver felt this section to be important in his discipline, which values rigorous quantitative analysis and methodology more highly than the disciplinary orientation of the journal, which is more interested in political analysis. *As he put it, "[XYZ Journal]* is not an [X] journal and they do not require a lot of empirical stuff" (E, author, September 11, 1998).

Oliver stated that he felt that the in-house editor played a major role in shaping the focus of the paper, in "put[ting] his own agenda on the paper" (R, LE, December 2, 1998), as he described it. The disciplinary orientation of the in-house editor led Oliver to emphasise certain aspects that he himself considered minor relative to other sections of the paper. "My article is something about [X] and this has not been the major focus of the journal," Oliver stated. "He [the in-house editor] is trying to make the argument that [X is significant]—[Y] may not be as interesting as covering as [X]."

This function of the reviewer and in-house editor in reorienting the main focus of the paper is similar to the situation described by Berkenkotter and Huckin (1995) in their case study of the biologist, whose reviewers insisted that she make the article "newsworthy" by situating it within the previous related research. In Oliver's case it is also a question of news value, but this was created not by putting the paper in the context of other work but by emphasizing the methodology and subject matter that is appropriate for readers of *XYZ Journal*. Because the journal had a less empirical leaning, indeed, the methodology, the literature review, and the empirical data were less important than analysis and interpretation, which were of most interest.

When Oliver was asked about the experience of working with the in-house editor, the important legitimate peripheral participation afforded by this activity came out strongly. "I learned a lot in terms of style," Oliver stated. "The editor was tough, and I think that when I write another article—the current article I am writing—I will be more focussed and more concentrated on the style rather than a lot of the content and stuff like that" (I, author, December 15, 1998). As with Berkenkotter and Huckin's (1995) biologist, the editorial experience enabled Oliver to appreciate the importance of the rhetorical dimension of the scholar's work, which may well be as important as the actual content—at least if one wants the results of one's research published.

Examples of editing: The extensive nature of the editing carried out on Oliver's paper makes it difficult to exemplify clearly. The following examples are indicative of some of the trans-formations of certain paragraphs (some key words have been changed to preserve anonymity). Three stages are provided for each of the examples: the original submitted version, the LE's revision, and the final published version. I emphasize, however, that the examples illustrate edit-ing only at the level of paragraph coherence (admittedly, a significant area where many changes were made). They do not show deletions and reorganisation, which were also important editorial changes made by the in-house editor, or the cumulative effect that extensive sections of such rewriting had on comprehensibility.

EXAMPLE 1

Author: The question is whether the media would continuously be a companion of pro-status quo camp during the late political transition or alter the Communist Party has taken over. What will be the treatment of the media upon the various interest groups when they entered the establishment after winning the district board elections?

LE: The macro question under review is whether the media continues to support the pro-status quo camp and the public after the Communist Party take-over of Hong Kong.

In-house editor: This article seeks to anticipate whether the media will continue to lean toward the pro-status quo camp and the public under Chinese rule.

EXAMPLE 2

Author: With people's aspiration of democracy and hence district boards' popularity in the subsequent elections, mass media were shown to have made a complete volte-face from outraging to following public opinion, to shape the various groups, especially status quo groups, as legitimate political entities for district board electioneering in the 1990s.

LE: With the peoples' aspiration of democracy and the ensuing parties' popularity in the elections, the mass media made a complete about-face from opposing the general public opinion (in the 80s) to following and endorsing it (in the 90s) with regard to their view of district boards as legitimate political entities.

In-house editor: Such democratic aspirations and the resulting popularity of the parties brought a complete about-face in the mass media in the 1990s, and they now endorsed various groups as legitimate political entities.

EXAMPLE 3

Author: In the campaigns, Beijing was contradicting itself by espousing the reforms be a "triple violator" but mobilizing pro-China figures to participate.

LE: In the campaigns waged, Beijing was contradicting itself by on the one hand espousing that the political reforms were a 'triple violation' and on the other hand by mobilizing pro-China figures to participate.

In-house editor: In the campaign, though, Beijing acted inconsistently, saying that Governor Patten's political reforms were void while simultaneously mobilizing pro-China figures to participate in the subsequent school elections.

The editing of content

One other important aspect of the editorial process is the need for the author to adapt the content to suit the priorities of the journal. In response to a specific request for examples of this type of editing via e-mail, Oliver mentioned a number of aspects of content that he had felt obliged to change. First, he felt that the journal wanted the conflictual aspect of Hong Kong-China relations to be emphasized; he had accordingly developed this theme more. Second, he stated that, in the interpretation of events, the journal "tended to attribute everything to China's interference" (F, author, September 11, 1998). He felt obliged to accommodate this tendency. Third, he considered that the main concern of the journal was "freedom in Hong Kong under the rein [sic] of China." In response to this last issue, he added a lengthy section describing Hong Kong's gradual democratic development before the handover, in order to satisfy what he described as the journal's desire "to make the point that Hong Kong's political development is interrupted by China's presence." These changes were in line with the analytical orientation of the journal, as opposed to the more empirical emphasis that Oliver had originally put on the paper. They also suggest, however, that the journal, or at least the in-house editor, had a particular political ideology to convey.

Discussion

This ethnographic investigation of the publication of a scholarly article by an NNS is ultimately a success story, insofar as Oliver achieved publication of his article. However, the process was fraught with difficulties, and at various stages Oliver's efforts might have been thwarted. Some of these difficulties were overcome through Oliver's prior knowledge of the publishing "game." He was knowledgeable enough about the initial rejection from the first journal not to give up but to try a second and then a third one. His disregard of the two separate suggestions by the editor of *XYZ Journal* to submit elsewhere was a wise move in the end. His willingness to cooperate with the in-house editor and accept radical cutting and rewriting also worked in his favour. Other possible impediments to success, however, were overcome by luck as much as judgement. Oliver was lucky in that, in the change of editorship of *XYZ Journal*, his was one of the few submissions taken on by the new editor. He was also lucky in that the single reviewer of his submission had the skill to see a publishable article in a manuscript that two nonspecialists (the LE and I) were unable to envision and that had what the reviewer described as "second language mistakes that interfere with clarity and obscure meaning" (reviewer, September 1997). He was furthermore lucky in that the journal staff devoted an immense amount of time and effort to editing his paper when the journal editor had earlier said they were not willing to do this. Finally, he was fortunate in being able to secure the services of the LE.

To what extent Oliver's difficulties were specific to his situation as an NNS is hard to say. It is of course true that native-English-speaking writers are likely to experience most, if not all, of Oliver's problems. It is equally true, however, that it is impossible to draw the line between content and form in writing. As the reviewer of Oliver's article noted, L2 mistakes do have the potential to interfere with clarity and obscure meaning (although some errors, such as subject-verb concord, are more transparent than others). In terms of the time put in working on a manuscript, as an NNS Oliver most likely had to put in more time than would an NS. Certainly, as far as the LE was concerned, Oliver's struggle represented "L2 challenges which seem far beyond those experienced by L1 scholars" (R, LE, December 2, 1998). On the other hand, one wonders if the editors of *XYZ Journal* would have been willing to put in so much time on a poorly presented manuscript if it had be written by an NS. Perhaps as an NNS Oliver was accorded a special privilege.

Considering Oliver's endeavour in terms of discourse community and legitimate peripheral participation sheds a considerable amount of light on the experience. As an NNS writer, Oliver was at two steps removed from a desirable situation with regard to these two phenomena. By living and working on the periphery, in Hong Kong, he was geographically removed from the discourse community and peripheral participation to which he is seeking access. But he was also linguistically removed insofar as he lacked the nativelike language proficiency that full membership of his target discourse community and peripheral participation demanded.

In Oliver's case, the geographical isolation was mitigated by the use of technology (e-mail), but, perhaps significantly, electronic communication began only when the journal was already committed to publishing Oliver's paper. The technology, it seems, is at the service of the gatekeeper, when the in-house editor requires rapid work on the paper, but not at the service of the supplicants, who are eager to receive news of progress on their submission. In any case, as already mentioned, for Oliver e-mail communication was "not as deep" as face-to-face conversation. In terms of literacy theory, in highlighting the important roles played by the LE and the in-house editor, the study has reiterated the mediated nature of academic writing, as previously highlighted by, for example, Prior (1998).

Conclusion

What might be done to alleviate the difficulties of nonnative-English-speaking scholars such as Oliver seeking to publish in international journals in English? In many ways Oliver is in a privileged position compared with other NNSs, having had great exposure to English at school and having done his graduate studies in the United States, with all of the opportunities for legitimate peripheral participation that that implies. Nonnative-speaking scholars who have had less exposure to English and less opportunity for peripheral participation than Oliver are presumably in a more difficult position when it comes to the international publication of their research.

One obvious point that needs addressing is the tendency of editors and reviewers to use the label *NNS* in their reviews and correspondence. The terms NS and *NNS* mark two ends of a continuum that mask a whole range of language competencies. English is the native scholarly language of many scholars internationally even though it is not strictly speaking their mother tongue; it is the language they have been educated in and the language in which they conduct a great part of their scholarly activity. Thus Oliver described himself as an NS of both Chinese and English, even though his English is perceived by others, including reviewers, as nonstandard. Nonstandard language needs to be pointed out to all contributors, but this can be done without distinguishing between NSs and NNSs. NNSs, of course, also have a responsibility to prepare their manuscripts to the best of their ability and to use any editorial assistance they may be able to find locally. Given the importance of disciplinary knowledge in editing (as indicated by the problems of the LE in this study), native-English-speaking writers might be better to work with a specialist in the discipline in addition to a nonspecialist NS.

A number of further recommendations come to mind with regard to the notions of discourse community and legitimate peripheral participation, which are so crucial in achieving success in writing for academic publication. Legitimate peripheral participation is likely to come about through the encouragement of attendance at international conferences and exchanges of scholars between the centre and the periphery. Similarly, international collaboration in research is likely to be beneficial.

If one were to identify a misapprehension on Oliver's part, it might be that, like the biologist in Berkenkotter and Huckin's (1995) study, he did not initially put a high value on the rhetorical dimension of his work; he was more interested in the ideas than in the format for their expression. Oliver's understanding of the importance of the discursive dimension of his work, as this case study has demonstrated and Oliver has acknowledged, came with the experience of submitting and editing journal papers. To this extent Oliver's experience, as reported in this case study, was beneficial not just in terms of getting the paper published but also in the opportunity for the peripheral participation and learning it afforded. (Oliver's experience in collaborating on this research project was also beneficial; he commented that he felt that what this article says was "essentially true" and that "the influence of research collaboration [as highlighted in the paper] is particularly important" (E, author, June 5, 1998). Like other academics, with each submission Oliver will know a little bit more about how to manage the process; however, editors, reviewers, and the academic community at large still have a duty to facilitate and optimise such learning.

In case the conclusions about the usefulness of informal legitimate peripheral participation to be drawn from this article might be construed as negative for the teaching of academic writing, I would like to stress that this is certainly not the case. As stated earlier, the notions of discourse community and legitimate peripheral participation do not preclude any role for formal instruction (Lave, 1998). In considering the sort of training that might be offered to people in Oliver's position, however, instead of being designed as a formal, teacher-fronted package, such instruction might better be envisioned as an opportunity for bringing together apprentice professionals to share their experiences and reflect together on their ongoing legitimate peripheral participation. In such a programme, young scholars would meet periodically to interact with their peers, receive a certain amount of formal instruction in academic writing, and be mentored by both subject and language specialists.[3] This training might be supported by individual mentoring sessions organized in some sort of writing "clinic" staffed by both language and subject specialists. Perhaps Oliver's experience might have been easier if his university had been able to offer him access to a centre where such opportunities were available.[4]

Notes

1 Coding conventions are as follows: E = e-mail message; FN = field notes; I = interview; R = report written by LE.
2 Oliver showed me one review that did actually have such a statement in the first two sentences. The review began as follows: "Obviously, this manuscript has not been written by a native speaker. There are many problems with language usage that would need to he corrected were this to be published." Oliver also showed me several other reviews that had similar statements, although not right at the beginning. The reviewer did then go on to say that extra efforts need to be made so that international contributions can be published. Nevertheless, initially the first two sentences must have been demoralising.
3 This idea is expressed in more general terms by Lave (1998, p. 250).
4 Hong Kong Polytechnic University has set up such a centre (Sengupta, Forey, & Hamp-Lyons, 1999). See also an account of a similar programme run at the University of Hong Kong for graduate student dissertation writing (Allison et al., 1998).

References

Allison, D., Cooley, L., Lewkowicz, J., & Nunan, D. (1998). Dissertation writing in action. *English for Specific Purposes*, *2*, 209–217.

Ball, S. J. (1988). Participant observation. In J.P. Keeves (Ed.), *Educational research methodology and measurement: An international handbook* (pp. 310–314). Oxford: Pergamon Press.

Bartholomae, D. (1985). Inventing the university. In M. Rose (Ed.), *When a writer can't write* (pp. 134–165). New York: Guilford Press.

Bazerman, C. (1980). A relationship between reading and writing: The conversational model. *College English*, *41*, 656–661.

Bazerman, C. (1985). Physicists reading physics: Schema-laden purposes and purpose-laden schema. *Written Communication*, *2*, 3–23.

Bazerman, C. (1988). *Shaping written knowledge: The genre and activity of the experimental article in science.* Madison: University of Wisconsin Press.

Belcher, D. (1994). The apprenticeship approach to advanced academic literacy: Graduate students and their mentors. *English for Specific Purposes*, *13*, 23–34.

Berkenkotter, C., & Huckin, T. N. (1993). You are what you cite: Novelty and intertextuality in a biologist's experimental article. In N. R. Blyler & C. Thralls (Eds.), *Professional communication: The social perspective* (pp. 109–127). Newbury Park, CA: Sage.

Berkenkotter, C., & Huckin, T. (1995). *Genre knowledge in disciplinary communication: cognition/culture/power.* Hillsdale, NJ: Erlbaum.

Berkenkotter, C., Huckin, T., & Akerman, J. (1988). Conventions, conversations, and the writer: Case study of a student in a rhetoric Ph.D. program. *Research in the Teaching of English, 22,* 9–44.

Bizzell, P. (1982a). Cognition, convention, and certainty: What we need to know about writing. *PRE/TEXT, 3,* 213–243.

Bizzell, P. (1982b). College composition: Initiation into the academic discourse community. [Review of *Four worlds of writing* and *Writing in the arts and sciences*]. *Curriculum Inquiry, 12,* 191–207.

Cameron, Deborah (2000). *Good to talk? Living and working in a communication culture.* London: Sage.

Casanave, C. P. (1995). Local interactions: Constructing contexts for composing in a graduate sociology program. In D. Belcher & G. Braine (Eds.), *Academic writing in a second language* (pp. 83–110). Norwood, NJ: Ablex.

Connor, U. (1999). Learning to write academic prose in a second language: A literacy autobiography. In G. Braine (Ed.), *Non-native educators in English language teaching* (pp. 29–42). Mahwah, NJ: Erlbaum.

Dias, P. (1994). Initiating students into discipline-based reading and writing. In A. Freeman & P. Medway (Eds.), *Learning and teaching genre* (pp. 193–206). Portsmouth, NH: Elsevier.

Dudley-Evans, T. (1991). Socialisation into the academic community: Linguistic and stylistic expectations of a Ph.D. thesis as revealed by supervisor comments. In P. Adams, B. Heaton, & P. Howarth (Eds.), *Socio-cultural issues in English for academic purposes* (pp. 41–51). London: Macmillan.

Flowerdew, J. (1999a). *Attitudes of journal editors to non-native speaker contributions.* Manuscript submitted for publication.

Flowerdew, J. (1999b). Problems in writing for scholarly publication in English: The case of Hong Kong. *Journal of Second Language Writing, 8,* 243–264.

Flowerdew, J. (1999c). *A text analysis of the introductions to two manuscript submissions written by Hong Kong academics.* Manuscript in preparation.

Flowerdew, J. (1999d). Writing for scholarly publication in English: The case of Hong Kong. *Journal of Second Language Writing, 8,* 123–145.

Flowerdew, J., & Dudley-Evans, A. (1999). *Genre analysis of editorial letters to international journal contributors.* Manuscript submitted for publication.

Geertz, C. (1973). *The interpretation of cultures.* New York: Basic Books.

Gosden, H. (1995). Success in research article writing and revisions: A social constructionist perspective. *English for Specific Purposes, 14,* 37–57.

Gosden, H. (1996). Verbal reports of Japanese doctoral students. *Journal of Second Language Writing, 5,* 109–128.

Kuhn, T.S. (1970). *The structure of scientific revolutions* (2nd ed.). Chicago: University of Chicago Press.

Lave, J. (1998). *Communities of practice.* New York: Cambridge University Press.

Lave, J., & Wenger, E. (1991). *Situated learning: Legitimate peripheral participation.* Cambridge: Cambridge University Press.

Li, X. M. (1999). Writing from the vantage point of an outsider/insider. In G. Braine (Ed.), *Non-native educators in English language teaching* (pp. 43–55). Mahwah, NJ: Erlbaum.

Myers, G. (1985). The social construction of two biologists' proposals. *Written Communication, 12,* 219–245.

Prior, P. (1998). *Writing/disciplinarity: A sociohistoric account of literate activity in the academy.* Mahwah, NJ: Erlbaum.

Sengupta, S., Forey, G., & Hamp-Lyons, L. (1999). Supporting effective English communication within the context of teaching and research in a tertiary institute: Developing a genre model for consciousness raising. *English for Specific Purposes, 18*(Supplement), S7–S22.

Swales, J. M. (1990) . *Genre analysis: English in academic and research settings.* Cambridge: Cambridge University Press.

Swales, J. M., & Feak, C. B. (1994). *Academic writing for graduate students.* Ann Arbor: University of Michigan Press.

Weissberg, R., & Buker, S. (1990). *Writing up research: Experimental research report writing for students of English.* Englewood Cliffs, NJ: Prentice Hall.

Chapter 20

TIM McNAMARA

LANGUAGE ASSESSMENT AS SOCIAL PRACTICE
Challenges for research (2001)

I Introduction

LANGUAGE TESTING IS FACING a fundamental challenge as a result of our growing understanding of the social character of its constructs and its practices. An awareness of language use as a social activity, of the socially derived nature of our notions of language, and of testing as an institutional practice, is causing language testers to look critically at their practices and the assumptions that underpin them.

Such a re-evaluation is at one level simply part of the natural ongoing process of the evolution of the field. Like any interdisciplinary area, language testing seeks to remain in touch with ideas in fields on which it draws for its concepts and methods. Among the most fundamental concepts in language testing are validity (Messick, 1989; Bachman, 1990) and the construct of language proficiency (Canale and Swain, 1980; Bachman, 1990; McNamara, 1996; among many others). Understanding of both of these concepts has in the past several years undergone a profound change. Established understandings of the construct of language proficiency have been challenged on the grounds of a variety of more socially oriented conceptions of language use (McNamara, 1997). More fundamentally, all such constructs can be seen as social constructions, following recent work within poststructuralism (Butler, 1990; 1993); the implications of this for language testing are now beginning to be explored (McNamara, 1999), and will be discussed below.

An associated and equally fundamental challenge arises from the debates about the epistemology of research in the social sciences, including applied linguistics, triggered by the advent of postmodernism (Pennycook, 1994). As language testing is arguably the most positivist in orientation of all areas of applied linguistics (Alderson and Hamp-Lyons, 1996; Hamp-Lyons and Lynch, 1998), and the most directly involved in issues of power and control (Shohamy, 1998; 2001a, 2001b), it is widely seen as potentially an intellectually and politically conservative domain. In this sense it is especially vulnerable to current intellectual critiques, and also has a particular obligation to respond constructively to them.

There is thus a lot of intellectual work to be done in absorbing the point and significance of recent debates for our field and in discovering new orientations for language testing research and

	TEST INTERPRETATION	TEST USE
EVIDENTIAL BASIS	Construct validity	Construct validity + Relevance/utility
CONSEQUENTIAL BASIS	Value implications	Social consequences

Figure 20.1 Facets of validity

practice as a result. This article begins with a brief outline of some areas of challenge to the status quo in language testing research from theoretical advances which emphasize the social and socially constructed nature of assessment. It begins with a discussion of the social dimension of validation research in the work of Messick. The discussion includes his now frequently cited concern for the social consequences of testing practice, but also considers the way in which Messick situates all test constructs in the realm of values, itself a social arena. The way in which test constructs can be seen as the embodiment of social values is illuminated in recent work in poststructuralism, and the work of the feminist and queer theorist Judith Butler is explored for its implications for language testing research. The article concludes with a discussion of how institutional needs in school-based assessment determine both what is to be assessed and the procedures for assessment in ways that may paradoxically be at odds with the needs of teachers and learners. It asks, what is the current role of language testing research in such settings, and how might this role be re-thought to provide greater support for teachers and learners? Any search for alternatives in language testing research will involve revisiting what is traditionally known as alternative assessment (Hamayan, 1995; Brown and Hudson, 1998) and interpreting its goals and rationale rather differently.

II Theoretical alternatives

1 Messick's theory of test validity: the social dimension

The fundamentally social nature of assessment is a key feature, and perhaps the most radical feature, of the classic validity framework of Messick (1989).[1] Messick distinguishes a number of facets of validity within a unified theory of validity (Figure 20.1). The first cell in the matrix emphasizes the need to gather evidence in support of the interpretations we make of scores, in terms of the constructs that we have proposed (for example, in a language proficiency test, the interpretation that individuals achieving different score have different degrees of proficiency). The second cell on the top line stresses the need for test constructs to be relevant and useful in the testing context. So far, neither of these appear to present a fundamental challenge to existing practice; rather, they inform it. Much of the best current language testing research is using an increasingly complex range of research techniques to carry out a broader set of investigations into the interpretation of test scores (Bachman, 2000).

The bottom row of the matrix has been seen as presenting new, or relatively unfamiliar, sets of considerations for testers. The bottom left cell of the matrix insists that all interpretations of test scores involve questions of value, that is, that we have no 'objective', 'scientific', value-free basis for this activity. This is, indeed, a radical and disturbing (or liberating) notion, and I discuss it further below. The final cell stresses the need to investigate what specifically happens when a test is implemented in terms of its impact; and the proper scope for this investigation is currently the topic of considerable debate (e.g., Davies, 1997).

While Messick and other writers have stressed that this is a unitary view of validity, it is also discussed componentially in terms of aspects or facets, as indicated by the cells in the matrix and its rows and columns. The way in which these different facets may be seen as part of a unitary whole becomes an issue. By including consideration of values and of social action in his discussion of validity, Messick has in a sense opened up the possibility of debate on such topics. On one reading of this matrix Messick appears paradoxically to restrict such debate. That is, if we proceed cell by cell, it appears that validity research on the evidential basis of test interpretation and test use (the top line of the matrix) may be conducted, or at least understood, independently of validity research on the consequential basis of these things (the bottom line), that is, it may proceed in a social and value vacuum. Messick reminds us that this is a progressive matrix, that every cell further on contains the preceding cell(s). This is normally taken to mean that construct validity is represented within each of the subsequent cells, that is, that we should read the matrix forwards, with each cell gathering up the next in snowball fashion. But that is not really what Messick is saying at all. The implication of the forwards reading is that by the time we reach the final cell, we will include the aspects of validity featured in all of the four cells. That is, the final cell is the most inclusive of all. Each cell of the matrix in other words represents an ever more encompassing circle, creating a sort of hierarchy. The most fundamental, or outer circle, which encompasses everything else, is the social one, and questions of social value will permeate all other aspects of validity research. This means that values will be understood in social terms, and constructs will be understood as embodying social values and meanings. This does not mean of course that research motivated by considerations related to the top two cells is any less important; nor does it obviate the practical need for the development of tests for selection, placement and achievement decisions. But it means that our thinking about these activities cannot be restricted to the technical: Messick requires us to engage explicitly with the fundamentally social character of assessment at every point.

The reception of Messick's framework within language testing has proceeded in a gradual and somewhat uncoordinated fashion. The initial emphasis in early discussions of the relevance of this framework for language testing (Bachman, 1990) was on the first cell of the matrix, on the need for empirical evidence of construct validity. In Bachman's ground-breaking work this led to an advocacy of the need for explicitness of test constructs and an explicit relationship between test construct and test method, resulting in the famous Bachman model. (In more recent work, Bachman and Palmer (1996) have, through their notion of test usefulness, moved forwards in the matrix, as it were.) Other researchers have tackled the matrix from the other direction, so to speak, and emphasized the question of the social consequences of test interpretation and use. While Bachman discusses the social consequences in his 1990 work, research in this area has been carried forwards very extensively since then, particularly by Lynch and Hamp-Lyons (1996), Lynch (this issue) and Shohamy (2001; this issue), by those interested in the ethics of language testing (Davies, 1997) and by researchers on washback in language testing (Alderson and Wall, 1993; Alderson and Hamp-Lyons, 1996; Wall, 1997; amongst others).

2 *Performativity: the value-laden character of test constructs*

The third cell of the matrix, the necessarily value-laden character of test constructs, has been relatively little discussed. The question of the value implications of test constructs is an elusive notion, and such values are seldom explicitly addressed in discussions of the validity of test constructs. Take the notion of language ability or language proficiency. In communicative testing, which – as Morrow (1979) was perhaps the first to point out – involves performance testing, we are required to estimate competence from performance. By competence we are here referring to underlying abilities, whose existence allows us to generalize (as we must) beyond the moment of assessment to the criterion behaviour that the assessment is used to predict. As Bachman (1990) has persuasively argued in his discussion of direct tests, the issue of generalizing from instances of performance in tests is often simply elided, in the mistaken belief that competence is directly observable in test performance. Moreover, as I have argued extensively elsewhere (McNamara, 1996; 1997; 1999), our existing models of performance are inadequately articulated, and the relationship between performance and competence in language testing remains obscure. In particular, the assumption of performance as a direct outcome of competence is problematic, as it ignores the complex social construction of test performance, most obviously in the case of interactive tests such as direct tests of speaking. I do not rehearse these arguments further here, but emphasize the potential of such an erasure of the social to lead to an unfortunate result: that the impression created by the joint action of the many participants in the language testing event (communicative partner, rater, test designer) is attributed solely to the performance of the candidate.

Theories of performance in language assessment may have much to learn from the notion of performativity developed in the work of the feminist poststructuralist and queer theorist Judith Butler (Butler, 1990; 1993). The term performative was introduced by Austin (1962: 6–7):

> In these examples it seems clear that to utter the sentence (in, of course, the appropriate circumstances) is not to describe my doing of what I should be said in so uttering to be doing or to state that I am doing it: it is to do it . . . . What are we to call a sentence or an utterance of this type? I propose to call it a performative sentence or a performative utterance, or, for short, 'a performative' . . . The name is derived, of course, from 'perform', the usual verb with the noun 'action': it indicates that the issuing of the utterance is the performing of an action – it is not normally thought of as just saying something.

Butler greatly extends Austin's notion of the performative. She exploits Austin's embedded notion of socially sanctioned (verbal) actions implying deeper, more abstract actions as a kind of metaphor for what she sees as the way in which our actions may construct a sense of our inner being or sense of self. She argues that a sense of our being in the world, or more specifically of our gender identity, is the product of socially sanctioned actions. This process of construction is social, and through it we create a shared sense of being through subjection to it. Such a process may not be easily available to our consciousness, particularly as an awareness of the process would destabilize or threaten the sense of being in the world that is thereby engendered.

This is a difficult idea, as a sense of our selves as male or female is something experienced as private and individual, and in some sense part of our 'true selves'. Love songs are full of references to 'a real man', 'a natural woman': how can these be fictions? The revelation or expression of our 'true selves' in intimacy is essentially private. How can our sense of this aspect of our selves be social, public, constructed?

Yet Butler insists that this inner sense of gender is created, or in her terms, is 'performed'. She rejects the conventional belief in actions expressing our inner being, our true selves, by contrasting what she calls 'expression' with what she calls 'performativity'. Expression is the term she uses for the conventional belief that our inner nature is given, and that our actions are the external manifestation of something 'inner'. Instead, she argues that through performativity we construct or create a sense of something 'inner' by our actions, actions that are performed as a result of social constraints and training. In rejecting the conventional notion that the outer is an expression of the inner, Butler argues that through performativity, we come to believe in the existence of an 'inner essence', which is in fact a result, an effect, a fiction.

Furthermore, because performativity tends to obscure its action because its result is a sense of inner self which is experienced as private and individual, the social origins of gender identity are also obscured. As the process remains invisible and unconscious, we are accordingly less conscious of the potential for investigating the origins and sources of these actions in social values and social ideologies.

In applying Butler's ideas to the field of language testing, we can begin to cast light on the third and fourth cells in Messick's matrix. Discussions of constructs in language testing and their manifestation in performance bear striking parallels to the conventional understanding of gender identity that Butler sets out to critique. We assume in language testing the existence of prior constructs such as language proficiency or language ability. It is the task of the language tester to allow them to be expressed, to be displayed, in the test performance. But what if the direction of action is the reverse, so that the act of testing itself constructs the notion of language proficiency? Are the constructs of language testing susceptible to a performative unveiling, to be revealed as social constructs serving social ideologies? Messick, whose discussion in his 1989 paper shows a deep awareness of postmodern epistemological critiques of the notion of a value-free social science, advocates exactly the sort of critique of the value-laden nature of psychological constructs represented by Butler in her chosen field.

Let us consider what it would mean for language testing research to view language testing constructs as performative achievements. Instead of taking constructs as givens, they would be subject to critical interrogation. Such work has hardly begun. It would include analysis of the social origins and derivations of test constructs, including:

- epistemological critiques of the notions of individuality and individual responsibility for performance that underlie much current work (on the notion of co-construction of performance, see Jacoby and Ochs, 1995; on the application of this notion to assessment of oral language, see McNamara, 1997);
- critical historical research on the provenance and genesis of test constructs and their epistemological foundations;
- policy analysis relevant to test constructs, for example the way 'competency' as a key construct in language testing has emerged within globalizing policy contexts (on policies informing the development of rating scales for reporting on language development of immigrant children in schools, see Moore, 1996; 1999);
- empirical analysis of the microgenesis of the activity of performativity, for example using discourse analytic techniques to reveal the jointly constructed nature of performance in face-to-face oral tests (on the inherent variability of oral tasks from the perspective of Activity Theory, see Coughlan and Duff, 1994; for the use of conversation analytic techniques to reveal the joint construction of performance in oral proficiency interviews, see Young and He, 1998; see also Brown, 1998, who reveals the attribution to candidates of features of the behaviour of interlocutors in oral language tests);
- studies of the institutionality of language testing, that is of the institutional and bureaucratic contexts in which language test constructs emerge, and the institutional ends that they serve

(for example, on the history of TOEFL, see Spolsky, 1995; on the way in which contrasting constructs of language proficiency serve the goals of competing social groups in a high-stakes secondary school language examination, see Elder, 1997).

An alternative research agenda for validation studies, and the exploration of appropriate alternative methodologies for conducting them, are thus urgent tasks facing our field.

III Competing demands in classroom-based assessment

Equally urgent is a related practical matter, which may in fact be understood in the light of the foregoing: a widespread perception that the needs of teachers and learners are not currently well served by assessment practice and by assessment research. In this part of the article I explain the nature of the problem and then go on to outline an alternative research orientation which is offered as a way forwards.

1 Demands as mutual imposition

My argument in this section is that classroom assessment is the site of competing demands which do not necessarily match the needs of learners and teachers. Ironically, one of these sets of demands comes from language testing researchers, concerned with particular types of validity evidence. Another is the demands made on classroom teachers by system-wide administrative needs for accountability and reporting. Table 20.1 illustrates the dilemma. We can see these demands in terms of mutual imposition; that is, the demands of one section will affect and possibly limit the achievability of the demands of the others. The group most at risk here are learners and teachers.

Let us look at the role of each group, beginning with the group in column 2, the policy makers and system managers, typically working in national and state departments of education and/or employment. This is the most overtly powerful group, and their demands are likely to prevail; they are increasingly interventionist in the interests of policy objectives such as efficiency, reform, modernization, globalization and the like. This intervention often takes the form of demands for greater accountability and more accurate reporting of outcomes of effort (Brindley, 1998; this issue). A favourite way of achieving these goals is the creation of over-arching state-mandated frameworks, scales and profiles which are proliferating in vocational and schoolbased language education. Examples of these are competency frameworks such as the

Table 20.1 Competing demands on classroom-based assessment

1 Validity demands	2 Managerialist demands	3 Teacher/learner demands
• intellectual defensibility of construct	• reporting	• meaningfulness in instructional process
• evidence of reliability	• accountability	• facilitation of learning
• other empirical evidence of validity		• enhanced quality of teaching
• concern for consequences		• minimization of administrative burden on teachers

Australian Certificate of Spoken and Written English (Hagan *et al.*, n.d.) and the Canadian Language Benchmarks (Citizenship and Immigration Canada, 1993; Peirce and Stewart, 1997), and proficiency scales such as the Common European Framework for Languages (Trim, 1997). Such frameworks often disguise their true managerial and policy-serving purpose as they are presented to teachers as solutions to some of their curriculum and assessment needs, and hence of benefit to learners (column 3). Teachers are often co-opted into the genesis of such scales (for a first-hand account, see McKenna, 1996), and consultation with teachers is used as part of an effort to 'validate' such scales, that is, to ensure their political acceptability, in other words their face validity. In fact, such schemes often create another burden for teachers, who are required to generate the assessment data required for management of educational systems, and can discourage teachers from viewing assessment positively (as if they needed further discouragement). While such frameworks draw on theories of language ability, and hence on the work of those in column 1, the intellectual heart of the schemes, the constructs, are often direct expressions of government policies (competency-based assessments are a good example). Such politically mandated constructs may be susceptible to influence from the findings of research only marginally; for example, the powerful validity arguments against the competency movement have fallen on deaf ears. It is not much help for empirical and analytic validity research to expose the limitations or even contradictions in framework-based constructs if they are amenable to modification only through political processes. Of course, the intellectual and moral weight of reasoned argument may have an effect in the longer term; an important study of the role of assessment specialists in the genesis and evolution of language assessment policy in the Australian context has been undertaken by Helen Moore (Moore, 1996; 1999).

Ironically, classroom-based assessment is in some ways not well served by many of the demands of language testing researchers (column 1). This is because, following the imperatives of the first cell of Messick's matrix, researchers make strenuous demands on the interpretability and comparability of assessments. The assessments most vulnerable to rigorous empirically based validation studies are complex, performance-based ones, as Lado (1961) realized many years ago. This is especially so if they are designed and conducted by teachers. It is easy to reveal the variability associated with task and rater factors in complex performance assessments, and to expose their subsequent unreliability (Brindley, 2000; 2001), which makes the information derived from them of limited usefulness in cases where the assessment decision bears some weight. Teachers who lack the training, expertise and resources to carry out validation research of this order are left powerless faced with such demands from researchers armed with rigorous notions of validity.

It may be argued that criterion-referenced language testing (Brown and Hudson, 1998) is immune from the criticism that language testing research is failing to meet the needs of teachers and learners, as it is specifically directed at classroom assessments and deals directly with achievement of learning objectives, and diagnostic assessment, both of them important for teachers. Even here, however, the techniques of analysis to be learned by teachers to validate assessments where judgement is involved (for example, in speaking and writing assessments) are formidably difficult, involving as they do such things as Generalizability Theory and Item Response Theory (Brown and Hudson, 1998). Moreover they are likely to reveal again the problematic character of teacher assessments described by Brindley.

2 Expanding the notion of assessment

The current structures appear then not to be meeting – or to be meeting in part only – the demands of the third group, teachers and learners. Making the needs of this group a priority would represent an alternative approach to assessment, not 'alternative assessment' as we currently know it, which is compatible at face value with a scales-and-frameworks approach. I am interested here particularly in what this alternative focus would mean for group 1 (researchers). I wish to make two suggestions.

First, such a focus would lead to a greater research emphasis on the implementation of assessment schemes, including an analysis of the impact of assessment reforms and a critique of their consequences. Excellent work is currently being done; for example, research is being carried out in Australia on how teachers understand and use scales and frameworks (Breen et al., 1997) and by those researching the washback of tests (see references above).

Secondly, assessment specialists can help more adequately to theorize and conceptualize alternative, more facilitative functions of assessment in classrooms. These would not replace but supplement the functions of placing students in appropriate groupings for learning, certifying achievement and the like. Such a step involves expanding our notion of assessment to include a range of activities that are informed by assessment concepts and that are targeted directly at the learning process.

Any deliberate, sustained and explicit reflection by teachers (and by learners) on the qualities of a learner's work can be thought of as a kind of assessment. While most performance assessment procedures require such reflection as a core component, it need not be restricted to those contexts in which formal reports or whole-class comparisons (class tests) are involved. Instead, teachers (and learners) can engage in systematic reflection on the characteristics of an individual performance as an aid to the formulation of learning goals in a variety of contexts.

In this kind of assessment activity, teachers are not involved in comparison of performances of different individuals, except in order to sharpen awareness of the characteristics or features of difference. We are not interested in who is relatively better or worse. We are not even involved in thinking of performances against a particular yardstick. Even where performances of the same individual at different points are compared, this is done largely descriptively and qualitatively and does not lead obviously into questions of score comparison, i.e., into the domain of measurement. This then means that the kinds of difficulties with subjective assessment that are exposed through careful validation research are not really an issue with this approach. From a certain perspective, each instance of this kind of assessment is unique; it does not always have to be fitted into a larger framework of comparison across individuals or across occasions (although such comparisons, particularly of progress over time, can facilitate consciousness of the nature of development, as suggested above). Nor does this kind of assessment activity necessarily involve record keeping and reporting to fulfil managerialist agendas. Teachers may of course choose to record some details of their reflections to help them see the 'bigger picture' of development over time, but this need not be formalized into a report.

An objection to the above may be that what I am talking about here is pedagogy, not assessment. Extending the notion of assessment in this way certainly blurs the boundary between assessment and pedagogy as they are conventionally understood. The claim of this kind of constructively critical reflection to be considered a form of assessment is based on the fact that it shares with assessment a number of features:

- It is deliberate and may be planned.
- It involves samples of performance.
- It makes reference to criteria derived from constructs of proficiency and its development (for teachers, such reflection on performance may be informed by the scales and frameworks constructed at the behest of managers).
- It leads to decisions about intervention and the targeting of learning efforts.

The role of the language testing researcher in aiding this process can include:

- working to develop the articulation of constructs in assessment frameworks in such a way that they are potentially of maximum benefit to teachers in this process of reflection and evaluation of the detail of individual performance;
- researching effective procedures for promoting critical reflection on learner performance by teachers, for example by developing techniques and opportunities for reflection that can be carried out in 'real time' during classroom activity, and comparing them with 'slowed down' procedures that require the recording of performance and subsequent analysis and evaluation for diagnostic purposes.

Learners too can engage in a process of deliberate sustained reflection on the quality of the products of their learning to date. This is one of the primary goals of the familiar area of self-assessment. Learner self-assessment has the goal of making learners more reflective, more aware, more responsible and more independent. Initially, this means encouraging learners to pay attention to their own performances and to develop ways of talking about them. We should not underestimate the task involved. We need research on the way in which an emerging metalanguage about their own performances can be developed with learners, building on their own terms for the things they notice. Learners may be very reluctant to consider their performances as objects at all. This is hardly surprising; most native speakers struggle to see their own language (that is, their own productive use) as an object. This is true even for highly educated speakers; ask any teacher trainer working with language teachers in initial training courses, and ask how much effort they have to put into developing the trainees' language awareness.

How might we go about helping learners become more self-aware of their development, for example in the speaking skill? Interviews and conferences with learners are common enough in the case of writing, but less common with speaking. Here again the use of audio and video recording can help make the learner an analyst and more accustomed to regarding the language performance as an object. Learners working in pairs may be encouraged to think about features of their performances. There are serious research opportunities here, as the activity I have in mind here can be seen as a possible extension of Merrill Swain's continuing project of research on the role and function of pair-work, considered from the perspective of sociocultural theory (Swain, 1999; Swain, 2001). Swain has studied how learners working in pairs on a task such as dictogloss, where they have to puzzle over the forms of language in a text reconstruction exercise, share and build on each other's awareness to come to an understanding.[2] The extension of this sort of activity to joint evaluation of the characteristics and qualities of performances certainly seems promising.

IV Conclusion

In this article I have attempted to draw attention to my sense of an important shift in our ways of thinking about assessment. There is an ongoing need for assessment to respond to the theoretical challenges presented by advances in validity theory and in the epistemological upheaval in the social and behavioural sciences. Related to this is a need to make our research more answerable to the needs of teachers and learners. There is a sense that the field is in fact moving and responding. A recent special issue of *Language Testing* was devoted to classroom assessment in the primary school, and there is ongoing vigorous discussion of the limits of the social responsibility of the language tester. But I have argued in this article that an alternative research agenda has scarcely been drawn up. We face an ongoing project of maintaining the relevance and utility of language assessment in the face of rapid and profound intellectual and political change.

Notes

1   This framework is familiar within language testing largely thanks to the work of Bachman (1990) and Bachman and Palmer (1996), who were among the first to appreciate the implications of Messick's work for language testing and who adopted Messick's approach to validity as the basis for their own monumental contribution.
2   While this kind of self-evaluation may not be familiar or indeed possible in all, even many, teaching and learning environments around the world, all discussions of self-directed learning and leaner autonomy face the same issue.

References

Alderson, J.C. and Hamp-Lyons, L. 1996: TOEFL preparation courses: a study of washback. *Language Testing* 13, 280–97.
Alderson, J.C. and Wall, D. 1993: Does washback exist? *Applied Linguistics* 14, 115–29.
Austin, J.L. 1962: *How to do things with words.* Oxford: Oxford University Press.
Bachman, L.F. 1990: *Fundamental considerations in language testing.* Oxford: Oxford University Press.
——— 2000: Modern language testing at the turn of the century: assuring that what we count counts. *Language Testing* 17, 1–42.
Bachman, L.F. and Palmer, A.S. 1996: *Language testing in practice: designing and developing useful language tests.* Oxford: Oxford University Press.
Breen, M., Barratt-Pugh, C., Derewianka, B., House, H., Hudson, C., Lumley, T. and Rohl, M. 1997: *Profiling ESL children: how teachers interpret and use national and state assessment frameworks, Volume 1: Key issues and findings.* Canberra: Department of Employment, Education, Training and Youth Affairs, 185–204.
Brindley, G. 1998: Outcomes-based assessment and reporting in language programs: a review of the issues. *Language Testing* 15, 45–85.
——— 2000: Task difficulty and task generalisability in competency-based writing assessment. In Brindley, G., editor, *Issues in immigrant English language assessment*, Volume 1. Sydney: National Centre for English Language Teaching and Research, Macquarie University, 45–80.
——— 2001: Investigating rater consistency in competency-based language assessment. In Brindley, G. and Burrows, C., editors, *Studies in immigrant English language assessment*, Volume 2. Sydney: National Centre for English Language Teaching and Research, Macquarie University, 59–80.
Brown, A. 1998: Interviewer style and candidate performance. Paper presented at the Language Testing Research Colloquium, Monterey, CA.
Brown, J.D. and Hudson, T. 1998: The alternatives in language assessment. *TESOL Quarterly* 32, 653–75.
——— 2002: *Criterion-referenced language testing.* Cambridge: Cambridge University Press.
Butler, J. 1990: *Gender trouble: feminism and the subversion of identity.* New York and London: Routledge.
——— 1993: *Bodies that matter: on the discursive limits of sex.* New York and London: Routledge.
Canale, M. and Swain, M. 1980: Theoretical bases of communicative approaches to second language teaching and testing. *Applied Linguistics* 1, 1–47.
Citizenship and Immigration Canada 1993: *Language. benchmarks: English as a second language for adults.* Ottawa: Citizenship and Integration Policy Division, Citizenship and Immigration Canada.
Coughlan, P. and Duff, P.A. 1994: Same task, different activity: analysis of a SLA task from an Activity Theory perspective. In Lantolf, J.P. and Appel, G., editors, *Vygotskian approaches to second language research.* Norwood, NJ: Ablex, 173–93.
Davies, A., editor, 1997: Special issue: ethics in language testing. *Language Testing* 14.
Elder, C. 1997: What does test bias have to do with fairness? *Language Testing* 14, 261–77.
Hagan, P., Hood, S., Jackson, E., Jones, M., Joyce, H. and Manidis, M. n.d: *Certificates in spoken and written English I-Ii, Iii, Iv.* 3rd edn, 3 vols. Sydney: NSW Adult Migrant English Service.
Hamayan, E. 1995: Approaches to alternative assessment. *Annual Review of Applied Linguistics* 15, 212–26.

Hamp-Lyons, L. and Lynch, B.K. 1998: Perspectives on validity: a historical analysis of language testing conference abstracts. In Kunnan, A.J., editor, *Validation in language assessment: selected papers from the 17th Language Testing Research Colloquium, Long Beach*. Mahwah, NJ: Lawrence Erlbaum, 253–76.

Jacoby, S. and Ochs, E. 1995: Co-construction: an introduction. *Research on Language and Social Interaction* 28, 171–83.

Lado, R. 1961: *Language testing: the construction and use of foreign language tests*. London: Longmans Green and Co.

Lynch, B.K. and Hamp-Lyons, L. 1999: Perspectives on research paradigms and validity: tales from the Language Testing Research Colloquium. *Melbourne Papers in Language Testing* 8, 57–93.

McKenna, A. 1996: The development of the National Reporting System as a social literacy event. MA thesis, University of Melbourne.

McNamara, T.F. 1996: *Measuring second language performance*. London and New York: Longman.

—— 1997: 'Interaction' in second language performance assessment: whose performance? *Applied Linguistics* 18, 446–66.

—— 1999: *Validity in language testing: the challenge of Sam Messick's legacy*. 1st Messick Memorial Lecture, Language Testing Research Colloquium (LTRC), Tsukuba, Japan, July.

Messick, S. 1989: Validity. In Linn, R.L., editor, *Educational measurement*. Third edition. New York: Macmillan, 13–103.

Moore, H. 1996: Telling what is real: competing views in assessing English as a Second Language development. *Linguistics and Education* 8, 189–228.

—— 1999: Bureaucratic and educational governmentalities in contact: cooperation and conflict. Paper presented as part of the Colloquium *How might applied linguists respond professionally to state agendas?*, American Association for Applied Linguistics Conference, Stanford, CT, March.

Morrow, K. 1979: Communicative language testing: revolution or evolution? In Brumfit, C.J. and Johnson, K., editors, *The communicative approach to language teaching*. Oxford: Oxford University Press, 143–57.

Peirce, B.N. and Stewart, G. 1997: The development of the Canadian language benchmarks assessment. *TESL Canada Journal* 14, 17–31.

Pennycook, A. 1994: Incommensurable discourses? *Applied Linguistics* 15, 1.15–38.

Shohamy, E. 1998: Critical language testing and beyond. *Studies in Educational Evaluation* 24, 331–45.

—— 2001a: *The power of tests: a critical perspective on the uses of language tests*. London: Pearson.

Shohamy, E. 2001b: Democratic assessment as an alternative. *Language Testing* 18 (4), 373–91.

Spolsky, B. 1995: *Measured words*. Oxford: Oxford University Press.

Swain, M. 1999: *Mediating second language learning through collaborative dialogue*. Paper given at the 12th AILA Conference, Tokyo, August.

—— 2001: Examining dialogue: another approach to content specification and to validating inferences drawn from test scores. *Language Testing* 18, 275–302. Based on the Samuel Messick Memorial Lecture, Language Testing Research Colloquium, Vancouver, March 2000.

Trim, J.L.M. 1997: The proposed Common European Framework for the description of language learning, teaching and assessment. In Huhta, A., Kohonen, V., Kurki-Suonio, L. and Luoma, S., editors, *Current developments and alternatives in language assessment: proceedings of LTRC 1996*. Jyväskylä: University of Jyväskylä and University of Tampere, 415–21.

Wall, D. 1997: Impact and washback in language testing. In Clapham, C.M. and Corson, D., editors, *Language Testing and Assessment*. [Volume 7 of *Encyclopaedia of Language and Education*]. Dordrecht, The Netherlands: Kluwer, 291–302.

Young, R. and He, A.W. editors, 1998: *Talking and testing*. Amsterdam: John Benjamins.

Chapter 21

PATRICIA A. DUFF, PING WONG, AND MARGARET EARLY

LEARNING LANGUAGE FOR WORK AND LIFE

The linguistic socialization of immigrant Canadians seeking careers in healthcare (2000)

I N   A N   E R A   C H A R A C T E R I Z E D   B Y an increasingly mobile labour force, changing populations, and transformations in the nature of work, work-related communication, and multiple literacies (Hull, 1997; New London Group, 1996; Taylor, 1997), teachers, scholars, government agencies, employers, and employees need to understand important issues surrounding the use of language(s) at work in order to provide suitable intercultural language training and support for employees and, perhaps, to modify workplace interaction and other aspects of work. However, second-language (L2) research has focused historically on either academic oral and written English as a Second Language (ESL) issues at the kindergarten to university levels, or on the grammatical development of uninstructed adults with little reference to their linguistic experiences at work or in the wider community (Ellis, 1994). Therefore, it is essential that more contextualized research be conducted in work-related programs with adult ESL learners, particularly as more programs are being established for ESL and skills training in (or for) workplaces in Canada and throughout the world (McGroarty, 1992; Roberts, Davies, & Jupp, 1992). Examining the experiences of individuals interacting in different languages (first language [L1], L2, or third language [L3]) in work environments and examining the new literacies and competencies required for work (Garay & Bernhardt, 1998) provides a basis for improving work conditions, productivity, mutual understanding, and cooperation among employees and management teams to the ultimate benefit of both workers and society. Research also reveals the social, cognitive, linguistic, and intercultural complexities of work and communication in times of intensive globalization.

This paper discusses research in ESL for work, identifying gaps in the existing literature and promising directions for new explorations. We then present a qualitative study conducted in one type of program for immigrant women and men in Western Canada seeking to become long-term resident care aides or home support workers.[1] We examine the linguistic and social processes at work in the education and integration of immigrant ESL speakers into the workforce and the broader community, the issues participants in such programs face, and the insights that can be gleaned for understanding language socialization in this context.[2] Of particular interest is the striking contrast observed in one such program between the instructional focus on medical and general English language proficiency, as well as nursing skills, and the actual communication requirements within both public and private institutions with large numbers of staff and patients (called residents) who do not speak English, and who, in the case of the elderly, may also face a number of other communication difficulties associated with ageing and illness. We also identify the restricted opportunities of many immigrant ESL learners to interact with English speakers before, during, and after language and skills programs, thus preventing them from becoming integrated more fully into English-speaking society. Finally, we highlight the importance of enabling immigrants to develop their English proficiency and marketable skills, which increases their self-esteem, social identity, independence, and overall integration.

Setting new agendas for research on language and literacy education and workplace communication with nonnative English-speaking adults

Wong (1998) identified four major thematic areas of research that have been done on the integration of immigrants into the workforce: (a) immigrant women and employment, which examines market/labour issues, women in the labour market, and barriers to improving job prospects; (b) access to training programs, including systemic, organizational, and personal barriers; (c) vocational ESL (VESL) and English for the workplace (e.g., curriculum issues, needs assessment, outcomes, the integration of language and content/skills, and workplace-ESL programs); and (d) immigrant settlement and identity issues, which covers issues of self-esteem, women's entry into the workforce, identities within family and society, and language and training as crucial aspects of settlement. Examples of previous research are found in Burnaby and Cumming (1992) and in the *English for Specific Purposes Journal* (1984, no. 3). Some highlights from research on English language education for work are reviewed below, and recommendations are made for future research.

The disadvantaged position of immigrants (particularly non-English-speaking and non-White women) in the labour force and their over-representation in low-paying service and manufacturing sectors (e.g., in hotel cleaning units and factories) and under-representation in white-collar occupations has been the focus of several Canadian studies (e.g., Beach & Worswick, 1993; Boyd, 1992; Buijs, 1993; Ng & Estable, 1987). Issues of a similar nature in Europe have been discussed by De Troy (1987) and Payne (1991). More recent studies have explored the difficulties, in terms of obstacles and barriers, that immigrant women especially face gaining access to training and employment for even low-status jobs (e.g., Kouritzen, 2000; Tisza, 1997; Wilson, 1998; Wong, 1998). However, relatively little qualitative research has tracked women who are in, or have completed, training programs or has examined the personal impact on the participants' lives, their families, and communities (Ng & Estable, 1987). Burnaby (1992) therefore called for more research into the lives of participants in these programs, before, during, and afterwards, and the relationships between the programs and what they enable students to achieve outside of class, namely in the workplace and society in general. Thus the actual implementation of workplace-oriented ESL curricula and concomitant linguistic socialization and acculturation processes require further research.

Furthermore, Cumming and Gill (1992) called for a greater focus on gender in understanding adults' opportunities and potential to learn a L2 and improve their personal circumstances. They described some of the factors preventing immigrant women from participating more fully in ESL (and/or skills) programs and noted high attrition rates in enrolments. Goldstein (1997), Peirce, Harper, and Burnaby (1993), and Harper, Peirce, and Burnaby (1996) researched some of these topics successfully in their studies of women in factories in Ontario, adding critical theoretical perspectives (see also Peirce, 1995). Many deterrents to participation in English workplace programs (EWP) and English use among coworkers were reported, including fear of income loss, resentment of peers, domestic pressures, and the need for affiliation and solidarity with compatriots (Goldstein, 1997; Peirce et al., 1993). In addition, Harper et al. (1996) noted that increased participation in EWP classes did not necessarily increase involvement in the company. Finally, taking a critical feminist approach, Rockhill (1991) conducted life history interviews with 35 Hispanic women in the United States, more than half of whom were recent immigrants. She underscored the tensions associated with English language and literacy education—the sometimes competing desires and threats immigrant women experience as they attempt to break out of the status quo:

> Contextualizing literacy, breaking it down into literacy and language practices, looking for differences between the experiences of men and women, and seeking to understand how these are related to cultural as well as gender differences, has led me to see three ideas as important to explicating immigrant women's educational experiences. The first is that literacy is women's work but not women's right; the second idea is that the acquiring of English is regulated by material, cultural and sexist practices that limit women's access to the "public," confining them to the private sphere of the home; the third idea is that literacy is both threat and desire.
>
> (p. 338)

More generally, in the United States, Canada, Australia, England, and other countries over the past 15 years, interesting initiatives have been taken to better understand the language, literacy, and numeracy needs of members of the labour force or those wishing to (re)enter the labour force, many of them ESL speakers. In addition, research funding has been earmarked specifically for such endeavours. In Canada, funding from the federal government for a trans-Canada Metropolis Project has focused on immigrant settlement issues in major cities; moreover, a new series of federal grants entitled the Valuing Literacy in Canada Program, administered by the Social Sciences and Humanities Research Council of Canada, has targeted adult (L1 and L2) literacy, with workplace, community, and family literacy as key areas. In Australia and the United States, concerted efforts have also been made to identify priorities for research with adult populations, both inside and outside of workplaces (e.g., Brindley et al., 1996; Center for Applied Linguistics, 1998). These studies have, for example, identified the need for more research on the assessment and measurement of adult ESL learners' progress and achievement, and on the impact of participation in adult ESL programs on the lives of participants and their families.

In summary, recommendations in many of the above-cited studies and reports call for increased contextualized, interpretive, and even critical studies of a qualitative nature examining the experiences, barriers, outcomes, and personal transformations associated with adult language and literacy education. They also discuss the marginalization of many ESL adults in terms of employment and educational opportunities and the need to examine the factors that promote or impede successful participation in language and skills programs and related occupations, as well as the broader social, political, and economic constraints that participants face. The study described below attempts to fill this gap and to suggest implications for future research and curriculum development.

The study

We report on a research project examining nonnative English speakers' (NNESs') participation in two related work-oriented programs sponsored by an immigrant services agency in Western Canada, together referred to as the Resident Care/Home Support Attendant (RC/HSAT) program(s). The programs combined ESL language skills and nursing skills to prepare students to work in the healthcare profession as long-term resident care aides, that is, to care for the elderly or others requiring extended care in nursing homes, hospitals, and private homes. Research on ESL/immigrant populations in long-term resident care is especially important in our view, since it is a field that employs large numbers of immigrant women and, as the baby boomer generation ages, will no doubt require even larger numbers of workers; in addition, the current shortage of nurses and doctors in Canada and the downsizing of healthcare facilities has received considerable recent media coverage, yet foreign-trained healthcare practitioners seeking employment in the field face many obstacles. Finally, clinical practice in resident care poses many linguistic and cultural challenges to all aspiring practitioners—immigrant and otherwise—connected with the technical, social, and cross-cultural aspects of providing care and communicating with elderly patients in multilingual work environments; interesting evidence of this is the growing number of publications on transcultural nursing (e.g., Andrews & Boyle, 1999; Luckmann, 1999). Research on language in healthcare occupations and workplaces is therefore extremely timely (for previous studies in this area, see Frank, 2000; Meyer & Bates, 1998; Svendsen & Krebs, 1984; Wilson, 1998; Wong, 1998).

In accordance with the recommendations for research with adult ESL students outlined above, our study involved two components: (a) research on nine former students from programs in 1995–96 and 1996–97, examining how their lives, employment status, and integration into Canadian society had changed over time as a result of participation in this workplace-oriented program; and (b) research on a current cohort of students, of whom 11 agreed to participate in this project over the 1997–98 period. The second study featured similar questions but had the added advantage of drawing upon introspective data from participants at different points in the program.

The study set out to uncover many kinds of information about one type of workplace-oriented ESL program. Three questions guiding the research reported here are: (a) Who were the participants and what were their perceived and real-life circumstances, threats, and desires in coming to the RCA/HSAT program?; (b) What was the nature of the language/literacy activities and socialization in which the participants engaged during their practical experience in workplace settings, as part of their practicums or their eventual employment as long term resident care aides?; and (c) What was the impact of the program on the lives of the participants? We were especially interested in examining the complexity of integration into Canadian society and the workforce for long-term and recent immigrant women learning ESL and their multilingual and multicultural experiences at work.

Following Rockhill (1991), the research incorporated feminist, interpretive approaches to studying the lives of women (and two men) moving from marginal positions in Canadian society toward the mainstream by also examining the threats, desires, and triumphs they reported in the process.[3] Furthermore, we sought new perspectives of a more general nature on the complexities of intercultural communication and language socialization at work.

In the following sections, the institutional context of the program and the structure of the RC/HSAT program are described and the research methods used in this study are discussed. We examine participants' motivations and expectations prior to the program, noting that constraints on participants' English language education and use prior to applying to the program were in many cases galvanizing factors for their enrolment and desire to become resident care aides. The main focus, however, is on the elements of linguistic socialization within the program. Of greatest interest is the powerful, yet sometimes contradictory, language socialization experienced within courses and in the practicum. For example, being a care aide requires high levels of technical or medical English proficiency; however, in some contexts, interpersonal English communication is far more central to the aides' daily interactions than is their medical English knowledge; and in other contexts, English plays only a very minor role, and body language and other forms of communication are vital, especially with non-English-speaking residents or those with language-related disabilities. We discuss briefly the outcomes of the programs and participants' success securing work, becoming more integrated within English-speaking society, and feeling that their circumstances, self-esteem, and roles and identities have changed and improved. Given the realities of life and work in multicultural and multilingual urban society where English may play only a minor role, we consider the implications for curriculum and program development in this area.

Institutional context: agency and program

The RC/HSAT program took place at a not-for-profit, government-funded institution called Immigrant Settlement Agency (ISA, a pseudonym), one of the largest settlement and serving agencies for immigrants and refugees in Western Canada. ISA has a training institute with Language Instruction for Newcomers to Canada (LINC) classes (Literacy to LINC 3), Adult Education English, occupational training, and employment skills programs, and a settlement house for refugees. In addition to the RC/HSAT program, there were occupational training programs for the hospitality industry, cooking, warehousing, painting and decorating, and office skills. The skills-training programs combine language and skills training and provide some allowances for training and transportation.

The RC/HSAT programs had been offered in one form or another for the past 10 years. The Project Manager, Janet (a pseudonym), had been with the program at ISA for 3 years and thus was very familiar with the institutional context and with current and former students included in this study.[4] The program involved 17 weeks of in-class instruction on nursing and ESL, and a 9-week practicum divided between two sites: 6 weeks at an extended care facility (an inner-city hospital) and 3 weeks at an intermediate care facility (a suburban nursing home). The program had a longstanding relationship with the two practicum sites, and all students received placements at both facilities, in turn. In addition to the practicum, the academic program included instruction on communications; basic principles of health, wellness, and ethics; home maintenance; anatomy, physiology, personal care skills, illness, and disease; equipment practice in a university hospital training lab; and first aid. Students' grades were determined by their practicum performance and other examinations. They attended their nursing ("skills") class for 4 hours each morning and ESL class for 2.5 hours in the afternoon. The morning instructor, Nancy, had considerable expertise in nursing and nurse education, and the afternoon instructor, Susan, was an experienced ESL teacher. Susan used nursing content in the assigned textbook for some of her instruction and general ESL materials the rest of the time. For logistical reasons, communication between instructors was not extensive.[5] However, Janet and other staff members (e.g., Mena, the practicum supervisor) provided crucial links between the two components of the program. The program could accommodate 16 students per year, from a pool of 50–60 applicants. Participants were screened on the basis of their level of English, their previous education and experience, their motivation and commitment to becoming health caregivers, and a number of other factors, such as employment status at the time of application. All applicants had to be landed immigrants or Canadian citizens. Home-Support (HS) participants from the past-cohort (1995–96) were required to be on social assistance at the time of application to be eligible for admission; for the combined RC/HSAT programs in 1996–98, applicants were required to be recipients of Employment Insurance (EI, formally known as Unemployment Insurance, UI) or "exhaustees," whose funding had been terminated. Some of the participants on EI, for example, had been laid off from jobs in the garment industry due to recent factory closures. Although the past (HS) and present (Resident Care) programs differed in certain respects, we refer to them as one program type (RC/HSAT) unless differences are specifically relevant to the analysis.[6]

Participants had learned about the program from friends, relatives, human resources offices, newspapers, and other sources. Most stated that they chose this program because of their desire to care for the elderly, an important service to society. The funding for the program was determined on a yearly basis by competitive government grants. The program was considered largely successful because of its deliberate integration of language and work skills, its accessibility to students whose English was not strong enough for other programs (such as college nursing programs) and the high rates of retention for students and employment for graduates.[7]

Data collection procedures

Data for this study come primarily from interviews with participants that were transcribed and analyzed for themes related to the three research questions. The 9 "past-cohort" students were interviewed once each, in most cases by telephone (see Wong, 1998);[8] and the 11 "present-cohort" students were interviewed individually at the beginning of their program, in focus groups during their clinical practicum, and then individually again at the end of the program. Thus, including the two focus groups, there were a total of 33 recorded interviews with students, each of which lasted an average of 30–45 minutes. Except for the telephone or focus group interviews (which took place at the hospital), interviews took place in a room at ISA. All participants provided their informed consent,[9] and students who chose not to participate, for whatever reason, were excluded from the study. We had hoped originally to conduct ongoing observations in the classroom and clinical settings in order to compare formal and informal language social-ization (i.e., in class versus the workplace) and to observe the linguistic and nonlinguistic negotiation of meanings in context, but were unable to obtain permission to do so because of the potential (or perceived) invasiveness of our presence in these institutional contexts. We did spend one morning observing the nursing class and were on site on several other occasions to speak with instructors and staff and to explain the study to members of the class; we also visited the university nursing lab when the class was there and attended the graduation ceremony for the ISA class at the end of the program.

We interviewed the language and skills instructors (Susan and Nancy), clinical practicum supervisor (Mena), project manager (Janet), and training institute director (Carl), and obtained program documents that helped contextualize our analysis. In addition, follow-up inquiries were made six months after the present-cohort program ended to find out about changes in the lives of the staff as well as recent programmatic changes. Therefore, our understandings of program and workplace language/communication processes, including socialization experiences, come primarily from students' and staff members' accounts rather than direct observation, with one unanticipated exception: when the ESL teacher became ill for several days, Wong was asked to serve as a substitute teacher (because she was already on staff in a different ESL program at ISA and was now acquainted with this program as well) and, as a result, she learned more about the participants, their level of English, and the nursing and ESL curriculum.

Women in ESL/healthcare education were our initial focus, reflecting realities associated with this profession (i.e., more women students and workers in long-term care) and our commitment to foregrounding the linguistic socialization of immigrant women into professional life and work. However, since both past- and present-cohorts had one male participant each who offered their own unique perspectives, those data are included as well.

Participants

The first research question set out to provide a description of the people in the study, their motivation for wanting to learn English and nursing to become care aides, their English language needs and competencies, and the tensions they faced seeking further education and employment. Of the 20 participants in the combined-cohort study, 18 were females and 2 were males (see Tables 21.1 and 21.2). Their ages generally ranged from early 30s to late 40s, although the present-cohort had 3 women in their early to mid-20s. Participants came from Hong Kong/People's Republic of China ($n = 8$), Philippines (3), Ethiopia/Eritrea (3), Central America (2), South America (1), Sri Lanka (1), Poland (1), and Vietnam (1). The majority (12) were married and had children. A smaller number were either single parents (3), single with no children (3), or recently married with no children (2). Family situation and previous employment help account for the challenges participants faced seeking access to professional programs and careers, in light of their child care and other family and work responsibilities. Also, although we didn't know all aspects of their personal histories, we had indications of the tribulations some had faced long before their immigration. The nursing instructor once remarked, "I need to remember to step back and understand some of these folks have lived lives and experiences [war, refugee camps] that I've only seen on CNN."

Some of the participants had already been in Canada for as long as 22 years (e.g., Anna), although most had been here for 10 years or less (the median length of Canadian residence was 6 years). They had various kinds and levels of academic or vocational training and work experience in their home or other previous countries; for example, in nursing (Karina, Madga, Yin, Min), medicine (Grace), home care (Rita, Fatima), teaching (Jan), secretarial and cashier services (Sofia, Maria, Chen), and bookkeeping (Juan). Once in Canada, they had been employed mostly in factory work (Juan, Jan, Grace, May, Min, Anna, Karina, with varying levels of responsibility), cleaning (Chen, Sofia), or public/private service-sector jobs (e.g., as clerks or nannies: Vida, Rita, Yin, Betty, Fatima). Tables 21.1 and 21.2 provide a comparison of participants' formal education and training, their occupations before coming to Canada, and their occupation in Canada prior to the ISA program. The tables also reveal that the present-cohort participants had, overall, more post-secondary college and university education and somewhat higher-status positions than the past-cohort students had (e.g., as medical doctor, factory manager, teacher, and nurse), both in their home countries and in Canada following their immigration (e.g., with higher-status factory positions); however, these differences are not great, and both cohort groups had experienced considerable downward occupational mobility from white- to blue-collar jobs.

Participants had studied ESL in Canada or in their countries of origin from a few months to several years. Although students with upper-intermediate or higher ESL skills were sought, as judged by a standard ESL test and interview (the present-cohort level being a bit lower than usual), records indicated that students spanned a range from lower-intermediate to advanced proficiency in English. ESL proficiency was just one of the factors taken into account in determining the suitability of applicants for admission to this program and for this career. Other qualities considered were presentation/personality, neatness, punctuality, attitudes/motivation, English communication skills and listening comprehension, sense of humour, flexibility, openness and honesty, commitment to the profession, and so forth.

Table 21.1 Description of research participants: past cohort (in alphabetical order, by pseudonym; male participant's name is asterisked)

Participant (N = 9)	Country of origin	Canadian immigration status	Years in Canada	Age	Marital status	Children and ages	Secondary education	Post-secondary training	Occupation in first or previous country	Occupation in Canada before HS/RCA
Alberto*	El Salvador	Citizen	20	Late 40s	Married	Two: 1,3	High school (Québec)	College, first year (El Salvador)	Student home support	Machine operator
Anna	Hong Kong	Citizen	22	Late 40s	Married	One: 26	Gr. 10 (Hong Kong)	—	—	Plastics factory worker
Fatima	Ethiopia	Citizen	8	Early 30s	Single	One: 4	Gr. 10 (Ethiopia)	—	Home support (Rome)	Cashier
Karen	Hong Kong	Landed immigrant	4	40s	Married	One: 18	Form 7 (Hong Kong)	Polytechnic, 1 yr, secret	Clerical officer	Office clerk
Karina	Sri Lanka	Landed	7	30s	Married	Three: 1,5,7	High school (Sri Lanka)	Nursing assistant	Nursing assistant	Stocking factory worker
Magda	Philippines	Landed	2	40s	Married	One: 10	High school (Philippines)	Nursing/ 4 yr B.Sc.	Registered nurse	Flyer stuffer
Rita	Philippines	Landed	5	Late 40s	Single	Four: 15–22	Gr. 10 (Philippines)	Nanny training	Caregiver to elderly (HK)	Nanny
Sofia	Poland	Landed	9	30s	Married	Two: 12, 14	Gr. 12 (Poland)	Nursing, 1st yr	Secretary	Cleaner
Yin	China	Landed	3	Early 30s	Single	None	Gr. 10 (China)	Nursing college	Registered nurse	Baby-sitter

Table 21.2 Description of research participants: present cohort (in alphabetical order, by pseudonym; male participant's name is asterisked)

Participant (N = 11)	Country of origin	Canadian immigration status	Years in Canada	Age	Marital status	Children and ages	Secondary education	Post-secondary training	Occupation in first or previous country	Occupation in Canada before HS/RCA
Betty	Eritrea	Citizen	9	30s?	Single	—	Gr. 12	Technical college, 1 yr	High school student	Convenience store clerk
Chen	PRC	Citizen	5	Mid-40s	Married	One: 18	Gr. 12	—	Accountant	Cleaner
Grace	PRC	Landed	1.5	40s?	Married	One: 10	Gr. 10	Medical university, 6+ yrs	GP at major hospital	Production worker
Jan	PRC	Landed	< 1	Late-40s	Married	One: 21	Middle school	Teachers' university	Manager, factory	Production worker
Juan*	Guatemala	Citizen	7	Late-30s	Married	Two: 7, 10	Gr. 12	University, public accounting (incomplete)	Bookkeeper	Factory production supervisor
Lily	PRC	Landed	2	Early-20s	Married	—	Gr. 12	Accounting: 2 yrs	Student (accounting/office skills)	Waitress
Maria	Chile	Citizen	8	Early-40s	Married	Two: 4–7	Gr. 12	Technical college	Secretary, private clinic	Home maintenance and nutrition
May	PRC	Citizen	14	Mid-40s	Married	Two: 12–24?	High school	—	Kindergarten teacher	Factory supervisor
Melanie	Eritrea	Citizen	4	Mid-20s	Married	—	High school (Canada)	—	High school student	Cashier
Min	Vietnam	Citizen	7	Mid-40s	Single	—	Gr. 11	1 yr nursing (on site)	Hospital nurse	Factory assembly
Vida	Philippines	Landed	5	Mid-30s	Single	One: 11 mo.	Gr. 12	B.Sc. agriculture; nanny program	Domestic helper and sales	Sandwich maker/nanny

Constraints on students' acquisition and use of English

Despite their current, and sometimes long-term, residence in Western Canada, students entering the program mentioned that they still had difficulties communicating in English and had relatively few opportunities to study ESL or to meet or develop friendships with native English speakers; consequently, they lacked confidence and feared public encounters in English. In this section, we recount some of their experiences and reflections on the acquisition and use of English prior to the program and the compensatory strategies they used.

First, students reported their distress at dealing with government agencies, using the telephone, and meeting with people in high-status positions or with interlocutors producing accented or highly technical English. The following account was not uncommon:

> It's difficult to listen and to speak. And, it's more difficult to speak out. I'm, some-sometimes I want I want to express my uh . . . my feeling, but I can't do it. It feels, it make me feel so dispress [depressed] . . .
>
> (Lily)

Like some of the other women in the study, May expressed her feelings of inadequacy and fear living in an English-dominant society with minimal knowledge of English:

> Before you know I . . . can't uh talk very well and cannot read or something very well. I cannot . . . step out to looking for job or talk to Western like uh that kind . . . Before I scared I can't do this I sometimes don't understand or sometimes I can't I can't do my language, like everything I can't do.

Maria from Chile explained:

> Before I felt like eh I didn't talk very well. I feel like . . . it's better if I don't talk too much because I don't know very well English and . . . I was . . . scared worried that the people will laugh . . . at me or . . . actually also in the phone . . . sometime I say "oh my God maybe they don't understand to me."

To compensate for restricted English oral proficiency, Lily and other participants developed functional communication strategies, such as asking interlocutors to speak slowly and repeat their utterances, and, in this way, they had been able to cope as long as they had:

> I will ask the person who is talking to to slow down. "Slow, can you repeat?" something and I maybe maybe I can write down the pronoun—the similar pronounce in the paper and after after the class, I ask the classmate. . . . I think [using English is] difficult in uh to the government office . . . Because they all—they always speak so fast. And also they use uh professional professional words I can't . . . understand. . . . If I don't understand "I am a, I am a ESL student, I can't catch the meaning, can you please repeat, it?" or "Can you can you say it easier?" [laugh]

Despite their acute desire to improve in English, some mentioned difficulties finding ESL tutors and opportunities to practice English prior to the program. Grace remarked: "I do not have have got people talk to me in English, teach me English. You know, sometimes you know the word, this word, this word, this word, but you don't know how to speak in sentence."

Another student, originally from Eritrea, echoed the same concern about her lack of contact with English speakers when she lived in Toronto where there were many people from her ethnic background. Similarly, Chinese students mentioned that their access to native English speakers was limited because of the size and vitality of the Chinese community on the West Coast. Lily recalled her isolation from English speakers and her difficulty even finding a native English speaker to interview for a class assignment:

> I always contact uh Chinese, Chinese I don't know where I can go to contact Canadians, [laugh] Sometimes I try to try to meet (this?) person in the library, but, I don't know why, every time I just catch Chinese. . . . You know, you know, last time, I actu—[our skills teacher] assign uh—give give us some assignment to do, interview an elderly person? I go to the library, I look around, [laugh] oh, where is the elderly? Then I catch a a a catch an elderly person, then I ask him, "Where do you come from?" Because his face look like a look like a English-speaking person. "I come from Hong Kong." I said "My God!" Then he speak Cantonese to me.

May expressed her desire to someday communicate more using English, even anticipating that her children might marry non-Chinese and she would need to communicate with them: "Even my children marry if some they don't know Chinese I can communication with them."

Thus, applicants to the RC/HSAT program were highly motivated to improve their L2 skills. Their time in Canada and previous ESL instruction had not equipped them with sufficient levels of comfort, confidence, or competence in speaking English in a wide range of public contexts. For some, this lack of ability (perceived or real) led to feelings of extreme isolation and insecurity. However, in addition to their desire for better L2 skills, they wanted to become care aides to gain (or change) occupational identities, to become better integrated into Canadian society, to have an opportunity to learn something new, and to build upon previous experiences they may have had in healthcare. We discuss these aspects in the following section.

Motivation to become care aides

Although being a care aide may not be considered a high-status role within the field of medicine or public health and, like nursing, is a heavily female-gendered profession, it was nonetheless already a step up for the participants in our study, a chance to move into the mainstream and improve their occupational status. Hence, learning English was important but not sufficient; learning something new and useful (content and marketable skills) was very attractive for those who had not studied for years. As Lily remarked, "Training can push you to learn, to think . . . just uh just talking about the language the English, you feel boring."

Salaries in resident care and home support, according to Wong (1998), are relatively good, paying up to $17 per hour in unionized facilities.[10] However, money was not the main motivator for most students either; it was more important to have an opportunity to learn English, to get a good job, and to have more contact with English-speaking Canadians. May recalled her interview to get into the program and how Janet emphasized that care aides need, above all, to want to help people:

> I passed because Janet's very good she said, "this course is not like uh your English very good, you have to everything like uh, you have to work like uh you like people.

You have to give back to society. You have to like that. Not like you want to make uh big money or something if. Money is important but you have to like uh help people." And I said, when she interview me, I said "I really like because my parents live with me. I care very good for them. Yeah. They live with me, almost nine years nine years. Yeah. I like those uh older people."

Lily, who had worked at a Chinese restaurant for years, also looked forward to having opportunities to deal with "real Canadians" and people from other cultures:

This my favourite job, it can help me to change my life . . . And to me to . . . go into the real Canadian's group. Yeah, I . . . am in there everyday. I communication with . . . come from different country people, so I know I know somebody about another country's culture or something. It's useful for me too in the future.

Students like Lily who had worked for years in jobs that did not require English were amazed and discouraged that after so many years their English proficiency was so limited. By then, some of them even had children attending English-medium universities. However, they sometimes faced opposition from spouses for whom it was not a priority to have their wives go to school and learn English. For example, May explained that she had worked in a blue-collar job for 12 years but still didn't know English. Desperate to study, she told her husband: "I want to study something, otherwise I'm just like a dummy." But with young children, her husband was reluctant to let her study for more than 2 months:

When I . . . finish that job, I feel like oh! I don't know English now. I only can speak a little bit oh everything I don't know how take exam take everything because . . . I didn't take ESL class . . . but when I have baby no one baby-sit. I think just stay home. Then I just like ah um my husband last time he got a night job and I have to look after two children at home. That's why go school when I almost fighting to my husband. "I want to study something, otherwise I'm just like a dummy, I don't want." He go, "Okay, just like got a one time's choice, night time twice a week." I got 2 months 2 months English and after that, no more.

Thus, May's desires also posed certain threats to her family. She explained that after her ESL class she got a job at a carbon company with "all those Western [Caucasian Canadian] people," where she started to learn English and remained for the next 5 years. It was only after she was laid off from another job that she thought, she might be able to improve her English and become a care aide, a job where she could work somewhat independently and help people. However, to reach a high-intermediate level of English would not be easy; and even after she took the ESL admission test she was afraid she had failed:

But I see English is uh need high intermediate and uh I think oh, oh I will fail, [laugh] Just went went to HS Education Centre they have 2 months start September to October 2 months and then I went to library free learning centre to just I don't know what I have to learn just okay I can pick this, pick that just everything I can do, I can learn, I just want to get in that course, maybe fail. Yeah, I think I got the English assessment it's not very good, I know. I forgot the body name. I know how to say but I don't know how to spell.

Magda, who had been a registered nurse in the Philippines, explained her disappointments and desires, related to the downward occupational mobility she had experienced:

> I was so desperate when I came here that I cannot practice my profession with, I mean, the length of experience that I had before. . . . I was really thankful when Janet gave me a chance to join the program, that I was able to go back again to the hospital.

Juan, whose wife had successfully completed the same program and had found employment, was highly motivated and also well informed about all that it entailed. Karen, who had been a clerk with a Chinese company, shared Lily's and May's desires to "get into the mainstream." Several participants had also been healthcare providers to ailing relatives or paying clients and felt they were well suited for the work. Others mentioned that they were looking to change careers after many years of other work or raising children. For some participants who had left behind extended families in their countries of origin, becoming a care aide was an opportunity to show compassion to people of their parents' or grandparents' generation, people with whom they missed having contact or who were now no longer living. Occasionally, participants also saw the program as providing an opportunity to gain relevant Canadian work experience and language training in order to get advanced-level education and employment in healthcare. However, the prospect of change and of returning to school also had attendant uncertainties; Anna, for example, who had been working at a plastics factory, had not been in school for nearly 35 years.

In summary, students cited a mixture of reasons for wanting to become care aides: they wanted to improve their English, study new content, become skilled, become more integrated in the English-speaking mainstream, get out of die house, have contact with seniors, serve society, work in healthcare once again (for those with previous experience), and gain secure jobs.

Experiences of linguistic socialization in healthcare settings

The second research question examines the nature of language use in the target workplaces and the continuing experiences of participants as they were socialized into the discourse and profession of care-giving. We divide our discussion of socialization into four categories: language connected with course work; the first practicum; the second practicum; and their eventual employment (if any) and role in their communities. We draw attention, in particular, to the remarkable contrasts across these four contexts of linguistic socialization and the resulting challenges faced by participants both during and after their programs.

The linguistic socialization that became of most interest to us was the "informal" type referred to by Scollon and Scollon (1995; Li, 2000), based on participants' compelling accounts of their field experiences in their two distinct practicum contexts—the inner-city hospital with frail, elderly immigrant residents, and the posh suburban facility with more affluent English-speaking residents—plus, in the case of graduates, their work experiences in private homes or other institutions. Informal socialization involved participants' ongoing observation and communication and other interactions with "residents," colleagues, supervisors, and people in the community, as opposed to their formal in-class linguistic experiences. Of course, the latter were also essential for the development of their professional identities and abilities, confidence, and English proficiency, although they are less central to the discussion in this paper. We discuss formal and informal aspects of language socialization, in turn, below.

Formal aspects of language socialization: English for nursing

In the nursing and ESL courses, students had particular difficulty with the technical English in lectures and nursing materials (using the text-book by Grubbs & Blasband, 1995). To illustrate the reading level, sections on Alzheimer's disease and digestion are shown below. (In these and other excerpts, deleted material is shown with three dots.)

> The resident with Alzheimer's Disease (AD) has a progressive nervous disorder that eventually destroys all mental function. It causes problems in thinking, communication, and behavior and causes physical deterioration resulting in death . . . Confusion, mood swings, depression, wandering, and poor judgment require special care that must be provided for the resident with AD.
>
> (p. 166)

> The major organs of the digestive system are the mouth, esophagus, small intestine, and large intestine (see Fig. 21–5). Accessory organs include the teeth, tongue, liver and gallbladder. The digestive system is also called the gastrointestinal or GI system. It is basically a long, continuous tube that begins at the mouth and ends at the anus (the opening to the rectum). . . .
>
> (p. 315)

Up to this point, many students had mentioned that composing complete sentences in English was problematic, so it was no wonder that the linguistic density of the medical texts and related in-class discussion were onerous. Even discussing simple bodily functions such as the elimination of wastes posed considerable linguistic and pragmatic challenges—yet care aides frequently needed to interact with their elderly or disabled residents in connection with those functions. Grace recalled: "Before came to this program, I just uh . . . know I—'I'm going to the bathroom.' But you . . . know the some words like uh 'seat,' but you don't know how to say . . . the detail." Nancy, the nursing instructor, cited the same example in her interview. In addition to being able to communicate grammatically, she pointed out that the students need to know sociolinguistically appropriate yet comprehensible terms to use with particular patients/residents. She explained that students have often already learned "the rough words" (e.g., for defecation or urination); however, they need to become comfortable using those terms with residents, which can be awkward for them. In addition, they need to consult their supervising nurse to find out what words their patient/resident uses for bathroom functions, so as not to be offensive. This is just one example of the complicated pragmatics of language use and language socialization in cross-cultural health education and healthcare.

Hence, navigating between technical, nontechnical, polite, and highly colloquial and functional oral English use with instructors, colleagues, patients/residents, residents' family members, and others was a major linguistic challenge, but one that Mena was confident the student care aides would be able to manage:

> When they are talking [with elderly hospital residents] sometimes it's better that you don't know the medical jargon . . . [They should] come down to their level and communicating the simple language that they would understand. . . . Although they are learning some terminology which is important from the whole, the way they are expressing themselves is in everyday terms. . . . I'm not trying to patronize them or anything. They have learned a lot of terminology which is important too. Disease for

instance. But I think that when they are talking and communicating with their client I don't think they'll have a problem with that at all [i.e., using nontechnical language].

During the practicum, however, some students still struggled with technical terminology:

> Many thing we can't know how to call that yeah if before that we can know everything they they have special names yeah because in hospital there there maybe some professional name. If if we can know this word before yeah so sometimes I ask help to ask . . . them which one how to call this one that one sometimes I was confused.
>
> (Chen)

In addition to the technical language of nursing and the colloquial language needs of patient care, our classroom observation revealed that the animated nursing lessons also contained many anecdotes and tips (e.g., related to elder care), rapid, colloquial speech, as well as academic register and considerable listening comprehension related to lectures by the teacher or guest speakers and videotapes explaining medical concepts. Nancy acknowledged that it was extremely challenging to cover all the material, even more so with a mixed-level ESL group such as the present-cohort. (Nancy had previously worked in nurse education with native English speakers at the college level.) She felt that the video and curriculum materials were far too difficult for the students and that, just as they were being stretched to learn the material, so too was she being socialized into appropriate levels of English language use with the group:

> Their levels of English are so broad . . . Because I'm teaching them medicalese which is a totally different language again . . . I've been in [the field] so long . . . I assume they know what [those words] mean. [So now] I think before I talk and I'll say okay I want to say this but how can I say it easier . . . and then in a way that they are not going to find aggressive or threatening and they will understand. . . .

The students worked very hard to master the language and content in time for the first practicum. In addition to speaking, listening, and reading skills, students were also required to develop skills for preparing written reports about patients/residents. Mena felt they needed additional work on both writing and grammar. Karina, a past-cohort graduate, also mentioned this point:

> In our working place we have to write reports for the other person, what happened with this client. Everything explain to the other person so other person won't have any problem to continue her work . . . So we have to write in order to understand. So we learned. Before that I don't very well, but I learned in this ESL.

Janet explained that report writing, oral presentations of the kind a care aide might make in a ward, language usage at various levels (with residents, colleagues, supervisors, family members, etc.), and other aspects of language were crucial aspects to be covered in the ESL course.

Besides the linguistic demands of the course material, Nancy felt that students needed to be taught how to ask for help with domestic tasks at home so they would have enough time and energy to devote to their studies. Therefore, language socialization also extended to the home sphere. She taught them to say: "Could you do this for me . . . you know I need your help."

She felt that if spouses were resistant, as they seemed to be in some cases, children could be asked to help first, then perhaps husbands might follow suit.

Another aspect of their prepracticum experience was dealing with cultural aspects of caregiving, learning from each other's different cultural orientations to physicality, intimacy, chastity, privacy, and so forth, and expectations regarding who cares for the elderly and ill (i.e., relatives vs. nonrelatives, males vs. females, high-status vs. low-status members of society). According to Nancy, even discussing certain topics in class with a male present (e.g., Juan) proved awkward at times for some of the women for cultural reasons. The staff were all very sensitive to these issues and to dealing with the participants as complex, whole, worthy individuals with their own sensibilities and cultured, gendered life experiences. Susan, the ESL instructor, explained that many of the women in the current-cohort had low self-esteem when they entered the program because of their circumstances, cultural background, and other factors. However, she said that, with the program's emphasis on the "whole person" (i.e., mental, physical, emotional, spiritual, social), students also became more aware of themselves as complete people with a variety of needs. As they discovered this concept they were transformed. Susan also had a special interest in voice—in conveying education and social status through one's own communication skills. She therefore emphasized pitch, tone, breathing, and voice training that would enhance the students' self-concept and the effectiveness and power of their communication.

Thus, instructors and students alike experienced less formal linguistic socialization at different levels, although probably none more so than the students themselves. In the following sections, we discuss specific and unique aspects of language socialization that participants experienced during their practical work experience at Central Hospital and Seaview Gardens (pseudonyms), respectively. Although both are considered excellent care facilities, the different communication requirements for apprentice care aides in each work setting were particularly intriguing.

First practicum: communication at its most rudimentary level

For the first practicum, all students were placed in a large inner-city institution, Central Hospital, for 6 weeks. They had already completed several months of ESL and nursing education and were eager to apply both their language and content skills. However, their experiences at the hospital ranged from shocking to exhilarating as they learned to deal with very sick and elderly residents who depended on them for almost all their needs and who, in some cases, would die soon. As Nancy anticipated correctly, "after they get into the practicum situation, they are going to have their socks blown off." What was perhaps more surprising and demanding than the heavy physical and emotional demands of working with this population were the enormous linguistic and cultural challenges in a workplace where 90% of the patients were ethnically Chinese. The students had not fully anticipated the difficulties they would have communicating with colleagues and patients who were not proficient in English, spoke varieties of Chinese that even the Mandarin and Cantonese speakers in the group could not understand, or who had conditions such as Alzheimer's, dementia, deafness, blindness, even toothlessness, making communication all the more difficult. Some students felt they needed to learn Cantonese but later found that the patients spoke Toisan (another southern Chinese dialect) instead. In focus groups, students spoke frankly about their experiences with linguistic socialization at Central Hospital. In the following section, we examine some of the concerns and experiences participants had, opportunities for verbal and nonverbal language socialization, and the lessons they learned as a result.

Learning ESL for a Chinese-dominant workplace

The overriding linguistic concern mentioned by participants was that they were immersed in a world of very elderly, frequently very ill, Chinese speakers with whom communication required much more than ESL proficiency or technical expertise. Chen, a Mandarin speaker who had left a cashier's position to take the RC/HSAT program because she could not communicate with her mainly Cantonese-speaking customers, found herself in a similar situation at Central Hospital:

> Because I speak uh Mandarin but most customer they speak Cantonese so so for the cashier I can't handle. [laugh] Yeah so I think it's a problem because um my English is not enough but also I have difficult for the Cantonese so I I think I have to learn some . . . because they say uh 90% the [Central Hospital] residents they are Cantonese . . . so I have to learn some some Cantonese . . . Because I think people they get sick they may hope the the the staff to help them to say the same language you can make them comfort.

By the end of the practicum, Chen reported that she had successfully learned to speak Cantonese with residents. Similarly, another Mandarin speaker, Grace, described how difficult it was to have to learn *both* English and Cantonese simultaneously in order to work effectively:

> They are Chinese but they speak in Cantonese right? They they couldn't understand English. I'm a Chinese but I speak Mandarin [laughs] so they can't understand English they can't understand Mandarin so it's really hard to communicate . . . I need to learn Cantonese. But my English is not good. I need to learning English and Cantonese too. It's too hard.

Juan, the only male in the present-cohort and a native Spanish speaker, discovered that he and his classmates were not the only ones having difficulty communicating with the elderly residents. Each student had a "buddy" who helped with language and skills. Juan's buddy, a Cantonese speaker who had lived in Canada for 17 years and was very proficient in English, had achieved different levels of communication with each resident. However the buddy's knowledge of Cantonese was insufficient to communicate with the Toisan-speaking patients. Therefore, Juan's language socialization included learning about Chinese dialects, (in)comprehensibility across different varieties and disabilities, and linguistic guesswork.

> From one lady he [my buddy] understand only 50%, another lady he understand 25%. And he explain me why, because what happens, it's lots of village, and every village has their own language. So even though he speaks Cantonese, he wasn't able to understand really each word. So he says, "I guessing. Maybe I think I have a word, I pick up a word, I get a clue, and I think, the rest I guessing" . . . And he start teach me everything, "Oh you do this, you do that" . . . So I feel okay now.

"Reading" and "writing" (on) physical bodies: nonverbal communication and compassion

Most of the present-cohort students stated that being able to understand and communicate using body language, to "read" and "write" visual (or kinetic, tactile) expressions (or texts) with patients, was both crucial and part of their linguistic socialization or apprenticeship. May, who spoke three varieties of Chinese fluently but not Toisan, found that, in the end, she resorted to very simple language (e.g., "Good?"), body language, and other nonlinguistic ways of meeting residents' fundamental needs. The feedback she received, in turn, sometimes indicated that the communication had been successful:

> But they say something, still can't understand. But. uh y'know for some . . . you don't [use] the language, you learn the body language. You touch him, massage with them, and they feel like love, very good. So most of the surface just uh physical care, eat, and body care, clean or something like that. But they need uh I think something like home, love, security, I think. . . . Even they cannot talk, they will "hi" like this [gestures] when see you, you care them 1 week or 2 weeks later right? They cannot say, but they can say "Hi," like, know you. They're very happy, the eyes very happy, not like . . . oh, mad right? . . . "You want this one?" You have to show it to them. Yeah. So, it's body language it's work, for them. They know some limit of English, you say "Good?" And you can get feedback from them. "Ah good" yeah.

One of the African participants, Melanie, reported feeling disadvantaged by not knowing (or being) Chinese but related one happy occasion when she was able to communicate successfully with a resident nonverbally, in connection with a photo of the woman's daughter. Later, the daughter praised Melanie: "You know, my mom, she said you are good care of her and keep going. . . ." Melanie said that the elderly mother "then hand me a banana or something, 'Take it, take it for you, eat, eat.' She's nice. You can communicate like that." Thus, Melanie received positive feedback from her resident despite communication obstacles. For some participants, however, it was frustrating not to receive from the patients any concrete linguistic or nonlinguistic feedback about whether they had satisfied their needs. Nevertheless, in the process, they also discovered levels of communication, compassion, empathy, and love that they had not expected:

> I can do okay for them even by body languages but I want to know from them if I did good thing or bad thing for them. That's the feeling I had . . . if you give someone a care you have to know how you did it from them. You have to get feedback from them.
>
> (Melanie)

> I was expecting y'know English speakers, but there are other languages, so it's hard to communicate. Especially from today, the one I got she's a blind and also deaf. Last time also I found the same, she's blind and deaf, so it's hard communicate but there is always a way to do something, so I was using my touching. So it's quite okay, [laughs]
>
> (Betty)

The need to resort to physical touch for communication was threatening to Juan's sense of masculinity at first, leading him to question his choice of this predominantly female occupation. But he then realized that such difficulties were merely interesting challenges that he could overcome; he could "jump the barrier" (and, indeed, he was considered by program staff to be an excellent care aide):

> I was thinking, What am I doing in a women's job or whatever, y'know? But after Monday I was okay. I'm really happy and I really like it. I enjoy this job, I love it actually. Because it's really challenging for me. And I found out, even I don't speak the

language, but with you give them love . . . we establish communication. Because then—somehow they let me know what they want. Even with just pointing fingers, or the eyes. Or for example if I'm cleaning a lady she's paraplegic, for example, right? She doesn't move anything. Stroke and everything, right? But when I feeding her, she doesn't want something, she just clench her mouth like that. I know she doesn't like it. But—so I switch something else, I explain it "We're gonna try the peach pie, or whatever." And she ate, so she liked eh. So I find out, if you give them love, we get love back. Um, I know the language is a barrier but . . . I can jump the barrier.

Other students also found that vast amounts of compassion were needed to deal with this special population and that, like Juan, compassion increased with experience and exposure. Betty described one elderly resident with whom she worked:

She surprised me. . . . I didn't expect like that you know special blind and deaf and also you know usual dementia . . . but you don't know that voice but I noticed that when she's hungry. . . you know you can see her mouth she always [imitates the movement and sound] like this you know . . . I feel like she's hungry always when she . . . Sometimes she yell but we don't hear that [voice] . . . even I call my friend they speak Cantonese uh but is uh she's Chinese . . . but nobody can understand cause she's deaf so . . . Yeah. I became very compassion . . . so my feeling actually changed a lot. I didn't expect myself like that. . . . when I saw those people I changed a lot.

The challenge of communicating in long-term care facilities is accorded a chapter in the students' textbook (Chapter 8), with short sections on aspects of verbal and nonverbal communication, communication barriers (e.g., speaking too quickly), communication impairments (e.g., aphasia and poor vision or hearing), and communication with residents' family and friends. Other topics covered briefly are guidelines for recording patient information, answering the telephone, and using the computer. However, the discussion of nonverbal communication strategies and ways of dealing with barriers and impairments, which proved to be a major preoccupation throughout the practicum, was limited to just five pages, many of which contained glossy photos (e.g., a worker cleaning a resident's eye glasses, another checking a hearing aid). Thus, the demographics in long-term care facilities and the attendant communication barriers (on both sides) and impairments (among residents) did not appear to be a central concern for the writers of this textbook.[11]

Unexpected utility of participants' first language with residents

Students were dismayed at how little English was used at Central Hospital and that their Chinese skills, if present, were of equally limited utility because of mutually unintelligible dialects or other conditions that interfered with normal communication. Rather, they learned to communicate through touch and by reading subtle physical cues provided by their residents. However, in a few instances, students' were pleasantly surprised that their first language proved useful. For example, Juan was amazed that in this largely Chinese institution an ethnically Chinese resident would understand Spanish:

I think it was 2 weeks ago in this floor was a gentleman, he's Chinese. But he speaks so many languages. One of them is Spanish. So I speaking to him in Spanish. He had stroke (that's why he?) he's speak partially, but still I can understand him. So I was actually surprised.

Likewise, Min, the only Vietnamese participant, was pleased to find someone she could speak to and comfort in her L1:

> I knew one lady, she came from Vietnam. And she—when my classmate told me "she can speak Vietnamese, you can to talk to her." When I came to talk to her, oh she so happy. Said, "Oh, you speak Vietnamese? Okay, I feel lonely, nobody talk to me." And then said . . . "when you have time just come talk to me, talk to me." And I didn't know, before I thought um she was um Chinese because she look like Chinese, eh? And after that, she look at me around, she expect, expect me to come to talk to her, y'know?

Thus, these multilingual students brought resources to their work that monolingual English speakers did not have, skills that were very much appreciated by residents and are likely to become increasingly important in the future, given recent demographic and immigration trends.

Communicating about death and grief

Finally, participants sometimes had to deal with death and grieving during the practicum, topics covered both in the course and in their textbook. They found this prior information—understanding the stages of grieving, for example—very helpful albeit emotionally difficult. They were encouraged to communicate their feelings about the death of residents in their daily debriefing sessions with their instructors, in their optional practicum journals, and in other discussions and reflections. It was an especially sad experience for those who had managed to overcome communication barriers and make emotional connections with residents who, within days or weeks, died. As Chen wrote very poignantly in her practicum journal,

> Death and dying always like a shadow to me. During the flu period, there were several patients died. It was a shock and a sadness to me. Sometimes, I think it is unfair and disappointed. We contribute our warm hearts, give our best care to them. Our patients start smiling and showing their satisfaction from our help. They know somebody cares them, concerns them, but they have gone without least hesitation, (fortunately not one of my patients died.) I remember a patient who was a very interesting lady lived in [room #x]. She liked giving points to staff depending on their appearances. She gave 6 points to the most beautiful staff with her laughing and a thumb. She gave me only 4 points and told me the reason which is my upper front part of body is as flat as a pancake. Such a funny and cheerful person whose life was taken away from flu! I suspected the value of life. In those days, her figure in a wheelchair with a pair of sunglasses was always in my mind, even in my dream. The 6-week [practicum] is a remembrance of my life.

To summarize, the first practicum entailed an exploration of language and multilingual/multiliterate socialization in one inner-city workplace setting inhabited by many minority group members. Students learned to use residents' L1 to a certain extent, or found others with whom they could communicate in a common L1, or learned to communicate through body language and through other expressions of compassion and care. Ironically, everyday English and the technical language of nursing that students had studied for months were not particularly helpful or necessary. Indeed, participants later reflected that spending more time at the practicum site during the early part of the course, well before the actual practicum, would have helped them understand more fully the demands of working in this type of setting.

Second practicum: life-affirming communication

The second practicum took place close to the end of the program and represented a completely different experience for the research participants, one with which they were extremely satisfied. It was not accidental that the second site, Seaview Gardens, was the exact complement of the first site in several ways: Unlike those at the inner-city hospital, these residents were typically independent, affluent, English-speaking Caucasians who were elderly but enjoyed reasonably good health, although there was a special unit for dementia care and many residents also suffered from Alzheimer's. Their major need was affection and companionship, someone to talk to. In marked contrast with the sterile institutional setting at Central Hospital, the atmosphere at Seaview was homey as residents had many of their personal belongings in their rooms (bedspreads, TVs, photo albums, etc.) reminding them of their former lives in their own homes. For the students, this was the perfect opportunity to meet the "real Canadians" from whom they had felt isolated for so long, to not only provide care but also to be appreciated and respected as whole people by them. In this section, we consider the language socialization of care aides at Seaview by focusing on the themes of gaining rapport and confidence through interactions with residents; learning English (vocabulary, communication skills, pragmatics) from residents; discovering compassion and empathy; understanding oneself and others as displaced but whole people; and forging connections.

Gaining rapport and confidence through interaction

Residents helped the students with their language needs, inquired about their lives, taught them things, and told them about their own lives. This was possible because they were almost all proficient in English. In addition, many of them had been working professionals and therefore represented a class of English-speaking Canadians that students admired but with whom they had had limited contact in the past. As a result, participants' English, self-esteem, and confidence improved. May recalled: "They all English very good and then their back background is very good. And most yeah some like uh teacher like a army force uh uh like . . . and some businessman . . . Very good and then they can teach you something." Betty found that she got to know the residents well, and they enjoyed her visits:

> I became like you know very close friends uh special like two people they used to expect me "oh gee you are late today I was waiting for you" you know they need somebody to talk so like like we are sitting here they just expect it like they need to talk. So the whole day talking . . . so it was good.

Juan reported:

> I was speaking a lot with the residents . . . so that's the most I remember because . . . I was they was telling me the the the lives you know . . . the situations you know. . . . And at Seaview most of them are English speaking people and they're very aware.

Although most of the residents spoke English, there were exceptions, but overall these proved less demanding than at the hospital. However, the same skills using body language proved invaluable, and the communication was sufficiently meaningful that participants maintained contact with residents even months after the practicum. Maria reported her interactions with a non-English-speaking Chinese resident at Seaview:

My resident . . . she didn't speak any English but . . . only with eh . . . body language but we understand each other very very well and so that was very nice. It was very very kind lady and . . . actually I go out to see them I went to see them last week. . . . Because I like . . . that place very very much.

Learning English from residents: vocabulary and communication strategies

Students had many opportunities to learn English from their residents. They found it especially helpful to be able to ask them about meanings of unfamiliar words, synonyms, slang, and appropriate ways of expressing themselves better in context. Grace said, "I always ask them how do you say this how do you say that. Because I need to learn how to say. Sometimes you can . . . I can I can read and write and sometimes I can write but I can't speak correct."

> I ask them sometimes I have some three different words same meaning but different . . . like uh unconscious? Uh um conscious and awareness. And uh the other one . . . is uh . . . yeah I forget. Sometimes uh say almost like a same right? But the different time different uh use. I just ask them "why use this why use that?" They they can tell me um "because uh this is for you know already you have to know . . . unconscious like such and such." (May)

Chen explained how communication with residents was a bidirectional process of adjustment and accommodation:

> It's difference between uh you talking with the the um senior people. Sometimes they say the maybe slang I don't know or . . . they express that another uh words but the same meaning so first time uh I . . . little bit confused and after that I listen again again then I understand. Uh for me the same problem uh sometimes I say something they don't understand. I change the word then other way they understand. Yeah so . . . I think I learned more now . . . about how to say is not uh from the the the book it's the people say . . . because if we uh say some very professional word they don't understand yeah if I say . . . "bowel movement" maybe they yeah "poop?"

Participants were also sometimes instructed by residents on how to initiate interactions by using speech acts that residents expected. May reported that her resident wanted care aides to ask her what she wanted (or liked) to do first and what next (e.g., for personal grooming), that they should not simply proceed and do what they wanted without consulting the resident:

> Like like like uh they teaching me . . . "you come here you always like ah you . . . you do something you like to do . . . [but] you have to ask me . . . what uh do I like to do? . . . And uh what . . . do you like do this first or do that first?".

Maria learned that she needed to overcome her nervousness and her tendency to speak too quickly because the residents could not understand her otherwise:

> I learned . . . to talk . . . slowly. Because . . . that was my nervous before when I talk in English I try to say everything fast. That was worse but I didn't know that. Now in the practicum with the resident I start to talk more slowly and more eh better

pronunciation. So . . . it's very very . . . eh helpful when you . . . talk slowly. Especially in this job. You need to talk slowly and explain very well because many people suffer . . . dementia or or they they don't . . . understand . . . So it helped.

Another student discussed the need for patience and empathy (by putting oneself in their shoes) in dealing with seniors who are prone to repeating themselves:

> When they talk something they . . . repeat again and again but I say some people they say "oh no you say you told me that almost a few um time" like I never . . . say that because I know their feelings if you you say that very unhappy. I just pretend they say "oh yeah" uh like uh I've heard this one first time. [laughs] Yeah . . . because I know the . . . the the senior people feelings sometimes very fragile. Yeah they . . . very easy to hurt . . . I'm very . . . patient and . . . because before that I only know the sympathy yeah. Now I after this class I know empathy. How to . . . to put your your shoes how to say this idiom? [Interviewer: Put yourself in their shoes?]

More than words: true communication

One of the Eritrean participants (Betty) was especially moved by residents' interest in herself, her country, and her education. She also realized that much of the residents' linguistic and nonlinguistic behaviour could be accounted for when she realized that they were homesick, confused, lonely, and disempowered in comparison with earlier, happier, healthier days. Interestingly, the students, who at the outset of the program had reported similar feelings and experiences of isolation, loneliness, and misunderstanding, were now the ones providing comfort for Canadians undergoing similar emotions, adjustments, and now marginalization—all through therapeutic discourse in English:

> We talk a lot of thing. They ask me. I answer for them. . . . Some people they talk about too about my country. You know it's good. We talk about education and a lot and some of them also they were . . . you know trying to help us. A special one I found her . . . said "okay . . . let me talk" you know it's good for you also to practice your English you know so . . . it you know they were saying like that . . . and also one of them she said "okay eh send for me a letter . . . write for me so we come eh a good friends.". . . You know like most of them they come . . . they you know they they miss their home. Yeah. They say "oh I don't know I'm here. I don't know what to do.". . . All that things uh we have . . . to I mean to satisfy them by communication but "it's okay, it's good, you know it's time for rest now" so . . . eh "just you know life change so it's okay.". . . Sometimes I heard a one lady she say . . . "I hate this food. I don't know how they cook those people blah blah" you know so . . . it means maybe she was a good . . . you know uh cooker at home but you know when she came here . . . everything it changed for her so she is always to talk about "food yuck what strange mm they don't know how to cook" she said then . . . so . . . you know life change so . . . you have to explain to them what you mean by talking . . . make them happy yeah.
>
> (Betty)

Participants also needed to learn to use English strategically to cheer residents up, to distract them during unpleasant procedures, and to engage them in various other ways.

Sometimes you find them very bad mood . . . they don't like to talk to you but you say "What happened today? ." And . . . you say "There are so many photographs there so" . . . you say "Who is this person?" "Oh he is my husband. He was nice." And . . . you know they remembered . . . They feel like lonely sometimes . . . If their family . . . I mean they don't come to visit them you know sometime they go to work or you know . . . they go away so . . . they need somebody just.

(Betty)

Finally, in her practicum journal Chen described two incidents of a similar nature that had a lasting impression on her. The first illustrates how she could use language and topics that residents had used to engage care aides (and sometimes distract them in the process) in such a way that they could carry on with necessary nursing tasks:

One of my residents had resistive and aggressive behaviours. She refused everything such as getting up from bed, changing clothes, washing for her. It was a challenge for me. I was trying to talk with her and find out what was her interesting topic. Through the talking, I found that she mentioned my hair several times which was "thick and too much" (she said that). After that, every time, I came to her room, I made her be distracted by my hair. During the hair talking, I helped her get up, washed for her, changed her clothes. I got my job done. She was happy as well.

The second example also demonstrates how Chen tried to find some common ground to comfort a lonely resident (much as Betty did with the photos), which made both happy.

There is another story which I always remember. Before Mother's Day, many residents received their cards and gifts from their children. Some of them were very proud to show me and let me read the cards for them. When we were laughing, I noticed one resident sitting behind us looked like upset. I came to her and talked with her. She was unhappy because she didn't get anything from her children. I was sitting with her and trying to comfort her. Finally, she gave me a hug and kissed me, called me "extra daughter." I was almost moved to tears.

Chen then concluded her journal entry with the declaration, "I love this job. I would like to devote my every effort to helping senior people."

In summary, the second practicum site exposed participants to a world of primarily educated, English-speaking local Canadians and their families (in some cases) in a home-like environment. The cohort groups invariably enjoyed the practicum experience, continuing to visit their residents after graduation or exchanging letters with them. They were given opportunities to ask residents about proper English usage, and they learned to negotiate meanings and to become better communicators—skills that transferred easily to the outside world. They gained acceptance from the residents who showed interest in them as whole people, just as they themselves demonstrated their genuine interest in the lives and experiences of residents. For residents who had unlimited time to chat, but no one to talk to, the participants had a captive, grateful audience, and vice versa. Unfortunately, however, ISA staff remarked that it was unlikely that graduates would obtain immediate employment in this facility, since it is one of the most desirable. Nevertheless, the practicum provided many excellent opportunities for both care-giving and language socialization; it increased students' confidence in their abilities and enhanced their identities as capable professionals and members of society who can make a tangible, worthwhile contribution.

Postprogram experiences: work, community, and self

The third research question deals with the impact of the RC/HSAT education and work in ESL/healthcare on the lives of the participants, an aspect of the study in which ISA staff members expressed particular interest. Many positive rewards associated with participation in the program were discussed in the preceding section. Students reported improvements in their English, growing empathy, compassion, and attunement to body language. They learned about Anglo-European-Canadian culture, as well as other languages and cultures. They found strength in themselves and brought happiness to others. In turn, instructors were justifiably proud of the students' many achievements. As Janet observed, by the end of the program students' faces looked different; they walked and carried themselves differently; and their sense of self-worth had increased. Ultimately, they had blossomed. Janet acknowledged that the programs also had a big impact on the instructors, an observation that was confirmed in our interviews with them.

The linguistic socialization experienced so fully by the participants in their courses and on the practicum continued naturally afterward, since language socialization is a lifelong process of learning, adjustment, and change mediated by language use in different contexts (Schieffelin & Ochs, 1986). Along with their ongoing acquisition and refinement of language and skills, they noted resultant experiences of accomplishment, validation, and service to the community.

English and nursing skills in the family and community

Many students reflected on changes in their language abilities that enabled them to function much better in mainstream Anglo-Canadian society. Min reported, with great satisfaction, that her dental assistant, whom she had known since her arrival in Canada, noticed how much her English had improved since her last visit. Min responded with characteristic modesty:

> She asked me . . . "Does the course uh teach you English?" I say "Of course" so she said she said "so now that your English is . . . um . . . very good now," . . . I say "I don't know I just take it but I know I can . . . I take this course I can un I understand um . . . the instructor say and understand . . . what . . . I do, something like that, so I think I have mind is okay."

Sofia remarked that her improved English skills enabled her to help others:

> The most important is improve English. I am able to speak. Sometimes I got some problems but I forgot some word. I don't use that much English, but I can speak. . . .I can go to interview find some job, or in the store. . . . In the bus, when somebody ask me something . . . I can help somebody who don't know English.

Karina explained how her English abilities gave her the confidence to search for a job:

> I know how to search job, because before I don't go. I need somebody. If I go some-where, I call someone, one of my friend or my husband: "Come with me, come with me, help me." Because I was backward, I don't have forward by myself. I don't have strongness . . . Like nervous. Now I don't have that. I, by myself, I go and ask.

Several students mentioned that they were able to apply their knowledge of healthcare to friends, family members, and even strangers in the community. Thus their new-found and hard-earned occupational identity had currency in their nonprofessional lives as well. May recalled her experiences giving advice to neighbours—and even strangers—whose fathers were struggling with physical limitations with which she now had experience:

> My neighbour . . . her father is uh Parkinson's yeah they don't know how to care. . . I just call them and I say "I learned that, I can help." And I do something how to do it uh teach them. And then they they they're very thanks uh yeah. I feel like I can give somebody I learn something I can give out and then when I saw one one time I went to Chinatown I saw a family wife husband and a daughter. Husband uh uh something stroke cannot walk and then the wife was just like a pulling for him like uh uh . . . very hardly and I just uh . . . when I saw them I said "uh I show you. You put this there and . . . here and then much easier for him and for you. And you can buy like a walker. And then like a off belt. You can pull him like that."

Janet noted another major function of the program in the lives of women: to help them overcome their isolation and increase their self-confidence and sense of accomplishment from having learned new skills. She also acknowledged that this new-found confidence, independence, and expertise could change their roles and status within the family—both locally and inter-nationally (which sometimes created tensions as well). Participants not only gained independence to help themselves and others outside the home, they also declared that their children were proud of them for going back to school to get an education, for securing a "career" and not just a "job." Whereas some students had once depended on their relatives (typically a husband or child) to help them interact with English-speaking professionals, they now were the ones tending to medical matters. Lily reported:

> Very . . . helpful this course to me, because now I can go to the me drugstores buy the medicine for myself or something. It's very easier now [laughs] because I know the language, I know the knowledge about the some of the medical, something like that . . . Yeah, I can go to see the English-speaking doctor or something.

Betty reported that, although her family still lived in Africa, she could help her grandma by providing her mother with healthcare information:

> I have grandma back home so I can understand you know I can tell to my mom . . . "uh how is my grandma?" My mom she said "oh your grandma you know she's getting old she's saying this this blah blah." I say "Oh mommy . . . this is like this," you know, I can tell her what I learned. "Yeah just try to handle like this for her . . ." you know, so it's very helpful for our life also.

In summary, students' improved English, nursing skills, and knowledge of how best to provide care to the elderly or infirm served them well at home and in the community. In addition, they reported that they finally felt less isolated and more connected with others. As two past-cohort students reported: "I feel is like, now the time that I work is not the money. I find out we get the relationship" (Anna); and "I can be helpful, not only for my family, financially . . . [but also] other, different people who needs me" (Sofia). Maria and Min, who reported being depressed before the program, looked on their circumstances—and specifically their feelings of connectedness and inner strength—more optimistically now:

> I was a little depressed [before] and I . . . want eh to come back to my country and I say no I cannot . . . .but in this moment I'm I feel like I can stay for a a for more years. And I can be part of this society and I can be like . . . any other Canadian person. I have my certificate . . . I can work . . . .of course I feel like an immigrant but uh I know I can I can live here like any any Canadian person . . . .It's very important this kind of course for an immigrant especially because . . . you feel like you are not at home . . . in another country so . . . it's very important that immigrant have contact with another people. Because if you are . . . in your own world you can . . . be crazy . . . I learned how to be a little bit . . . more relaxed . . . and how to communicate . . . be more patient with everybody . . . and know more the old people.
>
> (Maria)

> [I gained] high um self esteem. And I learned . . . asserturfyness something like that? [Interviewer: Assertiveness?] Yeah assertiveness. Before I go so mm . . . shy or something like that I don't want to speak up everything like that, now though . . . okay if I don't . . . know or I don't understand I just speak up or maybe . . . [Before] I look I'm felt sick . . . I don't know . . . so depressed . . . like . . . no energy you know? But when I started this course and then um . . . have something to do that lift me up . . . and now um . . . I think it's very different from the before this course and after this course I think myself I different . . . my . . . spirit . . . .but after that so I feel confident and when I took this course I learned something from . . . the book. I learned from . . . professional development. Yes I learned from . . . instructor right and . . . help me . . . uh stand up? . . . I feeling . . . like . . . different.
>
> (Min)

Thus, students' personal and professional identities changed during the programs, and they now felt like they belonged in Canada and could assert themselves and move on with their lives.

Some ongoing concerns: securing satisfactory employment

Despite the participants' overall satisfaction and optimism regarding their personal growth and feelings of value within society, a number reported barriers to obtaining full-time employment as care aides. Here we mention only a few, from past-cohort students who had already been in the job market for one or more years (see Wong, 1998). They reported, for example, that it was more difficult to find work in this field than it had been in other fields (e.g., manufacturing) or other cities (e.g., Toronto); that they needed contacts, connections, excellent working relationships with their immediate supervisors, and personal referrals to gain entry to sites; that the need to take temporary on-call positions and shift work was problematic, especially for mothers (and fathers, as Alberto mentioned); that the unpredictability of hours and therefore of income was difficult to manage; that childcare needs within their own families restricted their employability; that transportation across great distances posed problems; that college graduates were sometimes favoured over ISA graduates; and that a range of other factors, such as age, English proficiency, and race further hampered their progress seeking and obtaining good jobs. Although Janet had clearly emphasized to participants before the time of admission that full-time employment was normally not secured automatically and might take a few years, the reality was nonetheless disappointing for graduates. Among the 9 past-cohort students, for example, 3 were unemployed nearly 2 years after their completion of the program (1 of these was doing volunteer work), 2 were underemployed, and 4 reported having sufficient employment. Interestingly, only Alberto, the lone male in that group, had secured a permanent position—in a French-language facility. Juan, in the present-cohort, also secured full-time employment immediately. These findings are therefore consistent with Ng and Estable's (1987) report about the nature of work for many immigrant women and the length of time it takes to obtain meaningful, full-time employment.

In addition, 2 past-cohort graduates lamented that not enough English was spoken in their Chinese-dominant workplaces, causing their English proficiency to suffer. Many other graduates also reported that they seldom used English outside the workplace, except for with former classmates. Thus the continuing sense of isolation from the anglophone mainstream was an on-going issue for some graduates, much as it has been discussed elsewhere (e.g., Giles, 1987; Goldstein, 1997; Tollefson, 1985; Peirce, 1995).

Summary and conclusion

This paper has described a program combining ESL instruction and nursing skills for immigrants wishing to become long-term resident care aides. Taking an interpretive, qualitative approach and informed by feminist research perspectives, we interviewed the program participants (on several occasions, in some cases) and noted common themes as they prepared for and then experienced their practical clinical work. We framed our discussion of the practicum in terms of language socialization and described some of the challenges the students faced in their care of elderly residents with various physical and emotional difficulties. The most interesting and unexpected findings include the range and complexity of communication skills required of the study participants; the need to speak a language other than English or their first language; the need to use and interpret body language; the need to master both technical academic discourse (oral and written) and colloquial interpersonal skills; the opportunity to ask for and receive assistance with English from the residents; the need to engage and respond empathetically to their interlocutors; and the need to assess and meet their communication and other (physical, emotional) requirements.

Most current ESL and skills programs—indeed perhaps the majority of academic and vocational programs in English-speaking regions—assume that graduates will go on to work in English-dominant workplaces with others who can communicate as effectively or even more so (because of their level of English proficiency). However, this study revealed what was for us a startling phenomenon: The monolingual English workplaces for which program curricula and textbooks prepare students simply do not exist any longer in large cities in many parts of the "English-speaking world." As well, the advantages that monolingual English speakers may once have enjoyed working in those contexts can no longer be assured. In fact, those employees who have had more rather than less experience learning to communicate in another language, even if that learning process is still incomplete, and those who speak languages other than English may now have the greater advantage. In addition, while we noted in several situations that care aides (as with nursing assistants, nurses, and other medical workers) must be able to use, understand, and write in appropriate medical and technical terminology and conventions, much of their work involves nonverbal or at least nontechnical communication. Therefore, programs must continue to emphasize all three kinds of communication: technical English, nonverbal, and interpersonal English (and multilingual) communication. Students must be prepared for the demanding social and linguistic realities that await them and the communication barriers and impairments that require greater accommodation on the part of future caregivers, and must be able to learn different ways of conveying the same information depending on register, interlocutor, purpose, and so on. For this purpose, greater collaboration among nursing, ESL, and practicum instructors would be beneficial.

The two practicum settings were compared in terms of the opportunities for English language use, overall communication and the kinds of learning that took place in each. However, we also noted that, although students thrived in the suburban nursing home, the prospects of their securing positions in such a facility were very unlikely. As a result, their opportunities for ongoing, mutually fulfilling interaction with English-speaking residents such as they experienced at Seaview Gardens would be limited following their graduation. We discussed briefly the impact of the program and the practicum experiences on participants, noting their reported struggles with isolation, finding full-time employment, and being able to work well together with colleagues and residents. However, the rewards associated with this program and work were still significant. Participants remarked that they now saw themselves more as worthy, capable, multidimensional people and that their independence and English proficiency had improved, which facilitated their integration into mainstream society. Their families and friends were proud of them.

Nonetheless, a number of barriers still face immigrant women and men seeking training and employment in healthcare; in the case of resident care-giving, these barriers include: lack of adequate, affordable childcare; cultural views of women's role in home/society; access to programs based on linguistic and employment (i.e., EI) prerequisites; familial priority given to husbands to receive training before wives; low self-esteem and confidence, and so forth. We also found that the lives of the participants were improved immeasurably by participation in such programs, which reduced their social isolation in the community and increased their employability and confidence, their status at home, and their ESL skills and medical knowledge which were of use not only in the workplace but at home and in the community. However, many of the women had not realized how long it would take to secure full-time daytime employment in the city where ISA is located, as many positions are outside the city, part-time or substitute (on-call), and/or require work at night. These factors present many difficulties for women, who often bear primary responsibility for childcare and domestic tasks.

Finally, we highlighted that, for many of the participants, the successful use of language at work required learning more than English and requisite medical knowledge/skills. It involved learning to communicate with elderly patients who may not speak English themselves (e.g., at the inner-city hospital) and may have other communication difficulties associated with dementia, Alzheimer's, aphasia, and loss of sight or hearing. On the job, students learned to "read and write" through body language, through touch, compassion, some degree of guesswork, and a large measure of goodwill. They developed greater empathy and new understandings of themselves and the elderly within Canadian society.

More research of a longitudinal, ethnographic nature on language(s) and work is warranted to complement the kind of interview-based research reported here. Whereas our project was limited necessarily to indirect observation via narrative accounts by program staff and participants, as well as their written records, direct longitudinal observation of participants in programs, in practicum settings, and later in regular workplaces would permit a different kind of analysis. The processes of professional socialization, language development, intercultural and intergenerational communication, and, ultimately, social integration could be studied first-hand; this would also enable us to observe unfolding negotiations of meaning and the development of participants' multiple professional and personal identities and abilities by means of both critical incidents and more mundane everyday trials, triumphs, and incremental changes in communication with individual care aides, residents, and colleagues. Differences in workers' interactions with various individual residents and across different contexts could also be explored. In addition, ethnographic work would reveal the cultures and behaviours of care-giving in distinct settings in ways that interviews may reveal only partially as participants themselves may not be fully conscious or attuned to their own behaviours (verbal and nonverbal) and sociolinguistic circumstances. For all these reasons, ethnographic research and contextualized analyses of discourse would provide a more vivid, grounded account of learning, living, and working in this kind of program and resident care workplaces. The results of such research would have obvious pedagogical utility as well, as future staff and students could observe and discuss others' experiences, and program planners and teachers could use ethnographic resources for needs analysis and curriculum development.

To conclude, understanding the difficult, complex, changing language needs in the multilingual and multicultural workplace is urgent for practitioners, educators, social scientists, and policy makers. Hearing about the experiences of students, prior to, during, and after their program also highlights the personal human struggles facing new (and old) Canadians and provides opportunities for further action and improvements in assisting them with social integration as well as education. These accounts allow us to learn from the dedication, hard work, and successes of people who have so much to contribute to society but for whom the processes of settlement and integration into Canadian society sometimes take many years. Finally, they are a reminder to researchers and caregivers that public and private social institutions—in this case in healthcare—are no longer monolingual and monocultural and that effective English-medium skills and interaction are just one facet of successful communication in the new, more global, workplace.

Notes

1   Long-term resident care aides provide assistance to elderly or disabled individuals who reside at home or require long-term care at facilities such as hospitals and nursing homes.

2   For a theoretical discussion of language socialization, see, e.g., Duff (1995); Roberts (1998); Schecter & Bayley (1997); Schieffelin & Ochs (1986); Ochs (1996); and Willett (1995).

3   One reviewer sought further comment about the feminist nature of this work and our roles, positions, and identities within it. We considered our approach feminist for a number of reasons listed here, not the least of which is that it provides a useful lens or perspective through which to examine socio-educational phenomena affecting, and potentially empowering, vulnerable or marginalized populations, especially immigrant women: (a) We were a team of university women working collaboratively with a team of professional women in one institution, involving the participation of immigrant women and men in a primarily female profession; (b) We do not want to categorically assert that the women (or men) in the study were "oppressed" or "dominated" as is assumed in much feminist research (e.g., Lather, 1991; Olesen, 1994; Roman, 1992), since, in many cases, that is not how they characterized themselves; however, they did share certain challenges and vulnerabilities (e.g., related to long-term job prospects, income, security, power), whether staff members or students. Indeed, our original grant proposal was entitled "Socializing Language and Sociocultural Identity from the Margins: A Study of Immigrant Women Learning English as a Second Language for the Health Professions." And, although we have some misgivings about the labels *margin* and *mainstream*, which seem to further marginalise women and minority populations, to qualify for the programs the applicants had to be either on welfare or (un)employment insurance. The participants' employment histories, second language needs, relatively enclosed social networks, and sometimes downward occupational mobility upon immigration also confirmed the marginalization they had experienced and in many cases continued to experience after the ISA programs. Ironically, the two men in the study who were in the minority within the program and profession had challenges of their own in that regard; yet, equally ironically, they were also the most successful

in securing full-time employment; (c) We were very hopeful that the educational opportunities provided to the women (and men) in the study would also lead to an improvement in their personal, social, and professional circumstances; (d) Our method of primarily interviewing participants about their lived experiences and interpretations is consistent with the methods and aims of much feminist research, as was our desire to negotiate the terms of our/their involvement in a way that was open, sensitive to participants' concerns, and demonstrated reciprocity. For example, one member of our research team, Ping Wong, a second-generation Cantonese-speaking, Chinese-Canadian graduate student and part-time ESL instructor in another ISA program at the time of the study, conducted most of the individual interviews and was also asked to substitute for the ESL teacher in this program on occasion, after our research project was well underway. She also conducted her master's thesis on one part of the larger study (Wong, 1998). Wong was both accessible and nonthreatening to the participants, and the recent ESL experiences of some of her own family members (e.g., mother and older sisters) were very similar to those of some of the research participants who after many years had just gone back to school. The other two researchers, Duff and Early, have both worked with adult immigrant ESL learners and with ESL professionals working with immigrant, women in healthcare and other professions; they participated in focus group interviews, meetings with staff, and other aspects of the research. Early is an immigrant to Canada, and Duff has also lived and worked in various non-English-speaking communities. Thus none of us were insiders within the community of participants, but Wong provided an invaluable bridge into the ISA community. In summary, although feminist research encompasses a range of ontological, epistemological, and methodological approaches and positions, a feminist research perspective enabled us to examine the program and participants in a way that has generally not been used in the Workplace ESL or ESP literature.

4   Janet was involved in all aspects of the program (applying for funding, selecting participants, managing the program, liaising with practicum sites and others who were contacted when special concerns arose, and remaining in contact with graduates) and was deeply appreciated by the students and by our research team for her cooperation and assistance.

5   Nancy mentioned that it would have been beneficial to work more closely with Susan, ensuring that students learned the terminology of the 24-hour clock in their ESL class, for example. However, as Nancy was new to the position and had a full work load already, responsibilities as a single parent, and a different schedule from Susan, it was not easy to collaborate in this way. Similar difficulties have been reported elsewhere in the language-skills and language-content literature (Platt, 1993; Yogman & Kaylani, 1996).

6   The programs had been merged recently because of pressure from the federal (HRDC)/provincial government funding sources and because colleges had begun combining programs in anticipation of funding cuts.

7   The students are referred to as clients by program personnel, but we refer to them as students or participants here. The patients with whom they worked are referred to as residents.

8   Janet, who knew all the students personally, issued a cover letter together with our recruitment letter to explain the purpose of the study and to assure students that their participation was voluntary. In general, the face-to-face interviews were longer than the telephone interviews. The longest interview took place in a participant's home, where the atmosphere was more informal and conversational in tone.

9   They each received a small honorarium for their cooperation upon completion of the final interview.

10   Salaries vary considerably, however, depending on the type of position and institution: from $8–10/hr for home support (providing company for the elderly and helping with daily routines, including housework); $12–15/hr for personal care work (assisting clients with washing and dressing and/or helping clients with health problems); differences between union and non-union wages for facilities, the former being higher.

11   Note that most of the illustrations in the textbook also show White nursing assistants and residents, with a much smaller number of people from visible minorities (Black or Hispanic); no obviously Asian workers and residents are shown. The Florida-based authors may therefore assume their readers and intended clinical clientele comprise predominantly English-speaking Americans or possibly Spanish-English bilinguals.

References

Andrews, M. M., & Boyle, J. S. (1999). *Transcultural concepts in nursing care* (3rd ed.). Philadelphia: Lippincott.

Beach, C. M., & Worswick, C. (1993). Is there a double-negative effect on the earnings of immigrant women? *Canadian Public Policy*, *14* (1), 36–53.

Boyd, M. (1992). Immigrant women: Language, socioeconomic inequalities, and policy issues. In B. Burnaby & A. Cumming (Eds.), *Socio-political aspects of ESL* (pp. 141–59). Toronto: Ontario Institute for Studies in Education.

Brindley, G., Baynham, M., Burns, A., Hammond, J., McKenna, R., & Thurstun, J. (1996). *An integrated research strategy for adult ESL, literacy and numeracy.* Sydney, Australia: National Centre for English Language Teaching and Research, Macquarie University.

Buijs, G. (Ed.). (1993). *Migrant women: Crossing boundaries and changing identities.* Oxford: Berg Publishers, Ltd.

Burnaby, B. (1992). Official language training for adult immigrants in Canada: Features and issues. In B. Burnaby & A. Cumming (Eds.), *Socio-political aspects of ESL* (pp. 3–34). Toronto: Ontario Institute for Studies in Education.

Burnaby, B., & Cumming, A. (Eds.). (1992). *Socio-political aspects of ESL.* Toronto: Ontario Institute for Studies in Education.

Center for Applied Linguistics. (1998). *Research agenda for adult ESL.* Washington, DC: Center for Applied Linguistics.

Cumming, A., & Gill, J. (1992). Motivation or accessibility? Factors permitting Indo-Canadian women to pursue ESL literacy instruction. In B. Burnaby & A. Cumming (Eds.), *Socio-political aspects of ESL* (pp. 241–252). Toronto: Ontario Institute for Studies in Education.

De Troy, C. (1987). *The specific needs of immigrant women: Existing and recommended measures to fulfill them.* Luxembourg: Office for Official Publications of the European Communities.

Duff, P. (1995). An ethnography of communication in immersion classrooms in Hungary. *TESOL Quarterly, 29,* 505–536.

Ellis, R. (1994). *The study of second language acquisition.* Oxford: Oxford University Press.

Frank, R. A. (2000). Medical communication: Non-native English speaking patients and native English speaking professionals. *English for Specific Purposes Journal, 19,* 31–62.

Garay, M. S., & Bernhardt, S. A. (Eds.). (1998). *Expanding literacies: English teaching and the new workplace.* Albany, NY: State University of New York Press.

Giles, W. (1987). Language rights are women's rights: Discrimination against immigrant women in Canadian language training practices. *Resources for Feminist Research, 17*(3), 129–132.

Goldstein, T. (1997). *Two languages at work: Bilingual life on the production floor.* New York: Mouton de Gruyter.

Grubbs, P., & Blasband, B. (1995). *The long-term care nursing assistant.* Englewood Cliffs, NJ: Prentice Hall.

Harper, H., Peirce, B., & Burnaby, B. (1996). English-in-the-workplace for garment workers: A feminist project? *Gender and Education, 8,* 5–19.

Hull, G. (Ed.). (1997). *Changing work, changing workers: Critical perspectives on language, literacy, and skills.* Albany, NY: State University of New York Press.

Kouritzen, S. (2000). Immigrant mothers redefine access to ESL classes: Contradiction and ambivalence. *Journal of Multilingual and Multicultural Development, 21,* 14–32.

Lather, P. (1991). *Getting smart: Feminist research and pedagogy with/in the postmodern.* New York: Routledge.

Li, D. (2000). The pragmatics of making requests in the L2 workplace: A case study of language socialization. *Canadian Modern Language Review, 57,* 58–87.

Luckmann, J. L. (1999). *Transcultural communication in nursing.* Albany, NY: Delmar.

McGroarty, M. (1992). Second language instruction in the workplace. *Annual Review of Applied Linguistics, 13,* 86–108.

Meyer, P., & Bates, P. (1998). Literacy practices in the healthcare industry: The challenge for teachers. In M. S. Garay & S. A. Bernhardt (Eds.), *Expanding literacies: English teaching and the new workplace* (pp. 133–152). Albany, NY: State University of New York Press.

The New London Group. (1996). A pedagogy of multiliteracies: Designing social futures. *Harvard Educational Review, 66*(1), 60–92.

Ng, R., & Estable, A. (1987). Immigrant women in the labour force: An overview of present knowledge and research gaps. *Resources for Feminist Research, 17*(3), 29–33.

Ochs, E. (1996). Linguistic resources for socializing humanity. In J. Gumperz & S. Levinson (Eds.), *Rethinking linguistic relativity* (pp. 407–437). Cambridge: Cambridge University Press.

Olesen, V. (1994). Feminisms and models of qualitative research. In N. Denzin & Y. Lincoln (Eds.), *Handbook of qualitative research.* (pp. 158–174). Thousand Oaks, CA: Sage Publications.

Payne, J. (1991). *Women, training and the skills shortage: The case for public investment.* London: Policy Studies Institute.

Peirce, B. N. (1995). Social identity, investment, and language learning. *TESOL Quarterly, 29,* 569–576.

Peirce, B. N., Harper, H., & Burnaby, B. (1993). Workplace ESL at Levi Strauss: Dropouts speak out. *TESL Canada Journal, 10*(2), 9–30.

Platt, E. (1993). Vocational/VESL teacher collaboration: Some substantive issues. *English for Specific Purposes Journal, 12*(2), 139–157.

Roberts, C. (1998). Language acquisition or language socialization in and through discourse? Towards a redefinition of the domain of SLA. *Working Papers in Applied Linguistics* (Centre for Applied Linguistic Research, Thames Valley University), *4*, 31–42.

Roberts, C., Davies, E., & Jupp, T. (1992). *Language and discrimination: A study of communication in multi-ethnic workplaces.* New York: Longman.

Rockhill, K. (1991). Literacy as threat/desire: Longing to be SOMEBODY. In J. Gaskell & A. McLaren (Eds.), *Women and education* (2nd ed., pp. 333–349). Calgary, AB: Detselig Enterprises.

Roman, L. (1992). The political significance of other ways of narrating ethnography: A feminist materialist approach. In M. LeCompte, W. Millroy, & J. Preissle (Eds.), *The handbook of qualitative research* (pp. 555–594). San Diego, CA: Academic Press.

Schecter, S., & Bayley, R. (1997). Language socialization practices and cultural identity: Case studies of Mexican-descent families in California and Texas. *TESOL Quarterly, 31*, 513–541.

Schieffelin, B., & Ochs, E. (1986). Language socialization. *Annual Review of Anthropology, 15*, 153–191.

Scollon, R., & Scollon, S. W. (1995). *Intercultural communication: A discourse approach.* Cambridge, MA: Blackwell.

Svendsen, C., & Krebs, K. (1984). Identifying English for the job: Examples from health care occupations. *English for Specific Purposes Journal, 3*(2), 153–164.

Taylor, M. (Ed.). (1997). *Workplace education: The changing landscape.* Toronto: Culture Concepts.

Tisza, M. (1997). *Accessing language resources: A study of the enabling elements of an ESL program for immigrant women.* Unpublished MEd major paper, University of British Columbia, Vancouver.

Tollefson, J. (1985). Research on refugee settlement: Implications for instructional programs. *TESOL Quarterly, 19*, 753–764.

Willett, J. (1995). Becoming first graders in an L2: An ethnographic study of L2 socialization. *TESOL Quarterly, 29*, 473–503.

Wilson, S. (1998). *An evaluation of a longterm care aide/ESL program.* Unpublished master's thesis, The University of British Columbia, Vancouver.

Wong, F. P. (1998). *The impact of training and employment as a health care aide on immigrants' lives.* Unpublished master's thesis, University of British Columbia, Vancouver.

Yogman, J., & Kaylani, C.T. (1996). ESP program design for mixed level students. *English for Specific Purposes, 15*(4), 311–324.

Chapter 22

NANCY H. HORNBERGER

MULTILINGUAL LANGUAGE POLICIES AND THE CONTINUA OF BILITERACY
An ecological approach (2002)

Introduction

TWO SCENES from the year 2000:

18 July 2000, Johannesburg, South Africa. In the course of my two-week visit at Rand Afrikaans University, I meet early this Tuesday morning (7:30 A.M.) with a group of young pre-service teachers enrolled in a one-year Diploma in Education program. The university has been bilingual from its founding, offering instruction in Afrikaans and English in a parallel dual medium format; in the post-apartheid period, rapidly expanding numbers of speakers of diverse African languages have enrolled.

About 20 students attend this English Language Pedagogy class where I have been invited to speak about bilingual education. Their teacher Judy is present, as is my host Elizabeth. At one point, I mention my dissertation research which documented "classroom success but policy failure" for an experimental bilingual education program in Quechua speaking communities of Puno, Peru. The policy failure, I suggest, was at least partly due to some community members' resistance to the use of Quechua in school, which they had always regarded as a Spanish domain. Taking off from this, Judy asks what one can do about negative community attitudes which impede top-down language planning, citing the case of Black African parental demands for English-medium instruction in the face of South Africa's new multilingual language policy.

Later, when the discussion turns to the importance of the teacher's recognizing and valuing students' languages and cultures even if they're not the teacher's own, Elizabeth takes the opportunity to demonstrate one such practice. Students are instructed to break into small groups to talk to each other about bilingual education for two-three minutes in their own languages. The result: four Nguni speakers (one Zulu, one Xhosa, two Swati), two Gujarati speaking women, three Afrikaans speakers, and one Portuguese speaker (who talks with me) form groups, while the rest of the class members chat to each other in small groups in English. The students clearly enjoy this activity and it generates lively whole class discussion.

17 August 2000, La Paz, Bolivia. On the first day of a three-day *Taller de reflexión y análisis sobre la enseñanza de castellano como segunda lengua* (Workshop of reflection and analysis on the teaching of Spanish as a second language), the Vice-Minister of Education welcomes workshop participants, emphasizing to us that the key to the Bolivian Education Reform is Bilingual Intercultural Education, and the key to *that* is Spanish as a Second Language. In recent months, she tells us, questions have been raised about the Reform's attention to indigenous languages, and indigenous parents have begun to demand that their children be taught Spanish. Perhaps the Reform erred, she says, in emphasizing the indigenous languages to such a degree that bilingual education appeared to the public to be monolingual indigenous language education.

There are approximately 45 participants in the workshop: 15 technical experts from the Curricular Development Unit of the Ministry, a half-dozen representatives from PROEIB, the Andean regional graduate program in bilingual intercultural education at the University of San Simón in Cochabamba, Bolivia, another 8–9 Bolivian pedagogical experts, and about a dozen international specialists in bilingual and second language education (from Brasil, Chile, Ecuador, Mexico, Peru, Belgium, Germany, USA, and Sweden). Many of us had participated five years earlier in a similar workshop on the curriculum and materials for the teaching of the indigenous languages, principally the three largest languages Quechua, Aymara, and Guarani. The materials we reviewed then have been under implementation in the schools for a couple of years now.

Our charge this time is to review the Spanish as a Second Language curriculum and materials developed by the Curricular Development Unit and to make recommendations for improvement in design and implementation. Among the materials available for review are curricular guides, teaching modules for Spanish, bilingual modules for the content areas, cassette tapes and laminated posters, an 80 book class library, a literary anthology, and a series of six big books in Spanish, three of them based on traditional Quechua, Aymara, and Guarani folktales.

In the ensuing three days of intensive work across long hours (8 A.M. to 9 P.M.), discussions are remarkable for the honesty and integrity with which the Curricular Development Unit experts welcome critical scrutiny of their work. These experts worry about how best to teach Spanish to a school population which in many cases has little to no exposure to oral Spanish or to print media outside of the classroom; and so have opted for a richly communicative and literature-based curriculum design. Some of the second language experts are concerned that there is not enough explicit grammatical and lexical instruction and that the syllabus is not sufficiently incremental. Concerns from those who have seen the materials in use in the field are of a different nature. They ask questions like: what are the implications for second language learning of teachers' frequent code-mixing in class, code-mixing prompted by the desire to communicate with the students in a language they understand?; by the same token, what are the implications for maintaining and strengthening the indigenous languages if one and the same teacher teaches in both the indigenous language and Spanish?

As these scenes readily show, the one language–one nation ideology of language policy and national identity is no longer the only available one worldwide (if it ever was). Multilingual language policies which recognize ethnic and linguistic pluralism as resources for nation-building are increasingly in evidence. These policies, many of which envision implementation through bilingual intercultural education, open up new worlds of possibility for oppressed indigenous and immigrant languages and their speakers, transforming former homogenizing and assimilationist policy discourse into discourses about diversity and emancipation. This paper points to two broad sets of challenges inherent in implementing these new ideologies, as they are evident in two nations which undertook these transformations in the early 1990s.

Post-apartheid South Africa's new Constitution of 1993 embraces language as a basic human right and multilingualism as a national resource, raising nine major African languages to national official status alongside English and Afrikaans;[1] this, along with the dismantling of the apartheid educational system, has led to the burgeoning of multilingual, multicultural student populations in classrooms, schools, and universities nationwide. The Bolivian National Education Reform of 1994 envisions a comprehensive transformation of Bolivia's educational system, including the introduction of all thirty of Bolivia's indigenous languages alongside Spanish as subjects and media of instruction in all Bolivian schools. Yet, to transform a standardizing education into a diversifying one and to construct a national identity that is multilingual and multicultural constitute ideological paradoxes which are a challenge to implement.

Scholars are increasingly turning to the metaphor of ecology to think and talk about language planning, teaching, and learning in multilingual settings. In the first part of the paper, I explore salient themes of that metaphor—namely language evolution, language environment, and language endangerment—and argue that multilingual language policies are essentially about opening up ideological and implementational space in the environment for as many languages as possible, and in particular endangered languages, to evolve and flourish rather than dwindle and disappear. In the second half of the paper, I use my continua of biliteracy model as heuristic to consider two broad sets of challenges facing these multilingual language policies (as exemplified in the above scenes) and suggest that there is urgent need for language educators, language planners, and language users to fill those ideological and implementational spaces as richly and fully as possible, before they close in on us again.[2]

Multilingual language policies, ideology, and the ecology of language

The one nation–one language ideology, the idea that a nation-state should be unified by one common language, has held sway in recent Western history from the rise of the European and American nation-states in the 18th and 19th centuries on through the formation of independent African and Asian nation-states in mid-20th century and up to the present. Fishman wrote of the several score new members brought into the family of nations in the mid-20th century and of the nationistic and nationalistic ideologies underlying their choice of a national language: "nationism – as distinguished from nationalism – is primarily concerned not with ethnic authenticity but with operational efficiency" (Fishman, 1969: 113). In either case, emphasis was on choosing *a* national language, *one* national language, whether it were a Language of Wider Communication serving nationistic goals or an indigenous language serving nationalistic ones.

Yet the one language–one nation equation is increasingly recognized as an ideological red herring (Woolard & Schieffelin, 1994: 60–61). For one thing, it is a relatively recent phenomenon when seen against the backdrop of human history. Referring not only to the Greek, Roman, Aztec, and Inca empires of ancient times but also to the more recent Austro-Hungarian and Ottoman empires, May writes in his recent book on the politics of language that "empires were quite happy . . . to leave unmolested the plethora of cultures and languages subsumed within them – as long as taxes were paid" (May, 2001: 6).

Furthermore, in our day, twin pressures of globalization and ethnic fragmentation exert pressures on the one language–one nation ideology. May suggests that modern nation-states have had to reassess the limits of their sovereignty as a result of the rise of globalization and the "burgeoning influence of multinational corporations and supranational political organisations," while at the same time minority groups increasingly exert their rights "either to form their own nation-states . . . or for greater representation within existing nation-state structures" (May, 2001: 7). In like vein, Freeland notes that Latin American nations are particularly prone to two frequently mentioned effects of globalization from without and within: (1) the weakening of the state from the surge of transnational phenomena and (2) the weakening of the state from social and ethnic fragmentation (Freeland, 1996: 168). Certainly, African nations are similarly prone to these effects.

Gal suggests what might be considered a linguistic corollary to these pressures when she notes that global processes like colonization, the expansion of capitalism and transnational labor migration have replaced earlier processes of "dispersion of populations and the peopling of the world," such that: 1) the characteristic form of language change in the modern era is the coming together of languages; and 2) the former "relatively egalitarian linguistic diversity, based on small-scale languages whose speakers believe their own language to be superior, [has been changed] into stratified diversity: local languages are abandoned or subordinated to 'world languages' in diglossic relations . . ." (Gal, 1989: 356). All of this points to two countervailing trends working together to break apart the one language–one nation ideology: the rise of English as a global language, hence infringing on national languages; and the reclaiming of endangered indigenous, immigrant, and ethnic languages at local and national levels, hence undermining the ascendancy of national languages.

Ecology of language

As the one language–one nation ideology breaks apart, so too the language planning field increasingly seeks models and metaphors that reflect a multilingual rather than monolingual approach to language planning and policy. One such model is the continua of biliteracy (to be taken up below) and one such metaphor is the ecology of language; both are premised on a view of multilingualism as a resource. Ruiz (1984) like Fishman (1966a) before him, drew our attention to the potential of a language-as-resource ideology as an alternative to the dominant language-as-problem and language-as-right ideological orientations in language planning. Mühl-häusler argues that "language planning until the 1980s was based on the premise that linguistic diversity is a problem" (Mühlhäusler, 1996: 311–312), but that it is now undergoing a conceptual shift toward recognizing linguistic diversity as an asset.

Einar Haugen is generally credited for introducing the ecology of language in his 1970 paper by that title (Haugen, 1972). Haugen himself points to an earlier, 1964 paper by Carl and Frances Voegelin, who suggested that "in linguistic ecology, one begins not with a particular language but with a particular area, not with selective attention to a few languages but with comprehensive attention to all the languages in the area" (Voegelin & Voegelin, 1964: 2).[3] For his part, Haugen defines language ecology as "the study of interactions between any given language and its environment," going on to define the environment of the language as including both psychological ("its interaction with other languages in the minds of bi- and multilingual speakers") and sociological ("its interaction with the society in which it functions as a medium of communication") aspects (Haugen, 1972: 325). He emphasizes the reciprocity between language and environment, noting that what is needed is not only a description of the social and psychological situation of each language, but also the effect of this situation on the language (Haugen, 1972: 334). Haugen argues for the heuristic value of earlier biological, instrumental and structural metaphors in understanding the life, purpose, and form of languages and goes on to invoke the tradition of research in human ecology as a metaphor for an approach which would comprise not just the science of language description, but also concern for language cultivation and preservation (Haugen, 1972: 326–329). He concludes with a comprehensive catalogue of ecological questions which Mühlhäusler later repeats (Haugen, 1972: 336–337; Mühlhäusler, 1996: 3–4).

For my purposes here, I am primarily interested in three themes of the ecology metaphor which are salient to me in writings on the ecology of language; all of them are present in Haugen's original formulation. These are: that languages, like living species, evolve, grow, change, live, and die in relation to other languages and also in relation to their environment; for ease of reference, I will call these the *language evolution* and *language environment* themes. A third theme is the notion that some languages, like some species and environments, may be endangered and that the ecology movement is about not only studying and describing those potential losses, but also countering them; this I will call the *language endangerment* theme.[4]

In his 1996 book, *Linguistic Ecology*, Mühlhäusler advocates an ecological approach to languages which, like Haugen's approach, encompasses all three of these metaphorical themes. He argues that our focus must shift from consideration of "given," countable languages to one on human communication in a holistic sense (Mühlhäusler, 1996: 89) and proposes an approach which "investigates the support system for a structural ecology of language rather than individual languages" (Mühlhäusler, 1996: 312–313); that is, he argues for consideration of *language evolution*. He "sees the well-being of individual languages or communication networks as dependent on a range of language-external factors as well as the presence of other languages" (Mühlhäusler, 1996: 49) and claims that "the focus of inquiry should be upon the functional relationship between the factors that affect the general interrelationship between languages rather than individual factors impacting on individual languages" (Mühlhäusler, 1996: 313); that is, he calls for a focus on *language environment*. Writing from a concern for the decline and loss of linguistic heterogeneity in the world, Mühlhäusler argues for applying ecological theory to the goal of language maintenance (Mühlhäusler, 1996: 311–324); that is, he writes from a concern for *language endangerment*, in the sense of both studying and countering language loss. He applauds the ecological metaphor for being action-oriented and prefers the partial and local explanations of an ecological approach to the complex yet ultimately mechanical explanations of a systems metaphor (Mühlhäusler, 1996: 2).

Others writing on an ecological approach to language planning elaborate on one or more of the metaphorical themes. Kaplan and Baldauf's work elaborates on the *language evolution* and *language environment* themes. They emphasize that language planning activity cannot be limited to one language in isolation from all the other languages in the environment (Kaplan & Baldauf, 1997: 271). Their model representing the various forces at work in a linguistic eco-system includes "language modification constructs" (Kaplan & Baldauf, 1997: 289) or "language change elements" (Kaplan & Baldauf, 1997: 296) such as language death, survival, change, revival, shift and spread, amalgamation, contact, pidgin and Creole development, and literacy development, all processes of what I am here calling *language evolution*. With regard to *language environment*, the model also depicts agencies such as government and non-government organizations, education agencies, and communities of speakers, all of which have an impact on the multiple languages in the linguistic eco-system (Kaplan & Baldauf, 1997: 311). "Language planning . . . is a question of trying to manage the language ecology of a particular language to support it within the vast cultural, educational, historical, demographic, political, social structure in which language policy formulation occurs every day" (Kaplan & Baldauf, 1997: 13); "language planning activity must be perceived as implicating a wide range of languages and of modifications occurring simultaneously over the mix of languages in the environment – that is, implicating the total language eco-system" (Kaplan & Baldauf, 1997: 296).

Recent work by Phillipson & Skutnabb-Kangas (1996) and Ricento (2000) highlights the *language endangerment* theme of the ecology metaphor. Phillipson and Skutnabb-Kangas contrast two language policy options with regard to English worldwide: the diffusion of English paradigm characterized by a "monolingual view of modernization and internationalization" and the ecology-of-language paradigm which involves "building on linguistic diversity worldwide, promoting multilingualism and foreign language learning, and granting linguistic human rights to speakers of all languages" (Phillipson & Skutnabb-Kangas, 1996: 429). The juxtaposition of the linguistic imperialism of English over against multilingualism and linguistic human rights is clearly founded on a concern for the ongoing endangerment of many languages, displaced by one or a select few, and the need to counteract that endangerment and displacement. Mühlhäusler cites Pakir's (1991) term "killer languages" in reference to the displacing effect of imperial English as well as other languages such as Mandarin, Spanish, French, and Indonesian.

In parallel fashion, van Lier (2000) argues that an ecological approach to language learning emphasizes emergent language development; learning and cognition as explained not only in terms of processes inside the head, but also in terms of interaction with the environment; and learners' perceptual and social activity as, in a fundamental way, their learning. These three emphases can be understood as microlevel, sociocultural language learning parallels to the *language evolution, environment*, and *endangerment* themes in an ecological approach to language planning. Bringing sociocultural and sociolinguistic strands together in his ecological approach to literacy, Barton (1994: 29–32) provides a succinct and useful review of the use of the ecology metaphor in both psychological and social traditions in the social sciences.

Ricento argues that as the macro sociopolitical context of language planning has moved over the last several decades from decolonization through modernization and into the new world order, and as social science epistemologies have simultaneously moved from structuralism through critical theory and into postmodernism, so too the language planning field has moved from a focus on problem-solving through a concern for access and into an emphasis on linguistic human rights. In words that evoke the *language endangerment* and *language environment* themes outlined above, he suggests that the ecology-of-language paradigm may well be the conceptual framework for language planning in the future, precisely because of its emphasis on language rights and on connecting macro sociopolitical processes with microlevel patterns of language use (Ricento, 2000: 208–209).

In sum, an ecology of language metaphor captures a set of ideological underpinnings for a multilingual language policy, in which languages are understood to (1) live and evolve in an eco-system along with other languages (*language evolution*), (2) interact with their sociopolitical, economic, and cultural environments (*language environment*), and (3) become endangered if there is inadequate environmental support for them vis-à-vis other languages in the eco-system (*language endangerment*). All three of these ideological themes come into play in the following consideration of challenges facing the implementation of multilingual language policies in South Africa and Bolivia.

Multilingual language policies and the continua of biliteracy: implementation in classroom and community

The scenes from South Africa and Bolivia which opened this paper evoke broad sets of challenges at community and classroom levels. In the first instance, there are the challenges of confronting community attitudes favoring the language of power in the society, attitudes which are at odds with developmental evidence that children learn best from the starting point of their own language(s). There are also the challenges, at classroom level, of providing materials and inter-action in multiple languages which are not necessarily spoken by all participants. In the continua of biliteracy model, the latter challenges relate to media and content of biliteracy, and the former to biliteracy development and contexts.

The *continua of biliteracy* is a comprehensive, ecological model I have proposed as a way to situate research, teaching, and language planning in multilingual settings. The continua of bi-literacy model defines *biliteracy* as "any and all instances in which communication occurs in two (or more) languages in or around writing" (Hornberger, 1990: 213) and describes it in terms of four nested sets of intersecting continua characterizing the contexts, media, content, and development of biliteracy (Hornberger, 1989a; Hornberger & Skilton-Sylvester, 2000). Specific-ally, it depicts the development of biliteracy along intersecting first language, second language, receptive-productive, and oral-written language skills continua; through the medium of two (or more) languages and literacies whose linguistic structures vary from similar to dissimilar, whose scripts range from convergent to divergent, and to which the developing biliterate individual's exposure varies from simultaneous to successive; in contexts that encompass micro to macro levels and are characterized by varying mixes along the monolingual-bilingual and oral-literate continua; and with content that ranges from majority to minority perspectives and experiences, literary to vernacular styles and genres, and decontextualized to contextualized language texts (see Figures 22.1 and 22.2).

The notion of continuum conveys that all points on a particular continuum are interrelated, and the model suggests that the more their learning contexts and contexts of use allow learners and users to draw from across the whole of each and every continuum, the greater are the chances for their full biliteracy development and expression (Hornberger, 1989a: 289). Implicit in that suggestion is a recognition that there has usually *not* been attention to all points. In educational policy and practice regarding biliteracy, there tends to be an implicit privileging of one end of the continua over the other such that one end of each continuum is associated with more power than the other, for example written development over oral development

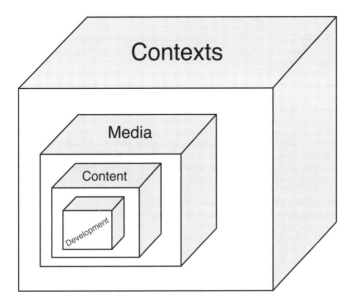

Figure 22.1 Nested relationships among the continua of biliteracy

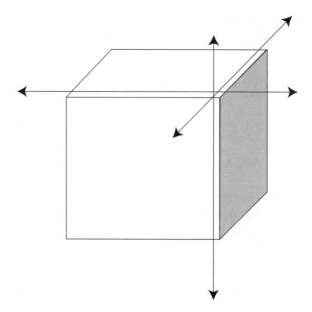

Figure 22.2 Intersecting relationships among the continua of biliteracy

(Figure 22.3 depicts the traditional power weighting assigned to the different continua). There is a need to contest the traditional power weighting of the continua by paying attention to and granting agency and voice to actors and practices at what have traditionally been the less powerful ends of the continua (Hornberger & Skilton-Sylvester, 2000).

As noted earlier, the continua of biliteracy model, like the ecology of language metaphor, is premised on a view of multilingualism as a resource. Further, as the above overview reveals, the continua of biliteracy model also incorporates the language evolution, language environment, and language endangerment themes of the ecology of language metaphor. The very notion of bi (or multi)-literacy assumes that one language and literacy is developing in relation to one or more other languages and literacies (*language evolution*); the model situates biliteracy development (whether in the individual, classroom, community, or society) in relation to the contexts, media, and content in and through which it develops (i.e. *language environment*); and it provides a heuristic for addressing the unequal balance of power across languages and literacies (i.e. for both studying and counteracting *language endangerment*).

Biliteracy development and contexts: language and power in the community

Judy asked what one can do about negative community attitudes toward South Africa's multilingual language policy, referring specifically to Zulu, Xhosa or other Black African parental demands for English-medium instruction for their children. The Bolivian Vice-Minister of Education suggested that the National Education Reform might have erred in placing too much emphasis on indigenous language instruction at the outset, while neglecting instruction in Spanish as a second language. In both cases, the zeal of educators and policy makers for teaching children literacy on the foundation of a language they already speak appears to be at odds with a popular demand for the language of power.

The challenge of popular demand for the societal language of power is a very real one in contexts all over the world, one not to be lightly dismissed. In terms of the continua model, case

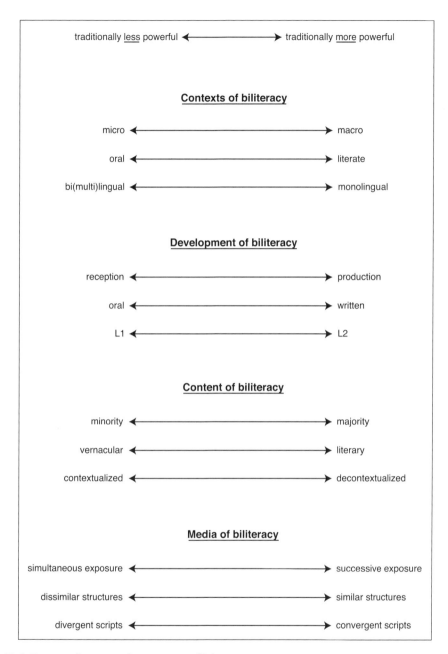

Figure 22.3 Power relations in the continua of biliteracy

after case shows that societal power relationships tend to favor the macro, literate, and mono-lingual ends of the context continua; and national policy and school curricula tend to focus primarily on second language, written, productive skills in biliterate development.

My dissertation study in Puno, Peru, in the 1980s had documented Quechua-speaking community members' resistance to the implementation of Quechua as a medium of instruction in the schools for ideological reasons largely having to do with Spanish being seen as the language of formal education and thereby of access to socioeconomic mobility and power (Hornberger, 1987, 1988a, 1988b). I concluded that unless the wider societal context could be geared toward valuing Quechua on a par with Spanish, "policy failure" was inevitable; the schools, however well they might implement bilingual education, could not on their own counteract deep-seated ideologies favoring Spanish. Those same, enduring ideologies are the ones that the Bolivian Vice-Minister indexed in her opening comments at the Workshop, referring to Quechua and Aymara speaking communities of Bolivia some twenty years after my study in Peru; these ideologies still thrive throughout indigenous communities of the Andes.

Several South African scholars have recently documented or made reference to a similar set of ideologies in Black African communities of South Africa. There, English is the language of power, undergirded not only by the worldwide hegemony of English but also by the heritage of apartheid education which left in its wake a deep suspicion of mother tongue education. Banda explores the paradox whereby black and coloured parents increasingly demand English medium instruction even while academics and researchers agree that English medium instruction is largely responsible for "the general lack of academic skills and intellectual growth among blacks at high school and tertiary levels" (Banda, 2000: 51); and he considers what would be needed to implement a truly additive bilingual policy. De Klerk undertook a survey and interview study in Grahamstown in the Eastern Cape Province, focusing on Xhosa-speaking parents' decisions to send their children to English-medium schools; among the reasons parents gave for choosing an English school for their children were the need for a better education, the recognition that English is an international language and the hope that English would open the door to more job opportunities for their children (de Klerk, 2000: 204–205).

Interestingly, both Bolivia and South Africa have opened up implementational space for popular participation in establishing school language policies, South Africa via the School Governing Boards and Bolivia via the Comités which are part of the Popular Participation provisions of the Education Reform. The goal is to empower parents to make their own decisions about what languages will be medium and subject of instruction in their children's schools. Yet, it would appear that the implementational space for popular participation is of little avail in advancing a multilingual language policy if it is not accompanied by popular participation in the ideological space as well.

In a study carried out in six newly integrated schools in Durban in Kwazulu-Natal Province, Chick and McKay (2001) found a pervasive English-only discourse (along with a decline of standards discourse and a one-at-a-time discourse of classroom interaction) affecting classroom teaching. English-only discourse was evident for example in principals' and teachers' rejection of the use of Zulu in classes other than in Zulu lessons, a practice for which they cited as reasons that students need to improve their English, that students need English for economic advancement, and that the African National Congress itself uses English as a means of reconciling rival ethnic groups (at odds with the ANC's publicly stated position) (Chick, 2000). Yet, the same study also found evidence of counter discourses, namely a multicultural discourse and a collaborative, group work discourse. "A number of teachers, primarily younger teachers, stated that they have discovered that the judicious use of Zulu in classrooms can be beneficial and are permitting the use of Zulu even when it runs counter to school policy" (Chick, 2000: 7); and one teacher in a former Indian elementary school had started doing more group work since attending an in-service workshop on Outcomes-Based Education, finding it advantageous in that quick progress can be made when "brighter and more fluent learners can explain to others exactly what is required" (Chick, 2000: 12). Chick attributes the emergence of these new discourses among teachers to the ideological space which the new language policies opened up (Chick, 2000: 13).

Similarly, while Bloch and Alexander acknowledge that the languages of South Africa are situated along the macro-micro context continuum with English at the most macro (powerful) end and the indigenous African languages clustered at the most micro (powerless) end, and with Afrikaans somewhere along the middle, they go on to make clear that what is at stake with the new multilingual language policy is the "gradual shift of power towards the languages of the majority of the people, who continue in linguistic terms to be treated as a social minority" (Bloch & Alexander, 2001: 5). They report on the work of their PRAESA[5] group at Battswood Primary School in Cape Town, where the "intention is to develop, try out, and demonstrate workable strategies for teaching and learning, using additive bilingualism approaches"; they see themselves as working at the "less powerful micro, oral, and multilingual ends [of the context continua] as [they] develop ways to challenge the power relations that exist at macro, literate, and mono-lingual English levels of the continua in the school and the wider society" (Bloch & Alexander, 2001: 10).

What then does the continua model tell us about what to do in cases such as those depicted in the opening vignettes? The work of Chick and McKay and of Bloch and Alexander is consistent with the argument from the continua model that what is needed is attention to oral, multilingual interaction at the micro level of context and to learners' first language, oral, and receptive language skills development (that is, to the traditionally less powerful ends of the continua of context and development). It is consistent as well with the "classroom success" story that my dissertation told alongside the "policy failure" account referred to above (Hornberger, 1987). That is, despite the ideological privileging of Spanish for school contexts, Quechua speaking children were seen then (and continue today) to clearly thrive from the greater participation in oral classroom interaction which receptive and productive use of their first language afforded them (Hornberger, 1988a, 1989b). In other words, what is needed is to find as many ways as possible to open up ideological spaces for multiple languages and literacies in classroom, com-munity, and society. The continua model is a heuristic to assist in that ecological endeavor. We turn now to consideration of the media and content through which this can be accomplished and the power imbalance among languages subverted.

Media and content of biliteracy: language and identity in the classroom

South African Professor Elizabeth encouraged her young pre-service teachers to speak and use their languages to discuss their own educational experiences and views in the classroom, thereby modeling a practice they might use with their own multilingual, multicultural students in the future. The Bolivian Curricular Development Unit experts sought to provide richly communi-cative and literature-based curriculum and materials for indigenous language speakers to learn Spanish, and raised questions about the implications of code-mixing practices in classroom interaction. In both cases, the negotiation of multiple languages, cultures, and identities among learners (and teachers), who bring different resources to the classroom, is at issue.

The challenge of negotiating across multiple languages, cultures, and identities is a very real one in classrooms all over the world, one not to be lightly dismissed. Yet, on the whole, edu-cational policy and practice continues blithely to disregard the presence of multiple languages, cultures, and identities in today's classrooms. In terms of the continua model, case after case shows that majority, literary, decontextualised contents and similar, convergent, standard language varieties as successively acquired media of instruction, are the established and expected norms in educational systems everywhere.

Multilingual language policies offer a stunning contrast to these expectations, opening up a space where minority, vernacular, contextualised contents and identities can be introduced and a range of media – including dissimilar, divergent, nonstandard varieties as well as visual and other communicative modes – can be employed simultaneously in instruction. Andean teachers in a course I taught on bilingual intercultural education wrote narratives about some of their experiences along these lines. One teacher opened up a Mother's Day celebration to a child's recitation of a Quechua poem and another opened up her language class to the dramatization of a local story, using local materials and local music. In each case, the results were an impressive display of the learners' talents, accompanied by greater intercultural understanding of all those involved. These teachers made use of media and content that have historically been excluded from the school, and thereby subverted the power imbalance among the languages and literacies in the school environment (Hornberger, 2000: 191–192).

Pippa Stein writes along these lines in recounting experiences with two projects she has worked on with pre-service and in-service language teachers in Johannesburg, both of which encourage students' use of a range of representational resources in their meaning making, including the linguistic mode in its written and spoken forms, but also the visual, the gestural, the sonic, and the performative modes (paraphrasing Kress & van Leeuwen, 1996). A reflective practitioner, she is exploring "ways of working as a teacher using certain pedagogies which re-evaluate the value of a resource in the classroom," specifically with the goal of ascribing equal value to resources brought by historically advantaged and historically disadvantaged students. Both the Performing the Literacy Archive Project and the Photographing Literacy Practices Project focus on literacy because "issues of literacy are at the heart of educational success in schools," but in them the students "explore meaning-making in multiple semiotic modes." Drawing on her reflections and on written and video documentation of the students' work over the several years she has done these projects with language teachers, Stein shows how these pedagogies "work with what students bring (their existing resources for representation) and acknowledge what [historically disadvantaged] students have lost." As she puts it, it is "the saying of the unsayable, that which has been silenced through loss, anger or dread, which enables students to re-articulate their relationships to their pasts. Through this process of articulation, a new energy is produced which takes people forward. I call this process of articulation and recovery re-sourcing resources" (Stein, 2004).

The PRAESA group has been carrying out another effort at including practices at the traditionally less powerful ends of the content and media continua as resources in instruction in their work at Battswood Primary School with 30 Xhosa and 19 English/Afrikaans bilingual children, as they have progressed from their first days in Grade One up to the present, their third year of primary school. Bloch and Alexander report on this work in the following terms: "Regarding the media of biliteracy, we encourage simultaneous exposure for the Xhosa and English speaking children to both languages with an emphasis on the children's first language . . . we are concentrating mainly on Xhosa and English, while at the same time not excluding Afrikaans. Our ongoing challenge, in terms of Xhosa language learning for the English/Afrikaans speakers is to try and inspire them enough, and teach the language in ways that motivate them to learn 'against the odds' of any real incentives which promote Xhosa as either necessary or even desirable in the wider society" (Bloch & Alexander, 2001: 12). As regards the content of biliteracy, "the teachers have had to move from the safety of the decontextualised content of a rigid phonics-based part-to-whole skills programme to face the real evidence of what their pupils actually know and can do, thereby drawing on contextualised, vernacular, minority (i.e. majority) knowledge" (Bloch & Alexander, 2001: 14–15).

To carry out these goals, they encourage oral, mother tongue and bilingual interaction; in grade one, the teachers sang many songs and did rhymes with the whole class, typing up the Xhosa rhymes and songs and putting them in plastic sleeves with an English one on one side and Xhosa on the other so that the children could serve as readers to each other. They use interactive writing and journal writing, with the English and Xhosa speaking teachers and PRAESA staff members writing back to the children in their respective languages, a strategy which has proved to provide powerful motivation for the children's use of both languages in their writing. The teachers read daily stories in both Xhosa and English, and have collected an adequate selection of Xhosa and English picture storybooks, which they encourage the children to read in bilingual pairs. The PRAESA group has begun to identify numerous strengths which such practices develop in the children, while simultaneously confronting the fact that most scholastic assessment tools do not measure the kinds of metalinguistic and interpretive skills which particularly stand out in these children.

What then does the continua model tell us about what to do in cases such as those depicted in the opening vignettes? The work of Stein and of Bloch and Alexander is consistent with the argument from the continua model that what is needed is attention to the diversity of standard and nonstandard language varieties, orthographies, and communicative modes and the range of contextualized, vernacular, minority knowledge resources that learners bring to the classroom (that is, to the traditionally less powerful ends of the continua of media and content). It is consistent as well with the on-the-ground experience of the Bolivian and South African educators who find that multilingual interaction in the classroom is inevitable and desirable if multilingual learners are to be encouraged to participate – in the classroom, in academic success, and, ultimately, in a truly democratic society. In other words, what is needed is to find as many ways as possible to open up implementational spaces for multiple languages, literacies, and identities in classroom, community, and society. The continua model is a heuristic to assist in that ecological endeavor.

Conclusion

Bloch and Alexander express the hope that "the window of opportunity will remain open for another few years and that the multiplication of such projects in different areas of South Africa involving all the different languages. . . . will shift the balance of power in favour of those for whom ostensibly the democratic transition was initiated" (Bloch & Alexander, 2001: 25). I share their optimism and their sense of urgency that we linguists and language educators must work hard alongside language planners and language users to fill the ideological and implementational spaces opened up by multilingual language policies; and as researchers to document these new discourses in action so as to keep those ecological policy spaces open into the future.

My sense of urgency about this is perhaps heightened because of recent accumulating events in my own country, where multilingual language policy spaces seem to be closing up at an accelerating rate and the one language–one nation ideology still holds tremendous sway. Analyzing the politics of official English in the 104th Congress of the United States, Joseph Lo Bianco writes of a U.S. discourse which he designates *unum* and which is all about opposing multilingual excess and national disunity, i.e. about homogenization and assimilationism. Also present, he found, was a discourse of *pluribus*, about diversity and emancipation, i.e. about language pluralism (Lo Bianco, 2001). Both discourses have arguably always been present in the

United States, waxing and waning with the times, an ideological tension captured succinctly in the U.S. motto, *E pluribus unum* "out of many one" from which Lo Bianco takes his designations.[6]

Though the United States traditionally has no national language policy, US language ideologies are evident in both national educational policy and state level language policies. In the latter half of the twentieth century, there have been ecological policy spaces for multilingualism and the discourse of *pluribus* in, for example, the national Bilingual Education Act, now of more than 30 years standing, and in state language policies such as Hawaii's recognition of Hawaiian and English or New Mexico's of Spanish and English. Since 1980, however, when Hayakawa first introduced a proposed English Language Constitutional Amendment in Congress, the discourse of *unum* has been gaining ground as a growing number of states have passed English-only legislation.

Even more recently, the pace has picked up. At the state level, under the infamous Unz initiative, California and Arizona voters passed antibilingual education referenda in 1999 and 2000, respectively. In these states, multilingual language policies were thereby reversed (or severely curtailed) for ideological reasons before implementation could be fully realized, documented, and tested. In the debates surrounding passage of Proposition 227 in California, it became clear that (1) the public had very little understanding of what bilingual education really is; and (2) much of what passed for bilingual education in California was in fact not. The ideological discourse of *unum* prevailed over that of *pluribus*, with very little attention to the facts of institutional implementation.[7] At the national level, under the Bush administration, the Bilingual Education Act is undergoing threat of revision which would gut its potential to provide multilingual education for thousands of children who speak English as a second language. Instead, the emphasis is on "moving them to English fluency" in a minimal number of years (National Association for Bilingual Education Action Alert, 23 April 2001; 3 May 2001). None of these trends bodes well for the pluralistic discourse of *pluribus* or a multilingual language ecology in the United States.

Happily, however, there is also a move afoot in recent years among U.S. linguists and language educators to help solidify, support, and promote longstanding grassroots minority language maintenance and revitalization efforts in the United States, under the rubric of "heritage languages."[8] The Heritage Language Initiative, which has among its priorities "to help the U.S. education system recognize and develop the heritage language resources of the country" and "to increase dialogue and promote collaboration among a broad range of stakeholders" (www.cal.org/heritage/), has thus far sponsored one national research conference in 1999 with plans for another in 2002 [see Wiley & Valdés (2000) for a selection of papers from the first conference]. In the intervening years, a working group of scholars was convened to draft a statement of research priorities now being circulated to researchers and policy-makers [available in Wiley and Valdés (2000) and at www.cal.org/heritage]; and a bi-national conversation on heritage/community languages between U.S. and Australian scholars took place in Melbourne (www.staff.vu.edu.au/languageconf/).

This Heritage Language Initiative, supported by both the Center for Applied Linguistics and the National Foreign Language Center, is at least in part about resolving the longstanding language policy paradox whereby we squander our ethnic language resources while lamenting our lack of foreign language resources. It further seeks to draw together and provide visibility and support for the myriad and ongoing bottom-up efforts at rescuing and developing U.S. indigenous and immigrant language resources [as documented in volumes such as Cantoni (1996); Henze & Davis (1999); Hornberger (1996); McCarty & Zepeda (1995, 1998) on U.S. indigenous languages; Fishman (1966b); Kloss (1977); Ferguson & Heath (1981); Garcia & Fishman (1997); McKay & Wong (1988, 2000); Pérez (1998) on U.S. (indigenous and) immigrant languages; Fishman (1991, 2000); May (1999) on cases around the world including U.S. indigenous and immigrant languages].

The Heritage/Community Language effort is one which, I believe, takes an ecological, resource view of indigenous, immigrant, ethnic, and foreign languages as living and evolving in relation to each other and to their environment and as requiring support lest any one of them become further endangered. As linguists and language educators, we need to fill as many ecological spaces as possible, both ideological and implementational, with efforts like these and the Andean and South African efforts mentioned above if we are to keep the multilingual language policy option alive, not only in Bolivia, South Africa, the United States, and Australia, but in all corners of our multilingual world.

Notes

1   The nine languages are: Ndebele, Northern Sotho, Southern Sotho, Swati, Tsonga, Tswana, Venda, Xhosa, and Zulu.
2   In my usage here, "language educators" includes linguists and researchers on language education, language teachers, language teacher educators, and others; "language planners" includes both top-down and bottom-up, organizational and individual agents of language planning; and "language users" includes learners, parents, community members, and others. In other words, I take an inclusive view of those who should be involved in the efforts described here.
3   Van Lier (2000) cites Trim (1959) as the first reference to ecology of language.
4   Huss, Camilleri & King, 2001; Liddicoat & Bryant, 2001; Maffi, 2001; Nettle & Romaine, 2000; Skutnabb-Kangas, 2000 posit an ecology of language in not only a metaphorical sense but also a literal one, explicitly linking the maintenance of linguistic and cultural diversity with the protection and defense of biological and environmental diversity. While I may share their views, that is not the focus of this paper.
5   PRAESA is the Project for the Study of Alternative Education in South Africa, directed by Neville Alexander and based at the University of Cape Town. The team at Battswood Primary School includes one PRAESA staff member (Carole Bloch), assisted sometimes by a post-graduate student, a Xhosa speaking teacher, Ntombizanele Nkence, and a resident Battswood teacher, Erica Fellies (Bloch & Alexander, 2001: 11).
6   Similarly, Cobarrubias identifies "linguistic assimilation" and "linguistic pluralism" as two typical language ideologies which have long co-existed in tension in the United States (Cobarrubias, 1983: 63).
7   Similarly, May (2000), analyzing the Welsh case, writes that minority language policy must overcome both institutional and attitudinal difficulties in order to be successfully implemented at state level. That is, the minority language must be institutionalized in the public realm and it must gain attitudinal support from majority language speakers.
8   While the term "heritage language" has been in use, particularly in Canada, since the early 1970s, a brief search in the *Linguistics and Language Behavior Abstracts* covering 1973 to 2001 shows that the term has been gaining significant ground in the U.S. only in the last decade and in particular the last five years. Of 120 references, 100 date from 1991 or later; 68 of these from 1997 or later. While the majority of references are still to Canada's heritage languages, there is a growing number of references to U.S. indigenous (e.g. Hawaiian, Navajo, Oneida, Siouan) and immigrant (e.g. Chinese, Korean, Italian, Spanish, Yiddish) languages. Meanwhile, as Colin Baker has noted, the term sometimes carries a negative connotation of pointing to the (ancient, primitive) past rather than to a (modern, technological) future (Baker & Jones, 1998: 509); for perhaps this reason and others, the preferred term in Australia is "community languages" (Clyne, 1991; Horvath & Vaughn, 1991).

References

Baker, Colin & Jones, Sylvia Prys (1998). *Encyclopedia of bilingualism and bilingual education*. Clevedon, UK: Multilingual Matters.
Banda, Felix (2000). The dilemma of the mother tongue: Prospects for bilingual education in South Africa. *Language, Culture and Curriculum*, *13*(1), 51–66.

Barton, David (1994). *Literacy: An introduction to the ecology of written language.* Oxford: Blackwell Publishers.

Bloch, Carole & Alexander, Neville (2001). A luta continua!: The relevance of the continua of biliteracy to South African multilingual schools. Paper presented at Third International Bilingualism Symposium, Bristol, UK, April.

Cantoni, Gina (Ed) (1996). *Stabilizing indigenous languages.* Flagstaff: Northern Arizona University Center for Excellence in Education.

Chick, Keith (2000). Constructing a multicultural national identity: South African classrooms as sites of struggle between competing discourses. Paper presented as Nessa Wolfson Colloquium, University of Pennsylvania, November.

Chick, Keith & McKay, Sandra (2001). Positioning learners in post apartheid South African schools: A case study of selected multicultural Durban schools. *Language and Education, 12* (4), 393–408.

Clyne, Michael (1991). *Community languages: The Australian experience.* Melbourne: Cambridge University Press.

Cobarrubias, Juan (1983). Ethical issues in status planning. In Juan Cobarrubias (Ed), *Progress in language planning* (pp. 41–86). Berlin: Mouton.

de Klerk, Vivian (2000). To be Xhosa or not to be Xhosa . . . that is the question. *Journal of Multilingual and Multicultural Development, 21*(3), 198–215.

Ferguson, Charles A. & Heath, Shirley Brice (Eds) (1981). *Language in the USA.* New York: Cambridge University Press.

Fishman, Joshua A. (1966a). Planned reinforcement of language maintenance in the United States; Suggestions for the conservation of a neglected national resource. In Joshua A. Fishman (Ed), *Language loyalty in the United States: The maintenance and perpetuation of non-English mother tongues by American ethnic and religious groups* (pp. 369–411). The Hague: Mouton.

Fishman, Joshua A. (Ed) (1966b). *Language loyalty in the United States: The maintenance and perpetuation of non-English mother tongues by American ethnic and religious groups.* The Hague: Mouton.

Fishman, Joshua A. (1969). National languages and languages of wider communication in the developing nations. *Anthropological Linguistics, 11*(4), 111–135.

Fishman, Joshua A. (1991). *Reversing language shift: Theoretical and empirical foundations of assistance to threatened languages.* Clevedon, UK: Multilingual Matters.

Fishman, Joshua A. (Ed) (2000). *Can threatened languages be saved? "Reversing language shift" revisited.* Clevedon, UK: Multilingual Matters.

Freeland, Jane (1996). The global, the national and the local: Forces in the development of education for indigenous peoples – the case of Peru. *Compare, 26*(2), 167–195.

Gal, Susan (1989). Language and political economy. *Annual Review of Anthropology, 18*, 345–367.

Garcia, Ofelia, & Fishman, Joshua A. (Eds) (1997). *The multilingual apple: Languages in New York City.* Berlin: Mouton.

Haugen, Einar (1972). *The ecology of language.* Stanford, California: Stanford University Press.

Henze, Rosemary & Davis, Kathryn A. (Eds) (1999). Authenticity and identity: Lessons from indigenous language education. *Anthropology and Education Quarterly, 30*(1) (entire issue).

Hornberger, Nancy H. (1987). Bilingual education success, but policy failure. *Language in Society, 16*(2), 205–226.

Hornberger, Nancy H. (1988a). *Bilingual education and language maintenance: A southern Peruvian Quechua case.* Berlin: Mouton.

Hornberger, Nancy H. (1988b). Language ideology in Quechua communities of Puno, Peru. *Anthropological Linguistics, 30*(2), 214–235.

Hornberger, Nancy H. (1989a). Continua of biliteracy. *Review of Educational Research, 59*(3), 271–296.

Hornberger, Nancy H. (1989b). Pupil participation and teacher techniques: Criteria for success in a Peruvian bilingual education program for Quechua children. *International Journal of the Sociology of Language, 77*, 35–53.

Hornberger, Nancy H. (1990). Creating successful learning contexts for bilingual literacy. *Teachers College Record, 92*(2), 212–229.

Hornberger, Nancy H. (Ed) (1996). *Indigenous literacies in the Americas: Language planning from the bottom up.* Berlin: Mouton.

Hornberger, Nancy H. (2000). Bilingual education policy and practice in the Andes: Ideological paradox and intercultural possibility. *Anthropology and Education Quarterly, 31*(2), 173–201.

Hornberger, Nancy H. & Skilton-Sylvester, Ellen (2000). Revisiting the continua of biliteracy: International and critical perspectives. *Language and Education: An International Journal, 14*(2), 96–122.

Horvath, Barbara M. & Vaughan, Paul (1991). *Community languages: A handbook.* Clevedon, UK: Multilingual Matters.

Huss, Leena, Grima, Antoinette Camilleri & King, Kendall (Eds) (2001). *Transcending monolingualism: Linguistic revitalisation in education.* Lisse, The Netherlands: Swets & Zeitlinger.

Kaplan, Robert B. & Baldauf, Richard B. (1997). *Language planning from practice to theory.* Clevedon, UK: Multilingual Matters.

Kaplan, Robert B., Baldauf, Jr., Richard B., Liddicoat, Anthony J., Bryant, Pauline, Barbaux, Marie-Thérèse & Pütz, Martin (2000). Editorial. *Current Issues in Language Planning, 1*(1), 1–10.

Kloss, Heinz (1977). *The American bilingual tradition.* Rowley, Massachusetts: Newbury House.

Kress, Gunther & van Leeuwen, Theo (1996). *Reading images: The grammar of visual design.* London: Routledge.

Liddicoat, Anthony J. & Bryant, Pauline (Eds) (2001). Language planning and language ecology: A current issue in language planning. *Current Issues in Language Planning, 1*(3) (entire issue).

Lo Bianco, Joseph (2001). What is the problem? A study of official English. Paper presented at the annual meetings of the American Association for Applied Linguistics, St. Louis, Missouri.

Maffi, Luisa (2001). *On biocultural diversity: Linking language, knowledge, and the environment.* Washington, DC: Smithsonian Institution Press.

May, Stephen (Ed) (1999). *Indigenous community-based education.* Clevedon, UK: Multilingual Matters.

May, Stephen (2000). Accommodating and resisting minority language policy: The case of Wales. *International Journal of Bilingual Education and Bilingualism, 3*(2), 101–128.

May, Stephen (2001). *Language and minority rights: Ethnicity, nationalism and the politics of language.* Essex, UK: Pearson Education.

McCarty, Teresa L. & Zepeda, Ofelia (Eds) (1995). Indigenous language education and literacy. *Bilingual Research Journal, 19*(1) (entire issue).

McCarty, Teresa L. & Zepeda, Ofelia (Eds) (1998). Indigenous language use and change in the Americas. *International Journal of the Sociology of Language,* 132 (entire issue).

McKay, Sandra Lee & Wong, Sau-ling Cynthia (Eds) (2000). *New immigrants in the United States: Readings for Second Language Educators.* New York: Cambridge University Press.

McKay, Sandra Lee & Wong, Sau-ling Cynthia (Eds) (1988). *Language diversity: Problem or resource?* New York: Newbury House.

Mühlhäusler, Peter (1996). *Linguistic ecology: Language change and linguistic imperialism in the Pacific region.* London: Routledge.

Nettle, Daniel & Romaine, Suzanne (2000). *Vanishing voices: The extinction of the world's languages.* New York: Oxford University Press.

Pakir, Anne (1991). Contribution to workshop on endangered languages, International Conference on Austronesian Linguistics, Hawaii (cited in Mühlhäusler 1996).

Pérez, Berths (Ed) (1998). *Sociocultural contexts of language and literacy.* Mahwah, New Jersey: Lawrence Erlbaum.

Phillipson, Robert & Skutnabb-Kangas, Tove (1996). English only worldwide or language ecology? *TESOL Quarterly, 30*(3), 429–452.

Ricento, Thomas (2000). Historical and theoretical perspectives in language policy and planning. *Journal of Sociolinguistics, 4*(2), 196–213.

Ruiz, Richard (1984). Orientations in language planning. *NABE Journal, 8*(2), 15–34.

Skutnabb-Kangas, Tove (2000). *Linguistic genocide in education – or worldwide diversity and human rights?* Mahwah, New Jersey: Lawrence Erlbaum.

Stein, Pippa (2004). Re-sourcing resources: pedagogy, history and loss in a Johannesburg classroom. In M. Hawkins (Ed), *Language learning and teacher education* (pp. 35–51). Clevedon, UK: Multilingual Matters.

Trim, John L.M. (1959). Historical, descriptive and dynamic linguistics. *Language and Speech,* 2, 9–25.

van Lier, Leo (2000). From input to affordance: Social-interactive learning from an ecological perspective. In J.P. Lantolf (Ed), *Sociocultural theory and second language learning* (pp. 245–259). Oxford: Oxford University Press, 35–51.

Voegelin, Carl F. & Voegelin, Frances M. (1964). Languages of the world: Native America Fascicle One. *Anthropological Linguistics, 6*(6), 2–45.

Wiley, Terrence & Valdés, Guadalupe (Eds) (2000). Heritage language instruction in the United States: A time for renewal. *Bilingual Research Journal, 24*(4) (entire issue).

Woolard, Kathryn A. & Schieffelin, Bambi B. (1994). Language ideology. *Annual Review of Anthropology, 23,* 55–82.

Chapter 23

CHRISTINA SCHÄFFNER

POLITICAL DISCOURSE ANALYSIS FROM THE POINT OF VIEW OF TRANSLATION STUDIES (2004)

1 Introduction: Political discourse analysis: topics and methods

POLITICAL DISCOURSE ANALYSIS is concerned with the analysis of political discourse. This may sound like a trivial statement, but it raises the following questions: what is political discourse? What are characteristic features of political discourse? With which methods can it be analysed? Political discourse has been described as 'a complex form of human activity' (Chilton and Schäffner 1997: 207), based on the recognition that politics cannot be conducted without language. Equally, the use of language in the constitution of social groups leads to what is called 'politics' in a broad sense. But how 'broad' can this sense be? In other words, what counts as 'politics', and subsequently as 'political discourse'?

It is generally acknowledged that the mass media play an important role in disseminating politics and in mediating between politicians and the public, also in a critical sense (cf. the concept of mediatisation of politics, Ekström 2001: 564). The topics which quality newspapers discuss in texts on their front pages, in editorials and comments should therefore be good examples of political texts. In February and March 2003, the topical political events which make the headlines in the mass media are the Iraq conflict and the Middle East crisis, topics which will easily be described as political ones by everybody. However, if we look back to see what made the headlines a year ago, the picture is different. For example, the main topic for *The Times* on 12 April 2002 was David Beckham's broken foot. The title of an article on page 1 was 'Beckham's foot becomes Blair's bone of contention', and the first sentences of the text are as follows:

> (1) Forget the Middle East. And who cares about next week's Budget? The one issue that had Tony Blair and his ministers on tenterhooks at yesterday's Cabinet meeting— together with the rest of the country—was David Beckham's foot.
>
> Such has become the national obsession with the broken bone in the England captain's left foot, sustained during Manchester United's European Cup quarter-final clash with Spain's Deportivo La Coruna on Wednesday night, that the Prime Minister interrupted the Cabinet meeting to declare that "nothing was more important" to the country's World Cup preparations than the state of Beckham's foot.

Another issue which made the headlines in *The Times* on the same day was that the German Chancellor Schröder had sued a journalist for saying he was dying his hair. This topic was even worth an editorial, in which a link was established between hair colour and the credibility of politicians. In another article on the same issue on the same day we read (*The Times* 12 April 2002, p.16):

(2) The Christian Democrat deputy Karl-Josef Laumann added to the Chancellor's fears when he said: "A man who colours his hair is certainly capable of trimming statistics."

Politologists have used the label 'politainment' (Dörner 2001) to describe this recent phenomenon of a symbiosis of politics and entertainment, i.e. the reduction of actual content to a minimum and the addition of aspects of entertainment to 'sell' politics. These examples show that 'politics' is indeed a rather wide and flexible notion. Seen from a functional perspective, we can say that any topic can become political, or politicised (cf. Muntigl 2002). In other words, what is considered 'political' depends on the participants in the communicative context. Nevertheless, there are some types of texts and forms of talk which are political in a more narrow, or prototypical sense. These are texts that either discuss political ideas, beliefs, and practices of a society or some part of it (e.g. textbooks, academic papers, essays), or texts that are crucial in constituting a political community or group (e.g. treaties, a manifesto of a political party, a speech by a politician).

It is mainly these 'prototypical' political texts that have been the object of discourse analysis. A range of analytic methods have been applied, including textual, pragmatic, discourse-historical, and socio-cognitive approaches, to a variety of phenomena of political discourse in the media and other domains (cf. the bibliography in Chilton and Schäffner 1997, also the contributions in Chilton and Schäffner 2002). In Chilton and Schäffner (1997: 211) we defined the task of political discourse analysis as to relate the fine grain of linguistic behaviour to politics, or political behaviour. Political situations and processes can be linked to discourse types and levels of discourse organisation by way of four strategic functions at an intermediate level. We proposed the following four functions: (i) coercion; (ii) resistance, opposition and protest; (iii) dissimulation; (iv) legitimisation and delegitimisation. Research can proceed both prospectively and retrospectively, i.e. an analyst can ask with which linguistic means a specific function can best be fulfilled in a particular context, or, s/he can start with the linguistic choices identified in a specific text and relate them to the strategic functions.

A retrospective analysis can also try to find an answer to the question of why a specific word, phrase, structure was chosen rather than some other possible one. If we look again at example (2) above, we notice that a direct quote from a German politician has been used. However, the reader is not provided with the exact words used by Karl-Josef Laumann, but with an English version of his original German statement which had been taken from a German newspaper. In other words, a process of translation was involved as an intermediary process for the production of the text as it was finally published in *The Times*. Translation is a very regular phenomenon for practically all types of political discourse. A few examples will suffice to illustrate this. In January and February 2003, the German news magazine *Der Spiegel* published translated extracts of the book *The Threatening Storm* by Kenneth Pollack, to accompany its reports about the Iraq crisis. It also published a series of essays on the same topic, written by intellectuals who argue for or against waging war, also commenting on each other's arguments (intertextuality). Among those intellectuals are John le Carré and Leon de Winter, and their essays are published in German translations. It is statements from the German versions that are taken up and commented on in the subsequent essays. A group of members of the AtlantikBrücke, a German-American friendship association, published *A Message to the People of the United States of America* in the *New York Times* on 16 February 2003, and a German version in the *Frankfurter Allgemeine Zeitung* on 22 February 2003. A Radio Address by President Bush of 7 March 2003 is made available on the Internet in a German translation produced by the German Press Agency *dpa*. The text of the UN Iraq Resolution 1414, adopted in November 2002, is valid in the six official languages of the UN (Arabic, Chinese, English, French, Russian and Spanish). A German translation is available on the Internet, and extracts in German are repeatedly quoted in speeches of German politicians and in articles in the mass media. A letter, signed by eight European heads of government and expressing support for the US policy towards Iraq, is published in several European newspapers (30 and 31 January 2003), each time in the local language. A political statement, entitled 'We Stand for Peace & Justice', is available on the Internet in the English original (www.zmag. org/wspj/index.cfm?language=eng) in March 2003 together with translations into Portuguese, Spanish, Turkish, French, Italian, and announcing translations into Korean, Macedonian, Dutch, Chinese, Polish, Greek, Japanese, Russian . . . to come.

What these examples illustrate is that political discourse relies on translation; translation is in fact part of the development of discourse, and a bridge between various discourses. It is through translation that information is made available to addressees beyond national borders; and it is very frequently the case that reactions in one country to statements that were made in another country are actually reactions to the information as it was provided in translation. As said above, political discourse analysis relates linguistic behaviour to political behaviour. The linguistic behaviour may well reflect evidence of mediated behaviour, i.e. mediated by translation. It is therefore important to take full account of the phenomenon of translation in analysing political texts. My claim is that so far Political Discourse Analysis has not yet paid sufficient attention to aspects of translation. In this paper, I want to argue that (i) the discipline of Translation Studies (TS) has much to offer to Political Discourse Analysis (PDA), and that (ii) TS and PDA already share certain concerns and concepts which should be exploited to the benefit of both disciplines. I will start with presenting a few examples of authentic cases of translations (political or politically relevant texts, mainly involving the language pair German and English) and comment on them from the point of view of Translation Studies. These examples concern political effects to the choice of specific translation solutions; the processes by which information is transferred via translation to another culture; and the structure and function of equally valid texts in their respective cultures. In short, these examples concern both the translation of politics and the politics of translation. After the discussion of examples, I will present some of the main issues that are being discussed in the discipline of Translation Studies, which has become a discipline in its own right. I will conclude with some comments on shared concern between Political Discourse Analysis and Translation Studies, thus pointing to scope for interdisciplinary cooperation.

2 Political discourse in translation

2.1 Lexical choice

One focus of attention in Political Discourse Analysis (PDA) and also in Critical Discourse Analysis (CDA) has been a critical reflection on the strategic use of political concepts, or keywords, for achieving specific political aims. There is widespread agreement in modern linguistics that meanings are not inherent to words, neither are they stable. It is rather the case that language users assign meanings in communicative contexts, and in this process of meaning construction the information presented in the text interacts with previously stored knowledge and mental models (cf. van Dijk 2002). Political concepts too are relative to the discourse of a cultural or political group, and thus contestable. The experiential and socio-cultural background of language users also needs to be taken into account when it comes to translation. The following extract from a newspaper article shows how a particular word that had been used in the translation led to an accusation of a politician.

(3) "Hungarian Prime Minister Viktor Orban has been accused of breaching EU entry criteria by using a term synonymous with Nazi-era Germany. [. . .] he used the word *Lebensraum* ('living space') in a debate about granting preferential treatment to ethnic Hungarians from neighbouring states. The term was notoriously used by Adolf Hitler, when he talked about providing Germany with 'living space' in the east.

    'This language is distasteful,' said Watson. 'The sentiments it betrays are incompatible with the Copenhagen criteria for entry into the EU.' [. . . But a spokeswoman for Orban said he had actually used the Hungarian word *eletter*. While this could be translated as *lebensraum* in German, it also corresponds to the English term 'room for manoeuvre; the spokeswoman added."

(*The European voice* 14–20 February 2002)[1]

This example reflects a case of multiple mediation: an English politician criticising a Hungarian politician with reference to a word that appeared in the translation into German. In his speech, Orban had recommended to link the economic living space (*élettér*) of Hungarians living across the border with that of the Hungarians living in Hungary, so that the national economy could perform better. Although '*élettér*' was and is used with reference to the politics of Hitler-Germany, the word does not exclusively belong to Nazi vocabulary. It is also used in other contexts, e.g. in the field of animal behaviour or in the name of a foundation (Magyar *Elettér* Alapitvany – Hungarian Living-space Foundation), without any negative associations in both cases).[2] Following the critical reactions abroad, also in Hungary itself the political sense of the word was reactivated. That is, a debate was initiated on the basis of a translation, and the lexical choice that had been made by the translator (deliberately? unaware of the association? under time pressure?) was exploited eventually to the advantage of politicians who are not in favour of admitting former Communist countries as new members to the European Union.

    There are, however, also cases where translators or interpreters had been instructed to use specific terms and avoid others. Translating and interpreting as the two main modes of mediated communication share certain features, but they also have their own distinctive characteristics (cf. e.g. Gile 2004).[3] In contrast to translators, interpreters are physically present at a communicative event and thus visible. However, both translators and interpreters operate in contexts which are shaped by social aims and ideologies, which is particularly obvious in the field of politics. For example, Hermann Kusterer, who interpreted at meetings between the first German Chancellor Konrad Adenauer and the French President Charles de Gaulle, reported that in 1962 he had been told by a German minister to avoid the word 'Union' whenever the French 'union' came up in speaking about the bilateral relations. He was required to use the synonym '*Zusammenschluß*' instead, which was less forceful as a political keyword. The reason was that the German government had considered it tantamount at that time of the Cuba missile crisis to put more emphasis on Germany's relations to the USA and not to France (*Frankfurter Rundschau* 22 January 2003). Political motivations were also the reason for the existence of two different German translations of the Quadripartite Agreement on West Berlin signed in 1971. The authentic texts were in English, French and Russian. The paragraph dealing with the relations between West Berlin and the Federal Republic of Germany says that the *ties will* be developed.

Ties (*liens* in the French version) had been translated as *Verbindungen* in the East German and as *Bindungen* in the West German version, with *Verbindungen* denoting relations that are not so tight as those denoted by *Bindungen* (see Kade 1980: 57ff). Although neither of the two German versions was a politically valid document, political decisions and practical steps were nevertheless justified with reference to the wording (i.e. *Bindungen* or *Verbindungen*).

That word choice in the context of politically sensitive issues is not only relevant with reference to the past can be seen in the following example. In reporting on the Middle East problem in April 2002, the German news magazine *Der Spiegel* published an interview with Mosche Kazaw, the President of Israel. On the following day, the British daily *The Times* reported on this interview, quoting selected passages. The aspect of information selection itself is of interest to Political Discourse Analysis (which passages have been selected and why?), as is the question of the discursive employment of the selected information (cf. the concepts of reformulation, recontextualisation, intertextuality, e.g. Sauer 1996, Fairclough 1995). I am interested in the recontextualisation from the point of view of translation.

(4) a. *Der Spiegel:* In Europa wird inzwischen sogar über Handelssanktionen debattiert.

Kazaw: Europa macht einen Fehler. Ich habe keine Angst vor ökonomischem Schaden. Aber Europa vergisst, dass wir gegen Terror kämpfen. Dem sollten sich die Europäer anschließen. Doch ihre Position ermutigt Terror. Sie haben das falsche Ziel im Visier. [. . .]

Der Spiegel: Deutschland denkt sogar über eine Teilnahme an einer internationalen Nahost-Schutztruppe nach. Können Sie sich deutsche Soldaten in Israel vorstellen?

Kazaw: Unsere Erfahrung mit Uno-Truppen ist nicht gut. Im Südlibanon marschieren die Hisbollah-Kämpfer einfach an den Blauhelmen vorbei und greifen uns an. Uno-Truppen können keinen Terror stoppen.

(*Der Spiegel* 15 April 2002)

The original question-answer schema has been turned into a reporting style in *The Times*, but some of Katzav's answers are presented as direct speech.[4]

(4) b. "Europe is making a mistake," Mr Katzav told the German news magazine *Der Spiegel*. "Europe forgets that we are fighting a war against terror which they should be part of. Yet their position encourages terror, they have the false target in their sights." [. . .] President Katzav said yesterday: "Our experience with United Nations troops is not good." He added that in southern Lebanon "Hizbollah fighters simply marched past the peacekeepers and attacked us. UN troops cannot stop terror."

(*The Times* 15 April 2002)

There is no reference in the texts as to the language in which the interview was actually conducted (it might well have been in Hebrew), but since the English text refers to the German one, the German version becomes the source text for the subsequent English text. A comparison of the English and the German version points to some interesting aspects. In the second quote, the use of present tense ('*marschieren . . . vorbei, greifen . . . an*') indicates repeated, regular behaviour, whereas the past tense in the English version ('marched past, attacked') reflects a single event. In the first quote, the addition of 'war' in the English version ('*dass wir gegen Terror kämpfen*' – 'we are fighting a war against terror') is indicative of ideological considerations. After September 11th, US-President Bush declared to fight a 'war' against worldwide terrorism, an announcement which was received critically in large circles in Europe. In Germany, for example, most politicians and the media objected to the use of '*Krieg*' ('*war*') and preferred to speak of the less dramatic '*Kampf*' ('fight'). In the case of the renewed violence in the Middle East in spring 2002, there was again a debate on the appropriateness of describing Palestinian suicide attacks on Israel as 'terrorism' and the Israeli government's military campaign in the West Bank as 'war against terrorism'. The Israeli government argued that they were entitled to speak of 'war against terrorism', which means that the English version has brought President Katzav's discourse in line with the official government discourse. Alternatively, if the German text too had been a translation from an interview conducted in Hebrew, it could be that '*Krieg*' had been avoided, equally signalling ideological considerations.

This example may look trivial, and, admittedly, the position of a politician usually becomes clear in a text as a whole, even if specific microstructures seem to have been 'toned down' or 'exaggerated'. But texts, including translations, fulfil functions in their social contexts, they are used – quoted, referred to, commented on – in other texts. It is in those intertextual and interdiscursive contexts where interpretations are often made solely on the basis of a translated version. Politicians, or political analysts, usually do not go back to the original text, neither do they request a detailed comparative analysis of the original text and the translation. Once produced, translations as texts lead a life of their own, and are the basis on which people acquire information and knowledge.

I will briefly illustrate how a political dispute on the future of the European Union between the UK and Germany in 1994 was caused by a translation (for a detailed discussion see Schäffner 1997). The case in point is the choice of 'hard core' for '*fester Kern*' in the English translation of a German document produced by the parliamentary group of the German Christian Democratic Union/Christian Social Union (CDU/CSU), with Wolfgang Schäuble (the then CDU parliamentary floor leader) and Karl Lamers as co-authors. In one of its sections, this document argued for the formation of an inner group of closely integrated EU member states which would lead the way to further EU integration. This inner group is referred to in the German original as '*ein fester Kern*', cf.:

(5) a. "Daher muß sich [. . .] der feste Kern von integrationsorientierten und kooperationswilligen Ländern, [. . .] weiter festigen.

Der feste Kern hat die Aufgabe, den zentrifugalen Kräften in der immer größer werdenden Union ein starkes Zentrum entgegenzustellen und damit die Auseinander-entwicklung [. . .] zu verhindern."

(Überlegungen zur Europäischen Politik, 1 September 1994, p. 7)

The document was translated by in-house translators in Germany and made available abroad. One day after its publication in Germany, an extract of the document was published in *The Guardian*, using the translation that had been produced in Germany. The authentic English translation of the extract above is as follows:

(5) b. "[. . .] that existing hard core of countries oriented to greater integration and closer cooperation must be further strengthened. [. . .]

The task of the hard core is, by giving the Union a strong centre, to counteract the centrifugal forces generated by constant enlargement and, thereby, to prevent [. . .] drifting apart."

(*Reflections on European Polity*, 1 September 1994, p. 7,
also *The Guardian*, 7 September 1994)

There were other issues raised as well in the total of fourteen typed pages of the document, but the highly controversial political debates that followed centred around the notion of 'hard core'. '*Fester Kern*' was to be interpreted in a positive way, suggesting a firm commitment to European integration. However, the choice of 'hard core' had significantly shifted the tone of the document in its English version. 'Hard core' is frequently associated with people and things that are tough, immoral and incorrigible. Therefore, the British Government and the media typically argued against any attempt of the core countries (and in particular Germany) trying to impose their ideas on all member states. In a keynote speech in The Netherlands on 7 September 1994, the then Prime Minister John Major, in responding to the document, said that he saw 'a real danger in talk of a hard core' and that there 'should never be an exclusive hard core either of countries or of policies' (*The Times* 8 September 1994).

As a consequence to the critical debates in the UK, the conceptual metaphor of the 'core' was discursively elaborated in German political discourse. When challenged that his idea of a '*Kerneuropa*' would mean that a few take the initiative in decision-making processes, thus leaving others outside, Schäuble linked it to another metaphor, the magnet, cf.:

(6) "Wir haben immer das Bild des Magnetfelds gebraucht: Der Kern zieht an und stößt nicht ab." (*Der Spiegel* 12 February 1996)

[We have always used the image of the magnetic field: the magnetic core attracts, it does not repel.—my translation, CS]

From a translational point of view it can be said that the translator had only accounted for the metaphorical expression ('*Kern* – core'), without reflecting about underlying conceptual metaphors (cf. Lakoff and Johnson 1980, Chilton 1996, Schäffner 2004a). The consequence was a – politically motivated – heated debate in Great Britain and in Germany, which ultimately resulted in a shift from an orientational metaphor (HAVING CONTROL IS BEING AT THE CENTRE) to a structural metaphor (THE EU IS A MAGNET). This example shows that translation solutions can have specific effects for international political discourse and equally for polity making.

2.2 Information selection and transfer

The media play an important role in disseminating information about political ideas and decisions of other countries. People will form their opinions on the basis of such reports, and political leaders too may take their decisions on the basis of information provided to them via the media. It is important that the information provided is reliable. If a quality newspaper reports about statements made by a politician, we usually accept that these statements have really been made. However, tracing the origin of statements provided in translation by the media can result in more or less surprising findings. As I have shown elsewhere (Schäffner 2001), comments attributed to the German Chancellor Gerhard Schröder had turned out to have been made by somebody else. In December 1999, a number of British newspapers reported about a policy statement made by Schröder on 3 December 1999 in the Bundestag, the lower house of parliament. In this statement, Schröder outlined the position which the German Government was going to take at the EU summit meeting in Helsinki in mid-December. One of the issues that was on the agenda of the Helsinki Summit meeting was tax harmonisation, which was favoured by the German Government but fiercely opposed by the UK Government. Before the summit, the media were reporting that a heated debate on the issue of a crossborder savings tax was to be expected. Their tenor in reporting about Schröder's speech was rather critical, for example, 'Schröder gave a fresh twist to the row with Britain' (*The Guardian* 4 December 1999), 'German fury at Blair over tax "intransigence" [. . .] the German Chancellor lashed out at Britain' (*Daily Telegraph* 4 December 1999). The most important point for all papers was that Schröder had threatened unilateral action if an EU-wide agreement could not be reached, quoting him verbatim:

(7) According to the German chancellor: "We will exert pressure at all levels to find an EU-wide solution. If that doesn't work then if necessary we should consider a national solution."

(The Guardian 4 December 1999)

It is exactly this statement, however, which was never made by Schröder. As can be seen from the stenographic records of that particular session of the Bundestag, the only reference to a solution without the UK came in the speech by Wolfgang Schäuble, who was speaking on behalf of the opposition party CDU, cf.:

(8) "Ich möchte zu erwägen geben, ob wir unseren britischen Freunden nicht sagen sollten: Wenn sie partout nicht wollen, daß wir in der Europäischen Union zu einer Harmonisierung der Besteuerung der Kapitaleinkünfte kommen, dann gehen wir diesen ersten Schritt im Rahmen der Eurozone—das ist flexibles Vorgehen—, dann harmonisieren wir die Besteuerung der Kapitaleinkünfte in der Eurozone.

[I would like to suggest to tell our British friends: If they do resist achieving harmonisation in capital taxation within the European Union, then we will take this first step within the Euro-zone—this is flexibility—then we will harmonise capital taxation in the Euro-zone."—my translation, CS]

However, it was not a national solution that was suggested by Schäuble, but one for the Euro-zone. Such a 'mistake' raises the question, how the media interpretation had come about. Schröder's polity statement had been translated into English by the translation service of the German government (made available on the Internet, Press release 7.12.99, www.bundesregierung.de/english). It is common practice that the translations are made available to journalists, and depending on the type of speech and the context in which it is made, this happens either before or after the actual delivery.[5] In this specific case, the journalists obviously did not refer to an official translation, for whatever reason. As a result, the readers of British newspapers were given information which was inaccurate. The choice of words such as 'row, fury, lash out' in the articles quoted contributed to the impression that Germany – once more – wanted to impose a decision on other EU member states. The Helsinki Summit did not reach an agreement on the tax package. It may well be that the style of reporting in Britain had contributed to Blair's tough negotiating position.

What this example reveals is that the selection of information, whether due to lack of linguistic competence or to carelessness, nevertheless fits into a traditional way of reporting about Germany in the UK press and seems to reveal deep-seated perceptions and stereotypes about the Germans. A more recent case can serve as another example of how pre-conceived notions can have an impact on text reception.

In April 2002, the German Government debated Germany's potential role in solving the Middle East conflict. The magazine *Der Spiegel* reported in a very detailed way how arguments made by Chancellor Schröder had been reported by the international press. On Monday, 8 April 2002, Schröder gave a talk in the German town Hannover to high-ranking military officers. He was asked whether it would be necessary for Europeans in general and for Germany in particular to show more engagement once a peaceful settlement in the Middle East had been reached. According to *Der Spiegel*, Schröder replied, in a vague style as characteristic of diplomatic discourse, that in order to give peace a chance, the United Nations would need to consider not only sending observers, but also whether it might become necessary to use military means, legitimated by the United Nations. He added that it would be premature to discuss the role that Germany might play in this respect.[6]

Der Spiegel goes on to say that at 5.59 pm the same day, the news agency *Reuters* reported that an international military action in the Middle East had become a possibility and that the participation of the German army could no longer be ruled out. Following this report, various newspapers ran articles on reactions to the 'German plan to send troops to Israel'. *The Times* had invited its readers to join the discussion on that issue. In one of the readers' letters that was published in response to the question 'Is Germany right to offer to send peacekeeping troops to Israel?' we read:

> (9) "The German suggestion of sending its troops to the Middle East makes my blood run cold. [. . .] One gets the feeling that they would like to finish the job that came close to reality half a century ago."
>
> *(The Times* 16 April 2002)

Although these examples may not represent prototypical instances of what is understood by 'translation', they nevertheless involve processes of mediated communication across languages and cultures. Journalists use information as provided by the (translation service of) news agencies, or they produce 'translations' themselves. In these contexts of mediated text production, it is not always the case that a complete target text is produced on the basis of a complete source text. It may as well be that, in view of specific needs, only extracts are selected for a translation process. But also in the case of complete texts, the conditions of text production and the purposes which the texts are to serve in their respective cultures must be taken into account. With the following example I want to illustrate that also supposedly identical texts reveal traces of culture-specific sensitivities.

2.3 *Illusion of identity*

The example is the policy document 'Europe: The Third Way/Die Neue Mitte' which was officially launched on 8 June 1999 in London and presented in English and in German as a joint paper by Tony Blair as leader of the British Labour Party and Gerhard Schröder as leader of the German Social Democratic Party (SPD). Both texts were presented to the public at the same time and as identical copies. The document argues for modernising Social Democracy, and its function is to mobilise party members to carry out this task.

The idea for a joint policy paper originated in the SPD, and the German side produced a draft outline which was largely written in German, with some paragraphs in English (i.e. those that dealt specifically with political developments in the UK). Based on this draft, the actual full text was then produced in English by New Labour, and then translated again into German. In the following revision stages, all paragraphs that were amended or added, by either side, were translated into the other language. That is, both the German and the English version of (parts of) the text functioned alternatively as source text and target text. The whole process of text production was done by a small team of political officials, led by Peter Mandelson, then Britain's trade minister, and Bodo Hombach, then head of the chancellery and a close aide of Schröder's.

The paper caused a stir in Germany, especially within the SPD itself and the trade unions, but it was hardly noticed in the UK. In comparing the textual profiles of the two versions, I was able to explain some of the reactions to the German text in Germany (for a detailed discussion see Schäffner 2003). Two examples will suffice here. The document argues for 'a newly defined role for an active state' in relation to industry, trade unions, and the people. In this new role, the state is to allow for sufficient flexibility and freedom for economy and businesses, and shall renounce its responsibility to provide welfare for everybody. The following paragraphs, which are slightly different in the English and in the German text, reflect different perceptions and ideological traditions in Britain and in Germany, cf.:

(10) a. "Our countries have different traditions in dealings between state, industry, trade unions and social groups, but we share a conviction that traditional conflicts at the workplace must be overcome. This, above all, means rekindling a spirit of community and solidarity, strengthening partnership and dialogue between all groups in society and developing a new consensus for change and reform. We want all groups in society to share our joint commitment to the new directions set out in this Declaration."

b. "Unsere Staaten haben unterschiedliche Traditionen im Umgang zwischen Staat, Industrie, Gewerkschaften und gesellschaftlichen Gruppen, aber wir alle teilen die Überzeugung, daß die traditionel len Konflikte am Arbeitsplatz überwunden werden müssen. Dazu gehört vor allem, die Bereitschaft und die Fähigkeit der Gesellschaft zum Dialog und zum Konsens wieder neu zu gewinnen und zu stärken. Wir wollen allen Gruppen ein Angebot unterbreiten, sich in die gemeinsame Verantwortung für das Gemeinwohl einzubringen." (Second and third sentence literally: This, above all, means regaining and strengthening society's willingness and ability for dialogue and consensus. We want to make an offer to all groups to join into the common responsibility for the public weal.)

'Community', 'community spirit' and 'partnership' are core concepts of the ideology of New Labour. Thinking in terms of communitarianism is identical with the rejection of a state interfering in a successful market economy, and also includes relying on initiatives of individuals (see also Fairclough 2000: 37ff). In Germany, however, with strong trade unions and corporate ownership patterns, there has always been a political culture of consultation with the aim of achieving consensus. Therefore, communitarianism and partnership would not have been interpreted as a new offer for society. The German text reflects the tradition of consultations among the main social forces, i.e. government, employers, trade unions, to work for the common good (and not inviting them immediately to share the commitment to the objectives as laid down in the Blair/Schröder paper, as the English text does).

The following extract too reflects a difference in the two versions. The German text accounts for the traditionally strong role of trade unions. It gives them assurance that they will be needed in a changed world, whereas the English text allows the inference that only modern (i.e. not 'old', left-wing) trade unions will be supported, cf.:

(11) a. "We support modern trade unions protecting individuals against arbitrary behaviour, [. . .]"

b. "Wir wollen, daß die Gewerkschaften in der Modernen Welt verankert bleiben. Wir wollen, daß sie den einzelnen gegen Willkür schützen [. . .]" (Literally: We want trade unions to remain anchored in the modern world. . . .)

As indicated above, it was in fact political officials who acted as translators. Their main argument for not employing professional translators was that they would not understand the subtleties and sensitivities involved in political discourse. However, had competent translators with specific subject expertise in the domain of politics been involved, the resulting political debate might not have been equally fierce. Be that as it may, the more or less subtle differences between the English and the German text reflect different ideological phenomena, both texts thus serving as windows onto ideologies in the two political cultures. The document, however, was presented as a joint paper, as evidence of Blair and Schröder 'speaking the same language'. To the addressees, therefore, the two versions gave only an illusion of identity (cf. Koskinen 2000).

What all these examples were meant to show is that textual features need to be linked to the social and ideological contexts of text production and reception. In other words, texts and discourses are framed by social and political structures and practices. This aspect links TS to PDA and CDA. Fairclough and Wodak (1997: 258) describe the aim of CDA as to make the 'ideological loading of particular ways of using language and the relations of power which underlie them' more visible. In CDA, this is usually done on the basis of discourse in one language and one culture. In the case of translation, however, textual features, ideological contexts, and underlying relations of power apply both to the source text and culture and to the target text and culture. The discipline of Translation Studies has developed concepts with which it is possible to describe and explain target text profiles, the translation strategies used, the appropriateness of those strategies, the conditions under which the translator operated, and the effects a text has had in its receiving culture. Some of these concepts have been 'imported' and incorporated into TS from neighbouring disciplines, especially (applied) linguistics, communication studies, discourse analysis, cultural studies, comparative literature. In the following section I will give a short overview of the emergence of modern Translation Studies, introduce some of the key concepts used, and present some of the current research interests. This presentation will be selective, in view of my aim to propose ways for cooperation between Political Discourse Analysis and Translation Studies.

3. Translation Studies as a discipline

Translation and interpreting as activities have existed for many centuries. Throughout history, translators have contributed to the development of alphabets and of national languages, to the development of national literatures, to the dissemination of knowledge, the advancement of science, and to the transmission of cultural values (cf. Delisle and Woodsworth 1995). The increasing need for translation and interpreting in a variety of domains resulted in the development of Translation Studies as an academic discipline in the second half of the 20th century. Theoretical principles have been formulated which are the basis for the description, observation, and teaching of translation. However, there is no unified theory and no general agreement on central concepts of the discipline. What we have instead is a multiplicity of approaches, each of which focuses on specific aspects, looks at the product or the process of translation from a specific angle, and/or analyses the socio-political causes and effects of translations (for an overview see Gentzler 1993, Stolze 1994, Baker 1998, Munday 2001, and the contributions in Venuti 2000). The label 'Translation Studies' traditionally covers research into both translating and interpreting, although more recently there have been attempts to highlight the specific profile of 'Interpreting Studies' (see the introductory chapter in Pöchhacker and Shlesinger 2002, and the contributions in Schäffner in 2004b). In the following discussion, I will focus on TS in the narrower sense, i.e. excluding interpreting research.

After the Second World War, a more systematic reflection on the nature of translation set in, very much influenced by (applied) linguistics. Translation was initially studied as a linguistic phenomenon, as a process of meaning transfer via linguistic transcoding, and consequently, Translation Studies was conceived as a linguistic discipline. Attempts were made to develop a 'science of translation' (e.g. Nida 1964), or a linguistic theory of translation (Catford 1965), whose aim it was to give a precise description of the equivalence relations between signs and combinations of signs in the source language (SL) and the target language (TL).

Since translation involves texts with a specific communicative function, the limitations of a narrow linguistic approach soon became obvious. Thus, from the 1970s, insights and approaches of text linguistics, pragmatics, discourse analysis, sociolinguistics, communication studies, were adopted to translation studies. Translation was defined as text production, as retextualising a SL-text according to the TL conventions. The text moved into the centre of attention, and notions such as textuality, context, culture, communicative intention, function, text type, genre, and genre conventions have had an impact on reflecting about translation (e.g. Reiss 1971, Hatim and Mason 1990, 1997, Neubert and Shreve 1992, Trosborg 1997). Texts are produced and received with a specific purpose, or function, in mind. This is the main argument underlying functionalist approaches to translation, initiated by Vermeer (1978) with his *Skopos Theory* (derived from the Greek word 'skopós', which means purpose, aim, goal, objective). The basic assumptions are as follows: translation is a specific kind of communicative action; each action has a specific purpose, and therefore, the most decisive criterion for any translation is its purpose (Skopos). Translation is a purposeful activity (Nord 1997), initiated by a translation commission and resulting in a target text (TT) which is appropriately structured for its specified purpose. The starting point for any translation is therefore not the (linguistic surface structure of the) source text (ST), but the purpose of the target text. The Skopos of the ST and the Skopos of the TT can be either identical or different, resulting in different, but equally valid, types of translation (cf. documentary and instrumental translation, equifunctional and heterofunctional translation, Nord 1997, overt and covert translation, House 1997). Since language and culture are interdependent, translation is transfer between cultures, a specific kind of culture-determined text production (cf. Reiss and Vermeer 1991). This complex translatorial action (Holz-Mänttäri 1984) is realised by a translator as an expert in text production for transcultural interaction.

It can be said that functionalist approaches are representative of the shift from linguistic and rather formal translation theories to a more functionally and socioculturally oriented concept of translation which set in in the 1970s. Another major impetus came with Descriptive Translation Studies, inspired by comparative literature. In a conference paper 1972, Holmes outlined the field of what he termed 'Translation Studies' (which has become the widely accepted term) and its two main objectives: (i) to describe the phenomena of translating and translations) as they manifest themselves in the world of our experience, and (ii) to establish general principles by means of which these phenomena can be explained and predicted (Holmes 1988: 71). Descriptive Translation Studies (DTS), as a distinct branch next to Theoretical Translation Studies (ThTS) and Applied Translation Studies, is subdivided into product-oriented, function-oriented, and process-oriented DTS.[7] In the early 1970s, descriptive analyses were still missing within the discipline, but once scholars started undertaking such research, they opened up the field of Translation Studies by introducing new questions and perspectives. For example, through comparative descriptions of translations of the same source text, either in one single language or in various languages, it could be shown how social and historical conditions, primarily in the recipient socio-culture, had influenced the translational behaviour. Translational behaviour is contextualised as social behaviour, with the act of translation, i.e. the cognitive aspects of translation as a decision-making process, embedded in a translation event, i.e. the social, historical, cultural, ideological context. Based on his descriptive analyses, Toury introduced the concept of norms as being central to both the act and the event of translating. Translational norms are understood as internalised behavioural constraints which embody the values shared by a community, and translation is thus defined as norm-governed behaviour (Toury 1995).

Identifying regularities in the behaviour of several translators at the same time in the same culture[8] can help to establish which particular general concept of translation prevailed in a particular community at a particular time. An empirical and historical perspective also allows to study the position of translated literature (central or peripheral) in a literature as a whole, and its function for that literature (cf. polysystem theory, Even-Zohar 1978; the 'Manipulation School', Hermans 1999). A norm-based theory of translation thus focuses on regularities of translation behaviour and the situational, or cultural features (norms) which may account for these regularities. The empirical data for DTS scholars are the translations (as facts of the target culture) themselves and also 'paratexts', e.g. reviews of translations, translator's prefaces, footnotes, the whole discourse on translation. DTS has thus paved the way to developing a history of translation and a sociology of translation (e.g. Simeoni 1998 who links his concept of the translator's habitus to Bourdieu's writings).

Since the early 1990s, the discipline of Translation Studies has been inspired to a consid-erable extent by Cultural Studies, anthropology, poststructuralist, postmodern, and postcolonial theories (Bassnett and Lefevere 1990: 12 speak of the 'cultural turn' in Translation Studies, stressing that 'translation has been a major shaping force in the development of world culture'). These approaches follow a number of different tendencies and agendas. But in spite of this, as Arrojo states, they share as 'common ground a radical distrust of the possibility of any intrinsic-ally stable meaning that could be fully present in texts [. . .] and, thus, supposedly recoverable and repeated elsewhere without the interference of the subjects, as well as the cultural, historical, ideological or political circumstances involved' (Arrojo 1998: 25). Translation is defined as a form of regulated transformation, as a socio-political practice, and some scholars recommend a translation method which signifies the difference (Venuti 1995) and which allows the reader to discover the cultural other. Venuti calls this recommended translation method 'foreignization' and sets it apart from 'domestication'. Translations are to represent glimpses into other worlds where reality is perceived differently, and this 'otherness', it is argued, needs to be respected and represented. Translation, via a method of foreignisation, thus becomes a form of political action and engagement ('engagement' also figures prominently in CDA; on the scope and limitations of engagement in respect of translation cf. Tymoczko 2000).

Empiricist-positivist traditions which regard translation as communication and thus as a symmetrical exchange between cultures have been criticised for ignoring power relations. Scholars have shown that translation often involves asymmetrical cultural exchanges (e.g. Tymoczko 1999, Niranjana 1992). Consequently, in postmodern theories, the traditional conception of the translator as an invisible transporter of meanings has been replaced by that of the visible interventionist. Translators are seen as being actively engaged in shaping com-municative processes. In this way, new fertile areas for research have been opened up, for example, the study of translation and power (e.g. Àlvarez and Vidal 1996, see also Lefevere's concept of *patronage* as manifestations of power –ideology, economy, status – which either promote or hinder reading, writing, and rewriting [translating] of literature, Lefevere 1992: 15), translation and identity (e.g. Venuti 1994), translation and gender (e.g. Simon 1996), translation and ideology (e.g. Caldaza Pérez 2003), translation and ethics (e.g. the special issue of *The Translator* 7:2, 2001).

Modern Translation Studies is no longer concerned with examining whether a translation has been 'faithful' to a source text (the notion of 'equivalence' is almost a 'dirty' word now).

Instead, the focus is on social, cultural, and communicative practices, on the cultural and ideo-logical significance of translating and of translations, on the external politics of translation, on the relationship between translation behaviour and socio-cultural factors. In other words, there is a general recognition of the complexity of the phenomenon of translation, an increased concentration on social causation and human agency, and a focus on effects rather than on internal structures. The object of research of Translation Studies is thus not language(s), as traditionally seen, but human activity in different cultural contexts (cf. Witte 2000: 26). The applicability of traditional binary opposites (such as source language/text/culture and target language/text/culture, content vs. form, literal vs. free translation) is called into question, and they are replaced by less stable notions (such as hybrid text, hybrid cultures, space-in-between, intercultural space, cf. the special issue of *Across* 2:2, 2001). It is also widely accepted nowadays that Translation Studies is not a sub-discipline of applied linguistics (or of comparative literature, cf. Bassnett and Lefevere 1990: 12) but indeed an independent discipline in its own right (cf. the debate on 'shared ground', Chesterman and Arrojo 2000 and responses in the subsequent issues of the journal *Target*). However, since insights and methods from various other disciplines are of relevance for studying all aspects of translation as product and process, Translation Studies is often characterised as an interdiscipline (cf. Snell-Hornby et al. 1992). In other words, translation itself being a crossroads of processes, products, functions, and agents, its description and explanation calls for a comprehensive interdisciplinary approach.[9]

It is the interest in human communicative activity in socio-cultural settings, especially the interest in texts and discourses as products of this activity, that Translation Studies and Critical/Political Discourse Analysis have in common. There is thus much to gain from disciplinary interaction. In the following section I will outline where such an interaction can be especially fruitful with respect to political discourse.

4 Translation studies and political discourse analysis: scope for interaction

With some of its roots in linguistics, Translation Studies has always used concepts and methods of linguistics, textlinguistics, pragmatics, and discourse analysis in its own disciplinary discourse. However, Discourse Analysis, Critical Discourse Analysis, and Political Discourse Analysis have not made use of Translation Studies concepts to a similar extent, although analyses were conducted on the basis of translations. For example, Donahue and Prosser (1997) present analyses of UN addresses by several world leaders. Many of those politicians addressed the United Nations assembly in their native tongues (usually simultaneously interpreted and the speeches also made available in translation). However, all the 'findings' of their analyses (which combine methods of discourse analysis and rhetorical analysis) have been arrived at solely on the basis of the English versions. The book is also intended as a textbook, with exercises for students. In one of those exercises, students are asked to compare the personal references as used in the addresses by the representatives of the two Korean states and to derive conclusions about the socio-cultural and ideological background—on the basis of the English versions. Looking for specific features in a text, and linking them to cultural issues, however, is risky if not applied to the original text itself. We can only come up with relevant results if we have knowledge about the system of personal references and personal pronouns in the Korean language. The analysis of the specific conditions of the production of the English versions, thus, needs to be an integral part of the 'toolkit' of discourse analysis.

As said above, translators work in specific socio-political contexts, producing target texts for specific purposes. This social conditioning is reflected in the linguistic structure of the target text.

That is, translations (as target texts) reveal the impact of discursive, social, and ideological conventions, norms and constraints. By linking translations (as products) to their social contexts, causes and effects of translations can be discovered (cf. Chesterman 1998). A causal model of translation allows for questions such as: What causal conditions (seem to) give rise to particular kinds of translations and translation profile features? What effects do given profile features (seem to) have, on readers, clients, cultures? (How) can we explain effects that we find by relating them to profile features and to causal conditions? Which translation strategies produce which results and which effects? Which particular socio-cultural and ideological constraints influence the translation polity in general and the target text production in particular?

CDA and PDA also mediate between linguistic structures as evident in a text and the social, political, and historical contexts of text production and reception. Scholars study the textual or discursive manifestations of power structures and ideologies and their specific linguistic realisations at lexical and grammatical levels (see the overview on issues and methods in CDA in Fairclough and Wodak 1997). These approaches link linguistic forms to social, and hence also to political activity. A translation perspective to political discourse can shed new light to understanding politics. In the concluding part of this paper, I will briefly outline which Translation Studies concepts and approaches could be useful to PDA, thus also indicating scope for cooperation.

4.1 Awareness of product features

In analysing texts as products of discursive actions, PDA researchers use either original texts or translations. In the latter case, full attention needs to be given to the nature of those texts, i.e. they need to be taken as what they are: translations, i.e. target texts operating in a new socio-cultural context and based on a source text which functioned in its original socio-cultural context. As translations they have their own profiles which came about by decisions that were taken by a translator who was working in specific conditions (cf. translation as norm-governed behaviour). We cannot tacitly assume that the target text is an exact copy of the source text, or that the source text fulfilled the same function. The translator may have used strategies to make the text correspond to the genre conventions that apply in the target culture, or to compensate for different background knowledge or sensibilities of the new addressees (cf. translation as purposeful activity). Admittedly, the examples I discussed above were extreme cases. Not all translations show differences to their source texts in such a drastic way, but I chose them deliberately to raise our awareness to the variety of factors that are involved in translation.

Before we start with an analysis of a translation then, we need to know whether we are dealing with an overt or a covert, a documentary or an instrumental translation, a text produced by a strategy of domestication or foreignisation. Commenting on textual features (the target text profile) and/or on discursive or socio-political effects, is very risky if we rely solely on the target text without having checked the conditions of text production and/or compared it to the source text (this is where the expertise of TS scholars could come in). It is particularly risky if the aim of the analysis is to illustrate linguistic or textual features, discursive practices, or manifestations of power structures and/or ideologies which apply to the original language and culture. For example, if we want to analyse the metaphors in the speech by the German Foreign Minister Joschka Fischer, delivered at Berlin Humboldt University on 12 May 2000 on the finality of European Integration, we might arrive at somewhat different results if we rely solely on the English translation. A detailed comparison between source text and target text reveals a number of cases where the metaphorical expression in the source text has been replaced by a more general expression in the target text (demetaphorisation as a legitimate translation strategy), cf. the following example, where the construction metaphor, which structures the original German text, is of less significance as a cohesive devise in the English translation.[10]

(12) a. "[. . .] müssen wir den letzten Baustein in das Gebäude der europäischen Integration einfügen [:..] bei diesem letzten Bauabschnitt der Europäischen Union [. . .]"

b. "[. . .] we must put into place the last brick in the building of European integration [. . .] this latest stage of European Union [. . .]"

Not everything which can be shown in the original text can be shown in the same convincing way in a translation. This is equally true for translations which we as scholars produce ourselves, primarily because the publication policy of, for example, a journal requests the paper to be in English. It happens regularly that only English versions of analysed data are provided, with the authors commenting that they tried to be as accurate as possible in producing a translation.[11] But even a close reproduction of the source text for illustrative purposes can actually conceal what is meant to be shown. For example, Hatim and Mason (1997) comment on cultural differences in the argumentative style in English and Arabic, with a preference for counter-argumentation and through-argumentation, respectively. A close translation from English into Arabic will thus not immediately reveal the argumentation pattern. For the function to be fulfilled, it may become necessary to turn an implicit counter-argument into an explicit one by adding a connector. From the point of view of Translation Studies, the tendency to publish in English only is dangerous since it limits the actual insights into textual structures and functions. It would always be better to provide the original text (and, if necessary, add a gloss into English) to prove what one wants to prove.

A product-oriented analysis can of course have as a legitimate aim to study precisely what translations, as texts in their own right, look like, independent of the source text. Translation profiles can be compared to authentic texts of the same genre, in order to find out to what extent they are similar or different in respect to genre conventions. As has been shown, it is often through translation that new genres are introduced into a culture or that genre conventions change (e.g. Zauberga 2001, who illustrates how advertising has emerged as a new genre in post-Communist Latvia, modelled on [translations from] English). If we ask for the causal conditions that gave rise to particular kinds of translations, we see that such changes often happen at times that are critical for the development of a culture. As Zauberga argues, a culture in the process of development or transition may be more open to input from outside and also more willing (or tolerant) to accept texts (including translations) which may look "strange" from the perspective of the linguistic system and discourse conventions of the receiving culture. At times of social change, translations may thus move from the periphery into the centre of a socio-cultural polysystem.

Conflicting genre conventions may also result in hybrid forms. For example, Tirkkonen-Condit (2001) illustrates this with English-language grant applications to the EU Commission as produced by Finns, either independently or as a result of a translation process. She describes these texts as 'a hybrid which vacillates between three norms: the Finnish rhetorical norm, the intended target norm (i.e. Anglo-American scientific rhetoric), and the hybrid target norm' of the EU (Tirkkonen-Condit 2001: 263). This EU-rhetoric can be imagined as having incorporated features from the various linguistic communities which participate in its functions. Describing such new, or hybrid, forms of texts and discourse in relation to the conditions under which they came about is of interest to both discourse analysis and TS; and the concepts and analytical tools available in both disciplines can be combined for this purpose.

4.2 Multilingual texts

The particular conditions and constraints in the context of the European Union offer a wide field for joint research. Due to the EU language policy, all official documents are translated into all official EU languages, i.e. all texts are equally authentic versions (cf. Wagner et al. 2002). Similarly, the political parties in the European Parliament produce joint documents, often combining parallel text production and translation. Studying such texts as products raises a number of issues which are of interest to both PDA and TS. A few examples, taken from the Manifestoes for the Elections to the European Parliament of 1999, adopted by the Party of European Socialists (PES) and the European Peoples Party (EPP), respectively, will suffice to indicate some of these points. The first two examples refer to conceptual metaphors and their linguistic realisations.

> (13) "Europa muß mit einer <u>Stimme</u> in der Welt <u>sprechen</u>.—We must <u>act</u> as one on the international <u>scene</u>.—Nous devons <u>parler d'une seule voix sur la scène</u> internationale." (EPP Manifesto 1999)

What we can see here is that different aspects of the common conceptual metaphor EUROPE IS A PERSON are made explicit in the texts. The German text has made the voice explicit (a part-whole metonymical relation), the English one introduces a theatre scene, i.e. the person as an actor, and the French text has both these aspects combined. The next example shows that conceptual metaphors may be culture specific at a more specific level, but culture overlapping (or maybe universal) at a more abstract level:

> (14) "Mit der Einführung des EURO haben wir einen großen <u>Schritt nach vorn getan</u>. Der EURO [. . .] Die EVP sieht darin den <u>Beginn</u> eines neuen Projektes, [. . .]—We have already <u>taken a great step forward</u> towards European integration by introducing the Single Currency. But the euro is [. . .] the <u>foundation stone</u> of what we intend to be a new era, [. . .]—Nous venons de <u>faire un rand pas</u> vers l'intégration européenne avec l'instauration de la monnaie unique. Mais l'euro [. . .] est <u>une étape sur la voie</u> d'une union politique, [. . .]" (EPP Manifesto 1999)

All three texts have a reference to a movement metaphor, POLITICS IS MOVEMENT TOWARDS A DESTINATION ('*Schritt nach vorn getan*, taken a step forward, *faire un pas*'). However, the beginning of a new project is conceptualised as the start of a construction process in the English text ('foundation stone'), whereas the French text continues the movement metaphor ('*une étape sur la vole*'), and the German text uses a more general expression ('*Beginn*'). All these different expressions can be seen as realisations of a more abstract conceptual metaphor PROGRESS IS GROWTH (cf. Schäffner in 2004a).

The analysis of translations can thus help to find out more about universal, culture-overlapping, and culture-specific metaphors, here in the field of political discourse. The combined expertise of PDA and TS may help to explain other observed differences, such as different lexical choices and omissions, which may point to ideological and socio-cultural values. In the following example, the English version operates on the left-right opposition. The German version, however, systematically avoids the use of these ideologically charged labels, cf.:

(15) a. "In this election the parties of <u>the Left</u> challenge those of <u>the Right</u> on two fronts. [. . .] We reject the posture of <u>the Right</u> [. . .] reject the short-sighted focus of <u>the Right</u> on narrow national interest [. . .] " (PES Manifesto 1999)

b. "Bei dieser Wahl werden <u>die sozialdemokratischen und sozialistischen Parteien</u> sich besonders in zwei Bereichen mit der Politik der <u>Konservativen</u> auseinander zu setzen haben. [. . .] wir lehnen <u>es</u> ab [. . .] wir lehnen die kurzsichtige Ausrichtung auf nationale Interessen ab [. . .]"

[Literally: In this election the Social-Democratic and Socialist parties will have to challenge the policies of the Conservatives especially in two areas. [. . .] we reject [. . .] we reject the short-sighted focus on narrow national interest [. . .]]

The concepts of intertextuality, interdiscursivity, and orders of discourse, which figure very prominently in PDA and CDA, are especially appropriate in explaining such differences. PDA and CDA aim at revealing the mediated connection between properties of text on the one hand, and socio-political or socio-cultural structures and processes on the other hand. Postmodern translation theories too link textual features to social conditions. The concept of orders of discourse, however, has not yet played a highly significant role in TS. The analytical tools of PDA and CDA also allow to show the 'different implications of different readings for social action' (Fairclough and Wodak 1997: 279). In a cross-cultural perspective, different social actions may be the result of different readings of an original text and its translation. Such culture-specific or ideology-specific readings are related to and determined by orders of discourse. The concepts of intertextuality and orders of discourse can thus also be fruitfully applied when it comes to translation evaluation and/or criticism. That is, what may look like a 'mistranslation' or a 'translation loss' at a first glance (or from a linguistic or text-specific point of view) will actually turn out to highlight the socio-political or ideological structures, processes, norms and constraints in which translations were produced (and received). Translation 'criticism' can thus contribute to revealing and 'criticising' socio-political practices and relationships.

4.3 *Process analysis*

To account for such phenomena as illustrated in examples (13)-(15), PDA and TS scholars could ask how those equally valid versions actually come about, i.e. researching the process instead of or in addition to the products. By studying the actual text production-cum-translation process one could find out which factors (linguistic, textual, cultural, legal, ideological . . .) have an impact on the final versions of the texts. From the point of view of Critical Discourse Analysis, Wodak (2000) traced changes in the textual surface structures in the drafting process of a polity paper in an expert committee. She discovered different types of transformation which result from recontextualisation, i.e. the succession of meetings at different times. In the following example, she records, among other changes, shifts from theme to rheme, a transformation of a nominal group ('public opinion') to actors ('people'), and the replacement of a mental process ('perceive') by a physical one ('grasp'):

(16) Text version (a):

"The breadth and urgency of the needed adaptations are indistinctly perceived by public opinion, which explains a widespread sense of unease."

Text version (b):

"It has been difficult for people to grasp the breadth and urgency of necessary adaptations. This explains a widespread sense of unease, inequality and polarisation."

(Wodak 2000: 100 ff)

However, she does not explicitly comment on the role of translation work in her analysis. It would also be interesting to see whether the same types of changes have been made in other language versions. Focussing on the specific impact of translation in this respect would surely contribute valuable insights by providing a missing link in the analysis. In this way, textual profiles could be systematically linked to the social conditions which governed their production. The recontextualisation in Wodak's example is still embedded in the same institutional macrosetting. Translations, as products, normally involve recontextualisation across cultures. Studying how presumably identical texts are received by their addressees in different cultures and what effects they have on readers and on cultures, would thus also be a valuable topic for research jointly done by PDA and TS scholars.

4.4 Politics of translation

Postmodern translation theories argue that the crossing of linguistic, geographical and political spaces and the resulting encounters with the other should lead to new modes of thinking, feeling, and experiencing the world. In reality, cultures have learned about each other to a large extent by means of translations. Over the centuries it has been fairly common that ideas and concepts, including political ideas and concepts, have travelled between cultures and nations. But not in each case has the experiencing of the other resulted in mutual understanding. As Pym (1998: 124) points out, the 'work of translators can effectively separate, rather than bridge cultures, flattening rather than pluralising the image of the other, edging towards transcultural mistrust rather than cooperative understanding'. In order to understand such phenomena, one needs to reflect about the politics of translation, which concerns questions such as: Who decides which texts get translated, from and into which languages? Where are the translations produced? Who chooses and trains translators, how many, for which language combinations? Following the attacks of September 11, for example, the FBI Director Robert S. Mueller III cited a critical need for translators, especially of Arabic. The FBI had 'suddenly' realised that they did not have sufficient numbers of translators who were able to deal with the documents. As *The Washington Post* (24 September 2001) pointed out, translators were required with competence in both the language and the underlying cultural and ideological aspects. Reading in early 2003 that the USA is training Iraqi dissidents in a camp in Hungary to become translators and interpreters to be deployed in Iraq after the end of the war (or, to use the official discourse of the Bush Administration, 'once the country has been liberated') can be interpreted as a change in the translation policy of the country.

In discussing the definition of political discourse at the beginning of this paper, I referred to four strategic functions (coercion; resistance, opposition, protest; dissimulation; legitimation and delegitimation) with which to link political situations and processes to discourse types and levels of discourse organisation. These functions can also be applied to translation, both at a macro-level and at a micro-level, in the following way:

Coercion: Power can be exercised through controlling access to information, e.g. selection of source texts to be made available in translation to the home culture (in view of topics, authors, cultures), checking the end product, using translations in the service of home agendas (i.e. the politics of translation, power relations, publishing strategies, censorship).

Resistance, opposition and protest: Many of the discourse strategies used by the powerful for coercion may be counter-deployed by those who regard themselves as opposing power. Translators themselves can be active in selecting source texts to be made available in translation, thus making the home audience appreciate the 'other', give voice to neglected or oppressed minorities (i.e. the politics of translation). Resistance can also mean resisting dominant translation practices and strategies and be innovative (cf. foreignisation, resistancy, norms, engagement).

Dissimulation: Quantitative or qualitative control of information, i.e. preventing people from receiving information by not allowing texts to be made available in translation; or providing only selected extracts of source texts in translation; or deliberately publishing inaccurate translations (i.e. politics of translation, ethics, and also translation of politics, since it may be political ideas from abroad which those in power do not wish their people to know about; cf. also the discussion about the translatability of the Koran—if translated, it is usually presented as a 'commentary' rather than a translation, Halliday 2001).

Legitimisation and delegitimisation: Positive self-presentation and negative presentation of the others, explicitly or implicitly, by using specific translation strategies, by using and abusing texts for purposes of national ideologies. For example, Kadric and Kaindl (1997) illustrate how the *Asterix* translations into Croatian reinforced negative feelings towards the former war-time enemy Serbia (i.e. politics of translation, ethics).

Translation, as product and as process, can highlight sociocultural and political practices, norms, constraints, which can be of particular relevance in the field of political discourse. Combining concepts and methods of modern Translation Studies and of Political Discourse Analysis can thus result in a more extensive study of political discourse.

Notes

1 The diacritic signs are missing in the Hungarian word, the correct spelling is '*élettér*'; and the German '*Lebensraum*' should be spelled with an initial capital letter in both occurrences.

2 I am grateful to my colleague Eva Szantho for providing this information. A two-volume German-Hungarian and Hungarian-German dictionary, published by Akadémiai Kiadó Budapest in 1983 and 1985, respectively, lists '*Lebensraum*' and '*élettér*' as a pair without any further information as to restricted use or associative senses.

3 In a somehow simplified way, *translation* denotes a written target-language reformulation of a written source text, whereas *interpreting* denotes a non-written re-expression of a nonwritten source text. Both translators and interpreters have to deal with problems raised by inter-linguistic, intercultural, and thematic issues. The main differences in the processes of translation vs. interpreting have to do with technical constraints (time, sources of information, working environment) (for details see Gile 2004). In this paper, the focus is on translation.

4 The German and the English texts reflect different transcription conventions for Hebrew proper names: Kazaw, Katzav.

5 If a speech is distributed before the event, there is the statement 'Check against delivery' on top of the text. In the case of a translation, the standard phrase is 'Advance translation'.

6 'Er teile die "in der Frage angedeutete Ansicht", so Schröder laut Wortprotokoll der Bundeswehr. Wenn der Frieden eine Chance erhalten solle, müsse man bei den Vereinten Nationen "nicht nur über Beobachter nachdenken", sondern auch darüber, ob es notwendig sei—"ich glaube, das wird man mit Ja beantworten

müssen"—,bei den Konfliktparteien eine friedliche Entwicklung "durch Druck von außen einzuleiten, auch zu trennen und dafür eben auch, legitimiert durch die Vereinten Nationen, militärische Mittel einzusetzen". Er, der Kanzler, könne "jedenfalls nicht völlig ausschließen, dass man sich mit einer solchen Frage befassen muss". Welche Rolle Deutschland darin zu spielen hätte, sollte "man nicht im Vorgriff diskutieren"' (*Der Spiegel* 15 April 2002).

7   Research into the actual cognitive processes of translation (the translation act) began in the mid-1980s with the study by Krings (1986), using Think-aloud protocols (TAPS) as research method.

8   More recently, the development of corpus studies has proved highly relevant for identifying such regularities in translational behaviour (e.g. Bowker and Pearson 2002).

9   Prunc (2002:267), however, warns that a broad concept of translation, which includes almost any kind of cultural transformation, could lead to the dissolution of Translation Studies as an independent discipline since it would lose its genuine object of research. He argues that the boom which was initiated by the 'cultural turn' could thus turn into a boomerang.

10   It is highly probable that the translator did not make these changes deliberately, with some hidden agenda behind. But this example also highlights the need for a systematic training in discourse analysis as part of translator training.

11   Cf. one author's comment in a recent issue of the journal *Discourse & Society*, 'special care has been taken in translating the transcriptions so that they are as "true to genre" as possible'.

References

Across Languages and Cultures. Special issue on Hybrid Texts and Translation (guest editors: Christina Schäffner and Beverly Adab), 2(2), 2001.

Álvarez, Román and Vidal, M. Carmen-África (eds). 1996. *Translation, Power, Subversion*. Clevedon: Multilingual Matters.

Arrojo, Rosemary. 1998. The revision of the traditional gap between theory and practice and the empowerment of translation in postmodern times. *The Translator* 4(1), 25–48.

Baker, Mona (ed.). 1998. *Routledge Encyclopedia of Translation Studies*. London and New York: Routledge.

Bassnett, Susan and Lefevere, André (eds). 1990. *Translation, History and Culture*. London: Pinter.

Bowker, Lynne and Pearson, Jennifer. 2002. *Working with Specialized Language. A Practical Guide to Using Corpora*. London and New York: Routledge.

Caldaza Pérez, Maria (ed.). 2003. *Apropos of Ideology. Translation Studies on Ideology—Ideologies in Translation Studies*. Manchester: St. Jerome.

Catford, J. C. 1965. *A Linguistic Theory of Translation*. London: Oxford University Press.

Chesterman, Andrew. 1998. Causes, translations, effects. *Target* 10(2), 201–230.

Chesterman, Andrew and Arrojo, Rosemary. 2000. Shared ground in translation studies. *Target* 12(1), 151–160.

Chilton, Paul. 1996. *Security Metaphors. Cold War Discourse from Containment to Common House*. New York: Lang.

Chilton, Paul and Schäffner, Christina. 1997. Discourse and Politics. In: Teun van Dijk (ed.). *Discourse Studies: A Multidisciplinary Introduction, vol. 2: Discourse as Social Interaction*. London: Sage, 206–230.

Chilton, Paul and Schäffner, Christina (eds). 2002. *Politics as Text and Talk. Analytic Approaches to Political Discourse*. Amsterdam and Philadelphia: Benjamins.

Delisle, Jean and Woodsworth, Judith (eds). 1995. *Translators Through History*. Amsterdam and Philadelphia: Benjamins, UNESCO Publishing.

Donahue, Ray T. and Prosser, Michael H. 1997. *Diplomatic Discourse: International Conflict at the United Nations—Addresses and Analysis*. Greenwich, Connecticut and London: Ablex Publishing Corporation.

Dörner, Andreas. 2001. *Politainment. Politik in der medialen Erlebnisgesellschaft*. Frankfurt a. M.: Suhrkamp.

Ekström, Mats. 2001. Politicians interviewed on television news. *Discourse & Society* 12(5), 563–584.

Even-Zohar, Itamar. 1978. *Papers in Historical Poetics*. Tel Aviv: Porter Institute for Poetics and Semiotics.

Fairclough, Norman. 1995. *Critical Discourse Analysis*. London: Longman.

Fairclough, Norman. 2000. *New Labour, New Language?* Routledge: London.

Fairclough, Norman and Wodak, Ruth. 1997. Critical discourse analysis. In: Teun van Dijk (ed.). *Discourse Studies: A Multidisciplinary Introduction. vol. 2: Discourse as Social Interaction*. London: Sage, 258–284.

Gentzler, Edwin. 1993. *Contemporary Translation Theories*. Routledge: London.

Gile, Daniel. 2004. Translation research vs. interpreting research: Kinship, differences and prospects for partnership. In: Christina Schäffner (ed.). *Translation Research and Interpreting Research: Traditions, Gaps and Synergies*. Clevedon: Multilingual Matters. 10–34.

Halliday, Fred. 2001. Words and States: The Politics of Language in the Middle East. Paper presented to seminar series at Oxford Centre for Islamic Studies, 10 October 2001 (draft manuscript).

Hatim, Basil and Mason, Ian. 1990. *Discourse and the Translator*. London: Longman.

Hatim, Basil and Mason, Ian. 1997. *The Translator as Communicator*. London: Routledge.

Hermans, Theo. 1999. *Translation in Systems. Descriptive and System-Oriented Approaches Explained*. Manchester: St. Jerome.

Holmes, James. 1988. *Translated! Papers on Literary Translation and Translation Studies*. Amsterdam: Rodopi.

Holz-Mänttäri, Justa. 1984. *Translatorisches Handeln. Theorie und Methode*. Helsinki: Suomalainen Tiedeakatemia.

House, Juliane. 1997. *Translation Quality Assessment. A Model Revisited*. Tübingen: Narr.

Kade, Otto. 1980. *Die Sprachmittlung als gesellschaftliche Erscheinung und Gegenstand wissenschaftlicher Untersuchung* (Übersetzungswissenschaftliche Beiträge 3). Leipzig: Enzyklopädie.

Kadric, Mira and Kaindl, Klaus. 1997. Astérix—Vom Gallier zum Tschetnikjäger: Zur Problematik von Massenkommunikation und übersetzerischer Ethik. In: Mary SnellHornby, Zuzana Jettmarova, and Klaus Kaindl (eds). *Translation as Intercultural Communication. Selected Papers from the EST Congress—Prague 1995*. Amsterdam and Philadelphia: Benjamins, 135–146.

Koskinen, Kaisa. 2000. Institutional illusions: Translating in the EU Commission. *The Translator* 6(1), 495.

Krings, Hans P. 1986. *Was in den Köpfen von Übersetzern vorgeht: Eine empirische Untersuchung zur Struktur des Übersetzungsprozesses an fortgeschrittenen Französischlernern*. Tübingen: Narr.

Lakoff, George and Johnson, Mark. 1980. *Metaphors We Live By*. Chicago: University of Chicago Press.

Lefevere, André. 1992. *Translation, Rewriting, and the Manipulation of Literary Fame*. London/New York: Routledge.

Munday, Jeremy. 2001. *Introducing Translation Studies. Theories and Applications*. London and New York: Routledge.

Muntigl, Peter. 2002. Politicization and depoliticization: Employment policy in the European Union. In: Paul Chilton and Christina Schäffner (eds). *Politics as Text and Talk. Analytic Approaches to Political Discourse*. Amsterdam and Philadelphia: Benjamins, 45–79.

Neubert, Albrecht and Shreve, Gregory M. 1992. *Translation as Text*. Kent and London: Kent State University Press.

Nida, Eugene. 1964. *Toward a Science of Translating: With Special Reference to Principles and Procedures Involved in Bible Translating*. Leiden: E. J. Brill.

Niranjana, Tejaswini. 1992. *Siting Translation: History, Post-Structuralism, and the Colonial Context*. Berkeley: University of California Press.

Nord, Christiane. 1997. *Translating as a Purposeful Activity. Functionalist Approaches Explained*. Manchester: St. Jerome.

Pöchhacker, Franz and Shlesinger, Miriam (eds). 2002. *The Interpreting Studies Reader*. London/New York: Routledge.

Prunc, Erich. 2002. *Einführungin die Translationswissenschaft. Band I. Orientierungsrahmen*. Graz: Institut für Translationswissenschaft.

Pym, Anthony. 1998. Lives of Henri Albert, Nietzschean Translator. In: Ann Beylard-Ozeroff, Jana Králová, and Barbara Moser-Mercer (eds). *Translators' Strategies and Creativity—Selected Papers from the 9th International Conference on Translation and Interpreting, Prague, September 1995*. Amsterdam & Philadelphia: Benjamins, 117–125.

Reiss, Katharina. 1971. *Möglichkeiten und Grenzen der Übersetzungskritik*. München: Hueber.

Reiss, Katharina and Vermeer, Hans J. 1991. *Grundlegung einer allgemeinen Translationstheorie*. Tübingen: Niemeyer.

Sauer, Christoph. 1996. Echoes from Abroad—Speeches for the Domestic Audience: Queen Beatrix' Address to the Israeli Parliament. *Current Issues in Language and Society* 3(3), 233–267.

Schäffner, Christina. 1997. Metaphor and interdisciplinary analysis. *Journal of Area Studies* 11, 57–72.

Schäffner, Christina. 2001. Attitudes towards Europe—mediated by translation. In: Andreas Musolff, Colin Good, Petra Points, and Ruth Wittlinger (eds). *Attitudes towards Europe. Language in the unification process*. Aldershot: Ashgate, 201–217.

Schäffner, Christina. 2003. Third ways and new centres—ideological unity or difference? In: Maria Caldaza Pérez (ed.). *Apropos of Ideology*. Manchester: St Jerome, 23–41.

Schäffner, Christina. 2004a. Metaphor and Translation: Some implications of a cognitive approach. *Journal of Pragmatics* 36, 1153–1269.

Schäffner, Christina (ed.). 2004b. *Translation Research and Interpreting Research: Traditions, Gaps and Synergies*. Clevedon: Multilingual Matters.

Simeoni, Daniel. 1998. The pivotal status of the translator's habitus. *Target* 10(1), 1–39.

Simon, Sherry. 1996. *Gender in Translation. Cultural Identity and the Politics of Transmission*. London: Routledge.

Snell-Hornby, Mary, Pöchhacker, Franz and Kaindl, Klaus (eds). 1992. *Translation Studies. An Interdiscipline*. Amsterdam and Philadelphia: Benjamins.

Stolze, Radegundis. 1994. *Übersetzungstheorien. Eine Einführung*, Narr: Tübingen.

The Translator. 2001 Special Issue on *The return to ethics*, guest editor: Anthony Pym, 7(2).

Tirkkonen-Condit, Sonja. 2001. EU project proposals as hybrid texts: Observations from a Finnish research project. *Across* 2(2), 261–264.

Toury, Gideon. 1995. *Descriptive Translation Studies and Beyond*. Amsterdam and Philadelphia: Benjamins.

Trosborg, Anna (ed.). 1997. *Text Typology and Translation*. Amsterdam and Philadelphia: Benjamins.

Tymoczko, Maria. 1999. *Translation in a Postcolonial Context*. Manchester: St. Jerome.

Tymoczko, Maria. 2000. Translation and political engagement. *The Translator* 6(1), 23–47.

van Dijk, Teun A. 2002. Political discourse and political cognition. In: Paul Chilton and Chistina Schäffner (eds). *Politics as text and talk. Analytic Approaches to Political Discourse*. Amsterdam and Philadelphia: Benjamins, 203–237.

Venuti, Lawrence. 1994. Translation and the formation of cultural identities. *Current Issues in Language and Society* 1(3), 201–217.

Venuti, Lawrence (ed.). 1995. *The Translator's Invisibility*. London: Routledge.

Venuti, Lawrence. 2000. *The Translation Studies Reader*. London: Routledge.

Vermeer, Hans J. 1978. Ein Rahmen für eine allgemeine Translationstheorie. *Lebende Sprachen* 23(2), 99–102.

Wagner, Emma, Bech, Svend, and Martínez, Jesús M. 2002. *Translating for the European Union Institutions*. Manchester: St. Jerome.

Witte, Heidrun. 2000. *Die Kulturkompetenz des Translators. Begriffliche Grundlegung und Didaktisierung*. Tübingen: Stauffenburg.

Wodak, Ruth. 2000. From conflict to consensus? The co-construction of a polity paper. In: Peter Muntigl, Gilbert Weiss, and Ruth Wodak (eds). *European Union Discourses on Un/employment. An Interdisciplinary Approach to Employment Polity-Making and Organizational Change*. Amsterdam and Philadelphia: Benjamins, 73–114.

Zauberga, Ieva. 2001. Discourse interference in translation. *Across* 2(2), 265–276.

Chapter 24

JANET MAYBIN AND JOAN SWANN

EVERYDAY CREATIVITY IN LANGUAGE
Textuality, contextuality, and critique
(2007)

Introduction

T HE AIM OF THIS PAPER is to explore everyday creativity in language, developing
and expanding on a body of research on this topic that has been influential within applied
linguistics in recent years. Research to date has done a great deal to establish the pervasiveness
of linguistic creativity across a range of everyday genres, to explore potential continuities
between everyday and literary creativity, and to consider also the purposeful nature of everyday
linguistic creativity—how this functions locally, in interactions. There is, however, rather less
in this tradition of enquiry that explores broader social, cultural, and critical dimensions of
creativity.

This article opens up the exploration of these sociocultural aspects of language creativity,
arguing for an analytical approach which integrates textual, contextual, and critical dimensions.
By 'textual', we mean text-intrinsic properties of creative language such as linguistic patterning
or the adoption of certain generic structures. The 'contextual' dimension takes into account the
ways such forms are used in particular sociohistorical and interpersonal contexts—we consider
different analytical formulations of 'context' below. By 'critical' we are referring to the potential
for linguistic creativity to foreground, in various ways, the kinds of critical/evaluative stances
that are evident in all language use.[1] We develop this analytic framework in the light of our
reading of recent work within applied linguistics on everyday uses of poetic language, as well as
linguistic anthropological research on performance. This latter, we would argue, includes a more
developed theorization of context, and some suggestions for addressing evaluation and critique.
We then draw on ideas from both of these research traditions in an analysis of four brief examples
of language creativity emerging from the flow of everyday interaction. Finally, we draw together
and review our analytic approach. We discuss the ways in which textual, contextual, and critical
dimensions may be differentially called up or highlighted by different sets of data, but argue that
these need to be treated as interrelated, in order to more fully understand everyday language
creativity and how it works.

Language creativity in applied linguistics

Contemporary researchers in applied linguistics have argued that, far from being restricted to
literary authors, media professionals, and other linguistically-skilled writers and speakers,

creativity is a pervasive feature of more routine uses of language. We take as examples of this position an early study by Tannen (1989) and more recent work by Cook (1997, 2000), Crystal (1998) and Carter (1999, 2004). Much of the focus here is on poetic forms in everyday discourse: the manipulation of linguistic form—rhyme, word play, metaphor, and other figures of speech—associated with the self-referential potential of language, and consistent with Jakobson's (1960) 'poetic function' and Mukarovsky's (1964) concept of poetic 'deviation'. Tannen and Carter also include aspects of repetition (e.g. speakers echoing one another's words and speech rhythms) that do not play so obviously with linguistic form; Tannen includes the creative construction of dialogue in narrative, which 'makes story into drama' (1989: 133); and Cook includes children's and adults' preoccupation with imaginary or fictional worlds.

Researchers have used different terms for this range of phenomena. Tannen echoes Jakobson in her use of the literary term *poetic*, with the argument that everyday conversation 'provides the source for strategies that are taken up by other, including literary genres. . .' (1989: 2). Carter refers to *creativity* and *literariness*. For Carter, creativity is a matter of degree, existing along a series of clines across 'everyday' and 'literary' texts, rather than as discrete sets of features associated with particular registers. The term *literariness* encapsulates the clinal nature of creativity. Cook and Crystal, on the other hand, refer to language *play* rather than literariness. On the face of it, these terms suggest different intellectual starting points and purposes. Carter, for instance, seeks to broaden the frame of literariness to include everyday linguistic practices, whereas Cook theorizes language play in terms of play more generally, but extends this to 'high culture' practices such as literature and ceremony. As we discuss below, however, there is also considerable commonality in the ideas addressed by all four writers, reflecting a consensus amongst linguists with interests in this area.

The pervasiveness of language creativity has immediate implications for policy and practice in several areas, including education. Crystal, for instance, points to what he terms the 'ludic gap' between the linguistic world of young children and the lack of playful uses of language in educational materials such as reading schemes. Cook argues that current orthodoxies in communicative and task-based approaches to English language teaching similarly ignore the potential of language play. Both authors suggest that language teaching, for learners of all ages, could be enhanced by the inclusion of a play element. The value of language play in language teaching and learning is borne out by some empirical research. For instance, studies of second language acquisition have pointed to the importance of an affective dimension in learning; the value of play in drawing attention to linguistic form; and play as a necessary part of advanced proficiency (e.g. Lantolf 1997; Sullivan 2000; Tarone 2000; Bell 2005). More fundamentally, the pervasiveness of creativity across communicative practices also poses broader theoretical challenges to conventional ideas about language, questioning, in particular, the primacy accorded to its transactional role. Carter speculates whether 'creative language may be a default condition, a norm of use from which ordinary, routine "non-creative" exchanges constitute an abnormal departure' (2004: 214). And Cook suggests: '[i]t might be that, both ontogenetically and phylogenetically, the first function of language is the creation of imaginative worlds: whether lies, games, fictions, or fantasies' (2000: 47).

Such ideas may be seen as part of a broader theoretical refocusing in contemporary applied and sociolinguistics, in which language users have come to be seen as constantly refashioning linguistic and other communicative resources rather than as reproducing static rules of language use. Kress (1998, 2003), for instance, has elaborated the concept of 'design' to account for the integration of different modes in the production and interpretation of texts. For Kress, design necessarily involves transformation, however slight, and creativity in this sense is therefore ordinary, or normal: 'it is the everyday process of semiotic work as making meaning' (2003: 40).

Similarly, contemporary sociolinguistic studies of speaking style (including style-shifting, code-switching and 'crossing') have focused on speakers' creative styling of the self and others in everyday life (Eckert 2000; Coupland 2001, 2007; Rampton 2001, 2005). And practice-based approaches to the study of literacy have emphasized the creative role of participants as active, strategic agents, using literacy practices to represent or create histories, social relationships, and social identities (Bloome *et al.*, 2005). Such work does not see the communicative strategies adopted by individuals as unconstrained, but there is an emphasis, nevertheless, on language users' creativity that is consistent with the more specific focus in Carter, Cook, Crystal, and Tannen on the routine use of literary, or literary-like practices.

While Carter, Cook, Crystal, and Tannen have a significant textual focus in their work, identifying formal characteristics associated with creative language, they also see creativity as rooted in, and deriving meaning from, particular contexts. Of particular interest here are the rather different ways 'context' has been conceived or, more accurately, the different aspects of context made available by particular approaches to language study. Carter's and Tannen's focus is on the empirical study of language use—in this case mainly audio recordings of spoken interaction. Tannen's longest recording (at 2.5 hours) is of a Thanksgiving dinner conversation between friends, at which she was a participant; other recordings were made by Tannen's students—again mainly informal interactions between family or friends. Tannen also includes stories she elicited, mainly from women in the USA and Greece. She therefore knows something of the setting in which interactions took place, characteristics of different speakers, or groups of speakers, and relations between speakers, although she will have a greater depth of understanding of some interactions than others. Across these mainly informal, friendly interactions, Tannen argues that strategies such as repetition and constructed dialogue function as 'involvement strategies', in that they both reflect and serve to create interactional and emotional involvement amongst participants.

Like Tannen, Carter (2004) identifies creative language use in his data as having to do with building solidarity and friendly relations, 'an affective convergence or commonality of viewpoint' (2004: 8), although he also notes that, in other contexts, it may be associated with disagreement or critiquing an established institutional order. Carter's data come from the Cambridge and Nottingham Corpus of Discourse in English (CANCODE), a substantial corpus of around five million words of spoken interaction. The data in CANCODE are classified according to 'context type' (distinguishing four categories of interpersonal relationship: transactional/public; professional; socializing; and intimate) and 'interaction type' (distinguishing 'non-collaborative' interactions, where one participant holds the floor; collaborative interactions concerned with the sharing of ideas; and collaborative interactions that are more task-oriented). Carter argues that, while creativity may occur across different types of interaction, it is associated particularly with the collaborative sharing of ideas between friends or family members.

Cook (2000) and Crystal (1998) are concerned not with the empirical study of interaction but with the analysis of texts that are (mainly) in the public domain – jokes, word games, children's rhymes and riddles, playground lore – including some from published sources. Cook and Crystal do consider the interactional function, or pragmatic use of language play: Crystal's focus is particularly on the establishment of rapport, whereas Cook considers more broadly the creation of solidarity or antagonism and competition, the preservation or inversion of the social order. However, with one or two exceptions, neither is concerned with specific instances of play emerging from particular contexts of utterance.

These studies reflect traditional conceptions of context, seen as something external to a text that affects its production and interpretation. This kind of model underpins the analysis of large, computerized corpora such as CANCODE. The model is necessarily rather static, but it affords the possibility for systematic comparisons between different speakers and settings. However, the attention paid by all researchers to the functions of creativity – for example building solidarity and friendly relations – also points to the potential of a more dynamic model, in which creativity is both contextualized and contextualizing. This dynamic model, with a focus on processes of contextualization (Gumperz 1982) rather than context in a more static sense, would foreground the essentially dialogic nature of everyday creativity, seeing creative episodes as jointly constructed between participants, incorporating and elaborating the voices of others. Carter, in particular, also acknowledges important sociocultural and sociohistorical dimensions in creativity – that conceptions of creativity are culturally/historically variable, and that new creativities may emerge to meet particular (changing) goals and purposes. These are points we develop further below.

Carter and Cook acknowledge that creativity may be used antagonistically or critically, although in Carter's own data, as in Tannen's, creativity is associated with solidarity. Our own proposal for a critical dimension to creativity builds on these linguists' interest in its interactional functions. We also draw on points from Mukarovsky (1970) and Vološinov (1973)[2] about the evaluative function of language art as a social sign. For Mukarovsky, the aesthetic function (which can be keyed, internally and externally, in relation to any object), organizes contact between individuals and the reality they find themselves in (1970: 23). Similarly, Vološinov argues that the socially evaluative stance of the poet organizes the choice of rhythm and other formal elements to depict subjects in a particular way and metaphor 'regroups values' (1973: 116). While Vološinov assumes a strong evaluative dimension underpinning all uses of language ('[t]here is no such thing as a word without evaluative accent' Vološinov 1973: 103), we want to argue that the use of creativity in language, because of its framing effect, may be particularly suited to foregrounding an evaluative function. We take this idea of 'framing' from the argument propounded within linguistic anthropology by Bauman and Briggs (1990) that, by drawing attention to themselves, artful language performances are framed and highlighted within the context of ongoing communication, thus intensifying communicative experience and holding the performance, and its contents, up for display and evaluation. Bauman and Briggs suggest that this framing also renders the performance more likely to be preserved as a coherent stretch of language and recontextualized in other future contexts. While linguistic anthropologists have, on the whole, focused on traditional oral performances, for example folk stories or plays, Bauman (1992) argues that all communicative acts involve a potential for performance, and that there is a continuum in terms of the relative dominance of this function which ranges from a sustained, full, formally recognized performance, for example in an opera, to a fleeting breakthrough into performance, for example when a child impresses peers with an exotic word (1992: 45). We would argue that performance, with its framing and intensifying effects, is keyed by more fleeting uses of poetic language within everyday interactions, which are also potentially recontextualizable (thus the retelling of anecdotes, jokes, and so on). Within this everyday poetics, the evaluative potential of creative language is foregrounded to varying degrees, as implicit or explicit critique. In the next section, we explore this point further through an examination of work in linguistic anthropology which focuses directly on spoken language performance and contextualization.

Contextualization and critique in linguistic anthropology

A seminal starting point for linguistic anthropologists interested in creativity in everyday texts, as for the applied linguists discussed above, has been Roman Jakobson's conception of the poetic function of language as characterized by a 'focus on the message for its own sake' (Jakobson

1960: 356): in other words where linguistic choices are motivated not only in terms of sense-making but, most importantly, to highlight and manipulate particular linguistic features (thus making linguistics rather than literature the primary disciplinary reference point for poetics). While Jakobson's work on what he calls 'equivalence', that is the patterned repetition of sounds or structures, has been highly influential in linguistic analysis that focuses on creativity at a textual level,[3] his notion of 'speech event' provided the basis for developing a more contextualized approach to studying oral language creativity within US linguistic anthropology and folklore. For Jakobson, there are six omnipresent factors in any speech event: an addresser, addressee, context, message,[4] contact, and code, each determining, respectively, the emotive, conative, referential, poetic, phatic, and metalingual functions of language, which are differentially hierarchically organized depending on the nature of the event. Jakobson's list of six factors was taken up and elaborated by Hymes in the context of his proposal for an alternative linguistics which could capture the performance-oriented, social and cultural dimensions of language in use and provide a theoretical alternative to Saussurean and Chomskyan abstractism (e.g. see Hymes 1977: 10). Hymes' anthropological interest and situated ethnographic approach were reflected in the elaborated list of components which he saw as omnipresent in a communicative event, which included setting, scene, channels, key, norms of interaction, norms of interpretation, and genres.

Hymes' retranslations of Native American poetry and narrative (e.g. Hymes 2004) and his analysis of oral and written narratives in English (Hymes 1996) are based on the premise that narratives are structured through poetic relationships of equivalence, which he argues are often disregarded in translations and are not addressed in Labovian structural analysis. For Hymes, meanings and evaluative functions in narrative are signalled textually by repetition and parallelism as well as by lexis and syntax. The rhetorical art of poetic patterning is fundamental to the organizing and representation of experience within narrative, and for its pragmatic effects. While the poetic function may be dominant in narrative, it is still (as Jakobson suggested) intimately connected with the other dimensions of the speech event and its meaning and significance are configured by the sociohistorical context. Thus, for example, Hymes (1996) argues that sociopolitical factors have led to a devaluing and delegitimizing of the narrative poetics of disempowered groups. Within education, he suggests, the identification of particular narratives as authoritative and cognitively superior is established through processes of framing and classification (see Bernstein 1996).

Bauman (1977, 1986) applied Jakobson's notion of the reflexive[5] dimension of creativity, whereby language draws attention to itself, to verbal performance where a creative display is framed and marked off from ongoing communicative practice. Bauman sees performance as:

> a mode of communication, a way of speaking, the essence of which resides in the assumption of responsibility to an audience for a display of communicative skill, highlighting the way in which communication is carried out, above and beyond its referential content. From the point of view of the audience, the act of expression on the part of the performer is thus laid open to evaluation for the way it is done, for the relative skill and effectiveness of the performer's display. It is also offered for the enhancement of experience, through the present appreciation of the intrinsic qualities of the act of expression itself. Performance thus calls forth special attention to and heightened awareness of both the acts of expression and the performer. Viewed in these terms, performance may be understood as the enactment of the poetic function, the essence of spoken artistry.
>
> (Bauman 1986: 3)

Bauman lists a number of ways in which such creative verbal performances may be keyed, including a combination of textual and contextualizing features (e.g. formal stylistic devices, special prosodic patterns of tempo, stress, and pitch, paralinguistic features of voice quality and vocalization, and appeals to tradition). While these 'keys' can be looked for in any verbal performance, Bauman stressed that their enactment will depend very much on specific, local contextual and motivational factors.

Bauman (2002) acknowledges his debt to Erving Goffman's analysis of framing (Goffman 1974), pointing out that the metacommunicative notion of framing is 'a fundamentally reflexive concept'. Goffman's dramaturgical metaphors for social interaction rituals, the differences between front stage and back stage behaviours (often exploited in humour), the possibilities for the rekeying of frames and the socially strategic use of face work and footing in the interactive presentation of the self, all point to what Goffman suggests is an essentially creative use of language in everyday interactions (Goffman 1969, 1972, 1974). Goffman's ideas have been suggestive for linguists like Carter and Tannen who are interested in creativity within everyday talk (cf. arguments for language use as intrinsically creative referred to earlier above), and have contributed to the development of the theory of performance within linguistic anthropology.[6]

Linguistic anthropologists and applied linguists interested in creativity have also been influenced by a contemporary of Jakobson's, whose work has more recently become prominent. While Bakhtin's ideas are now pervasive within literary studies, his project to incorporate the formal properties of language, and its evaluative functions, within a 'translinguistics' grounded in the communicative practices of everyday life makes his work particularly appealing to researchers seeking to combine linguistics, ethnography, and social theory. Bakhtin can be read as addressing language creativity through three interrelated sets of concepts, within a framework acknowledging the essentially evaluative function of language. First, the concept of dialogicality (the intrinsic addressivity and responsivity of all texts, see Vološinov 1973 and Bakhtin 1981) can be used to explore the interactive aspects of creative language, both within the context of immediate dialogue, and through more distal intertextual referencing. Secondly, Bakhtin's notion of heteroglossia, the co-existence and struggle between diverse social languages and between centripetal and centrifugal forces (Bakhtin 1981, 1984), can be used to explore the artful juxtaposition or dialogic positioning of social languages within texts, and their animation in double-voicing. Thirdly, his notion of speech genres (Bakhtin 1986), defined both formally from within and externally through recognition, practice, and evaluation, and his ideas about the incorporation and transformation of primary within secondary genres (e.g. the orchestration of everyday talk in narrative), can be used to address generic intertextuality and hybridity in both spoken and written texts.

Bakhtin's ideas about dialogicality, diverse voices and genre have been taken up by Bauman and Briggs (e.g. Bauman and Briggs 1990; Briggs and Bauman 1992; Bauman 2004) in their discussion of the dialectic between performance and its wider sociohistorical and sociopolitical context. Moving away from the conceptualizations within earlier performance studies of text and context, Bauman and Briggs (1990) argue for a more processual conceptualization of contextualization. Performances, because of their framing and intensity, are intrinsically more amenable to being decontextualized and recontextualized or transformed into a new context. Foregrounding these processes is an important part of examining the sociopolitical context of creative language use, because it enables questions to be asked about the differential access to texts and to different kinds of legitimacy to use or reuse them, how individuals gain these rights to particular modes of verbal display and to their transformation, and the social value attached to the texts themselves. All these processes involve issues of power and authority and are 'culturally constructed, socially constituted and sustained by ideologies' (Bauman and Briggs

1990: 76). (See also Shuman 1986 on story-telling rights amongst teenagers, and Rampton 2005 on language crossing.)

Within this linguistic anthropological tradition, there is still an important focus on the 'message for its own sake', with keyed performances being seen as more detachable and amenable to recontextualization. But the poetic organization of lines, verses, and stanzas in conversational narratives (Hymes 1996), or generic intertextuality (Bauman 2004), or the stylization of voices (Rampton 2001, 2005) are also seen as intensifying the potential for evaluation and critique. The evaluative function of narrative, the manipulation of the 'intertextual gap' between generic expectations and an individual performance (Briggs and Bauman 1992), the framing and transformation of reported discourse in parody and irony, can be used by participants for both local and more substantive critical purposes. Thus, the work of Hymes, Bauman, Briggs, and other linguistic anthropologists, and their application of theoretical ideas from Jakobson, Bakhtin and Goffman, suggest ways of extending the insights into dimensions of creativity which we identified as incipient in the work by the applied linguists reviewed above.

Analysis: identifying and accounting for language creativity

In this section we draw on insights from applied linguistics and linguistic anthropology in the analysis of everyday creativity in language. We look at four extracts taken from different communicative contexts: a family picnic, a research interview, an online chatroom, and a school classroom. While these examples illustrate a range of different poetic features, they all demonstrate reflexivity at formal, interactional, and sociohistorical levels (Bauman 1992). Our argument is that ideas developed within linguistic anthropology in relation to oral performances such as storytelling may help in the understanding of performances that arise, often fleetingly, in everyday interaction. We draw also on the work of linguists such as Carter and Cook in considering the local, interactional/interpersonal practices within which such episodes are embedded. Across these four examples we seek to show how a combination of different analytical dimensions – textual, contextualized, critical – extends our understanding of language creativity and how this works.

Example 1 Conversational joking

This first example comes from an interaction in which one of us (JS) was a participant. A family is having a picnic in the park and throwing scraps to pigeons. They discuss a somewhat bedraggled pigeon who has driven away another bird.

1   A: He might look scruffy but he's seen off that one over there
2   B: Obviously a thug amongst pigeons
3   C: Al Capigeon
4   D: The godfeather
     [Laughter overlaps C & D]

This is a classic example of interactional poetics, similar to episodes analysed by Carter (2004). The word play in the extract (lines 3 and 4) may be analysed textually, in terms of its manipulation of linguistic form – a blend of *pigeon* and *Al Capone*, and a near pun based on *the godfather* – and as an instance of reflexivity at the formal level, in which language structures are highlighted, with the potential to draw attention to themselves. These poetic forms are also dialogically accomplished, in terms of their immediate co-construction: *the godfeather* is a response to *Al Capigeon*, itself a response to *thug amongst pigeons* which, in turn, builds on *seen off that one over there*; an intertextual reference to US gangsters and gangster movies, humorously recontextualized within the world of parks and pigeons; and presentation to an audience (also co-participants) whose laughter ratifies the humour.

Wordplay between participants is embedded within (is responsive to and constitutive of) a particular set of social relations. Speakers are family members who habitually interact together. There is no serious threat to face if the joke falls flat, which may be one reason why joking is common amongst these speakers. Potential hierarchies are, here, de-emphasized partly through collaborative humour (although playful teasing is also common elsewhere). Reflexivity is then evident at an interactional level: the salience afforded to poetic forms arguably foregrounds speakers' friendly relations, representing these in a temporarily heightened form.

There is also a significant sociohistorical dimension to the word 'play'. Participants' appreciation of this depends on joint cultural reference points: common knowledge of gangsters, without which it would not be successful. The working of the wordplay *as humour* also depends upon time and place. In contemporary Britain it is possible, and not uncommon, to make joking intertextual references to early twentieth-century US gangsters – perhaps less so about more recent violent crime.

Example 2   A conversational narrative

The extract below comes from a research interview conducted by one of us with 11-year-old Lee and his friend Geoffrey (Maybin 2006). While not strongly keyed as a public performance (the audience consisted of Geoffrey and Maybin), Lee's story nevertheless involves the framing of personal experience which is held up for reflection and critique. The data also demonstrate how the aesthetic, interactive, and critical functions of creative language are closely intertwined.

Lee's story has been transcribed as a series of lines and verses, following Hymes (1996). Lines are identified rhythmically and correspond to clauses (treating line 1 as including a false start). Verses mainly consist of two sets of paired lines with lines 9 and 18 seen as evaluative asides (Labov 1972).

(1)   Yesterday I was on, I was walking with my mum,
(2)   we walked past this bush,
(3)   and there was this nest
(4)   and it was fallen down on the floor,
(5)   and I goes 'Mum look, there's a nest on the floor',
(6)   and I goes 'Mum can I go and have a look at it?'
(7)   and I went over there
(8)   and there was four baby chicks in it, little chicks,
(9)   I think they were Willow Warbler
(10)   and my mum said 'Climb up and put them back in the tree',
(11)   so, and I had some bread,
(12)   eaten some bread,
(13)   so I fed it bits of bread,
(14)   cause she had to go to the phone,
(15)   and em she waited
(16)   and I put it back up in the tree
(17)   and its mum's with it now.
(18)   Yea, cause someone, someone had pulled the nest down, out of the tree.

In terms of text structure, following Labov (1972), this story includes an orientation, complication, and resolution, together with two evaluative asides: line 9 'I think they were Willow Warbler' (apparently displaying the narrator's expert knowledge) and line 18, which also functions as a coda, 'Yea, cause someone, someone had pulled the nest down, out of the tree'. In addition, there is the rhythm and patterning of repetition at various levels, for example at the level of sound in bush/nest, fallen/floor, and parallelism, for example between lines 5 and 6. These relationships of equivalence, as well as the sequence of clauses, organize the narrative and shape its meaning (Hymes 1996). This story acts as a shared reference point in the subsequent conversation: following on line 18 above, Geoffrey and Lee go on to refer disapprovingly to other boys who knock nests down and smash eggs, and to a girl who 'nicks' birds which then die.

Setting Lee's story within its broader dialogical context highlights how the three-part structure in lines 11–13 'and I had some bread, eaten some bread, so I fed it bits of bread' is not only an example of repetition within a story but also of repetition across stories. Lee's story mirrored one told earlier in the interview by Geoffrey about a stray cat, which ended with a similar three part linked structure 'it eat a bit, it eat a bit, only a little bit'. Geoffrey's story was also about kindness to lost, vulnerable creatures and, while the specific ornithological details in Lee's story and the possibility of finding a nest with chicks intact on the ground may be questioned, Lee strengthens the evaluative function of his story through linking it to his friend's in terms of both structure and content. At the same time, through confirming a shared valuing of kindness to small creatures which the boys subsequently contrast with the behaviour of other children, Lee reflexively displays and affirms their friendship (cf. Goodwin 1990; Coates 1996).

Example 3 Online chat

The example below comes from an online chatroom.[7] The discussion was sparked off by media coverage in 2005 of Prince Charles's forthcoming marriage with Camilla Parker-Bowles, and illustrates how the role of textual creativity in expressing a critical stance in the online context can be closely intertwined with its role in building, maintaining, and repairing social relations.

10/04/2005 03:03	Glowworm	. . .The HRH stripped from Diana—she'd served her purpose, now given to that dirty common adulterer
		A plague of locusts on the windors seems the camilla/charles supporters can truly empathise, from experience???
		'Let he who is without sin throw the first stone'
		Well I've chucked mine👍
10/04/2005 03:50	Orca	Good grief.
		Well I suppose you can't do any harm tapping away on a keyboard. Care in the community is great, isn't it?
10/04/2005 09:34	Boxer	Glowworm, while respecting your views, nowhere did I mention Diana, nor compare Camilla with her, nor mention the Royalty as such. It seems to me that Camilla has been maligned for years, not so much because of adultery but because of her looks.

Don't get me wrong, I was once angry beyond belief that the "Dream Marriage" came adrift, because, like many, I was hoping for a happy ending. It was cruel to see it end the way it did, and people wanted to blame someone.

Camilla, in retrospect, has behaved impeccably throughout and perhaps now she has suffered enough for her "dirty common adultery". Let them live peacefully and happily.

Orca 🗡

10/04/2005 10:11	S'fari	LOL

Why and how on earth do people get so worked up about another couple of people doing what loads of other people the world over do ?

<"a plague of locusts on the windors"> (sic)

<"angry beyond belief">

Good grief indeed

10/04/2005 10:58	Castaway	Surely Charles is just resurrecting a Royal Tradition.

. .

Marry a suitable princess and produce an heir.

Keep as many mistresses as you like.

Divorce or behead your wife

Marry one of your mistresses

Repeat from step 2.

10/04/2005 11:04	Boxer	☻

Wasn't one of Camilla's ancestors a mistress to Charles II? ☺

10/04/2005 11:11	Castaway	I think that's how most of the aristocracy was created Boxer. . .. .

If your mistress falls pregnant give the illegitimate offspring a title and some land to keep them quiet.

The affordances of the chatroom medium, where speech-like communication is recorded in writing and participants can scroll backwards and forwards to check and extract text, produce a characteristically reflexive, heteroglossic texture (Goddard 2003). At the textual level in the example above, S'fari (10:11) recontextualizes phrases from three previous turns to strengthen his/her own criticism of people who get 'so worked up' about the behaviour of the British royal family. S'fari signals critical distance from Glowworm and Boxer's positions through the use of inverted commas and echoes Orca's 'Good grief' in 'Good grief indeed', which in this new context is transformed into a criticism of both Glowworm and Boxer. Following S'fari's posting, Castaway (10:58) switches generically to a list: a double-voiced, ironic set of instructions for royals. This receives an appreciative response from Boxer (11:4), who also picks up and extends Castaway's historical point.

The chatroom participants use metaphors, double-voicing, recontextualization, and generic intertextuality to express particular critical positions and also to convey social alignments. Creative textual forms are implicated in the delicate interactional work to manage participants' face (Goffman 1969), in the light of expressions of strong feeling that could threaten the fabric of the online conversation. There is frequent hedging and mitigation and Castaway's parody serves not only to frame and hold up for evaluation a particular critical stance against the behaviour of the British Royals, but also to release some of the tension generated by the previous discussion between Boxer, Glowworm, and S'fari. Castaway redirects critical attention outside the group in a humorous manner which mitigates possible offence to pro-Royalists. Throughout the conversation, emoticons are also exploited to attend to the 'face' of others: Glowworm's mitigating (3.03), Boxer's for Orca (9.34) and Boxer's (11.04) expressing appreciation of Castaway's parody and contributing to the restoration of a more positive atmosphere in the chatroom. Emoticons, of course, can also be double voiced: Boxer's (11.04) produces and parodies the very over-reaction to royal affairs which S'fari was criticizing.

Example 4 Classroom talk

Example 4 comes from a British primary school classroom in which children are working on a computer activity that addresses a moral dilemma.[8] Kate's friend, Robert, has stolen some chocolates for his sick mother and Kate believes stealing is wrong. The children need to decide what Kate should do about this. Here, three children discuss whether Kate should tell her mother. The children have been taught certain strategies to explore ideas in discussion (e.g. giving reasons for their views, asking for others' opinions and their reasons for these), and these are evident in their talk. (The extract comes from a more extended analysis of children's talk in this context in Swann 2007.)

1	Gemma:	I think she should tell her parents[(.) (xxxx)
		D is rocking back and forwards on his seat
2	Dan:	[no (you always think that)
3	Emily:	em why do you don't why don't you think that
4	Dan:	cos she (said) a promise and can't break a promise
5	Emily:	Gemma
6	Gemma:	I think it's (.) I think she should tell her parents because (.) right
		Slow, thinking as she speaks
7	Dan:	steal[ing is wrong
		Slightly whining voice quality
8	Gemma:	[stealing
9		((laughter))
10	Emily	I think she (.) should not tell her parents. . . etc.

Note: The following conventions are used in this transcript: Square brackets mark the beginning of overlapping speech; (.) represents a brief pause; (you always. . .) single curved brackets mark an uncertain transcription; (xxxx) represents an unclear utterance that could not be transcribed; ((laughter)) double brackets are used for non-speech sounds.

This is an example of relatively formal, schooled talk in which speakers are discussing a set topic, adopting interactional conventions they have been taught. These interactional constraints represent what might be expected to be a relatively hostile environment for linguistic creativity, or at least one that is not conducive to the often playful use of poetic language evident in informal interactions such as Examples 1 and 3. When such playful language does occur, it tends to involve a very brief shift of frame, as in Dan's turn 7 above. Dan has earlier disagreed with Gemma's view that Kate should tell her parents of Robert's theft. His utterance at turn 7 (formally, a completion of Gemma's turn) is lightly keyed as ironic by his tone of voice. This is an instance of double-voicing in Bakhtin's terms, in which Dan repeats, and ironically recontextualizes, a view expressed by Kate herself, displayed on the computer screen.

Dan's speaking turn bears all the hallmarks of performance: it is framed and highlighted, keyed as distinctive from the surrounding interaction; it is a reflexive display of wit to an audience, responded to by laughter; it is also critically reflexive, interrupting and humorously subverting official activity and official social relations. It is, however, the most fleeting of performances, with Emily reinstating the official discursive frame at turn 10.

Discussion: developing an analytic framework

We have suggested earlier, and tried to demonstrate in the section above, that analyses of everyday creativity need to take account of three broad and interrelated analytical dimensions, which we termed textual, contextualized, and critical. The four data extracts analysed above all show creative episodes emerging from the flow of interaction, whether this is face-to-face or online in a chatroom. In these episodes, creative language is unplanned and unrehearsed, constructed on the hoof, whether it represents a brief, even fleeting (re)framing in which the interaction is temporarily keyed as artful/creative, or forms part of a more sustained creative interchange. It may take a range of textual forms, which reflexively draw attention to themselves, enhancing the experience and pleasure of participants and attracting evaluative/aesthetic judgements. This is consistent with Jakobson's poetic function, and Bauman's extension of this in his definition of performance. This is not, however, only art for art's sake: creative language is also used for a range of interactional and social ends, highlighted in contextualized and critical dimensions of analysis.

Textual, contextualized, and critical dimensions reflect different analytical focuses, foregrounding different aspects of creativity—see Table 24.1 for a schematic representation. A textual dimension, for instance, provides a focus on creativity as:

- adopting, adapting, and playing with, a range of linguistic forms – word play, figures of speech, echoing or transforming others' words, etc. (evident in all the examples above);
- contingent upon, and sometimes creatively deploying, or playing with, the affordances of particular genres, modes, etc. (the adoption of a narrative format in example 2; the possibility of cut and paste citation, and the use of emoticons for evaluation in example 4).

Many textual strategies may be recast as repetition, or near repetition at various levels (sounds, grammatical structures, words and phrases, reported speech, narrative themes), supporting Tannen's (1989: 2) and Cook's (1994) judgement that repetition underlies other forms of creativity.

A contextualized dimension focuses on the contextual embeddedness of such textual strategies, and their potential for recontextualization to particular interactional and aesthetic effect. Language creativity is, in this sense:

- interwoven with a range of shifting communicative purposes – getting on with others, scoring a point, negotiating particular identities, etc. (all the examples above);

Table 24.1 Dimensions of analysis

Dimension	Focus	Examples
Textual	Linguistic forms and structures, at word/sentence level and above; may also include formal multimodal analysis	Word play; narrative structure; voice quality used to enhance the point of an ironic or playful comment; placement of emoticons in electronic chat
Contextualized	How language is used by participants in specific interactions, and/or how it shapes, responds to, and is shaped by particular sociocultural and socio-historical contexts (the balance varies in different analyses)	Joint construction of a narrative, or word play, and how this is responded to by others; the cultural understandings necessary to make sense of a joke; economic, social, and technological conditions associated with contemporary electronic creativity
Critical	Creativity as necessarily evaluative, with the potential for more developed critique of social relations/positions and associated values	Conversational narrative that indexes a speaker's moral stance; joking that subverts or critiques authority, the potential of poetic language to call attention to a critical stance

- both responsive to and constitutive of particular contexts and sets of social relations (again, evident in all examples);
- dialogically co-constructed, in the sense that participants may jointly contribute to a creative episode (e.g. interactional joking in example 1); and in the sense that speakers are designing what they say for an audience, who may themselves construct an episode as creative in their evaluation (general laughter in examples 1 and 4; Boxer's grin in example 3);
- dialogical also in that episodes are intertextually framed, and that speakers may creatively call up and recontextualize utterances from prior contexts (the reference to gangsters in example 1; reported speech, and the mirroring of another story in example 2; direct citation from other posts in example 3 and educational software in example 4);
- historically and culturally contingent – something that is possible here and now because of the availability of particular social, cultural, economic, technological, etc. resources – e.g. contemporary electronic communication and the communicative conventions that have grown up around this (example 3); relying on joint cultural reference for their understanding (all examples).

A critical analytical dimension provides an additional focus on creativity as:

- critical in the sense that, like all language use, linguistically creative episodes are necessarily evaluative, reflecting and constructing a certain evaluative stance, or stances (all examples);
- because they are framed and highlighted within communication, such episodes also have the potential for more developed, heightened critique (constructing a shared critical moral

position in example 2; the humorous critique of the royal family in example 3; the fleeting
subversion of classroom values in example 4).

'Critical', in this sense, does not necessarily suggest critique of more powerful social positions
or established values. Various forms of language creativity may be drawn on to reinforce, play
along with or subvert authority, or (as in example 3 above), to balance critique with mitigation.
    Textual, contextualized, and critical dimensions may be differentially called up by particular
sets of data. We suggest, however, that the three dimensions are not actually discrete (textual
forms need to be interpreted in context, and also serve to (re)fashion contexts, social relations,
evaluative standpoints, etc.), and that it is necessary to take all three into account, to the extent
that this is analytically possible, in order to understand everyday creativity and how this works.
    Some issues, however, remain unresolved within this framework. First, the analytical
identification of context is notoriously problematical. For instance, through recontextualization and intertextual referencing, speakers are pointing towards contexts away from the here
and now and the significance of these connections cannot be fully recovered from an analysis
restricted to the current exchange. However, suggesting that we cannot analyse the function and
significance of a specific utterance without addressing the dialogic chains with which it is
associated raises the question of how far a researcher should, or is able to, follow these chains
in order to produce a valid interpretation. More generally, stressing the importance of a
contextualized dimension raises the question, which applies to both more static and more
dynamic models, of how far the analyst needs, or is able, to go in identifying contextual information. There is also a methodological question about whether one is recovering aspects of context
that are significant for the speakers themselves, or constructing context in terms of the
theoretical preconceptions and research purposes of the analyst. Indeed, it is doubtful whether
these two can ever be fully teased apart.
    Secondly, while we have discussed the need for an evaluative, critical dimension in the
analysis of everyday creativity, we have not addressed a somewhat different area of evaluation,
which relates to the value, as art, of specific instances of language creativity. The idea of clines
of creativity or literariness is one way in which such notions of value may be addressed, where
different forms of poetic language (for instance) may be seen as having more, or less literary
value. A contextualized approach, by contrast, would tend to see creativity as contextually
(sociohistorically, interpersonally, or generically) specific, so that it makes little sense to
compare conversational word play with a published poem in terms of their literary value. What
we have here, rather, are different creativities. We can say word play 'works' within an interaction (in that people laugh, or continue the wordplay, or fall silent) but it is pointless to try to
judge wordplay according to its literary merit – that is not what it is about (Carter 2007; Semino
2007).
    Creativity in everyday language may be identified in different ways – according to certain
formal characteristics, for instance, or cognitive effects, or conformity to sociocultural conventions and expectations.[9] Our own focus on creativity in terms of Jakobson's poetic function
in language, and Bauman's, Hymes', and Bauman and Briggs' conceptions of performance allows
the inclusion of a wide range of otherwise disparate texts, genres and practices. While these
differ formally, functionally and in terms of their sociohistorical framing, they have in common
a focus on creative language use as a reflexive practice in which speakers/writers assume responsibility for presentation to an audience, and which is also subject to evaluation by the audience.
We have cited others who take different approaches. Tannen, Carter, Cook, and Crystal seem
to have a stronger focus on linguistic form; and Tannen's and Carter's examples of speakers
echoing one another's words would not necessarily be creative in our sense of the term.

We mentioned also Kress's conception of design, which would reframe all language use as creative. The boundaries around creativity in everyday language, then – what should count as the object(s) of research – are by no means settled and will no doubt continue to shift as the subject receives further discussion.

Notes

1   Our use of the term 'critical' here, referring to a critical/evaluative stance evident in an utterance, which may be the focus of analysis, is different from the use of 'critical' to refer to approaches to the study of language that reflect an overt critical (political) stance on the part of the analyst (as in Critical Discourse Analysis). In this paper we retain a conceptual distinction between these two uses. They are linked, however, in that the critical evaluative dimension of an utterance, in the first sense of the term, is likely to be of interest to a critical researcher.

2   There is controversy about whether works published under Vološinov's name were in fact written by Bakhtin.

3   This includes stylistic studies of literary texts (e.g. Short 1996; Leech and Short 2007) and media texts (e.g. Cook 2001), as well as the work on everyday talk discussed above.

4   Jakobson is here referring to the message form, rather than its content.

5   The idea of reflexivity corresponds here to the poetic function of language, in which language draws attention to itself and is subject to evaluation by an audience. The term does not suggest that speakers consciously reflect on their language use, and in fact this is unlikely within spontaneous interaction.

6   Note however that Bauman's conception of performance is different from that of Goffman. Goffman (1969: 26) defines performance as 'all the activity of a given participant on a given occasion which serves to influence in any way any of the other participants'. While there is still an emphasis on audience here, for Goffman all interactions constitute performances in which participants necessarily express themselves and impress others. This contrasts with Bauman's more specific concern with performance as something that is set off from ongoing interaction, dependent on the assumption of responsibility to an audience for a display of communicative skill.

7   We are grateful to Sarah North for supplying these data.

8   This example comes from data collected by Neil Mercer and colleagues as part of their research on children's use of exploratory talk in science and maths lessons. We are grateful to Neil Mercer for permission to re-analyse data from this project.

9   This is similar to a three-way distinction established by Carter (1999, 2004) in relation to the identification of literary or creative language.

References

Bakhtin, M. 1981 [1935]. 'Discourse in the novel' in M. Holquist (ed.): *The Dialogic Imagination: Four Essays by M. M. Bakhtin*, trans. C. Emerson and M. Holquist. Austin, TX: University of Texas Press.

Bakhtin, M. 1984 [1929]. *Problems of Dostoevsky's Poetics*, ed. and trans. C. Emerson. Manchester: Manchester University Press.

Bakhtin, M. 1986 [1953]. 'The problem of speech genres' in C. Emerson, and M. Holquist (eds): *Speech Genres and Other Late Essays*, trans. V. W. McGee. Austin, TX: University of Texas Press.

Bauman, R. 1977. *Verbal Art as Performance*. Rowley, MA: Newbury House.

Bauman, R. 1986. *Story, Performance and Event*. Cambridge: Cambridge University Press.

Bauman, R. 1992. 'Performance' in R. Bauman (ed.): *Folklore, Cultural Performances and Popular Entertainments*. New York: Oxford University Press.

Bauman, R. 2001 [1975]. 'Verbal art as performance' in A. Duranti (ed.): *Linguistic Anthropology: A Reader*. Oxford: Blackwell Publishing.

Bauman, R. 2002. 'Disciplinarity, reflexivity and power', *Journal of American Folklore* 115/455: 92–128.

Bauman, R. 2004. *A World of Others' Words: Cross-cultural Perspectives on Intertextuality*. Oxford: Blackwell Publishing.

Bauman, R. and C. Briggs. 1990. 'Poetics and performance as critical perspectives on language and social life', *Annual Review of Anthropology* 19: 59–88.

Bell, N. 2005. 'Exploring L2 language play as an aid to SLL: A case study of humour in NS–NNS interaction', *Applied Linguistics* 26/2.

Bernstein, B. 1996. *Pedagogy, Symbolic Control and Identity: Theory, research, critique*. London: Taylor and Francis.

Bloome, D., S. P. Carter, B. M. Christian, S. Otto, and N. Shuart-Faris. 2005. *Discourse Analysis and the Study of Classroom Language and Literacy Events: A Microethnographic Perspective*. London: Lawrence Erlbaum Associates.

Briggs, C. and R. Bauman. 1992. 'Genre, intertextuality and social power', *Journal of Linguistic Anthropology* 2/2: 131–72.

Carter, R. 1999. 'Common language: Corpus, creativity and cognition', *Language and Literature* 8/3: 195–216.

Carter, R. 2004. *Language and Creativity: The Art of Common Talk*. London/New York: Routledge.

Carter, R. 2007. 'Creativities across texts and values', Paper presented at an AHRC-funded seminar on *Transitions and Transformations: Exploring Creativity in Everyday and Literary language*. The Open University, Milton Keynes, UK, 16 March.

Coates, J. 1996. *Women Talk: Conversation Between Women Friends*. Oxford: Blackwell Publishers.

Cook, G. 1994. 'Repetition and knowing by heart: An aspect of intimate discourse', *English Language Teaching Journal* 48: 133–42.

Cook, G. 1997. 'Language play, language learning', *English Language Teaching Journal* 51/3: 224–31.

Cook, G. 2000. *Language Play, Language Learning*. Oxford: Oxford University Press.

Cook, G. 2001 (2nd edn.). *The Discourse of Advertising*. London: Routledge.

Coupland, N. 2001. 'Language, situation and the relational self: Theorising dialect style in socio-linguistics', in P. Eckert and J. R. Rickford (eds): *Style and Sociolinguistic Variation*. Cambridge and New York: Cambridge University Press.

Coupland, N. 2007. *Style: Language Variation and Identity*. Cambridge and New York: Cambridge University Press.

Crystal, D. 1998. *Language Play*. Harmondsworth: Penguin.

Eckert, P. 2000. *Linguistic Variation as Social Practice*. Oxford: Blackwell Publishers.

Goddard, A. 2003. '"Is there anybody out there?" Creative language play and "literariness" in Internet Relay Chat (IRC)', in A. Schorr, W. Campbell, and M. Schenk (eds): *Communication Research and Media Science in Europe: Perspectives for Research and Academic Training in Europe's Changing Media Reality*. Berlin: Mouton de Gruyter.

Goffman, E. 1969. *The Presentation of Self in Everyday Life*. London: Penguin.

Goffman, E. 1972. *Interactional Ritual: Essays on Face to Face Behaviour*. London: Penguin.

Goffman, E. 1974. *Frame Analysis: An Essay on the Organisation of Experience*. Harmondsworth: Penguin.

Goodwin, M. H. 1990. *He-Said-She-Said: Talk as Social Organisation Among Black Children*. Bloomington: Indiana University Press.

Gumperz, J. J. 1982. *Discourse Strategies*. Cambridge: Cambridge University Press.

Hymes, D. 1975. 'Breakthrough into performance', in D. Ben-Amos and K. S. Goldstein (eds): *Folklore: Performance and Communication*. The Hague: Mouton.

Hymes, D. 1977. *Foundations in Sociolinguistics: An Ethnographic Approach*. London: Tavistock.

Hymes, D. 1996. *Ethnography, Linguistics, Narrative Inequality: Towards an Understanding of Voice*. London: Taylor and Francis.

Hymes, D. 2004 (2nd edn.). *In Vain I Tried to Tell You: Essays in Native American Ethnopoetics*. Lincoln: University of Nebraska Press.

Jakobson, J. 1960. 'Closing statement: Linguistics and poetics', in T. A. Sebeok (ed.): *Style in Language*. Cambridge, MA: M.I.T. Press.

Kress, G. 1998. 'Visual and verbal modes of representation in electronically mediated communication: the potentials of new forms of text', in I. Snyder (ed.): *Page to Screen*. London: Routledge.

Kress, G. 2003. *Literacy in the New Media Age*. London: Routledge.

Labov, W. 1972. *Language in the Inner City*. Philadelphia: University of Philadelphia Press.

Lantolf, J. 1997. 'The function of language play in the acquisition of L2 Spanish', in W. R. Glass and A. T. Pérez-Leroux (eds): *Contemporary Perspectives on the Acquisition of Spanish. Volume 2: Production, Processing and Comprehension*. Somerville: Cascadilla Press.

Leech, G. and M. Short. 2007 (2nd edn.). *Style in Fiction: A Linguistic Introduction to English Fictional Prose*. London: Longman.

Maybin, J., 2006. *Children's Voices: Talk, Knowledge and Identity*. Basingstoke: Palgrave and Macmillan.

Mukarovsky, J. 1970 [1936]. *Aesthetic Function, Norm and Value as Social Facts*, trans. M. E. Suino. Ann Arbor, MI: University of Michigan.

Mukarovsky, J. 1964 [1932]. 'Standard language and poetic language', in P. Garvin (ed.): *Prague School Reader on Esthetics, Literary Structure and Style*. Washington, DC: Georgetown University Press.

Rampton, B. 2001. 'Critique in interaction', *Critique of Anthropology* 21/1: 83–107.

Rampton, B. 2005 (2nd edn.). *Crossing: Language and Ethnicity among Adolescents.* Manchester: St Jerome Press.

Semino, E. 2007. 'Metaphor and creativity across genres', Paper presented at an AHRC-funded seminar on *Transitions and Transformations: Exploring Creativity in Everyday and Literary Language.* The Open University, Milton Keynes UK, 16 March.

Short, M. 1996. *Exploring the Language of Poems, Plays and Prose.* London: Longman.

Shuman, A. 1986. *Storytelling Rights: The Uses of Oral and Written Texts among Urban Adolescents.* Cambridge: Cambridge University Press.

Street, B. 1993. 'Culture is a verb: Anthropological aspects of language and cultural process', in D. Graddol, L. Thompson, and M. Byram (eds): *Language and Culture: British Studies in Applied Linguistics*, 7. Clevedon: Multilingual Matters.

Sullivan, P. N. 2000. 'Playfulness as mediation in communicative language teaching in a Vietnamese classroom', in J. P. Lantolf (ed.): *Sociocultural Theory and Second Language Learning.* Oxford: Oxford University Press.

Swann, J. 2007. '*Designing "educationally effective" discussion*', Language and Education 21(4): 342–59.

Tannen, D. 1989. *Talking Voices: Repetition, Dialogue and Imagery in Conversational Discourse.* Cambridge: Cambridge University Press.

Tarone, E. 2000. 'Getting serious about language play: Language play, interlanguage variation and second language acquisition', in B. Swierzbin, F. Morris, M. Anderson, C. Klee, and E. Tarone (eds): *Social and Cognitive Factors in SLA: Proceedings of the 1999 Second Language Research Forum.* Somerville: Cascadilla Press.

Vološinov, V. N. 1973 [1929]. *Marxism and the Philosophy of Language*, trans. L. Matejka and I. R. Titunik. Cambridge, MA: Harvard University Press.

Vološinov, V. N. 1976 [1927]. 'Discourse in life and discourse in art', in I. R.Titunik and N. H. Bruss (eds): *Freudianism: A Marxist critique*, trans. I. R. Titunik. New York: Academic Press.

Chapter 25

ANETA PAVLENKO

"I'M VERY NOT ABOUT THE LAW PART"

Non-native speakers of English and the Miranda Warnings (2008)

I N T H E P A S T F E W Y E A R S, the scope of inquiry in the fields of applied linguistics and TESOL has widened to an unprecedented degree. Until recently, the two fields were predominantly preoccupied with classroom teaching, but they have begun to address a larger array of real-world concerns, many of which have direct implications for the classroom (e.g., Cook & Kasper, 2005; McGroarty, 2003). This article addresses one such real-world issue, namely, the inability of the U.S. legal system to address language issues affecting nonnative speakers (NNSs) of English. In 1978, *TESOL Quarterly* published an article titled "Limited English Speakers and the Miranda Rights" by Eugène Brière that became a classic in the field of forensic linguistics. Brière (1978) analyzed the linguistic complexity of the Miranda warnings and described a set of tests administered to a speaker with limited English skills. The test scores revealed that the speaker did not have sufficient proficiency to understand his Miranda rights. And yet, almost 3 decades later, many NNSs of English, even those with low proficiency, are still read their rights exclusively in English.

The present article takes off from where Brière's (1978) study ended and pursues three interrelated goals: (a) to show that the Miranda warnings are difficult to understand for speakers at more advanced levels of proficiency than the participant in Brière's (1978) study, (b) to argue that police cautions, such as the Miranda warnings, should be presented both in English and in the native language to NNSs of English, regardless of their proficiency levels, and (c) to motivate designers of adult ESL curricula to incorporate at least one module that introduces common legal terms, concepts, and speech events, such as police cautions. In view of the fact that more and more TESOL professionals are becoming involved in court cases as linguistic experts, I also aim to familiarize the TESOL community with the research and arguments about police cautions in the fields of law and forensic linguistics.

I begin with an overview of studies that consider comprehension of police cautions by NNSs of English. Next, I discuss a case in which I testified as an expert witness with regard to the defendant's ability to understand the Miranda warnings. What makes this case particularly interesting is that the NNS in question had a high level of interactional competence and at the time of her interrogation was a student in a U.S. university. Yet I intend to show that, despite her interactional competence, she was unable to fully understand her Miranda rights and interpreted signing the waiver of rights as a routine procedure for witnesses, an interpretation that was facilitated by the detective in charge of the interrogation. I will end by discussing the implications of this case study for the treatment of NNSs by the U.S. legal system and for ESL curricula.

Nonnative speakers of English and police cautions

In Common law countries, such as the United Kingdom, United States, or Australia,[1] police are required to inform suspects of their rights through scripted cautions, whose form and meaning may vary slightly, even within the same jurisdiction. Hollywood movies and TV shows often portray such cautions in the scenes where guns are drawn and a heroic policeman shouts at the wrongdoer: "You are under arrest! You have the right to remain silent!" When presented outside of such context and not preceded by the utterance "you are under arrest," however, police cautions are not necessarily identified as such and not easily understood by NNSs of English.

Several studies and case reviews carried out in the United Kingdom (Cotterill, 2000), in the United States (Berk-Seligson, 2000; Brière, 1978; Connell & Valladares, 2001; Einesman, 1999; Roy, 1990; Shuy, 1997, 1998; Solan & Tiersma, 2005), and in Australia (Eades, 2003; Gibbons, 1990, 1996, 2001, 2003) show that NNSs of English are at a considerable disadvantage when processing police cautions because of the linguistic and conceptual complexity of these texts and their cultural specificity. These difficulties may be further compounded by the use of untrained interpreters, including police officers and family members (Berk-Seligson, 2000, 2002; Connell & Valladares, 2001; Einesman, 1999, Nakane, 2007; Russell, 2000).

The focus of the present article is on the U.S. caution, commonly known as the Miranda warnings or the Miranda rights (for an in-depth discussion of the history of and the issues surrounding the Miranda warnings, see Einesman, 1999; Leo & Thomas, 1998; Shuy, 1997; Solan & Tiersma, 2005). This caution came about as a result of the 1966 Supreme Court ruling in the case of *Miranda v. Arizona* which expanded the Fifth Amendment privilege against self-incrimination from the courtroom to the police station, requiring police officers to inform suspects of their constitutional rights prior to questioning.[2] The warnings do not need to be given in any specific way; the Miranda standard is satisfied as long as the rights are reasonably conveyed. To comprehend the Miranda warnings correctly, individuals being questioned must understand that they are suspects in the police investigation and that they have all of the following rights: (a) the right to remain silent, (b) the right to an attorney, and (c) the right to have an attorney present during questioning. Suspects must also understand that exercising these rights will not lead to harmful consequences, and that waiving the rights may in fact lead to harmful consequences, such as the suspects' own testimony being used against them in court. In other words, the suspects must understand (d) that anything they say can be used against them in a court of law, and (e) that if they cannot afford an attorney, an attorney will be furnished to them free of charge both prior to and during questioning.

The Supreme Court summarized the waiver requirements in *Moran v. Burbine:* "First, the relinquishment of the right must have been voluntary in the sense that it was the product of a free and deliberate choice rather than intimidation, coercion, or deception. Second, the waiver must have been made with a full awareness of both the nature of the right being abandoned and the consequences of the decision to abandon it" (Solan & Tiersma, 2005, pp. 75–76). If the warnings are not adequately presented, the court may deem that the Miranda rights were not waived voluntarily, knowingly, and intelligently. As a result, the court may suppress the statements made by the suspect as improperly obtained, excluding them from the entire court proceedings.

Overviews of cases where the validity of the waiver was questioned show that in some cases the defendants' statements were indeed subsequently suppressed. For instance, in *United States v. Short*, the court found the waiver invalid because the defendant, a West German national, had only been in the United States for 3 months before questioning and spoke and understood English poorly (Einesman, 1999). In *United States v. Garibay*, the court found the waiver invalid because of the defendant's English language difficulties, low IQ, and the fact that he was not advised of his rights in his native language, Spanish, nor provided an interpreter (Einesman, 1999). Roy's (1990) analysis of a case where the Puerto Rican defendant was denied an interpreter, both during the reading of the Miranda warnings and in court, helped to overturn the conviction on appeal.

The absence of an interpreter is not the only rationale for overturning the waiver; other cases involve a faulty translation (see also Berk-Seligson, 2000, for an overview of cases where the waiver was overturned because law enforcement used incompetent or ad hoc interpreters, including children and relatives). In the case of *People v. Mejia-Mendoza*, the Supreme Court of Colorado found that the translation of the Miranda rights into Spanish was embellished and inaccurate and ruled that the government did not properly advise the defendant of his rights (Connell & Valladares, 2001; Einesman, 1999). In turn, in *United States v. Pham*, a California Superior Court suppressed the testimony of the defendant because the jail nurse who translated his testimony from Vietnamese failed to translate his statements "I want to go back to jail" and "I don't want to say any more," which were effectively invocations of his right to silence (Figueroa, 2005).

However, in the majority of the cases where NNSs of English were advised of their rights in their native language, the validity of the waiver has been upheld, despite the suspects' lack of familiarity with the U.S. criminal justice system. For example, in *People v. Márquez*, the California Supreme Court found the waiver valid, even though the defendant claimed that he could not understand the police officer's Spanish (Berk-Seligson, 2000). Similarly, in *People v. González*, the Supreme Court of New York ruled that discrepancies in the translation of the Miranda rights did not matter because the detective interpreter managed to convey the substance of the rights (Berk-Seligson, 2000). In *State v. Leu-thavone*, the Supreme Court of Rhode Island ruled that translating the rights into Laotian satisfied the requirement of a voluntary, knowing, and intelligent waiver (Dinh, 1995). And in *United States v. Yunis*, the District of Columbia Circuit Court of Appeals ruled that the defendant's waiver was valid because the rights were read to him in both English and Arabic, and he was also shown a written Arabic translation of the rights and gave both an oral and written waiver (Einesman, 1999).

In several other cases, the waivers were found valid based on the simple fact that the suspect could communicate in English. For instance, in *United States v. Alaouie*, the court found the Miranda waiver valid because the officer "took special care to thoroughly explain" the rights and because the defendant responded in English and did not use an interpreter at trial (Einesman, 1999, p. 11). In *United States v. Bernard S.*, the court found a juvenile defendant's waiver valid because the defendant had studied English through the Grade 7, answered questions in English, and responded in English that he understood the rights. Thus the validity of the waiver was upheld, despite the fact that the Apache-speaking defendant was unable to read or write English and required an interpreter during trial (Einesman, 1999; see also Solan & Tiersma, 2005). Several legal scholars have expressed concern over the lack of standard for what is considered adequate English proficiency for the purposes of understanding the Miranda rights, pointing out inconsistencies in decisions made by various courts (Connell & Valladares, 2001; Einesman, 1999; Roy, 1990; Solan & Tiersma, 2005).

Linguists also take issue with decisions such as the one made in the case of *Bernard S.* and argue that an understanding of the Miranda warnings requires more than a basic level of English proficiency. Brière's (1978) analysis of the language of the Miranda rights reveals that for native speakers of English, the Miranda text has a Grade 8 level of reading difficulty with 50% comprehension and a Grade 13 level of difficulty with 100% aural comprehension. This and other analyses of the linguistic and conceptual complexity of the Miranda warnings (Brière, 1978; Shuy, 1997, 1998) identify the following features of the text that make it difficult for NNSs of English and for English speakers with limited educational background:

(a) Syntactic complexity, seen in the high number of embedded clauses, that is, clauses introduced by *and*, *but*, *or*, *when*, *if*, *so*, *before*, *to*, and *that*, within a single sentence; commonly, the deeper the embedding, the more likely a NNS of English will either fail to understand the sentence or rely on alternative cues to understand the gist of it (see also Gibbons, 2001). In the case discussed in this article, the Miranda Warning Form required the NNS of English to process six layers of embedding:

    1.   *If* you cannot afford
    2.   *to* hire a lawyer,
    3.   [then] one will be appointed
    4.   *to* represent you
    5.   *before* any questioning
    6.   *if* you wish one.

(b) The presence of medium- and low-frequency terms, such as *afford*, *appointed*, and *discontinue*, and legal terms such as *the court of law* and *waiver of rights* (for frequency information, see *Collins COBUILD English Dictionary*, 1995).
(c) Reliance on the privilege against self-incrimination and the notion of rights specific to the Common law system adopted in the United States.
(d) Lack of logical progression in the order of decisions that need to be made: remain silent, consider legal representation, and discontinue the interview. As pointed out by forensic linguist Roger Shuy (1998): "clients do not realize that their first action is to be represented by a lawyer before considering their speaking/silence options" (p. 55).

Participation of interpreters does not always alleviate these problems. Forensic linguists and legal scholars identify the following factors that may lead to errors and inaccuracies in the online translation of police cautions: (a) the use of ad hoc interpreters and translators that do not have any professional training in working with legal discourse; (b) cross-linguistic and cross-cultural differences that make an accurate rendering of the cautions very challenging; (c) false cognates, such as the Spanish verb *apuntar* (to point to) that can be erroneously used instead of the correct verb *otorgar* (to appoint); (d) long segments and arbitrary turn boundaries which strain the interpreters' ability to render accurate translation and may lead to omissions; (e) interference from interpreters' own understanding of the meaning and legal implications of the cautions; and (f) difficulties in rendering a written text in a face-to-face speech mode (Berk-Seligson, 2000; Connell & Valladares, 2001; Nakane, 2007; Russell, 2000).

To sum up, NNSs of English have difficulty understanding the Miranda warnings because of the warnings' linguistic and conceptual complexity, their use of low-frequency terms, and the lack of logical progression. NNSs' understanding may also be impeded because they are unfamiliar with the Miranda rights, police procedure, and the U.S. criminal justice system.

The use of interpreters or locally created translations is not a viable solution, either. As Berk-Seligson (2000) argues, in translation of the Miranda rights, problems can emerge "even when the interpreter is a highly competent professional and has no conflict of interest with respect to the person who is being questioned" (p. 232). I will return to this issue at the end of the article to argue for standardized translation of the Miranda warnings.

Present study

The present case study examines a videotape and a transcript of a police interrogation of a 22-year-old Russian national, Natasha, a suspect in the murder of another Russian national, Marina.[3] As mentioned earlier, two aspects of Natasha's case distinguish it from the cases just reviewed. The first is Natasha's high level of interactional competence in English. The second is the fact that although the defendants in the cases mentioned earlier were aware of their status as suspects, Natasha believed that she was being interviewed as a witness in the case.

Natasha was born in 1982 and grew up in Moscow. She began to study English in Grade 2 but, in her own words, for the first few years her "knowledge of the language was pure zero" and she received 3s and 2s (Russian equivalents of Cs and Ds) in her English class. When she was in Grade 8, her parents hired an English tutor who gave her private lessons for two school years, from 1995 to 1997. According to Natasha, she acquired most of her knowledge of English grammar through these lessons. In 1998–1999 Natasha spent a year in the United States as a high school exchange student. In her own words: "I could not understand anybody speaking to me and nobody understood a word of what I was saying. For the first 6 months I had problems separating words in the sentences" (p. 4; page numbers refer to the language-learning history that Natasha wrote at my request). She did not take any ESL classes, and it is not clear whether her school actually had an ESL program. Nevertheless, Natasha's speaking ability improved during her stay and her verbal SAT score increased from 420 in the fall of 1998 to 480 in the spring of 1999.

On her return to Moscow, Natasha graduated from high school and entered college. Because she did not perform well on her entrance exam in English, she decided to take French in college. In her 3rd year, in the fall of 2002, Natasha transferred to a U.S. university where she majored in finance and management. When she began her university course work, she "experienced extreme difficulties" with English (language-learning history, p. 6). Because she could not understand her professors, she would often attend all three sections of the same course. During her 2 years at the university she spent most of her time with Russian-speaking friends and made two trips to Russia, during a winter and a summer break.

On December 30, 2004, Natasha was invited to the police headquarters for an interview with Detective S. The interview was conducted in English, and at no point was Natasha offered the services of an interpreter or translations of the English forms. At the end of the interview, she was charged with first degree murder on the basis of circumstantial evidence and detained in a women's correctional facility.[4] Natasha's lawyers questioned the validity of her waiver of rights and filed a motion to suppress the interview. In September of 2005, I was invited as an expert witness to examine the transcripts and to give a professional opinion as to whether Natasha waived her Miranda rights voluntarily, knowingly, and intelligently. The lawyers selected me for two reasons: my expertise in the field of SLA and the fact that I too was a native speaker of Russian. I placed my findings in an expert witness report and presented them at the suppression hearing. After the hearing, Natasha kindly signed a consent form that allowed me to use the data for this research article.

Data analysis

To analyze Natasha's linguistic proficiency at the time of her police interrogation, I examined the following data: (a) a transcript of a phone conversation between Natasha and Detective S on December 30, 2004 (9 pages); (b) a videotape and a transcript of a 5-hour interrogation of Natasha by Detective S on December 30, 2004 (134 pages); (c) Natasha's university transcripts; (d) Natasha's TOEFL and SAT scores; and (e) a language-learning history written in English by Natasha at my request. In other cases, researchers have also administered English language proficiency tests to the defendants (Brière, 1978; Roy, 1990). In the present case, however, testing Natasha's proficiency directly would have been inappropriate because by the fall of 2005 she had spent almost a year in the all-English-speaking environment of the women's correctional facility, and by that time her English proficiency and understanding of legal terms and concepts would not have been identical to her knowledge in December 2004. Consequently, I had to design my own methodology to proceed with the analysis of her proficiency at that time.

To determine Natasha's linguistic proficiency at the time of the interrogation, I examined phonological, morphosyntactic, and lexical properties of Natasha's speech and her conversational strategies, as seen in the videorecording and the transcripts of the phone conversations. I have also analyzed phonological, morphosyntactic, and lexical features of the speech of her interlocutors and their conversational strategies that either facilitated or impeded Natasha's comprehension of questions addressed to her. In addition, I have considered her standardized test scores and university grades.

To analyze Natasha's familiarity with police procedure and her understanding of legal vocabulary, I have examined her questions and comments about legal terms and procedures throughout the interview. To examine whether Russian concepts and cultural frames influenced her performance, I have analyzed language transfer, that is, the influence of Russian on her speech in English.

To analyze how the Miranda Warning Form, a written version of the Miranda warnings, was presented to Natasha and how she signaled her understanding or lack thereof during the interrogation process, I have performed a discourse analysis of the conversational strategies used by Detective S to introduce the form and of the strategies used by Natasha to refer to her Miranda rights. This analysis draws on Leo's (1992) work on deceptive interrogation and on Galasinski's (2000) work on the pragmatics of deception.

My analysis of Natasha's performance also draws on Cummins' (1979, 1984) theoretical framework that differentiates between *basic interpersonal communicative skills* (BICS) and *cognitive academic language proficiency* (CALP) in children with limited English proficiency. BICS, more recently reconceptualized as *interactional competence* (Young, 1999), are used in contexts that support understanding with, for example, verbal and nonverbal cues and instant feedback. CALP is used in context-reduced environments that require higher order thinking skills, such as analysis, synthesis, and evaluation. Eades (2003) underscores the importance of a similar distinction for understanding why defendants, who may appear quite fluent in answering basic biographical questions, are unable to participate in more complex exchanges or, for that matter, process complex legal texts. In accordance with this reasoning, in what follows I adopt the distinction between interactional competence, on the one hand, and linguistic and conceptual competence, on the other, with conceptual competence limited here to a set of legal concepts. EFL learners do not always develop interactional competence before they develop linguistic competence, and some NNSs have high levels of fluency in academic or professional discourses and low levels of interactional competence. The distinction between the two types of competence is not limited to NNSs: Many native speakers may also experience difficulties processing complex texts. What is important for my argument is the relative independence between the levels of interactional competence and levels of linguistic and conceptual competence necessary to process legal texts and exchanges.

Results

Natasha's linguistic proficiency

Throughout the interview, Natasha's pronunciation was fully comprehensible to native speakers of English interacting with her.[5] At the same time, she displayed several segmental and suprasegmental features that contributed to the overall perception of a Russian accent, including an absence of the short-long vowel differentiation and of diphthongs, vowel fronting after glides (in words like *worst* and *work*), and Russian intonation patterns. Her listening comprehension was fully adequate and comprehension difficulties observed during the interrogation did not stem from perceptual or parsing difficulties but from gaps in her lexical and morphosyntactic knowledge.

In the area of morphosyntax, Natasha displayed a preference for simple sentence structure; a typical pattern for her is the following: "He doesn't speak English. That's a very easy here. We live in a Russian area" (interrogation transcript,[6] p. 3). Trying to avoid relative clauses, she produced sentences such as "She had like boyfriend very looking like Michael. Looking like him" (p. 20). It is difficult to judge her comprehension of complex sentences because the detectives interacting with her used mostly simple sentence structure, repetition, and paraphrasing.

Natasha also displayed numerous transfer errors that stem from differences between the Russian and English morphosyntactic systems. Among these errors were (a) omission of subject pronouns, which is acceptable in Russian but not in English; for example, in a comment about her parents she said, "Know no English" (interrogation transcript, p. 2); (b) erroneous tense assignment: Because Russian has a single present tense, she substituted present simple for present progressive and stated that her sister "learns English at school" (p. 3) instead of *is studying English;* (c) omission and incorrect assignment of articles because Russian has no articles, for example, "I never had the dog" (p. 14); "there was a police" (p. 31); and "I have a Adidas shoes" (p. 33); (d) omission and incorrect assignment of prepositions, driven by Russian preposition usage, for example, "pays more attention on chemistry" (p. 3); "I went on the taxi" (p. 10); "I was waiting him at his car" (p. 28); "and he just says me" (p. 29). She also exhibited difficulties with negation, seen in statements such as "I'm very not about the law part. I mean it's not know" (p. 15).

At times, morphosyntactic difficulties interfered with Natasha's comprehension during the interrogation. For instance, she interpreted a question in simple present referring to her parents' occupation as a question in present progressive referring to the parents' activities at this point in the day:

EXTRACT 1

Detective W:	what do your parents do?
Natasha:	sleep.
Detective W:	no (.) I mean (.) what do they do for a <u>living</u>?

(For transcription conventions, see appendix.)

In the area of the lexicon, Natasha favored high frequency words and exhibited several types of lexical difficulties: (a) word-finding difficulties, for example, "like renting a cassette, like tape or videocassette" (interrogation transcript, p. 12); (b) incorrect uses of words, collocations, and lexical phrases, for example, "she's targeting to be a . . . she is targeting to be a doctor of medicine" (p. 3; instead of *she wants to become a doctor*); "I was figuring like how to transport myself better" (p. 27); "I knew I had to make a lot of walking" (p. 33); "it was occasionally in his car" (p. 26; meaning *accidentally*).

In some contexts, Natasha was unable to find English equivalents of Russian words and appealed to Russian loan words that her interlocutors could not understand, for example, "there are like Russian kind of events, *slyot*, it's the, um, people getting together about like, I'm not sure, 3,000 people or something" (interrogation transcript, p. 10); "mobile phone" (p. 42, *mobil'nyi telefon* or *mobil'nik* is a common Russian term for a cell phone). In other contexts, she exhibited forward lexical transfer, using English words in the meanings of their Russian equivalents. For instance, she consistently used the word *company* to mean a specific group of people, "our group," "our crowd," "their group," as would its Russian translation equivalent *kompaniia*, for example, "they were there, it was their company. And then somebody was arranging a party and, uh, they invited that company" (p. 10); "he was really lucky like to get out of that company" (p. 12).

In terms of comprehension, throughout the interview Natasha displayed difficulties understanding medium and low frequency words:

EXTRACT 2

Detective S: you had the tan coat on?=
Natasha: =what?
Detective S: tan coat?
Natasha: what kind (.) what's tan coat?

EXTRACT 3

Detective M: I have to take pictures of your injury (.) all right?
Natasha: of <u>what</u>?
Detective M: your injury (.) the bruises [points toward her body]
Natasha: OK.

Natasha's ability to avoid or repair communication breakdowns through clarification questions, paraphrasing, and circumlocution, and her willingness to communicate and to joke in English suggest a high level of BICS or interactional competence. She did not, however, display a similarly high level of academic success, which relies on CALP. In her language learning history, Natasha mentions extreme difficulties she had with academic English in her university studies. This self-perception is borne out by her scores and by her university transcripts. To begin with, her score of 230 out of 300 on the computer-based version of the TOEFL places her at about the 50th percentile among all the TOEFL takers in the year 2001–2002 (Educational Testing Service, 2003). Natasha's verbal SAT scores of 420 and 480 out of 800 are also relatively low (for comparison, mean scores for the majority of the freshmen admitted to her university are between 660 and 760, only 2% have verbal scores below 500). Her grades are also on the low side: At the time of her arrest, Natasha's cumulative grade point average (GPA) was 2.81

on a 4.0 grade point system and her record displays five C grades (with A+ being the highest and F the lowest possible grade). She also had two incomplete grades and a record of withdrawals from four classes due to comprehension difficulties. The A grades she earned came from two classes on Russian literature (where she had a native speaker advantage), a French class and a low-level class on industrial relations. What is particularly notable is that her grade record showed almost no improvement between the fall of 2002 (B, B+, C) and the fall of 2004 (B, B+, C+).

Overall, Natasha's performance reflects a High-Intermediate (also referred to as Intermediate-High) level of proficiency as described in the *American Council of Teachers of Foreign Language Guidelines* (Breiner-Saunders et al., 2000, p. 16). Speakers at this level can handle uncomplicated routine tasks, exchange basic information related to school, work, and recreation, and produce discourse at paragraph length, using major time frames. Their performance is marked by errors, hesitation, and first language transfer. Nevertheless, they can generally be understood by native speakers unaccustomed to dealing with nonnative speakers.

The lacunae in Natasha's lexical and morphosyntactic knowledge compromise her ability to process decontextualized information. This ability can, however, be enhanced by familiarity with a particular domain of knowledge. Consequently, the next step in my analysis is to examine Natasha's familiarity with legal terms and concepts, referred to here as *conceptual competence*.

Natasha's conceptual competence

The analysis of the video recording and the transcript of the interrogation shows that Natasha is comfortable using low-frequency and culture-specific terms in domains with which she has had personal experience, such as academics (e.g., *GPA, postdoc*), computers (e.g., *computer memory device*), immigration (e.g., *visa, immigrants, refugees, employment authorization*), finance (e.g., *credit card, credit history, customer service*), and service industry (e.g., *calling plan, airport shuttles*). She commented on this selective ability when talking to Detective W: "Especially like in finance kind of field, I mean, I would understand this [a text] perfectly" (interrogation transcript, p. 1).

On the other hand, as mentioned earlier, she displayed a lack of familiarity with several medium- and low-frequency words (e.g., *tan, injury, drawing, hot tub, speed dial*). In particular, she had difficulties understanding words and concepts related to the criminal justice system, a domain with which she had not had any experience prior to the interrogation. She acknowledged this lack to Detective S: "I'm very not about the law part. I mean, it's not know" (interrogation transcript, p. 15). Two terms that she did not seem to understand are *detained* and *waiver of rights*. In her language-learning history, Natasha stated that, at the time of the interrogation, she "did not know the meaning of the word 'detained'. I honestly thought that everyone invited to Police Department for questioning is detained for the time of the questioning" (language-learning history, p. 2). Because she thought she understood the term, she did not question its meaning. *Waiver* is another word that is commonly difficult for learners of English, because, according to the *Collins COBUILD English Dictionary* (1995), its usage falls outside of the 75% of the most frequently used spoken and written English words (see also Stygall, 2002). It is possible that Natasha did not question the meaning of the *waiver of rights* because she was satisfied with her general inference that it had something to do with rights, and, as a witness, she did not see the need for further clarification.

When Natasha finally realized that she was a suspect, she began to ask more questions and exhibited a lack of understanding of terms such as *bail* or *search warrant*:

EXTRACT 4

Detective W: so then once the judge (.) uhm (.) they discuss the charges (.) the judge sets bail
               to make sure that you show up for court (.) with something like [this
Natasha: [sets what?=
Detective W: =bail is (.) uhm uh (.) you post money,
Natasha: oh.

EXTRACT 5

Detective W: this is a copy Natasha of the search warrant that they did from (.) uh (.) that's
               from [[the city]].
Natasha: what (.) what is this?
Detective W: it's a search warrant that was done in [[the city]] on your apartment.

Natasha also appeared to be unfamiliar with the term *trial*, nor did she have any knowledge about the timeline between the arrest and the trial:

EXTRACT 6

Natasha: so how long does it usually take from this point to the real (.) [like,
Detective W: [like a trial?
Natasha: right (.) when I can be defended and,=
Detective W: =it can take a long time (1.5) it can take six months.
Natasha: up to six months or <u>longer</u>?
Detective W: it could take six months or longer (.) I mean (.) it can take a long time.
Natasha: <u>why</u> (.) <u>why</u> is the time difference?

In sum, it appears that at the time of the interrogation Natasha had very little knowledge of the U.S. criminal justice system and of legal terminology. In the absence of this domain-specific knowledge, she relied on the partial understanding she derived from the meanings of separate words and from the verbal and nonverbal cues provided by her interlocutors. Let us then examine the cues provided by Detective S to guide her comprehension.

Presentation of the Miranda Warning Form by Detective S

Although other detectives periodically appeared in the room, Detective S was in charge of the interrogation and he was the one questioning Natasha. He applied what is commonly known as the sympathetic approach to interrogation (Berk-Seligson, 2002); namely, he established rapport with Natasha, engaged in social talk, expressed interest in her Russian background and continuously flattered her appearance and intelligence. He also used a number of deception strategies in presenting the Miranda Warning Form and Natasha's role in the interview.

In contemporary police interrogations, physical coercion has been replaced by manipulation, persuasion, and deception, and these are all legitimate interrogation strategies. I will consider the use of these strategies through the lens of Galasinski's (2000) theory of deception, which was developed in the context of American and British politics but which is applicable to police interrogation as well. Galasinski differentiates between three types of *deception*: (a) deception by concealment or omission of information (the police are not obligated to reveal everything they know about the case); (b) deception through explicit misinformation (the police can misrepresent the nature of the evidence they have); and (c) deception through implicit misinformation that contributes to the interlocutor's acquiring or continuing a belief that suits the purposes of the deceiver (the police may imply that they have a strong case against the suspect without stating so). Furthermore, deception is not limited to the discussion of the case against the suspect—it may also be used in the presentation of the Miranda warnings (Leo, 1992). In the present case, all three types of deception outlined by Galasinski (2000) were used to misrepresent (a) the purpose of the questioning and (b) the nature of the Miranda warnings.

The misrepresentation of the nature and purpose of questioning is, according to legal scholar Richard Leo (1992), one of the most fundamental and overlooked deceptive strategies used by the police. The Court in *Miranda* posited that "warnings must be given only to a suspect who is in custody or whose freedom has otherwise been significantly deprived" (Leo, 1992, pp. 66–67). Nevertheless, Detective S appealed to explicit and implicit misinformation to recast the interrogation of a suspect as an interview of a witness.

On December 30, 2004, Detective S called Natasha, whom he had met previously in the course of the investigation. They chatted for several minutes about her ski trip to the mountains. Then he invited Natasha to come to police headquarters, repeating several times that his goal was to find out more about Natasha's former boyfriend Michael, whose most recent girlfriend Marina was the murder victim in the case:

EXTRACT 7

Detective S: Yeah, I just wanted, there are some things I found out, I guess, um, some things about Michael, um, just some things about, you know, relationship with, you know, as far as just finding out some interesting things about him. Um . . . Kinda wanted to just touch base with you. (telephone conversation transcript, p. 2)

EXTRACT 8

Detective S: [. . .] I, I, just because of things that are, I really want to talk to you about Michael. I mean, there are just some things we've been finding out about him and some, some very interesting stuff about him and, you know, stuff that's been going on so I'd really like to talk to you today about it. (p. 4)

EXTRACT 9

Detective S: Like I said, there were just some things that came up about Michael that are pretty interesting. I'd just like to find out a little bit more about him. (p. 5)

Even though Natasha was already a suspect by that point and her house was being searched for evidence, Detective S repeatedly framed their encounter as an informal conversation about Michael. He also signaled the informality of the interview implicitly, through mitigators and colloquialisms, such as "some things," "some stuff," "kinda," "a little bit more," and "touch base."

Detective S also misrepresented and trivialized the Consular Notification form and the Miranda Warning Form. Leo (1992) also identifies this strategy as a common approach, whereby "some investigators very consciously recite the warnings in a trivializing manner so as to maximize the likelihood of eliciting a waiver" (p. 67). Using a perfunctory tone and ritualistic behavior, the investigators effectively convey "that these warnings are little more than a bureaucratic triviality" (Leo, 1992, p. 67). Detective S, however, went beyond common trivialization, misrepresenting the nature of the documents in question, all the while urging Natasha to trust him.

The following transcript segments illustrate the conversational strategies Detective S used to present the documents as a formal procedure rather than as a warning that Natasha is a suspect and must be conscious of her rights. The first exchange took place early in the interrogation, with Detective S speaking in a very friendly tone and maintaining direct eye contact with Natasha:

EXTRACT 10 (DUE TO PRODUCTION CONSTRAINTS, CONVERSATION
TRANSCRIPTS DO NOT APPEAR IN THEIR ORIGINAL FORMAT)

1	Detective S:	you're from <u>Russia</u> [gestures with both hands toward Natasha] (.)
2		originally (.) you're here in the United States, [gestures with both hands
3		toward himself] (.) you're going to school, [once again gestures toward
4		Natasha with both hands] =
5	Natasha:	=uh-huh=
6	Detective S:	=uhm (.) Russia [points away with his left hand] has its <u>la:ws</u> (.) and all
7		that kind of stuff [dismissive left hand wave] (1.0) and of course we
8		[points to himself] have all the stuff in here (.)=
9	Natasha:	[keeps nodding] =OK=
10	Detective S:	uhm (.) there's some <u>things</u> because of us just sitting and talking [makes a
11		circular gesture with both hands] (.) that I have to do (.) just to (.) I've got
12		to <u>read</u> (.) I'm gonna <u>read</u> something to you here and then I've got to <u>read</u>
13		something else to you just to, =
14	Natasha:	= [smiles] It's like with a procedure, right?=
15	Detective S:	= [smiles] you <u>got</u> it (.) the <u>procedure</u> (.) <u>perfect</u>. [laughs] (.) here (.) let
16		me just put this in front of you so you can see it and I can see it, [places the
17		document on the table so that they both can see it]

Both here and later on, Detective S repeatedly used first person pronouns with modal verbs: "I have to do" (line 11), "I've got to read" (lines 11–12), "I'm gonna read something" (line 12), "I've got to read something else" (lines 12–13). This personalization strategy served to shift attention from Natasha to the detective, making him the agent in this event and framing the documents as something Detective S was obligated to present rather than something that Natasha had to make decisions about. He also used hedging, mitigation, and colloquialisms, referring to important laws and regulations as "all that kind of stuff" (lines 6–7), "some things" (line 10), and "something" (lines 12, 13) to downplay their importance.

To signal her comprehension of this framing, Natasha volunteered the term *procedure*, which Detective S enthusiastically accepted. It is important to note here that the term *procedure* is a partial cognate of the Russian term процедура (*protsedura*) which refers to routine procedure. The Russian word is commonly used to refer to routine procedures and repeated medical treatments, such as regular vitamin shots. This lexical choice suggests that Natasha understands the process of signing the waiver of rights as a formalized procedure and not as an actual decision to be made.

After asking Natasha whether she needs reading glasses, Detective S introduced the first form he has to familiarize her with, Consular Notification:

EXTRACT 11

[Both Detective S and Natasha are looking at the document while talking]

1	Detective S:	because of your <u>nationality</u> (.) we are required to notify your country's
2		<u>consular</u> (.) representatives here in the United States that you have been (.)
3		°well° (.) arrested or detained (.) [waves his left hand in a dismissive
4		manner] °you're just here with us° (.) after your consular officials are
5		notified (.) they may call or <u>visit</u> you. (.) you're <u>not</u> required to accept
6		their assistance but they may be able to help you obtain legal counsel and
7		may contact your <u>family</u> and visit you in (.) in detention among other
8		things (.) we will be <u>notifying</u> your country's consular officials as soon as
9		possible (.) °I'm just <u>reading</u> that to you° [makes another dismissive left
10		hand gesture]
11	Natasha:	OK=
12	Detective S:	=OK?=
13	Natasha:	=I mean (.) is that <u>really</u> necessary?
14	Detective S:	well as far as your consular notification? (.) well (.) just like it says
15		(.) it says actually (.) see this [points to the document] (.) mandatory.
16		[raises both hands with palms up in a gesture that commonly signifies
17		helplessness]
18	Natasha:	like to (.) you want to speak with me (.) you need to do that?
19	Detective S:	yeah, exactly (.) just for us sitting here talking. =
20	Natasha:	=OK.=
21	Detective S:	=so (.) I guess the (.) you know (.) U.S. and all their protections and
22		all that kind of stuff.

Here, Detective S reads Natasha a document that could potentially arouse her suspicions because the consulate needs to be notified only if she is arrested or detained. To minimize the impact of the document and to avoid alerting her to the fact that she is a suspect, Detective S used several verbal and nonverbal strategies. To begin with, he inserted "well" immediately before the words "arrested or detained" (line 3) and follows on line 4 with an implied parenthetical negation, "You're just here with us" (which in fact could be consistent with being in custody). He further deemphasized the words "arrested or detained" (line 3) by using a casual tone and a lack of stress, accompanied by a dismissive wave of his hand. After the statement about notifying her country's officials as soon as possible, Detective S said, "I'm just reading that to you" (line 9), stressing the word *reading* (similar to Extract 10, line 12) and waving his hand to signal that the preceding text has a ritualistic quality that is not to be taken seriously. It is interesting that, whereas in the preceding segments Detective S positioned himself nonverbally as a representative of the United States (e.g., gesturing toward himself when talking about the United States), in this segment he verbally dissociated himself from the "U.S. and all their protections" (line 22). In doing so, he positioned himself as a reasonable adult, somewhat ironic about "all their protections" yet obligated to follow the "mandatory" (line 15) guidelines.

Natasha made two attempts to clarify her status, although she did not ask directly if she was a suspect or a witness. First, she asked whether this document is really necessary if they are just talking (line 13). Detective S offered an evasive answer, stating that the notification is mandatory (lines 14–15), but he did not address Natasha's status, implying that the document is mandatory for witnesses as well. When Natasha repeated her question (line 18), he asserted that signing the document is necessary "just for us sitting here talking" (line 19). In the absence of independent knowledge about legal procedures, Natasha relied on his answers and his casual tone of voice to infer that the situation was nonthreatening, and she displayed this understanding through her friendly and calm demeanor. Then Detective S introduced the next document, the Miranda Warning Form:

EXTRACT 12

1	Detective S:	there's another one I have to do.=
2	Natasha:	=OK [smiles and nods] =
3	Detective S:	=I want to read you that one, (.) OK? [Natasha nods] (.) then we'll we'll
4		get by all of that (.) and then you will sit (.) and I'll have my <u>coffee</u> (.) and
5		you can have some more <u>water</u> (.) what do you think?
6	Natasha:	all right.=
7	Detective S:	= OK [laughs] (.) here let me read this one to you (.) uhm, if there's any
		part of this that you don't understand let me know=
8	Natasha:	=OK=
9	Detective S:	=OK (.) this is who I work for, [[county]] Police Department (.) and this
10		says Miranda Warning Form (.) and this is just your name (.) and then
11		there are some numbers I'll fill in [dismissive hand gesture] [there
12	Natasha:	[you like read
13		this for everybody (.) not the (.) for foreigners only?
14	Detective S:	this is when we're sitting and talking (.) anybody (.) whether [it's
15	Natasha:	[like
16		Michael signed this?=
17	Detective S:	=to sit and talk at some point (.) Michael signed this (.) yes, Georgy, uh,
18		George [[short segment omitted here, to prevent identification]]
19	Detective S:	we do this for [[state]] (.) I mean (.) people in the United States too.=
20	Natasha:	=OK, so they do the same thing?
21	Detective S:	yeah, [nods several times]

Here, Detective S once again appealed to personalization strategies to frame the new form as something relevant for him, as well as for the state and for "people in the United States" (line 19), rather than for Natasha. He continued to use a casual and friendly tone, making references to Natasha's friends and creating rapport. The tone and the rhythm of the delivery, his gestures, and the focus on trivial details ("this is just your name and then there are some numbers I'll fill in there," lines 10–11), all served to signal that the form is yet another formality to get through, and then the two can get down to the important business of drinking coffee and water (lines 4–5).

Natasha was clearly unfamiliar with the Miranda warnings, despite the fact that by the time of the interrogation, she had lived in the United States for 3 years and had a class on the American government system in her first semester of high school. As seen on the videotape, there was not a flicker of recognition on her face at the sound or sight of the word *Miranda*, which should have warned her that she was a suspect. Instead she asked whether this form is read to everyone or foreigners only and whether Michael (a law student) and her other friends had also signed this form. Her questions revealed that she was not familiar with the Miranda warnings, that she did not understand the purpose of the document, and that she did not know who is supposed to sign it, and when they usually sign it.

It was at this point that Detective S committed his most egregious act of deception by explicit misinformation when he stated that "anybody" who sits down to talk to the police signs this form and that all of Natasha's friends had signed it (lines 14, 17–18). In reality, Michael, who was also a suspect at some point had indeed signed the form, but other friends who were interviewed as witnesses did not have to. During cross-examination at the suppression hearing, Detective S admitted that he had lied about this to Natasha. Together, his explicit statements and mitigation strategies served to create an impression that signing the new form was also a formality. Then Detective S placed the form in front of Natasha and read the text to her, carefully enunciating each word:

EXTRACT 13

1	Detective S:	you have the right to remain silent. (.) anything you say can and will be
2		used against you in a court of law. (.) you have the right to talk to a lawyer
3		and to have him present with you while you are being questioned (.) if you
4		cannot afford to hire a lawyer (.) one will be appointed to represent you
5		before any questioning if you wish one (.) if at any time during this
6		interview you wish to discontinue your statement you have the right to do
7		so (.) do you understand each of these rights I have explained to you?
8		[Natasha nods] (.) OK, <u>good</u>. (.) having these rights in mind do you wish
9		to talk to us now?=
10	Natasha:	=right (.) of course,=
11	Detective S:	=OK (.) let me give you [that.
12	Natasha:	[°how can you be silent if you brought me here
13		to talk?°=
14	Detective S:	=let me get you to sign right there on the top line (.) <u>thank you</u>.

Looking closely at Natasha's facial expression during the reading of the document, one could see that the phrase "you have the right to remain silent" (line 1) did not alarm her or conjure any negative associations. Her follow-up question, "How can you be silent if you brought me here to talk?," signaled that she did not understand her right to silence. Although this lack of under-standing could have also been displayed by some native speakers of English, in Natasha's case it was particularly acute because she grew up in Russia, a country that traditionally accorded little importance to the notion of individual rights. Detective S ignored the question and the lack of understanding it signaled. Instead of explaining to Natasha that she was in fact entitled to refuse to talk, he displayed concern for the proper filling out of the document.

To sum up, I argue that Detective S misrepresented the nature and the purpose of questioning and the nature and the purpose of the documents signed by Natasha using three discursive strategies: personalization, hedging/mitigation, and explicit misrepresentation or lying. In doing so, he appealed to three types of deception outlined by Galasinski (2000): (a) deception by concealment or omission of information (Natasha was not told that she was being questioned as a suspect); (b) deception through explicit misinformation (statements that all who come to the police station to talk have to sign the Miranda Warning Form and that all of Natasha's friends did so); and (c) deception through implicit misinformation that contributes to the interlocutor's acquiring or continuing a belief that suits the purposes of the deceiver (trivialization, minimization, and misrepresentation of the Miranda Warning Form as a harmless routine procedure).

Natasha's understanding of her rights

Because Natasha did not know much about the U.S. criminal justice system or the legal terminology, she was very susceptible to Detective S's misrepresentation of the interview and the documents shown to her. Natasha did not understand that she was a suspect and not a witness until an hour and a half into the interrogation, when she asked Detective S directly: "So you mean I killed the persons?" (interrogation transcript, p. 55), "So you're saying I'm involved? You're saying I killed somebody? That's what you are saying?" (p. 57). If Natasha had been able to identify the Miranda Warning Form for what it was, she would have asked these questions immediately. Furthermore, if, as the prosecution argued, she understood the rights presented to her earlier and chose to speak regardless, this would have been the time to invoke her rights and to discontinue the interview. Instead, she proceeded with the conversation for several more minutes and only then began making attempts to invoke her rights, which Detective S either ignored or purposefully misinterpreted:

EXTRACT 14

Natasha:	I really don't like this=
Detective S:	=it's, it's because people feel that way, OK? (.) about people that are (.) that were close to them (.) OK?

In Extract 14, Natasha's utterance responded to a series of statements made by Detective S that implicated her in the murder of Marina. Her use of the present tense suggests that she resents these implications. Detective S reframed her discomfort as one with Michael's having a new girlfriend, rather than one with his interrogation.

A little later, Natasha again communicated her discomfort:

EXTRACT 15

Detective S:	you needed to do something to <u>protect</u> yourself (.) you needed to do something to <u>defend</u> yourself (.) you needed [to
Natasha:	[it seems like I need to defend myself [. . .] [laughs] =
Detective S:	=well (.) against this <u>person</u> (.) against this (.) against <u>Marina</u> (.) is that what happened? (.) did she actually do something to <u>you</u>? (.) did she hit <u>you</u> first? [did she
Natasha:	[I don't know (.) I don't know the girl.

Once again, Natasha's use of the present tense suggests that she is talking about the need to defend herself at the moment, against the accusations made by Detective S. Detective S however reframed her comment as related to Natasha's interaction with the murder victim.

Eventually, 3 hours into the interrogation Natasha asked if they could stop talking:

EXTRACT 16

1	Natasha:	can I ask you a question?=
2	Detective S:	=please.=
3	Natasha:	=like I'm <u>really</u> tired (.) is it possible to like stop it at this point?
4	Detective S:	to do (.) you want a couple of (.) do you want me to step out for a couple

```
 5                          of moments and [you
 6    Natasha:                            [for today=
 7    Detective S:   =you want (1.0) a couple of moments? (.) you want the rest of the day?
 8                          what would you like?
 9    Natasha:        the rest of the day.=
10    Detective S:   =the rest of the day? OK.
11    Natasha:        can I go home?
12    Detective S:   I (.) let me walk out and we'll (.) we'll work something out for you.
```

It was clear that Natasha did not understand that she had the right to silence; instead she asked for permission to stop talking (line 3). Detective S took advantage of her inability to invoke her rights unambiguously and pretended that he did not understand her intent, asking if he should just step out for a couple of minutes (lines 4–5). When she clearly stated "for today" (line 6), he repeated in a more irritated tone "You want a couple of moments? You want the rest of the day? What would you like?" (lines 7–8) in an intent to discourage her from stopping, and he eventually continued the interrogation (notably, the court ruled to suppress the transcript from this point forward).

Natasha was also unclear about her right to an attorney. It may be relevant to point out that in Russia it is not customary to have an attorney present during the interrogation. Instead, she kept repeating: "I do need to help myself. I want to help myself but I don't know how. I don't know how at this point" (p. 97). Eventually, she remembered reading about attorneys in the Miranda Warning Form and realized that this information was relevant to her present situation. She did not however have a full understanding of the right and asked another clarification question:

EXTRACT 17

```
Natasha:        I have a question (.) like you remember those rights in the papers?
Detective S:    yes.
Natasha:        so (.) I mean (.) at this point I need a lawyer I guess?=
Detective S:    =that's entirely up to you, Natasha.
```

Just as he ignored her initial attempts to invoke her right to silence, Detective S ignored Natasha's indirect invocation of her right to an attorney because she worded it as a question. Rather, he treated it as a genuine question and stated that the responsibility for this decision was hers. Natasha then repeatedly asked for permission to make a phone call to her father in Russia because she needed his help to find and hire a lawyer. Detective S ignored her requests and continued to intimidate and badger her into talking to him:

EXTRACT 18

```
 1    Natasha:       [visibly upset] so (.) can I ask my father if I (.) if I can afford a lawyer (.)
 2                          and if I cannot what (.) how much is a lawyer? like how [much . . .
 3    Detective S:                                                                                  [I have no idea
 4                          [in an assertive tone of voice] (.) let me ask you [this
 5    Natasha:                                                                              [I don't like all this
 6    Detective S:                                                                              [a lawyer for after
 7                          today or for right now today while we're talking?=
```

8	Natasha:	=like it should be the same person, right?=
9	Detective S:	=do you want (.) do you want to keep talking with me <u>right now</u>?=
10	Natasha:	=I do want to keep talking with you=
11	Detective S:	=OK=
12	Natasha:	=but the little things that I say (.) like with this paper and (.) I mean I
13		could (1.0) throw it away or something (.) <u>right</u>? (.) but it's mostly <u>natural</u>
14		way of things like (.) and you are trying to say that because of this [paper
15	Detective S:	[in an emphatic assertive manner] [I have
16		to ask you this (.) I have to ask you this (.) do you want to keep
17		talking with me <u>right now</u>?=
18	Natasha:	=I mean=
19	Detective S:	=do you [want
20	Natasha:	[I feel like unprotected talking with you. I'm telling you
21		the truth.
22	Detective S:	You feel like you're protected?=
23	Natasha:	=I'm not protected=
24	Detective S:	=<u>Not protected</u>? [faking surprise]
25	Natasha:	[crying] not protected (.) unprotected (.) like I'm (.) I'm telling you the
26		<u>truth</u> (.) the whole truth (.) I told you (.) I went I tried (.) like I walked
27		around the apartment (.) I (.) I mean (.) but I never inside (.) I'm telling
28		you (.) and you are like not listening to me (.) you're trying to push me if
29		I'm like (.) I didn't go inside.
30	Detective S:	what did you do when you left that day?

Throughout this conversation, Natasha tried to communicate to the best of her ability that she felt unprotected in this interrogation (lines 20, 23, 25) and that she wanted an attorney (lines 1, 2, 8). Her questions show that she did not understand that she can simply request an attorney and that one will be provided to her free of charge. Rather, she said she hoped that her father can hire an attorney for her (line 1).

According to U.S. law, if an individual undergoing custodial interrogation requests an attorney or invokes his or her right to silence, the interrogation must cease until an attorney is present. It is important to note, however, that the suspect must unambiguously request counsel during the interrogation, and this rule clearly disadvantages NNSs of English who may not know how to communicate an unequivocal request (Einesman, 1999; Shuy, 1997). Einesman (1999) cites several cases where NNSs' questions such as "Do you think I need a lawyer?" and "I can't afford a lawyer but is there any way I can get one?" were not found to be unambiguous requests for counsel. Detective S took advantage of the fact that Natasha's invocations were ambiguous and, despite her repeated statements about feeling unprotected, proceeded with the interrogation (line 30). As indicated earlier, however, the court suppressed the transcript from an earlier point where Natasha asked if it was possible for them to stop (Extract 16).

Natasha represents an outstanding example of an intelligent, well-educated NNS of English whose proficiency is sufficient to maintain social conversations and minimal academic perform-ance but not to process complex texts in an unfamiliar domain. Her interactional competence hindered rather than helped in the interrogation process because it led her to rely on verbal and nonverbal cues provided by Detective S. Unaware that police officers are permitted to deceive suspects during the interrogation, Natasha assumed that Detective S was telling the truth and that the information he provided was correct. Consequently, she viewed herself as a witness and the Miranda Warning Form as a routine form signed by all witnesses. As seen in her questions about the right to silence and the right to an attorney later in the interrogation, she did not fully understand her rights when the Miranda Warning Form was presented to her. Yet she did not ask any questions about them because Detective S led her to think of the form as a trivial and routine procedure. I also did not see any evidence that Natasha understood what it meant to waive her rights when she signed the waiver of rights. Consequently, based on my analysis of the data provided to me, I concluded that, in my professional opinion, Natasha did not sign the Miranda Warning Form "with a full awareness of both the nature of the right being abandoned and the consequences of the decision to abandon it" (Einesman, 1999, p. 11) and thus did not waive her rights voluntarily, knowingly, and intelligently.

Conclusion

As Einesman (1999) rightly points out, the Court that decided *Miranda v. Arizona* in 1966 could not foresee how profoundly the demographic composition of the United States would change in the coming years. Yet the decision coincided in time with a major change in U.S. immigration policy, the 1965 Immigration and Nationality Act that eliminated previous national origin quotas and opened the country once again to immigrants from all over the world. This and subsequent immigration legislation led to a major influx of immigrants and refugees into the country. By 2000, 18% of the total population aged 5 and over, or 47 million people, reported that they spoke a language other than English at home, up from 11% in 1980 and 14% in 1990. California had the largest percentage of NNSs of English (39%), followed by New Mexico (37%), Texas (31%), New York (28%), Hawaii (27%), Arizona (26%), and New Jersey (26%) (United States Census Bureau, 2000).

These demographic changes are not unique to the United States—they are happening in other English-speaking countries, in particular the United Kingdom and Australia. To ensure linguistic rights of NNSs of English, Australian authorities have recently begun cooperating with local linguists. Thus, translations of police cautions have been tape-recorded in 15 indigenous languages (Mildren, 1999). And in New South Wales, public critiques of police interview procedures have led the local police to revise their procedures and cautions in consultation with their most outspoken public critic, forensic linguist John Gibbons (see Gibbons, 2001, 2003).

It is my hope that the U.S. legal system will follow suit in ensuring the linguistic rights of NNSs of English. To do so, we need to move away from debating what constitutes sufficient English proficiency to understand the Miranda rights. Rather, NNSs of English at all levels of proficiency should have the information presented to them in English and in their native language in one of three formats: (a) standardized written translations of the Miranda warnings, created on either the federal or state level by committees consisting of certified court interpreters, forensic linguists, and legal experts; (b) tape recordings of the same translated texts (for suspects with low levels of literacy); or (c) oral translations by certified court interpreters in cases where written or tape-recorded translations are temporarily unavailable. Solan and Tiersma (2005) further argue that these translations should not be literal, rather they should "convey the content in a way that is understandable to speakers of the language in question" (p. 84).

Meanwhile, the ESL establishment can do its part to ensure that NNSs of English are not penalized for their lack of language proficiency or understanding of the U.S. legal system and incorporate modules that familiarize the learners with the Common law system, introduce basic legal terms and concepts, and offer hands-on practice with common legal forms, such as the Miranda Warning Form. Invited speakers from the legal and law enforcement communities could talk about individual rights in the police interview process, interactional norms that accompany a routine traffic stop, a witness interview, or interrogation of a suspect, permissibility and limits on deception in police interviews, and ways in which one could get legal aid. Useful materials for such courses can be found in textbooks created for teaching legal English (e.g., Lee, Hall & Hurley, 1999). Students' understanding can also be enhanced through discussions of examples from popular fiction and the media, including films, such as *Twelve Angry Men*, and television shows, such as *Boston Legal*, that illustrate the functioning of the jury system or the presumption of innocence. Finally, just as they talk about cross-cultural differences in cuisine or holiday celebrations, students should be encouraged to research and reflect on differences between the Common law system adopted in the United States and the one adopted in their native country. In this way, the module could become an intrinsic part of a larger discussion of the rights guaranteed by the U.S. constitution to U.S. citizens as well as to those who find themselves, however temporarily, on American soil.

Appendix

Transcription conventions

(.)	short pause, less than 1 second
(2.0)	timed long pause (in the example, two second pause)
=	utterances latched onto the preceding or following turn
[	simultaneous or overlapping speech
<u>good</u>	emphasis
goo:d	vowel lengthening
good?	rising intonation, as in a question
good,	rising intonation, suggesting intention to continue speaking
good.	falling (utterance final) intonation, full stop
°good°	change in voice used to mark parenthetical comments
[. . .]	inaudible or incomprehensible word or utterance
[laughter]	transcriber's description (e.g., laughter, smiling, nodding, gestures, etc.)
[[county]]	words taken out of the transcription to prevent identification of the case

Notes

1 Common law derives from English law and is adopted in the United States, the United Kingdom (apart from Scotland), Australia, New Zealand, most of Canada, and former Anglo-American colonies. Common law is case based; that is, court decisions become precedents for future decisions. Most countries have legal systems based on Civil law, which developed out of Roman law. Civil law is code based; that is, legislation is seen as the primary source of law and courts make decisions by drawing analogies from statutory provisions. In criminal cases, the differences between the two systems are expressed in the way investigations, arrests, and trials are conducted. In the Common law system, the state has the burden to prove guilt, which is decided at trial, whereas in the Civil law system, guilt is determined primarily in the pretrial process, and at the trial the accused must disprove that he or she is guilty.

2 It is important to note that the warnings are read only to suspects, not to witnesses.

3 To preserve confidentiality, all names have been changed.

4 The case has been retried, and the outcome of the trial is not yet known; however, Natasha's guilt or innocence are incidental to the purpose of this article because linguistic rights should be accorded to all NNSs of English.

5 Throughout, my analysis addresses exclusively the level of proficiency that Natasha displayed during her interrogation by police on December 30, 2004.

6 Throughout, page numbers are given based on the official interrogation transcript.

References

Berk-Seligson, S. (2000). Interpreting for the police: Issues in pre-trial phases of the judicial process. *Forensic Linguistics*, 7, 212–237.

Berk-Seligson, S. (2002). The Miranda warnings and linguistic coercion: The role of footing in the interrogation of a limited-English-speaking murder suspect. In Cotterill, J. (Ed.), *Language in the legal process* (pp. 127–143). New York: Palgrave Macmillan.

Breiner-Sanders, K., Pardee, L., Miles, J., & Swender, E. (2000). ACTFL proficiency guidelines—Speaking. Revised 1999. *Foreign Language Annals*, 33(1), 13–18.

Brière, E. (1978). Limited English speakers and the Miranda rights. *TESOL Quarterly*, 12, 235–245.

Collins COBUILD English Dictionary. (1995). London: Harper Collins.

Connell, J., & Valladares, R. (2001). Cultural factors in motions to suppress. 25-MAR Champion, 18. Retrieved January 15, 2005, from Westlaw, pp. 1–13.

Cook, G., & Kasper, G. (Eds.). (2005). Applied linguistics and real-world issues [Special issue]. *Applied Linguistics*, 26(4).

Cotterill, J. (2000). Reading the rights: A cautionary tale of comprehension and comprehensibility. *Forensic Linguistics*, 7, 4–25.

Cummins, J. (1979). Cognitive/academic language proficiency, linguistic interdependence, the optimal age question, and some other matters. *Working Papers on Bilingualism*, 19, 197–205.

Cummins, J. (1984). Wanted: A theoretical framework for relating language proficiency to academic achievement among bilingual students. In C. Rivera (Ed.), *Language proficiency and academic achievement*. Clevedon, England: Multilingual Matters.

Dinh, Ph. (1995). Self-incrimination clause requires that suspects understand plain meaning of Miranda rights before making valid waiver—State v. Leuthavone. *Suffolk University Law Review*, 619. Retrieved January 15, 2005, from Westlaw, pp. 1–6.

Eades, D. (2003). Participation of second language and second dialect speakers in the legal system. *Annual Review of Applied Linguistics*, 23, 113–133.

Educational Testing Service. (2003). TOEFL test and score data summary. Princeton, NJ: Author. Available from www.ets.org/Media/Research/pdf/TOEFLSUM-0203.pdf

Einesman, F. (1999). Confessions and culture: The interactions of Miranda and diversity. *Journal of Criminal Law and Criminology*, 90, 1–47. Retrieved January 15, 2005, from Westlaw, pp. 1–33.

Figueroa, T. (2005). Obstacles arise when interrogating non-English speakers. *North County Times*, January 22, 2005. Retrieved December 27, 2005 at www.nctimes.com/articles/2005/01/24/news/top_stories/22_08_521_22_05.txt

Galasinski, D. (2000). *The language of deception: A discourse analytical study*. Thousand Oaks, CA: Sage.

Gibbons, J. (1990). Applied linguistics in court. *Applied Linguistics*, 11, 229–237.

Gibbons, J. (1996). Distortions of the police interview process revealed by video-tape. *Forensic Linguistics*, 3(2), 289–298.

Gibbons, J. (2001). Revising the language of New South Wales police procedures: Applied linguistics in action. *Applied Linguistics*, 22, 439–469.

Gibbons, J. (2003). *Forensic linguistics: An introduction to language in the justice system*. Oxford: Blackwell.

Lee, D., Hall, C., & Hurley, M. (1999). *American legal English: Using language in legal contexts*. Ann Arbor: University of Michigan Press.

Leo, R. (1992/1998). From coercion to deception: The changing nature of police interrogation in America. Reprinted in R. Leo, & G. Thomas III (Eds.), *The Miranda debate: Law, justice, and policing* (pp. 65–73). Boston: Northeastern University Press.

Leo, R., & Thomas, G., III. (Eds.). (1998). *The Miranda debate: Law, justice, and policing*. Boston: Northeastern University Press.

McGroarty, M. (Ed.). (2003). Language contact and change [Special issue]. *Annual Review of Applied Linguistics*, 23.

Mildren, D. (1999). Redressing the imbalance: Aboriginal people in the criminal justice system. *Forensic Linguistics*, 6, 137–160.

Nakane, I. (2007). Communicating the suspect's rights: Problems in interpreting the caution in police interviews. *Applied Linguistics*, 28, 87–112.

Roy, J. (1990) The difficulties of limited-English-proficient individuals in legal settings. In Rieber, R. & W. Stewart (Eds.), *The language scientist as expert in the legal setting: Issues in forensic linguistics* (pp. 73–83). New York: The New York Academy of Sciences.

Russell, S. (2000). "Let me put it simply . . .": The case for a standard translation of the police caution and its explanation. *Forensic Linguistics, 7,* 26–48.

Shuy, R. (1997). Ten unanswered language questions about Miranda. *Forensic Linguistics, 4,* 175–196.

Shuy, R. (1998). *The language of confession, interrogation and deception.* Thousand Oaks, CA: Sage.

Solan, L., & Tiersma, P. (2005). *Speaking of crime: The language of criminal justice.* Chicago, IL: University of Chicago Press.

Stygall, G. (2002) Textual barriers to United States immigration. In J. Cotterill (Ed.), *Language in the legal process.* (pp. 35–53). New York: Palgrave Macmillan.

United States Census Bureau. (2000). United States Census 2000. Retrieved December 29, 2005, from www.census.gov/main/www/cen2000.html

Young, R. (1999). Sociolinguistic approaches to SLA. Annual Review of Applied Linguistics, 19, 105–132.

Chapter 26

GUY COOK, MATT REED, AND ALISON TWINER

'BUT IT'S ALL TRUE!'

Commercialism and commitment in the discourse of organic food promotion (2009)

THIS ARTICLE DISCUSSES the findings of a one-year research project investigating the language of organic food promotion in Britain in 2006, the thinking of those behind it, and public reactions to it. As in earlier projects on food controversies (Cook and O'Halloran 1999; Cook et al. 2004; Cook et al. 2006), a key element of our approach is to combine corpus linguistics, close textual analysis, interviews, and focus group discussions to arrive at a rich understanding of the language used, its origins and effects. The project is therefore neither an exercise in textual analysis alone, nor an investigation of opinions and ideas without reference to how these are realized linguistically. By combining approaches, we hope to contribute to the development of a multi-perspective discourse analytic methodology, as advocated by, *inter alia*, Stubbs (1996), Widdowson (2004), Wodak et al. (1999).

1 Background: the organic food landscape

The 2000s have witnessed an unprecedented boom in organic business worldwide, and in the United Kingdom particularly (Sahota 2007). This expansion has led both to diversification and to an overall change in character. Organic food products are now no longer the domain only of those who believe in them for reasons of principle, but can be found in all types and scales of food production and retail: from major supermarkets, to small, independent, and committed producers selling directly to their customers. There are also non-profit-making organizations campaigning for organics, arguing for its positive environmental, health, and social effects. We shall distinguish in this article between 'corporate' and 'independent' organic sectors, and we shall use the term 'organic movement' to embrace both this independent sector and campaign organizations.

Since its inception, there has always been a multiple political identity in the organic movement (Reed 2001). Nevertheless, some general political and economic implications of contemporary support for organics can be identified. Firstly we can say that, whereas in the past, organic farming often involved material sacrifice, and for many an acceptance of a more frugal lifestyle for reasons of principle, recent commercial successes have seen some organic producers and retailers become highly profitable, and likely to be seen more as models of commercial entrepreneurial success than political commitment (Wright and McCrea 2007). Secondly, the organic movement as a whole, whether left or right, rich or poor, can be characterized as opposed to large-scale globalized economic distribution chains, and supportive of more localized community-based production and consumption. These two characteristics may of course be in conflict. Some writers have gone as far as to criticize the organic food movement for joining the corporate food industry it initially opposed (Guthman 2004; Pollan 2006; Fromartz 2006).

Many organic farmers, however, continue to perceive the production and retail of organic produce as a form of environmental campaigning. Their attempt to change economic and social organization through the market-place necessarily involves a degree of engagement with corporate capitalism on its own terms. Many campaigners see consumer action rather than legislation as the way to limit corporate irresponsibility and promote in its place environmental protection, fair trade, community-based production, localized distribution networks, and ethical employment practices (Tormey 2007). They hope to exert pressure on the large food corporations who, in response to the market, now also produce and promote organic foods, though they cannot by definition adopt the small-scale production and localized distribution networks advocated by their opponents.

Changes in the market for organics have been accompanied by changes in the organic movement's promotional strategies. Thus the fast-moving interaction between the corporate and independent organic sector is not only of economic and political interest, but also for discourse analysis. Organic food promotion can provide key insights into the degree to which political and commercial persuasive language may be converging or remaining distinct (Moloney 2006). This article considers the communicative strategies of committed advocates of organic farming when they take on the corporate food establishment literally in its own terms: using words to promote products. Do they adopt the same linguistic and rhetorical strategies as their opponents, or develop a different marketing discourse of their own? And if they do adopt standard marketing language, and the beliefs that go with it, does this have implications for the integrity of their campaigns?

Our work is unusual as discourse analysis for its combination of corpus analysis to identify significant and typical language choices in a database of texts, with an investigation of why the creators of those texts used language in the way that they did, and how their target audience reacted to their choices. Despite a recent attempt to marry interviewee perceptions of pronoun use to corpus analysis (Harwood 2006, 2007), this is a neglected dimension of contemporary discourse analysis, where the tendency is to focus either on texts in isolation, as in much corpus analysis and arguably some systemic functional linguistics (Widdowson 1997), or on the users' perceptions of what is happening in communication, as in ethnography, without integrating findings with corpus-based descriptions of large amounts of data. Despite some well-documented limitations in the reliability of both interview and focus group data, which we address below, we believe our integrated approach can uncover significant trends in the direction and development of food marketing discourse, which in turn reflects major social and political developments.

2 Data

To these ends, we collected and analyzed three datasets:

1. A 500,000-word machine-readable corpus of organic food promotion texts including product labels and packaging, newsletters, adverts, reports, press releases, with a balance between multiple and independent retailers, farm types, and the British nations and regions. A 250,000-word machine-readable corpus of promotional material for non-organic food was

also collected for comparison. Corpus analysis software (Wordsmith Tools 4.0) identified frequent words and collocations, as well as statistically significant words referred to as 'keywords' (Scott 2005).[1] Results guided the selection of typical texts for close analysis and for discussion with focus groups and interviewees.

2. Transcriptions of interviews with sixteen stakeholders responsible for the communicative strategies of organizations promoting organic food. These included representatives of influential lobby groups, certification agencies, organic producers and retailers, food writers, and major supermarkets.

3. Transcriptions and recordings of eight focus groups (representing a variety of ages, incomes, ethnic and family profiles)[2] who explored product labels and a promotional leaflet. Focus group discussions and interviews were transcribed in full to allow greater attention to linguistic detail (Myers 2004: 44; Myers and McNaghten 1999). They were also coded for content using qualitative software (Atlas.ti), allowing identification of themes not always revealed through corpus analysis.

3 The language of organic food promotion

3.1 Supermarkets

As an aim of our project was to evaluate to what extent the organic movement has adopted the marketing practices of corporate retail, a good starting point is an example of current organic packaging by Tesco, the UK's largest supermarket: 'Tesco organic baby new potatoes'. The 'degradable packaging' for this product is largely transparent, allowing the customer to see the potatoes inside. A black rectangle with bright green leaves in the right-hand half (common across the product line), prominently displays the wording:

(1) TESCO
     Organic
     Baby new potatoes
     A specially selected new potato, delicious with chopped mint or chives
     BOILED POTATOES ARE LOWER IN FAT THAN PASTA OR RICE
     HIGH IN FOLIC ACID
     Organic certification UK4.
     Grown to strict organic standards

The place of origin is given as Egypt,[3] although a black rectangle on the back includes a photo-graph of rolling green countryside (presumably English and definitely not Egyptian), and the words:

(2) These organic baby new potatoes have been sourced to guarantee consistent availability and quality.
     Tesco farmers work with nature, helping to maximize wildlife on their farms and growing wild flowers to discourage pests.
     The beneficial effects of working with the environment leads to the best tasting, healthy crops that Tesco customers expect.
     Tesco organic produce meets the standards laid down by the law in the European Union and by the UK government.

There is also smaller print information about preparation, storage, and nutrition, etc.

This wording and presentation have characteristics which we found through our corpus analysis to be typical of high-profile corporate organic food promotion. There is patterning of language fulfilling a poetic function (Jakobson 1960), exemplified here by the alliterative 'specially selected' and 'chopped mint or chives', and the similar rhythms of 'organic/baby new potatoes' and 'delicious/with chopped mint or chives'. As in poetry, line breaks are determined by factors other than reaching the margin (Cook 2001: 126). Imagery is sensual and tactile: 'baby', 'delicious', 'specially selected', 'chopped'. The back panel, though no doubt factually correct, deploys vague language (Channell 1994; Cutting 2007), which distracts from issues of detail. Thus describing the food as 'sourced' avoids giving particulars of relations between retailer and supplier, as does 'Tesco farmers' – a phrase which presumably includes both organic and non-organic farmers. The claims that they 'work with nature', 'help [. . .] to maximize wildlife', 'discourage pests' are far from specific. The fourth paragraph, though perhaps impressive on a casual reading, is somewhat superfluous: if organic produce did not meet these legal standards it could not be sold as organic.

This packet then exemplifies certain typical features of corporate organic food promotion. Another common tactic is to offer a story of production, naming the farmer,[4] and focusing upon small-scale traditional farming methods, with particular emphasis on animal welfare. We can exemplify this with another supermarket package: 'Waitrose 12 Organic English Pork Chipolatas'. The pastel-shaded packaging features a picture of two smiling pigs. Wording on the front includes:

(3) Waitrose organic Chipolatas are made from selected cuts of belly and shoulder of pork from organically reared, English pigs. The pork is coarsely chopped and blended with herbs and spices to produce succulent and full flavoured chipolatas. Our organic pigs are reared outside with freedom to root and roam on selected farms in Norfolk and Lincolnshire.

And on the back:

(4) James Keith supplies Waitrose exclusively, with pigs from his farm in Norfolk. The pigs are reared outdoors throughout their lives in small family groups and fed on a balanced cereal diet with vitamins and minerals. Warm shelters and straw bedding protect them from winter, while mud baths keep them cool in summer. James' expertise, care and commitment to the more extensive nature of organic farming ensures we deliver consistently high quality and traceable sausages.

Here again, as on the Tesco label, we have poetic forms ('root and roam') and sensual semantics ('coarsely chopped . . . succulent and full-flavoured').

A recurrent theme in British organic food promotion is an idealized rural idyll of non-industrial farming, using bucolic imagery presumably designed to appeal to the predominantly urban British population. We found words denoting farm realia to be significantly frequent in organic promotion across the sector. A corpus comparison of words on packaging showed the following among the first 250 organic-corpus keywords using the non-organic corpus as a reference:

pollen, land, animals, poultry, birds, cattle, feed, chickens, flour, broiler, broilers, manure, clover, livestock, pollination, insects, pasture, earth, flours, flock, grass, compost, grazing, seed, sheep, bees, landscape, moorland, fed, farmer, mountain, fields, hedges, wheatgrass, grass, feeding.

In contrast, non-organic corpus keywords indicate an imagery which is predominately in the kitchen rather than on the farm. Organic food promotion seems to have reconceptualized the relation between farm and customer, refocusing on the point of production rather than of retail or consumption. This innovative focus appears to have originated in smaller retailers, where close relations with producers lend it credibility, and then to have been copied by supermarkets, in a process of discourse appropriation.

In keeping with this emphasis on the physical experience of being on the farm is an imagery which is sensual and tactile ('Warm shelters. . . . straw bedding . . . mud baths'), and an almost anthropomorphic depiction of animals and their relations to humans ('bedding', 'baths', 'freedom', 'family groups', the picture of smiling pigs). Related to this sensuality, is an emphasis on pleasurable sensation, particularly 'tastiness'. Words referring to taste (*flavour, taste, tastiness*) and further modifying them (*delicate, delicious, distinctive, flavoursome, full, intense, mouth-watering, natural, peppery, real, succulent, superb, sweet, tangy, tasty, unique, wonderful*) are notably frequent in our organic corpus. Often they occur in expanded noun phrases (NPs) with a proliferation of pre- and post-modifiers, such as the 20-word NP on a Duchy ready-made meal packet:

(5) This flavoursome recipe is made from [tender pieces of organic British chicken breast marinated in organic cider with a fresh butter glazed apple and cider sauce].

Such abundance of modification arguably represents iconically the extravagance it recommends:

(6) (Duchy New Handmade Fudge)
Our new fudge has [an indulgent and smooth texture, with a melt-in-the-mouth sensation]. It is [the perfect sweet treat for your sweetheart this Valentine's Day]. . .

Such combinations of an emphasis on sensation with verbal excess can be found in smaller producers of organic food promotion, too.

Personal information about producers and their farms, often using first names to create a pseudo familiarity, lends itself to another common marketing technique: an apparently dialogic style in which the product is described as though producer and consumer were in direct face-to-face conversational interaction, even when there is no interactive dialogue or intimate relationship between sender and receiver. (This common technique in persuasive market discourse is described by Fairclough [1992] as 'synthetic personalization'.) Though not evident in the Tesco packaging, and only minimally in the Waitrose packaging ('our' in 'our organic pigs'), this tactic is common in other supermarket packaging, and is present across the sector, particularly favored by box schemes:

(7) (Organic box scheme)
Food should tell a story and, because we know what it is, we can tell you: from farm to table, the Riverford way.

As shown in other research on public relations and marketing language (Swales and Rogers 1995; Koller 2007a, 2007b, 2009; Mulderrig 2006, 2007; Cook 2004: 62–75, 2007, 2008), this foregrounding of the interpersonal (Halliday 1973: 22–46) is reflected in a very high incidence of first and second person pronouns.[5] The word form *we* is the 12th most frequent word in our organic corpus.[6] The word form *you* is 27th.[7] By contrast, the third-person pronouns *he* (position 268), *she* (position 786), *they* (position 38) are comparatively rare. The atmosphere of personal interaction is also created by a preference for contractions over full forms (*don't* not *do not*) and familiar over formal lexis (*Mums* not *Mothers*) and phrasing (*fork out, weird and wonderful*).

3.2 Common characteristics of corporate and independent organic food promotion language

Analysis of supermarket own-brands in our corpus suggests that they have certain common characteristics, of which the two labels analyzed above are illustrative. Their language (outside the obligatory factual information relating to ingredients, nutrition, expiry, etc.) tends to be poetic, vague, sensual and 'earthy', story-telling, and conversational, with emotive appeals to a rural idyll and animal welfare. These same typical characteristics are found in promotional language across the independent organic sector, from – least surprisingly – the large organic brands such as Yeo Valley, through the box schemes, to the smallest organic producers.

When it comes to story telling, rural imagery, personalization, and dialogue, however, the echoes across texts from different types of organic food promotion are striking. Thus the Waitrose description above is uncannily similar to this newsletter extract from a large and successful organic box scheme, delivering organic produce directly to customers' doorsteps:

(8) (Box-scheme newsletter)
Other pigs trot about playfully, following us to sniff our clothes with their wet noses and chew our trainers (. . . .) There are roomy huts to give the pigs shade, and during the summer Will makes sure they get plenty of mud to wallow in, which gives their skin a protective 'sunscreen'. (. . . . .) The cows have shiny, healthy coats

Or to this description in the Web pages of a small-scale organic pork producer:

(9) Oxford Sandy and Black pigs are renowned for their excellent temperament and mothering abilities, their friendly nature and hardiness. They produce succulent pork, fine bacon and excellent ham. The pigs are free range with plenty of space to roam, grazing on lush grass, foraging and generally enjoying themselves. Because the herd is organic, their diet is completely natural and free from hormones, growth promoters and antibiotics.

They have sheds for shelter, and build nests in the long grass to farrow and create pig shaped depressions in damp places for wallowing in mud. They spend much of their time rooting through the grass, digging for tasty morsels, and making trenches to sunbathe. The piglets are naturally weaned by their mothers, and stay in family groups.

And this last company also provides a striking and humorous example of pseudo face-to-face interaction in print:

(10) OK—now concentrate—there are questions later! We have some sows that are 50% Wild Boar and 50% OSB, and some sows that are 75% Wild Boar and 25% OSB. This means that some of the piglets are 75% Wild Boar and some are 87.5% Wild Boar. With me so far? Sometimes we cross a Wild Boar X sow to Scratchy, the OSB Boar. You can work that one out yourself! The result? Fantastically tasty pork! Just in case you are wondering, the Wild Boar Boar (*sic*) is called Nigel. No, we did not name him. No, he does not come to call.

While it might be tempting to assume that such similarities emanate from the larger corporate promotional strategies and are picked up by smaller producers in the belief that this must be 'marketing that works', there is also the possibility of influence in both directions, with the supermarkets appropriating strategies from the independent sector as well as vice versa, and/or of writers arriving at similar strategies independently.

We are arguing that certain linguistic characteristic can be found in both corporate and independent sales material. More surprisingly, perhaps, some of these characteristics can be found even in noncommercial advocacy. Thus a leading campaign organization's point-of-contact Web page and leaflet entitled '10 Reasons to Eat Organic' (whose ordering of arguments is discussed in Section 4.4) uses the following headings:

(11)   1. Top for taste
       2. It's healthy
       3. No nasty additives
       4. Avoids pesticides
       5. GM-free
       6. Reliance on drugs removed
       7. No hidden costs
       8. High standards
       9. Care for animals
      10. Good for wildlife and the environment

These make use of alliteration ('top for taste', 'no nasty additives') and colloquial conversational forms ('it's' and 'nasty'). The leaflet is also vague, as exemplified in the explanatory paragraph under the first heading:

(12)   Many people buy organic food because they believe it tastes better than non-organic. This could be because organic fruit and vegetables tend to grow more slowly and have a lower water content, which may contribute to the fuller flavour some people experience. A poll in 2005 showed that quality and taste of food are important to more people than low prices.

Using techniques common in marketing, this formulation carefully avoids any unequivocal claim through vague quantifiers ('many people', 'some people', 'more people'), modal hedges ('could be because', 'tend to', 'may contribute') and lack of detail ('a poll in 2005') in ways which make the 'small print' effectively undermine the heading. These are points to which we will return later in our discussion of focus group reactions to organic food promotion.

4 Interviewee beliefs

In the textual analyses so far, a number of questions arise which cannot be answered by corpus or close textual analysis alone. What is the history of a linguistic choice and style? Are corporations appropriating the discourse of smaller organizations, or vice versa? How factually accurate are descriptions of named people and places? It is to gain insight into questions such as these that we have supplemented textual analysis with interview data. We recognize however that the process of asking writers and others responsible for communications, to introspect on and self-report their own creative processes, has inevitable pitfalls and problems. There is the possibility of dishonest responses; there are inevitable memory limitations, lack of a linguistics metalanguage, and of conscious access to subconscious linguistic processing (Cabello and O'Hora 2002; Jourdenais 2001). Nevertheless, asking those with direct or indirect responsibility for the content and communicative strategy of texts can, we believe, provide some significant insights into why language is used in the ways that it is, and while these may not be infallibly reliable, they may be the only resource available to the discourse analyst for this purpose.

An interview with the author of Extract (8) for example revealed that not only had she visited the farm in question, met Will the farmer, and had her trainers nibbled by the piglets, but also that her writing skills had been developed in journalism rather than marketing, and that the newsletters she is now writing are direct stylistic descendants of a genre developed by the box-scheme founder, at a time when organic retail was not so commercially viable. All this raises the issue that while texts may be very similar on the surface, their genesis, and indeed their truthfulness, may be very different. In this the smaller producers have an edge over the supermarkets, for in a climate where personal touch, small-scale production and product traceability are selling points, they can adopt such a stance both convincingly and truthfully. This is not to say however that supermarket claims are false. In an interview which we conducted with the communications director of a leading campaign organization, he responded to insinuations that the Waitrose description was mere supermarket 'spin' by assuring us of the existence of the named farmer, and exclaiming, in the phrase we have used in the title of this article:

(13) But it's all true!

4.1 Interviewee attitudes to language

Access to writers of corporate promotional material can be difficult, and as we have found in earlier projects, campaigners are more willing to talk to researchers than are those working for larger businesses, especially supermarkets. At the other end of the spectrum, smaller producers can also be unforthcoming and unwilling to talk in detail about their own promotional material/business, perhaps through lack of confidence. Nevertheless, our interview data capture the different types of organic food promoters described in Section 1 above, and includes informants from:

* major supermarkets: an organic brand manager, a copy writer, an organic buyer
* independent brands: manager for organic bread supplier
* box schemes: a managing director, a lead copy writer
* campaign organizations: a director of communications, a chief executive, a campaign head, a PR and media manager, an information officer, a copy writer of campaign material
* smaller producers: farmers with farm shops (not recorded)
* others: wine and food writer, food consultant, market researcher

As with the texts we analyzed, we found elements of surprising uniformity of opinion among those responsible for them across the organic sector, from the largest supermarkets to the smallest producers and campaigners. Particularly striking was the convergence of thinking about how to influence the public between those responsible for campaign point-of-contact literature and supermarket promotion.

Even among those directly concerned with communication strategy, there was often general reluctance or inability to focus upon linguistic choices such as synonyms (*delicious* versus *succulent* versus *tasty*). They preferred to discuss propositional content, whether it is true, legal, and accurate, and whether it is what consumers want to hear:

(14) (Technical manager, supermarket supplier)
we need to make sure it's legal, it's clear, and it's also got the right selling message on.

Questions about commercial promotion tended to be answered with reference to visual design and positioning in store, rather than language:

(15) (Supermarket buyer)
Three years ago it was an electric blue sky, and a bright green . . . which kind of looks . . .

(16) (Supermarket brand manager)
I think the first most important thing which we then changed last year was where it is actually positioned.

Where there was focus on language in response to specific questions, it tended to be brief and dismissive:

(17) (Supermarket food writer)
I know this packaging and I know that, yes succulent's a difficult word but how the hell do you give the sense of flavor without words like that?

4.2 Interviewee beliefs about consumers

There was a general assumption that consumers were:

a. less interested in fact than 'feeling' and more emotional than rational:

(18) (Wine and food writer)
not all consumers are [concerned about factual correctness] because you know you want to have a nice feeling about the thing you've bought, you're buying into, emotion you're buying into, building your self esteem is one of the sorts of things you do when you shop.

b. primarily self-interested (note the convergence here between super market and campaign organization):

(19) (Campaign organization policy officer)
at the end of the day most people don't buy organic food because it is better for the environment you know, people aren't that altruistic, they are not going to dig deep into their pockets and pay extra like a pound for their tomatoes just because it's less polluting.

(20) (Supermarket brand manager)
what we have discovered is that for many people it's about taste and health as the reasons for buying organic food. And the kind of worry, care for the environment has a slightly lower motivation for the majority of people.

c.   would not pay attention to wording:

   (21) (Supermarket brand manager)
         in reality you know people don't have a lot of time to read the packaging

4.3 Interviewee beliefs about successful communication strategies

There was a general belief that arguments for organic food should mirror consumer preferences, and the main determiner of communication strategy should be market research. This was true of campaigners, who might aspire to lead rather than follow opinion, as well as commercial organizations:

(22) (Campaign organization copy writer)
      Well the order changed and I changed it because we did some research, . . . that showed that most people bought on taste, that was the main reason and at the time taste was right at the bottom and I just thought we need to put that at the top because that will hopefully engage people . . .

There was unquestioning belief in conventional marketing effectiveness, with themes and wording being described as 'buttons' and 'triggers' for consumer response:

(23) (Campaign communication team)
      that word organic is a trigger for many people, our research tells us

(24) (Supermarket food writer)
      I spend a lot of my time making sure that what I write is factually accurate so to speak, but also hopefully presses those nice touchy, feely buttons which I actually think is part of the reason why consumers buy organic.

4.4 Arguments

The effects of such beliefs about consumers and how to influence them can be seen in the nature and prioritization of arguments for organic food. Possible lines of argument are claims of benefits to health, the environment, and economic and political structures, and eating pleasure. In choosing among these, one might expect those with purely commercial interest in organics to prioritize arguments relating directly to customer self-interest, while those whose support for organic farming is partly political might foreground those arguments relating to social issues. What we find instead, however (with some exceptions to be discussed below), is that across the sector 'tastiness' is now foregrounded by supermarkets, campaign groups, and many smaller retailers as the dominant argument in favor of organic food, followed by health and then environmental benefit. Arguments about the sociopolitical benefits of smaller scale production and localized retail have become comparatively rare, and are confined to smaller producers and campaign organizations. Thus the re-design of 'Tesco Organic' has recently demoted environmental arguments in favor of 'tastiness'. Smaller companies have long adopted similar strategies ('Taste is top of our agenda' as one box scheme puts it).

   Surprisingly, given their noncommercial environmentalist missions, campaign organizations also prioritize taste in their point-of-contact literature. The leaflet '10 Reasons to Buy Organic' has elevated 'Top for taste' to first reason, and relegated 'Good for wildlife and the environment' to tenth, making no reference at all to the positive social effects of promoting small independent farms, local produce, and fair rates for producers.

Reasons for this elevation of 'tastiness' are several. As a subjective quality, it is less refutable than health or environmental claims, and is thus a 'safer bet'. Indeed, health claims may be in second place only because they are more contestable:

(25) (Supermarket brand manager)
     taste isn't a claim, whereas health is a claim, legally.

It also perhaps lends itself to short 'poetic' copy of the kind analyzed above, and being less factual and objective by nature, is in some senses easier to write about than medical, environmental, or political arguments, which beg substantiation through factual evidence. Yet our interview data suggest that the main reason for the prominence of 'tastiness' is an uncritical acceptance both by corporations and across the organic movement of the received marketing wisdom that self-interest rather than social and environmental concern are the main motivators of attitudes to food.

4.5 An exception

Among our interviewees, the managing director and the lead copy writer of a highly successful organic box scheme proved to be exceptions to the above generalizations. Although winners of marketing and business awards, they sought to distance themselves both from conventional marketing language:

(26) (Box scheme writer)
     We try to stay clear as much as possible of the supermarket, supermarkety type phrases like, you know, delicious, succulent pork chops

and to maintain a commitment to providing substantive information:

(27) (Box scheme MD)
     So it's not just a fluffy story. We do give facts. So for example we did a newsletter about air freight last week and you know I insisted that there was a sentence that said, we don't ever air freight.

They thus distinguished themselves carefully from supermarkets, emphasizing:

(28) (Box scheme MD)
     our job is to keep educating people about what it is they're eating.

in contrast to the frank view expressed by one of our supermarket interviewees that:

(29) (Supermarket brand manager)
     I don't think supermarkets in general educate people about what organic is and what it isn't, and what's allowed and what isn't allowed. I think it's actually the media that does that, and the Soil Association or bodies like the Soil Association.

These interviewee claims can be borne out by text analysis. Point-of-contact literature maintains references to environmental and social benefits, and is accompanied by quick links to factual information where required.

For this box scheme, these strategies are accompanied by exponential growth, suggesting that it is not necessary to follow the usual promotional strategies to achieve commercial success. They rely too on the power of peer networks, as well as their own marketing. These promotional departures seem to echo the alternative the box schemes offer to conventional retail, illustrating perhaps how a dislocation between supermarkets and people's aspirations (discussed in the next section) can have discoursal as well as commercial consequences.

5 Focus groups

Like interviews, focus group discussions of texts have limitations as a reliable source of discourse analytic evidence. They face the paradox that participants are being asked to read and reflect upon wording which is normally read very casually (O'Halloran 2003). In addition, group dynamics can develop, often under the influence of one or two dominant personalities, which do not necessarily reflect the individual views of group members, and as with interviewees, participants generally lack a metalanguage for discussion of linguistic detail. Nevertheless, as with interviews, we have regarded focus groups as a flawed but available means of gaining insight.

The faith of our interviewees in orthodox marketing language described above, and their related belief in the carelessness and emotional gullibility of consumers, was not borne out by our focus groups, suggesting that those in the organic movement who adopt such language use may not be actually furthering their cause as successfully as they assume.

Our eight focus groups were recruited to represent a variety of ages, incomes, ethnic, and family profiles. Each group met on two occasions. In the first session they discussed packages for organic food products from supermarkets (including a Tesco Organic package similar to Extract (2), the Waitrose sausages packaging which includes Extracts (3) and (4), and the Duchy ready-meal quoted from in Extract (5); in the second session they discussed the '10-Reasons to Buy Organic' leaflet). As in the discussion above, packages were selected to exemplify firstly highly professional large-scale marketing, and represent different price profiles, product types, and marketing styles. The leaflet exemplified campaigning material.

5.1 Focus group reactions to organic food promotional language

Discussions indicated that our participants pay least attention to poetic descriptions, and preferred to assess factual statements such as ingredients. Where they focused (or were asked to focus) upon more rhetorical elements, of the kind identified as typical of supermarket language, their reactions were far from uniformly favorable. Words such as 'succulent' and 'chopped', which our interviews suggest have been confidently chosen to attract readers, frequently had the opposite effect:

(30) (Focus Group 30 Nov 06, 00.58.08)
I wouldn't buy something that said the word succulent on it because that for me conjures up the image of fat and I would just think, 'oh no I don't want that' (. . .)

(31) (Focus Group 3–1, 00.42.21)
I don't like these words that remind me that these animals are butchered, so – no it's true, it does jar because you have got these happy organic pigs and then you have got words like – cuts and coarsely chopped and succulent is a bit dodgy as well (. . .)

(32) (Focus Group 5–1, 00.14.54)
      Words like coarsely chopped and things don't help!

(33) (Focus Group 30 Nov 06, 00.18.40)
      That is the sort of thing that irritates me, it is just bacon for god's sake.

5.2 Focus group distrust of supermarkets

Related to this rejection of flamboyant descriptions was widespread distrust of retailers, drawing upon other independent sources of information, suggesting that organic food purchasing may happen despite, rather than because of, its promotional strategies.

Opposition was expressed toward supermarkets, although that is where most participants shop:

(34) (Focus Group 13 Nov 06, 00.06.26)
      And also I don't trust supermarkets anyway to be honest with you, I don't and the fact that if, and you can quote me, on the tape for this,—for example I know they have space specific things don't they, that say, it isn't grown within a certain range or something or other, a chemical is being used all that kind of stuff. I don't believe that for a minute, I don't believe if supermarkets are going to make some money out of it, I don't trust them—I do trust the more locally grown stuff but not supermarkets. (. . .)

Yet while many participants did not trust supermarkets, they were not necessarily convinced by organic alternatives, suggesting that if there is copying of high-pressure marketing, it may be misguided. For example, the first reason cited on the 10 Reasons leaflet is supported by evidence from a 'recent poll'. All focus groups, regardless of age or socioeconomic background, queried the validity of this evidence:

(35) (Focus Group 6–2, 00.00.40)
      I think they are almost a bit disgraceful really to start off with a poll you have conducted yourself with no sort of reference to sample size or no independent source.

This initial skepticism set the tone for discussion of later points in the leaflet. One bullet point claims that organic food is healthier because it has 'No Nasty Additives' (a phrase deploying both alliteration and colloquial lexis), but the accompanying text explains that of the 290 additives permissible in the EU, 32 can be used in organic food, eliciting comments such as:

(36) (Focus Group 4–2, 00.30.27)
      I think it is the conflicting information, people are always skeptical about it and it says no nasty additives, you think oh great . . . that for me is like well you are trying to gain my trust here and you are trying to be up front and be honest, then just say 'reduction of additives' or 'healthier style' rather than that.

Reason 8 is 'High Standards', backed up with the vague, emotive claim that 'Organic food comes from *trusted* sources' which are 'inspected *at least* once a year' (our emphases). Rather than satisfying curiosity or offering reassurance this point raised questions. For all groups this account lacked the rigor they hoped for in an inspection system:

(37) (Focus Group 6–2, 00.39.01)

I mean I am a bit worried about things like trusted sources because what they are saying is they are trusted because they inspect them once a year, is that enough?

Overall focus group discussions suggested a degree of immunity to marketing and promotional language, distrust of organizations, especially supermarkets, and some considerable fatalism and cynicism about the food chain in general.

6 Conclusion

Our combination of corpus and textual analysis with interviews and focus groups has enabled us to gain insights which would not be available from any of these data sources in isolation. To give a small example: the word 'succulent' identified as unusually frequent in our corpus, elicited from our interviewees when asked to comment on it an allegiance to standard behaviorist perceptions of marketing (in which the right stimulus will evoke the targeted response), while our focus groups' actual response to this same word suggested a growing cynicism and distrust of marketing discourse, and the emergence of a new stance on the social implications of different regimes of food production and distribution. Thus a small linguistic item can reflect major changes in the power relations between corporations and their publics.

By juxtaposing evidence of producer beliefs with reader responses against a background of corpus-informed textual analysis, we have suggested that contemporary marketing beliefs about how PR language works may be seriously flawed. While a good deal of marketing practice is based upon partial (often in-house) research following an inappropriate behaviorist psychological paradigm, market research surveys with limited questions, or vague folk beliefs about 'how language works', we have used a principled and independent linguistic approach based on in-depth open-ended interviews and discussions to reveal beliefs and opinions about how specific linguistic choices may or may not actually work. Despite the limitations of interview and focus group data as a reliable insight into intention and response, our findings strongly suggest that across very different kinds of producers and receivers, conventional approaches to marketing language, at least in the area of food, may not work in the way they are believed to, though it is often in the interests of those who produce them to persuade their paymasters that they do. The upshot of this is that a change of direction in promotional language might be more effective, not only for those bent on profit alone, but significantly for those with more altruistic and socially responsible intent. Indeed, it may be that certain directions in promotional language would not be accessible to corporate marketers, who have more to hide, in that their produce is not local, not environmentally friendly, and not the fruit of just labor and trade relations.

Despite reference to some categories of consumer (such as 'deep green' for consumers who always buy organic), our interviewees generally shared a derogatory view of their audience as a homogeneous 'public', quite different from themselves, who are ill-informed, gullible, emotional, selfish, careless, and easily manipulated. Our findings, on the contrary, show a critical and fact-oriented information-age readership, who, even when they do not know relevant facts, are aware of questions to ask and ways of assessing answers, judging communications for example as much by what they know about the sender as about the topic (e.g., they judge Tesco rather than the potatoes). Interviewees also implied that product presentation is the main factor in motivating purchase, and did not consider the possibility that in some cases goods may be bought in spite of rather than because of their presentation. Our findings also suggest a deep dislocation between purchasing behavior and attitudes to those purchases, especially among those who shop mostly in supermarkets (i.e., almost everybody, and certainly almost everybody in our focus groups) reflecting dissatisfaction and mistrust of these corporate retailers – a finding which has also been borne out in research which shows that while people may shop in a given supermarket, they are not happy with the fact that they do (Clarke et al. 2007).

While it is true therefore that purchasing behavior and attitude are not necessarily the same (Padel and Foster 2005), and that from a supermarket point of view it is the former that matters rather than the latter, the two are nevertheless not unconnected. Our findings suggest that changes in attitude may be building up a sufficient head of steam to create a 'tipping point' when a change in attitude does lead to a change in behavior. With regard to food purchase and consumption, this tipping point may be closer for more people than the multiple retailers suppose. Not only marketers but also most campaigners thus seem to be misjudging the food market in their assumptions that the many different 'publics' can all continue to be easily manipulated by the kinds of texts described in this article. Food has moved in people's consciousness out of the category of fast-moving consumer goods (FMCGs as they are known in marketing) and its purchase is now perceived as a way of expressing identity (both individual and cultural), concern about the environment and social justice, and a political stance. Food has become an area of symbolic value indicative of philosophical and political conviction which, like religious and philosophical beliefs, while not unsusceptible to manipulation, cannot be as easily shifted as marketers suppose. Corporations are perceived for what they are, and their language as an expression of that identity.

Notes

1   Using each corpus as a reference corpus for the other, and each corpus against 'BNC baby' (a four-million word sample of the British National Corpus) as a reference corpus.
2   The eight groups, recruited in Milton Keynes and Nottingham, were: (i) aged 16–18, (ii) aged 35–60 social groups A/B, (iii) aged 35–60 social groups C1/C2/D, (iv) parents of children aged 2–12, (v) aged 19–34 without children, (vi) over 60s, (vii) organic consumers aged 19–34, (viii) non-organic consumers aged 19–34.
3   This applies to the package we used. Other Tesco organic baby new potatoes are from other countries.
4   Sometimes other family members are named too, with reference to earlier generations if the farm is inherited. Farmers are typically male, couples heterosexual, and families nuclear.
5   Unusually, pronouns also appear high in keyword lists against noncommercial corpora, and also in poetry and song (Cook 2007). The fact that first- and second-person pronouns do not appear high in keywords using our non-organic corpus as a reference corpus shows that this form of address is the norm in both.
6   Even without the contractions *we'd, we'll, we've, we're*, or the other forms of the lemma *we*, namely *our* (position 17) and *us* (position 70).
7   Even without the contractions *you're, you'll, you'd* (56 occurrences in total), or the other forms of the lemma *you*, especially *your* (position 52).

References

Cabello, F. & D. O'Hora. 2002. Addressing the limitations of protocol analysis in the study of complex human behavior. *International Journal of Psychology and Psychological Therapy* 2(2). 115–130.
Channell, J. 1994. *Vague language*. Oxford: Oxford University Press.
Clarke, I., M. Kirkup & H. Oppewal. 2007. Are consumers getting what they REALLY want? Initial findings from a major survey of consumer satisfaction with their local selection of grocery stores. (ESRC/EPSRC RES-331–25–0017). commission.org.uk/inquiries/ref2006/grocery/pdf/third_party_submissions_ other_org_ advanced_institute.pdf (accessed 4 October 2007).
Cook, G. 2001. *The discourse of advertising*, 2nd edn. London: Routledge.
Cook, G. 2004. *Genetically modified language*. London: Routledge.
Cook, G. 2007. 'This we have done.' The different vagueness of poetry and PR. In J. Cutting (ed.), *Vague language explored*, 21–40. London: Palgrave.

Cook, G. 2008. Advertising and public relations. In R. Wodak & V. Koller (eds), *Handbook of applied linguistics, volume 4: Communication in the public sphere*, 113–138. Berlin & New York: Mouton de Gruyter.

Cook, G. & K. O'Halloran. 1999. Label literacy: Factors affecting the understanding and assessment of baby food labels. In T. O'Brien (ed.), *Language and literacies, BAAL Studies in Applied Linguistics 14*, 145–157. Clevedon: British Association for Applied Linguistics in association with Multilingual Matters.

Cook, G., E. Pieri & P. T. Robbins. 2004. 'The scientists think and the public feels': Expert perceptions of the discourse of GM food. *Discourse and Society* 15(4). 433–449.

Cook, G., P. T. Robbins & E. Pieri. 2006. 'Words of mass destruction': British newspaper coverage of the GM food debate, and expert and non-expert reactions. *Public Understanding of Science* 15(1). 5–29.

Cutting, J. (ed.). 2007. *Vague language explored*. London: Palgrave.

Fairclough, N. 1992. *Discourse and social change*. Cambridge: Polity.

Fromartz, S. 2006. *Organic, INC*. Orlando, FL: Harcourt.

Guthman, J. 2004. *Agrarian dreams. The paradox of organic farming in California*. Berkley: University of California Press.

Halliday, M. A. K. 1973. *Explorations in the function of language*. London: Arnold.

Harwood, N. 2006. (In)appropriate personal pronoun use in political science: A qualitative study and a proposed heuristic for future research. *Written Communication* 23(4). 424–450.

Harwood, N. 2007. Political scientists on the functions of personal pronouns in their writing: An interview-based study of 'I' and 'we'. *Text & Talk* 27(1): 27–54.

Jakobson, R. 1960. Closing statement: Linguistics and poetics. In T. A. Sebeok (ed.), *Style in language*, 350–377. Cambridge, MA: MIT Press.

Jourdenais, R. 2001. Cognition, instruction and protocol analysis. In P. Robinson (ed.), *Cognition and second language instruction*, 354–375. Cambridge: Cambridge University Press.

Koller V. 2007a. Identity as metaphor: Communicating notions of the self through corporate branding discourse. Paper delivered at the 40th annual meeting of the British Association for Applied Linguistics, University of Edinburgh.

Koller, V. 2007b. 'The world's local bank': Glocalisation as a strategy in corporate branding discourse. *Social Semiotics* 17(1): 111–131.

Koller, V. 2009. Corporate self-presentation and self-centredness: A case for cognitive critical discourse analysis. In H. Pishwa (ed.), *Language and social cognition*, Berlin & New York: Mouton de Gruyter.

Moloney, Kevin. 2006. *Rethinking public relations: The spin and the substance*, 2nd edn. London: Routledge.

Mulderrig, J. 2006. *The governance of education: A corpus-based critical discourse analysis of UK education policy texts 1972–2005*. Lancaster: Lancaster University doctoral thesis.

Mulderrig, J. 2007. Textual strategies of representation and legitimation in New Labour policy discourse. In G. Rikowski, A. Green & H. Raduntz (eds), *Marxism and education: Renewing dialogues Vol. 1*, 135–150. Basingstoke: Palgrave Macmillan.

Myers, G. 2004. *Matters of opinion. Talking about public issues*. Cambridge: Cambridge University Press.

Myers, G. & P. McNaghten. 1999. Can focus groups be analysed as talk? In R. S, Barbour & J. Kitzinger (eds), *Developing focus group research: Politics, theory and practice*, 173–185. London: Sage.

O'Halloran, K. 2003. *Critical discourse analysis and language cognition*. Edinburgh: Edinburgh University Press.

Padel, S. & C. Foster. 2005. Exploring the gap between attitudes and behaviour. Understanding why consumers buy or do not buy organic food. *British Food Journal* 107(8). 606–625.

Pollan, M. 2006. *The omnivore's dilemma. The search for a perfect meal in a fast-food world*. London: Bloomsbury.

Reed, M. 2001. Fight the future! How the contemporary campaigns of the organic movement have arisen from their compositing of the past. *Sociologia Ruralis* 41(1). 131–146.

Sahota, A. 2007. The international market for organic and fair trade food and drink. In S. Wright & D. McCrea (eds), *The handbook of organic and fair trade marketing*, 1–28. Oxford: Blackwell.

Scott, M. 2005. Help menu. *Wordsmith tools*. Oxford: Oxford University Press (accessed 5 July 2006).

Stubbs, M. 1996. *Text and corpus analysis*. Oxford: Blackwell.

Swales, J. & P. Rogers. 1995. Discourse and the projection of corporate culture: The mission statement. *Discourse and Society* 6(2). 233–242.

Tormey, S. 2007. Consumption, resistance and everyday life: Ruptures and continuities. *Journal of Consumer Policy* 30(3). 263–280.

Widdowson, H. G. 1997. The use of grammar, the grammar of use. *Functions of Language* 4(2). 145–168.

Widdowson, H. G. 2004. *Text, context, pretext*. Oxford: Blackwell.

Wodak, R. R. de Cillia, M. Reisigl & K. Liebhart. 1999. *The discursive construction of national identity*, A. Hirsch & R. Mitten (trans.). Edinburgh: Edinburgh University Press.

Wright, S. & D. McCrea (eds). 2007. *The handbook of organic and fair trade food marketing*. Oxford: Blackwell.

NOTES FOR STUDENTS AND INSTRUCTORS

Study questions

1 What do the concepts of *discourse community* and *peripheral participation* mean?
2 According to McNamara, what role can the language tester play in addition to constructing valid and useable assessments?
3 What is *language socialization*?
4 What does Continua of Biliteracy mean?
5 How does Process Analysis help to connect Translation Studies and Political Discourse Analysis?
6 What is Linguistic Creativity? According to Maybin and Swann, what can a critical approach to linguistic creativity reveal?
7 What are BICS (basic interpersonal communicative skills) and CALP (cognitive academic language proficiency)? What is the difference between interpersonal competence and linguistic and conceptual competence? How are these concepts played out in Pavlenko's case study?
8 In what way are commercial and political discourses converged according to Guy et al? Why has the adoption of standard marketing language not been particularly effective on the consumer?

Study activities

1 Conduct a case study in a community or an organisation (e.g. school, hospital, commercial company, public institution). Find out if there is any language policy, explicit or implicit. Are these policies consistent with the language policies of the wider society or of the nation? What are the attitudes of the people in the community or the organization? Are there tensions and conflicts between the policies and actual language practices of the individuals?
2 How do different agencies of language socialization (e.g. family, school, workplace, media) impact on individuals' language ideologies and practices?

3   Observe the people around you and what they do in everyday life. Is everyone equal in terms of linguistic knowledge and skills? How are individuals' access to resources affected by their linguistic knowledge and skills? Can everyone have equal linguistic knowledge and skills, and why?

Further reading

Flowerdew, John, 2001, *Academic Discourse*, Harlow: Longman, is an introductory text on academic discourse.

Flowerdew, John and Peacock, Matthew (eds), 2001, *Research Perspectives on English for Academic Purposes*, Cambridge: Cambridge University Press, investigates the theoretical issues and pedagogical concerns of academic discourse.

Bhatia, Vijay, Flowerdew, John and Jones, Rodney, 2007, *Advances in Discourse Studies*, Oxford: Routledge, features discussion questions, classroom projects and case studies.

McNamara, Tim, 2000, *Language Testing*, Oxford: Oxford University Press, is a concise introduction to core issues in language testing.

McNamara, Tim, and Roever, Carsten, 2007, *Language Testing: the social dimension*. Oxford: Blackwell, focuses on the social aspects of language testing, including assessment of socially situated language use and societal consequences of language tests.

Duff, Patricia, 2010, Language socialization into academic discourse communities. *Annual review of applied linguistics*, 30, 169–192, is a review article of the key issues in language socialization with specific reference to academic discourse.

Duff, Patricia and Labrie, Normand (eds), 2000, Languages and Work. *Canadian Modern Language Review*, 57, 1, is a special issue on workplace communication.

Duff, Patricia and Li, Duanduan (eds), 2009, Indigenous, Minority, and Heritage Language Education in Canada. *Canadian Modern Language Review*, 66 (1), is a special issue containing case studies of minority language education.

Duff, Patricia and Hornberger, Nancy (eds), 2008, *Language Socialization: encyclopedia of language and education*, Volume 8, Boston: Springer, is a major reference collection of state-of-the-art surveys of the field.

Hornberger, Nancy, 2003, *Continua of Biliteracy: an ecological framework for educational policy, research and practice in multilingual settings,* Clevedon: Multilingual Matters, offers a comprehensive yet flexible model to guide educators, researchers and policy-makers in designing, carrying out and evaluating educational programmes for the development of bilingual and multilingual learners, each programme adapted to its own specific context, media and contents.

Hornberger, Nancy and McKay, Sandra Lee, 2010, *Sociolinguistics and Language Education*, Cleveland: Multilingual Matters, covers topics such as nationalism and popular culture, style and identity, creole languages, critical language awareness, gender and ethnicity, multimodal literacies, classroom discourse, and ideologies and power.

Chilton, Paul and Schaffner, Christina (eds), 2002, *Politics as Text and Talk: analytic approaches to political discourse,* Amsterdam: Benjamins, is a collection of articles that investigates the use of language in political situations.

Schaffner, Christina (ed.), 2002, *The role of discourse analysis for translation and translator training*. Clevedon: Multilingual Matters, discusses the role of discourse analysis for translation and translator training.

Maybin, Janet and Swann, Joan (eds), 2006, *The Art of English: everyday creativity,* Basingstoke: Palgrave, examines ideas about creativity and explores the link between creativity and literary language. Chapters examine poetic language, narrative and performance in conversation, and a range of written genres (from graffiti and text messages to online chat).

Pavlenko, Aneta and Blackledge, Adrian (eds), 2003, *Negotiation of Identities in Multilingual Contexts*, Clevedon: Multilingual Matters, highlights the role of language ideologies in the process of negotiation of identities and shows that in different historical and social contexts different identities may be negotiable or non-negotiable.

Pavlenko, Aneta, Blackledge, Adrian, Piller, Ingrid and Teutsch-Dwyer, Marya, 2001, *Multilingualism, Second Language Learning and Gender,* Berlin: Mouton de Gruyter, focuses on the issue of gender in multilingualism and second language learning.

Cook, Guy, 2001, *The Discourse of Advertising* (2nd edition), Oxford: Routledge, focuses on contemporary advertising in the context of changes in communication.

Cook, Guy, 2004, *Genetically Modified Language: the discourse of arguments for GM crops and food*, Oxford: Routledge, presents a critical analysis of the language of the GM debate, and how it influences policy and opinion.

Cook, Guy, 2000, *Language Play Language Learning*, Oxford: Oxford University Press, demonstrates the extent and importance of language play in human life and discusses the implications for applied linguistics and language teaching.

Other publications of interest include:

On language testing, citizenship, and learning:

Shohamy, Elana, 2001, *The Power of Tests: a critical perspective on the uses of language tests*, Harlow: Longman.

Extra, Guus, Spotti, Massimiliano, and Van Avermaet, Piet (eds), 2009, *Language Testing, Migration and Citizenship: cross-national perspectives*, London: Continuum.

Osler, Audrey and Starkey, Hugh, 2004, *Citizenship and Language Learning*, Stoke-on-Trent: Trentham Books.

On workplace and professional communication:

Grin, François, Sfreddo, Claudio and Vaillancourt, François, 2010, *The Economics of the Multilingual Workplace*, Oxford: Routledge.

Gunnarsson, Britt-Louise, 2009, *Professional Discourse*, London : Continuum.

On linguistic diversity and language teaching:

Wiley, Terrence G., 2005, *Literacy and Language Diversity in the United States* (2nd edition), Delta Publishing Company.

Edge, Julian, 2009, *(Re-)Locating TESOL in an Age of Empire*, Basingtoke: Palgrave.

On language policy and management:

Spolsky, Bernard, 2003, *Language Policy*, Cambridge: Cambridge University Press.

Spolsky, Bernard, 2009, *Language Management*, Cambridge: Cambridge University Press.

Phillipson, Robert, 2003, *English-Only Europe? Challenging Language Policy; Language Policy Challenges*, Oxford: Routledge.

Shohamy, Elana, 2006, *Language Policy: hidden agendas and new approaches*, Oxford: Routledge.

On language, politics, and power:

Joseph, John, 2006, *Language and Politics*, Oxford: Routledge.

Simpson, Paul, and Mayr, Andrea, 2009, *Language and Power*, Oxford: Routledge.

Fairclough, Norman, 2010, *Critical Discourse Analysis: the critical study of language* (2nd edition), Harlow: Longman.

On language and the law:

Coulthard, Malcolm, 2007, *An Introduction to Forensic Linguistics: language in evidence*, London: Routledge.

Gibbons, John, 2003, *Forensic Linguistics: an introduction to language in the justice system*, Oxford: Blackwell.

Schane, Sanford A., 2006, *Language and the Law*, London: Continuum.

Shuy, Roger, 2005, *Creating Language Crimes: how law enforcement uses (and misuses) language*, New York: Oxford University Press.

On language, communication and the new media:

Crystal, David, 2006, *Language and the Internet*, Cambridge University Press.

Baron, Naomi, 2010, *Always On: language in an online and mobile world*, Oxford: Oxford University Press.

Myers, Greg, 2009, *The Discourse of Blogs and Wikis,* London: Continuum.

Thurlow, Crispin, Lengel, Laura and Tomic, Alice, 2004, *Computer Mediated Communication: an introduction to social interaction online*, London: Sage.

On linguistic landscape:

Jaworski, Adam and Thurlow, Crispin, 2010, *Semiotic Landscapes: language, image, space*, London: Continuum.
Shohamy, Elana and Gorter, Durk, (eds), 2008, *Linguistic Landscape: expanding the scene*, Oxford: Routledge.

On language and globalization:

Fairclough, Norman, 2006, *Language and Globalisation*, London: Routledge.
Blommaert, Jan, 2010, *The Sociolinguistics of Globalisation*, Cambridge: Cambridge University Press.
Coupland, Nikolas (ed.), 2010, *Handbook of Language and Globalisation*, Oxford: Blackwell.

On approaches to discourse analysis:

Scollon, Ron and Wong Scollon, Suzie, 2003, *Discourses in Place: language in the material world*, Oxford: Routledge.
Scollon, Ron and Wong Scollon, Suzie, 2004, *Nexus Analysis: discourse and the internet*, Oxford: Routledge.
Jones, Rodney and Norris, Sigrid, 2005, *Discourse in Action: introducing mediated discourse analysis*, London: Routledge.

On public discourse:

Myers, Greg, 2004, *Matters of Opinion: talking about public issues*, Cambridge: Cambridge University Press.

LI WEI AND ZHU HUA

DOING APPLIED LINGUISTICS
Methodological considerations

DOES APPLIED LINGUISTICS HAVE a methodology? Does it need one? How would an applied linguistics methodology be different from that of, say, formal linguistics, or pedagogy, sociology and psychology? Having presented a range of studies in this Reader with very different questions, databases and analyses, it is worth considering the broader issue of methodology.

1 Method and methodology

First of all, let us remind ourselves of the distinction between method and methodology. There is quite a lot of confusion about the meanings of these two terms. *Methods* refer to specific techniques of collecting and analysing data. For example, a survey questionnaire is a method, and ethnographic fieldwork is another. Sometimes people use methods to refer to tools or instruments, for instance, a computer software for analysing data, or multiple choice questions (MCQs). Students are often very concerned about choosing the right method for their research project, and they want to learn how to do it, be it doing an interview or using a data bank. But the method chosen for a particular research project depends on the methodology, which is the underlying logic of methods. More precisely, *methodology* is the principle or principles that determine how specific methods or tools are deployed and interpreted. In one sense, applied linguistics could be considered a methodology in itself. As we discussed in the General Intro-duction, applied linguistics is concerned with real-world problems in which language plays a central role. Such a problem-solving approach distinguishes applied linguistics from other methodologies where the main concern may be hypothesis testing or theorization.

There are various ways of characterising different research methodologies. People often think of research methodology in terms of a quantitative versus qualitative dichotomy. In general terms, *quantitative methodology* aims to uncover facts and truths in an objective way by delineating patterns or structures, whereas *qualitative methodology* attempts to interpret meanings of and relationships between objects in context. For instance, a language class could be regarded as an object for investigation. A quantitative approach might focus on how the class

is structured, what are the key components of the class, and what role does each component play
in the structuring of the class in terms of frequency and regularity. A qualitative perspective, on
the other hand, would most likely be asking what is the definition of a class in comparison
with some other event, how are the different components of a class (e.g. participants, topic,
setting) related to each other, and why a particular language class takes place in the way it
does. Quantitative methodology is used a great deal in science disciplines, while qualitative
methodology is more common in the humanities and arts. The social sciences often use both:
there are social scientists who are more interested in the what and how questions and adopt a
quantitative perspective, while others are more concerned with the how and why questions and
lean towards a qualitative methodology. Applied linguistics as a problem-solving approach does
on the surface seem to lean towards the qualitative perspective, although there are also plenty
of applied linguists who are interested in facts and figures and therefore adopt a quantitative
methodology.

Perhaps a better way to understand the differences in the various methodologies is to look
at the objectives of the research. Creswell (2003: p. 6) proposed a classification, which he terms
as 'worldviews in research' (see Table below). Such a classification helps us to think of research
methodologies in more practical ways and avoids the quantitative versus qualitative dichotomy
and the potential confusions between methodology and methods. One can use specific quantitative
or qualitative methods and techniques, or a combination of the two, within each of these
methodological perspectives.

2 The process of research

Whatever methodology one chooses to adopt, there are certain steps one needs to take in
conducting a research project. These typically include:

- defining the research question or questions
- collecting evidence
- analyzing and presenting findings

Four worldviews used in research

Postpositivism	Constructivism	Advocacy and participatory	Pragmatism
• Determination • Reductionism • Empirical observation and measurement • Theory verification	• Understanding • Multiple participant meanings • Social and historical construction • Theory generation	• Political • Empowerment and issue oriented • Collaborative • Change oriented	• Consequences of actions • Problem centered • Pluralistic • Real-world practice oriented

Source: Creswell (2003). Reprinted with permission of Sage Publications.

2.1 Defining the research question

Defining the research question is a crucial first step. The question has to be researchable, which means:

- there are potentially different answers to it;
- there is evidence available for the researcher to answer the question with.

In defining the research question, consideration should be given to both the feasibility and ethics of pursuing research. As Lorch (n.d.) points out,

- some things *do not* get researched because the question is not of interest, in fashion, relevant to current theories and models;
- some things *cannot* get researched because of a lack of data or resources, e.g. time, human resources, research tools;
- some things *should not* get researched because of ethical issues, e.g. dignity and welfare, consent, anonymity, risk.

The most common ways of finding research questions are through personal experience or reading other people's work. These two ways also often go hand in hand with each other. Many applied linguists come into the field because of professional and personal interests. Some may have taught languages in different parts of the world, to different groups of learners, at different levels, and they are interested in researching questions that are directly related to their work experience. Others may themselves be multilingual, have raised children in diverse linguistic and cultural environments, worked in a particular institution, e.g. multinational corporates, the media, translation and interpreting services, and would like to gain knowledge and understanding of the key issues in these domains. Most of the people entering applied linguistics with professional or personal interests tend to have a better idea of the broad area or topic they want to research into, rather than a specific, researchable question. For example, they may say that they are interested in researching heritage language schools, or intergenerational communication in multilingual families, or attitudes towards certain languages in a particular community. To make the journey from such broad areas of interests to specific research(able) questions is not always an easy or straightforward process. This is where critical reading of the literature comes in.

2.1.1 LITERATURE REVIEW

A good literature review serves two closely related purposes:

- to make the reader understand why you are doing what you are doing and in the way you are doing it; and
- to prepare your own argument.

So, a good literature review should be more than a clear summary of what has been done on the topic or area you are interested in. It should also be a synthesis of the existing knowledge of the topic or area. A summary is a recap of the important information of the source, but a synthesis is a re-organization, or a reshuffling, of that information. While a summary merely presents other people's work, a synthesis should have the reviewer's voice at the front and centre. References to other sources need therefore to be woven into the reviewer's own points. This is what many instructors mean when they ask their students to be 'critical' in the literature review, i.e. they want the students to state their own positions on what they have read and summarized. It may be useful, then, to try and trace the intellectual progression of the field, including major debates.

A good literature review should cover the following:

- What has been done on the topic or area of interest? Are you interested in exactly the same topic or area, or in something that is similar but different?
- What are the questions asked by the other researchers? Can you ask the questions in a different way? Do you have other questions to ask?
- From what methodological perspective did they ask the questions: post-positivism, constructivism, advocacy and participatory, or pragmatism? What methodology would you use?
- What methods and data did they use in answering the questions? Can you improve on the research design and method? Is there other evidence that you can provide to address the questions?
- How did the researchers interpret their results and what argument did they put forward on the basis of their data analysis? Do you agree with their analysis? Are there other ways of interpreting the data?

In other words, a good, critical review should show that you not only have read extensively the existing work in the field but also understood the methodology and arguments, by pointing out the strengths and weaknesses, by comparing the results of different studies and by evaluating them with reference to your own interests. Once you have answered the above questions, you are likely to have a research question or even a set of questions for your own project.

On a more practical level, try to avoid giving too many direct quotes in the literature review. Extensive quotation gives the impression of the reviewer not having a critical view on the issue of concern. However, if you want to emphasize a point of your own and use a quote from other people to back it up, it is perfectly acceptable. In the meantime, paraphrasing a source that is not your own needs to be done with great caution. It is crucial to represent the original author's information or opinions accurately. If you are not sure, it would be better to use a direct quote. Misrepresenting other people's work can cause problems for all concerned. See Mallon (1989), Sherman (1992), Pennycook (1996), Pecorari (2003), and Sutherland-Smith W. (2005) for discussions of the issue of plagiarism in applied linguistics.

The literature review should help you not only to understand other researchers' methodological perspectives, but also to choose your own stance. In formatting your research questions, you should be clear whether you are most interested in finding facts and figures, patterns and structures, in understanding the relationships, contexts and consequences, in devising a practical solution to a problem, or in initiating change either in the situation that you are researching or in your personal and professional life. As has been discussed above, different methodological perspectives require different designs, methods and tools for collecting and analysing evidence.

2.1.2 IN NEED OF A HYPOTHESIS?

Before we move onto the issue of research design, there is a frequently asked question by students embarking on their first research project: *Do I need a hypothesis*? Most often, students who think that they are doing qualitative research, describing what is happening in a particular situation – say, migrant workers speaking different languages seeking health care or legal aid in places where nobody understands them, or European teachers who speak English as their third or fourth language but teaching it in the Far East – claim that they do not have a hypothesis. This is a misunderstanding of the concept of hypothesis. Yes, a hypothesis can mean something that is taken to be true for the purpose of argument or investigation, and as such, it generally forms the basis of experiments to establish its plausibility. But it can also mean a tentative explanation for an observation or a phenomenon. Having reviewed the relevant literature on a research topic, one should know what explanations other people have offered, and these explanations can then be used as hypotheses for new research projects. It does not matter if the actual research project involves a set of tightly controlled laboratory experiments, or extended fieldwork and participant observation, or a large number of interviews and questionnaires; it is always advisable to have an argument and a tentative explanation in advance. As yourself: *what do I expect to find? How do I explain whatever I find?* Answers to these questions will prepare you for an argument or a theory, which is the key to research; a mere description without explanation, however detailed and systematic, is not enough. Furthermore, good research should problematize what has been taken for granted, formulating questions that have broader implications, looking at things in a new, different way.

2.2 Collecting evidence

2.2.1 RESEARCH DESIGN

It is often said that a research project only really begins when one starts to collect evidence or data. Many students are anxious about the amount of data they collect and whether the data they have collected is 'good enough'. To ensure that the data one has are of sufficient quantity and quality, one needs to consider carefully a number of design issues. The first and foremost is: 'given this research question (or theory), what type of evidence is needed to answer the question (or test the theory) *in a convincing way*?' (de Vaus, 2001, p. 9, original emphasis). Using an analogy, de Vaus compares the role and purpose of research design in a project to knowing what sort of building one is planning (such as an office building, a factory for manufacturing machinery, a school, etc.). One can normally get a sense of what kind of evidence or data are appropriate for the research question by reviewing existing studies – what evidence did other researchers use to support their arguments? More specifically, one can ask the following questions:

1   Is the primary aim of the study to compare two or more individuals, situations, behaviours, or to focus on just one? (etic vs. emic)
2   Is the data collected and analysed in numerical form or not? (quantitative vs. qualitative)
3   Is the data collected under controlled conditions or not? (experimental vs. non-experimental)

4   Is the study conducted over a period of time or at one point in time? (longitudinal vs. non-longitudinal)
5   Does the study involve one single participant, a small group of participants or a large number of participants? (case study vs. group study)

The terms in brackets after each of the above questions are different types of research design. An *etic* study is often known as a comparative study, which involves comparing one individual, or situation, or behaviour, with another. The challenge facing an etic design is the issue of comparability. Ideally comparison should be made on a 'like-for-like' basis, but in reality, comparative studies often encounter practical difficulties. The other approach is what has been referred to as *emic* whereby researchers try to explore and discover patterns and meanings *in situ*. Two principles guide the emic study: one is 'holism', which requires that the issues being investigated are not divorced from the historical, social, cultural and ideological contexts; the other is the principle of 'emergence', which requires that structures and meanings are discovered rather than predetermined and assigned. Emic and etic designs provide different perspectives, but they are neither exclusive of each other nor irreconcilable. Instead, they are often taken as inter-dependent stages of an enquiry and a 'continuous circle of research activity' (Berry, 1999). At the starting point, a researcher may set out to test whether an argument or observation true to one situation applies to another situation. This may then set the agenda for an in-depth study from within that situation. When ample and extensive studies on several cases have been carried out separately, a researcher may attempt to compare and integrate what has been learned about a common phenomenon in different situations.

The use of numerical data lies behind the difference between quantitative and qualitative research design. A quantitative study is essentially about explaining phenomena and identifying trends and patterns by collecting and analysing data numerically, while a qualitative design is an umbrella term that covers a variety of methods which focus on the meaning of the phenomenon being investigated and do not involve numerical data. Quantitative research, when it is supported by statistical analysis, can give research findings additional confidence and help to discover the relationship between variables (e.g. whether two variables are causal or correlational). It can handle a large quantity of data and therefore the finding can be more representative. The potential disadvantages of quantitative research include decontextualization of patterns and meanings by reducing data to numbers, and neglect of certain subtleties in the data. Compared with quantitative studies, a qualitative design has the advantage of offering an opportunity to gather richer and more detailed data and carry out in-depth analysis of data. Special cases or individual differences can be highlighted, and interpretation can be more nuanced. The disadvantages of qualitative research include that the data may be less representative and generalizations may be less clear, and that data collection and interpretation may be subject to researchers' positions and backgrounds. Quantitative and qualitative can be combined in mixed method designs.

Experimental studies collect data under controlled conditions. The purpose of the 'control' is to keep everything except for the variables under investigation, as similar or comparable as possible so that the experimental results can be reliably attributed to the changes in variables. Among variables under investigation, a distinction is usually made between dependent and independent variables. Independent variables are those that have an effect on other variables and a change in their value or state would lead to a change in other variables, while dependent variables are those which change as a result of changes in other variables.

In a typical *experimental design*, a researcher starts with formulating a hypothesis between the dependent variable and independent variables and then decides on the subject sampling criteria, instrument, treatment and procedures. There are many variations of experimental designs depending on how many groups of subjects are involved, whether the groups are identical or different, whether the groups are doing different things or doing the same thing under different conditions, and how many times data will be collected from each group. Some researchers refer to the type of experimental design in which subjects are not randomly allocated as a quasi-experimental design. This type of experimental design is often used in evaluation studies in which random assignment is neither possible nor practical. Experimental design helps to discover the relationship between variables. The results are easier to process and interpret. However, behaviours under experimental conditions may not be the same as those in naturally occurring social contexts. And control over the variables can be difficult in actual practice.

In a *non-experimental design*, researchers do not manipulate conditions. This design is suitable for research questions which aim to explore the phenomena in a more natural manner, such as spontaneous interaction, to find out opinions, attitudes or facts or to assess current conditions or practice. Non-experimental design can afford to sample a larger population, and can collect a large amount of data efficiently, hence can be more representative or in-depth. However, it may be difficult to establish the causal link between variables. And the data can be difficult to process and analyze.

Longitudinal design refers to studies in which data are collected from a small number of subjects over a period of time. Longitudinal studies are suitable for answering research questions which aim to explore changes and development over time or to evaluate the effectiveness of a training programme or the impact of an experience. The main advantages of longitudinal study design include its sensitivity to sequential development and changes; opportunities to examine individual differences; and the possibility of collecting a large amount of data from every participant over time and hence providing detailed information. Yet, longitudinal studies are often time-consuming, vulnerable to participants' attrition, subject to practice effect (the more times a participant is observed over the same task, the better or worse they would become) and inconsistency between each data collection.

Cross-sectional design refers to the type of studies in which data is collected at one point in time from a large number of subjects either grouped together according to age or other variables such as length of stay in a new country. Cross-sectional studies can be used to explore the relationship between various variables, for example, the correlation between the degree of appropriateness in using a speech act by an English-as-a-foreign-language learner and the length of stay in an English-speaking country; or to describe the developmental pattern of a particular feature or skill such as the development of Intercultural Communicative Competence. Cross-sectional design can generate a large quantity of data in a short period of time. Multiple subjects can be sampled and therefore be more representative. Relationships between variables can be established more clearly. However, it has the disadvantage of not being sensitive to developmental patterns and changes, or to individual differences. It requires consistency in data collection from different subjects.

Case study design is an in-depth investigation of, usually, a single subject. It can be used to describe the linguistic or communicative behaviour of an individual member of a group, to refute a claim by providing counter-evidence, or alternatively to show what is possible as positive evidence. It provides rich and in-depth data, and allows for close observation and intensive study. Its main limitation is its lack of generalizability. *Group study* involves a group of individuals instead of one subject. It can be an in-depth investigation as in the case study. It has the advantage of being capable of providing generalizable data. But it demands consistency across different individuals. Single case study and group study are very often combined with longitudinal and cross-sectional designs. For example, a case study can be conducted longitudinally, and a group study can be done cross-sectionally.

There are two further types of research that are increasingly popular in applied linguistics, namely, *action research* and *critical research*. Action research belongs to the pragmatist and the advocacy and participatory methodological perspectives. It is a *reflective process* of *problem solving*. Some people think of action research as case studies. It is true that most often action research is done on a case by case basis. But the key to action research is that it is aimed at improving the way the individuals involved in the research process address issues and solve problems. Action research can also be undertaken by larger organizations or institutions, assisted or guided by researchers, with the aim of improving their strategies, practices, and knowledge of the environments within which they practice. Kurt Lewin, who is believed to have coined the term *action research*, described it as 'a comparative research on the conditions and effects of various forms of social action and research leading to social action' that uses 'a spiral of steps, each of which is composed of a circle of planning, action, and fact-finding about the result of the action' (1946). Action research has been particularly popular among language teaching professionals who wish to improve their own as well as their organization's professional practice through the reflective research process.

Critical research cuts across the constructivist, the advocacy and participatory as well as the pragmatist methodological perspectives. Critical research has two rather different origins and histories, one originating in literary criticism and the other in sociology. This has led to the rather literal use of 'critical theory' as an umbrella term to describe theoretical critique. Starting in the 1960s, literary scholars, reacting against the literary criticism in the previous decades which tried to analyze literary texts purely internally, began to incorporate into their analyses and interpretations of literary works semiotic, linguistic and interpretive theory, structuralism, post-structuralism, deconstruction, psychoanalysis, phenomenology, hermeneutics, as well as feminist theory, critical social theory and various forms of neo-Marxist theory. With the expansion of the mass media and popular culture in the 1960s and 70s, social and cultural criticism and literary criticism began to be intertwined in the analysis of popular cultural phenomena, giving rise to the field of Cultural Studies. Critical research in the sociological context, on the other hand, arose from a trajectory extending from the non-positivist sociology of Weber, the neo-Marxist theory of Lukács, to the so-called Frankfurt School of social theorists, most notably Horkheimer and Habermas. It is underpinned by a social theory that is oriented towards critiquing and changing society in its totality, in contrast to traditional theories oriented only to understanding or explaining it. It was intended to be a radical, emancipatory form of social research and concerned itself with 'forms of authority and injustice that accompanied the evolution of industrial and corporate capitalism as a political-economic system' (Lindlof & Taylor, 2002, p. 52). A newer, postmodern version of the critical social theory focuses on what has been called the 'crisis of representation' and rejects the idea that a researcher's work is considered an 'objective depiction of a stable other'; instead, it tries to politicize social problems 'by situating them in historical and cultural contexts, to implicate themselves in the process of collecting and analyzing data, and to relativize their findings' (Lindlof & Taylor, 2002, p. 53). Meaning itself is seen as unstable due to the rapid transformation in social structures and as a result the focus of the research is centered on local manifestations rather than broad generalizations.

Critical research has been particularly appealing to some applied linguists because of the shared interests in language, symbolism, text and meaning. In the 1970s and 1980s, Jürgen Habermas redefined critical social theory as a theory of communication, i.e. communicative competence and communicative rationality on the one hand, distorted communication on the other. Applied linguists who adopt the critical research perspective have focused on the processes of synthesis, production, or construction by which the phenomena and objects of human communication, culture and political consciousness come about. This is reflected in much of the discussion on language ecology, language rights, and linguistic imperialism, as well as on gender and ethnicity in language learning and language use (e.g. Pennycook, 2001; Sealey and Carter, 2004).

2.2.2 THE RESEARCHER'S IDENTITY

As we have said earlier, the choice of research design depends first and foremost on the research question one wants to address. There are, however, practical considerations too. For example, how much time does one have for data collection? A longitudinal study by its very nature requires a substantial period of time. Are there sufficient resources for distributing and analysing questionnaires for a quantitative study on a sizeable population? Another important consideration is the relationship between the researcher and the researched. As many applied linguists carry out participatory research, we get involved with real people in real situations. Our own identities as researchers, our linguistic profile, ethnic origin, age, gender and education background can have a significant and noticeable effect on the way other people react to us. And our own beliefs, values and ideologies can also impact on the way we interpret and present our findings.

Elsewhere Li Wei (2007) talked about two related examples from work with the Pakistani and Chinese communities in Tyneside in the north-east of England. Suzanne Moffatt, a white female researcher of university education, was a non-native speaker of Panjabi who was particularly interested in the bilingual behaviour of young children at the critical kindergarten stage, when they were faced with their first extensive exposure to English. She had previously travelled to Pakistan and had extensive personal contacts within the Pakistani community in Tyneside, partly due to her job as a community speech therapist. Nevertheless, it was impossible to claim the identity of a community member on the grounds of ethnic origin and religious beliefs. She had the further difficulty of having to deal with the male members of the community who tended to be heads of the household. Subsequently she decided to concentrate on a variety of situations in kindergarten and infant school, where she doubled as a teacher's helper and was, in fact, accepted as such. Her social role was quite clear and she was able to carry out a participant observation study which gave her systematic evidence of the language switching behaviours of young incipient bilinguals (for a fuller description of this study and discussions of the findings, see Moffatt, 1990).

In the meantime, Li Wei was interested in the language shift from Chinese monolingualism in the grandparent generation to English-dominant bilingualism in the British-born children's generation which was taking place within the Tyneside Chinese community. Although he was of the same ethnic origin as members of the local Chinese community, his first language was Mandarin and he had only a working knowledge of Cantonese, the lingua franca of the community. Like Suzanne Moffatt, Li Wei had built up extensive personal contacts within the community during a three-year period of residence in Tyneside prior to our study. Because he was the only Chinese in the area who had a degree in English language and literature at the time, he was often asked by the families to help with English language problems when they went to see their doctors and solicitors. He also taught in the Chinese community language school and helped organize Mandarin Chinese and English language classes there. Where Li Wei's situation differed from that of Suzanne Moffatt was that he did have access to the family setting which was usually closed to outsiders. However, he did also have certain difficulties which Suzanne Moffatt did not encounter. Intra-generational interaction among Chinese adults was normally exclusively in Chinese, and intergenerational communication between adults and children was in both English and Chinese. Since Li Wei was accepted by most families as a friend of the parent generation, his use of English was confined to conversations with the British-born children. Most adults refused to speak to him in English, even if it meant that they sometimes had to switch to Mandarin, a non-native variety of Chinese to them, to accommodate his needs. Indeed, the assessments of the English language abilities of the adult Chinese in Tyneside had to be carried out by a non-Chinese researcher (see further discussions in Li Wei, 1994; Milroy, Li Wei and Moffatt, 1993). The main point that we want to make with these two related examples is that there is no point in trying to conceal the 'incompatible' aspects of one's identity in data collection. Instead, we should take into consideration the effect of the researcher's identity during data analysis and make it explicit in the discussions of the findings.

More importantly perhaps, applied linguistics research can never be truly 'value-free'. To continue with the Tyneside example, during Li Wei's fieldwork in the Chinese community, he came across two groups of community leaders with rather different views: one group wanted to emphasize the problems and disadvantages of being speakers of a 'minority' language in an English-dominant environment; they wanted the central and local governments to provide more support by funding community language schools, translating policy documents and public notices into their language and providing bilingual assistants in public services. In contrast, the other group of community leaders wanted to highlight the success story of the Chinese community: their self-reliance and self-efficiency, assimilation into the mainstream society and harmonious relationships both within the community and with other social groups. Both groups tried to influence the research agenda by giving only the examples that they thought would support their views. We have also encountered researchers who had already decided even before the study began that bilingual children, especially those from an ethnic minority background, would have serious difficulties at school because their English was not up to standard. They then set out to find evidence only to confirm their ideas. It is therefore necessary both for those who are planning a research project and those who are reading published results to be aware of the possible ideological influences on the findings and claims of the research.

2.2.3 DATA COLLECTION

The data that applied linguists are interested in can be broadly identified into two categories: interactional and non-interactional data. As has been discussed in the General Introduction, applied linguistics research should have language as its main focus. This does not mean, however, that it has to be language-in-interaction; it could be language attitude, language awareness, motivations and strategies for language learning, language policy, language assessment, etc. In fact, interactional data only constitutes the database for a small proportion of applied linguistics.

Interactional data consist of a continuum with elicited conversation and naturally occurring conversation at each end, according to the degree of naturalness. Conversation can be elicited through a range of methods and techniques such as discourse completion tasks, recall protocols, or role play. The key issue for the interaction obtained through elicitation is its comparability to naturally occurring interaction. For naturally occurring conversation, the key issue is how to capture it (using observation sheet vs. audio-visual recording, for example) and how to strike the balance between details and analytical approach (interactional or conversation analysis). In addition to elicited and recorded conversation, conversation data are also available in a number of other sources such as data banks, the internet, and other mass and social media. These methods are discussed in detail in Zhu Hua (2011).

The so-called *non-interactional data* are data about language practices rather than samples of language practices themselves. Surveys, questionnaires, interviews, self-reports, standard assessments, laboratory experiments can all be used to collect non-interactional data. They are often used to collect large amounts of information from sizeable populations. With the exception of self-reports, the researcher normally has an expectation of what the responses (i.e. data, findings) would be. They are therefore more often used to test hypotheses or verify existing findings and claims. Some applied linguists are also interested in critical analysis of public discourse or media language.

Ethnography is sometimes used as a data collection technique when the researcher is particularly interested in exploring the meaning of a phenomenon. Ethnography is in fact more of a methodology than a method; it is a holistic approach to social phenomena and social practices, including linguistic practices, with specific references to both historical and present contexts. Ethnography requires rich data, often collected through a combination of different means including recordings, interviews and questionnaires. But the key data collection method for ethnography is *in situ* observation. Observation enables the investigator to describe events, actions, behaviours, language use, etc., in detail and to interpret what has happened in context. During observation, researchers make field notes of what they see in as much detail as possible. There are different types of observations, depending on the researcher's role and visibility in the event under study. Researchers can either actively take part in observation and have maximum contact with the people being studied or remain as unintrusive as possible. The main advantages of ethnographic observation are that it allows the researcher to uncover information previously unknown, to gain an in-depth description, and to capture a series of events and processes over time. The challenges are several: researchers may have biases in selecting what to note down; it is difficult to differentiate describing from interpreting what has happened; documenting an event while observing and participating in activities can be a demanding task.

There is a huge amount of published literature on specific techniques and tools for collecting data. Some of the key references and useful guides are listed in the Further Reading.

2.3 Analysing and presentation findings

Data analysis follows closely from research design. It is advisable to consider how you intend to analyse and present the findings during the design stage of the research process. If you have collected interactional data, transcription is the key first step towards analysis. There are different techniques of transcribing language-in-interaction, for example, Conversation Analysis (CA) specifies a set of conventions for sequential analysis. There are also computer software and other new technologies to assist you in transcribing interactional data, including non-verbal communication and multimodality data. However, most people do not follow a specific set of transcription conventions tightly. And most people do not transcribe everything that has been recorded. It could be argued that one cannot transcribe everything after the event has taken place anyway. There are, therefore, certain decisions one has to make in transcribing interactional data: what is to be transcribed and what is to be left out; what gets highlighted or emphasized and how. What should be done to ambiguous elements, e.g. when it is not clear who the speaker was, or what was being referred to. As Ochs (1979) remarked over thirty years ago, such decisions in transcription are also theoretical decisions that would affect the way data is interpreted.

Quantitative data are most often analyzed through statistics and presented in various figures, tables, graphs and diagrams. There are ample guide books for students on how to do quantitative and statistical data analysis. Qualitative data, on the other hand, are usually presented in discursive accounts, with quotations and samples of actual data. For both quantitative and qualitative data analysis, accuracy and accountability is paramount. We are talking about accountability to the participants, to the situation that has been investigated, to the researcher him or herself, as well as to the wider audience. The researcher should be truthful and honest not only in describing what they have observed but also explaining what their ideological stance may be, what they expected to find, and how their identity and relationship with the people they studied impacted on the findings.

3 Ethical considerations

Research involving human subjects must be carried out in accordance with accepted ethical standards and studies in applied linguistics are not an exception. The key considerations are:

(a) Justification: the proposed research will achieve worthwhile objectives and the time and resources needed for the research are justifiable. Participants' welfare and public responsibility are paramount. Where the project may potentially put the participants at risk, either physically or psychologically, care must be taken to ensure that the benefits of the project outweigh the risks. Appropriate support mechanisms need to be provided to minimize any potential risk. Where there is a possible conflict of interest (e.g. the work is to be carried out in the same organization or sponsored by an organization), again a case must be made.

(b) Access to participant(s): this includes issues of participants' privacy, the need to reduce invasiveness of the presence of researchers, and issues of confidentiality and anonymity, etc.

(c) Informed consent: when seeking consent, participants need to be fully informed about the aim and nature of the project and any potential risks. They should be made aware of their rights in the project such as the right to withdraw anytime, the right to refuse to answer any question, the right to ask any question, etc. With young and school-age children and vulnerable populations such as patients, consent must be sought from their parents, guardians, carers or schools (if the research is carried out on the school premises or with the assistance from the school).

Other ethical concerns relevant to studies in applied linguistics include:

(d) Participants' language ability: whether participants' language ability is sufficient for them to understand the informed consent form.

(e) Cross-cultural differences in ethics: there may be differences in the ethical considerations between the culture in which the research is carried out and the culture from which participants come. This issue is particularly relevant to studies on Study Abroad and intercultural interactions. It is important to anticipate any potential differences and clarify any misunderstandings.

Most educational institutes have an ethics committee which oversees the ethical approval and a set of ethical approval procedures. Students must check with the procedure and seek approval before carrying out data collection. In addition, ethical guidelines are provided by some professional bodies or research journals. For example,

- TESOL Quarterly Research Guidelines are available at www.tesol.org/s_tesol/seccss. asp?CID=476&DID=2150
- British Association for Applied Linguistics (BAAL) has a set of recommendations for good practice in applied linguistics student projects www.baal.org.uk/about_goodpractice_ stud.pdf
- British Education Research Association (BERA) ethical guidelines are available at www.bera.ac.uk/ethics-and-educational-research-philosophical-perspectives/

Wray & Bloomer (2006) also provides useful information on the differences between confidentiality and anonymity and data protection laws.

4 Some suggestions to instructors

Nowadays research training is a compulsory component of applied linguistics programmes. As Lorch (n.d.) points out, research training often has several competing objectives:

- To facilitate a theoretical understanding of what research is;
- To provide an introduction to the research sub-areas of applied linguistics;
- To survey the types of methodology used in practice and their rationales;
- To develop practical skills needed to carry out research.

There is a need to satisfy these multiple and potentially incongruent objectives within a limited period of contact hours. It may be useful to consider a two-step approach to research training: one at the outset of the students' studies and the second at the time students begin to develop plans for their own research.

A crucial aspect of the initial training is critical analysis in order to develop the ability to evaluate the strengths and weakness of research assumptions, data analysis and interpretation; identify inadequacies, fallacies, or lack of plausibility, and select the strongest elements of existing viewpoints to provide a synthesis. At the same time students need to develop a theoretical appreciation of the research process and gain an understanding of the different benefits of pursuing formal research. This should include training in:

- A systematic process of inquiry
- A set of procedural conventions
- A method for organizing observations
- A means of evaluating findings

Comparing several published studies and writing book reviews can be very useful exercises for this initial phase of research training.

Once the students are ready to plan their own projects, training can be given to specific research designs, data collection methods, transcription, quantitative and qualitative data analyses, and presentation. Research methods training should equip students with an under-standing of a multiplicity of methods, their respective advantages and disadvantages, and both the feasibility and ethics of choosing a specific method. Helping the students to learn to draw conclusions from their own data is another key element of the research training.

Group discussions of individual student projects can be very beneficial. They provide a good opportunity for students to become acquainted with different methods, develop academically supportive relationships and share good practice. They can also enable the students to become progressively reflective, interpretive, analytical and critical, which is not only the key to applied linguistics as a field of enquiry but also to themselves in their own professional practice.

Applied linguistics often prides itself as a multidisciplinary field. As the articles in this Reader show, there is a whole range of approaches that can be, and has indeed been, adopted. Applied linguists are also interested in a wide range of language phenomena in diverse social contexts. All of these give the impression to the outsider that applied linguistics is a diffused field with no clear focus or coherent perspective. For the future of applied linguistics, methodological considerations should be given priority both in research and in training.

References

Berry, John, 1999, Emics and etics: a symbiotic conception. *Culture & Psychology* 5, 165–171

Creswell, John, 2003, *Research Design: qualitative and quantitative and mixed methods.* London: Sage

de Vaus, David, 2001, *Research Design in Social Research.* London: Sage

Lewin, Kurt, 1946, Action research and minority problems. *Journal of Social Issues,* 2(4): 34–46

Li Wei, (ed.) 2007, *The Bilingualism Reader* (2nd edition). Oxford: Routledge

Li Wei, 1994, *Three Generations Two Languages One Family: language choice and language shift in a Chinese community in Britain.* Clevedon: Multilingual Matters

Lindlof, Thomas, and Taylor, Bryan, 2002, *Qualitative Communication Research Methods* (2nd edition). London: Sage

Lorch, Marjorie, n.d., Turning students into researchers: introduction to research methods in applied linguistics. Subject Centre for Languages, Linguistics and Area Studies. www.llas.ac.uk/resources/gpg/2273

Mallon, Thomas, 1989, *Stolen Words: forays into the origins and ravages of plagiarism.* New York: Ticknor and Fields

Milroy, Lesley, Li Wei, and Moffatt, Suzanne, 1993, Discourse patterns and fieldwork strategies in urban settings. *Journal of Multilingual and Multicultural Development,* 12: 287–300

Moffatt, Suzanne, 1990, Becoming bilingual: a sociolinguistic study of the communication of young mother tongue Panjabi-speaking children. Unpublished Ph.D. thesis, University of Newcastle upon Tyne

Ochs, Elinor, 1979, Transcription as theory. In E. Ochs and B. Schieffelin (eds), *Developmental Pragmatics.* New York: Academic Press, pp. 43–72

Pecorari, Diane, 2003, Good and original: plagiarism and patchwriting in academic second-language writing. *Journal of Second Language Writing,* 12: 317–345

Pennycook, Alastair, 1996, Borrowing others' words: text, ownership, memory, and plagiarism. *TESOL Quarterly,* 30(2): 201–230

Pennycook, Alastair, 2001, *Critical Applied Linguistics: a critical introduction*, London: Lawrence Erlbaum Associates

Sealey, Alison, and Carter, Bob, 2004, *Applied Linguistics as Social Science*, London: Continuum

Sherman, Jane, 1992, Your own thoughts in your own words. *ELT Journal*, 46(2): 190–198

Sutherland-Smith, Wendy (2005) Pandora's box: academic perceptions of student plagiarism in writing. *Journal of English for Academic Purposes*, 4: 83–95

Zhu Hua, 2011, *The Language and Intercultural Communication Reader*. Oxford: Routledge

NOTES FOR STUDENTS AND INSTRUCTORS

Study questions

1 What is the difference between method and methodology?
2 What are the key methodological perspectives according to Creswell's Worldview classification?
3 What are the main advantages and disadvantages of the different research designs – etic vs. emic, quantitative vs. qualitative, experimental vs. non-experimental, longitudinal vs. cross-sectional, single case study vs. group study?
4 What is action research?
5 What is critical research?
6 How can the identity of the research affect data collection and data analysis?
7 What are the key ethical considerations in applied linguistics research?

Study activities

1 Choose two recently published studies on a topic in applied linguistics. Compare the way the researchers ask the questions and design the studies. Is there any difference? How do they justify the questions and the designs?
2 Choose a study that has used a mixed design, e.g. longitudinal and cross-sectional, quantitative and qualitative. What is the added value of the mixed design, i.e. what are the things that a single design is unable to reveal? Are there any contradictions in the findings by different research designs? If yes, how does the researcher interpret them?
3 Carry out an observational study in an everyday situation. How does your own identity affect the relationship with the people you are observing, your perspective on what you observe, and how you interpret what you observe? What ethical issues do you need to consider for the study?

Further reading

There are literally hundreds of books on research methodology, research design and methods of data collection and analysis. Publishers such as Sage and Palgrave specialize in books on research methods.

Creswell, John, 2003, *Research design: qualitative and quantitative and mixed methods,* London: Sage, which has been referred to in this chapter provides a useful overview of different methodological perspectives in research design.

Hunston, Susan and Oakey, David 2009, *Introducing Applied Linguistics: concepts and skills,* Oxford: Routledge, is a concise, introductory text that introduces students to the key concepts faced when studying applied linguistics as well as the study skills needed for academic reading and writing.

Dörnyei, Zoltan, 2007, *Research Methods in Applied Linguistics: quantitative, qualitative, and mixed methodologies,* Oxford: Oxford University Press, offers a practical guide to different designs and methods in applied linguistics.

Paltridge, Brian and Phakiti, Aek, 2010, *Continuum Companion to Research Methods in Applied Linguistics,* London: Continuum, is a useful one-volume guide for students. The book includes: qualitative and quantitative methods; research techniques and approaches; ethical considerations; sample studies; a glossary of key terms; and, resources for students. It also looks at various topics in applied linguistics in depth, including gender and language, language and identity, pragmatics, vocabulary, and grammar.

Perry, Fred Lehman, 2005, *Research in Applied Linguistics: becoming a discerning consumer,* Oxford: Routledge, is an introduction to the foundations of research methods, with the goal of enabling students and professionals in the field of applied linguistics to become not just casual consumers of research who passively read bits and pieces of a research article, but discerning consumers able to effectively use published research for practical purposes in educational settings.

Other introductory texts on research methods in applied linguistics include:

Larsen-Freeman, Diane and Long, Michael, 1991, *An Introduction to Second Language Acquisition Research,* London: Longman.

Nunan, David, 1992, *Research Methods in Language Learning,* Cambridge: Cambridge University Press.

Dean, James and Rodgers, Theodore, 2003, *Doing Second Language Research,* Oxford : Oxford University Press.

Mackey, Alison and Gass, Susan, 2005, *Second Language Research: methodology and design,* Oxford: Routledge.

Practical guides to specific methods include:

Dörnyei, Zoltán, 2002, *Questionnaires in Second Language Research: construction, administration and processing,* Hove: Psychology Press.

Duff, Patricia, 2008, *Case Study Research in Applied Linguistics,* Mahwah, NJ: Lawrence Erlbaum Associates.

Burns, Anne, 2009, *Doing Action Research in English Language Teaching,* Oxford: Routlege.

Guides on quantitative and statistical methods in applied linguistics include:

Hatch, Evelyn and Lazaraton, Anne, 1991, *The Research Manual: design and statistics for applied linguistics,* Boston: Heinle & Heinle.

Larson-Hall, Jenifer, 2009, *A Guide to Doing Statistics in Second Language Research Using SPSS,* Oxford: Routledge.

Baayen, R. Harald, 2008, *Analyzing Linguistic Data: a practical introduction to statistics,* Cambridge: Cambridge University Press.

Li Wei and Moyer, Melissa (eds), 2008, *The Blackwell Guide to Research Methods in Bilingualism and Multilingualism,* Oxford: Blackwell, has a comprehensive coverage of research designs and methods ranging from sampling, recording and transcription to laboratory experiments and brain imagining techniques. The examples are drawn from studies of bilingualism and multilingualism.

Wray, Alison and Bloomer, Aileen, 2006, *Projects in Linguistics: a practical guide to researching language* (2nd edition), London: Hodder Arnold, provides advice on research projects in different areas of linguistics and useful information on the differences between confidentiality and anonymity and data protection laws.

Bitchener, John, 2009, *Writing an Applied Linguistics Thesis or Dissertation: a guide to presenting empirical research,* Basingtoke: Palgrave, introduces first-time thesis writers to the process of writing up empirical research.

Resources

The section contains lists of key references, handbooks, book series, journals, corpora, professional associations and websites in applied linguistics.

1 Key references

Due to the vast number of articles published in applied linguistics, the following lists contain predominantly books and collections of articles, especially those that are published since 2000. Relevant handbooks are listed in 2, book series in 3, and journals in 4.

Language teaching (general)

Brown, H.D., 2006, *Principles of Language Teaching and Learning* (5th edition), Harlow: Pearson.
Carter, R. and Nunan, D. (eds), 2001, *The Cambridge Guide to Teaching English to Speakers of Other Languages*, Cambridge: Cambridge University Press.
Celce-Marcia, M. (ed.), 2001, *Teaching English as a Second or Foreign Language* (3rd edition), Boston: Heinle & Heinle.
Widdowson, H.G., 2003, *Defining Issues in English Language Teaching*, Oxford: Oxford University Press.

Language teaching (approaches)

Norton, B. and Toohey, K. (eds), 2004, *Critical Pedagogies and Language Learning*, Cambridge: Cambridge University Press.
Cook, V., 2008, *Second Language Learning and Language Teaching*, London: Arnold.
Doughty, C. and Williams, J. (eds), 1998, *Focus on Form in Classroom Second Language Acquisition*, Cambridge: Cambridge University Press.
Edbert, J.E. and Hanson-Smith, E. (eds), 1999, *CALL Environments: research, practice and critical issues*, Alexandra, VA: TESOL.
Ellis, R., 2003, *Task-Based Language Teaching and Learning*, Oxford: Oxford University Press.
Kramsch, C. (ed.), 2002, *Language Acquisition and Language Socialization: ecological perspectives*, London: Continuum.
Larsen-Freeman, D. and Cameron, L., 2008, *Complex Systems and Applied Linguistics*, Oxford: Oxford University Press.
Nunan, D., 2004, *Task-Based Language Teaching*, Cambridge: Cambridge University Press.
O'Keefe, A., McCarthy, M., and Carter, R., 2007, *From Corpus to Classroom: language use and language teaching*, Cambridge: Cambridge University Press.

Richards, J. and Renandya, W. (eds), 2002, *Methodology in Language Teaching: an anthology of current practice*, Cambridge: Cambridge University Press.
Richards, J. and Rodgers, T., 2001, *Approaches and Methods in Language Teaching*, Cambridge: Cambridge University Press.
Young, R., 2009, *Discursive Practice in Language Learning and Teaching*, Oxford: Blackwell.
van den Branden, K., 2006, *Task-Based Language Education*, Cambridge: Cambridge University Press.

Language teaching (skills and structures)

Anderson, N., 2008, *Reading*, New York: McGraw-Hill.
Blachowicz, C. and Ogle, D., 2008, *Reading Comprehension: strategies for independent learners* (2nd edition), New York: Guilford.
Block, C. and Parris, S., 2008, *Comprehension Instruction: research-based best practices* (2nd edition), New York: Guilford.
Carter, R., Hughes, R. and McCarthy, M.J., 2001, *Exploring Grammar in Context*, Cambridge: Cambridge University Press.
Celce-Marcia, M. and Olshtain, E., 2000, *Discourse and Context in Language Teaching*, Cambridge: Cambridge University Press.
Cook, V. and Bassetti, B. (eds), 2005, *Second Language Writing Systems*, Clevedon: Multilingual Matters.
Day, R.R. and Bamford, J., 1998, *Extensive Reading in the Second Language Classroom*, Cambridge: Cambridge University Press.
Ferris, D. and Hedgecock, J., 2005, *Teaching ESL Composition: purpose, process and practice* (2nd edition), Mahwah, NJ: Lawrence Erlbaum.
Flowerdew, J. (ed.), 2005, *Academic Discourse*. Harlow: Longman.
Flowerdew, J. and Miller, L., 2005, *Second Language Listening: theory and practice*, Cambridge: Cambridge University Press.
Grabe, W., 2009, *Reading in a Second Language: moving from theory to practice*, Cambridge: Cambridge University Press.
Grabe, W. and Stoller, F., 2002, *Teaching and Research Reading*, Harlow: Longman.
Han, Z.-H. and Anderson, N. (eds), 2009, *Second Language Reading: research and instruction*, Mahwah, NJ: Lawrence Erlbaum.
Hinkel, E. and Fotos, S. (eds), 2002, *New Perspectives on Grammar Teaching in Second Language Classrooms*, Mahwah, NJ: Lawrence Erlbaum.
Hudson, T., 2007, *Teaching Second Language Reading*, Oxford: Oxford University Press.
Hyland, K., 2004, *Disciplinary Discourses: social interactions in academic writing*, Ann Arbor: The University of Michigan Press.
Koda, K., 2005, *Insights into Second Language Reading*, Cambridge: Cambridge University Press.
Krashen, S., 2004, *The Power of Reading* (2nd edition), Portsmouth, NH: Heinemann.
Kroll, B. (ed.), 2003, *Exploring the Dynamics of Second Language Writing*, Cambridge: Cambridge University Press.
Larsen-Freeman, D., 2003, *Teaching Language: from grammar to grammaring*, Boston: Heinle & Heinle.
Lynch, T., 2009, *Teaching Second Language Listening*, Oxford: Oxford University Press.
Nation, I.S.P., 2001, *Learning Vocabulary in Another Language*, Cambridge: Cambridge University Press.
Nation, I.S.P., 2009, *Teaching ESL/EFL Reading and Writing*, Oxford: Routledge.
Pressley, M., 2006, *Reading Instruction that Works* (3rd edition), New York: Guilford.
Schmitt, N. (ed.), 2004, *Formulaic Sequences*, Amsterdam: Benjamins.
Schmitt, N., 2000, *Vocabulary in Language Teaching*, Cambridge: Cambridge University Press.
Silva, T. and Matsuda, P.K. (eds), 2001, *On Second Language Writing*, Mahwah, NJ: Lawrence Erlbaum.
Swales, J., 2004, *Research Genres: explorations and applications*, Cambridge: Cambridge University Press.

Language teaching (learner-related issues)

Benson, P., 2001, *Teaching and Researching: autonomy in language learning*, Harlow: Pearson.
Cohen, A.D. and Macaro, E. (eds), 2007, *Language Learning Strategies*, Oxford: Oxford University Press.
Dornyei, Z., 2001, *Teaching and Researching Motivation*, Harlow: Longman.
Griffiths, C. (ed.), 2009, *Lessons from Good Language Learners*, Cambridge: Cambridge University Press.

Macaro, E., 2001, *Learning Strategies in Foreign and Second Language Classrooms*, London: Continuum.

O'Malley, J.M. and Chamot, A.U., 1990, *Learning Strategies in Second Language Acquisition*, Cambridge: Cambridge University Press.

Oxford, R.L., 1990, *Language Learning Strategies: what every teacher should know*, Boston: Newbury House.

Language teaching (classroom)

Cole, K.M. and Jane Zuengler, J., 2007, *The Research Process in Classroom Discourse Analysis: current perspectives*, Oxford: Routledge.

Gibbons, P., 2006, *Bridging Discourses in the ESL Classroom: teachers, students and researchers*, London: Continuum.

Hall, J.K. and Verplaetse, L.S. (eds), 2000, *Second and Foreign Language Learning Through Classroom Interaction*, Oxford: Routledge.

Luk, J.C.M. and Lin, A.M.Y., 2006, *Classroom Interactions as Cross-cultural Encounters: native speakers in EFL lessons*, Oxford: Routledge.

Mackay, S.L., 2006, *Researching Second Language Classrooms*, Mahwah, NJ: Lawrence Erlbaum.

Rex, L.A. and Schiller, L., 2009, *Using Discourse Analysis to Improve Classroom Interaction*, Oxford: Routledge.

Runesson, U., 2009, *Classroom Discourse and the Space of Learning*, Mahwah, NJ: Lawrence Erlbaum.

Seedhouse, P., 2005, *The Interactional Architecture of the Language Classroom*, Oxford: Blackwell.

Walsh, S., 2006, *Investigating Classroom Discourse*, Oxford: Routledge.

Language teaching (teacher-related issues)

Burns, A. and Richards, J., 2009, *Cambridge Guide to Second Language Teacher Education*, Cambridge: Cambridge University Press.

Cohen, A.D. and Weaver, S.J., 2006, *Styles and Strategies-Based Instruction: a teachers' guide*, Minneapolis: Centre for Advanced Research on Language Acquisition, University of Minnesota.

Dornyei, Z., 2001, *Motivational Strategies in the Language Classroom*, Cambridge: Cambridge University Press.

Ellis, R., 2001, *Form Focused Instruction and Second Language Learning*, Oxford: Blackwell.

James, P., 2001, *Teachers in Action: tasks for in-service language teacher education and development*, Cambridge: Cambridge University Press.

Johnson, K.E., 2009, *Second Language Teacher Education*, Oxford: Routledge.

Tomlinson, B. (ed.), 2003, *Developing Materials for Language Teaching*, London: Continuum.

Language teaching (assessments)

Alderson, J. C., 2000, *Assessing Reading*, Cambridge: Cambridge University Press.

Alderson, J.C., 2005, *Diagnosing Foreign Language Proficiency: the interface between learning and assessment*, London: Continuum.

Brown, H.D., 2004, *Language Assessment: principles and classroom practice*, White Plains, NY: Pearson.

Buck, G., 2001, *Assessing Listening*, Cambridge: Cambridge University Press.

Chapelle, C.A. and Douglas, D., 2006, *Assessing Language Through Computer Technology*, Cambridge: Cambridge University Press.

Douglas, D., 2000, *Testing Language for Specific Purposes: theory and practice*, Cambridge: Cambridge Univerity Press.

Ekbatani, G. and Pierson, H., (eds), *Learner-Directed Assessment in ESL*, Mahwah, NJ: Lawrence Erlbaum.

Gottlieb, M. and Nguyen, D., 2007, *Assessment and Accountability in Language Education Programmes*, Philadelphia, PA: Caslon Publishing.

Hughes, A., 2003, *Testing for Language Teachers*, Cambridge: Cambridge University Press.

Luoma, S., 2004, *Assessing Speaking*, Cambridge: Cambridge University Press.

McKay, P., 2006, *Assessing Young Language Learners*, Cambridge: Cambridge University Press.

McNamara, T. and Roever, C., 2006, *Language Testing: the social dimension*, Oxford: Blackwell.

Purpura, J., 2004, *Assessing Grammar*, Cambridge: Cambridge University Press.

Read, J., 2000, *Assessing Vocabulary*, Cambridge: Cambridge University Press.

Shohamy, E., 2001, *The Power of Tests*, Harlow: Longman.

Weigle, S.C., 2002, *Assessing Writing*, Cambridge: Cambridge University Press.

Culture and politics in language teaching and learning

Alderson, C., 2009, *The Politics of Language Education: individuals and institutions*, Clevedon: Multilingual Matters.
Corbett, J., 2003, *An Intercultural Approach to English Language Teaching*, Clevedon: Multilingual Matters.
Guilherme, M., 2002, *Critical Citizens for an Intercultural World: foreign language education as cultural politics*, Clevedon: Multilingual Matters.
Hellermann, J., 2003, *Social Actions for Classroom Language Learning*, Clevedon: Multilingual Matters.
Holliday, A., 2005, *The Struggle to Teach English as an International Language*, Oxford: Oxford University Press.
Kramsch, C., 2002, *Language Acquisition and Language Socialization*, London: Continuum.
Lantolf, J. and Thorne, S., 2006, *Sociocultural Theory and the Genesis of Second Language Development*, Oxford: Oxford University Press.
Norton, B., 2000, *Identity and Language Learning: gender, ethnicity and educational change*, Harlow: Longman.
Zhu Hua, Seedhouse, P., Li Wei and Cook, V. (eds), 2007, *Language Learning and Teaching as Social Inter-Action*, Basingstoke: Palgrave.

Identity in language learning

Block, D., 2007, *Second Language Identities*, London: Continuum.
Breen, M. (ed.), 2001, *Learner Contributions to Language Learning*, Harlow: Longman.
Lin, A. M. Y. (ed.), 2006, *Problematizing Identity: everyday struggles in language, culture and education*, Mahwah, NJ: Lawrence Erlbaum.
Mantero, M., 2006, *Identity and Second Language Learning: culture, inquiry, and dialogic activity in educational contexts*, Norwood, NJ: Information Age Publishing.
Menard-Warwick, J., 2009, *Gendered Identities and Immigrant Language Learning*, Clevedon: Multilingual Matters.
Norton, B. and Pavlenko, A. (eds), 2004, *Gender and English Language Learners*, Alexandria, VA: TESOL.
Pavlenko, A., Blackledge, A., Piller, I. and Teutsch-Dwyer, M., 2001, *Multilingualism, Second Language Learning and Gender*, Berlin: Mouton de Gruyter.

Minority learners

Block, D., 2006, *Multilingual Identities in a Global City: London stories*, London: Palgrave.
Canagarajah, S., 2002, *Critical Academic Writing and Multilingual Students*, Ann Arbor: University of Michigan Press.
Edwards, J., 2009, *Language Diversity in the Classroom*, Clevedon: Multilingual Matters.
Leung, C. and Creese, A. (eds), 2010, *English as an Additional Language: approaches to teaching linguistic minority students*, London: Naldic/Sage.
Menard-Warwick, J., 2009, *Gendered Identities and Immigrant Language Learning*, Clevedon: Multilingual Matters.
Ramirez, D., Wiley, T.G., de Klerk, G., Lee, E. and Wright, W.E., 2005, *Ebonics: the urban education debate* (2nd edition), Clevedon: Multilingual Matters.
Wiley, T.G., Lee, J.S. and Rumberger, R.W., 2009, *The Education of Minority Immigrants in the United States*, Clevedon: Multilingual Matters.

Language-in-education policy

Canagarajah, S. (ed.), 2005, *Reclaiming the Local in Language Policies and Practices*, Mahwah, NJ: Lawrence Erlbaum.
Crawford, James, *At War with Diversity: U.S. language policy in an age of anxiety*, Clevedon: Multilingual Matters.
Lin, A.M.Y. and Martin, P. (eds), 2005, *Decolonisation, Globalization: language-in-education policy and practice*, Clevedon: Multilingual Matters.
Tollefson, J.W., 2001, *Language Policies in Education: critical issues*, Oxford: Routledge.

Second language acquisition

Block, David, 2003, *The Social Turn in Second Language Acquisition*, Edinburgh: Edinburgh University Press.

de Bot, K., Lowie, W. and Verspoor, M., 2005, *Second Language Acquisition: a resource book*, Oxford: Routledge.

DeKeyser, R. (ed.), 2007, *Practice in a Second Language*, Cambridge: Cambridge University Press.

Dornyei, Z., 2005, *The Psychology of the Language Learner: individual differences in second language acquisition*, Mahwah, NJ: Lawrence Erlbaum.

Dornyei, Z., 2009, *The Psychology of Second Language Acquisition*, Oxford: Oxford University Press.

Ellis, N.C. and Larsen-Freeman, D. (eds), 2006, *Language Emergence: implications for applied linguistics*. A special issues of *Applied Linguistics*, 27.

Ellis, R., 2008, *The Study of Second Language Acquisition* (2nd edition), Oxford: Oxford University Press.

Gass, S. and Selinker, L., 2008, *Second Language Acquisition: an introductory course* (3rd edition), Mahwah, NJ: Lawrence Erlbaum.

Han, Z.-H., 2004, *Fossilization in Adult Second Language Acquisition*, Clevedon: Multilingual Matters.

Han, Z.-H., (ed.) 2008, *Understanding Second Language Process*, Clevedon: Multilingual Matters.

Han, Z.-H. and Odlin, T., 2006, *Studies in Fossilization in Second Language Acquisition*, Clevedon: Multilingual Matters.

Housen, A. and Pierrard, M. (eds), 2005, *Current Issues in Instructed Second Language Acquisition*, Berlin: Mouton de Gruyter.

Lantolf, J.P., 2000, *Sociocultural Theory and Second Language Learning*, Oxford: Oxford University Press.

Lightbown, P.M. and Spada, N., 2006, *How Languages Are Learned* (3rd edition), Oxford: Oxford University Press.

Macaro, E. (ed.), 2010, *The Continuum Companion to Second Language Acquisition*, London: Continuum.

Mackey, A. (ed.), 2007, *Conversational Interaction in Second Language Acquisition*, Oxford: Oxford University Press.

Mitchell, R. and Myles, F., 2004, *Second Language Learning Theories* (2nd edition), London: Arnold.

Ortega, L., 2007, *Second Language Acquisition*, London: Hodder Education.

Paradis, M., 2009, *Declarative and Procedural Determinants of Second Languages*, Amsterdam: Benjamins.

Piennemann, M., 1998, *Language Processing and Second Language Development: processability theory*, Amsterdam: Benjamins.

Ritchie, W. and Bhatia, T. (eds), 2009, *The New Handbook of Second Language Acquisition*, Bingley: Emerald.

Schumann, J.H., Crowell, S.E., Jones, N.E., Lee, N., Schuchert, S.A. and Wood, L.A., 2004, *The Neurobiology of Learning: perspectives from second language acquisition*, Mahwaw, NJ: Lawrence Erlbaum.

Van Patten, B., 1996, *Input Processing and Grammar Instruction in Second Language Acquisition*, Norwood, NJ: Ablex.

Van Patten, B. and Williams, J., 2006, *Theories in Second Language Acquisition: an introduction*, Oxford: Routledge.

White, L., 2003, *Second Language Acquisition and Universal Grammar*, Cambridge: Cambridge University Press.

New approaches to language relevant to language learning

Goldberg, A., 2006, *Constructions at Work: the nature of generalisation in language*, Oxford: Oxford University Press.

Leeuwen, T. van, 2005, *Introducing Social Semiotics*, Oxford: Routledge.

Tomasello, M., 2003, *Constructing a Language: a usage-based theory of language acquisition*, Cambridge, MA: Harvard University Press.

Wodak, R. and Meyer, M. (eds), 2002, *Methods of Critical Discourse Analysis*, London: Sage.

Wray, A., 2002, *Formulaic Language and the Lexicon*, Cambridge: Cambridge University Press.

General references

Biber, D., Johansson, S., Leech, G., Conrad, S. and Finega, E. (eds), 1999, *Longman Grammar of Spoken and Written English*, Harlow: Longman.

Crystal, D., 2003, *The Cambridge Encyclopaedia of the English Language* (2nd edition), Cambridge: Cambridge University Press.

Davies, A., 2005, *A Glossary of Applied Linguistics*, Edinburgh: Edinburgh University Press.
Johnson, K. and Johnson, H. (eds), 1999, *Encyclopedic Dictionary of Applied Linguistics*, Oxford: Blackwell.
Richards, J. and Schmidt, R. (eds), 2010, *Longman Dictionary of Language Teaching and Applied Linguistics*, 4th edition, Harlow: Longman.

2 Handbooks

Handbooks of Applied Linguistics, published by Mouton de Gruyter under the general editorship of Karlfried Knapp and Gerd Antos, contain nine volumes:

1   Communicative Competence of the Individual
2   Interpersonal Communication
3   Communication in the Professions
4   Communication in the Public Sphere
5   Foreign Language Communication
6   Multilingualism and Multilingual Communication
7   Intercultural Communication
8   Technical Communication
9   Language and Communication: Diversity and Change

Encyclopaedia of Language and Education, published by Springer under the general editorship of Nancy Hornberger, contains ten volumes:

1   Language Policy and Political Issues in Education
2   Literacy
3   Discourse and Education
4   Second and Foreign Language Education
5   Bilingual Education
6   Knowledge about Language
7   Language Testing and Assessment
8   Language Socialization
9   Ecology of Language
10 Research Methods in Language and Education

Four single-volume handbooks provide comprehensive and in-depth surveys of the field:

Davies, A. and Elder, C. (eds), 2004, *Handbook of Applied Linguistics*, Oxford: Blackwell.
Kaplan, R., 2010, *The Oxford Handbook of Applied Linguistics*, second edition, Oxford: Oxford University Press.
Simpson, J., 2011, *The Routledge Handbook of Applied Linguistics*, Oxford: Routledge.
Spolsky, Bernard, and Francis M. Hult (eds), 2007, *Handbook of Educational Linguistics*, Oxford: Blackwell.

Other relevant handbooks include:

Aarts, B. and McMahon, A. (eds), 2006, *Handbook of English Linguistics*, Oxford: Blackwell.
Bhatia, T.K. and Ritchie, W.C. (eds), 2003, *Handbook of Bilingualism*, Oxford: Blackwell.
Coulmas, F. (ed.), 1998, *Handbook of Sociolinguistics*, Oxford: Blackwell.
Coupland, N. (ed.), 2010, *Handbook of Language and Globalisation*, Oxford: Blackwell.
Doughty, C.J. and Long, M. (eds), 2003, *Handbook of Second Language Acquisition*, Oxford: Blackwell.
Fitch, K. and Sanders, R.E. (eds), 2005, *Handbook of Language and Social Interaction*, Mahwah, NJ: Lawrence Erlbaum.
Fletcher, P. and MacWhinney, B. (eds), 1996, *Handbook of Child Language*, Oxford: Blackwell.
Hickey, R. (ed.), 2010, *Handbook of Language Contact*, Oxford: Blackwell.
Hinkel, E. (ed.), 2005, *Handbook of Research in Second Language Teaching and Learning*, Mahwah, NJ: Lawrence Erlbaum.
Holm, J. and Meyerhoff, M., 2003, *Handbook of Language and Gender*, Oxford: Blackwell.
Horn, L. and Ward, G. (eds), 2005, *Handbook of Pragmatics*, Oxford: Blackwell.

Joshi, R. and Aaron, P. (eds), 2006, *Handbook of Orthography and Literacy*, Mahwah, NJ: Lawrence Erlbaum.
Kachru, B., Kachru, Y. and Nelson, C. (eds), 2006, *Handbook of World Englishes*, Oxford: Blackwell.
Kroll, J.F. and De Groot, A.M.B. (eds), 2005, *Handbook of Bilingualism: Psycholinguistic Approaches*, Oxford: Oxford University Press.
Long, M. and Doughty, C. (eds), 2009, *Handbook of Language Teaching and Testing*, Oxford: Wiley-Blackwell.
Robinson, P. and Ellis, N. (eds), 2008, *Handbook of Cognitive Linguistics and Second Language Acquisition*. Oxford: Routledge.
Schiffrin, D., Tannen, D. and Hamilton, H.E., (eds) 2001, *Handbook of Discourse Analysis*, Oxford: Blackwell.

3 Book series

Cambridge Applied Linguistics contains titles such as:

Cognition and Second Language Instruction
Computer Applications in Second Language Acquisition
Corpora in Applied Linguistics
Criterion-Referenced Language Testing
Critical Pedagogies and Language Learning
Culture in Second Language Teaching and Learning
Evaluating Second Language Education
Exploring the Dynamics of Second Language Writing
Exploring the Second Language Mental Lexicon
Feedback in Second Language Writing
Focus on Form in Classroom Second Language Acquisition
Immersion Education
Interactive Approaches to Second Language Reading
Interfaces Between Second Language Acquisition and Language Testing Research
Language Program Evaluation
Language Transfer
Learning Strategies in Second Language Acquisition
Learning Vocabulary in Another Language
Modelling and Assessing Vocabulary Knowledge
Network-Based Language Teaching: Concepts and Practice
Practice in a Second Language
Pragmatics in Language Teaching
Reading in a Second Language
Researching and Applying Metaphor
Research Perspectives on English for Academic Purposes
Second Language Needs Analysis
Second Language Vocabulary Acquisition
Second Language Writing (Cambridge Applied Linguistics)
Task-Based Language Education
The Learner-Centred Curriculum
Understanding Expertise in Teaching

Cambridge Handbook for Language Teachers contains the following:

Communicative Activities for EAP
Dialogue Activities
Dictation
Dictionary Activities
Extensive Reading Activities for Teaching Language
Intercultural Language Activities
Keep Talking
Language Activities for Teenagers
Laughing Matters
Learner Autonomy

Learning One-to-One
Lessons from Nothing
Literature in the Language Classroom
Personalizing Language Learning
Pictures for Language Learning
Planning Lessons and Courses
Pronunciation Practice Activities
Stories
Teach Business English
Teaching Adult Second Language Learners
Teaching English Spelling
Teaching Large Multilevel Classes
Teaching Listening Comprehension
Testing Spoken Language
Using Authentic Video in the Language Classroom
Using Folktales
Using Newspapers in the Classroom
Using the Board in the Language Classroom
Working with Images
Working with Words

Other series published by Cambridge University Press include *Cambridge Language Assessment, Cambridge Language Education, Cambridge Teacher Training and Development.*

Oxford Applied Linguistics contains the following:

A Cognitive Approach to Language Learning
Analysing Learner Language
Complex Systems and Applied Linguistics
Context and Culture in Language Teaching
Conversational Interaction in a Second Language
English as a Lingua Franca: Attitude and Identity
Formulaic Language: Pushing the Boundaries
Individual Freedom in Language Teaching
Language Learner Strategies
Language Play Language Learning
Language Testing in Practice
Lexical Phrases in Language Teaching
Linguistics Imperialism
Literacy and Second Language Oracy
Research Methods in Applied Linguistics
Resisting Linguistic Imperialism in English Teaching
Sociocultural Theory and Second Language Learning
Sociocultural Theory and the Genesis of Second Language Development
Task-Based Language Learning and Teaching
The Phonology of English as an International Language
The Psychology of Second Language Acquisition
The Struggle to Teach English as an International Language

Oxford Handbooks for Language Teachers contains titles on:

Communication in the Language Classroom
Doing Second Language Research
Doing Task-Based Teaching
ESOL: A Critical Guide
Exploring Learner Language
From Experience to Knowledge in ELT
How Languages Are Learned

Intercultural Business Communication
Teaching American English Pronunciation
Teaching Business English
Teaching English as an International Language
Teaching English Overseas
Teaching Second Language Listening
Teaching Second Language Reading
Teaching the Pronunciation of English as a Lingua Franca
Teaching Young Language Learners

Oxford University Press also publishes a series, *Oxford Introductions to Language Study*, and other series on teacher education and professional development.

Other book series include:

ESL & Applied Linguistics Professional Series, formerly by Lawrence Erlbaum, now Routledge, Taylor & Francis
Education Linguistics, Springer
Research and Practice in Applied Linguistics, Palgrave Macmillan
AILA Applied Linguistics Series, Benjamins
Penguin English Applied Linguistics Series, Penguin
Studies in Applied Linguistics, Equinox

4 Journals

There are many high quality journals that are published in and for specific regions. The following are international journals:

Applied Linguistics
Computer-Assisted Language Learning
ELT Journal
English for Specific Purposes
International Journal of Applied Linguistics
International Journal of Bilingual Education and Bilingualism
International Journal of Corpus Linguistics
International Review of Applied Linguistics in Language Teaching
Journal of Applied Linguistics
Journal of English for Academic Purposes
Journal of Second Language Writing
Language Acquisition
Language and Education
Language Awareness
Language, Culture and Curriculum
Language, Identity and Education
Language Learning
Language Teaching
Language Teaching Research
Language Testing
Linguistics and Education
Modern Language Journal
Second Language Research
Studies in Second Language Acquisition
System
TESOL Quarterly

Two annual publications are:

Annual Review of Applied Linguistics
Applied Linguistics Review

5 Corpora

Bank of English

www.titania.bham.ac.uk/docs/svenguide.html#Getting%20Connected
>A corpus collected at University of Birmingham, currently containing a 450 million word corpus of present-day English and a subcorpus aimed at teaching consisting of 56 million words. The COBUILD series of dictionaries and grammars are built on this corpus.

British National Corpus

http://corpus.byu.edu/bnc/
>A corpus collected by Oxford University Press, Longman, Chambers, the British Library and the University of Oxford and Lancaster. It contains both spoken and written British English.

The Corpus of Contemporary American English (COCA)

www.americancorpus.org/
>The largest corpus of American English. It contains over 400 million words.

Cambridge Learner Corpus (CLC)

www.cambridge.org/elt/corpus/learner_corpus2.htm
>As part of the Cambridge International Corpus, CLC has been compiled by Cambridge University Press and Cambridge ESOL. It contains a large collection of examples of English writing from anonymized exam scripts written by students taking Cambridge ESOL English exams around the world. It currently contains over 30 million words from over 95,000 students speaking 130 different first languages.

Cambridge International Corpus (CIC)

www.cambridge.org/elt/corpus/international_corpus.htm
>A very large collection of English texts, compiled by Cambridge University Press over the last ten years with the primary purpose for writing language textbook books for learners of English. It has a number of subsets of corpora on spoken English in the UK and in North America, business English, legal English, financial and academic English.

Longman Corpus Network

www.pearsonlongman.com/dictionaries/corpus/index.html
>A database of 330 million words from a wide range of real-life sources such as books, newspapers and magazines. Longman dictionaries are compiled using the database.

International Corpus of Learners' English

http://cecl.fltr.ucl.ac.be/Cecl-Projects/Icle/icle.htm
>One of the first learners' English corpora, currently containing over 3 million words of writing by learners of English from 21 different language backgrounds.

French Learner Language Oral Corpora

www.flloc.soton.ac.uk/
>A comprehensive list of French Learner corpora including Linguistic Development Corpus, Progression Corpus, Salford Corpus, Brussels Corpus, Reading Corpus, Newcastle Corpus, UEA Corpus, etc.

English as a Lingua Franca in Academic Settings (ELFA)

www.uta.fi/laitokset/kielet/engf/research/elfa/
> A joint research project between University of Tampere and University of Helsinki in Finland. The project has compiled a corpus of spoken academic English in intercultural contexts.

Vienna-Oxford International Corpus of English (VOICE)

www.univie.ac.at/voice/page/index.php
> A database containing 1 million words of spoken ELF interactions among speakers from 50 different first languages (mainly, though not exclusively, European languages).

Michigan Corpus of Academic Spoken English (MICASE)

http://micase.elicorpora.info/
> A collection of nearly 1.8 million words of transcribed speech (almost 200 hours of recordings) at the University of Michigan in Ann Arbor. It contains data from a wide range of speech events such as lectures, classroom discussions, lab sections, seminars, and advisory sessions and locations across the university.

Talk bank

http://talkbank.org/
> An interdisciplinary project containing a number of sample databases within each of the subfield of communication such as aphasiabank, CHILDES, BilingBank, CABank, DementiaBank, and PhonBank. Its primary aim is to set up a system for sharing and studying conversational interactions.

CHILDES

http://childes.psy.cmu.edu/
> The child language component of the TalkBank system. It contains transcript and media data collected from conversations between young children and their playmates and caretakers in different languages.

6 Professional associations

International Association of Applied Linguistics (www.aila.info/)

America

American Association for Applied Linguistics (www.aaal.org/)
Center for Applied Linguistics (www.cal.org/)
Canadian Association of Applied Linguistics (www.aclacaal.org/)
Asociación Mexicana de Lingüística Aplicada (www.cele.unam.mx/amla/)
Asociación de Lingüística y Filología de América Latina/Associação de Lingüística e Filologia da América Latina (www.mundoalfal.org/)

Europe

Association Belge de Linguistique Appliquée (www.abla.be/)
Asociación Española de Lingüística Aplicada (www.aesla.uji.es/)
Association Finlandaise de Linguistique Appliquée (www.cc.jyu.fi/~kmantyla/afinla/!index.html)
Association Française de Linguistique Appliquée (www.afla-asso.org/)
Associazione Italiana di Linguistica Applicata (www.aitla.unimo.it/)

Association Néerlandaise de Linguistique Appliquée (www.aila.info/about/org/ic.htm#SG)
Association Norvegienne de Linguistique Appliquée (www.hf.ntnu.no/anla/)
Association Suédoise de Linguistique Appliquée (www.nordiska.su.se/asla/)
Association Suisse de Linguistique Appliquée (www.vals-asla.ch/cms/)
British Association for Applied Linguistics (www.baal.org.uk/)
Estonian Association of Applied Linguistics (www.eki.ee/rakenduslingvistika/)
Gesellschaft für Angewandte Linguistik (www.gal-ev.de/)
Greek Applied Linguistics Association (www.enl.auth.gr/gala/)
Irish Association for Applied Linguistics (www.iraal.ie/)

Oceania

Applied Linguistics Association of New Zealand (www.victoria.ac.nz/lals/about/alanz/alanz.html)
Applied Linguistics Association of Australia (www.latrobe.edu.au/alaa/)

Asia

Asian Association of TEFL (Asia TEFL) (www.asiatefl.org/)
Applied Linguistics Association of Korea (www.alak.or.kr/)
China English Language Education Association (www.celea.org.cn/)
Hong Kong Association for Applied Linguistics (www.haal.hk/)
Japan Association of College English Teachers (www.jacet.org/index.html)
Linguistic Society of the Philippines (www.dlsu.edu.ph/inside/organizations/lsp/default.asp)
Singapore Association for Applied Linguistics (www.saal.org.sg/)

Others

Israel Association of Applied Linguistics (www.tau.ac.il/~ilash/)
Southern African Applied Linguistics Association (www.saala.org.za/)

7 Websites

All the professional associations have their websites which contain useful information. In addition:

Center for Applied Linguistics at Washington DC has a useful website: www.cal.org.

The Linguist List, http://linguistlist.org, provides up-to-date information about conferences, publications and exchanges of views among linguists of all interests.

ethnologue.com is a searchable database of language resources.

Vivian Cook, one of the leading scholars in the field of applied linguistics, runs a website: http://homepage.ntlworld.com/vivian.c/Vivian%20Cook.htm, which contains very useful information and bibliography on various topics in applied linguistics.

www.appliedlinguistics.org/ (Applied Linguistics.Org) provides useful information on applied linguistics, language acquisition and language teaching.

Index